T0125244

"The Law," "The State," and
Other Political Writings,
1843–1850

The Collected Works of Frédéric Bastiat
Jacques de Guenin, General Editor

*The Man and the Statesman: The Correspondence and Articles on Politics*

*"The Law," "The State," and Other Political Writings, 1843–1850*

*Economic Sophisms and "What Is Seen and What Is Not Seen"*

*Miscellaneous Works on Economics: From "Jacques-Bonhomme" to Le Journal des Économistes*

*Economic Harmonies*

*The Struggle Against Protectionism: The English and French Free-Trade Movements*

*Frédéric Bastiat*

# "The Law," "The State," and Other Political Writings,

## 1843–1850

FRÉDÉRIC BASTIAT

Jacques de Guenin, *General Editor*
*Translated from the French by*
Jane Willems and Michel Willems
*with an introduction by*
Pascal Salin

*Annotations and Glossaries by*
Jacques de Guenin, Jean-Claude Paul-Dejean,
and David M. Hart

*Translation Editor*
Dennis O'Keeffe

*Academic Editor*
David M. Hart

Liberty Fund

This book is published by Liberty Fund, Inc., a foundation established
to encourage study of the ideal of a society of free and responsible individuals.

𒀝𒂼𒄀

The cuneiform inscription that serves as our logo and as a design element
for Liberty Fund books is the earliest-known written appearance of the word "freedom"
(*amagi*), or "liberty." It is taken from a clay document written about 2300 B.C.
in the Sumerian city-state of Lagash.

© 2012 by Liberty Fund, Inc.

All rights reserved
Printed in the United States of America

22 23 24 25 C 6 5 4 3 2
24 25 26 27 28 P 8 7 6 5 4

Cover art: Image of the village of Mugron, France, the town where Bastiat spent most
of his adult life, from a postcard at www.communes.com/www.notrefamille.com.

Library of Congress Cataloging-in-Publication Data

Bastiat, Frédéric, 1801–1850. [Selections. English. 2012]
The Law, the State, and other political writings, 1843–1850 /
Frédéric Bastiat; Jacques de Guenin, general editor;
translated from the French by Jane Willems and Michel Willems;
with an introduction by Pascal Salin;
annotations and glossaries by Jacques de Guenin and David M. Hart;
translation editor Dennis O'Keeffe.
p. cm. — (Collected works of Frédéric Bastiat)
Includes bibliographical references and index.
ISBN 978-0-86597-829-4 (hbk.: alk. paper) — ISBN 978-0-86597-830-0 (pbk.: alk. paper)
1. Economics. 2. Law. 3. Property. 4. France—Politics and government—1830–1848.
5. France—Politics and government—1848–1852. I. Guenin, Jacques de. II. Title.
HB105.B3A25 2012
330—dc23 2012010907

LIBERTY FUND, INC.
11301 North Meridian Street
Carmel, Indiana 46032
libertyfund.org

# Contents

# General Editor's Note

*The* six-volume Collected Works of Frédéric Bastiat will be the most complete compilation of Bastiat's works published to date, in any country or in any language. The main source for the translation is the *Œuvres complètes de Frédéric Bastiat,* published by Guillaumin in the 1850s and 1860s.[1]

Although the Guillaumin edition was generally chronological, the volumes in this series have been arranged thematically:

> *The Man and the Statesman: The Correspondence and Articles on Politics*
> *"The Law," "The State," and Other Political Writings, 1843–1850*
> *Economic Sophisms and "What Is Seen and What Is Not Seen"*
> *Miscellaneous Works on Economics: From "Jacques-Bonhomme" to Le Journal des Économistes*
> *Economic Harmonies*
> *The Struggle Against Protectionism: The English and French Free-Trade Movements*

There are four kinds of notes in this volume: footnotes by the editor of the Guillaumin edition (Prosper Paillottet), which are preceded by "(Paillottet's note)"; footnotes by Bastiat, which are preceded by "(Bastiat's note)"; new editorial footnotes, which stand alone (unless they are commenting on Paillottet's notes, in which case they are in square brackets following Paillottet's note); and source notes, which are given after the title of each article. The source note consists of (1) the volume number and the beginning page number as the work appears in the *Œuvres complètes;* (2) the original French title; and (3) the date and place of original publication.

In the text, Bastiat (as Paillottet does in the notes) makes many passing refer-

---

1. For a more detailed description of the publication history of the *Œuvres complètes,* see "Note on the Editions of the *Œuvres complètes*" and the bibliography.

ences to his works, for which we have provided an internal cross-reference if the work is found in this volume. For those works not in this volume, we have provided the location of the original French version in the *Œuvres complètes* (indicated in a footnote by "*OC,*" followed by the Guillaumin volume number, beginning page number, and French title of the work).

In addition, we have made available two online sources for the reader to consult. The first source is a table of contents of the seven-volume *Œuvres complètes* and links to PDF (Portable Document Format) facsimiles of each volume. The second source is our "Comparative Table of Contents of the Collected Works of Frédéric Bastiat," which is a table of contents of the complete Liberty Fund series.[2] Here, the reader can find the location of the English translation of the work in its future Liberty Fund volume. These contents will be filled in and updated as the volumes are published and will eventually be the most complete comparative listing of Bastiat's works.

In order to avoid multiple footnotes and cross-references, a glossary of persons, a glossary of places, and a glossary of subjects and terms have been provided to identify those persons, places, and terms mentioned in the text. The glossaries will also provide historical context and background for the reader as well as a greater understanding of Bastiat's work. If a name as it appears in the text is ambiguous or is found in the glossary under a different name, a footnote has been added to identify the name as it is listed in the glossary.

Finally, original italics as they appear in the Guillaumin edition have been retained.

*Jacques de Guenin*
*Saint-Loubouer, France*

---

2. These two sources can be found at http://oll.libertyfund.org/person/25.

# Note on the Translation

*In* this translation we have made a deliberate decision not to translate Fré-déric Bastiat's French into modern, colloquial American English. Wherever possible we have tried to retain a flavor of the more florid, Latinate forms of expression that were common among the literate class in mid-nineteenth-century France. Bastiat liked long, flowing sentences, in which idea followed upon idea in an apparently endless succession of dependent clauses. For the sake of clarity, we have broken up many but not all of these thickets of expression. In those that remain, you, dear reader, will have to navigate.

As was the custom in the 1840s, Bastiat liked to pepper his paragraphs with exclamations like "What!" and aphoristic Latin phrases like *Quid leges sine moribus?* (What are laws without customs?). We have translated the latter and left most of the former as a reminder that Bastiat wrote in a by-gone age when tastes were very different. We have also kept personal names, titles of nobility, and the like in their original French if the persons were French; thus, "M." instead of "Mr."; "Mme" instead of "Mrs."; "Mlle" instead of "Miss"; and "MM" instead of "Messrs."

In the glossaries and footnotes, we have translated the French titles of works referred to by Bastiat or cited by the editors only if the work is well known to English-speaking readers, such as Montesquieu's *Spirit of the Laws* or Rousseau's *The Social Contract*.

Because many of the pamphlets in this volume were originally given as speeches in the Chamber of Deputies (Bastiat was elected to the Constitu-ent Assembly in April 1848 and to the Legislative Assembly in May 1849) and because Bastiat did not live to edit them into a final publishable form, the language can be at times rather colloquial and informal. One needs to remember that the speeches were given in the heat of the revolutionary moment, when France was undergoing considerable upheaval and the liberal forces Bastiat represented were under siege from both the conservatives and the protectionists on the right and the socialists on the left. Other essays in the volume were prepared for publication in such journals as *Le Journal des débats, Le Journal des économistes,* or *Le Libre-échange* and were thus in a more polished form. A handful of writings in the volume were published privately by Bastiat as "pamphlets," which he handed out to his friends, or were submissions to parliamentary committees on various topical matters. Thus, the language he used varied considerably from pamphlet to pamphlet depending on its raison d'être. It is therefore possible that both the original French editor (Paillottet) as well as the translation in this edition have given too final a form to what were in fact ephemeral *pamphlets du jour*.

Concerning the problematical issue of how to translate the French word *la liberté*—whether to use the more archaic-sounding English word *liberty* or the more modern word *freedom*—we have let the context have the final say. Bastiat was much involved with establishing a free-trade movement in France and to that end founded the Free Trade Association (Association pour la liberté des échanges) and its journal *Le Libre-échange*. In this context the word choice is clear: we must use *freedom* because it is intimately linked to the idea of "free trade." The English phrase "liberty of trade" would sound awkward. Another word is *pouvoir,* which we have variously translated as "power," "government," or "authority," again depending on the context.

A third example consists of the words *économie politique* and *économiste*. Throughout the eighteenth century and most of the nineteenth, in both French and English the term *political economy* was used to describe what we now call "economics." Toward the end of the nineteenth century as economics became more mathematical, the adjective "political" was dropped and not replaced. We have preferred to keep the term *political economy* both because it was still current when Bastiat was writing and because it better describes the state of the discipline, which proudly mixed an interest in moral philosophy, history, and political theory with the main dish, which was economic analysis; similarly, with the term *économiste.* Today one can be a free-market economist, a Marxist economist, a Keynesian economist, a mathematical economist, or an Austrian economist, to name a few. The qualifier before the noun is quite important. In Bastiat's day it was assumed that any "economist" was a free-market economist, and so the noun needed no adjectival qualifier. Only during the 1840s, with the emergence of socialist ideas in France and Germany, did there arise a school of economic thinking that sharply diverged from the free market. But in Bastiat's day this had not yet become large enough to cause confusion over naming. Even in 1849, when Gustave de Molinari published his charming set of dialogues, *Les Soi-*

*rées de la rue Saint-Lazare,* between three stock characters—the socialist, the conservative, and the economist—it was perfectly clear who was arguing for what, and that the economist was, of course, a laissez-faire, free-market economist.

A particularly difficult word to translate is *l'industrie,* as is its related term *industriel.* In some respects it is a "false friend," as one is tempted to translate it as "industry" or "industrious" or "industrial," but this would be wrong because these terms have the more narrow modern meaning of "heavy industry" or "manufacturing" or "the result of some industrial process." The meaning in Bastiat's time was both more general and more specific to a particular social and economic theory current in his day.

The word *industry* in the eighteenth century had the general meaning of "productive" or "the result of hard work," and this sense continued to be current in the early nineteenth century. *Industry* also had a specific meaning, which was tied to a social and economic theory developed by Jean-Baptiste Say and his followers Charles Comte and Charles Dunoyer in the 1810s and 1820s, as well as by other theorists such as the historian Augustin Thierry. According to these theorists there were only two means of acquiring wealth: by productive activity and voluntary exchanges in the free market (that is, by "industrie"—which included agriculture, trade, factory production, and services) or by coercive means (conquest, theft, taxation, subsidies, protection, transfer payments, or slavery). Anybody who acquired wealth through voluntary exchange and productive activities belonged to a class of people collectively called *les industrieux,* in contrast to those individuals or groups who acquired their wealth by force, coercion, conquest, slavery, or government privileges. The latter group were seen as a ruling class or as "parasites" who lived at the expense of *les industrieux.*

Bastiat was very much influenced by the theories of Say, Comte, and Dunoyer and adopted their terminology regarding *industry.* So to translate *industrie* in this intellectual context as "production" (or some other modern, neutral term) would be to ignore the resonance the word has within the social and economic theory that was central to Bastiat's worldview. Hence, at the risk of sounding a bit archaic and pedantic we have preferred to use *industry* in order to remain true to Bastiat's intent.

Bastiat uses the French term *la spoliation* many times in his writings. It is even used in the title of two of his pamphlets (found in this volume), "Propriété et spoliation," published in July 1848 in *Le Journal des débats;* and "Spoliation et loi," published in May 1850 in *Le Journal des économistes.*

The *Oxford English Dictionary* defines *spoliation* as "the action of ruining or destroying something" and "the action of taking goods or property from somewhere by illegal or unethical means"—from the Latin verb *spoliare* (strip, deprive). In using this term, Bastiat is making the point that there is a distinction between the two ways in which wealth can be acquired, either through peaceful and voluntary exchange (i.e., the free market) or by theft, conquest, and coercion (i.e., using the power of the state to tax, repossess, or grant special privileges). Some earlier translations of Bastiat use the older word *spoliation;* the word *plunder* is also used on occasion. In our translation we have preferred to use *plunder.* Another possible translation for *spoliation* is "exploitation," which carries much the same meaning but has an unfortunate association with Marxist theories of "capitalist exploitation."

A final note on terminology: in Bastiat's time, the word *liberal* had the same meaning in France and in America. In the United States, however, the meaning of the word has shifted progressively toward the left of the political spectrum. A precise translation of the French word would be either "classical liberal" or "libertarian," depending on the context, and indeed Bastiat is considered a classical liberal by present-day conservatives and a libertarian by present-day libertarians. To avoid the resulting awkwardness, we have decided by convention to keep the word *liberal,* with its nineteenth-century meaning, in the translations as well as in the notes and the glossaries.

*David M. Hart*

# *Note on the Editions of the* Œuvres complètes

*The* first edition of the *Œuvres complètes* appeared in 1854–55, consisting of six volumes.[1] The second edition, which appeared in 1862–64, was an almost identical reprint of the first edition (with only minor typesetting differences) but was notable for the addition of a new, seventh volume, which contained additional essays, sketches, and correspondence.[2] The second edition also contained a preface by Prosper Paillottet and a biographical essay on Bastiat by Roger de Fontenay ("Notice sur la vie et les écrits de Frédéric Bastiat"), both of which were absent in the first edition.

Another difference between the first and second editions was in the sixth volume, which contained Bastiat's magnum opus, *Economic Harmonies*. The first edition of the *Œuvres complètes* described volume 6 as the "third revised and augmented edition" of *Economic Harmonies*. This is somewhat confusing but does have some logic to it. The "first" edition of *Economic Harmonies* appeared in 1850 during the last year of Bastiat's life but in an incomplete form. The "second" edition appeared in 1851, after his death, edited by "La Société des amis de Bastiat" (most probably by Prosper Paillottet and Roger de Fontenay) and included the second half of the manuscript, which Bastiat had been working on when he died. Thus the edition that appeared in the first edition of the *Œuvres complètes* was called the "third" edition on its title page. This practice continued throughout the nineteenth century, with editions of *Economic Harmonies* staying in print as a separate volume as

---

1. *Œuvres complètes de Frédéric Bastiat, mises en ordre, revues et annotées d'après les manuscrits de l'auteur* (Paris: Guillaumin, 1854–55). 6 vols.: vol. 1, *Correspondance et mélanges* (1855); vol. 2, *Le Libre-échange* (1855); vol. 3, *Cobden et la Ligue ou L'Agitation anglaise pour la liberté des échanges* (1854); vol. 4, *Sophismes économiques. Petits pamphlets I* (1854); vol. 5, *Sophismes économiques. Petits pamphlets II* (1854); vol. 6, *Harmonies économiques* (1855). [Edited by Prosper Paillottet with the assistance of Roger de Fontenay, but Paillottet and Fontenay are not credited on the title page.]

2. Vol. 7: *Essais, ébauches, correspondance* (1864).

well as being included as volume 6 in later editions of the *Œuvres complètes*. By 1870–73, therefore, when the third edition of the *Œuvres complètes* appeared, the version of *Economic Harmonies* in volume 6 was titled the "sixth" edition of the work.

Other "editions" of the *Œuvres complètes* include a fourth edition, 1878–79, and a fifth edition, 1881–84. If there was a sixth edition, the date is unknown. A seventh edition appeared in 1893, and a final edition may have appeared in 1907. (For a complete listing of the editions of the *Œuvres complètes* that were used in making this translation, see the bibliography.)

*David M. Hart*
*Academic Editor*

# *Acknowledgments*

*This* translation is the result of the efforts of a team comprising Jane Willems and Michel Willems; Dr. Dennis O'Keeffe, Professor of Social Science at the University of Buckingham and Senior Research Fellow at the Institute of Economic Affairs in London, who carefully read the translation and made very helpful suggestions at every stage; Dr. David M. Hart, Director of the Online Library of Liberty Project at Liberty Fund, who supplied much of the scholarly apparatus and provided the translation with the insights of a historian of nineteenth-century European political economy; Dr. Aurelian Craiutu, Professor of Political Science at Indiana University, Bloomington, who read the final translation and contributed his considerable knowledge of nineteenth-century French politics to this undertaking; Dr. Robert Leroux of the University of Ottawa for additional assistance with the translation; and Dr. Laura Goetz, senior editor at Liberty Fund, who organized and coordinated the various aspects of the project from its inception through to final manuscript.

I would also like to acknowledge the contribution of Mr. Manuel Ayau (1925–2010), a Liberty Fund board member whose support and enthusiasm for the translation project was crucial in getting it off the ground.

This volume thus has all the strengths and all the weaknesses of a voluntary, collaborative effort. My colleagues and I hope that Bastiat would approve, especially as no government official was involved at any stage.

*Jacques de Guenin*
*General editor*
*Founder of the Cercle Frédéric Bastiat*

# Introduction

*The* pamphlets and articles in this volume clearly show Frédéric Bastiat to be a keen observer and analyst of the political and economic problems of his time. Many of the pamphlets were written while he was an active politician, a position he held unfortunately for only a short period of time. Bastiat was elected to the Constituent Assembly in April 1848 and then to the Legislative Assembly in May 1849 but died on Christmas Eve in 1850, at the age of forty-nine.[1]

Despite his brief life, Bastiat was a privileged witness to a particularly unsettled period of French history: after the Revolution of 1789 came a period of political chaos, followed by the Napoleonic Empire, the return of the monarchy in 1815, a revolution in 1830, and another one in 1848, at which date the Second Republic was founded and universal suffrage adopted for the first time in French history. It was also during this period that the "bourgeoisie" became an increasingly influential social class that made possible, after the death of Bastiat, the takeoff of economic growth under Emperor Napoléon III and the beginnings of industrialization in Britain and France. These were the events that provided the background for Bastiat's numerous writings on economics and politics.

## THE POLITICAL PAMPHLETS AS MODELS
## OF APPLIED ECONOMICS

Bastiat was both a thinker and an actor in public affairs. He was a politician who was inspired by both economic and ethical principles, which is a

---

1. It is not clear exactly what killed Bastiat. We know from his correspondence that he had a painful throat condition of some kind, which was probably tuberculosis but could also have been throat cancer. Whatever it was that finally killed him, Bastiat died at the peak of his powers as a writer and a politician.

rare occurrence, whether then or now. Next to Bastiat "the economist," who wrote such monumental theoretical works as *Economic Harmonies* (1850), we have Bastiat the "political pamphleteer," who wrote in response to the political and economic battles of the moment.[2] To those economists who dream of attempting to implement their ideas, political life might seem attractive; however, only a very few, like Bastiat, are lucky enough to get that opportunity. While France was wracked by wave after wave of revolutionary change between 1848 and 1850, Bastiat had the chance to present his ideas in speeches to the Assembly, in broadsides handed out in the street, as essays in popular journals, and as articles in academic journals.

Throughout the pamphlets, Bastiat demonstrates how the combination of careful logic, consistency of principle, and clarity of exposition is the instrument for solving most economic and social problems. He does not hesitate to present facts and even statistics to his readers, but he does so in a manner that is understandable and coherent because the material is analyzed through the filter of rigorous economic theory.[3]

In this volume the reader will find discussions covering a wide variety of topics, such as the theory of value and rent (in which Bastiat made pathbreaking contributions), public choice and collective action, regulations, taxation, education, trade unions, price controls, capital and growth, and the balance of trade, many of which topics are still at the center of political debate in our own time. Far from being dry and technical discussions of abstruse matters, all Bastiat's pamphlets are written with such outstanding limpidity that reading them is a joy.

## EYEWITNESS TO POLITICAL AND ECONOMIC UPHEAVALS (1848–50)

After a period as a successful provincial magistrate, Bastiat was elected in the immediate aftermath of the February revolution of 1848 to the Constituent Assembly in Paris. He represented his home *département* (the Landes,

---

2. A future volume will contain Bastiat's "economic" pamphlets, better known as *Economic Sophisms,* but it must be understood that in Bastiat's writing there is no hard and fast barrier between politics, ethics, and economic theory. He moves from one to the other with great ease.

3. See, for example, the interesting way in which Bastiat is able to explain the poverty of vine growers in his province by referring to the effects of taxation and protectionism in "Discourse on the Tax on Wines and Spirits," p. 328.

located in the southwest region of France) and became active in opposing both the socialism of the left and the authoritarianism of the right. As a classical liberal advocate of natural rights, universal franchise, the ultraminimalist state, and absolute free trade, Bastiat was not completely at home on the right or on the left side of the Assembly, though he often sat on the left because of his opposition to many of the establishment's policies. On the right sat the monarchists, militarists, large landowners, supporters of the very limited voting franchise, and business interests who advocated tariff protection and subsidies. Occupying the left were the republicans, democrats, socialists, and advocates of state-supported make-work schemes and other subsidies to the poor. As some of his speeches indicate, Bastiat could cleverly play off one side against the other, appealing to the right in his attacks on socialism but appealing to the left in his support of the republic and his criticism of state subsidies to the rich.

In 1846 a key economic reform occurring in Britain caught Bastiat's attention: Prime Minister Robert Peel's abolition of the Corn Laws.[4] The repeal of these laws eliminated many price controls on imported food stuffs and thus lowered the cost of food for those British consumers who were the least well off. The person behind the successful repeal was Richard Cobden whose organization, the Anti–Corn Law League, mobilized British opinion and forced Peel to act as he did. Bastiat, impressed with this popular and successful movement, very much wanted to emulate Cobden's success by organizing a homegrown French free-trade movement and spent much of his time during the mid-1840s trying to bring this about, with disappointing results.[5]

TOWARD the end of his life, as a deputy in the Constituent Assembly and then in the Legislative Assembly, Bastiat became immersed in the struggles against the rise of socialist groups from the left and the opportunistic, interventionist policies of other groups on the right. Many of his pamphlets from this period were economic in nature and designed to alert people to the dangers of growing government intervention in the economy and attacks on the rule of law. The pamphlets are period pieces to the extent that they

4. See the entry for the "Anti–Corn Law League" in the Glossary of Subjects and Terms.

5. A future volume will contain Bastiat's writings on the free-trade movements in Britain and France.

reflect the day-to-day or week-to-week battles for liberty fought by Bastiat in the Assembly (he served on a budget committee and thus had access to important economic data). However, they are also timeless works of applied economic theory that still stand today as insightful, informative, and even exemplary forms of their kind.

## Republicanism and Universal Suffrage

Bastiat was a "sincere" republican in the sense that he favored a republican system of government (as opposed to a monarchical one) and, more precisely, because he favored universal suffrage. Yet he was also aware of the dangers of unrestrained democracy if it were allowed to violate the people's rights to property ("plunder") and liberty ("slavery"). In his famous pamphlet "The Law" (1850) Bastiat explains that the law, far from being what it ought to be, namely the instrument that enabled the state to protect individuals' rights and property, had become the means for what he termed "spoliation," or plunder.

As the will and the capacity to legislate became commonplace—the result of universal suffrage—plunder, too, became commonplace. Bastiat's views on law and plunder are both modern and prophetic, given that democracy was a relatively new experience in France. Like his contemporary Alexis de Tocqueville, Bastiat was an astute observer of the society of his time as well as a visionary of what unrestrained democracy might lead to, as the following passage shows:

> Whatever the disciples of the Rousseau school think, those who say that they are *very advanced* and whom I believe to be *retarded* by twenty centuries, *universal* suffrage (taking this word in its strictest sense) is not one of the sacred dogmas with regard to which any examination or even doubt is a crime.[6]

Bastiat points out the logical contradiction of the Rousseauean lawmakers who believed that ordinary citizens are naturally inclined to make bad choices in their own lives (but not in choosing their political representatives apparently), so that they must be deprived of their freedom, whereas the elected rulers of society would necessarily be inclined to make good choices

6. "The Law," p. 112. Italics in the original.

concerning the lives of others: "And if humanity is incapable of making its own judgments, why are people talking to us about universal suffrage?"[7]

Bastiat concludes with a sad commentary on the effects that unbridled democracy has had in France, writing that although the French people "have led all the others in winning their rights, or rather their political guarantees, they nevertheless remain the most governed, directed, administered, taxed, hobbled, and exploited of all peoples."[8]

In the pamphlet "Plunder and Law"[9] (1850), written before "The Law" appeared, Bastiat had already expressed his uneasiness concerning the idea of universal suffrage:

> Following the February revolution, when universal suffrage was proclaimed, I hoped for a moment that its great voice would be heard to say: "No more plunder for anyone, justice for all!" . . . No, by bursting into the National Assembly, each class came to make the law an instrument of plunder for itself according to the principles they upheld. They demanded progressive taxes, free credit, the right to work, the right to state assistance, guaranteed interest rates, a minimum rate of pay, free education, subsidies to industry, etc., etc.; in short, each wanted to live and develop at other people's expense.[10]

We thus find in Bastiat's writings clear statements about the dangerous confusion that exists between two opposite concepts of the law, "law and legislation"—to use the words of the twentieth-century Nobel Prize–winning economist Friedrich Hayek (1899–1992). *Legislation* is the output of the political process; it is an instrument of plunder and it breeds a war of all against all. But *law,* properly conceived, is, as Bastiat states, "the common power organized to obstruct injustice and, in short, the law is justice"[11]—a straightforward but striking formula that encapsulates a whole body of theory.

In witnessing these processes at work in the French assemblies of 1848 and 1849, Bastiat was led to some important theoretical insights into the nature of the state itself. He most clearly expressed these views in another pam-

---

7. Ibid., p. 140.
8. Ibid., p. 140.
9. See "Plunder and Law," p. 266.
10. Ibid., p. 273.
11. "The Law," p. 142. Italics in the original.

phlet, "The State," which he wrote in that most revolutionary year of 1848 and from which comes perhaps his best-remembered quotation: "*The state is the great fiction by which* everyone *endeavors to live at the expense of everyone else.*"[12]

## STATE EDUCATION

In his writings Bastiat gives a lot of attention to the problem of education. A good example is his opposition to the importance placed upon the teaching of Latin in the school curriculum. In his own education Bastiat had attended a progressive school that emphasized modern languages and practical subjects. He was opposed to learning Latin and reading the works of the famous Latin authors because, in his view, Roman civilization was based on slavery and the glorification of war and the state; commerce, individual rights, and natural law were ignored or downplayed.

In a submission to the Mimerel Commission in 1847,[13] Bastiat opposed the politicalization of the teaching of economics in higher education. Apart from the fact that political economists were not granted their own faculty but had to teach within the schools of law, the commission at first wanted to abolish the teaching of political economy altogether. Eventually it relented and recommended that if the political economists must teach, they should be required by the state to soften their relentless criticism of protection by giving "equal time" to protectionist ideas—an early version of "teaching the debate," if you will. Bastiat naturally opposed this measure. His view of state education became so severe that he saw no other option than its complete abolition. His pamphlet "Baccalaureate and Socialism" (1850) was written expressly in order to explain an amendment he had proposed to the National Assembly: he dared to ask that the state-run universities no longer be the sole grantors of degrees, thereby ending the state's monopoly over the awarding of such degrees.[14]

12. "The State," p. 97. Italics in the original.
13. See "The War Against Chairs of Political Economy," pp. 277–81.
14. Bastiat failed in his effort, and it is only recently that France conceded some autonomy to the universities.

## HAYEK AND SPONTANEOUS ORDER

Two of the themes Bastiat pursues in the pamphlets are his advocacy of the "harmony" and justice of freely acting individuals in the marketplace and his criticism of state intervention and "plunder" to create authoritarianism or socialism. Friedrich Hayek called these opposing worldviews "spontaneous order" and "constructivism," respectively.

During the 1840s a new socialist movement sprang up in France, and it would play a significant role during the upheavals of the 1848 revolution.[15] Bastiat's writing on this topic[16] places the reader at the very center of the debates that explain the historical evolution of France and of a great part of the world. Similarly, as Hayek has persuasively argued, Bastiat is at the very center of the fundamental debates of political philosophy.[17]

The coexistence since the eighteenth century of both these streams of thought (the classical liberal and the socialist) has arguably been the source of the ambiguity in the meaning of the words *liberty* and *property* during the French Revolution and its aftermath. One can see this conflict played out in the various versions of declarations of rights that emerged periodically during the Revolution, beginning with the famous Declaration of the Rights of Man and of the Citizen (1789).

Bastiat criticized such thinkers as Fénelon, Montesquieu, Rousseau,

15. See the entries for "Saint-Simon, Claude Henri de Rouvroy," "Fourier, François-Marie Charles," and "Blanc, Louis," in the Glossary of Persons.

16. In a similar way, Gustave de Molinari, in *Les Soirées de la Rue Saint-Lazare* (1849), presented a fascinating debate among a socialist, a conservative, and an economist. The latter, who supports individual freedom, opposes both the socialist and the conservative, both of whom think in constructivist terms and, incidentally, frequently agree with each other. The real opposition is not between left and right but between the constructivists—whether "conservative" or "socialist"—and the "liberals."

17. It is interesting that in several chapters of his book *The Counter-revolution of Science* Hayek explored the ideological situation in France in the nineteenth century, which seemed particularly strange to him. He stressed the paradox of a country in which one could find some of the most eminent representatives of both liberalism and positivism. Concerning the latter, he pointed out the importance of the scientistic prejudice that led to the appearance in the late eighteenth and early nineteenth centuries of "social engineers," who modeled their discipline on that of the physical and natural sciences.

Mably, and Robespierre, who had done much to inspire modern enlightened public opinion. Bastiat objected to their claims that property rights are created by the state and are thus "conventional" and not "natural," that is, existing prior to any man-made law. Rousseau comes in for particularly harsh criticism by Bastiat for the distinction he makes between "individual liberty" (which Rousseau regards as "natural") and "property" (which Rousseau considers purely conventional).

According to Bastiat, this false distinction led Rousseau to conclude that the state had the right to enact legislation establishing the right to work, the right to get relief (welfare), and the right to impose progressive taxation. Robespierre, one of the leaders of the French Revolution, especially during the 1793–94 Reign of Terror, had been directly influenced by Rousseau, whom Bastiat quotes in "Baccalaureate and Socialism": "Property is the right held by each citizen to enjoy and dispose of possessions that are guaranteed to him *by the law*."[18] In Bastiat's view, if property were not a natural right that existed prior to the state, then the state (or whoever temporarily controlled the organs of the state) could define what "property" was and legislate to create any kind of society it desired.

THE French revolutionaries of the 1790s and the 1840s had tried to apply what Bastiat called the "communist principle" to the formation of declarations of rights and constitutions and to the development of government policies regarding price controls, make-work schemes, and other economic interventions by the state. Such an extreme form of despotism frightened many French citizens in the 1790s. These citizens, seeking security and stability, turned toward a Roman-inspired form of despotism,[19] such as that offered by Napoléon Bonaparte.

After lurching from the radicalism of the Jacobins to the militaristic dictatorship of Napoléon and to the conservatism of the restored Bourbon monarchy, the French people seemed to have settled upon a form of po-

18. "Baccalaureate and Socialism," p. 209. Italics in the original.

19. Napoléon's dictatorship had also inspired Benjamin Constant (1767–1830) to reflect on the differences between ancient and modern notions of liberty and the dangers of military conquest and political usurpation. See "The Spirit of Conquest and Usurpation and Their Relationship to European Civilization" (1814) and "The Liberty of the Ancients Compared with That of the Moderns" (1819) in Benjamin Constant, *Political Writings*.

litical armistice after the July revolution, with the forces of revolution and counterrevolution achieving a kind of temporary balance. Bastiat, however, unhappily believed that the French continued to educate their youth with the ideas of Rousseau and Caesar, thus trapping them in a maze that began with dreams of utopia, followed by experimentation in an attempt to create this utopia on earth, and then finally political reaction after these dreams inevitably fell apart. In its incarnation in the revolutionary period this maze began with the ideas of Rousseau, was followed by the revolutionary communism of Robespierre and his followers, and ended in the military despotism of Napoléon. In 1848 it looked to Bastiat as if France were going to repeat this pattern all over again, this time under the influence of the new socialist movement that had sprung up in the 1840s.

## Peace, Liberty, and Taxes

In the pamphlet "Peace and Freedom or the Republican Budget" (1849), Bastiat's skill as a writer and thinker enables him to rapidly turn the mundane topic of the national budget into one of principle and high theory. He quickly goes beyond strict budgetary considerations to reach a high level of theoretical analysis and, in so doing, provides an original and audacious contribution to the field of tax theory. In fact, he may be the first author to support the idea that "taxes kill taxes"—in other words, the concept known in our own time as the Laffer Curve.

In this text Bastiat blames both the "financiers," who try to obtain fiscal equilibrium by taxing people, and the so-called advanced republicans, who make so many promises to their constituents that an increase in taxes is unavoidable. Bastiat believed that it was important to secure the stability of the young republic by alleviating the tax burden on the people, thus inducing them to "love the republic." For Bastiat, in order for public finance to blossom, the rational thing to do would be to decrease tax rates, not increase them, because, for the state, "*taxing more* is to *receive less*."[20] Bastiat does not hesitate to write that even if there is a budget deficit, taxes must be reduced, as much out of principle as out of the recognition that economic hardship has been so severe that the people have to receive some relief. As he put it, such a solution "is not boldness, it is prudence"![21]

---

20. "Peace and Freedom or the Republican Budget," p. 294. Italics in the original.
21. Ibid., p. 305.

## THE LEFT, TAXES, AND TRADE UNIONS

In Bastiat's lifelong quest to instill into the French people the ideals of liberty, peace, and prosperity—that is, those principles today associated with the conservative right—Bastiat sat on the parliamentary benches with the left. His political position is more easily understood if one remembers that, in his time, those who sat on the right in the Assembly were mainly conservatives, not classical liberals. They were nostalgic for the *ancien régime* of the pre-1789 period, namely the era of the monarchy and aristocratic class privileges. In fact, Bastiat was very critical of the efforts made by the wealthiest and most politically connected individuals to protect their own interests by manipulating the power of the legislature and the state. Like his friend and colleague in England Richard Cobden, Bastiat passionately believed that in advocating for free markets, low taxes, and free trade he was defending the interests of the poor.

The difficulty of Bastiat's balancing act in the Assembly between left and right can clearly be seen in the reaction to two of his speeches: "Discourse on the Tax on Wines and Spirits" (1849) and "The Repression of Industrial Unions" (1849).

In the first speech Bastiat, who represented an agricultural district in which the production of wine was particularly important, attempts to convince his colleagues that the farmers in his locality have to bear an unfair tax burden. He defends the interests of his constituents without compromising what he rightly considers to be the lessons of sound economic theory. What is particularly striking in this speech is the fact that he receives applause from those sitting on the left's benches. Bastiat points out that poor people suffer the most from state interventionism and that politically influential businessmen are able to induce the state to pass laws giving them protection from foreign competition, with the result that higher prices are created for ordinary consumers.

Bastiat concludes therefore that liberalizing trade and freeing up markets benefit the poor. Note that in Bastiat's time, as in ours, it was a commonly held view that liberals (in the classical sense of the word) supported business interests over the interests of ordinary consumers. It is fascinating to discover that when Bastiat gave this speech, both the champions of the poor and the supporters of the republic (the left) seemed to understand what he was saying and to approve it. Unfortunately, the applause he received in the Assembly was not followed up by any concrete legislation to bring about the reforms he advocated.

In the second speech, "The Repression of Industrial Unions," Bastiat opposes legislation that restricts the right of workers to form the unions proposed by the right. Bastiat explains why both businessmen and workers must be granted the freedom to form trade unions; he argues that "the word *union* is synonymous with association"[22] and that human freedom implies the right to associate with whomever and for whatever purpose one chooses. In addition, Bastiat strongly supports the right to strike, since an individual can legitimately decline to sell his or her work and "when it [an action] is innocent in itself, it cannot become guilty because it is carried out by a large number of individuals."[23] He further proclaims, "For what is a slave if not a man obliged by law to work under conditions that he rejects?" This sentence was greeted in the Assembly with repeated shouts of "Hear! Hear!" from the benches of the left.

Contrary to frequently held modern views, Bastiat's belief is that a consistent (classical) liberal is necessarily against all forms of slavery and is in favor of the right to associate and also to strike, with the important condition that violence is not used. Thus, the state should not forbid trade unions and strikes, but it should punish those who use violence in any strike-related activity. On the basis of these clear principles of individual liberty, Bastiat supported the proposal to allow the creation of trade unions, concluding that "only principles have the power to satisfy people's minds, to win over their hearts, and to unite all serious minds."[24]

## The Economists, the Socialists, and Legal Plunder

According to Bastiat and the liberal, free-trade political economists of his time, there was only one school of economics, that of *Les Économistes*.[25] On the other hand, there were many schools of socialism, all of which opposed the ideas of *Les Économistes*. The reason for this difference is straightforward in Bastiat's view: true economists are concerned with principles, and if people agree on principles they cannot express conflicting or incoherent statements. On the contrary, socialists want to rebuild human nature and each school has its own recipe for changing society. Bastiat expresses this view clearly in "Justice and Fraternity" (1848): "I believe that what radically

---

22. "The Repression of Industrial Unions," p. 349. Italics in the original.
23. Ibid., p. 350.
24. Ibid., p. 361.
25. See the entry for "*Les Économistes*" in the Glossary of Subjects and Terms.

divides us is this: political economy reaches the conclusion that only universal justice should be demanded of the law. Socialism, in its various branches and through applications whose number is of course unlimited, demands in addition that the law should put into practice the dogma of fraternity."[26]

For Bastiat, the approaches of the political economists and the socialists are incompatible with each other because socialism necessarily impinges upon individual rights whenever one wants to redistribute wealth by using constraint. The main criterion for evaluating human actions is to ask whether an act is made freely or whether it is obtained by violence. According to Bastiat, legal violence is the most dangerous of human actions because it is wielded without any risk to the politicians and their supporters; moreover, it is even considered virtuous because politicians use it in the name of brotherhood and solidarity. Bastiat's consistency in opposing all forms of coercion, whether legal or not, separates him from most of his contemporaries.

## FREEDOM TO EXCHANGE

It is not surprising that Bastiat frequently opposes protectionist measures and pleads the case for free trade, but what is surprising is the broad range of arguments he uses to make his case. He draws his arguments from many fields of inquiry, such as economics, history, philosophy, and ethics. He reminds us that he was the founder of the Association pour la liberté des échanges (the free-trade association) and not the "association for commercial freedom" or the "association for the gradual reform of tariffs." The "association for commercial freedom" would suggest support for only a narrowly based interest group that worked in the area of "commerce." Likewise, the "association for the gradual reform of tariffs" would be inappropriate in Bastiat's view because it would imply a willingness to compromise with those groups who benefited from protection at the expense of the broad mass of consumers who suffered from it. Thus, he chose for his organization the more general and somewhat abstract name "Association pour la liberté des échanges," explaining that "the term *free trade* implies the *freedom to dispose of the fruits of your work,* in other words, *property,*"[27] and this property could be in the form of wine, cotton cloth, gold bullion, or ideas.

Bastiat also makes a striking comparison between slavery and protection-

26. "Justice and Fraternity," pp. 60–61.
27. "Protectionism and Communism," p. 237. Italics in the original.

ism: "If I use force to appropriate all the work of a man for my benefit, this man is my slave. He is also my slave if, while letting him work freely, I find a way through force or guile to take possession of the fruit of his work."[28] In his battle with both conservatives and socialists Bastiat wanted to make the rhetorical and philosophical point that protectionism was just another form of that age-old means of granting privileges to one group at the expense of the liberty and property of another group. Thus he gave "this new form of servitude the fine title of *protection*."[29]

## CONCLUSION

Throughout the writings in this volume, we discover the personality of Bastiat. He is a keen observer and analyst of the times and a passionate politician who rushes into many debates with the hope of changing the course of history during the crucial period in which he lived. It is as if he somehow anticipated that he had only a very short time left to live.

The time between his election to the Assembly in early 1848 and his death on Christmas Eve in 1850 was a scant twenty months. During this period he carried out his parliamentary duties, wrote numerous pamphlets, and worked feverishly to complete his magnum opus, *Economic Harmonies*.[30] His aim was to convince as many people as possible that liberal economic theory is the only way to evaluate political decisions rationally and to help bring about the creation of a free, prosperous, and peaceful society.

*Pascal Salin*

My thanks to David M. Hart for his editorial contributions and his insights into the history of this period.

---

28. Ibid., p. 250.
29. Ibid., p. 250. Italics in the original.
30. A future volume in this series will contain Bastiat's *Economic Harmonies*.

## Frédéric Bastiat Chronology

| | |
|---|---|
| 1801 | Born in Bayonne, 30 June. |
| 1808 | Death of mother. Moves to Mugron with father, grandfather, and Aunt Justine. |
| 1810 | Death of father. |
| 1814–18 | Attends school at Sorèze. |
| 1819–25 | Works in Bayonne for his Uncle Monclar. |
| 1825 | Death of grandfather. Inherits part of his estate. |
| 1830 | The "three glorious days," 27–29 July. Louis-Philippe becomes "king of the French." |
| 1831 | Appointed county judge. |
| 1833 | Elected to the General Council of the Landes. |
| 1840 | Travels to Spain and Portugal. |
| 1844 | *On the Influence of French and English Tariffs on the Future of the Two Peoples.* |
| 1845 | Travels to Paris and London. |
| | *Cobden and the League.* |
| | *Economic Sophisms* (first series). |
| 1846 | Founds the Association pour la liberté des échanges. |
| | *To the Electors of the District of Saint-Sever.* |
| | Founds weekly journal *Le Libre-échange.* |
| 1847 | *Economic Sophisms* (second series). |
| 1848 | Revolution, 22–24 February. The republic is proclaimed. |
| | Elected to the Constituent Assembly, 23 April. |
| | Founds *La République française* and *Jacques Bonhomme.* |
| | *Property and Law.* |
| | *Justice and Fraternity.* |
| | *Property and Plunder.* |
| | *The State.* |
| | Louis-Napoléon elected president of the republic, 10 December. |

1849   Elected to the Legislative Assembly, 13 May.
       *Protectionism and Communism.*
       *Capital and Rent.*
       *Peace and Freedom, or the Republican Budget.*
       *Parliamentary Incompatibilities.*
       *Damned Money.*
       *Free Credit.*
1850   *Economic Harmonies.*
       *Plunder and Law.*
       *The Law.*
       *Baccalaureate and Socialism.*
       *What Is Seen and What Is Not Seen.*
       Departure for Rome, September.
       Dies in Rome, 24 December.


An expanded and detailed version of the life and works of Bastiat can be found at oll.libertyfund.org/person/25.

## Map of France Showing Cities Mentioned by Bastiat

Cartography by Mapping Specialists, Madison, Wisconsin.

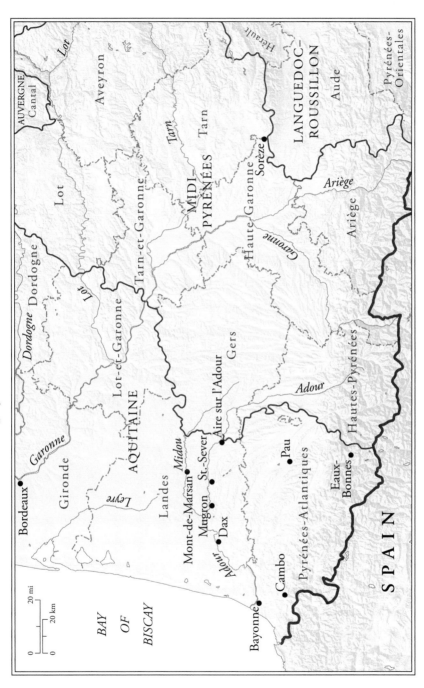

Map of Southwestern France

Cartography by Mapping Specialists, Madison, Wisconsin.

"The Law," "The State," and

Other Political Writings,

1843–1850

# → 1 ←

## Reflections on the Petitions from Bordeaux, Le Havre, and Lyons Relating to the Customs Service[1]

[vol. 1, p. 231. "Réflexions sur les pétitions de Bordeaux, Le Havre et Lyon, concernant les Douanes." April 1834. n.p.]

Free trade will probably suffer the fate of all freedoms; it will be introduced into our legislation only after it has taken hold of our minds. For this reason, we should applaud the efforts of the traders in Bordeaux, Le Havre, and Lyons even if the only effect of these efforts in the immediate future is to draw public attention to the matter.

However, if it is true that a reform has to be generally understood to be firmly established, it follows that nothing can be more disastrous than something that misleads opinion. And nothing is more likely to mislead it than writings that clamor for freedom on the basis of the doctrines of monopoly.

It would doubtless require a great deal of temerity for a simple farmer to disturb, through bold criticism, the unanimous chorus of praise that welcomed the demands of French trade both inside and outside France. No less would be needed to confirm his decision to do so than a firm conviction, I would even say a certainty, that such petitioning would be as disastrous in its effects on the general interest, and in particular on the agricultural interests of France, as its doctrinal effects would be on the progress of economic science.

In speaking out in the name of agriculture against the customs plans presented by the petitioners, I feel the need to begin by declaring that what

1. Following the July revolution, the government initiated a debate on the future of the protectionist system introduced under the restoration. Some politicians were in favor of the progressive introduction of commercial freedom, while some lobbies, using various sophisms, argued for a partial freedom that would not hurt their own business. One such lobby was composed of traders from Bordeaux, soon joined by traders from Le Havre and Lyons. Bastiat responded in a Bordeaux newspaper with the above article.

arouses my complaints in these plans is not the liberal element in their *premises,* but the *exclusive* content of their *conclusions.*

They demand that all protection be removed from *primary products,* that is to say from agricultural work, but that protection be maintained for the manufacturing industry.

I have come not to defend the protection that they are attacking but to attack the protection that they are defending.

Privilege is being claimed for a few; I come to claim freedom for all.

Agriculture owes its *cosseted sales* to the monopoly it exercises and its *unfairly priced purchases* to the monopoly to which it is subject. If it is just to relieve it of the first of these, it is no less so to free it from the second.[2]

To wish to deliver us to universal competition without subjecting manufacturers to the same situation is to damage our sales without relieving our purchases and to do just the opposite for manufacturers. If this is *freedom,* may I then have a definition of *privilege?*

It is up to agriculture to reject such attempts.

I make so bold here as to call upon the petitioners themselves and especially M. Henri Fonfrède. I urge him to refute my complaints or to support them.

I will show:

1. That, between the plan of the petitioners and the government system, there is community of principle, error, aim, and means;
2. That they differ only in one additional error for which the petitioners are responsible;
3. That the aim of this project is to set up an unjust privilege in favor of traders and manufacturers to the detriment of farmers and the general public.

§1.   *Between the petitioners' proposals and the protectionist system there is community of principle, error, aim, and means.*

What is the protectionist system? Let us hear M. de Saint Cricq's views on this.

"Work constitutes the wealth of a people, since on its own it has created material things that we need, and because general affluence consists in an abundance of these things." This is the principle.

---

2. (Paillottet's note) See vol. 2, pages 25ff. (*OC,* vol. 2, p. 25, "De l'influence du régime protecteur sur la situation de l'agriculture en France.")

"But it is necessary for this abundance to flow from the nation's work. If it were based on foreign work, domestic work would stop immediately." This is the error.

"Therefore, what should a farming and manufacturing country do? Limit its market to the products of its territory and its industry." This is the aim.

"And to do this, limit through duties, and prohibit as necessary, the products of the territory and industry of other peoples." This is the means.

Let us compare this approach with that of the petition from Bordeaux.

The petition divides all goods into four categories. The first and second cover food products and *raw materials that have not yet undergone any human transformation. In principle a wise economy would require that these two categories not be taxed.*

The third category is made up of objects that have undergone some preparatory work. This preparation enables *a few duties to be levied on them.* It can be seen, therefore, that according to the doctrine of the petitioners, *protection* begins as soon as *national* work begins.

The fourth category is made up of *finished products that can under no circumstances be useful to national work.* We consider these, says the petition, to be the most properly taxable.

Thus the petitioners claim that foreign competition damages national work; this is the error of the protectionist regime. They demand protection for work; this is the aim of the protectionist regime. They make this protection consist of duties on foreign work; this is the means used by the protectionist regime.

§2. *These two systems differ through one additional error for which the petitioners are responsible.*

However, there is an essential difference between these two doctrines. It lies entirely in the greater or lesser extension given to the meaning of the word *work.*

M. de Saint-Cricq extends it to cover everything. He therefore wishes to protect everything.

"Work constitutes the *entire* wealth of a people," says he. "The protection of the agriculture industry, the *entire* agriculture industry, the manufacturing industry, the *entire* manufacturing industry, is the cry that will always resound around this chamber."

The petitioners regard as work only that which is done by manufacturers, and therefore they accord the favors of protection only to this.

"*Raw materials have not yet undergone any human transformation, and in principle they should not be taxed.* Manufactured objects *can no longer be useful to national work; we consider these to be the most properly taxable."*

This gives rise to three questions which require examination: 1. Are raw materials the outcome of work? 2. If they are not something else, is this work so different from the work done by factories that it would be reasonable to subject them to opposing regimes? 3. If the same regime suits all types of work, should this regime be one of free trade or one of protectionism?

1. Are raw materials the outcome of work?

And precisely what are, I ask you, all the articles that the petitioners include in the first two categories of their proposals? What are *all types of wheat, flour, farm animals, dried and salted meat, pork, bacon, salt, iron, copper, lead, coal, wool, skins, and seeds,* if they are not outcomes of work?

What, it will be said, is an iron ingot, a ball of wool, or a bushel of wheat if not a product of work? Is it not *nature* that *creates* each?

Doubtless, nature creates the elements of all these things, but it is human work that produces their value. It is not given to men, to manufacturers, any more than to farmers, to create or make something out of nothing, and if by *work* you mean *creation,* all our work would be nonproductive and that of traders more so than any other!

The farmer therefore does not claim to have created wool, but he does claim to have produced *value,* by which I mean that through his work and expenditures he has transformed into wool substances that in no way originally resembled wool. What else does the manufacturer do when he converts wool into fabric?

In order for men to clothe themselves in fabric, a host of operations is necessary. Before the intervention of any human work, the true raw materials of this product are air, water, heat, light, and the gases and salts that have to be included in its composition. An initial operation converts these substances into fodder, a second into wool, a third into thread, and a fourth into a garment. Who would dare to say that no part of this operation constitutes work, from the first furrow of the plough that starts it to the final stitch that completes it?

And since, for greater speed in the completion of the end product—the garment—the work is divided among several categories of workers, you wish, through an arbitrary distinction, to determine that the sequence of these tasks should be the reason for their importance, so that the first does not even deserve the title of work and the last, work par excellence, should be the only one worthy of the *favors* of monopoly! I do not believe that one could push the spirit of system and partiality any further than this.

The farmer, people will say, unlike the manufacturer, has not done everything himself. Nature has helped him and, while there is some work involved, not everything in wheat is work.

But everything in its *value* is work, I repeat. I agree that nature has contributed to the material growing of the grain; I agree that this growth is exclusively its work; but you have to agree that I have obliged nature to do this by my work, and when I sell you wheat, I am not being paid for *the work of nature but for my own work*.

And, in this respect, manufactured objects would not be the products of work either. Are not manufacturers also helped by nature? Do they not make use of the weight of the atmosphere when using steam engines, just as I use its humidity with the help of the plough? Did they create the laws of gravity, of the transmission of force, and of affinity?

You will agree, perhaps, that wool and wheat are the product of work. But coal, you will say, is certainly the work, and only the work, of nature.

Yes, nature has made coal (for it has made everything), *but work has created its value*. Coal has no value when it is a hundred feet below ground. You have to find it, and this is work. It has to be taken to market, and this is work of a different kind; and mark my words, the price of coal in the marketplace is nothing other than the sum of all the wages paid for all the work of extraction and transport.

The distinction people have tried to make between raw materials and manufactures is therefore theoretically empty. As the basis for an unequal distribution of privilege, it would be iniquitous in practice, unless one wished to claim that although both are the result of work, the importing of one category is more useful than the other in the development of public wealth. This is the second question I have to examine.

2. Is it more advantageous to a nation to import so-called raw materials than manufactured objects?

Here I have to combat a very firmly entrenched belief.

"The more abundant the raw materials," says the Bordeaux petition, "the more manufactures increase in number and expand." "Raw materials," it says elsewhere, "provide endless opportunity for the work of the inhabitants of the countries into which they are imported." "Since raw materials," says the petition from Le Havre, "are the basic units of work, they have to be subject to a different regime and *immediately* admitted at the *lowest rate of duty.*"[3] "Among other articles whose low price and abundance are a necessity," states the petition from Lyons, "manufacturers all mention raw materials."

Doubtless it is advantageous for a nation that so-called raw materials should be abundant and at a low price; but I ask you, would it be advantageous for that nation if manufactured objects were high priced and few in number? In both cases this abundance and cheapness must be the fruit of free trade or this scarcity and high price must be the fruit of monopoly. What is supremely absurd and iniquitous is to want the abundance of the one to be due to free trade and the scarcity of the other to be due to privilege.

It will still be insisted and said, I am sure, that the duties that *protect* the work of factories are demanded in the general interest and that to import articles *that require no further human intervention* is to lose all the profit of labor, etc., etc.

Note the terrain into which the petitioners are being drawn. Is this not the terrain of the protectionist regime? Could M. de Saint-Cricq not produce a similar argument against the importation of wheat, wool, coal, and all materials that are, as we have seen, the products of work?

To refute this latter argument and prove that the import of foreign products does not damage national work is therefore to demonstrate that the regime of competition is just as suitable for manufactured objects as for raw materials. This is the third question I have asked myself.

In the interests of brevity, may I be allowed to reduce this demonstration to one example that includes them all?

An Englishman may export a pound of wool to France in a variety of forms, as a fleece, as thread, as fabric, or as a garment, but in all cases he will not import an equal quantity of value, or, if you like, of work. Let us suppose that this pound of wool is worth three francs raw, six francs as thread, twelve francs as fabric, and twenty-four francs when made into a garment. Let us also suppose that in whatever form the exportation is made the payment is made in wine, for, after all, it has to be made in something and nothing stops us from supposing that it will be in wine.

If the Englishman imports raw wool, we will export three francs' worth of wine; we will export six francs' worth if the wool arrives as thread, twelve

---

3. (Paillottet's note) The same petition wanted the protection of manufactured objects to be reduced, not immediately, but at an unspecified time and not to the lowest rate of duty but to a rate of 20 percent.

francs' worth if it arrives as fabric, and finally, twenty-four francs' worth if it arrives in the form of a garment. In this last case, the spinner, the manufacturer, and the tailor will have been deprived of work and profit, I know; one sector of *national work* will have been discouraged to the same extent, as I also know; but another sector of work that is *equally national,* wine making, will have been encouraged in precisely the same proportion. And since the English wool can arrive in France in the form of a garment only to the extent that all the workers who combined to produce it in that form are superior to French workers, all things considered, the consumer of the garment will have gained an advantage which may be considered to be a net one, both for him and for the nation.

Change the nature of the goods, the stage of their evaluation, and their source, but think the matter through clearly and the result will always be the same.

I know that people will tell me that the payment might have been made not in wine but in cash. I will draw attention to the fact that this objection could equally well be advanced against the importation of a primary product as against that of a manufactured product. Besides, I am sure that it would not be made by any trader worthy of the name. As for the others, I will limit myself to saying to them that money is a domestic or foreign product. If it is the former, we can do nothing better than to export it. If it is the latter, it must have been paid for out of national work. If we acquired it from Mexico, exchanging it for wine for example, and we then exchanged the wine for an English garment, the result is still wine exchanged for a garment, and we are totally in line with the preceding example.

§3.  *The petitioners' plan is a system of privileges demanded by trade and industry at the expense of agriculture and the general public.*

That the petitioners' plan creates unjust privileges that benefit manufacturers is a fact that, I believe, is only too well proved.

However, it is doubtless not so clear how it also grants privileges to trade. Let us examine this.

All other things being equal, it is to the public's advantage for raw materials to be used on the very site of their production.

For this reason, if people in Paris want to consume eau-de-vie from Armagnac, it is in Armagnac, not in Paris, that the wine is distilled.

It would, however, not be impossible to find a hauler who prefers to transport eight barrels of wine than one barrel of eau-de-vie.

It would not be impossible either for a distiller to be found in Paris who preferred to import the primary rather than the finished product.

It would not be impossible, if this came within the field of protectionism, for our two industrialists to come to an understanding to demand that wine be allowed to enter the capital freely but that eau-de-vie be *taxed* with heavy duties.

It would not be impossible that, when they sent their demand to the protectionist authority, in order to conceal their selfish outlooks the better, the hauler would mention only the interests of the distiller and the distiller only those of the hauler.

It would not be impossible for the protectionist authority to see an opportunity to acquire an industry for Paris in this plan and to increase its own importance.

Finally, and unfortunately, it would not be impossible for the good people of Paris to see in all this only the *extended* views of those enjoying protection and the protectionist authority and to forget that, in the final instance, it is on them that the costs and contingencies of protectionism always fall.

Who would wish to believe that the petitioners from Bordeaux, Lyons, and Le Havre, following the clamor of generous and liberal doctrines, would achieve by common accord a similar result and a totally identical system organized on a grand scale?

"It is mainly in this second category (the one that includes materials *that have not yet undergone any human transformation*)," the petitioners from Bordeaux say, "that the mainstay of our merchant navy is to be found.... In principle, a wise economy would require that this category, as well as the first, not be liable to duty. The third might have *duties levied* and the fourth we consider to be the most appropriate to the levying of duties."

"Whereas," say the petitioners from Le Havre, "it is *essential* to reduce raw materials *immediately* to the *lowest rate* of duty, so that industry can in turn put to work the *naval forces* that supply it with its initial and essential means of work...."

The manufacturers could not be more polite to shipowners. For this reason, the petition from Lyons requests the free introduction of raw materials to prove, it is said, "that the interests of manufacturing towns are not always in opposition to those of coastal ones."

Do we not seem to hear the Parisian hauler, whom I mentioned before, formulating his request thus: "Whereas wine is the principal element I transport, in principle it should not be liable to duty; as for eau-de-vie, this can have *duty levied on it*. Whereas it is essential to reduce wine immediately to the lowest rate of duty so that the distiller can use my vehicles, which supply him with the initial and essential element of his work ..." and to hear the distiller requesting the free import of wine to Paris and the exclusion of eau-de-vie, "to show that the interests of distillers are not always in opposition to those of haulers."

In sum, what would be the results of the system being proposed? They are these:

It is at the price resulting from competition that we, the farmers, sell our primary products to manufacturers. It is at the price resulting from monopoly that we buy it back from them.

If we work in circumstances that are less favorable than those of foreigners, so much the worse for us. In the name of freedom we are condemned.

But if manufacturers are less skillful than foreigners, so much the worse for us. In the name of privilege we are condemned once more.

If people learn to refine sugar in India or weave cotton in the United States, it is the raw sugar and cotton in the form of fiber that will be transported *in order to use our naval forces* and we, the consumers, will pay for the pointless transportation of the residues.

Let us hope that, for the same reason and in order to supply lumberjacks *with the initial and essential element of their work,* we will bring in firs from Russia with their branches and bark. Let us hope that gold from Mexico will be imported in mineral form. Let us hope that, in order to have leather from Buenos Aires, herds of cattle will be transported.

It will never come to that, people will say. And yet it would be rational. But this so-called rationality borders on absurdity.

Many people, I am convinced, have adopted the doctrines of the protectionist regime in good faith (and certainly what is happening is scarcely likely to change their minds). This does not surprise me in the least; what does surprise me is that, when doctrines have been adopted with regard to one point, they are not adopted with regard to everything, since error also has its own logic. As for me, in spite of all my efforts, I have not been able to find a single objection that can be made to the regime of absolute exclusion that cannot be applied equally to the *practical* system of the petitioners.

# → 2 ←
## The Tax Authorities and Wine[1]

[vol. 1, p. 243. "Le Fisc et la vigne." January 1841. n.p.]

The production and sale of wines and spirits must of necessity be affected by the treaties and laws on finance that are currently the subject of deliberations in the chambers.

We will endeavor to set out:

1. The new obstacles that the draft law dated 30 December 1840 is threatening to impose on the wine-producing industry;
2. Those obstacles implicit in the formal rationale that accompanies this draft;
3. The results to be expected from the treaty signed with Holland;
4. The means by which the wine-producing industry might succeed in freeing itself.

§1. *The legislation on wines and spirits is a clear departure from the principle of equality of duties.*

At the same time it places all the classes of citizen whose industry it regulates in a separate, heavily taxed category, it creates among these very classes

---

1. Taxes on wine and spirits were very detrimental to the Chalosse. Introduced in 1806, twice withdrawn and reestablished between 1814 and 1816, the taxes did not change much until 1840, when the European crisis led to greater government spending. On 30 December 1840 a bill for taxes on wines and spirits in order to lower the deficit was presented to parliament. Being from a wine-producing region, Bastiat was somewhat concerned for himself, because he had some vines on his own property; however, as a member of the General Council, he was even more concerned by a law that was very hard on the local farmers, whose main crop was grapes for wine producing. This study was presented to the General Council in 1841. See "On the Wine-Growing Question," p. 25 in this volume. See also the entry for "Wine and Spirits Tax" in the Glossary of Subjects and Terms.

inequalities of a second order: all are placed outside common law; each is held at varying degrees of distance.

It appears that the minister of finance has taken not the slightest notice of the *radical inequality* we have just pointed out, but on the other hand he has shown himself to be extremely shocked by the *secondary inequalities* created by the law: he considers as *privileged* the classes that have not yet suffered from all of the rigors it imposes on other classes. He is devoted to removing these nice differences not by relaxing them but by making them worse.

However, in pursuit of *equality* thus understood, the minister remains faithful to the traditions of the creator of the institution. It is said that Bonaparte originally established tariffs that were so moderate that the receipts did not cover the costs of collection. His minister of finance drew to his attention the fact that the law annoyed the nation without providing the treasury with funds. "You are an idiot, M. Maret," replied Napoléon. "Since the nation is complaining about a few impositions, what would it have done if I had added heavy taxes to them? Let us first accustom them to the exercise; later we can adjust the tariff." M. Maret realized that the great captain was no less an able financier.

The lesson has not been lost, and we will have the opportunity of seeing that the disciples are preparing the reign of *equality* with a prudence worthy of the master.

The principles on which the legislation on wines and spirits is based are clearly and energetically expressed in three articles flowing from the law dated 28 April 1816:

> Art. 1. Each time wine, cider, etc., is taken away or put somewhere else, a *circulation duty* will be paid. . . .
> Art. 20. In towns and villages with a total population of two thousand people and more[2] . . . the treasury will levy an *entry duty* . . . , etc. . . .
> Art. 47. When the wine, cider, etc., is sold retail, *a duty* of 15 percent of the said sales price will be levied. . . .

In this way, each *movement* of wine, each *entry,* and each *retail sale* lead to the payment of a duty.

Side by side with these rigorous and, one might say, strange principles, the law establishes a few exceptions.

---

2. (Bastiat's note) This figure varied at times.

With regard to *circulation duty:*

> Art. 3. The following will not be subject to the duty levied under Art. 1:
> 1. Those wines and spirits that an owner has transported from his press or a public press to his cellars or storehouses;
> 2. Those that a sharecropper, farmer, or holder of a long-term lease for rent hands over to the owner or receives from him by virtue of official leases or customary use;
> 3. The wine, cider, or perry[3] that is dispatched by an owner or farmer from the cellars or storehouses in which his harvest has been deposited, and provided that it is the produce of the said harvest, whatever place it is sent to and the standing of the person to whom it is sent.
>
> Art. 4. The same exemption will be granted to traders, wholesalers, brokers, middlemen, agents, distillers, and retail traders, for the wines and spirits they have had moved from one to another of their cellars situated within the confines of the same *département.*
>
> Art. 5. The transport of wines and spirits that are removed for dispatch abroad or to the French colonies will equally be exempt from circulation duty.

The entry duty did not allow any exceptions.
With regard to *retail duty:*

> Art. 85. Owners who wish to sell the wines and spirits they produce at retail will be granted a discount of 25 percent on the duties they will have to pay. . . .
>
> Art. 86. However, they will be subject to all the obligations imposed on professional retailers. Notwithstanding this, inspections by agents will not take place within their domiciles provided that the premises on which their wines and spirits will be sold at retail are separate from these.

Thus, to summarize these exceptions:

Exemption from circulation duty for the wines of their harvest that owners send from their own property to their own property elsewhere *throughout the entire territory of France;*
Exemption from the same duty for the wine that traders, merchants, retailers, etc., have had transported from one to another of their cellars situated in the same *département;*

---

3. An alcoholic drink made from pear juice.

Exemption from the same duty for wine that is exported;

A discount of 25 percent of the retail duty for owners;

Exemption from inspection visits by agents within their own domiciles where the premises on which this sale is made are separate from these.

Now, here is the text of the draft law put forward by the minister of finance:

Article 13. Exemption from circulation duty on wines and spirits will be allowed only in the following cases:

1. For wines which the harvester has transported from his press to his cellars and storehouses or from one to another of his cellars, *within the confines of the same village or a bordering one;*

2. For wines and spirits that a farmer or the holder of a long lease hands over to his owner or receives from him, *within the same limits of a single village,* by virtue of official leases or customary use.

Article 3 of the law dated 28 April 1816 and Article 3 of the law dated 17 July 1819 are repealed.

Article 14. Wines and spirits from their harvest that owners have transported from one part of their own property to another, outside the limits laid down in the preceding article, will be exempt from circulation duty, provided the owners acquire the necessary permit and are subject at the place of destination to all the obligations imposed on wholesale merchants with the exception of the payment of a license.

Article 25. The provision of Article 85 of the law dated 28 April 1816, which allows to owners who sell at retail the wines and spirits of their own production an exceptional discount of 25 percent of the retail duty that they have to pay, is repealed.

We would greatly exceed the limits we have set ourselves if we carried out a comprehensive examination of the points raised by the draft law, and we will have to limit ourselves to a few short observations.

First, does Article 13 of the draft law repeal Articles 4 and 5 of the 1816 law? An affirmative answer appears to result from the following absolute phrase: *Exemption will be allowed only if . . .* , which implies the exclusion of all categories not listed in the remainder of the disposition.

However, a negative answer may be concluded from the disposition that ends Article 13, since, by repealing only Article 3 of the 1816 law, it apparently maintains Articles 4 and 5.

In this last case we consider that there is a certain anomaly in reserving for traders and retailers *within the confines of the département* a right that is restricted for owners to *the limits of a village.*

Second, since the new measures aim to increase revenue, we should no doubt expect them to be burdensome for taxpayers. It is possible, however, for these measures to exceed their aim and lead to disadvantages out of all proportion to the advantages hoped for.

In effect, these measures deal a deathblow to large-property owners through Article 13 and to small-property owners through Article 20.

As long as exemption from circulation duty was limited to the confines of a *département,* it could have resulted only in exceptional evils. The ownership of vineyards in several *départements* is rare, and where this occurs owners will have cellars in each of these *départements.* However, it is very frequent for an owner to have vineyards in several neighboring villages that do not border on one another; and in general, in this situation, it is in his interest to gather his harvest into the same cellar. The new law obliges him either to increase the number of his buildings, making surveillance more difficult, or to bear the cost of circulation duty for a product that is already very heavily taxed and whose sale will perhaps take place only several years later.

And what will the exchequer gain? Very little, unless the owner, as M. de Villèle hopes, drinks all his wine to recover the duty a little earlier.

It will doubtless be said that Article 14 of the draft will counteract this disadvantage. We will wait and examine the spirit and effect of this later.

On the other hand, small owners draw a very considerable advantage from retail sales: that of keeping their wooden barrels from year to year. From now on, they will be obliged each year to make an outlay often in excess of their means to buy them. I will say without hesitation that this disposition contains the cause of total ruin for a great many small owners. The purchase of wooden barrels is not something that they can avoid or delay doing. When the harvest arrives, it is essential, whatever the price, to acquire the wood in which to store it; and if the owner does not have the money, he is at the mercy of the sellers. Wine producers have been seen to offer half their harvest to obtain the means to house the other half. Retail sales would avoid this extreme situation, one that will often recur now that this possibility will in practice be forbidden to them.

The two modifications or, as the minister puts it, the two *improvements* to existing legislation, which we have just been analyzing, are not the only ones contained in the draft law dated 30 December. There are two others on which we ought to make a few comments.

Article 35 of the law dated 21 April 1832 had converted the *circulation, entry, and retail* duties into a *single tax,* levied at the entrance to towns, thus allowing free circulation within these towns and abolishing customs investigations.

According to Article 16 of the draft, this single tax will now replace only the entry and retail duties, with the circulation and license duties continuing to be levied as they were in 1829, so that one could say of it, in chorus with the singer,

> That this *single* tax will have two sisters.

Another difficulty arises here. In order to establish the single tax (1832 law, Article 36), "The sum of all the annual yields, from all the duties to be replaced, is to be divided by the total value of annual production."

Since circulation and license duties are no longer included in those *to be replaced,* they should not be part of the dividend; this being so, since the quotient will be correspondingly lower, the general public will be subject to the old barriers, with no benefit for the treasury.

The implication is that if the minister intends the yield of current taxation to be maintained, circulation and license duties will be levied twice, once directly by virtue of the new law and a second time through the *single tax,* since they are included as elements in the calculation of this tax.

Last, a fourth modification introduces a new basis for conversion of spirits into liqueurs.

This is not all. The minister makes it clearly felt that it will not be long before he raises the tariff on wines and spirits to the levels of 1829. Many distinguished authorities, he said, considered that it was the right time to cancel the exceptions allowed in 1830.

Many other such authorities consider that if the minister refrains from making a formal proposal in this respect, it is to allow the Chamber of Deputies the honor of this initiative.

We will now leave the reader to measure the space that separates us from the July revolution. Ten years have scarcely elapsed, and here we are with our legislation on wines and spirits shortly to be indistinguishable from that under the empire or restoration, except for an increase in charges and severity.

§2. *If only this growth in severity had as its aim just the current interest of the tax authorities, we could at least hope that it satisfies their requirements in full. But it does not even leave us this illusion, and by proclaiming that they wish a particular dispensation to carry the day, the tax authorities are warning us that we have to expect new requirements until such time as this dispensation has been fully implemented.*

"We have considered it just (says the "statement of the reasons") to restrict the exemption to circulation duty in favor of owners to the just limits within which it might be legitimately claimed; that is to say, to restrict it to the products of their harvest which they intend for their consumption and that of their family, in the actual place of production. Beyond this, it was a *privilege* that nothing justified and that *violated the principle of the equality of duties. For the same reason,* we propose to cancel the discount of 25 percent to the wine producer who sells the wines of his production at retail."

Now, from the instant the government has *the equality of duties* as its aim, with the understanding that this language means the subjection of all the classes affected by the law on wines and spirits to the full total of the obstacles weighing on the most maltreated class, then for as long as this aim is not reached, the most rigorous measures can be only the prelude to still more rigorous measures.

We should fear it above all in the knowledge that the master[4] has carried out and recommended a pitiless but prudent tactic in this connection.

We have seen that the 1816 law extended the owner's exemption from circulation duty *to the entire territory of France.*

Shortly afterward it was restricted to the *limits of the département* or to bordering *départements* (law dated 25 March 1817, Article 81).

Later it was reduced to the limits of bordering districts (law dated 17 July 1819, Article 3).

Now, the proposal is being made to circumscribe it to the *limits of a* village or bordering villages (draft law, Article 13).

One step further and it will have totally disappeared.

And this step undoubtedly will be taken, for while these successive restrictions have circumscribed the *privilege,* they have not destroyed it. There still remains one case in which the harvester consumes a wine that *has circulated* without paying *circulation duty,* and it will not be long before it is said

4. Napoléon Bonaparte.

that *this is a totally unjustified privilege, which violates the principle of equality of taxes.* At the level of application, therefore, the tax authorities have compromised with *principle* but have also, in principle, made clear their intent, and is it not enough for once that they have come down from the *district* to the *commune* without stopping at the *canton?*

Let us be quite sure, therefore, that the reign of *equality* is coming and that in a short time there will be no exceptions at all to this principle. *On each removal or displacement* of wine, cider, or perry,[5] duty will be levied.

But should this be said? Yes, we will be expressing our entire thoughts, even though we may be suspected of giving way to exaggerated distrust. We believe that the tax authorities have perceived that, when the circulation duty is extended to all without exception, *equality* will have reached only half of its career; it will still subject owners to the yoke of *customs inspection.*

We consider that in Article 14 the tax authorities have sown the seed of this secret intention.

What other aim could this measure have?

Article 13 of the draft restricts the exemption from circulation duty to the *limits of the village commune.*

The rationale is careful to declare that anything *exceeding* this exemption is *a privilege that is totally unjustified.*

And Article 14 immediately restores the right that Article 13 removed from us; it gives it back without limits, provided that the owner subjects himself to the obligations imposed on wholesale merchants.

A concession like this is designed to arouse our mistrust.

This floury sack bodes no good.[6]

Note the specific character of this Article 14.

First, it appears to be a corrective. Article 13 may have seemed rather harsh; Article 14 comes to offer some consolation.

Second, it goes somewhat further than sugar-coating the pill; it hides the pill and hints at the customs inspection without referring to it explicitly.

---

5. See p. 12, note 3.

6. This line is probably from Molière's comedy *Les Fourberies de Scapin* (1671). Scapin is a servant who extorts money from his wealthy and aristocratic patrons in a complex comedy about love and social station. A "sack" plays an important role in the subterfuge as Scapin fools the father Géronte into hiding in the sack while Scapin proceeds to hit it with a stick at periodic intervals. See *Œuvres complètes de Molière*, vol. 5, pp. 548–49, where there is a similar passage to Bastiat's quotation.

Last, it pushes prudence to the point of being *optional;* it goes even further, it makes Article 13 *optional.* How can we complain? Can we not escape circulation duty by taking refuge in customs inspections and find shelter against customs inspections in circulation duty?

Let us hope we are mistaken! However, we have witnessed an increase in the tariff, and we have witnessed an increase in circulation duty; we are right to worry that customs inspections will increase, too. As the teller of fables told us: "What is small will grow large . . . , *provided that God keeps it alive.*"[7]

The gradual progress toward *equality* is also shown in the development of retail duty.

We have seen that current legislation allows owners two forms of exemption in this respect: first, by giving them a discount of 25 percent on the duty; second, by exempting the owner from home inspections when the point of sale is in a different location.

For the moment, current legislation merely limits itself to calling for the withdrawal of the first of these exemptions. However, the principle of equality is not satisfied, since owners continue to enjoy a privilege denied to café owners, that is to say, the privilege of not having to open their houses, their bedrooms, and their cupboards to the gaze of customs agents, always provided that, in order to sell their wine, they rent premises on an official lease.

§3.   *If we redirect our gaze to France's external relations and how these relate to the sale of wine, we will find scarcely any grounds to console us for the internal regime that burdens our industry.*

We cannot examine here all the matters that relate to this huge subject. We have to limit ourselves to a few considerations on a question currently being negotiated, a trade treaty with Holland.

After having announced during the session on 21 January that according to this treaty: "Our wines and spirits in barrels will be exempt from any customs duty upon entry into Dutch territory; should they be imported in bottles, they will enjoy a discount of three-fifths of the duty on wine and half for spirits," the minister exclaimed:

"You will be aware, sirs, that in all sales negotiations carried out by the government, one of its most pressing considerations has always been to expand as far as possible the market for our wine production by opening up new outlets in foreign countries. It is with particular satisfaction that we

---

7. From Jean de La Fontaine's poem "Le Petit poisson et le pêcheur."

submit to your approval the means of relieving the sufferings of a sector of trade that is so worthy of our solicitude."

From this pompous preamble, who would not think that our wines are going to enjoy considerable sales in Holland?

To measure the amplitude of the concessions that our negotiators obtained from the Dutch government, you ought to know that foreign wines and spirits are subject to two different import duties in Holland: *customs duty* and *excise duty*.

If you consult the table at the end of this article,[8] you will see that the Dutch government has combined its reductions so cleverly that our luxury trade (wine in bottles) enjoys a tax relief of 10½ percent for the Gironde and 21 percent for the Meuse, and our essential trade (wine in barrels) 12 percent for the east and 1⅓ percent for the west of France. This fine outcome has caused such *great satisfaction* in our negotiators that they have been quick to reduce by 33⅓ percent the duties on cheese and white lead[9] made in Holland.

§4.    *When a significant sector of the population considers itself to be oppressed, it has just two means of regaining its rights: revolutionary means and legal means.*

It appears that successive governments in France have vied with one another to instill in the wine-producing classes a disastrous prejudice to the effect that their sole hope of escape lies in revolutions.

As a matter of fact, the 1814 and 1815 revolutions at least won the wine-producing classes a great many promises, and we see from the actual text of the laws of the time that the Restoration claimed to be keeping indirect taxation only as an exceptional resource, which was essentially temporary (law dated 1816, Article 257; and law dated 1818, Article 84).

Scarcely had this empowerment consolidated somewhat, however, when its promises evaporated along with its fears.

The 1830 revolution,[10] to do it justice, promised nothing, but it did effect some notable tax relief (laws dated 17 October and 12 December 1830).

We can already see that it was thinking not only of returning to the old legislation but also of giving it an aspect of rigor that was unknown in the great days of the Empire and the Restoration.

8. "Droits d'Entrée en Hollande" (Import Duties in Holland).
9. In French, *céruse*. Refers to a white lead pigment used in cosmetics.
10. See the entry for "Revolution of 1848" in the Glossary of Subjects and Terms.

Thus, in troubled times, the tax authorities make promises, compromise, and relax their severity.

In peaceful times, they retract their concessions and march on to new conquests.

We repeat that we are surprised that the authorities do not fear that this comparison will strike people's minds and that they will not draw this deplorable conclusion: "Legal means are killing us."

This would certainly be the most dreadful of errors; and experience, which may be invoked in this regard, proves on the contrary that no reliance should be placed on promises and alleviations wrung through fear from a tottering government.

A government newly come to power may well, under pressure of circumstances, temporarily renounce part of its revenues; but too many charges weigh on the new government for it to abandon totally the intention of regaining them. More than any other government, has it not certain ambitions to satisfy, persons to reassure, prejudices to overcome? Domestically, a government newly come to power has given rise to jealousy, bitterness, and miscalculations; does it not have to develop some apparatus for policing and repression? Externally, it arouses fear and mistrust; does it not have to surround itself with walls and increase its fleets and armies?

Therefore, seeking relief through revolution is an illusion.

However, we believe, and strongly, that the wine-producing population can, through an intelligent and persevering use of legal means, succeed in improving its situation.

We draw its attention in particular to the resources offered by the *right of association*.

For the last few years, manufacturers have acknowledged the advantage of being represented by special delegations to the government and the chambers. Manufacturers of sugar, woolen cloth, and linen and cotton fabrics have their committee of delegates in Paris.

In this way, no tax or customs measure likely to affect these industries can be passed without enduring the crucible of a long and rigorous inquiry, and everyone is aware how much the domestic producers of sugar owe the success of their struggle to the vigor of their *association*.

If the manufacturing industry had not introduced the system of delegation, perhaps it would have fallen to the wine-producing industry to set the example. But what is certain is that the wine-producing industry cannot refuse to enter the arena into which others have gone before. It is only too clear that inquiries in which its voice is not heard are incomplete and further that it has everything to lose in leaving the field open to interests that are often rivals.

In our opinion, each wine-producing area ought to have a committee in the town that is located at the heart of its commercial activities. Each of these committees would nominate a delegate, and the association of delegates in Paris would form the *central committee*.

Thus, the basin of the Adour and its tributaries, those of the Garonne, the Charente, the Loire, the Rhone, and the Meuse, and the *départements* that make up the Languedoc, Champagne, and Burgundy would all have their own delegates.

We have had discussions with several people in this institution without encountering a single one who disputed the usefulness of our proposed legislation, but we have to answer a few objections they made to us.

We have been told:

"The wine-producing industry has its natural delegates in its deputies.

"It is difficult to obtain the assistance of such a large number of interested parties, the majority of whom are scattered throughout the countryside.

"The financial situation of France does not allow any hope of the abolition of indirect taxation; besides, indirect taxation has indisputable advantages alongside a great many disadvantages."

1. Are deputies delegates of the wine-producing industry?

Clearly, when an electoral body invests a citizen with legislative functions, it does not reduce this mission to matters pertinent to industry. Other considerations determine its choice, and we should not be surprised if a deputy, even when he represents a wine-producing *département,* has not beforehand made an in-depth study of all the questions relating to the trade in and the duties on wines and spirits. Even less, once he has been nominated, can he concentrate his attention exclusively on a single interest when so many serious matters claim it. Therefore, in the special committees that deal with sugar, iron, and wine, he can see nothing but an advantage in having available the information and documents which would otherwise be physically impossible for him to seek out and coordinate on his own. Besides, the precedents established by the manufacturers remove any value from this objection.

2. It is also said that it is difficult to obtain long-lasting assistance from people scattered about the country.

We, for our part, believe that this difficulty is exaggerated. It would doubtless be insurmountable if active and painstaking assistance were to be expected from each person concerned. But, in situations like these, the most active participate on behalf of the others, and towns act on behalf of the countryside. This does not cause a problem when their interests are identical, and since there is a wine-producing committee in Bordeaux, there is no reason why there should not be one in Bayonne, Nantes, Montpellier, Dijon, or Marseilles, and from these to a central committee there is just one further step to take. It is when difficulties are exaggerated that nothing is achieved. It is certainly easier for three hundred manufacturers of sugar rather than several thousand manufacturers to reach agreement and organize themselves. However, just because something does not happen by itself it should not be concluded that it cannot be done. It should even be recognized that if the masses find it harder to organize themselves, they acquire through organization an unstoppable momentum.

3. Last, the objection is made that France's financial situation rules out any hope that it would be able to give up the income from consumption tax.

But that again is to circumscribe the question. Does the organization of a central committee establish in advance that its sole mission would be to pursue the total abolition of this tax? Would it have nothing else to do? Do customs questions relating to wine not arise every day? In the discussions that resulted in the treaty with Holland, are people sure that the intervention of the committee would have had no influence on the terms of this treaty? And, as for indirect taxation, is there nothing between total abolition and the total maintenance of the current regime? Do not the method of collection, the means of preventing or repressing fraud, and pertinent powers and jurisdictions offer a vast scope for reform?

Moreover, it should not be thought that everything has been said with regard to the principal question. It is not our place to formulate an opinion on the consumption tax; there are leading authorities and great examples both for and against it. Consumption tax is the rule in England and the exception in France. Well, now! This problem has to be settled. If the system is bad in principle, it has to be abolished; if it is deemed to be good, it has to be improved, its exceptional character has to be removed, and it has to be made both less heavy and more productive by *its being generalized.* Here, perhaps, lies the solution to the great ongoing debate between the tax authorities and the taxpayer. And who can say that the movement of minds generated by the setting up of industrial committees and the regular exchanges of views made either between them or by their agency, between the general public and the government, will not hasten this solution?

## Import Duties in Holland

| | Unit | CUSTOMS DUTIES | | | | EXCISE DUTIES | | | | | Total of Current Import Duties | Duties Modified by Treaty | Difference |
|---|---|---|---|---|---|---|---|---|---|---|---|---|---|
| | | Main Duty | Importers | Stamp Duty | Total | Main Duty | Additional Amounts | Importers | Stamp Duty | Total | | | |
| | hectol. | fr. c. | fr. c. | fr. c. | fr. c. | fr. c. | fr. c. | fr. c. | fr. c. | fr. c. | fr. c. | fr. c. | |
| **WINES** By Sea | | | | | | | | | | | | | |
| In Barrels | " | " 21 | " 03 | " 43 | " 67 | 26 71 | 6 68 | 3 47 | 3 68 | 40 54 | 41 21 | 40 54 | 1 ⅖ |
| In Bottles | " | 12 29 | 1 60 | " 43 | 14 32 | 26 71 | 6 68 | 3 47 | 3 68 | 40 54 | 54 86 | 46 28 | 10 ½ |
| By Land | | | | | | | | | | | | | |
| In Barrels | " | 6 57 | " 85 | " 43 | 7 85 | 26 71 | 6 68 | 3 47 | 3 68 | 40 54 | 48 39 | 40 54 | 12 |
| In Bottles | " | 19 67 | 2 85 | " 43 | 22 66 | 26 71 | 6 68 | 3 47 | 3 68 | 40 54 | 63 26 | 49 67 | 21 ½ |
| **SPIRITS** | | | | | | | | | | | | | |
| In Barrels | " | 2 12 | " 27 | " 43 | 2 82 | 42 40 | 10 60 | 5 51 | 5 85 | 64 36 | 67 18 | 64 26 | 4 ⅕ |
| In Bottles | " | 9 84 | 1 28 | " 43 | 11 55 | 42 40 | 10 60 | 5 51 | 5 85 | 64 36 | 75 91 | 70 12 | 7 ⅔ |

# ⇥ 3 ⇤
## On the Wine-Growing Question

[vol. 1, p. 261. "Mémoire présenté à la société d'agriculture, commerce, arts et sciences, du département des Landes sur la question vinicole." 22 January 1843. n.p.]

Memoir Presented to the Société d'agriculture, commerce, arts, et sciences du département des Landes on the Wine-Growing Question (22 January 1843)

*Sirs,*

In one of your previous sessions you set up a commission to investigate the causes of the hardship afflicting the wine-growing sector of the *département* of the Landes and the means by which it would be possible to combat this.

Circumstances have not allowed me to transmit to the commission the work it entrusted to me. I regret this most sincerely, since the contribution of the enlightened men that form the commission would have made it more worthy of you. Although I am bold enough to believe that my ideas are not so very different from those that they would have authorized me to submit to you, I must nevertheless assume full responsibility. . . .

Sirs, proving first of all that the hardship experienced by our wine-growing people is genuine and presenting a living picture of this to you would both satisfy the logical order of this report and win over your interest and goodwill for it. I am only too ready to sacrifice this consideration to the desire not to intrude on your time too much, since, ready as I am to admit unreservedly and without fear of being wrong that we are not all in agreement on the causes of the decline of the industry we are discussing, there is at least no disagreement between us on the fact that this decline exists.

A detailed analysis of all the causes that have contributed to this unfortunate result would also lead to amplifications that are too wide-ranging. We would need first of all to examine those causes that are beyond our means of action. One of these is competition from the southeast of France, which is growing daily, encouraged by the gradual improvement in our transport systems. Another is the relative inferiority that appears to be the lot of regions that, like the Chalosse, are not structured to replace cultivation using manpower with that using oxen.

We would then need to distinguish the causes of suffering for which the producer himself is responsible. Has he devoted enough time to improving his cultivating and wine-producing procedures? Has he been farsighted enough to limit his planting? Has he been clever enough to adapt his products to the changes that may have been noted in the needs and tastes of consumers? Have efforts been made, through the choice and blend of grape varieties or other means, to substitute quality for the quantity of wine produced, insofar as outlets are limited, since this might have restored the balance of income to a certain extent? And has the Société d'agriculture itself not been too sparing of encouragement to an agricultural sector from which a third of our population earns its living, while being only too ready to encourage the introduction of exotic plants, whose success is more than uncertain?[1]

Finally, we need to list those causes of our hardship that must be laid at the door of government measures whose effect has been to hinder the production, circulation, and consumption of wine, and this would lead me to examine the special influence on our region of direct taxes, indirect taxes, city tolls, and customs regulations.

I will limit the scope of this report to the last three of these causes of our sufferings, first because they are much the most immediate determinants of our decline and second because I consider that they are susceptible to present or future changes, which public opinion may hasten or delay at will through demonstrations for or against them.

Before discussing this subject, I have to say that it has been examined with impressive intellectual talent, along with several other economic questions, by one of our colleagues, M. Auguste Lacome of Le Houga,[2] in a paper that was read during one of your previous sessions. The author assesses the situation of vineyard owners with equal sagacity and impartiality. By granting concessions that were perhaps too great, he acknowledges that the ever-increasing needs of the country, the communes, and the factories make

---

1. The society recommended the introduction of rapeseed, tobacco, and mulberries for the rearing of silkworms.
2. Le Houga is a village close to the eastern border of the Landes in the Gers *département*.

it unlikely that our public charges will be reduced. He asks the question whether, supposing this to be so, it is just to give satisfaction to all interests at the expense of the interests of wine alone and, after establishing that this is as contrary to natural justice as it is to the letter of the law, he seeks to find out by what means the resources requested up to now from our sector might be replaced. Going down this route and directing his meditations to practical use is to show genuine capability and the ability to rise above the crowd of critical souls who limit themselves to the facile task of criticizing what is wrong without suggesting a remedy. I will not take the liberty of deciding whether the author has always succeeded in indicating the proper sources from whom compensation for the tax on wines and spirits should be requested; I will limit myself to suggesting that the general public should be enabled to judge this by including Lacome's paper in our *Annals*.

Sirs, I am approaching the subject I propose to discuss. Has the triple chain of gross impositions that our wines encounter through city dues, indirect taxes, or customs tariffs, depending on whether they seek outlets in towns, nationwide, or through export sales, affected production or caused the burdens that have given rise to our complaints?

It would be very surprising if there were conflicting opinions on this.

What has become of the many commercial houses in Bayonne whose sole activity in days gone by was to export our wines and spirits to Belgium, Holland, Prussia, Denmark, Sweden, and the towns of the Hanseatic League? What has become of the inland navigation system, which we have seen so active and which incontestably gave rise to the many concentrations of population established on the left bank of the Adour? What has become of the proliferating trade investment in a product that because of its property of improving with age would under normal conditions increase in value with time, a product that was effectively a savings bank for our forefathers, spread a comfortable existence among the working classes of the time, and was the traditionally acknowledged source of all the wealth that still survives in Chalosse? All of that has disappeared together with freedom of production and trade.

In the face of this twin assault on our property by the protectionist regime and overbearing taxation, faced with a burden so straightforwardly explained by the obstacles that block our domestic and foreign outlets, nothing surprises us more than the haste with which the tax authorities seek to find the cause of our sufferings elsewhere, unless it is the credulity of the general public in being taken in by their sophisms.

This, however, is what we witness every day. The tax authorities claim that too many vines have been planted and each person repeats, "If we are suffering, it is not because we lack trade or because the weight of taxes is suffocating us, but because we have planted too many vines."

I have in previous times attacked this assertion, but it expresses an opinion that is too widespread and the tax authorities have made it too deadly a weapon against us for me not to return to my refutation in a few words.

First of all, I would very much like our opponents to set the limits they intend to impose on the growing of vines! I never hear reproaches made that wheat, flax, or orchards invade too high a proportion of our territory. The comparison of supply and demand and costs compared with sale prices are the limits between which the expansion or contraction of industries operates. Why would vine growing, contrary to this general law, extend more widely as it becomes more ruinous?

People will say all that is theory. Well then, let us see what the facts reveal.

Through the offices of a minister of finance,[3] we learn that the wine-growing area of France was 1,555,475 hectares in 1788 and 1,993,307 hectares in 1828. The increase is therefore in the ratio of 100 to 128. In the same period of time, the population of France, which according to Necker[4] had been 24 million, increased to 32 million, a ratio of 100 to 133. The cultivation of vines, far from expanding unreasonably, has not even kept up with the increase in numbers of the population.

We could check this result through research into consumption if we had statistical data relating to this. As far as we know, this has been done only for Paris and has provided the following result:

| | Population | Total Consumption | Consumption per Inhabitant |
|---|---|---|---|
| 1789 | 599,566[5] | 687,500 hectoliters[6] | 114 liters |
| 1836 | 909,125[7] | 922,364 hectoliters[8] | 101 liters |

3. (Bastiat's note) M. de Chabrol, "Report to the King."
4. Jacques Necker.
5. (Bastiat's note) Mémorial de chronologie [The Chronological Gazette].
6. (Bastiat's note) Lavoisier.
7. (Bastiat's note) Annuaire du bureau des longitudes [The Yearbook of the Longitudes Office].
8. (Bastiat's note) Ibid.

Thus, sirs, it is undeniable that in this half-century and while all branches of production have made such remarkable progress, the most natural thing we produce has remained at the very least stationary.

We should conclude that the so-called encroachment of vines is based on allegations as contrary to logic as to fact, and after we have been assured that we are not mistaken in attributing our suffering to the administrative measures that have limited all of our outlets, let us examine the character and effects of these measures more closely.

At the top of the list, we should place the indirect tax on wines and spirits and the duties on circulation, dispatch, consumption, license, transportation, entry, and retail—a sorry and incomplete list of the subtle inventions by which the tax authorities are paralyzing our industry and greedily extracting from it, *indirectly,* more than one hundred million every year. Far from giving any hint of a foreseeable lessening in these rigors, they redouble them from year to year and although, in 1830, they were obliged in a revolutionary spirit,[9] so to speak, to agree to a reduction of forty million, a reduction that has ceased to be noticeable, they have never allowed a session to be completed without expressing their regret and complaining about it.

It has to be said that the wine-producing populations have rarely brought a practical business attitude to bear in their efforts to escape from this regime of arbitrary exceptions. Driven by the more immediate impact of their own sufferings or by the necessities of the time, either they have demanded, vehemently, the total abolition of all consumption taxes, or they have bowed unreservedly under a system they considered monstrous but irremediable, thus swinging from blind confidence to cowardly demoralization.

The pure and simple abolition of indirect contributions is obviously an illusion. Demanded in the name of equality of duties, it implies the abolition of all consumption taxes, from those imposed on salt and tobacco to those bearing on wines and spirits, and what bold reformer would succeed in decreasing budgeted public expenditure immediately to the level of budgeted income reduced to the four headings of direct taxation? No doubt the time will come, and we should hasten its coming through our efforts as well as our hopes, when private industry, with a morale lifted by experience and expanded by a sense of association, will encroach on the domain of public

9. Bastiat is making a joke here about how the revolution accidentally forced a temporary reduction in taxes because of turmoil and confusion. See also the entry for "Revolution of 1848" in the Glossary of Subjects and Terms.

services; and government, reduced to its essential function, the maintaining of internal and external security, will require only the resources to meet this sphere of activity, thus enabling a host of taxes that undermine the liberty and equality of our citizens to be removed from our financial system. But how far from this trend are the views of those who govern us and the all-powerful forces of public opinion! We are being drawn inexorably and perhaps providentially in opposite directions. We ask everything from the state: roads, canals, railways, encouragement, protection, monuments, education, conquests, colonies, and military, maritime, and diplomatic supremacy; we want to civilize Africa and Oceania and what else? Like England, we are obeying a force for expansion that is directing all our resources to be centralized in the hands of the state; we cannot therefore avoid seeking, like England, the exercise of power in taxes on consumption, the most fruitful, regularly increasing, and even the most tolerable of all taxes, when properly understood, since it is then mingled with the act of consumption itself.

But should we conclude from this that all is well with the current situation, or at least that our ills are irremediable? I do not think so. On the contrary, I think that the time has come to subject indirect taxation, still in its infancy, to a revolution similar to that which the land register and equalization have brought to taxes on land.

I in no sense aspire here to the formulation of an entire system of indirect taxes, since this would require knowledge and experience, which I am far from possessing. However, I hope that you will not find it out of place for me to lay down a few principles if only to give you a glimpse of the huge field awaiting your consideration.

I have said that indirect taxation was still in its infancy. Perhaps it will be felt that it is somewhat presumptuous to judge a work of Napoléon in this way. However, it must be realized that a tax system is always of necessity imperfect at its outset, since it is established under the influence of some urgent need. Is it to be imagined that if a need for funds gave rise to a land tax in a country in which this type of public revenue was unknown, it would be possible at the first try to achieve the perfection that has been achieved in France only at the cost of fifty years of work and a hundred million of expenditure? How therefore could indirect taxation, so complicated in nature, have achieved from its inception the final degree of perfection?

A rational law for a good system of consumer taxes would be this: *make the tax as comprehensive as possible with regard to the number of objects it falls on and as moderate as possible with regard to its level.*

The closer indirect taxation gets in practical terms to these two rules, the more it will fulfill the conditions that ought to be found in an institution of this kind:

1. Make each person contribute in accordance with his wealth;
2. Avoid damaging production;
3. Hinder the movements of industry and commerce as little as possible;
4. Curtail profits and consequently the incidence of fraud;
5. Avoid imposing restrictions that make arbitrary exceptions of any specific class of citizen;
6. Follow unswervingly all the fluctuations of public wealth;
7. Adapt with the greatest flexibility to all the distinctions that a sensible policy can establish between products, depending on whether they are essentials or convenience products and luxuries;
8. Get involved, readily, in cultural mores by emphasizing with regard to public opinion the respect with which it does not fail to enshrine everything that is undeniably useful, moderate, and just.

It appears in this case that our financial system has been based on the diametrically opposing principle, namely the *limitation of the number of objects taxed and the maintenance of the tax on a high level.*

A choice has been made, from a thousand products, of two or three—salt, wine and spirits, and tobacco—and these have been heavily burdened.

Once again, it could scarcely have been otherwise. The head of state, desperate for money, has not been concerned with perfection or justice. He has been concerned with making funds flow into the treasury *abundantly and easily,* and since he had a force capable of overcoming all resistance, he had only to pick a *product that was eminently taxable* and inflict repeated blows on it.[10]

With regard to us, the public, wines and spirits must have been the first to come to his mind. They are universally used and promise abundant resources. They are difficult to transport and could hardly escape the attention of the tax authorities. They are produced by a scattered population, which is apathetic and inexperienced in public conflict, and their collection did

10. (Bastiat's note) "It has been acknowledged that, of all the products that can be taxed, wines and spirits yield the most [taxes] and are the *easiest* to collect." M. de Villèle.

not seem likely to subject the authorities to insurmountable resistance. The Decree dated 5th Ventôse[11] in the Year XII was passed accordingly.

However, two opposing principles can produce only opposing consequences; it could not therefore be denied that indirect taxes such as those instituted by the Decree of Year XII[12] are a perpetual violation of the rights and personal interests of citizens.

Indirect taxation is unjust simply by virtue of the exceptions it makes.

It offends equity because it raises as much from the wages of a workman as from the income of a millionaire.

Indirect taxation is bad economics because by raising too much revenue it limits consumption, affects production, and tends to restrict the very source that feeds it.

It is not good policy, since it encourages fraud and is incapable of either preventing or repressing fraud without encircling the activities of production with formalities and obstacles laid down in the most barbarous code that has ever dishonored the legislature of a great people.

If, therefore, men of goodwill and intelligence, the councils of the *départements* and districts, the Chambers of Commerce, the societies for agriculture, the committees of industrialists and wine producers, these lobby groups that fashion public opinion and draw up material for legislation, wish to give their work in this context a useful and practical direction, if they wish to achieve results that reconcile the collective requirements of

---

11. See the entry for "Republican calendar" in the Glossary of Subjects and Terms.

12. It is not clear to what decree Bastiat is referring. Year XII of the Republican calendar would place it sometime in 1804, which was the year the Constitution of Year XII (18 May 1804) was decreed, creating the new empire of Napóleon. In April 1803 duties were enacted on the importation of cotton goods, and all French protective duties were codified in February and April 1806. Soon after becoming emperor, Napóleon passed a number of decrees putting in place his continental blockade against Britain (the Berlin Decree of November 1806 and the Milan Decree of November 1807).

Bastiat might also have had in mind a passage from Jean-Baptiste Say's *Traité d'économie politique,* which refers to a decree of May 1812 and states that "whenever a maximum of price has been affixed to grain, it has immediately been withdrawn or concealed. The next step was to compel the farmers to bring their grain to market and prohibit the private sales. These violations of property, with all their usual accompaniments of inquisitorial search, personal violence, and injustice, have never afforded any considerable resource to the government employing them. In polity as well as morality, the grand secret is not to constrain the actions but to awaken the inclinations of mankind. Markets are not to be supplied by the terror of the bayonet or the saber." (Say, *A Treatise on Political Economy,* bk. 1, chap. 17, p. 101.)

our civilization and the interests of each industry and class of citizen, they should not have recourse to a puerile list of unattainable requirements and still less should they give way to sterile discouragement. They should work with perseverance toward the fertile principle we have just set out, with all its just and practical consequences.

The second cause of the decline in wine producing is the regime of city tolls. In the same way that indirect taxes hinder the general circulation of wine, city tolls drive the wine trade away from population centers, that is to say, its major markets of consumption. This is the second barrier placed by the spirit of taxation between the seller and the purchaser.

Except for the fact that city tolls are applied to specific locations, they are a branch of indirect taxation, and for this reason their proper basis in terms both of yield and of justice is the one we have just assigned to this kind of tax: *generalization with regard to its area of operation, limitation with regard to the intensity of its application.* In other words, such tolls must cover everything but must subject each product to a duty too small to be noticed. City tolls are all the more properly held to this principle of good administration and equity in that unlike combined duties they do not even have the trite excuse of being hard to collect. However, we see that the principle of taxing only certain key products has won in this instance and that highly populated towns base half, three quarters, and even all of their revenues on wines and spirits alone.

If the tariffs of city tolls were left to the sovereign decision of municipal councils, wine-producing *départements* would be able to retaliate against manufacturing *départements.* All the working groups of the population would then be seen to engage in an internal customs conflict, a huge turmoil, but one from which the common sense of the general public would probably sooner or later, by way of negotiation, cause the application of the principle we have invoked. It is unquestionably to avoid these domestic disorders that the central power has been given the authority to regulate the tariffs of city tolls, an authority that is an essential part of the franchises of towns and of which they have been deprived for the benefit of the state only on condition that the state is responsible for keeping an even balance between all the various interests.

What use has the state made of this excessive prerogative? If there is one product that the state ought to have protected and removed from municipal rapacity, that product is wine, which already provides the community with so many and such heavy tributes, and yet it is precisely wine that it allows to be overburdened. What is more, a law has set limits to these extortions; a vain barrier

> For the crucible of decrees
> Has evaporated the law.[13]

Would we be showing ourselves to be too demanding if we asked that the tariffs of city tolls be gradually reduced to a maximum not exceeding 10 percent of the value of the goods?

The protectionist regime is the third cause of our hardship, and perhaps the one that has most immediately caused our decline. It is therefore worth your particular attention, especially since it is currently the subject of a lively debate between all of the interests concerned, at the end of which debate your opinion and wishes cannot remain far apart.

Customs duties originated as a means of creating revenue for the state. They are an indirect tax, a giant national toll; and as long as they retain this characteristic it is an act of injustice and bad management to remove them from this rule governing any consumer taxes: *universality and reasonableness of the tax*.

I would go even further: as long as the customs service is a purely *fiscal* institution, it is in its interest to tax not only imports but also exports, under the twin consideration that the state is thus creating for itself a second source of revenue that costs nothing to collect and that is borne by foreign consumers.

However, it has to be said that it is no longer *tax* but *protection* that is the aim of our customs measures, and in order to judge them from this point of view, we would have to go into arguments and developments which have no place in this report. I will limit myself therefore to considerations that have a direct bearing on our subject.

The idea that dominates the protectionist system is this: if we succeed in creating a new form of industry in our country or in giving new impetus to an industry that already exists, we will be increasing the mass of *work* and consequently the *wealth of the nation*. Now, a simple way of causing a product to be made within is to prevent its coming in from outside. From this we get prohibitive or protectionist duties.

---

13. From "Le Ventru, aux électeurs de 1819," a satirical song by Pierre Jean de Béranger. See Béranger, *Chansons*, pp. 301–3. In the song Béranger mocks in turn the electors, the prefects, the mayors, the clergy, the conservative Ultras, and the liberals.

This system would be based on reason if it were in the power of a decree to add something to the wherewithal of production. But there is no decree in the world that can increase the number of hands or the fertility of the soil of the nation, add a cent to its capital or an additional ray to its sunshine. All that a law can do is to change the combinations of action that these means exercise over each other, substitute an artificial direction for the spontaneous direction of production, and force it to solicit the services of a miserly agent instead of a generous one: in a word, to divide it, scatter it, mislead it, and set it against greater obstacles but never to increase it.

Allow me a comparison. If I said to someone, "You have just one field and you grow cereals in it, part of which you sell to purchase flax and oil. Do you not see that you depend on two other farmers? Divide your field into three; divide your time, your advance payments, and your strength into three and grow olive trees, flax, and cereals together." This man would probably have good arguments to put against me, but if I had authority over him I would add: "You do not know your own interests; I forbid you, under pain of paying me huge taxes, to purchase oil and flax from anyone whomsoever." I would oblige this man to diversify his crops, but would I have increased his well-being? That is the prohibitionist regime. It is a bad pruning of the industrial tree, which, while adding nothing to its sap, diverts the tree from growing fruit in favor of *suckers*.

In this way, in each zone protectionism encourages the production of *consumable* value but discourages to the same degree *tradable* value, from which we must rigorously conclude—and this is what brings me back to the decline of wine producing in France—that protectionist tariffs cannot promote the production of certain objects we obtain from abroad without restricting the industries that supply us with the means of trade, that is to say, without causing hindrance and suffering to that production that harmonizes best with the climate, the soil, and the gifts of the inhabitants.

And, sirs, do not the facts once again energetically support the rigor of these deductions? What is happening on either side of the Channel? On the other side, with this nation that nature has endowed so profusely with the wherewithal and the ability needed for the development of manufacturing industry, it is precisely the population of the workshops that is devoured by destitution, misery, and starvation. Language has no expression to describe such hardship; goodwill is powerless to relieve it, and the laws are powerless to repress the disturbances to which it gives rise.

On this side of the Channel, a clear sky and generous sun should generate inexhaustible sources of wealth at every corner of the territory. Well then! It is exactly the wine-producing population that offers the vision of destitution, a sad mirror of the destitution that reigns in the workshops of Great Britain.

Doubtless the poverty of French vineyard owners is less widely trumpeted than that of English workmen. Its ravages are not felt by turbulent urban masses, and it is not proclaimed by the thousand outlets of the press morning and evening, but it is no less real. Travel through our sharecropping farms and you will see families in straitened circumstances, their food mere corn and water, people whose entire consumption does not exceed ten centimes per day per person. Half of this may be supplied to them, apparently as a loan but in effect as a gift from the owner. For this reason, the fate of the owner is relatively no better. Enter his house, one that is falling down, with furniture handed down from generation to generation bearing witness to the struggle that exists, an incessant and bitter struggle against the attractions of well-being and modern comforts that surround him and that he keeps out. Initially you will be tempted to see a ridiculous side to these constant privations, this ingenious parsimony, but take a closer look and you will soon see its sad and touching and, I might say, almost heroic side, for the thought that sustains him in this painful conflict is the ardent desire to keep his sons up to the level of his ancestors, to avoid descending from generation to generation down to the lowest ranks of the social scale, an intolerable suffering from which all his efforts will not spare him.

Why therefore are these people, who are so rich in iron and fire, so rich in capital and productive abilities, whose men are active, persevering, and as constant as the cogs of their machines, dying of want on piles of coal, iron, and fabric? Why are these other people with fertile land and generous sun succumbing to deprivation surrounded by their vines, silk, and cereals? Solely because an economic error incorporated in the protectionist regime has forbidden them to trade mutually in their various riches. Thus, this deplorable system, already ruined on theoretical grounds by economic science, also has ranged against it the terrible argument of the facts.

It is therefore not surprising that we are witnessing the start of a reaction in favor of liberal ideas.[14] These ideas have arisen in the highest of our intel-

14. Bastiat is referring to the first glimmers of liberal economic reform in the 1820s and 1830s. See also the entries for "Huskisson, William," and "Tanneguy Duchâtel, Charles Marie," in the Glossary of Persons.

ligent minds, and, before rallying the forces of public opinion, they have penetrated the sphere of power, in England with Huskisson and in France with M. Duchâtel.[15]

Doubtless, the government is generally in no great hurry to hasten the development of public freedoms. There is, however, one exception to be made in favor of free trade. It can never be through ill will but only through systematic error that those in power paralyze this freedom. They are only too aware that if the customs service were brought back to its original purpose—the creation of public revenue—the treasury would gain, the task of the government would be made easier because of its neutrality in the face of industrial rivalries, and peace between nations would have its most powerful guarantee in the trade relations between peoples.

———

We should therefore not be surprised by the trend toward favoring free trade that is becoming apparent in the high circles of governments in Prussia, Austria, Spain, England, Belgium, and France, in the guise of customs unions, trade, commercial treaties, etc., etc.[16] These are all steps toward the *holy alliance of peoples.*

Unquestionably, one of the most significant official demonstrations of this trend is the treaty negotiated two years ago between France and England.[17] At that time if the wine-producing industry had kept an eye on its genuine interests, it would have glimpsed, and through its share of influence hastened, a prosperous future of which it probably had no idea. In effect, at no time had such brilliant prospects been open to southern France. Not only was England lowering the duties she had imposed on our wines, but

15. (Bastiat's note) I am not so much referring to the minister, with whose acts I am not familiar, but to the political writer who is a well-known member of the Adam Smith School.

16. See the entry for "Zollverein" in the Glossary of Subjects and Terms.

17. In the early 1840s there began what is called an "entente cordiale" between France and England following the tensions that arose because of the Eastern Crisis of 1840 (when war broke out between Egypt and the Ottoman Empire). Lord Aberdeen and Guizot wanted to improve relations with a new trade treaty, but tensions remained over such issues as the Franco-Belgian customs union, Franco-British rivalry over Spain, and the suppression of the slave trade. In 1842 Sir Robert Peel began to move in the direction of unilateral trade liberalization, which would result in the repeal of the Corn Laws in 1846. In 1842 he began to remove prohibitory duties on raw materials and foodstuffs, such as the removal of import and export duties on wool.

through an innovation of incalculable effect she was also replacing the fixed duty that was so disadvantageous to ordinary wines with a progressive duty which, while maintaining a reasonably high tax on luxury wine, reduced very considerably the duty on lower-quality wine. This meant that not only a few aristocratic cellars but also the farms, workshops, and cottages of Great Britain were open to our production. No longer was it just the Aï, Laffitte, and Sauterne[18] that had the privilege of crossing the Channel; the entire wine-producing districts of France were suddenly faced with twenty million consumers. I will not try to calculate the effect of a revolution on this scale and its influence on our vineyards, merchant navy, and trading towns, but I do not think anyone can doubt that, under the sway of this treaty, production, revenue, and investment in land in our *département* would have increased rapidly and prodigiously.

From another point of view, the principle of a progressive rate of duty was a fine victory and a step toward the general adoption of an ad valorem tax, the only just and equitable system that conforms to the true principles of science. A uniform duty is by nature aristocratic; it allows for the maintenance of a few relationships only, and only between high-born producers and consumers. A progressive duty based on value would bring the popular masses of all nations into relations of common interest.

However, France could not lay claim to such advantages without opening its market to some of the products of English industry. The treaty was likely, therefore, to be resisted by manufacturers. This was not slow to manifest itself in a clever, persevering, and desperate way. The producers of coal, iron, and fabric made their grievances plain and did not limit themselves to passive opposition. Associations and committees were organized within each industry; permanent delegates were given the mission of winning acceptance for special interests by ministries and chambers. Abundant and regular subscriptions assured the support of the most widely distributed newspapers to this cause and, through their pages, gained the sympathy of public opinion, which was misled. It was not enough to cause the treaty to fail to be concluded temporarily; it had to be made impossible, even at the risk of a general conflagration, and to this end the patriotic pride that is such a sensitive fiber in French hearts had to be unceasingly inflamed. Since that time, we have seen these groups stir up, with devilish Machiavellianism, all the

18. Bordeaux wines.

long-dormant jealousies of the nation and finally succeed in sabotaging all the negotiations started with England.

A short time afterward, the governments of France and Belgium developed the idea of merging the economic interests of the two nations.[19] Once again this was a source of hope for the industries of the south and a source of alarm for the manufacturing monopoly. This time, circumstances were not favorable for the monopoly; working against it were the interest of the masses and the industries in trouble, as well as the influence of the government and every popular instinct, quick to see in the customs union the prelude to and guarantee of a closer alliance between these two children of the same fatherland. Journalists who had supported it with regard to the English question were of little succor in the Belgian case for fear of being discredited in the eyes of the general public. All they could do was either counter the customs union through insinuations made with a great deal of oratorical circumspection or retreat into shameful neutrality.

However, the neutrality of the newspapers in the most important question to be raised in France at the present time could not be maintained for very long. The monopoly had no time to lose; it needed a prompt and vigorous demonstration to bring about the failure of the customs union and continue to keep our south of France under their heel. This was the mission that an assembly of delegates, which became famous under the name of the deputy who was its president (*M. Fulchiron*), accomplished successfully.

What were the wine-producing interests doing in the meantime? Alas! They scarcely managed laboriously to produce a few shadows of association. When they should have gone into combat, committees were recruited with difficulty in the depths of a province. With no organization, resources, order, or mouthpiece, is it surprising that they were defeated for the second time?

But it would be foolish to lose heart. It is not in the power of a few

19. Under the influence of the liberal revolution in France in 1830, which ushered in the July Monarchy of Louis-Philippe, Belgium broke away from the Netherlands and became independent with its own constitution and monarch, Leopold of Saxe-Coburg. There was a two-way battle in trade policy between the nations who favored free trade, the Netherlands and Great Britain, on the one hand, and the more-protectionist nations of France and Belgium on the other. Britain eventually removed most of its trade barriers unilaterally in 1846, and in 1860 France and Britain signed a free-trade treaty, the Cobden-Chevalier Treaty. In 1861–62 Britain, France, and Belgium signed a similar free-trade treaty. At the same time the German states were gradually adopting a common external tariff and removing internal German trade restrictions as part of the Zollverein (or Customs Union), which expanded in 1833.

fleeting intrigues to bury major social questions in this way and to reverse permanently the trends that are leading to the unity of human destinies. These questions may be restricted for a time, but they rise up again and these trends regain strength; at the time I am speaking to you, these questions have already been referred to our national assemblies by the speech from the throne.

Let us hope that this time the committees of wine producers will not be absent from the battlefield. Privilege has immense resources; it has delegates, finance, and supporters who have more or less declared themselves in the press. It is strong in the unity and swiftness of its movements. Let the cause of freedom be defended by the same means. It has truth and immense numbers in its favor; let it also acquire *organization*. Let committees rise up in all the *départements* and join with the central committee in Paris. Let them increase their financial and intellectual resources. May they finally help the central committee to carry out the difficult mission of being a powerful support for the government if it moves toward establishing free trade and an obstacle if it yields to the exactions of the special interests of a privileged industrial sector.

But is it part of your portfolio to give support to this task?

Well, sirs, is not your title the *Société d'agriculture et commerce*? Are you not summoned from all corners of the land as being the men most familiar with the knowledge relating to these two branches of public wealth? Do you not recognize that, since they are exhausted by disastrous measures, they no longer provide not just well-being but even subsistence for the population, and are you not allowed to take such dearly held interests under your wing and do what Chambers of Commerce are doing every day? Are you not a society to be taken seriously? Is the extent of your attributions legally limited to the inspection of some foreign plant, imaginary fertilizer, or common sector of speculative agronomy? And is it enough for a question to be serious for you to waive your credentials immediately?

I am convinced that the Société d'agriculture would not wish to reduce its influence to this degree. I have the honor of proposing that it adopt the following resolution:

## DRAFT RESOLUTION

The Société d'agriculture des Landes, taking note of the hardship afflicting the people of the Chalosse and Armagnac, who are particularly devoted to the cultivation of vines;

Acknowledging that the principal causes of this hardship are indirect taxation, city tolls, and the protectionist regime;

With regard to indirect taxation, the Society considers that the owners of vineyards, for as long as the state in order to meet its expenditures cannot forfeit its current revenues, cannot hope that a source of revenue as important as this be cut without replacing it with another, but nevertheless the Society still supports the vineyard owners' just protestations against the regime of arbitrary exceptions in which this system of taxation has placed them. It does not consider it impossible that a means of reconciling the requirements of the treasury, the interest of the taxpayers, and the truth of the principle of the equality of charges might be found in an extension of this type of tax at a reasonable level and with a less-complicated method of collection.

It is through a similar deviation from the laws of equity that city tolls were authorized to base themselves almost exclusively on wines and spirits. By reserving the right to sanction the tariffs decided by vote in the communes, it appears that the aim of the state must have been to prevent city tolls, overwhelmed with the industrial hostility aroused, from becoming between provinces what the customs system is between nations, a perpetual ferment of discord. However, it is in that case difficult to explain how the state can have tolerated and seconded the coalition of the interests of all the towns against one single sector of production. All the abuses of city tolls would be prevented if the law restored their franchises to the communes and intervened in the arrangement of the tariffs only to set them at a general, uniform limit that would not be exceeded to the disadvantage of any product, without distinction.

The Society also attributes the decline of wine producing in the *département* of the Landes to the absolute stoppage of exports of wines and spirits through the port of Bayonne, an effect that the protectionist regime could not fail to produce. It has also gained the hope of a speedy improvement in our external outlets from the recent words of the king of the French.[20]

The Society does not pretend that the obstacles that the spirit of monopoly will put in the path of the accomplishment of this benefit do not exist. It will point out that by temporarily turning the action of tariffs to the advantage of a few industrial firms, France never intended to relinquish the right to use customs dues for a purely fiscal purpose; rather, far from this, France has always proclaimed that *protection* was by its very nature temporary. The time has come at last when private interests should be subjugated to the in-

---

20. Louis-Philippe.

terests of consumers, industries suffering hardship, the maritime commerce of trading towns, and the overall interest of peace between nations of which trade is the surest guarantee.

The society expresses the wish that future treaties should, as far as possible, be founded on the principle of duties proportional to the value of the goods, which is the only true and fair system and the only one that is able to extend to all classes the benefits of international trade.

Foreseeing all the debates that are bound to take place between rival industries when the reform of the customs system takes place, the society believes it would be abandoning the cause that it has just taken under its patronage if it left the *département* of the Landes without the resources to take part in the combat which is being prepared.

Consequently, and in the absence of special committees, whose support it regrets not being able to lean upon in these circumstances, it has decided that the Commission of Wine Producers, which has already been nominated in the session of 17 April 1842, will continue its functions and will communicate with the committees for the Gironde and Paris.

Copies of this resolution will be sent through the good offices of the secretary of the Society to the minister for trade, to the Commissions of the chambers involved, and to the secretariat of the committees of wine producers.

# $\Rightarrow 4 \Leftarrow$
## Property and Law

[vol. 4, p. 275. "Propriété et loi." Originally published in the 15 May 1848 issue of *Le Journal des économistes*.]

The confidence of my fellow citizens has given me the title of *legislator*.

I would certainly have declined this title if I had understood it as Rousseau did.

"He who dares undertake to provide institutions to a people," he said, "must feel that he is capable, so to speak, of changing human nature, of transforming each individual who, of himself, is a perfect and solitary whole, into a part of a much greater whole from which this individual is to receive to a certain degree his life and being; of changing the physical constitution of man in order to strengthen it, etc., etc. If it is true that a great prince is a rare man, what is to be said of a great legislator? The first has only to follow the model that the second has put forward. The second is the inventor of the machine, while the first is only the workman who assembles it and makes it work."[1]

Since Rousseau was convinced that the social state was a human invention, he had to place law and the legislator on a high pedestal. Between the legislator and the rest of the human race, he saw the distance or rather the abyss that separates the inventor from the inert matter of which the machine is made.

According to him, the law ought to transform people and create or not create property. According to me, society, people, and property existed before the laws, and, to limit myself to a particular question, I would say: It is not because there are laws that there is property, but it is because there is property that there are laws.

The opposition of these two systems is radical. The consequences that

---

1. Rousseau, *Du contrat social,* bk. 2, chap. 7.

result from them are constantly divergent; let me therefore set out the question clearly.

I warn you first of all that I am taking the word *property* in a general sense and not in the restricted sense of *landed property*. I regret, and probably all economists regret with me, that this word involuntarily awakens in us the idea of possession of land. What I mean by *property* is the right the worker has over the value he has created through his work.

That having been said, I ask myself whether this right is a creation of the law or if it is not, on the contrary, prior to and higher than the law, whether it was necessary for the law to give birth to the right of property or whether, on the contrary, property was a fact and right that existed before the law and that had given rise to it? In the first case the mission of the legislator is to organize, amend, and even eliminate property if he thinks this right; in the second his powers are limited to guaranteeing it and ensuring that it is respected.

From the preamble to a draft constitution issued by one of the greatest thinkers of modern times, M. Lamennais, I quote:

> The French people declare that they acknowledge rights and duties that predate and are greater than all the positive laws and that are independent of them.
>
> These rights and duties, directly handed down by God, are summarized in the triple dogma expressed by these sacred words: equality, liberty, fraternity.

I put the question whether the rights of property are not among those that, very far from deriving from positive law, predate the law and are its raison d'être.

This is not, as might be thought, a slight or pointless question. It is a vast and fundamental one. The answer to it is of the highest concern to society, something you will be convinced of, I hope, once I have compared the origins and effects of the two opposing theoretical systems.

Economists consider that *property*, like the *person*, is a providential fact. The law does not give existence to one any more than to the other. Property is a necessary consequence of the constitution of man.

In the full sense of the word, man is *born a property owner*, since he is born with needs whose satisfaction is essential to life, with organs and faculties whose exercise is essential to the satisfaction of these needs. These faculties are merely an extension of the person, and property is just an extension of these faculties. To separate man from his faculties is to make him die; to separate man from the product of his faculties is once again to make him die.

There are political writers who are greatly preoccupied with finding out how God ought to have made man. For our part, we study man as God has made him. We ascertain that he cannot live without satisfying his needs, that he cannot provide for his needs without work, and that he cannot work if he is not *certain* of applying the fruits of his work to his needs.

This is why we consider that property is a divine institution and that its *safety and protection* are the object of human law.

It is so true that property predates the law that it is acknowledged even by primitive people who have no laws or at least no written laws. When a savage has devoted his work to building himself a hut, no one disputes his possession or ownership of it. Doubtless another savage who is stronger than he can drive him out but not without angering and alarming the entire tribe. It is actually this abuse of strength that gives rise to association, agreement, and the *law,* which places public force in the service of property. Therefore the law arises out of property, a far cry from property arising from law.

It can be said that the principle of property is even recognized by animals. The swallow tends her young family with care in the nest she has built with her own efforts.

Even plants live and thrive by assimilation, by *appropriation*. They *appropriate* substances, the elements of air and salts that are within their reach. You have only to interrupt this phenomenon for them to dry up and die.

In the same way, men live and develop through *appropriation*. Appropriation is a natural and providential phenomenon that is essential to life, and *property* is only appropriation that has become a right through work. When work has rendered *assimilable* and *appropriable* substances that were not so, I really do not see how it can be claimed that, in law, the phenomenon of appropriation has to be attained for the benefit of an individual other than he who has carried out the work.

It is in view of these primordial facts, necessary consequences of the very constitution of man, that the law intervenes. Since the aspiration toward life and development may induce a strong man to despoil a weak one, thus violating the rights of production, it has been agreed that the strength of all would be devoted to the prevention and repression of violence. The purpose of the law is therefore to ensure respect for property. It is not property that is conventional but law.

Let us now seek the origin of the opposing theoretical system.

All of our past constitutions proclaimed that *property* is sacred, which appears to assign to our coming together as a society the purpose of the free development either of individuals or of particular associations by means of work. This implies that property is a right that predates the law, law's only objective being to guarantee *property*.

I wonder, however, whether this declaration has not been introduced into our charters instinctively, so to speak, by virtue of catchwords, of language spoken long ago, and above all I wonder whether it is at the root of all social convictions.

Now, if it is true, as people say, that literature is the expression of society, doubts may be raised in this connection, since it is certain that never have political writers, after having respectfully saluted the principle of property, so often called for the intervention of the law, not in order to have property respected but to amend, alter, transform, fine-tune, weigh down, and organize property, credit, and labor.

Now, this supposes that an absolute power over people and property is attributed to the law and consequently to the legislator.

This may distress us but it should not surprise us.

From where do we draw our ideas on these subjects, especially our notion of law? In Latin books and in Roman law.

I have not studied my Roman law, but it is enough for me to know that this is the source of our ideas to be able to assert that these ideas are erroneous. The Romans had to regard property as purely conventional, a product and an artificial creation of the written law. Obviously, the Romans could not, as political economy does, go back to the constitution of man and perceive the relationship and necessary links between these phenomena: needs, faculties, work, and property. This would have been a suicidal error. How could they, who lived by pillage, all their property being the fruit of plunder and their means of existence based on the labor of slaves, have brought into their legislation, without shaking the foundations of their society, the notion that the true title of property was produced by work? No, they could neither say this nor think it. They had to have recourse to the following empirical definition of property: *jus utendi et abutendi*,[2] a definition that relates only to effects and not to causes or origins, since they were clearly obliged to keep the origins dark.

It is sad to think that the science of law in our country and in the nine-

---

2. "The right of using and abusing."

teenth century is still at the level of ideas that the presence of slavery must have inspired in the classical world, but there is an explanation for this. The teaching of law is a monopoly in France, and monopoly rules out progress.

It is true that jurists do not mold the entire range of public opinion, but it has to be said that university and church education is a marvelous preparation for the young people of France to receive the erroneous notions of jurists on these subjects since, as though the better to make sure of this, for the ten finest years of our life, it plunges us all into this atmosphere of war and slavery that enveloped and permeated Roman society.

Let us not therefore be surprised to see reproducing itself in the eighteenth century this Roman idea that property is a mere convention and a legal institution, that far from law being a corollary of property, it is property that is a corollary of law. We know that according to Rousseau not only property but also society as a whole was the result of a contract, an *invention* originating in the mind of the legislator.

"Social order is a sacred right which forms the basis of all the others. However, this right *does not come from nature*. It is therefore based on *conventions*."[3]

Thus, the right that is the basis of all the others is purely *conventional*. Therefore *property,* which is a subsequent right, is also *conventional. It does not come from nature.*

Robespierre was imbued with the ideas of Rousseau. From what the pupil had to say on property, we can recognize the theories and even the form of oratory of the master.

> Citizens, I will first of all put before you a few articles which are necessary to complete your theory of *property*. Let no one be alarmed by the use of this word. You souls of mud, who esteem only gold, I do not wish to touch your treasures, however tainted their source. . . . For my part, I would prefer to be born in Fabricius's hut than in Lucullus's palace, etc., etc.[4]

I will draw to your attention here that when you analyze the notion of property, it is irrational and dangerous to make this word a synonym

3. Rousseau, *Du contrat social,* bk. 1, chap. 1.

4. Gaius Fabricius Luscinus was a Roman ambassador and consul (282 B.C.) renowned for his probity, incorruptibility, and parsimonious life. He was much admired by Cicero as a model of good behavior. Lucius Licinius Lucullus (117 B.C.–57 B.C.) was a successful Roman general who amassed a huge fortune during his twenty years of military service. He used his wealth to build sumptuous palaces, libraries, and gardens in Rome.

of opulence and in particular of ill-gotten opulence. Fabricius's cottage is just as much an item of property as Lucullus's palace. However, may I draw the reader's attention to the following sentence, which sums up this entire outlook?

> In defining liberty, this primary need of man, the most sacred of the rights he *holds from nature,* we have correctly stated that its limit lies in the rights of others. Why have you not applied this principle to property, *which is a social institution,* as though the eternal laws of nature were less inviolable than the *conventions* of mankind?

Following these introductory remarks, Robespierre establishes the principles in these terms:

> Article 1: Property is the right of each citizen to enjoy and dispose of the portion of goods which is guaranteed to him by the law.
> Article 2: The right to property is limited, like all others, by the obligation to respect the rights of others.[5]

In this way, Robespierre contrasts *liberty* and *property.* These are two rights with different origins: one comes from nature; the other is a social institution. The first is *natural,* the second *conventional.*

The common limit that Robespierre places on these two rights ought, it would seem, to have led him to think that they have the same source. Whether it is a question of liberty or property, respecting others' rights is not to destroy or alter that right; it is to acknowledge and confirm it. It is precisely because property is a right that predates the law just as liberty does that both exist only on condition that they respect the rights of others, and the mission of the law is to ensure that this limit is respected, which means that it recognizes and maintains the very principle of it.

---

5. Bastiat is quoting from a speech Robespierre gave in the National Convention on 24 April 1793. In this speech Robespierre argues that the Convention in its deliberations on a new Declaration of the Rights of Man and the Citizen (which it passed in June) was too favorable to the natural right of property and did not give adequate attention to the "social" and "moral" aspects of property. He gave his own formulation in four articles, two of which Bastiat quotes above. The third and fourth articles, which Bastiat did not quote, are quoted here: Article 3: "He (the citizen) can harm neither the security, liberty, existence, nor property of others." Article 4: "All possession, all exchange (traffic) which violates this principle is illicit and immoral." Robespierre then offers his own proposal for a Declaration of Rights, which is turned down by the Convention as too radical. (*Œuvres de Maximilien Robespierre,* vol. 3, pp. 352–53.)

Be that as it may, it is certain that Robespierre, following Rousseau's example, considered property to be a social institution, like a convention. In no way did he link it to its true justification, which lies in work. It is the right of disposal of the portion of goods *guaranteed by the law,* he said.

I have no need to remind you here that through Rousseau and Robespierre the Roman notion of property has been transmitted to all our so-called socialist schools. We know that the first volume by Louis Blanc on the Revolution[6] is an extravagant eulogy to the Geneva philosopher and to the leader of the Convention.

Thus, this idea that the right of property is a social institution, that it is an invention of the legislator, a creation of the law, in other words, that it is unknown to man in a state of nature, this idea, say I, has been transmitted from the Romans to us through the teaching of law, classical studies, the political writers of the eighteenth century, the revolutionaries of '93, and the theorists of organization of today.[7]

Let us now move on to the consequences of the two theoretical systems that I have just contrasted beginning with the jurist view.

The first step is to open a limitless field to the imagination of utopian thinkers.

This is obvious. Once we establish the principle that property takes its existence from the law, there are as many possible means of organizing production as there are possible laws in the minds of dreamers. Once we establish the principle that the legislator is responsible for arranging, combining, and molding both people and property at will, there is no limit to the imaginable means by which people and property can be arranged, combined, and molded. Right now, there are certainly more than five hundred projects on the organization of production circulating in Paris, not counting an equal number of projects on the organization of credit. Doubtless these plans con-

---

6. Bastiat is referring to Blanc's *Histoire de la Révolution française.* The first and second volumes appeared before the revolution of 1848 broke out.

7. Bastiat distinguishes between the "revolutionaries of 1789" and the "revolutionaries of 1793." By the former he means the liberals and constitutional monarchists, such as the Girondin group, who wanted to replace the monarchy and the ancien régime with a new regime limited by a constitution and the rule of law. By the latter he means the radical Jacobins around Robespierre, who used the Terror to eliminate their enemies and to introduce socialist legislation between 1793 and 1795. (See also the entry for "Girondins" in the Glossary of Subjects and Terms and the entry for "Robespierre, Maximilien de," in the Glossary of Persons.)

tradict one another, but they have in common the fact that they are based on this consideration: the law has created the right of property; the legislator is the absolute master in disposing of workers and the fruits of their work.

Among these projects, those that have attracted the greatest public attention are those by Fourier, Saint-Simon, Owen, Cabet, and Louis Blanc. However, it would be madness to think that these five methods of organization are the only ones possible. Their number is boundless. Every morning a new one may be hatched, more attractive than yesterday's, and I leave you to imagine what would happen to the human race if, when one of these inventions was imposed on it, another more-specious one was suddenly revealed. The human race would be reduced to the choice of either changing its way of carrying on every morning or continuing forever down a path known to be erroneous, just because it had once set out on this path.

A second consequence is to arouse the thirst for power in all dreamers. Let us suppose that I have thought out a system for organizing work. Setting out my system and expecting people to adopt it if it is a good one would be to suppose that the prerogative of action lies with them. However, in the system that I am examining the principle of action lies with the legislator. "The legislator," as Rousseau says, "must feel that he has the strength to transform human nature."[8] This being so, my ambition should be to become a legislator in order to impose the social order of my devising.

It is also clear that systems based on the idea that the right to property is a social institution all lead either to the most highly concentrated privilege or the most fundamental communism, depending on the good or bad intentions of the inventor. If he has sinister designs, he will make use of the law to enrich a few at the expense of all. If he obeys philanthropic impulses, he will want to equalize the level of well-being, and to do this he will think of stipulating that each person should legally share equally of the products created. It remains to be seen whether, under these conditions, it is possible to engage in production.

With regard to this, the Luxembourg Palace[9] recently offered us an extraordinary sight. A few days after the February revolution, in the middle of the nineteenth century, did we not hear a man who was more than a minister, a member of the provisional government, a civil servant invested with

---

8. Rousseau, *Du contrat social et autres œuvres politiques,* p. 260.

9. The Luxembourg Palace was the seat of the Government Commission for the Workers, created on 20 February 1848. Louis Blanc was the president and François Vidal, the secretary.

unlimited revolutionary authority speak in the name of liberty and coldly ask whether, in distributing salaries, it was a good thing to take account of the strength, talent, activity, and skill of the worker, that is to say the wealth he produced, or whether it was not better to disregard these personal virtues and their beneficial effect and in future give everyone the same pay. The question amounts to this: will a meter of cloth sold by a lazy man be sold for the same price as two meters offered by someone who is industrious? And, something that beggars belief, this man has proclaimed that he preferred profits to be uniform, whatever the work offered for sale, and in his wisdom he has decided that although *two* equals *two* by nature, they would in future *be by law only one.*

That is what happens when we act on the basis that the law is stronger than nature.

His audience apparently grasped the fact that the very constitution of man rose up against such an arbitrary decision and that people would never allow one meter of cloth to claim the same remuneration as two meters. If this were to be so, the competition that he wished to abolish would be replaced by another form of competition a thousand times more deadly: everyone would compete to work the least and demonstrate the least activity since, by law, the reward would be always guaranteed and equal for all.

However, Citizen Blanc had foreseen the objection and, to prevent this sweet do-nothing, alas so natural to man when work is not rewarded, he had thought of setting up a *post* in each commune on which would be inscribed the names of those who were lazy. However, he did not say whether there would be inquisitors to uncover the sin of laziness, courts in which to judge it, and gendarmes to execute the sentence. It should be noted that utopians never concern themselves with the huge machine of government indispensable for putting their legal machinery in motion.

Since the delegates in the Luxembourg Palace were rather incredulous, Citizen Vidal, Citizen Blanc's secretary, appeared to complete his master's thought. Using Rousseau's example, Citizen Vidal suggested nothing less than changing the nature of man and the laws of Providence.[10]

It has pleased Providence to place within each individual certain *needs* and their consequences and *faculties* and their consequences, thus creating

---

10. (Paillottet's note) See vol. 1 for the report on the work by M. Vidal on the *Distribution of Wealth* and vol. 2 for the reply to five letters published by M. Vidal in the journal *La Presse*. (*OC,* vol. 1, p. 440, "De la répartition des richesses"; and vol. 2, p. 147, "L'Organisation et liberté.")

*personal interest,* in other words, an instinct for preservation and a love of development that is the mainspring of the human race. M. Vidal will be changing all that. He has looked at the work of God and seen that it was not good. Consequently, starting from the principle that the law and the legislator can do anything, he will be abolishing *personal interest* by decree and replacing it by *point of honor.*

Men will no longer work to live, to provide for and raise their families, but to obey a *point of honor,* to avoid the *hangman's noose,* as though this new motive were not still a *personal interest* of another kind.

M. Vidal constantly refers to what the question of honor encourages armies to do. But alas! Everything must be stated clearly, and if the wish is to regiment workers we should be told whether the military code, with its thirty transgressions carrying the death penalty, would become the labor code!

An even more striking effect of the disastrous principle which I am endeavoring to combat here is the uncertainty it always holds suspended, like the sword of Damocles, over production, capital, trade, and industry. This is so serious that I dare to claim the reader's entire attention.

In a country like the United States, where the right of property is placed above the law, and where the sole mission of the forces of public order is to have this natural right respected, every individual may with total confidence devote his capital and strength to production. He has no need to fear that his plans and arrangements will be upset by the legislative power from one minute to the next.

But when on the contrary, on the principle that it is not work but the law that is the basis of property, all the creators of utopias are allowed to impose their arrangements generally and through the authority of decrees, who can fail to see that all the farsightedness and prudence that nature has implanted in men's hearts are being turned against industrial progress?

Where is the bold speculator now who would dare to set up a factory or take on a business? Yesterday, it was decreed that people would be allowed to work for only a given number of hours.[11] Now it is being decreed that the payment for this type of work will be fixed, and who can predict what will be decreed tomorrow, the day after tomorrow, and the days after that? Once the legislator has set himself at such an incommensurable distance from other

---

11. The decree of 2 March (1848) appeared in the first few weeks of the new regime that came to power following the February revolution of 1848. The decree limited working time to ten hours a day in Paris and eleven hours in the provinces.

men and in all conscience thinks that he can dispose of their time, work, transactions, everything that is *property*, what man in all the land will have the slightest knowledge of what constraints he and his profession will be placed under tomorrow by the law? And in such circumstances, who will be able or want to undertake anything?

I certainly do not deny that, among the innumerable systems to which this erroneous principle will give rise, many and perhaps the majority will be based on benevolent and generous intentions. But what is to be feared is the principle itself. The manifest aim of each individual arrangement is to equalize well-being. But the even more manifest effect of the principle on which these arrangements are based is to equalize deprivation; I cannot put this too plainly, it will reduce affluent families to the ranks of the poor and decimate poor families through illness and starvation.

I admit that I am afraid for the future of my country when I consider the gravity of the financial difficulties that this dangerous precedent will make even worse.

On 24 February, we found a budget that exceeds the proportions that France can reasonably achieve and what is more, according to the current minister of finance, with nearly a billion francs in debts that are for immediate repayment.

Because of this situation, already alarming enough, expenditure has steadily increased and revenue steadily decreased.

That is not all. Two types of promises have been tossed with a boundless prodigality to the general public. According to one lot, they are going to be given a countless mass of institutions that are beneficial but expensive. According to the second lot, all taxes will be reduced. In this way, on the one hand the numbers of day nurseries, asylums, primary schools, free secondary schools, workshops, and industrial pensions will be increased. The owners of slaves will be indemnified and the slaves themselves paid damages. The state will found credit institutions, lend workers their instruments of work, double the size of the army, reorganize the navy, etc., etc., and on the other hand it will abolish the salt tax, city tolls, and all the most unpopular contributions.

Certainly, whatever idea one has of the resources of France, it has at least to be admitted that such resources must increase if they are to meet twin aspirations that are so vast in scale and so contradictory in appearance.

But, in the midst of this extraordinary movement, which might be considered beyond human strength even when the entire energy of the country is being directed toward productive work, a cry can be heard: *the right to property is a creation of the law*. Consequently, the legislator can issue, at any time and in accordance with the theoretical systems with which he is imbued, decrees that overturn all the arrangements made by industry. Workers are not the owners of any object or thing of value because they have created these through their work but because the laws in effect today guarantee this. Tomorrow's law may withdraw this guarantee, at which time property will no longer be legitimate.

I ask you, what is bound to happen? Capital and production are terrified; they can no longer count on the future. Under the influence of a doctrine like this, capital will hide, flee, and be reduced to nothing. And what will then happen to the workers, these very workers for whom you profess such a lively, sincere, but so unenlightened affection? Will they be better fed when farming production has ceased? Will they be better clothed when no one dares start up a factory? Will they be more fully occupied when capital has vanished?

And taxes, where will you obtain these? And the financial position, how will this be restored? How are you going to pay the army? How will you pay your debts? What money will there be to lend for investment in machinery? With what resources will you support the charitable institutions whose existence it is so easy to decree?

I hasten to abandon these somber considerations. It remains for me to examine the consequences of the opposite principle that prevails today, namely, the "economists' principle,"[12] the principle that attributes the right of property to labor [*travail*] and not to the law; the principle that says that property existed before the law; the sole mission of the law is to ensure respect for property wherever it is and wherever it is formed, in whatever manner in which the worker has created it, either in isolation or in association, provided that he respects the rights of others.

First, just as the jurists' principle virtually implies slavery, that of the economists espouses *liberty*. Property, the right to enjoy the fruit of your labor, the right to work, develop yourself, and exercise your faculties as you please without the intervention of the state except in its protective role, that is liberty. And I still cannot understand why the many partisans of opposing persuasions allow the word *liberty* to remain on the republican flag. It is said

12. Bastiat uses the expression "le principe économiste," which is the name that the free-market political economists gave themselves in France, for example, *Le Journal des économistes*. See also the term "*Les Économistes*" in the Glossary of Subjects and Terms.

that some of them have removed it and substituted the word *solidarity*. Such people are more frank and consistent. However, they should have put *communism,* not *solidarity,* since the solidarity of interests, like property, exists outside the law.

It also implies *unity*. We have already seen this. If the legislator creates the right to property, there are as many ways for property to exist as there may be errors in the minds of utopians, that is to say, an infinite number. If, on the other hand, the right to property is a providential fact that predates any human legislation and the aim of human legislation is to ensure its respect, there is no place for any other arrangements.

It is also *security,* and this is perfectly clear: if a people fully acknowledge that each person has to provide for his means of existence but also that each person has a right to the fruit of his work that predates and is higher than the law, also that human law has been necessary and has intervened only to guarantee to all the freedom to work and the property of the fruit of that work, it is clearly evident that a totally secure future opens out before human activity. It no longer has to fear that legislative power will through successive decrees stop its efforts, disrupt its arrangements, and bring to nothing its forecasts. Within the shelter of this security capital will spring up rapidly. The rapid increase in capital, for its part, is the sole reason for growth in the value of labor. The working classes will therefore become better off and will themselves contribute to providing new sources of capital. They will be increasingly capable of freeing themselves from wage-labor,[13] becoming partners in the businesses, founding their own businesses, and recovering their dignity.

Last, the eternal principle that the state should not be a producer but should provide security for producers would inexorably lead to economy and order in public finances. The implication is that only this principle makes it possible to establish a good foundation and just distribution for taxes.

In fact, we should never forget that the state has no resources of its own. It has nothing and it owns nothing that it does not take from workers. Therefore, when it interferes in everything, it substitutes the grim and expensive activity of its agents for private activity. If, as happens in the United States, people came to realize with regard to this matter that the mission of the state is to provide a perfectly safe context for all, the state would be able to

---

13. That is, workers paid by the hour.

accomplish this mission with a few hundred million. This saving, combined with economic prosperity, would at last make it possible to establish a single direct tax which would bear only on actual *property,* of whatever kind.

But for this contingency we would have to wait until a few experiences, sometimes cruel ones, had somewhat diminished our faith in the state and increased our faith in humanity.

I will end with a few words on the *Free Trade* Association. It has often been reproached for this title. Its opponents have rejoiced, and its supporters have regretted, what both have considered to be a fault.

"Why cause alarm in this way?" say its partisans. "Why emblazon a *principle* on your flag? Why do you not limit yourselves to demanding those wise and prudent alterations to the customs tariff that time has made necessary and experience has shown to be opportune?"

Why? First, because, in my view at least, free trade has never been a matter of customs and tariffs but a question of right, justice, public order, and property. Second, because privilege, in whatever form it is manifested, implies a negation or scorn for property. Third, because state intervention to level out fortunes, increasing some shares at the expense of others, is *communism,* just as one drop of water is water just as the entire ocean is water.

Fourth, because I foresaw that once the principle of property has been undermined in one form, it would soon be attacked in a thousand different forms. Fifth, because I did not quit my solitude to pursue a partial amendment of the tariffs, which would have implied my adherence to the false notion that *law predates property,* but to fly to the aid of the opposite principle, compromised by protectionism. Finally, because I was convinced that the landowners and capitalists had themselves, with the tariff, sown the seed of the *communism* that terrifies them now, since they were demanding additional profits *from the law* at the expense of the working classes. I could see clearly that the working classes would not be slow to demand, in the name of equality, the benefits of the *law applied to leveling out well-being,* which is *communism.*

Let people read the first statement of principles issued by our Association, the program drawn up in a preparatory session on 10 May 1846; this will convince them of our central approach.

> Trade is a natural right, like property. Every citizen who has created or acquired a product should have the option either of using it immediately or of selling it to someone anywhere in the world who is willing to give him what he wants in exchange. Depriving him of this faculty, when

he is not using it for a purpose contrary to public order or morals and solely to satisfy the convenience of another citizen, is to justify plunder and violate the laws of justice.

It also violates the conditions of order, since what order can exist within a society in which each economic activity, with the assistance of the law and the powers of government, seeks success by oppressing all the others? We placed this question so far above that of tariffs that we added the following:

> The undersigned do not dispute society's right to establish, on goods that cross the border, taxes intended to meet common expenditure, provided that they are determined by the needs of the treasury.
>
> However, as soon as the tax loses its fiscal nature and is aimed at discouraging foreign products—to the detriment of the tax authorities themselves—in order to raise the price of a similar home product artificially and thus hold the community to ransom for the benefit of a particular class of people, it then becomes protection or rather plunder, and these are the ideas and practices that the Association is seeking to discredit and remove totally from our laws.

Of course, if we had pursued only the immediate modification of the tariffs, if we, as was claimed, had been the agents only of a few commercial interests, we would have taken care not to emblazon on our flag a word that implies a principle. Does anyone believe that I did not foresee the obstacles that this declaration of war against injustice would raise for us? Did I not know full well that by scheming, concealing our aim, and hiding half of our thought we would arrive more quickly at this or that partial victory? But how would these triumphs, which are fleeting anyway, have identified and safeguarded the great principle of property which we ourselves would have kept in the shadows and ruled out?

I repeat, we were asking for the abolition of the protectionist regime, not as a good government measure but as justice, as the achievement of freedom, as the rigorous consequence of a right that is higher than the law. We should not conceal behind its outward form that which we most desire.[14]

The time is coming when it will be recognized that we were right in not agreeing to insert a catch, a trap, a surprise, or an ambiguity in the title of our

---

14. (Paillottet's note) See in vol. 1 the letter dated January 1845 and addressed to M. de Lamartine on the *Right to Work*. (*OC*, vol. 1, p. 406, "Du droit au travail.")

Association but rather a frank expression of an eternal principle of order and justice, since only principles have power. They alone are the flame of intelligent minds or the rallying point for misguided convictions.

Recently, a universal shiver of terror has run through the entire territory of France. At the single word *communism,* every soul has become alarmed. Seeing the strangest systems appear in broad daylight and almost officially, and subversive decrees issued in succession, which may be followed by even more subversive ones, everyone has asked himself where we are all going. Capital has become terrified, credit has fled, work has been suspended, and the saw and hammer have been stopped in mid task as though a disastrous and universal electric current had suddenly paralyzed both mind and arm. Why? Because the principle of property, whose essence has already been compromised by the protectionist regime, has suffered further violent shocks as a consequence of the first. Because the intervention of the law with regard to industry and *as a way of adjusting values and redistributing wealth,* an intervention of which the protectionist regime was the first manifestation, is threatening to reveal itself in a thousand known or unknown forms. Yes, I say it loud and clear; it is the landowners, those who are considered to be property owners par excellence, who have undermined the principle of property, because they have called upon *the law* to give their lands and products an artificial value. It is the capitalists who have suggested the idea of leveling out wealth *by law. Protectionism* was the forerunner of *communism;* I will go even further, it was its first manifestation. For what are the suffering classes asking for now? Nothing other than what the capitalists and landowners have asked for and obtained. They are asking for the *intervention of the law* to balance, adjust, equalize wealth. What the capitalists and landowners have done by means of customs, the poor want to do by way of other institutions, but the principle is always the same: *to take from some people on the basis of legislation to give the proceeds to others,* and certainly, since it is you, property owners and capitalists, who have had this disastrous principle accepted, you should not complain if those more unfortunate than you claim the benefit. They have at least a right to it that you did not.[15]

But at last our eyes are being opened, and we see toward what abyss this initial blow against the essential conditions of public safety is driving

---

15. (Paillottet's note) See vol. 2 for a group of articles on the question of subsistence and, following this, *Protectionism and Communism.* (*OC,* vol. 2, pp. 63ff., "Subsistances"; and vol. 4, p. 504, "Protectionisme et communisme.")

us. Is this not a terrible lesson, clear proof of the chain of cause and effect through which at long last the justice of providential retribution is appearing, when we now see the rich terrified out of their wits by the invasion of a false doctrine whose iniquitous foundations they themselves laid and whose consequences they thought they could peacefully turn to their own profit? Yes, protectionists, you have been the promoters of communism. Yes, landowners, you have destroyed in people's minds the true concept of property. It is political economy that disseminates this concept; and you have proscribed political economy because, in the name of the right to property, it opposed your unjust privileges.[16] And when they have seized power, what has also been the first thought of these modern schools of thought that so terrify you? It is to eliminate political economy, since economic science is a constant protestation against the legal *leveling out* that you have sought and others are seeking today, following your example. You have asked the law for things that are far and away beyond what may be demanded of the law. You have asked it not for security (which would have been your right) but for *added value* on what belongs to you, which could not be given to you without damaging the rights of others. Now the folly of your claims has become universal folly. And if you wish to stave off the storm that threatens to engulf you, you have just one means left. Acknowledge your mistake; renounce your privileges; restrict the law to its own powers and limit the legislator to his role. You have abandoned us and you have attacked us, probably because you did not understand us. At the sight of the abyss you have opened up with your own hands, make haste to come over to our side and adopt our propaganda in favor of the right to property by, I repeat, giving this word its widest meaning, including in it both the faculties of man and all that they are able to produce, whether in production or trade!

The doctrine that we are defending arouses a certain mistrust because of its extreme simplicity; it limits itself to asking the law for security for all. People find it hard to believe that the mechanics of government can be reduced to these proportions. What is more, since this doctrine encloses the *law* within the limits of *universal justice,* some reproach it for excluding fraternity. Political economy does not accept this accusation. That will be the subject of another article.

16. (Paillottet's note) See vol. 5, *Plunder and Law—The War Against Chairs of Political Economy.* (*OC,* vol. 5, p. 16, "Guerre aux chaires d'économie politique.")

# → 5 ←
## *Justice and Fraternity*[1]

[vol. 4, p. 298. "Justice et fraternité." Originally published
in the 15 June 1848 issue of *Le Journal des économistes*.]

On a great many points the Economists[2] are in opposition to a number of
schools of socialism, which claim to be more *advanced* and which are, I readily agree, more active and popular. Our adversaries (I do not wish to call
them detractors) are the communists; the followers of Fourier and Owen;
MM Cabet, Louis Blanc, Proudhon, and Pierre Leroux; and many others.

What is very strange is that these schools differ among themselves at least
as much as they differ from us. It is therefore necessary (1) that they admit
a common principle that we do not admit and (2) that this principle lends
itself to the infinite diversity among them that we observe.

I believe that what radically divides us is this:

Political economy reaches the conclusion that only universal justice
should be demanded of the law.

Socialism, in its various branches and through applications whose num-

---

1. The slogan "liberté, égalité, fraternité" is deeply associated with the ideals of the
French Revolution, yet before it became the official motto of France (probably during
the Third Republic) many other combinations of ideals were used for polemical effect
by various groups: law, nation, unity, property, justice, and so on.

In 1790 Robespierre wanted the slogan "liberté, égalité, fraternité" used on the
uniforms of the National Guard, but he was defeated. In a well-known engraving by
Paul André Basset (1796), the words "Unité, indivisibilité de la République. Liberté,
égalité, fraternité ou la mort" [Unity, indivisibility of the Republic. Liberty, equality,
fraternity or death] were used. The slogan was revived during the 1848 revolution and
was incorporated into the new constitution decreed by the National Assembly on
28 October 1848, where Article 4 of the Preamble stated, "Elle a pour principe la liberté,
l'égalité et la fraternité. Elle a pour base la famille, le travail, la propriété, l'ordre public"
(It has for its principle liberty, equality, fraternity. It has as its foundation family, work,
property, public order).

2. See the entry for "*Les Économistes*" in the Glossary of Subjects and Terms.

ber is of course unlimited, demands in addition that the law should put into practice the dogma of fraternity.

Well, what is the result? Following Rousseau, socialism accepts that the entire social order is encompassed by the law. We know that Rousseau based society on a contract. On the very first page of his book on the Revolution,[3] Louis Blanc says: "The principle of fraternity is that which, viewing the members of the extended family as interdependent, at some point tends to organize various forms of society, *the work of man,* on the model of the human body, the work of God."[4]

Starting from this point, that society is *the work of man,* the work of the law, socialists are inevitably led to the conclusion that nothing exists in society that has not been ordered and arranged in advance by the legislator.

Therefore, seeing that political economy limits itself to demanding from the law justice everywhere and for all, that is, universal justice, they have concluded that it did not acknowledge fraternity in social relationships.

The reasoning for this is strict. "Since society is contained in law," they say, "and since you ask the law only for justice, you are therefore excluding fraternity from the law and consequently from society."

From this have come the imputations of rigidity, coldness, hardness, and lack of feeling that have been heaped on economic science and those who profess it.

But is the leading premise admissible? Is it true that all of society is encompassed in the law? It can be seen immediately that if it is not, then all these imputations collapse.

Now! To say that positive law, which always acts with authority, through constraint, resting on the force of coercion, with the bayonet and dungeon as sanctions and ending with some laid-down penalty; to say that law, which cannot decree affection, friendship, love, self-denial, selflessness, or sacrifice therefore cannot decree that which epitomizes them, namely fraternity: is this to wipe out or deny these noble attributes of our nature? Certainly not; it is to say only that society is wider than the law; that a number of acts take place and a host of feelings are stirring outside and above the law.

For my part, in the name of science, I protest with all my strength at this wretched interpretation, according to which, because we acknowledge that the law has limits, we are accused of denying everything that is outside

3. Blanc, *Histoire de la Révolution française* (1847).
4. Ibid., vol. 1, pp. 9–10.

these limits. Ah! Whether people believe or not, we too salute with ardor the word *fraternity* which came down from the peak of the sacred mountain eighteen centuries ago and is emblazoned forever on our republican flag. We too wish to see individuals, families, and nations come together, help one another, and come to each other's assistance in the difficult journey through mortal life. We too feel our hearts beat faster and our tears flow at the recounting of generous acts, whether they shine in the lives of simple citizens or bring together and mingle different classes and especially when they precipitate predestined peoples to occupy pioneering positions in progress and civilization.

And will we be reduced to talking about ourselves? Well, then! Let our actions be scrutinized. Certainly, we are very willing to admit that the host of political writers, who these days wish to stifle everything, including the sentiment of personal self-interest, in people's hearts and who show themselves to be so merciless toward what they call individualism, whose mouths are so incessantly filled with words like *selflessness, sacrifice,* and *fraternity,* exclusively adhere to the sublime motives they advise others to observe, that they give examples as well as advice and are careful to align their conduct with their doctrine. We are very pleased to take their word for it that they are full of disinterestedness and charity, but finally we should be allowed to say that from this point of view we are not afraid of comparison.

Each one of these Deciuses[5] has a plan that intends to achieve the happiness of humanity, and all appear to say that if we oppose them it is because we fear either for our wealth or for other social advantages. No, we oppose them because we hold their ideas to be false and their projects to be as puerile as they are disastrous. Because if it were proved to us that it is possible to bring down happiness on earth permanently through an artificial organization or by decreeing fraternity, there are those among us who, although they are economists, would joyfully sign such a decree with their last drop of blood.

However, it has not been proved to us that fraternity can be imposed. Whenever and wherever it occurs, it arouses such lively sympathy in us because it acts outside any legal constraint. Fraternity is either spontaneous or it does not exist. To decree it is to annihilate it. The law may indeed *oblige* men to remain just; in vain will it endeavor to *oblige* them to be devoted to others.

5. See the entry for "Decius, Gaius Messius Quintus," in the Glossary of Persons.

It is not I, incidentally, who have invented this distinction. As I said just now, eighteen centuries ago these words were uttered by the divine founder of our religion:

> *The law says: Do not unto others as you would not have them do*
> *unto you.*
> *And I say to you: Do unto others as you would have them do unto you.*

I believe that these words set the limits that divide justice from fraternity. I believe that they also trace the demarcation line, one that I will not say is absolute and impassable but theoretical and rational, between the circumscribed field of the law and the limitless region of human spontaneity.

When a large number of families, all of which in order to live, develop, and improve themselves need to work either in isolation or in association, pool part of their strengths, what can they demand of this common strength other than the protection of all the individuals, all their work, all their property, all their rights and interests? Is this anything other than universal justice? Obviously the rights of each person are limited by the absolutely identical rights of all the others. The law cannot therefore do anything other than to recognize this limit and see that it is respected. If it allowed some people to infringe it, this would be to the detriment of some of the others. The law would be unjust. It would be even more unjust if, instead of tolerating this infringement, it ordered it.

Let us take property, for example. The principle is that what each person achieves through his work belongs to him, whether this work is comparatively more or less clever, persevering, or apposite and consequently more or less productive. If two workers wish to combine their strengths in order to share the product in accordance with agreed proportions or exchange their products with each other, or if one wishes to make the other a loan or a gift, what does the law have to do with this? Nothing, I think, other than require the fulfilling of agreements and prevent or punish misrepresentation, violence, or fraud.

Does this mean that the law will forbid acts of selflessness and generosity? Who could even think this? But will it go so far as to order them? This is precisely the point that separates economists from socialists.

If the socialists mean that, in extraordinary circumstances and emergencies, the state has to store up a few resources, assist in certain misfortunes, and smooth over certain transitions, for God's sake, we would agree. This has been done and we would like it done better; however, there is a point along this path that should not be exceeded, the point at which governmental foresight destroys individual foresight by taking its place. It is perfectly clear that organized charity would, in such a case, do much more permanent harm than temporary good.

But we are not dealing here with exceptional measures. What we are investigating is this: is the mission of the law, viewed from a general and theoretical position, to determine the limits of *preexisting* mutual rights and see that they are respected, or to provide happiness to people directly by provoking acts of selflessness, self-denial, and mutual sacrifice?

What strikes me in this last theoretical viewpoint (and it is to this issue that I will be frequently returning in this hastily written article) is the uncertainty that it causes to hover over human activity and its results, the unknown before which it places society, an unknown whose nature is to paralyze all of its strength.

We know what justice is and where it is. It is a fixed and immovable point. Let the law take it as its guide, and everyone knows what is expected of him and acts accordingly.

But what is the fixed point of fraternity? What are its limits? What form does it take? Obviously it is infinite. Fraternity, in sum, consists in making a sacrifice for another, *working* for another. When it is free, spontaneous, and voluntary I can understand it and I applaud it. My admiration for sacrifice is all the greater where it is total. But when this principle, that fraternity will be imposed by law, is propounded within society, that is to say in good French, that the distribution of the fruits of work will be made through legislation, with no regard for the rights of the work itself, who knows to what extent this principle will operate, what form a caprice of the legislator will give it and in what institutions a decree will bring it into existence from one day to the next? Well, I ask whether society can continue to exist in these conditions.

Note that sacrifice, by its very nature, is not, like justice, something that has a limit. It can extend from the gift of a small coin thrown into a beggar's plate to the gift of life, *usque ad mortem, mortem autem crucis.*[6] The Gospels, which taught fraternity to men, explained it through its counsels. It tells us: "When someone strikes you on the right cheek, offer the left cheek. If

6. "[Christ became obedient for us] unto death, even the death of the cross." (Philippians 2:8.)

someone wants to take your jacket give him your coat as well."[7] It went further than just explaining fraternity to us; it has given us the most complete, touching, and sublime example of it on the summit of Golgotha.

Well then! Will it be said that legislation has to push the achievement of the dogma of fraternity through administrative measures to this point? Or will it stop somewhere along the way? But to what extent will it stop and in accordance with what rule? Today, this will depend on one vote, tomorrow on another.

The same uncertainties hover over the form. It is a question of imposing sacrifices on some for the benefit of all or on all for the benefit of some. Who can tell me how the law will deal with this? For it cannot be denied that the number of formulae for fraternity is infinite. Not a day goes past when five or six appeals do not reach me through the post and all of them, please note, are completely different. Truly, is it not folly to believe that a nation can experience a degree of moral tranquillity and material prosperity when the principle is admitted that, from one day to the next, the legislator can toss the nation in its entirety into the one of the hundred thousand molds of fraternity that has gained its favor momentarily?

May I be allowed to contrast the most striking consequences of the economic and socialist systems?

First of all, let us imagine a nation that adopts justice, universal justice, as the basis for its legislation.

Let us suppose that its citizens tell their government: "We will take responsibility for our own lives. We will take charge of our work, our transactions, our education, our progress, and our religion. For your part, your sole mission will be to contain us within the limits of our rights in all respects."

In truth, we have tried so many things that I would like the whim to take hold of my country, or any country around the globe, to try this at least. Certainly, it cannot be denied that the mechanics are of amazing simplicity. Each individual will exercise all of his rights as he sees fit, provided that he does not infringe the rights of others. The test would be all the more interesting if, in point of fact, the peoples that came the closest to each other under this system exceeded all the others in security, prosperity, equality, and

---

7. Luke 6:29. The King James version states: "And unto him that smiteth thee on the *one* cheek offer also the other; and him that taketh away thy cloke forbid not *to take thy* coat also."

dignity. Yes, if ten years of life were left to me, I would willingly give nine of them to witness for a year an experiment of this nature in my country. For here, it seems to me, is what I would be fortunate enough to witness.

In the first place, each individual would be certain of his future as far as this could be affected by the law. As I have pointed out, literal justice is something that is so constraining that legislation that had only this in view would be almost immutable. It could be changed only with regard to the means of achieving a single aim ever more closely: to ensure that people and their rights were respected. Thus each person could undertake all sorts of honest enterprises without fear or uncertainty. All careers would be open to all; each person would be free to exercise his faculties freely, according to his self-interest, liking, aptitude, or circumstances. There would be no privileges or monopoly, nor restrictions of any sort.

Next, since all the forces of government would be applied to preventing and redressing willful misrepresentations, frauds, misdemeanors, crimes, and violence, it is to be believed that government forces would achieve these all the more since they would not be dispersed as they are today over a host of objects that are foreign to their essential prerogatives. Our opponents themselves will not deny that preventing and eliminating injustice is the principal mission of the state. Why then is it that the valuable art of prevention and elimination has made so little progress in our country? It is because the state neglects it in favor of the thousand other functions for which it has been made responsible. This is why security is far from being the distinctive characteristic of French society. It would be total under the regime which I am for the moment analyzing: security in the future, since no utopia could impose itself by means of government power; security in the present, since this power would be exclusively devoted to combating and abolishing injustice.

I must at this point say something about the consequences that security engenders. First of all, property will be totally guaranteed in its variety of forms: land and movable assets; industrial, intellectual, and manual property. It is now protected from attack by wrongdoers and, what is more, from attack by the law. Whatever the nature of the services rendered by workers to society or between themselves, or traded externally, these services will always have their *natural value*. This value will still be much affected by events, but at least it can never be affected by the whims of the law or the needs of taxation, intrigues, claims, or parliamentary entanglements. The price of things and work will thus suffer minimally from fluctuations, and when all of these conditions obtain simultaneously it would be impossible for industry not to develop, wealth not to increase, or capital not to accumulate with prodigious rapidity.

Now, when capital increases, its uses compete among themselves; its remuneration decreases, or in other words interest rates fall. They bear less and less on the price of products. The share of capital in the national product decreases continuously. This factor of production, now being more widely distributed, comes within the reach of a greater number of men. The price of consumer goods is relieved of the whole part no longer set aside for capital; things become cheaper and this is an essential and prime condition for the liberating of the working classes.[8]

At the same time and for the same reason (the rapid accumulation of capital), earnings will of necessity rise. Capital, in fact, yields absolutely nothing if it is not put to use. The larger this source of earnings is and the more it is put to use in relation to a given number of workers, the more earnings will rise.

In this way, the necessary result of this clear-cut regime of strict justice, and consequently of freedom and security, is to raise the suffering classes in two ways, first of all by making life cheaper and second by raising the level of earnings.

It is impossible for the fate of workers to be naturally and doubly improved without their moral condition being elevated and purified. We are therefore proceeding along the path of equality. I am not talking only about equality before the law, which is obviously implied since it excludes any form of injustice, but actual equality, both physical and moral, that results from the fact that the remuneration of labor increases in the same proportion as the income from capital decreases.

If we cast an eye on the relationships of this people with other nations, we will see that they all favor peace. Arming itself against any form of aggression is its sole policy. It does not threaten nor is it threatened. It has no diplomatic service and still less any armed diplomatic force. Since by virtue of the principle of universal justice no citizen is able to call upon the law in his own self-interest to intervene to prevent another citizen from buying or selling abroad, the commercial relationships enjoyed by these people will be free and extensive. No one will argue that such relationships are not a

---

8. (Paillottet's note) See the pamphlet titled *Capital and Rent* in vol. 5, and see chap. 2 of *Economic Harmonies* in vol. 6. (*OC*, vol. 5, p. 23, "Capital et Rente"; and vol. 6, chap. 7, p. 228, "Capital.")

contributory factor to maintaining peace. They are a genuine and valuable system of defense, which will make arsenals, fortresses, navies, and standing armies almost pointless. Thus, all the forces of this people will be directed toward productive work, an additional cause of an increase in capital with all its consequences.

It is easy to see that within this people, the government has been reduced to very slender proportions and the wheels of administration to their simplest form. What does this mean? Giving government the sole mission of maintaining justice between the citizens. Well, this can be done at little cost, and even in France today it costs only twenty-six million. Therefore this nation will to all intents and purposes not pay any taxes. It is even certain that civilization and progress will tend to make the government ever more simple and economic, since the more justice results from sound social habits, the more it will be apposite to reduce the force organized to impose it.

When a nation is crushed by taxes, nothing is more difficult, and I might even say impossible, than to distribute them equitably. Statisticians and financiers no longer aspire to do so. However, there is something that is even more impossible, and that is to restrict the taxes to the rich. The state can have a great deal of money only by draining everybody's resources, especially those of the masses. But in the simple regime to which I am devoting this humble argument, a regime that requires only a few tens of millions, nothing is easier than an equitable distribution. A single contribution, proportional to the property realized, raised in the family and at no cost within municipal councils, will be enough. There will be no more of the tenacious tax system or voracious bureaucracy that are the dank moss and vermin of the social body, no more of the indirect contributions, the money snatched by force or guile, the tax traps set on all the paths of work, the harassments that hurt us even more because of the freedoms they withdraw from us than because of the resources of which they deprive us.

Do I need to show that order would be the inevitable result of a regime like this? Where would disorder come from? Not from destitution; it would probably be unknown in the country at least as a chronic occurrence; and where temporary and accidental suffering did on occasion occur, no one would dream of turning against the state, the government, or the law. At present, when it is accepted in principle that the state has been set up to distribute wealth to everyone, it is natural that it should be asked to account for this commitment. To fulfill it, the state increases the number of taxes and causes more destitution than it relieves. New demands from the public, new taxes from the state, and we can go only from one revolution to the next. But if it was fully understood that the state should take from workers only what was absolutely essential to protect them from all forms of fraud and violence, I cannot see from what quarter disorder would arise.

There are some who will think that society would be very dismal and gloomy under such a simple regime that is so easy to set up. What would become of great political action? What use would statesmen be? Would not national representation itself, reduced to improving the civil and penal codes, cease to offer the spectacle of passionate debates and dramatic combats to the avid curiosity of the public?

This curious reservation comes from the idea that government and society are one and the same thing, an erroneous and disastrous idea if ever there was one. If they were really identical, simplifying government would in effect be to demean society.

But would the mere fact that government would limit itself strictly to maintaining justice take something away from the initiative of the citizens? Is their action even today restricted within limits set by the law? Would it not be possible for them, provided that they did not depart from the principles of justice, to form an infinite variety of alliances or associations of all kinds—religious, charitable, industrial, farming, and intellectual, indeed not excluding even political associations like those of the followers of Fourier and Cabet? On the contrary, is it not certain that a wealth of capital would encourage all these activities? The only thing would be that each person would join voluntarily at his own risk. What people want, through the intervention of the state, is to share in the risks and expenses of the public.

It will doubtless be said: "In this sort of regime, we can clearly see justice, economy, freedom, wealth, peace, order, and equality, but we do not see fraternity."

Once again, does the human heart contain only what the legislator has put there? Was it necessary for fraternity to issue from the electoral urn for it to appear on earth? Does the law forbid you to practice charity because it imposes only justice on you? Do you believe that women would cease to be selfless and have a heart open to pity because selflessness and pity were not commanded by the Code? And which is the article of the Code that tears young girls from the embraces of their mothers and propels them toward the distressing asylums in which the hideous wounds of the body and even more hideous wounds of the mind are displayed? Which is the article of the Code that determines vocations to the priesthood? To which written law or government intervention are we to relate the founding of Christianity, the zeal of the apostles, the courage of the martyrs, the good deeds of Fénelon or Francis de Paule,[9] the self-denial of so many men who in our time have risked their lives for the triumph of the popular cause.[10]

Every time we judge an act to be good and fine, we want it to become more widespread, and this is natural. However, when we see within society a force before which everything bows down, our first thought is to have it collude with us in decreeing and imposing the act in question. But what is important is to know whether we are not in this way depreciating both the nature of this force and the nature of the act which from being voluntary has been made obligatory. As far as I am concerned, I cannot get into my head that the law, which is a force, can usefully be employed for anything other than curbing wrongs and maintaining rights.

I have just described a nation in which this would be so. Let us now suppose that within this people the opinion became prevalent that the law

9. The religious order known as the Minims was founded by the Italian priest Francis of Paola (1416–1507) in 1435. The order was severely weakened by the French Revolution and is now defunct.

10. (Paillottet's note) In practical terms, men have always distinguished between a *contract* and a purely benevolent act. I have on occasion been pleased to observe the most charitable man, the most selfless heart, and the most fraternal soul that I know. The parish priest of my village raises love for his fellow men and particularly for the poor to an exceptional level. It goes so far that when he has to extract money from the rich in order to assist the poor, this fine man is not very scrupulous in his choice of means.

He had brought a nun in her seventies to his house, one of those that the Revolution had scattered around the world. In order to give an hour's entertainment to his lodger he, who had never touched a playing card, learned to play piquet, and it was a sight for sore eyes to see him pretending to be enthusiastic about the game so that the nun was persuaded that she was being helpful to her benefactor. This lasted for fifteen years. But it is what turned an act of simple condescension into one of heroism. The good nun was suffering from a generalized cancer that caused an abominable odor to emanate from her and of which she was unconscious. In spite of this, the priest was never seen to take tobacco during the game for fear of making the unfortunate patient aware of her situation. How many people received the cross on 1 May and would be incapable of doing for one day what my old priest did for fifteen years?

Well then! I observed this priest and was able to ascertain that when he made a contract, he was as vigilant as any trader in the Marais. He defended his territory, watched out for the weight, the measure, the quality, and the price and considered that he was not in the slightest bound to confuse charity and fraternity in the affair.

Let us therefore strip the word *fraternity* of all the false, puerile, and high-flown trappings that have lately been added to it. [Unpublished rough draft by the author, written around the end of 1847.]

would no longer be limited to imposing justice but would aim to impose fraternity as well.

What would happen? It will not take me long to tell you since the reader has only to redo the scenario by reversing the foregoing picture.

First of all, a terrible uncertainty and a deadly insecurity would hang over the entire domain of private activity since fraternity can take on thousands of unknown forms and consequently thousands of decrees that cannot be anticipated. A host of draft regulations will threaten established relationships each day. In the name of fraternity some will demand the *uniformity of* earnings, and at a stroke the working classes will be reduced to the condition of Indian castes. Skill, courage, assiduity, and intelligence will not be enough to redress their situation; the lead weight of the law will weigh down upon them. This world will be for them like Dante's *Inferno:* "Lasciate ogni speranza, voi ch'entrate chi!"[11] In the name of fraternity, another will demand that work be reduced to ten, eight, six, or four hours, and production will grind to a halt. As there will be no more bread to assuage hunger or cloth to keep out the cold, a third inspiration will demand the missing bread and cloth be replaced by *obligatory paper money.* "Is it not with écus that we buy these things? Increasing the number of écus," he will say, "will increase the amount of bread and cloth. Increasing the amount of paper will increase the number of écus. Let us do this." A fourth will demand that competition be abolished, a fifth that personal self-interest be abolished. Someone else wants the state to provide work; another, education; and yet another, pensions for every citizen. Yet another person wants to bring down every king on this earth and decree universal war in the name of fraternity. I will stop there. It is perfectly clear that going down this road we will find an inexhaustible source of utopias. They will be rejected, people will say. This may be so, but it is *possible* that they will not, and this would be enough to create *uncertainty*, the greatest scourge of work.

Under this regime, it will be impossible to build up capital. It will become scarce, expensive, and concentrated. This means that earnings will decrease and that inequality will create an ever-deepening abyss between the classes.

Public finances will not be slow to descend into total confusion. How could it be otherwise when the state is responsible for supplying everything to everyone? The people will be crushed by taxes, and loan upon loan will be taken out. Once the present has been exhausted, the future will be devoured.

---

11. "All hope abandon, ye that enter here!" (Dante, *Inferno III,* line 9.)

Finally, since it will be accepted in principle that the state is responsible for producing fraternity in favor of its citizens, the entire people will be seen to be transformed into supplicants. Landed property, agriculture, industry, commerce, the merchant navy, and industrial companies will all clamor to receive favors from the state. The treasury will literally be pillaged. Each individual will have good reason to prove that legal fraternity has to be seen from the following angle: the advantages for me and the burdens for others. Everyone will devote his efforts to extracting some shred of *fraternal* privilege from the legislature. Despite having the best founded claims, the suffering classes will not always have the most success; their numbers will constantly increase, however, which will lead to our being able to go nowhere save from one revolution to the next.

In a word, we will witness the progress of the entire sad spectacle of which a few modern societies are offering us a foretaste since they have adopted this disastrous idea of *legal fraternity*.

I have no need to say that this notion is rooted in generous sentiments and pure intentions. It is indeed because of this that it attracted the sympathy of the masses so quickly and also that it opens an abyss beneath our feet if it is wrong.

I add that I personally would be happy if someone proved to me that it is not wrong. Good heavens, if universal fraternity could be decreed and this decree effectively given the sanction of government; if, as Louis Blanc would wish it, the spring of personal self-interest could be made to disappear from this world through the vote; if, through legislation, that article in the program of *La Démocratie pacifique* titled *No More Egoism* could be achieved; and if we could organize for the state to give everything to everyone without receiving anything from anyone, then let all this be done. I would certainly vote for the decree and rejoice that humanity had achieved perfection and happiness via such a short and easy route.

But, it has to be said, such notions appear illusory and futile to the point of puerility. It is not surprising that they have awakened hopes in the classes that work, suffer, and have no time to reflect. But how can they mislead leading political writers?

At the sight of the sufferings that overwhelm many of our brothers, these political writers thought that they could be laid at the door of the *freedom* that is justice. They started with the idea that the system of freedom and strict justice had been tested legally and had failed. They concluded that the time had come to make legislation take a further step forward and that it ought, in a word, to become imbued with the principle of *fraternity*. This has given rise to the schools of the followers of Saint-Simon, Fourier, communism, and Owen; to attempts to organize work; to declarations that the state owes subsistence, well-being, and education to all its citizens; that it should be generous, charitable, involved in everything, and devoted to all; that its mission is to give milk to babies, educate young people, ensure work for the able-bodied and pensions for the weak; in a word, that it should intervene directly to alleviate all forms of suffering, satisfy and anticipate every need, supply capital to all enterprises, enlightenment to all minds, balm to every wound, asylums to all misfortunes, and even help end the sacrifice of French blood to all the oppressed around the world.

Once again, who would not wish to see all these benefits flow over the world from the *law* as though from an everlasting source? Who would not be happy to see the state assume responsibility for every trouble, every precaution, every responsibility, every duty, and every arduous and weighty burden that the impenetrable design of Providence has placed on humanity, and reserve for the individuals who make it up the attractive and easy side of things: the satisfactions, enjoyments, certainties, peace, rest, a present that is always assured and a future full of gaiety, wealth without care, a family without responsibility, credit without surety, and an existence without effort?

Certainly, we would all like that, *if it were possible*. But is it possible? That is the question. It is not easy to grasp what people mean by the state. I find, in the perpetual personification of the state, the strangest and most humiliating mystification of all. What in fact is this state that takes on itself all virtues, all duties, and all liberalities? From where does it draw these resources that we urge it to shower such bounty on individual people? Is it not from the individuals themselves? How then can these resources grow when they pass through the hands of a parasitic and voracious intermediary? It is not clear, on the contrary, that this system is such that it will absorb a great deal of useful effort and reduce the workers' share of income by an equivalent amount? Do we not also see that workers will abandon to it, along with part of their well-being, part of their freedom?

From whatever point of view I consider human law, I cannot see that we can reasonably ask of it anything other than justice.

Take religion, for example. Certainly, it would be desirable for there to be just one belief, one faith, and one religion in the world, on condition that it was the *true faith*. But however desirable unity may be, diversity, that is to say research and discussion, is even better for as long as the infallible sign by which this *true faith* will be recognized does not shine out before men's intelligence. The intervention of the state, even where it took fraternity as a pretext, would therefore be an oppression, an *injustice* if it claimed to be establishing unity, for who would guarantee that the state, unbeknown to itself perhaps, would not work to stifle truth in favor of error? Unity must result from the universal consent of freely held convictions and the natural attraction that truth exercises over the minds of men. All that we can therefore ask of the law is freedom for all forms of belief, whatever anarchy may result in the thinking world. For what does this anarchy prove? That unity is not at the origin but at the end of intellectual evolution. It is not the point of departure; it is a result. The law that would impose it would be unjust, and if justice does not necessarily imply fraternity, it will at least be agreed that fraternity excludes injustice.

The same is true of teaching. Who will not agree that, if we could reach consensus on the best form of teaching possible with regard to the subject and method, then a single methodology or one imposed by government would be preferable since, on this assumption, only error could be excluded by law. But for as long as this criterion has not been found, as long as the legislator or the minister of public education does not bear the irrefutable sign of infallibility on his forehead, the best chance for the true method to be discovered and absorb the others lies in diversity, tests, experience, and individual effort, all directed by the concern for *success,* in a word, freedom. The worst option is a uniform system of education by decree since, under this regime, error will be permanent, universal, and irremediable. Therefore, those who, spurred on by a sentiment of fraternity, demand that the *law* should direct and impose a system of education should be aware that they are running the risk that the law will direct and impose only error and that legal prohibition may attack truth by way of the intelligent minds who believe that they possess it. Well, I ask you, is it genuine fraternity that has recourse to force to impose or at least risk imposing error? Diversity is feared and stigmatized as anarchy, but it is the inevitable result of the very diversity of intelligent minds and convictions and besides, it tends to be reduced by discussion, study, and experience. In the meantime, by what right is one system valued above the others by law or political fiat? Here again, we find that this alleged fraternity, which invokes the law or legal constraint, is in opposition to justice.

I could make the same remarks with regard to the press, and in truth I find it hard to understand why those who demand a uniform education imposed by the state do not also demand the same thing for the press. The press is a form of education too. The press allows discussion because it lives by it. It therefore also contains diversity and anarchy. Why not, in accordance with these ideas, create a ministry of publicity and make it responsible for inspiring all the books and journals in France? Either the state is infallible, in which case we could not do better than to submit to it the entire domain of intelligent thought, or it is not, in which case it is no more rational to hand over education to it than to the press.

If I consider our relationships with foreigners, in this case, too, I see no rule except justice, so prudent, solid, and acceptable to all that it is capable of becoming a law. To submit these relationships to the principle of legal, obligatory fraternity is to decree perpetual and universal war, for it would become an obligation for us to place our forces and the blood and treasure of our citizens at the service of anyone who claimed them with regard to any cause that arouses the sympathy of the legislator. What a singular form of fraternity! A long time ago Cervantes personified its ridiculous vanity.

But it is above all with regard to work that the dogma of fraternity seems to me to be dangerous, where, contrary to the idea that is the essence of this sacred word, plans are made to incorporate it into our codes, accompanied by the penal dispositions that sanction any positive law.

*Fraternity* always implies the idea of selflessness and sacrifice, and because of this it arouses tears of admiration whenever it occurs. If it is said, as some socialists do say, that acts of fraternity are *profitable* to their author, there is no need to decree them; men do not need a law to induce them to make a profit. Besides, this point of view degrades and much tarnishes the notion of fraternity.

Let us therefore leave it its character, summed up in these words: *a voluntary sacrifice inspired by fraternal sentiment.*

If you make fraternity a legal prescription, whose acts are prescribed and made obligatory by the industrial code, what remains of this definition? Only one thing: sacrifice, but an involuntary sacrifice, one that is forced, determined by a fear of punishment. And in good faith, what is a sacrifice of this nature, imposed on one person for the benefit of another? Is this fraternity? No, it is injustice. The word must be spoken; it is legal plunder, the worst form of plunder, since it is systematic, permanent, and unavoidable.

What was Barbès doing when in the session on 15 May he introduced a tax of a billion in favor of the suffering classes? He was putting your principle into practice. This is so true that the proclamation by Sobrier, which comes to the same conclusion as the speech by Barbès, starts with this pre-amble: "The consideration that fraternity must no longer be an empty word but must be revealed through actions entails the following: capitalists, iden-tified as such, will pay, etc."

You who are protesting, what right have you to blame Barbès and So-brier? What have they done apart from being slightly more consistent than you and taking your own principle a little further?

I say that when this principle is introduced into legislation, even when it first makes just a timid appearance, it paralyzes capital and labor, for nothing guarantees that it will not develop further indefinitely. Do we need so many reasoned arguments to show that where men are no longer certain of enjoy-ing the fruit of their work they no longer work or work less? You should be fully aware that insecurity is the major cause of paralysis of investment. It drives investment away and prevents it from building up, and then what happens to those very classes whose sufferings are allegedly being relieved? I sincerely think that this phenomenon alone is enough to make the most prosperous of nations descend rapidly to a level below that of Turkey.

The sacrifice imposed on some in favor of others through the operation of taxes obviously loses its fraternal character. Who therefore gains the merit for it? Is it the legislator? The only cost to him is casting a ball into an urn. Is it the tax collector? He obeys for fear of losing his job. Is it the taxpayer? He pays in self-defense. To whom therefore will be attributed the merit that selflessness implies. Where is the morality to be found?

Extralegal plunder arouses total aversion and turns against itself all the forces of public opinion, making them agree with the notions of justice. Legal plunder, on the other hand, is accomplished without disturbing con-sciences, which leads only to a weakening of a moral sense within a people.

With courage and prudence, we can avoid the plunder that is contrary to law. Nothing can protect us from legal plunder. If someone tries it, what dreadful sight is set before society? A plunderer armed by the law against a victim resisting the law.

When on the pretext of fraternity the law imposes mutual sacrifices on citizens, human nature does not for this reason lose its rights. Each person strives to contribute little to the sacrificial heap and to receive a great deal from it. However, in this struggle, are the most unfortunate the ones that gain most? Certainly not, those who gain the most are the most influential and the greatest schemers.

Are union, agreement, and harmony at least the fruit of fraternity as we have understood it? Doubtless, fraternity is the divine chain that in the long run will bind in unity all individuals, families, nations, and races. But this is on condition that it remains as it is, that is to say, the most free, spontaneous, voluntary, meritorious, and religious of sentiments. Its mask will not accomplish the prodigy, and it will be in vain that legal plunder adopts the name of fraternity with its features, formulae, and insignia. Legal plunder will always be just a principle of discord, confusion, unjust claims, terror, deprivation, inertia, and hatred.

A serious objection is made. We are told: "It is true that freedom and equality before the law constitute justice. But strict justice remains neutral between the rich and the poor, the strong and the weak, the scholar and the ignorant, the owner and the proletarian, the fellow countryman and the foreigner. However, *since self-interests are by nature antagonistic,* leaving men their freedom and allowing only just laws to intervene between them is to sacrifice the poor, the weak, the ignorant, the proletarian, and the athlete who presents himself unarmed for the combat."

"What could result from this freedom of production on which so much hope had been banked," said M. Considérant, "from this celebrated principle of *free competition,* which was thought to be so strongly endowed with the characteristics of democratic organization? The only result would be collective enthrallment of the propertyless masses, who are also without manufactured weapons or the wherewithal of production or education, in a word, their general subservience to the class that is well endowed with power over production and well armed to boot. It is said that 'the lists are open, each individual is called to combat and the conditions are the same for all combatants.' Very well, only one thing has been forgotten, and that is that on this great battlefield some are educated, seasoned, equipped, and armed to the teeth, that they possess a major procurement system, equipment, ammunition, and weapons of war and occupy all the positions; whereas the others are deprived, naked, ignorant, and famished and, in order to scrape a daily living for themselves and their wives and children, are obliged to implore their opponents themselves to give them work of sorts and a meager wage."[12]

What, are we comparing work with war? These arms that are being called capital, which consist in procurements of all sorts and which can never be

12. (Paillottet's note) See "Property and Plunder" hereafter, including the final note. [See "Property and Plunder," p. 147 in this volume.] See also in vol. 2 the reply to a letter from M. Considérant. (*OC,* vol. 2, p. 134, "La résponse à une lettre de M. Considérant.")

employed for other than conquering rebellious nature, are being assimilated through a deplorable sophism with the bloody weapons which in combat men turn against one another! It is obvious that it is too easy to calumniate the industrial order by using the vocabulary of war to decry it.

The profound and irreconcilable disagreement on this point between socialists and economists consists in this: The socialists believe in the inherent antagonism of self-interests. The economists believe in natural harmony or rather in the necessary and progressive harmonization of self-interests. This sums it all up.

From the premise that self-interests are naturally antagonistic, socialists are led by the force of logic to seek an artificial organization for self-interests or even to stifle the sentiment of self-interest in the hearts of men if they can. This is what they tried to do in the Luxembourg Palace. However, although they are crazy enough, they are not strong enough and it goes without saying that, having ranted against individualism in their books, they sell their books and behave exactly like common mortals in ordinary daily life.

Well, if interests were naturally antagonistic, then justice, freedom, and equality before the law probably should be trampled underfoot. The world would need to be remade or, as they say, *society would need to be reconstructed,* according to one of the innumerable plans they are always inventing. Self-interest, an unruly principle, should be replaced by legal, imposed, involuntary, and obligatory *selflessness,* in a word, organized plunder, and since this new principle would arouse only infinite repugnance and resistance, attempts would first be made to have it accepted under the dishonest misnomer of fraternity, after which the law would be invoked, which would mean force.

But if Providence has not erred, if it has arranged things in such a way that personal interests under the law of justice naturally achieve perfectly harmonious agreements, if, as M. de Lamartine says, they arrive through freedom at a form of justice with which despotism could never supply them, if the equality of rights is the most certain and direct way to equality in fact, well then, all that we can ask of the law is to provide justice, freedom, and equality, just as all that we ask is the removal of obstacles so that the drops of water that make up the ocean find their own level.[13]

---

13. In December 1844, Lamartine wrote in his journal *Le Bien public* an article titled "On the Right to Work," in which he said, "There is no other organization of work than its freedom; there is no other distribution of income than work itself paying its

And that is the conclusion reached by political economy. It does not seek this conclusion, it finds it, but it is happy to find it since, in the end, is it not highly satisfactory for the spirit to see harmony in freedom where others are reduced to demanding it from despotism?

The words full of hatred with which socialists often address us are really very strange! What then! If by mischance we were mistaken, should they not deplore this? What are we saying? We say: After mature consideration, it has to be acknowledged that God has done well, so that the best conditions under which progress can occur are justice and freedom.

Socialists think we are mistaken; that is their right. But they should at least be sorry about this, for if our error is proved it implies that it is urgent to substitute the artificial for the natural, arbitrary systems for freedom, and contingent and human inventions for eternal and divine design.

Let us imagine that a chemistry professor comes and tells us: "The world is threatened with a major catastrophe; God has not taken sufficient precautions. I have analyzed the air escaping from human lungs and seen that it is no longer fit to breathe, so that, calculating the volume of the atmosphere, I can predict the day when it will be totally corrupted and when humanity will perish by consumption unless it adopts the artificial means of respiration that I have invented."

Another professor comes forward and says: "No, humanity will not perish in this way. It is true that the air that is used for animal life is no longer fit for this use, but it is fit for plant life and that exhaled by plants is fit for humans to breathe. An incomplete study led people to believe that God made a mistake; more detailed research has shown that He included harmony in His work. Men can continue to breathe as nature intended."

What would people have said if the first professor had covered the second with insults, saying: "You are a chemist with a heart that is hard, dry, and cold. You are preaching a dreadful laissez-faire; you do not like humanity, as is shown in your demonstrating the uselessness of my breathing apparatus"?

This encapsulates our entire quarrel with the socialists. Both our camps want harmony. They seek it through the countless theoretical systems they want imposed on people by law; we find it in the nature of people and things.

This would be the right place to demonstrate that self-interest leads to

---

accomplishments and doing itself a justice that your arbitrary systems do not do." See also "Bastiat's Political Writings: Anecdotes and Reflections," pp. 410–12, and the entry for *"Le Bien public"* in the Glossary of Subjects and Terms.

harmony, since this is the entire question, but to do this would require me to give a course in political economy and the reader will forgive me for not doing so right now.[14] I will say only this: If political economy succeeds in recognizing the harmony of personal interests, it is because, unlike socialism, it does not stop at the immediate consequences of phenomena, but proceeds to their subsequent and final effects. That is its whole secret. The two schools differ exactly as the two chemists I have just mentioned do; one sees part of the picture and the other the whole. For example, when the socialists are prepared to take the trouble to follow the effects of competition right to the end, that is, right up to the consumer, instead of stopping at the producer, they will see that competition is the most powerful agent for equality and progress, whether it occurs inside the country or comes from abroad. And it is because political economy finds what constitutes harmony in this definitive effect that it says: In my field, *there is a lot to learn and little to do.* A lot to learn because the sequence of effects can be followed only with great application; little to do since the harmony of the entire phenomenon comes from the final effect.

I have had the opportunity of discussing this question with the eminent man that the revolution has raised to such great heights.[15] I told him: As the law acts through constraint we can ask only justice of it. He thought that nations could also expect fraternity of it. Last August, he wrote to me: "If ever in a crisis I find myself at the helm of events, your idea will be half of my creed." I sent him this reply: "The second half of your creed will stifle the first, since you cannot establish legal fraternity without establishing legal injustice."[16]

I will end by saying to the socialists: If you believe that political economy rejects association, organization, and fraternity, you are mistaken.

---

14. (Paillottet's note) Several chapters of *Economic Harmonies* had by this point already been published in the *Le Journal des économistes* and the author was shortly to continue this work.

15. Lamartine, then member of the provisional government and minister of foreign affairs.

16. (Paillottet's note) In August 1847, at the time when a public meeting was being prepared in Marseilles in favor of free trade, Bastiat met M. de Lamartine there and had a long discussion on free trade and then on freedom of all sorts, a fundamental axiom of political economy. See the note following the speech given in Marseilles in vol. 2 (*OC*, vol. 2, p. 311, "Sixième discours, à Marseille"). See also in vol. 1 the two letters to M. de Lamartine, vol. 1, p. 406, "Un Économiste à M. de Lamartine," and p. 452, "Seconde lettre à M. de Lamartine."

Association! And do we not know that this is society itself in the constant throes of improvement?

Organization! And do we not know that it makes all the difference between a heap of heterogeneous elements and nature's masterpieces?

Fraternity! And do we not know that this is to justice what impulses of the heart are to cold calculations of the mind?

We agree with you on this; we applaud your efforts to spread on the field of humanity the seed that will bear fruit in the future.

But we oppose you from the instant you call the law and taxes, that is to say, constraint and plunder, into play, since, apart from the fact that this recourse to force shows that you have more faith in yourselves than in the genius of humanity, this recourse is enough, in our view, to change the very nature and essence of the teaching that you are endeavoring to put into practice.[17]

17. (Paillottet's note) "There are three levels for humanity: the lowest, plunder; the highest, charity; and a middle level, justice.

"Governments only ever exercise one action, of which the sanction is force. Well, it is permissible to oblige someone to be just but not to force him to be charitable. When the law wishes to achieve by force what the moral law succeeds in doing through persuasion, far from lifting itself to the level of charity, it descends to the sphere of plunder.

"The proper sphere of the law and government is justice."

These ideas of the author were written in his handwriting in an autograph album sent to him in 1850 by the Literary Society on the occasion of the London Exhibition. We are reproducing the passage here because we consider that it summarizes the preceding pamphlet.

> # → 6 ←
> *Individualism and Fraternity*

[vol. 7, p. 328. "Individualisme et fraternité."
Possibly June 1848. n.p.]

A systematic view of history and the destiny of mankind, which seems to me to be as erroneous as it is dangerous, has recently been produced.[1]

According to this system, the world is divided into three principles: *authority, individualism,* and *fraternity.*

Authority relates to the aristocratic eras, individualism to the reign of the bourgeoisie, and fraternity to the triumph of the people.

The first of these principles is above all incarnated in the pope. *It leads to oppression by stifling personality.*

The second, inaugurated by Luther, *leads to oppression through anarchy.*

The third, *announced by the thinkers in La Montagne,* has given birth to true freedom by shrouding men in the ties of harmonious association.

As the people have been the masters in only one country, France, and for a short period, in '93, we still know the theoretical value and practical attractions of fraternity only through the attempt so noisily made at it at that time. Unfortunately, *union and love,* personified in Robespierre, *were only half able to stifle individualism, which reappeared the day after 9 Thermidor.*[2] *It still prevails.*

What is *individualism,* then? The author of the work to which we are referring defines it as follows:

"The principle of individualism is that which, taking man out of society, makes him the sole judge of what surrounds him and of himself, gives him

---

1. Bastiat is possibly referring to the first two volumes of a history of the French Revolution (*Histoire de la Révolution française,* 1847) that the socialist Louis Blanc had published just prior to the outbreak of the February Revolution of 1848. (See also the entry for "Blanc, Louis," in the Glossary of Persons.)

2. Date of the arrest of Robespierre (27 July 1794). He was guillotined the following day.

an exalted view of his rights without indicating his duties, abandons him to his own resources, and, with regard to all matters of government, proclaims the system of laissez-faire."[3]

That is not all. Individualism, the driving force of the bourgeoisie, was bound to invade the three major branches of human activity: religion, politics, and industry. From this sprang three major individualist schools: the school of philosophy, with *Voltaire as its leading light,* which by demanding freedom of thought *led us to a profound moral anarchy;* the school of politics, founded by Montesquieu, which, *instead of political freedom, brought us an oligarchy based on a property franchise;* and the school of economists, *represented by Turgot, which, instead of economic freedom, bequeathed us competition between rich and poor to the advantage of the rich.*[4]

We see that up to now humanity has been very poorly inspired and that it has gone wrong at every turn. This has not, however, been through lack of warnings, since the principle of *fraternity* has always issued its protests and reservations through the voices of Jean Huss,[5] Morelli, Mably, and Rousseau and through the efforts of Robespierre.

But what is fraternity? "The principle of fraternity is that which, considering the members of the extended family as being interdependent, tends to organize the various forms of society, the work of man, in line with the model of the human body, the work of God, and bases the power of government on persuasion and the voluntary acquiescence of the heart.[6]

This is M. Blanc's system. What makes it dangerous in my view, apart from the brilliance with which it is set out, is that in it the true and the false are intermingled in proportions that are difficult to determine. I have

---

3. (Bastiat's note) Blanc, *Histoire de la Révolution française,* vol. 1, p. 9. [Bastiat is quoting from the 1847 edition of Blanc's work.]

4. (Bastiat's note) Blanc, *Histoire de la Révolution française,* vol. 1, pp. 350–51. [Bastiat is again quoting from the 1847 edition of Blanc's work. In this passage Bastiat is summarizing Blanc's critique of eighteenth-century theories of individualism.]

5. Jan Hus.

6. (Paillottet's note) As Bastiat had not finished copying the passage of the book he is dealing with by hand in his manuscript, I have had to make good this lacuna and present the whole sentence. With regard to the last few words, I make so bold as to say that they imply a contradiction with the thought of achieving any form of social system through the intervention of the state, that is to say, by force. Those who put forward social systems they have invented do not limit themselves, any more than Robespierre does, to claiming to *persuade* or to obtain the *voluntary acquiescence of the heart,* and have no greater justification than he in assuming the flag of freedom.

no intention of studying it in all its symmetrical ramifications. In order to respect the requirements of this booklet, I will consider it principally from the point of view of political economy.

I must admit that when it is a question of setting out the principles which, in a given era, were the driving force of the social body, I would like them expressed in terms less vague than *individualism* and *fraternity*.

*Individualism*[7] is a new word that has been simply substituted for *egoism*. It is an exaggeration of the concept of personality.

Man is essentially a sympathetic creature. The more his powers of sympathy are concentrated on himself, the more of an egoist he is. The more they embrace his fellow men, the more of a philanthropist he is.

Egoism[8] is thus like all other vices, like all other prevarications; that is to say, it is as old as man himself. This can also be said of philanthropy. In all eras, under all regimes, and in all classes, there have been men who were hard, cold, self-centered, and who related everything to themselves, and others who were good, generous, humane, and selfless. I do not think that we can make one of these states of mind the basis of society any more than we can anger or gentleness, energy or weakness.

It is therefore impossible to accept that from a fixed date in history, for example, from the time of Luther, all the efforts of the human race have been systematically, and so to speak providentially, devoted to the triumph of individualism.

On what basis can it be held that an exaggerated sense of self was born in modern times? When ancient people pillaged and ravaged the world, reducing those they conquered to slavery, were they not acting under the influence of an egoism of the highest degree? If, in order to ensure victory, overcome resistance, and escape the frightful fate they reserved for those they called savages, alliances of warriors felt the need to join forces, if individuals were even disposed to make genuine sacrifices to this end, was egoism thereby any less egoism for being collective?

I would say the same thing with regard to domination by theological authority. Whether force or guile is used to achieve the servitude of men, whether their weakness or credulity is exploited, does not the very fact of unjust domination reveal a feeling of egoism in those who dominate? Did not Egyptian priests who imposed false beliefs on their fellow men in order

---

7. See "Bastiat's Political Writings: Anecdotes and Reflections," pp. 407–8.
8. Ibid., p. 408.

to make themselves masters of their actions and even of their thought seek *personal* advantage through the most immoral means?

As nations became stronger they rejected plunder achieved by force. They progressed toward moral propriety and the production and economic freedom attending it, and yet some people profess to find in freedom of production the primal manifestation of selfishness!

But you who do not want production to be free must want it constrained, for there is no halfway house. Yes, there is, you say, association. This is to misunderstand words, for as long as association is voluntary, production remains free. It is not an abandonment of freedom to enter into agreements or voluntary associations with your fellow men.

As men became more enlightened, they reacted against superstition, false beliefs, and opinions that were imposed. And there you go again discovering in *free inquiry* a second sign of selfishness.

But you who do not accept either authority or free examination, what would you put in its place? Fraternity, you say. Will not fraternity put into my mind either totally preconceived ideas or ones it has itself elaborated?

So you do not want men to examine opinions critically! I can understand this intolerance in theologians. They are logically consistent. They say: Seek the truth in everything, *traditus est mundus disputationibus eorum,*[9] when God has not revealed it. Where He has said: This is the truth, it would be absurd for you to want to examine it critically.

However, by what right do modern socialists refuse us the free inquiry they use so widely? They have just one means of curbing our minds and that is to claim to be inspired. A few of them have tried, but up to now they have not shown us their qualifications to be prophets.

Without calling into question their intentions, I say that at the basis of these doctrines there is the most irrational of all despotisms and consequently of *all individualisms*. What is more tyrannical than to want to regiment our work and minds, leaving aside, indeed not even invoking, any supernatural authority? It is not surprising that we end up seeing in Robespierre the archetype, the hero, and the apostle of fraternity.

If selfishness is not the exclusive motivation of a period in modern history, no more is it the principle that guides one class to the exclusion of all the others.

In moral sciences a certain symmetry in presentation is often taken for the truth. Let us be wary of superficial appearance.

---

9. "And the world has been handed over to their discussions."

This is how the notion that modern nations are made up of three classes—the aristocracy, the bourgeoisie, and the common people—has gained credibility. Therefore, it is concluded that there is the same antagonism between the two lower classes as between the two upper ones. The bourgeoisie, it is said, has overthrown the aristocracy and taken its place. With regard to the common people, it constitutes another form of aristocracy and will, in turn, be overthrown by it.

For my part, I see only two classes in society: conquerors who fall on a country, taking possession of the land, the wealth, and legislative and judiciary power; and a common people that has been overcome, that suffers, works, grows, breaks its chains, reconquers its rights, and governs itself more or less well, or very badly, for a long time, is taken in by a great many charlatans, is often betrayed by its own members, learns through experience, and gradually achieves equality through freedom and fraternity through equality.[10]

Each of these two classes obeys an indestructible sense of itself. But if this disposition deserves the name "selfishness," it is certainly in the case of the conquering and dominating class.

It is true that within the common people there are men who are more or less rich in infinite variation. But the difference in wealth is not enough to make up two classes. As long as a man of the common people does not turn against the common people themselves to exploit them, as long as he owes his wealth only to work and an ordered and economic life, despite the few riches he acquires and the limited influence that these riches give him, he will remain a member of the common people and it is a misuse of terminology to claim that he has entered another class, an aristocratic class.

If this were so, see what the consequences would be. An honest artisan who works hard and plans for the future, who imposes severe privations on himself, who increases the number of his customers because of the confidence he inspires, who gives his son a rather fuller education than the one he received himself, would be on the way to joining the bourgeoisie. This is a man to be distrusted, a nascent aristocrat, an *egoist*.

If, on the contrary, he is lazy, dissipated, improvident, if he totally lacks the dynamism necessary for making a few savings, we can then be certain that he will remain one of the common people. He will adhere to the principle of fraternity.

And now, how will all these men retained in the ranks of the lowest of

10. See "Note on the Translation," pp. xiii–xiv, and also "Bastiat's Political Writings: Anecdotes and Reflections," pp. 409–10.

society through improvidence, through vice, and only too often, I admit, because of misfortune understand the principle of equality and fraternity? Who will be their defender, their idol, their apostle? Do I need to name him? . . .

Abandoning the theater of polemics, I will endeavor, as far as my strength and time allow, to consider egoistical individualism and *fraternity* from the point of view of political economy.

I will begin by declaring very frankly that the concept of the individual, of self-love, the instinct of self-preservation, the indestructible desire within man to develop himself, to increase the sphere of his action, increase his influence, his aspiration to happiness, in a word, individuality, appears to me to be the point of departure, the motive and universal dynamic to which Providence has entrusted the progress of humanity. It is absolutely in vain that this principle arouses hostility in modern socialists. Alas! Let them look into themselves; let them go deep into their consciences and they will rediscover this drive, just as we find gravity in all the molecules of matter. They may reproach Providence for having made man as he is and, as a pastime, seek to find out what would happen to society if the divinity, accepting them as counselors, changed his creatures to suit another design. These are dreams for distracting the imagination, but it is not on these that social sciences are founded.

There is no feeling that is so constantly active in man or so dynamic as the sense of self.

We can differ in the way we conceive happiness or seek it in wealth, power, and glory or the terror we inspire, in the responsiveness of our fellow men, in the satisfaction of vanity or the crown of election, but continue to seek it we do and we cannot stop ourselves from doing so.

From this it must be concluded that *egoistic individualism,* which is the sense of self taken in its unfavorable meaning, is as old as the concept itself, since there is not one of his qualities, above all the one most inherent in its nature, that man cannot abuse and has not abused through the ages. To claim that the sense of self has always been held within just limits, except since the time of Luther and among the bourgeoisie, can be considered only a form of wit.

I think that the contrary thesis, in any case a more consoling one, could with more reason be held, and here are my arguments.

It is a sad truth, but one born of experience, that men in general give full rein to the sense of self and consequently abuse it up to the point at which they can do so with impunity. I say in general, since I am far from claiming that the inspiration of conscience, natural benevolence, or religious prescriptions have not often been enough to prevent personality from degenerating into egoism. However, it can be stated that the general obstacle to the exaggerated development or abuse of the sense of self is not in us but outside us. It is in the other personalities who surround us and react when we upset them to the point of keeping us in check, if you will excuse the expression.

This having been said, the more a gathering of men finds itself surrounded by weak or credulous beings and the less it finds obstacles in them, the more the concept of personality has to grow stronger in them and break the bounds that reconcile it with the general good.

Thus we see the peoples in classical times desolated by war, slavery, superstition, and despotism, all manifestations of egoism in men stronger or more enlightened than their fellows. It is never through action on itself in obedience to the moral laws that the concept of personality is confined within its just limits. To restrict it to these, it has been necessary for force and enlightenment to become the common heritage of the masses; and it is just as necessary that individualism, when manifested through force, is brought to a halt by a superior force, and when manifested through deceit, perishes through lack of support from public credulity.

Perhaps it will be thought that the representation of personalities as in a state of virtually perpetual antagonism containable only by a balance of force and enlightenment constitutes a very gloomy doctrine. It would follow that, as soon as this balance is disturbed, as soon as a people or a class realizes that they are endowed with irresistible force or an intellectual superiority that might make other peoples or classes subservient to them, the sense of self is always ready to exceed its limits and degenerate into egoism and oppression.

It is not a question of knowing whether this doctrine is gloomy, but whether it is true and whether the constitution of man is not such that he has to win his independence and security by the development of his strength and intelligence. *Life is a conflict.* This has been true up to now, and we have no reason to believe that that will ever cease to be the case as long as man carries within his heart this sense of self that is so ready to exceed its limits.

The socialist schools endeavor to fill the world with hopes that we cannot prevent ourselves from considering to be illusory, precisely because they take no account, in their trivial theories, of this indelible disposition and the unchangeable nature that drives it, if it is not contained, toward its own exaggeration.

We search in vain in their mathematical systems of series and harmonies for the obstacle to the abuse of personality, for we will never find it. The socialists appear to us to be revolving ceaselessly in this vicious circle: if all men wish to be selfless, we have found social forms that will maintain fraternity and harmony between them.

For this reason, when they come to propose something which appears to be practical, we always see them dividing humanity into two parts: on the one hand, the state, the ruling power which they take to be infallible, impeccable, and free from any egoistic character; on the other, the people who no longer need plans for the future or any guarantees as to their security.

To carry out their plans, they are reduced to entrusting the ruling of the world to a power that is drawn, so to speak, from outside humanity. They invent a word: the *state*. They suppose that the state is a being that exists in itself, that possesses an inexhaustible amount of wealth independent from society's wealth, and that by means of this wealth the state can provide work for everyone and ensure everyone's existence. They take no heed of the fact that the state can only give back to society goods that it started off taking from it, and that it can actually give back only a part of these; nor furthermore, that the state is made up of men endowed with the sense of self, which in them just as in those being governed is inclined to degenerate into abuse; nor that one of the greatest temptations enticing one personality to offend others occurs when the man concerned is powerful and able to overcome resistance. In truth, although they have never expressed many views on this subject, the socialists probably hope that the state will be supported by institutions, by education, by foresight, and by close and severe supervision of the masses. However, if this is to be so, the masses have to be enlightened and far-sighted, and the system of governance that I am examining tends precisely to destroy the foresight of the masses since it makes the state responsible for supplying all necessities, combating all obstacles, and providing for everyone.

But, people will say, if the sense of self is indestructible, if it has the disastrous tendency to degenerate into abuse, if the force that represses it is not within us but exterior to us, if it is contained within just limits only by the resistance and reaction of other selves, if the men who exercise power do not escape this law any more than those on whom power is exercised, so that society can be maintained in good order only by the constant vigilance of all its members over each other and in particular by those governed over those who govern, then radical antagonism is irremediable. We have no other safeguards against oppression than a sort of balance among all the

egoisms that keep one another in check; and fraternity, the principle that is
so comforting, whose very name touches and softens hearts, that is capable
of realizing all the hopes of all men of goodwill, uniting men through the
bonds of friendship, this principle, proclaimed eighteen centuries ago by a
voice that almost all of humanity has held to be divine, would be banished
forever from the world.

God forbid that this should be our thought. We have ascertained that the
sense of individuality is a general human law, and we believe that this fact is
beyond doubt.

It is now a matter of knowing whether the fully understood and constant
interest of a man, a class, or a nation is radically opposed to the interest of
another man, class, or nation. If this is so, it has to be stated with sorrow
but truthfully that fraternity is just a dream, since it must not be expected
that each person will sacrifice himself for others, and if this happened, we
cannot see how humanity would gain, since the sacrifice of each one would
be equivalent to the sacrifice of the entire human race; this would constitute
universal misfortune.

But if, on the contrary, by studying the action that men exercise over one
another, we discover that their general interests concur, that progress, morality, and the wealth of all are conditions for the progress, morality, and wealth
of each individual, we will then understand how the concept of individuality
is reconciled with that of fraternity.

There is one condition, however. It is that this agreement does not
consist in a vain proclamation but is clearly, rigorously, and scientifically
demonstrated.

When this happens, as this demonstration is better understood and in-
culcated in a greater number of intelligent minds, that is to say, as enlightenment and moral science progress, the principle of fraternity will extend
further and further throughout the human race.

Well, this is the comforting demonstration that we think we can make.

First of all, what should we understand by the word *fraternity*?

Should we, as it is said, take this word literally? And does it imply that we
should love everyone currently living on the surface of the globe as we love
the brother who was conceived in the same womb and fed on the same milk
and whose cradle, games, emotions, sufferings, and joys we have shared? Obviously this is not the meaning of the word that we should accept. No man
could exist for more than a few minutes if each sorrow, each setback, or each
death that occurred around the world had to arouse in him the same emo-

tion as if it concerned his brother, and if the socialist gentlemen are adamant on this point (and they are very adamant . . . when it applies to others), they have to be told that nature is much less demanding. It is useless for us to beat our breasts or indulge in the affectation of *words*, so commonly seen these days; we will never, fortunately, be able to raise our sensitivity to this height. If nature does not allow this, morality forbids it, too. We all have to fulfill our duties toward ourselves, those close to us, our friends, our colleagues, and all those whose existence depends on us. We are also responsible to our profession and for the functions entrusted to us. For most of us these duties take up all our time, and it is impossible for us to be able always to have a thought for and make our *immediate* aim the general interests of humanity. The question is to establish whether the scheme of things, resulting from the way men organize themselves and their perfectibility, does not lead to individual interests becoming increasingly merged with the general interest, and whether we are not brought by observation and perhaps by experience to desire the general good and consequently to contribute to it. In this case, the code of fraternity would arise from the very sense of self to which at first sight it is opposed.

Here, I need to return to a fundamental idea, one I have already discussed in this book[11] in the articles titled "Competition" and "Population."

With the exception of blood relationships and acts of pure selflessness and self-sacrifice, I think it can be said that the whole economy of a society is based on exchanged services.

However, to anticipate any misinterpretation, I have to say a word on self-sacrifice, which is the voluntary sacrifice of the sense of self.

Economists are accused of not taking self-sacrifice into account and perhaps despising it. Please God, we will never fail to recognize the power and grandeur in self-sacrifice. Nothing that is great and generous, nothing that arouses fellow feeling and admiration in men can be accomplished ex-

11. It is not clear to what book Bastiat is referring here. He published only three book-length works before his death: *Cobden and the League* (1845), *Economic Sophisms* (1847), and *Economic Harmonies* (1850). The last was only partially completed when it was first published and contained only the first ten chapters. A more complete edition was published in 1851, after his death. Chapter 10 of *Economic Harmonies* was titled "Competition," and chapter 16 was titled "Population." This essay appeared with no date or place of publication and may have been written in June 1848. Bastiat thus may be referring to a draft of the *Economic Harmonies,* which he was writing at the time this essay appeared.

cept through selflessness. Man is not just an intelligent mind, and he is not merely a calculating being. He has a soul, and in this soul there is a germ of fellow feeling which may be developed until it attains universal love, to the point of the most absolute sacrifice, at which point it produces the generous actions that, when narrated, bring tears to our eyes.

However, economists do not think that everyday events in our lives, the daily and constant actions that men carry out to keep themselves alive and fed and to develop themselves can be based on the principle of self-sacrifice. Well, these acts and transactions that are freely negotiated are the very ones that are the subject of political economy. The field is sufficiently large to constitute a science. Men's actions relate to a variety of sciences: when they give rise to dispute, they are subject to the science of law; when they are subject to the direct influence of the established authority, they relate to politics; and when they call for the effort we consider virtue, they concern morality or religion.

None of these sciences can do without the others and even less contradict them. However, we should not require one of them to embrace the others totally. And although economists have little to say about self-sacrifice since this is not their subject, we dare to assert that their biographies in this respect can bear comparison with those of writers who have embraced other doctrines. In the same way as priests have little to say about value and competition because these things are only indirectly concerned with the sphere of their predications, they buy and sell just like common mortals. This can also be said of socialists.

Let us say, then, that in human actions, those that form the subject of economic science involve the *exchange of services*.

Perhaps people will find that this is to disparage the science. However, I sincerely believe that it is substantial, although simpler than is supposed, and that it is entirely based on these vulgar notions: *give me this and I will give you that; do this for me and I will do that for you.* I cannot conceive of any other forms of human transaction. The intervention of cash, merchants, and middlemen may complicate this elementary system and obscure our view of it. It is nonetheless typical of all economic acts.

# → 7 ←
## The State

[vol. 4, p. 327. "L'État." Originally published in the 25 September 1848 issue of *Le Journal des débats*.]

I would like someone to sponsor a prize, not of five hundred francs but of a million, with crowns, crosses, and ribbons for whoever can provide a good, simple, and understandable definition of the words "the state."

What a huge service this person would be doing to society!

The state! What is this? Where is it? What does it do? What ought it to be doing?

All we know about it is that it is a mysterious being and is definitely the one that is most solicited and most tormented and is the busiest; the one to whom the most advice is given; the one most accused, most invoked, and most provoked in the world.

For, sir, I do not have the honor of knowing you, but I will bet ten to one that for the last six months you have been constructing utopias; and if you have been doing so, I will bet ten to one that you are making the state responsible for bringing them into existence.

And you, madam, I am certain that in your heart of hearts you would like to cure all the suffering of humanity and that you would not be in the slightest put out if the state just wanted to help in this.

But alas! The unfortunate being, like Figaro, does not know whom to listen to nor which way to turn. The hundred thousand voices of the press and the tribune are all calling out to this being at once:

Organize work and the workers.
Root out selfishness.
Repress the insolence and tyranny of capital.
Carry out experiments on manure and eggs.
Criss-cross the country with railways.
Irrigate the plains.

Reforest the mountains.

Set up model farms.

Set up harmonious workshops.

Colonize Algeria.

Provide children with milk.

Educate the young.

Succor the elderly.

Send the inhabitants of towns to the country.

Bear hard on the profits of all industries.

Lend money interest free to those who want it.

Liberate Italy, Poland, and Hungary.

Breed and improve saddle horses.

Encourage art and train musicians and dancers for us.

Prohibit trade and at the same time create a merchant navy.

Discover truth and toss into our heads a grain of reason. The mission of the state is to enlighten, develop, expand, fortify, spiritualize, and sanctify the souls of peoples.[1]

"Oh, sirs, have a little patience," the state replies pitifully. "I will try to satisfy you, but I need some resources to do this. I have prepared some projects relating to five or six bright, new taxes that are the most benign the world has ever seen. You will see how pleased you will be to pay them."

At that, a great cry arises: "Just a minute! Where is the merit in doing something with resources? It would not be worth calling yourself the state. Far from imposing new taxes on us, we demand that you remove the old ones. You must abolish:

The tax on salt;[2]

The tax on wines and spirits;

Postage tax;

<hr>

1. (Paillottet's note) This last sentence is from M. de Lamartine. The author quotes it again in the pamphlet that follows. (*OC*, vol. 4, p. 342, "La Loi." [The sentence itself is found on p. 387.])

2. Before the Revolution of 1789 the salt tax was known as the "gabelle." Because of its symbolic association with the ancien régime, it was much hated and was one of the first things abolished after the Revolution. However, it soon returned as a more straightforward "salt tax." See Coquelin, "Gabelle," in *Le Dictionnaire de l'économie politique,* vol. 1, pp. 814–15.

City tolls;[3]
Trading taxes;[4]
Mandatory community service."[5]

In the middle of this tumult, and after the country has changed its state two or three times because it has failed to satisfy all these demands, I wanted to point out that they were contradictory. Good heavens, what was I thinking of? Could I not keep this unfortunate remark to myself?

Here I am, discredited forever, and it is now generally accepted that I am a man without heart or feelings of pity, a dry philosopher, an individualist, a bourgeois, and, to sum it up in a single word, an economist of the English or American school.

Oh, excuse me, you sublime writers whom nothing stops, not even contradictions. I am doubtless mistaken, and I most willingly retract my statements. I do not ask for more, you may be sure, than that you have genuinely discovered, independently from us, a bountiful and inexhaustible being that calls itself THE STATE, which has bread for every mouth, work for every arm, capital for all businesses, credit for all projects, oil for all wounds, balm

3. The word Bastiat uses is "octrois," a form of hated taxes during the pre-Revolutionary period. An *octroi* was a consumption tax levied by a town or city in order to pay for the activities of the communal administration. It was much abused during the ancien régime because it was "farmed out" to private contractors. Although the *octroi* was abolished in the early years of the Revolution, it was reintroduced by the city of Paris in 1798. See Esquirou de Parieu, "Octrois," in Coquelin, *Dictionnaire de l'économie politique,* vol. 2, pp. 284–91.

4. The word Bastiat uses is "patentes," direct taxes imposed on any individual who carried out a trade, occupation, or profession. The *patentes* were first imposed in 1791 by the Constituent Assembly and were completely reformulated in 1844.

5. The French word used here is "prestations," which is an abbreviation of "prestations en nature" (or "obligatory services in kind"), according to which all able-bodied men were expected to spend two days a year maintaining roads in and around their towns. The *prestations* were a reform of the much-hated and burdensome compulsory labor obligations known as the "corvée," dating from the ancien régime. The *corvée* was abolished by Turgot in 1776; however, it returned, as did the "gabelle" (salt tax), in a less onerous form during the Consulate period under Napoléon, only to be abolished again in 1818. Under the law of 1824 the modern form of the *prestations* was introduced, whereby the compulsory labor was used only for local roads. A further modification took place in 1836, when the labor service could be commuted to the payment of a monetary equivalent. See also Courcelle-Seneuil, "Prestations," in Coquelin, *Dictionnaire de l'économie politique,* vol. 2, pp. 428–30.

for all suffering, advice for all perplexities, solutions for all doubts, truths for all intelligent minds, distractions for all forms of boredom, milk for children, wine for the elderly, a being that meets all our needs, anticipates all our desires, satisfies all our curiosity, corrects all our errors and all our faults, and relieves us all henceforth of the need for foresight, prudence, judgment, wisdom, experience, order, economy, temperance, and activity.

And why would I not desire this? May God forgive me, but the more I reflect on this, the more the convenience of the thing appeals to me, and I too am anxious to have access to this inexhaustible source of wealth and enlightenment, this universal doctor and infallible counsellor that you are calling THE STATE.

This being so, I ask you to show it to me and define it for me, and this is why I am proposing the establishment of a prize for the first person who discovers this phoenix. For in the end, people will agree with me that this precious discovery has not yet been made, since up to now all that has come forward under the name of THE STATE has been overturned instantly by the people, precisely because it does not fulfill the somewhat contradictory conditions of the program.

Does this need to be said? I fear that we are, in this respect, the dupes of one of the strangest illusions ever to have taken hold of the human mind.

Man rejects pain and suffering. And yet he is condemned by nature to the suffering privation brings if he does not embark upon the pain of work. All he has, therefore, is a choice between these two evils. How can he avoid both? Up to now, he has only found and will only ever find one means, that is, to *enjoy the work of others,* to act in such a way that pain and satisfaction do not accrue to each person in accordance with natural proportions, but that all pain accrues to some and all satisfaction to the others. From this we get slavery or even plunder, in whatever form it takes: wars, imposture, violence, restrictions, fraud, etc., all monstrous forms of abuse but in line with the thought that has given rise to them. We should hate and combat oppressors, but we cannot say that they are absurd.

Slavery is receding, thank heaven, and on the other hand, our aptitude for defending our property means that direct and crude plunder is not easy to do. However, one thing has remained. It is this unfortunate primitive tendency within all men to divide into two our complex human lot, shifting pain onto others and keeping satisfaction for themselves. It remains to be seen in what new form this sorry tendency will manifest itself.

Oppressors no longer act directly on the oppressed using their own forces. No, our conscience has become too scrupulous for that. There are still tyrants and victims certainly, but between them has placed itself the intermediary that is the state, that is to say, the law itself. What is more calculated to silence our scruples and, perhaps more appealing, to overcome our resistance? For this reason, we all make calls upon the state on one ground or pretext or another. We tell it, "I do not consider that there is a satisfactory relation between the goods I enjoy and my work. I would like to take a little from the property of others to establish the balance I desire. But this is dangerous. Can you not make my task easier? Could you not provide me with a good position? Or else hinder the production of my competitors? Or else make me an interest-free loan of the capital you have taken from its owners? Or raise my children at public expense? Or award me subsidies? Or ensure my well-being when I reach the age of fifty? By these means I will achieve my aim with a perfectly clear conscience, since the law itself will have acted on my behalf and I will achieve all the advantages of plunder without ever having incurred either its risks or opprobrium!

As it is certain, on the one hand, that we all address more or less similar requests to the state and, on the other, it is plain that the state cannot procure satisfaction for some without adding to the work of the others, while waiting for a new definition of the state I think I am authorized to give my own here. Who knows whether it will not carry off the prize? Here it is:

*The state is the great fiction by which everyone endeavors to live at the expense of everyone else.*

For today, as in the past, each person more or less wants to profit from the work of others. We do not dare display this sentiment; we even hide it from ourselves, and then what do we do? We design an intermediary, we address ourselves to the state, and each class in turn comes forward to say to it, "You who can take things straightforwardly and honestly, take something from the general public and we will share it." Alas! The state has a very ready tendency to follow this diabolical advice as it is made up of ministers and civil servants, in short, men, who like all men are filled with the desire and are always quick to seize the opportunity to see their wealth and influence increase. The state is therefore quick to understand the profit it can make from the role that the general public has entrusted to it. It will be the arbiter and master of every destiny. It will take a great deal; therefore a great deal will remain to it. It will increase the number of its agents and widen the circle of its attributions. It will end by achieving crushing proportions.

But what we should clearly note is the astonishing blindness of the general public in all this. When happy soldiers reduced the conquered to slavery, they were barbaric, but they were not absurd. Their aim, like ours, was to live at someone else's expense, but they did not fail to do so like us. What ought we to think of a people who do not appear to have any idea that reciprocal pillage is no less pillage because it is reciprocal, that it is no less criminal because it is executed legally and in an orderly fashion, that it adds nothing to public well-being, and that, on the contrary, it reduces well-being by everything that this spendthrift of an intermediary that we call the state costs us?

And we have placed this great illusion at the forefront of the Constitution to edify the people. These are the opening words of the preamble:

> France has set itself up as a republic in order to . . . call all its citizens to an increasingly higher level of morality, enlightenment, and well-being.

Thus, it is France, *an abstraction,* that calls French citizens, *real persons,* to morality, well-being, etc. Is it not wholeheartedly going along with this strange illusion that leads us to expect everything from some energy other than our own? Does it not give rise to the idea that there is, at hand and outside the French people, a being that is virtuous, enlightened, and rich that can and ought to pour benefits over them? Is it not to presume, quite gratuitously of course, that there is between France and the French, between the simple, abbreviated, abstract name of all these unique individuals and these individuals themselves, a relationship of father and child, tutor and pupil, teacher and schoolchild? I am fully aware that it is sometimes metaphorically said that the fatherland is a tender mother. However, to catch a constitutional proposition in flagrant inanity, you need to show only that it can be inverted, not without inconvenience but even advantageously. Would accuracy have suffered if the preamble had said:

> The French people have set themselves up as a republic in order to call France to an increasingly higher level of morality, enlightenment, and well-being?

Well, what is the value of an axiom in which the subject and attribute can change places without causing trouble? Everyone understands that you can say: "Mothers suckle their children." But it would be ridiculous to say: "Children suckle their mothers."

The Americans had another concept of the relationship between citizens and the state when they placed at the head of their Constitution these simple words:

> We the people of the United States, in order to form a more perfect union, establish justice, insure domestic tranquility, provide for the common defense, promote the general welfare, and secure the blessings of liberty to ourselves and our posterity, do ordain, etc.[6]

Here we have no illusions, no abstraction from which its citizens ask everything. They do not expect anything other than from themselves and their own energy. They place no expectations on anything other than themselves and their own energy. Or they place their expectations only on themselves and their own energy.

If I have taken the liberty of criticizing the opening words of our Constitution, it is because it is not a question, as one might believe, of wholly metaphysical subtlety. I claim that this personification of the state has been in the past and will be in the future a rich source of calamities and revolutions.

Here are the public on one side and the state on the other, considered to be two distinct beings, the latter obliged to spread over the former and the former having the right to claim from the latter a flood of human happiness. What is bound to happen?

In fact, the state is not and cannot be one-handed. It has two hands, one to receive and the other to give; in other words, the rough hand and the gentle hand. The activity of the second is of necessity subordinate to the activity of the first. Strictly speaking, the state is able to take and not give back. This has been seen and is explained by the porous and absorbent nature of its hands, which always retain part and sometimes all of what they touch. But what has never been seen, will never be seen, and cannot even be conceived is that the state will give to the general public more than it has taken from them. It is therefore a sublime folly for us to adopt toward the state the humble attitude of beggars. It is radically impossible for the state to confer a particular advantage on some of the individuals who make up the community without inflicting greater damage on the community as a whole.

The state therefore finds itself, because of our demands, in an obvious vicious circle.

If the state refuses to supply the services being demanded of it, it is accused of impotence, lack of willpower, and incapacity. If it tries to provide them,

6. We have used the original English wording for the words of the Constitution.

it is reduced to inflicting redoubled taxes on the people, doing more harm than good, and attracting to itself general dislike from the other direction.

Thus there are two hopes in the general public and two promises in the government: *a host of benefits and no taxes*. Hopes and promises that, since they are contradictory, can never be achieved.

Then is this not the cause of all our revolutions? For between the state, which is hugely generous with impossible promises, and the general public, which has conceived unattainable hopes, have come two classes of men, those with ambition and those with utopian dreams. Their role is clearly laid out by the situation. It is enough for these courtiers of popularity to shout into the people's ears: "The authorities are misleading you; if we were in their place, we would shower you with benefits and relieve you of taxes."

And the people believe this, and the people hope, and the people stage a revolution.

No sooner are their friends in power than they are required to fulfill these promises. "So give me work, bread, assistance, credit, education, and colonies," say the people, "and notwithstanding this, deliver me from the clutches of the tax authorities as you promised."

The new *state* is no less embarrassed than the former state since, when it comes to the impossible, promises may well be made but not kept. It tries to play for time, which it needs to bring its huge projects to fruition. First of all, it tries a few things timidly: on the one hand, it expands primary education a little; second, it makes slight modifications to the tax on wines and spirits.[7] But the contradiction still stands squarely before it; if it wants to be philanthropic it is obliged to maintain taxes, and if it renounces taxation it is also obliged to renounce philanthropy.

These two promises always, and of necessity, block each other. Making use of borrowing, in other words consuming the future, is really a current means of reconciling them; efforts are made to do a little good in the present at the expense of a great deal of evil in the future. However, this procedure evokes the specter of bankruptcy, which chases credit away. What is to be done then? The new state in this case takes its medicine bravely. It calls together forces to keep itself in power, it stifles public opinion, it has recourse to arbitrary decisions, it calls down ridicule on its former maxims, and it declares that administration can be carried out only at the cost of being unpopular. In short, it proclaims itself to be *governmental*.

7. 1830.

And it is at this point that other courtiers of popularity lie in wait. They exploit the same illusion, go down the same road, obtain the same success, and within a short time are engulfed in the same abyss.

This is the situation we reached in February.[8] At that time, the illusion that is the subject of this article had penetrated even further into the minds of the people, together with socialist doctrines. More than ever, the people expected the *state,* in its republican robes, to open wide the tap of bounty and close that of taxation. "We have often been misled," said the people, "but we ourselves will see to it that we are not misled once again."

What could the provisional government do? Alas, only what has always been done in a like situation: make promises and play for time. The government did not hesitate to do this, and to give their promises more solemnity they set them in decrees. "An increase in well-being, a reduction of work, assistance, credit, free education, farming colonies, land clearance, and at the same time a reduction in the tax on salt, on wine and spirits, on postage, on meat, all this will be granted . . . when the National Assembly meets."

The National Assembly met, and since two contradictory things cannot be achieved, its task, its sad task was to withdraw as gently as possible and one after the other all the decrees of the provisional government.

However, in order not to make the disappointment too cruel, a few compromises simply had to be undertaken. A few commitments have been maintained, and others have been started to a small degree. The current government is therefore endeavoring to dream up new taxes.

At this point, I will move forward in thought to a few months in the future and ask myself, with iron in my soul, what will happen when a new breed of agents goes into the countryside to raise the new taxes on inheritance, on income, and on farming profits. May the heavens give the lie to my presentiments, but I can still see a role in this for the courtiers of popularity.

Read the latest Manifesto of the Montagnards,[9] the one they issued regarding the presidential elections. It is a bit long, but in the end it can be briefly summarized thus: *The state must give a great deal to its citizens and*

8. Revolution of 1848.

9. During the Second Republic deputies on the extreme left adopted the name "Montagnards" (or Mountain), which had first been used during the French Revolution by Robespierre and his supporters. See also the entry for "La Montagne" in the Glossary of Subjects and Terms and the entry for "Robespierre, Maximilien de," in the Glossary of Persons.

*take very little from them.* This is always the same tactic, or if you prefer, the same error.

The state owes "free instruction and education to all its citizens."

It owes:

"General and vocational education that is as appropriate as possible to the needs, vocations, and capacities of each citizen."

It must:

"Teach him his duties toward God, men, and himself; develop his sensibilities, aptitudes, and faculties; and in short, give him the knowledge needed for his work, the enlightenment needed for his interests, and a knowledge of his rights."

It must:

"Make available to everybody literature and the arts, the heritage of thought, the treasures of the mind, and all the intellectual enjoyment that elevates and strengthens the soul."

It must:

"Put right any accident, fire, flood, etc. (this *et cetera* says far more than its small size would suggest), experienced by a citizen."

It must:

"Intervene in business and labor relations and make itself the regulator of credit."

It owes:

"Well-founded encouragement and effective protection to farmers."

It must:

"Buy back the railways, canals, and mines," and doubtless also run them with its legendary capacity for industry."

It must:

"Stimulate generous initiatives, encourage them, and help them with all the resources needed to make them a triumphant success. As the regulator of credit, it will sponsor manufacturing and farming associations liberally in order to ensure their success."

The state has to do all this without prejudicing the services which it currently carries out; and, for example, it will have to maintain a constantly hostile attitude toward foreigners since, as the signatories of the program state, "bound by this sacred solidarity and by the precedents of republican France, we send our promises made on high and our hopes soaring across the barriers that despotism raises between nations: the right we wish for ourselves we also wish for all those oppressed by the yoke of tyranny. We want our glorious army to continue to be, if necessary, the army of freedom."

As you can see, the gentle hand of the state, that sweet hand that gives and spreads benefits widely, will be fully occupied under the Montagnard government. Might you perhaps be disposed to believe that this will be just as true of the rough hand that goes rummaging and rifling in our pockets?

Don't you believe it! The courtiers of popularity would not be masters of their trade if they did not have the art of hiding an iron fist in a velvet glove.

Their reign will certainly be a cause for celebration for taxpayers.

"Taxes must reach the superfluous, not the essentials," they say.

Would it not be a fine day if, in order to shower us with benefits, the tax authorities were content to make a hole in our superfluous assets?

That is not all. The aim of the Montagnards is that "taxes will lose their oppressive character and become just a fraternal act."

Good heavens! I was well aware that it is fashionable to shove fraternity in everywhere, but I did not think it could be inserted into the tax collector's notice.

Coming down to detail, the signatories of the program say:

"We want the taxes levied on objects of first necessity, such as salt, wines and spirits, *et cetera,* to be abolished immediately;

"The land tax, city tolls, and industrial licenses to be reformed;

"Justice free of charge, that is to say, a simplification of the forms and a reduction in the fees" (this is doubtless intended to milk the stamp duty).

Thus, land tax, city tolls, industrial licenses, stamp duty, salt tax, tax on wine and spirits,[10] and postage would all go. These gentlemen have found the secret of giving feverish activity to the *gentle hand* of the state while paralyzing its *rough hand.*

Well then, I ask the impartial reader, is this not childishness and, what is more, dangerous childishness? What is to stop the people mounting revolution after revolution once the decision has been taken not to stop doing so until the following contradiction has been achieved: "Give nothing to the state and receive a great deal from it"?

Do people believe that if the Montagnards came to power they would not be victims of the means they employed to seize it?

Fellow citizens, since time immemorial two political systems have con-

10. See the entry "Wine and Spirits Tax" in the Glossary of Subjects and Terms.

fronted one another and both have good arguments to support them. According to one, the state has to do a great deal, but it also has to take a great deal. According to the other, its twin action should be little felt. A choice has to be made between these two systems. But as for the third system, which takes from the two others and which consists in demanding everything from the state while giving it nothing, this is illusionary, absurd, puerile, contradictory, and dangerous. Those who advocate it to give themselves the pleasure of accusing all forms of government of impotence, and of thus exposing them to your blows, those people are flattering and deceiving you, or at the very least they are deceiving themselves.

As for us, we consider that the state is not, nor should it be, anything other than a common force, instituted not to be an instrument of mutual oppression and plunder between all of its citizens, but on the contrary to guarantee to each person his own property and ensure the reign of justice and security.[11]

11. (Paillottet's note) See chapter 17 of the *Harmonies* in vol. 6 and the small work dated 1830 titled "To the Electors of the *Département* of the Landes," in vol. 1. (*OC,* vol. 6, p. 535, "Services privés, service publique"; and vol. 1, p. 217, "Aux électeurs du département des Landes.)

## → 8 ←

## *The State (draft)*

[vol. 7, p. 238. "L'État." Originally published as a draft dated 11–15 June 1848, in the first issue of *Jacques Bonhomme*.[1]

"There are those who say, 'A financial man, such as Thiers, Fould, Goudchaux, or Girardin, will get us out of this.' I think they are mistaken."

"Who, then, will get us out of this?"

"The people."

"When?"

"When the people have learned this lesson: since the state has nothing it has not taken from the people, it cannot distribute largesse to the people."

"The people know this, since they never cease to demand reductions in taxes."

"That is true, but at the same time they never cease to demand handouts of every kind from the state."

"They want the state to establish nursery schools, infant schools, and free schools for our youth, national workshops for those that are older, and retirement pensions for the elderly."

"They want the state to go to war in Italy and Poland."

"They want the state to found farming colonies."

"They want the state to build railways."

"They want the state to bring Algeria into cultivation."

"They want the state to lend ten billion to landowners."

---

1. This piece is a rough draft of Bastiat's best-known pamphlet, "The State," published in September 1848 (see "The State," pp. 93–104 in this volume. For more details on Bastiat's journalistic activity during the revolution of 1848, see "Bastiat's Political Writings: Anecdotes and Reflections," pp. 401–7 in this volume.

"They want the state to supply capital to workers.

"They want the state to replant the forests on mountains.

"They want the state to build embankments along the rivers.

"They want the state to make payments without receiving any.

"They want the state to lay down the law in Europe.

"They want the state to support agriculture.

"They want the state to give subsidies to industry.

"They want the state to protect trade.

"They want the state to have a formidable army.

"They want the state to have an impressive navy.

"They want the state to . . ."

"Have you finished?"

"I could go on for another hour at least."

"But what is the point you are trying to make?"

"This. As long as the people want all of this, they will have to pay
for it. There is no *financial man* alive who can do something with
nothing."

*Jacques Bonhomme* is sponsoring a prize of fifty thousand francs to be
given to anyone who provides a good definition of the word *state,* for that
person will be the savior of finance, industry, trade, and work.

# → 9 ←
## The Law

[vol. 4, p. 342. "La Loi." Bastiat wrote this pamphlet while vacationing with his family in Mugron. June 1850. n.p.]

The law corrupt? The law—and in its train all the collective forces of the nation—the law, I repeat, not only turned aside from its purpose but used to pursue a purpose diametrically opposed to it! The law turned into an instrument of all forms of cupidity instead of being a brake on them! The law itself accomplishing the iniquity it was intended to punish! This is certainly a serious occurrence if it is true, and one to which I must be allowed to draw the attention of my fellow citizens.

We hold from God the gift that encompasses them all: life; physical, intellectual, and moral life.

However, life is not self-supporting. He who has given it to us has left us the job of looking after it, developing it, and improving it.

To do this, He has provided us with a set of exceptional faculties and immersed us in a milieu of diverse elements. It is through the application of our faculties to these elements that the phenomena of *assimilation* and *appropriation* take place, through which life proceeds along the circle allocated to it.

Existence, faculties, and assimilation—in other words, personality, freedom, and property—this is man in a nutshell.

It may be said that these three things, leaving aside any demagogical hairsplitting, precede and supersede all human legislation.

It is not because men have enacted laws that personality, freedom, and property exist. On the contrary, it is because personality, freedom, and property are already in existence that men enact laws.

What is the law, then? As I have said elsewhere, it is the collective organization of the individual right of legitimate defense.[1]

---

1. (Paillottet's note) See vol. 5, the last two pages of the pamphlet titled "Plunder and the Law." (*OC*, vol. 5, p. 1, "Spoliation et loi.") [The last two pages are 14 and 15.] [See also "Plunder and Law," p. 275 in this volume.]

107

Each of us certainly holds from nature and God the right to defend our person, our freedom, and our property, since these are the three elements that constitute or preserve life, elements that are mutually complementary and that cannot be understood independently of one another. For what are our faculties if not an extension of our personality, and what is property if not an extension of our faculties?

If each person has the right to defend, even by force, his person, his freedom, and his property, several people have the right to join together, to form an understanding and organize themselves into a common force in order to provide lawfully for this defense.

Collective right therefore roots its principle, its raison d'être, and its legitimacy in individual right, and common force cannot rationally have any other aim or mission than those of the individual forces for which it is a substitute.

Thus, since force on the individual level cannot legitimately be aimed at the person, freedom, or property of another individual, by the same argument force cannot legitimately be used collectively to destroy the person, freedom, or property of either individuals or classes.

This is because such misuse of force would in either case be a contradiction of our premises. Who would dare to say that we were given such power not to defend our rights, but to reduce the equal rights of our fellows to nothing? And if this is not true for each individual acting in isolation, how can it be true for collective power, which is nothing other than the organized union of the power of individuals?

Therefore, if there is one thing that is clear, it is this: law is the organization of the natural right of legitimate defense. It is the substitution of collective for individual power to facilitate action in the area in which individuals have the right to act, that is to say, to do what they have the right to do. It serves to guarantee the integrity of persons, freedoms, and property; to maintain each person within his right; and to ensure the reign of justice among all.

And if there were a people constituted on this basis, I consider that order would prevail both in fact and in theory. I consider that this people would have the simplest, the most economical, the least heavy, the least felt, the least culpable, the most just, and hence the most solid government imaginable, whatever its political form.

For, under such a regime, each person would fully understand that he had full enjoyment as well as full responsibility for his existence. Provided that each person was respected, work was free, and the fruits of work protected against any unjust infringement, no one would have any cause to take issue with the state. So long as we were happy, we would not, it is true, have to thank it for our success; however, should we be unhappy, we would no more attribute this to the state than our farmers would attribute hail and frost to it. Its only effect on us would be the inestimable benefit of security.

We can also state that, thanks to the noninterference of the state in private affairs, needs and satisfactions would develop naturally. We would not see poor families seeking literary education before they had bread. We would not see towns growing in population at the expense of the countryside or the countryside at the expense of towns. We would not see those large-scale migrations of capital, labor, or populations triggered by legislative measures, migrations that render the very sources of existence so uncertain and precarious and which increase the responsibility of governments to such a great extent.

Unfortunately, the law is far from being limited to its proper role. It is far from deviating from it only according to neutral and questionable opinions. It has done worse: it has acted against its own purposes; it has destroyed its own aim; it has concentrated on abolishing the justice which it should have put in command and effacing the boundaries between various rights that its mission was to uphold. It has placed collective power at the disposal of those who wish to exploit persons, freedom, or the property of others without risk or scruple; it has converted plunder into right in order to protect it and legitimate defense into crime in order to punish it.

How has this corruption of the law come about? What have its consequences been?

The law has become corrupt under the influence of two very different causes: unintelligent selfishness and bogus philanthropy.

Let us take the first of these.

Protecting and developing oneself is an aspiration common to all men to the extent that if each person enjoyed the free exercise of his faculties and the free disposition of his attendant products, social progress would be constant, uninterrupted, and unerring.

However, there is another disposition that is just as common to them. That is to live and grow, when they can, at the expense of others. This is not a fortuitous allegation from someone with a bitter and pessimistic turn of mind. History gives examples of such a disposition through the constant wars, migrations of populations, oppression by religious leaders, universal slavery, industrial fraud, and monopolies with which its annals are filled.

This disastrous disposition arises from the very constitution of man, in the primitive, universal, and invincible sentiment that propels him toward well-being and makes him flee suffering.

Man can live and enjoy life only by assimilation and personal appropriation, that is to say, by a constant application of his faculties to things or by work. Hence property.

However, in practice, he can live and enjoy life by assimilating or appropriating to himself the product of the faculties of his fellow men. Hence plunder.

Well, since work is in itself a burden and since man by his nature is drawn to escape burdens, it follows, and history is there to prove it, that wherever plunder is less burdensome than work, it triumphs over work. This happens without religion or morality being able to stop it.

When, then, will plunder cease? When it becomes more of a burden or more dangerous than work.

It is very clear that the aim of the law has to be to oppose the powerful obstacle of collective power to this disastrous tendency and that it has to be on the side of property against plunder.

But the law is, in the majority of cases, established by one man or a class of men. And since the law has no existence without the sanction or support of an overwhelming force, the very probable result is that this force is finally placed in the hands of those who make the laws.

This inevitable phenomenon, combined with the disastrous tendency we have noted in men's hearts, explains the almost universal corruption of the law. It can be seen how, instead of being a brake on injustice, the law becomes an instrument and the most invincible instrument of injustice. It can be seen that, depending on the power of the legislator, to his profit and to varying degrees, the law destroys personality by slavery, freedom by oppression, and property by plunder among the bulk of mankind.

It is in the nature of men to react against the iniquity of which they are the victims. Therefore, when plunder is organized by law for the benefit of the classes that make it, all the classes that have been plundered attempt, by either peaceful or revolutionary means, to have a say in the making of laws. Depending on the level of enlightenment which they have attained, these classes may set themselves two very different aims when they pursue the acquisition of their political rights; they may either wish to stop legal plunder or they may aspire to take part in it.

Woe and misery three times over to any nation in which this last thought dominates the masses at the time when they in turn take the helm of the legislative power!

Up to now, legal plunder has been exercised by the minority over the majority as can be seen in those peoples in which the right to pass laws is concentrated in just a few hands. However, it has now become universal and equilibrium is being sought in universal plunder. Instead of the injustice existing in society being rooted out, it has become generalized. As soon as underprivileged classes recover their political rights, their first thought is not to rid themselves of plunder (that would suppose that they had an enlightenment that they cannot have) but to organize a system of reprisals against other classes and to their own detriment, as though it is necessary for a cruel retribution to strike them all, some for their iniquity and others for their ignorance, before the reign of justice is established.

No greater change or misfortune could therefore be introduced into society than this: to have a law that has been converted into an instrument of plunder.

What are the consequences of an upheaval like this? Volumes would be needed to describe them all. Let us content ourselves with pointing out the most striking.

The first is to erase from people's consciences the notion of the just and the unjust.

No society can exist if respect for the law does not prevail to some degree, but the surest means of ensuring that laws are respected is for them to be worthy of respect. When law and morality contradict one another, citizens find themselves in the cruel quandary of either losing their notion of morality or losing respect for the law, two misfortunes that are equally great and between which it is difficult to choose.

It is so deeply ingrained in the nature of law to ensure that justice reigns, that law and justice are inseparable in the eyes of the masses. We all have a strong disposition to consider what is legal to be legitimate, to the extent that many people mistakenly consider all forms of justice to be founded in law. It is therefore enough for the law to order and consecrate plunder for plunder to appear just and sacred in the understanding of many. Slavery, restrictions, and monopoly find their defenders not only in those who benefit from them but even in those who suffer from them. Try to put forward a few doubts about the morality of these institutions, and you will be told, "You are a dangerous innovator, a utopian, a theoretician, and a despiser of laws; you are undermining the base on which society is built." Do you give courses on morals or political economy? Official bodies will be found to express the following resolution to the government:

"That such subjects should be taught in the future *no longer* from the sole point of view of free trade (of freedom, property, and justice), as has been done so far, but also and above all from the point of view of the facts and the legislation (contrary to freedom, property, and justice) which govern economic life in France.

"That in the chairs in public universities whose salaries are paid for by the treasury, the professor should rigorously refrain from undermining in the slightest the respect due to the laws in force,[2] etc."

So that if there is a law that sanctions slavery or monopoly, oppression or plunder in any form, it cannot even be mentioned, since how can it be discussed without undermining the respect it inspires? What is more, it will be mandatory to teach morals and political economy from the point of view of this law, that is to say, on the premise that it is just merely because it is the law.

Another effect of this deplorable corruption of the law is that it gives an exaggerated weight to political passions and conflicts and in general to politics itself.

I could prove this proposition in a thousand ways. I will limit myself to comparing it, as an example, with a subject that has recently been in the minds of all: universal suffrage.

Whatever the disciples of Rousseau think, those who say that they are *very advanced* and whom I believe to be *retarded* by twenty centuries, *universal* suffrage (taking this word in its strictest sense) is not one of the sacred dogmas with regard to which any examination or even doubt is a crime.

Major objections may be made to it.

First of all, the word *universal* hides a crude sophism. There are in France thirty-six million inhabitants. In order for the right of suffrage to be *universal* it would have to be recognized for thirty-six million electors.[3] The most

---

2. (Bastiat's note) The General Council for Agriculture, Industry, and Trade. (Session on 6 May 1850.)

3. Under France's restrictive eligibility rules for voting only the wealthiest taxpayers were allowed to vote. Under King Charles X (1824–30) fewer than 100,000 taxpayers were able to vote out of a total population of about 32 million. By 1848 the increase in the size of the wealthy merchant and industrial classes had increased the number of voters to about 200,000 out of a total population of 36 million. By contrast, in England restrictions on voter eligibility were determined by the value of land one owned. The First Reform Bill of 1832 increased the size of the electorate from 435,000 to 652,000 out of a total population of 13 million.

generous account recognizes only nine million. Three out of four people are therefore excluded, and what is more they are excluded by the fourth. On what basis is this exclusion founded? On the principle of incapacity. Universal suffrage means the universal suffrage of those capable. There remains this practical question: who is capable? Are age, sex, and criminal record the only signs from which we can recognize incapacity?

If we look closely, we quickly see the reason the right of suffrage rests on the presumption of capacity, since the widest system differs in this respect from the most restricted system only by the appreciation of the signs from which this capacity can be recognized, which does not constitute a difference of principle but of degree.

This reason is that the elector does not stipulate for himself but for everybody.

If, as republicans of Greek and Roman hue claim, the right of suffrage was granted to us with life, it would be iniquitous for adults to prevent women and children from voting. Why should they be prevented from doing so? Because they are deemed to be incapable. And why is incapacity a reason for exclusion? Because the elector is not alone when given responsibility for his vote; because each vote commits and affects the entire community; because the community has the perfect right to demand a few guarantees with regard to the acts on which their well-being and existence depend.

I know what a possible answer might be. I also know what a possible reply to it might be. This is not the place to settle a controversy of this nature. What I want to draw attention to is that this controversy (as well as most political questions), one that so agitates whole nations, inflaming them and causing such distress, would lose almost all its importance if the law had always been what it ought to have been.

In fact, if the law limited itself to ensuring that all persons, freedoms, and properties were respected, if it were merely the organization of the individual right of legitimate defense, the obstacle, brake, and punishment that opposed all forms of oppression and plunder, would you believe that we would argue much, between citizens, as to whether suffrage was more or less universal? Do you believe that it would call into question the greatest of our benefits, public peace? Do you believe that the excluded classes would not wait patiently for their turn? Do you believe that the admitted classes would guard their privilege jealously? And is it not clear that, since personal interest is identical and common, some would take action without very much inconvenience on behalf of the others?

But if this fatal principle were to be introduced, if under the pretext of organization, regulation, protection, and subsidy the law *would be able to take from some to give to others,* to draw upon the wealth acquired by all classes to increase that of one class—sometimes that of farmers or manufacturers, traders, shipowners, artists, or actors—then, to be sure, in this case, there is no class that would not claim with reason that it too should have a hand in making the law, that would not fervently demand the right to vote and demand its eligibility to receive benefits and that would not overthrow society rather than be denied those benefits. Beggars and vagabonds themselves will prove to you that they have incontestable rights to it. They will say to you, "We never buy wine, tobacco, or salt without paying the tax, and part of this tax is given by law as premiums and subsidies to men who are richer than we are. Others use the law to raise the price of bread, meat, iron, and cloth artificially. Since each one exploits the law to his advantage, we want to exploit it too. We want it to enact the *right to assistance,* which is the share of plunder for the poor. To do this, we have to be electors and legislators in order to organize widespread alms for our class, just as you have organized widespread protectionism for yours. Do not tell us that you will provide our share and that, in accordance with M. Mimerel's proposal, you will throw us the sum of six hundred thousand francs to keep us quiet and as a bone to gnaw. We have other claims, and in any case we wish to decide for ourselves, just as the other sectors have decided for themselves!"

What can we say in reply to this argument? Yes, as long as the accepted principle is that the law can be diverted from its proper mission, that it can violate property instead of upholding it, each class will want to make the law, either to defend itself against plunder or to organize it for its own benefit. The political question will always be prejudicial, dominant, and absorbing; in a word, people will be beating on the door of the legislative palace. The conflict will be no less bitter within it. To be convinced of this, it is scarcely necessary to look at what is going on in the debating chambers in France and England; all you need to know is how the question is being put.

Is there any need to prove that this odious perversion of the law is a constant source of hatred and discord, which may go so far as to cause social disruption? Just look at the United States. This is one country in the world in which the law most faithfully fulfills its role to uphold the freedom and property of each person. It is therefore the one country in the world in which social order appears to be based on the most stable foundations. However, within the United States itself there are two questions, and only two questions, which have threatened political order from the outset. What are these two questions? Slavery and tariffs, that is to say, precisely the only two questions in which, contrary to the general spirit of that republic, the law has taken on the character of a plunderer. Slavery is a violation of the rights of the person sanctioned by the law. Protectionism is a violation of the right of property perpetrated by the law. Certainly it is very remarkable that, in the middle of so many other discussions, this twin *legal scourge,* a sorry inheritance from the old world, is the only one that may lead and perhaps will lead to the breakup of the Union. Indeed, no more significant fact can be imagined within society than this: *The law has become an instrument of injustice.* And if this fact leads to such momentous consequences in the United States, where it is just an exception, what will it lead to in this Europe of ours, where it is a principle, a system?

M. de Montalembert, referring to the reasoning behind a famous proclamation by M. Carlier, said, "We must make war on socialism." And by socialism, according to the definition by M. Charles Dupin, we have to understand that he meant plunder.

But what form of plunder was he wishing to talk about? For there are two forms. There is *plunder outside the law* and there is *legal plunder.*

As for plunder against the law, which we call theft or fraud and which is defined, provided for, and punished by the Penal Code, I really do not think this can be cloaked in the name of socialism. It is not this that systematically threatens the very foundations of society. Besides, the war against this sort of plunder has not waited for a signal from M. de Montalembert or M. Carlier. It has been waged since the beginning of time. France had already provided for it a long time before the February revolution, long before the apparition of socialism, by a whole apparatus of magistrates, police, gendarmes, prisons, convict settlements, and scaffolds. It is the law itself that wages this war, and what we should be hoping for, in my opinion, is that the law will always retain this attitude with regard to plunder.

But this is not the case. Sometimes the law takes the side of plunder. Sometimes it plunders with its own hands, in order to spare the blushes, the risk, and the scruples of its beneficiary. Sometimes it mobilizes the whole system of magistrates, police, gendarmes, and prisons to serve the plunderer and treats the victim who defends himself as a criminal. In a word, there is *legal plunder,* and it is doubtless to this that M. de Montalembert is referring.

Such plunder may be just an exceptional stain on the legislation of a people; and in this case the best thing to do, without undue oratory and lamentation, is to remove it as quickly as possible, in spite of the outcry from those it favors. How do we recognize it? That is easy; we need to see whether the law takes property owned by some to give to others what they do not own. We need to see whether the law carries out an act that a citizen cannot carry out himself without committing a crime, for the benefit of one citizen and at the expense of others. Make haste to repeal a law like this; it is not only an iniquity, it is a fruitful source of iniquity, for it generates reprisals, and if you are not careful an exceptional act will become widespread, more frequent, and part of a system. Doubtless, those who benefit from it will make a loud outcry; they will invoke *acquired rights*. They will say that the state owes their particular product protection and support. They will claim that it is a good thing for the state to make them richer because, as they are richer, they spend more and thus rain down earnings on their poor workers. Be careful not to listen to these sophists for it is exactly by the systematizing of such arguments that *legal plunder* becomes systematic.

This is what has happened. The illusion of the day is to make all sectors richer at each other's expense; this is generalizing plunder on the pretext of *organizing* it. Well, legal plunder can be carried out in an infinite number of ways. This gives rise to an infinite number of plans for organizing it, through tariffs, protectionism, premiums, subsidies, incentives, progressive taxes, free education, the right to work, the right to assistance, the right to tools for work, free credit, etc., etc. And all of these plans, insofar as they have legal plunder in common, come under the name of socialism.

Well, what type of war do you wish to wage against socialism, thus defined and as it forms a body of doctrine, if not a doctrinal war? Do you find this doctrine wrong, absurd, or abominable? Refute it. This will be all the easier the more erroneous, absurd, or abominable it is. Above all, if you wish to be strong, start by rooting out from your legislation everything relating to socialism that has managed to creep into it—no small task.

M. de Montalembert has been reproached for wanting to turn brute force against socialism. This is a reproach from which he should be cleared, since he formally stated, "The war against socialism should be in accordance with the law, honor, and justice."

But how has M. de Montalembert not seen that he has placed himself in a vicious circle? Do you want to oppose socialism by means of the law? But it is precisely socialism that invokes the law. It does not aim to carry out plunder against the law, but legal plunder. It is of the law itself that socialism claims to be the instrument, like monopolists of all stripes, and once it has the law on its side, how do you hope to turn the law against it? How do you hope to bring it within striking power of your courts, your gendarmes, or your prisons?

So what do you do? You want to prevent socialism from having any say in making laws. You want to keep it out of the legislative chamber. I dare to predict that you will never succeed in this while laws are being passed inside the chamber on the principle of legal plunder. It is too iniquitous and too absurd.

It is absolutely necessary for this question of legal plunder to be settled, and there are just three alternatives:

That the minority plunders the majority;
That everyone plunders everyone else;
That no one plunders anybody.

You have to choose between partial plunder, universal plunder, and no plunder at all. The law can pursue one of these three alternatives only.

*Partial plunder.* This is the system that prevailed for as long as the electorate was *partial* and is the system to which people return to avoid the invasion of socialism.

*Universal plunder.* This is the system that threatened us when the electorate became *universal* with the masses having conceived the idea of making laws along the same lines as their legislative predecessors.

*Absence of plunder.* This is the principle of justice, peace, order, stability, conciliation, and common sense that I will proclaim with all my strength, which is, alas, very inadequate, and with my lungs until my final breath.

And sincerely, can anything else be asked of the law? Can the law, with compulsion as its essential sanction, be reasonably employed for anything other than ensuring everyone his right? I challenge anyone to cause the law to step outside this circle without diverting it and consequently without turning compulsion against right. As this would be the most disastrous, the most illogical social upheaval imaginable, we really have to acknowledge that the true solution of the social problem, so long sought after, is encapsulated in these simple words: *law is organized justice.*

Well, we should note this clearly: to organize justice by law, that is to say, by compulsion, excludes the idea of organizing by law or compulsion any manifestation of human activity: labor, charity, agriculture, trade, industry, education, the fine arts, or religion, for it is impossible for any of these secondary organizations not to destroy the essential organization. In effect, how can we imagine compulsion impinging on the freedom of citizens without undermining justice, without acting against its own goal?

Here I am coming up against the most popular preconception of our age. Not only do we want the law to be just, we also want it to be philanthropic. We are not content for it to guarantee each citizen the free and inoffensive exercise of his faculties as they apply to his physical, intellectual, and moral development; we require it to spread well-being, education, and morality directly across the nation. This is the seductive side of socialism.

However, I repeat, these two missions of the law are contradictory. A choice has to be made. A citizen cannot simultaneously be free and not free. M. de Lamartine wrote to me one day, "Your doctrine is only half of my program. You have stopped at freedom; I have reached fraternity." I replied to him, "The second half of your program will destroy the first." And in effect it is totally impossible for me to separate the word *fraternity* from the word *voluntary*. It is impossible for me to conceive a fraternity that is enforced *by law* without freedom being destroyed *by law* and justice trampled underfoot *by law*.

Legal plunder is rooted in two things: the first, we have seen, is human selfishness, the other bogus philanthropy.

Before going any further, I think I have to explain myself as to the word *plunder*.

I do not take it to mean, as is only too often the case, something that is vague, undetermined, approximate, or metaphorical; I am using it in its properly scientific meaning, and as expressing the opposite idea to that of property. When a portion of wealth passes from the person who has earned it, without his consent and without compensation, to one who has not created it, whether this is by force or fraud, I say that property is undermined and that there is plunder. I say that it is exactly this that the law should be repressing everywhere and always. If the law is carrying out the very act that it should be repressing, I say that there is plunder nonetheless and even, socially speaking, with aggravating circumstances. Only in this case it is not the beneficiary of the plunder who is responsible for it, it is the law, the legislator, or society; and that is what constitutes the political danger.

It is unfortunate that this word has offensive overtones. I have tried in vain to find another, for at no time and still less today do I wish to cast an irritating word into the cauldron of our disagreements. For this reason, whether you believe it or not, I declare that I do not intend to query either the intentions or the morality of anyone whomsoever. I am attacking an idea that I consider to be false and a practice that appears to me to be unjust, and all this is so far beyond our intentions that each of us takes advantage of it unwittingly and suffers from it unknowingly. It is necessary to write under the influence of the party spirit or out of fear to cast doubt on the sincerity of protectionism, socialism, or even communism, which are only one and the same plant at three different stages of its development. All that can be said is that plunder is more visible in protectionism[4] because of its partiality and in communism because of its universality. From this it follows that of the three systems socialism is still the most vague, the most indecisive, and consequently the most sincere.

Be that as it may, agreeing that legal plunder has one of its roots in bogus philanthropy is obviously to exonerate its intentions.

This being understood, let us examine what the popular ambition that claims to achieve the general good through general plunder is worth, where it comes from, and where it will lead.

Socialists tell us, "Since the law organizes justice, why should it not also organize labor, education, or religion?"

Why? Because it could not organize labor, education, or religion without disorganizing justice.

Note therefore that law is compulsion, and that consequently the domain of the law cannot legitimately exceed the legitimate domain of compulsion.

When the law and compulsion hold a man in accordance with justice, they impose on him nothing other than pure negation. They impose only an abstention from causing harm. They do not interfere with his personality, his freedom, or his property. All they do is safeguard the personality, freedom, and property of others. They remain on the defensive; they defend the equal rights of all. They carry out a mission whose harmlessness is obvious, whose usefulness is palpable, and whose legitimacy is uncontested.

This is so true that, as one of my friends brought to my notice, to say that

---

4. (Bastiat's note) If in France protection were granted only to a single sector, for example to ironmasters, it would be so absurdly plunderous that it would be impossible to maintain it. For this reason, we see all forms of protected industry forming leagues, making common cause, and even recruiting each other to the extent that they appear to be embracing the whole of *national labor*. They feel instinctively that plunder is as concealed as it is generalized.

*the aim of the law is to ensure the reign of justice* is to use an expression that is not strictly true. What should be said is: *The aim of the law is to prevent injustice from reigning.* In reality it is not justice that has its own existence, it is injustice. The one results from the absence of the other.

But when the law, through the offices of its essential agent, compulsion, imposes a way of working, a method of teaching or the contents of the latter, a faith or a creed, it is no longer acting negatively but positively on men. It substitutes the will of the legislator for their own will. Their role is no longer to question themselves, make comparisons, or plan for the future; the law does all that for them. Intelligence becomes a superfluous attribute; they cease to be men and lose their personality, their freedom, and their property.

Try to imagine a form of labor compulsorily imposed that does not infringe freedom or a transmission of wealth forcibly imposed that does not infringe property. If you do not succeed, then you must agree that the law cannot organize economic production without organizing injustice.

When, from the confines of his office, a political writer surveys society, he is struck by the spectacle of inequality that greets him. He weeps over the sufferings that are the lot of so many of our brothers, sufferings that appear even more saddening when contrasted with luxury and opulence.

Perhaps he should ask himself whether such a state of society has not been caused by former plunder carried out by conquest and by current plunder carried out by means of the law. He should ask himself whether, given that all men aspire to well-being and improving their lot, the reign of justice is not enough to achieve the greatest activity of progress and the greatest amount of equality that are compatible with the individual responsibility ordained by God, as the just reward for virtue and vice.

He does not even give this a thought. His thoughts go to deals, agreements, and organizations that are either legal or artificial. He seeks a remedy in perpetuating or exaggerating the situation that has produced the misfortune.

The fact is, outside justice, which, as we have seen, is just a genuine negation, is there a single one of these legal agreements that does not include the principle of plunder?

You say, "Here are men who lack wealth," and you turn to the law. But the law is not a breast that fills by itself or whose milk-bearing ducts draw from elsewhere than society. Nothing enters the public treasury in favor of a citizen or a class other than that which other citizens and other classes have been *forced* to put in. If each person draws out only the equivalent of what he has put in, it is true that your law is not plunderous, but it does nothing for those men that *lack wealth,* it does nothing for equality. It can be an instrument for equality only to the extent that it takes from some to give to others, and in this case it becomes an instrument of plunder. If you look at the protection of tariffs, production subsidies, the right to profit, the right to work, the right to assistance, the right to education, progressive taxes, free credit, or social workshops from this point of view, you will always find at their root legal plunder and organized injustice.

You say, "Here are men who lack enlightenment," and you turn to the law. But the law is not a torch that spreads its own light far and wide. It hovers over a society in which there are men with knowledge and others without, citizens who need to learn and others who are willing to teach. It can do only one of two things: either it allows this type of transaction to operate freely and permits this type of need to be freely satisfied, or it can constrain people's wishes in this respect and take from some to pay teachers who will be responsible for educating the others free of charge. But in the second case it cannot do this without freedom and property being violated, signifying therefore legal plunder.

You say, "Here are men who lack morality or religion," and you turn to the law. But the law is compulsion and do I need to say how violent and crazy it is to use force in this connection?

For all its theories and strivings it appears that socialism, however indulgent it is toward itself, cannot avoid catching a glimpse of the fiend that is legal plunder. But what does socialism do? It cleverly shrouds the legal plunder from all eyes, even its own, under the seductive names of fraternity, solidarity, organization, and association. And because we do not ask so much of the law since we require only justice of it, socialism presumes that we are rejecting fraternity, solidarity, organization, and association and hurls the epithet *"Individualist!"* at us.

Socialism ought to know, therefore, that what we are rejecting is not natural organization, but forced organization.

It is not free association, but the forms of association that socialism claims to have the right to impose on us.

It is not spontaneous fraternity, but legal fraternity.

It is not providential solidarity, but artificial solidarity, which is only an unjust displacement of responsibility.

Socialism, like the old politics from which it stems, confuses government with society. For this reason, each time we do not want something to be done by the government, socialism concludes that we do not want this thing to be done at all. We reject education by the state; therefore we do not want education. We reject state religion; therefore we do not want religion. We reject equality established by the state; therefore we do not want equality, etc., etc. It is like accusing us of not wanting men to eat because we reject the growing of wheat by the state.

How in the world of politics has the strange idea become dominant of having the law generate things that it does not encompass: Good in its positive aspect, wealth, science, and religion?

Modern political writers, particularly those of the socialist school, base their various theories on a common hypothesis, definitely the strangest and most arrogant hypothesis that the human brain has ever devised.

They divide humanity into two parts. All men minus one form the first and the political writer all on his own forms the second and by far the most important part.

In effect, they begin with the premise that men do not have within themselves either a principle of action or any means of discernment; that they lack initiative; that they are made of inert matter, passive molecules, and atoms deprived of spontaneity; and that they are at most a form of plant life that is indifferent to its own mode of existence and willing to accept an infinite number of more or less symmetrical, artistic, and developed forms from an external initiative and hand.

Each of them then quite simply supposes that he is himself, wearing the hats of organizer, prophet, legislator, teacher, and founder, this driving force and hand, this universal dynamo and creative power whose sublime mission is to gather together in society the scattered stuff of humanity.

From this given starting point, just as each gardener according to his whim prunes his trees into pyramids, umbrellas, cubes, cones, vases, fruit-tree shapes, distaffs, or fans, each socialist, according to his vision, prunes poor humanity into groups, series, centers, subcenters, honeycombs, and social, harmonious, or contrasting workshops, etc., etc.

And just as the gardener needs axes, saws, sickles, and shears in order to prune his trees, the political writer needs forces that he can find only in the laws in order to marshal his society: customs laws, tax laws, laws governing assistance or education.

It is so true that the socialists consider humanity to be material that can be modeled to fit social templates that if by chance they are not certain of the success of these arrangements, they claim at least a part of humanity as *material for experimentation.* We know just how popular the idea of *trying out all their systems* is among them, and we have already seen one of their leaders[5] come in all seriousness to ask the Constituent Assembly to give them a commune with all its inhabitants in order for them to carry out tests.

In this way, every inventor makes a small-scale model of his machine before making it full scale. In this way, chemists sacrifice a few reagents and farmers a little seed and a corner of a field in order to test an idea.

But what incommensurable distance there is between a gardener and his trees, the inventor and his machine, the chemist and his reagents, and the farmer and his seed! This is the very distance that the socialist quite sincerely believes separates him from humanity.

We should not be surprised that nineteenth-century political writers consider society to be an artificial creation resulting from the genius of the legislator.

This idea, the fruit of a classical education, has dominated all the thinkers and great writers of our country.

All have seen the same relationship between humanity and the legislator as there is between clay and the potter.

What is more, while political writers have agreed to acknowledge a principle of action in the hearts of men and a principle of discernment in their intelligence, they have thought that this was a fatal gift from God and that humanity, under the influence of these two stimuli, was progressing inexorably toward its downfall. They have assumed that left to its own devices humanity would concern itself with religion only to end up with atheism, with education only to achieve ignorance, and with work and trade only to end up in destitution.

Fortunately, according to these same writers, there are a few men known as rulers and legislators who have received contrary tendencies from heaven not only for themselves but also on behalf of all the others.

Although human propensity is toward evil, the propensity of these few is toward good; although humanity marches on toward darkness, they aspire to the light; and although humanity is drawn to vice, they are attracted to virtue. And assuming this, they lay claim to force to enable them to substitute their own propensities for those of the human race.

All you have to do is to open at random a book on philosophy, politics, or history to see how deeply rooted in our country is the idea that human-

5. Victor Considérant.

ity is mere inert matter that receives alike life, organization, morality, and wealth from government, an idea born of study of the classics and having socialism for its offspring—or, what is worse, that humanity itself is drawn toward degradation and is saved from this slippery slope only by the mysterious hand of the legislator. Classic conventionalism shows us everywhere that behind a passive society there is an occult power that, going by the names of the law and the legislator, or under the cloak of the more convenient, vaguer word *one*,[6] moves humanity, brings it to life, enriches it, and infuses it with morality.

*Bossuet:*

> One of the things that *one* (who?) imprinted most strongly on the minds of the Egyptians was love of their country. . . . *No one was allowed* to be of no use to the state; each person had his work assigned to him by law and this was passed from father to son. No one could have two employments or change his own . . . but there was one obligatory communal activity, namely the study of the laws and conventional wisdom. Ignorance of the religion and policies of the country was not excused under any circumstances. Besides, each occupation had its own coinage assigned to it (by whom?). . . . Among good laws, the best was that everyone was fed (by whom?) with a view to his being observed. Their traveling traders filled Egypt with marvelous inventions and saw to it that they were aware of almost everything that might make life easier and more peaceful.

According to Bossuet, therefore, men draw nothing from themselves whether it be patriotism, wealth, activity, wisdom, inventions, agriculture, or science; all these they received by way of the laws or from their kings. All they had to do was to let themselves go. Bossuet takes his argument to such a pitch that he corrects Diodorus for having accused the Egyptians of rejecting wrestling and music. How could that be possible, he says, since these arts had been invented by Trismegistus?

Similarly, in Persia:

> One of the principal cares *of the prince* was to ensure that agriculture flourished. . . . Just as there were specific responsibilities laid down for directing the armies, so there were specific responsibilities for supervis-

---

6. The French word *on* has no real equivalent in English and is translated as "one," "we," "you," "they," or "people," depending on the context. We have chosen "one" in this context. In this passage, by Bossuet, Bastiat asks "who" and "by whom" these decisions were made for Egyptian society. It is not Bossuet who is asking this.

ing agrarian labor. . . . The respect for royal government that was inspired among the Persians reached excessive proportions.

Although the Greeks had highly developed minds, they were no less powerless as to their lot in life, to the point that, left to their own devices, they would not have risen, as do dogs or horses, to the heights of the simplest games. The agreed classical tradition is that everything comes from outside the people.

> The Greeks, naturally full of intelligence and courage, *had been developed* from the start by the kings and colonies that came from Egypt. It is from them that they learned to exercise their bodies, run races on foot, on horseback, or in chariots . . . The best thing the Egyptians taught them was to be docile and to let themselves be formed by laws enacted for the public good.

*Fénelon:* Brought up on the study and admiration of antiquity and a witness to the power of Louis XIV, Fénelon could scarcely escape from the idea that humanity is passive and that both its misfortunes and prosperity, its virtues and vices came to it because of external action exercised on it by the law or by the person who makes the law. Thus, in his utopian Salente,[7] he subjects men with all their personal interests, faculties, desires, and goods to the absolute discretion of the legislator. Whatever the circumstances, they never judge for themselves; it is the prince who judges for them. The nation is just a formless entity of which the prince is the soul. In him are united the thought, the foresight, the very principles of all forms of organization and progress, and consequently all responsibility.

To prove this assertion, I would need to copy the entire tenth book of *Télémaque.*[8] I refer the reader to this and am content to quote a few passages taken at random from this famous poem, the quality of which, in every other respect, I am the first to acknowledge.

With that surprising credulity that characterizes the classics, Fénelon accepts the general happiness of the Egyptians, in spite of the authority of

---

7. Fénelon published *Les Aventures de Télémaque* in 1699. It is the story of Telemachus's search for his father in the company of Mentor, who instructs the young Telemachus on the virtues required by a prince. They come across the fictitious city of Salentum (Salente in French), which has been corrupted by luxury and military despotism. Only the dictatorship of an enlightened legislator could reform Salentum according to Fénelon. The complete works of Fénelon were published in multivolume editions in 1830 and again in 1848–52: *Œuvres complètes de Fénelon.*

8. Telemachus.

reason and facts, and attributes it not to their own wisdom but to that of their kings.

> We cannot look at the two banks without glimpsing opulent towns, country houses with pleasant situations, land that each year is covered with a golden harvest without any fallow period, grasslands full of herds, farmers bowed under the weight of the fruit that overflows from the bosom of the land, or shepherds who cause the sweet sounds of their flutes and pipes to be echoed round about. *Happy are the people,* said Mentor, *who are led by a wise king.*
>
> Mentor then pointed out to me the joy and abundance that extended over the entire country of Egypt in which up to twenty-two thousand towns could be counted, the justice exercised in favor of the poor against the rich, the proper education of children who were trained in obedience, work, sobriety, and love of arts and letters, the exact observance of all religious ceremonies, disinterestedness, a desire for honor, fidelity to men, and fear of the gods that every father inculcated into his children. He never tired of admiring such fine order. *Happy are the people,* he said to me, *whom a wise king leads thus.*

Fénelon creates an idyll of Crete that is even more attractive. Then he adds, through the words of Mentor:

> All that you see in this marvelous island is the fruit of Minos's laws. The education whose provision he ordered for children makes the body healthy and strong. The laws make them accustomed first of all to a life that is simple, frugal, and physically taxing. They assume that all sensual pleasure makes body and mind soft. They never offer them any other pleasure than that of being invincible through virtue and gaining a great deal of glory. Here, they punish three vices that go unpunished in other peoples: ingratitude, dissimulation, and greed. They never need to repress ostentation and dissipation since these are unknown in Crete. They do not allow valuable furniture, magnificent clothes, delicious feasts, or gilded palaces.[9]

This is how Mentor prepares his pupil to grind down and manipulate the people of Ithaca, doubtless with the most philanthropic of intentions, and for greater safety he gives him an example of this in Salente.

9. In this passage we translate the French word *on* as *they.* Bastiat again wants to show that the ruling elite imposes restrictions on its citizens. He changes the quotation by Fénelon slightly to make this point. See also note 6, p. 124.

This is how we are given our first notions of politics. We are taught to treat men almost in the way Olivier de Serres teaches farmers to treat and mix their soil.

*Montesquieu:*

To maintain the spirit of trade, all laws need to encourage it, and the details of these same laws should be framed to divide up wealth as trade increases it, in such a way as to put each poor citizen in sufficient comfort to be able to work like the others, and each rich citizen in such a state of mediocrity that he needs to work to conserve or acquire.

The laws thus dispose of all wealth.

Although in democracy genuine equality is the soul of the state, this is, however, so difficult to establish that an extreme punctiliousness in this respect is not always suitable. It is sufficient that *one* establishes a quota that reduces or sets the differences at a certain level. After this, it is up to particular laws to equalize inequality, so to speak, through the charges they impose on the rich and the relief they give to the poor.

This again advocates the equalization of wealth by the law and by force.

In Greece, there were two forms of republic. One form was military, exemplified by Sparta; the other was commercial, exemplified by Athens. In the former, they *wanted* its citizens to be idle; in the latter, they *sought* to instill a love of work.

I would ask people to give some attention to the extent of the genius these legislators demonstrated in seeing that by upsetting all the accepted customs, by confusing all the virtues, they would be demonstrating their *wisdom* to the universe. Lycurgus, combining robbery with a spirit of justice, the most severe slavery with the heights of freedom, the most atrocious sentiments with the greatest moderation, gave his town stability. He appeared to remove from it all resources, arts, trade, money, and city walls. There was ambition with no hope of being better off. The Spartans had natural sentiments and were neither child, husband, nor father. Even modesty was removed from chastity. *It is along this route that Sparta was led to greatness and glory. . . .*

We have also seen this extraordinary situation that was observed in the institutions in Greece in *the dregs and corruption of modern times.* An honest legislator has formed a people in which probity appears to be as natural as bravery was in the Spartans. Mr. Penn is a genuine Lycurgus and, while Mr. Penn's object was peace in the same way that Lycurgus's was war, they resemble one another in the singular path in which they set *their* people, in the influence they had on free men, in the preconceptions they overcame, and in the passions they subdued.

Another example is Paraguay.[10] Those who regard the pleasure of governing as the sole good thing in life have wished to make it a crime against *society,* but it will always be a fine thing to *govern men while making them happy.* . . .

*Those who wish to establish similar institutions will set up the communality of assets* of Plato's republic, the respect for the gods that he demanded, the separation from foreigners in order to preserve customs, with the city, not the citizens, carrying out trade. They will give us our arts without our luxury and our needs without our desires."

However much popular enthusiasm cries, "It is by Montesquieu, so it is marvelous! It is sublime!" I will have the courage of my convictions and say: What? You have the effrontery to find that beautiful?

It is dreadful! Abominable! And these quotations that I could increase in number show that in Montesquieu's view people, freedom, property, and the entire human race are just materials suited to the exercise of the legislator's sagacity.

*Rousseau:* Although this political writer, the supreme authority for democrats, bases the social edifice on the *general will,* no one has accepted as completely as he does the hypothesis of the total passivity of the human race in the presence of the legislator.

While it is true that a great prince is a rare person, how much more so is a great legislator? The former has only to follow the model that the latter has to put forward. The latter is *the mechanic who invents the machine,* while the former is the worker who gets on it and makes it go.[11]

And what is the role of men in all this? The machine that you get on and make go, or rather the raw material out of which the machine is made!

10. Between 1609 and their expulsion from Latin America in 1767, the Jesuits organized among the native people of Paraguay a community based on Christian and communist principles. The Jesuits' aim was to Christianize the native people, organize the social and economic life of the communities, and create "the kingdom of God on earth." Bastiat rejected the idea of these communities, just as he did the contemporary attempts to create utopian socialist communities in Europe and America in the 1830s and 1840s, on the grounds that the communities owned property, in particular land, in common; sought an equality of ownership; and strictly regulated the free market.

11. Rousseau, *Du contrat social,* bk. 2, chap. 7, "The Legislator."

Thus, between the legislator and the prince and between the prince and his subjects there is the same relationship as between the agronomist and the farmer and the farmer and the soil. At what height above humanity, therefore, do we place the political writer who governs the legislators themselves and teaches them their job in such imperative terms as the following?

> Do you want to give consistency to the state? Reduce the distance between the extreme levels as far as is possible. Do not allow either wealthy people or paupers.
>
> Is the soil hard to till or infertile or the country too small to hold its inhabitants? *Turn toward* industry and the arts whose productions you can trade for the goods you lack. . . . Do you *lack* inhabitants where the land is good? Concentrate on farming, which increases the number of men, and *turn away* from the arts, which will succeed only in reducing the population of the country. . . . Are you concerned with shorelines that are broad and accessible? *Cover the sea* with ships and you will have a brilliant and short existence. Does the sea bathe only inaccessible rocks on your shoreline? Remain savages and eaters of fish; your life will be more peaceful, perhaps better, and certainly happier. In a word, apart from the maxims common to all, each people carries within it a cause that orders it in a particular way and makes its legislation proper to it alone. This is why in former times the Hebrews and more recently the Arabs have had religion as their principal object, the Athenians letters, Carthage and Tyre trade, Rhodes naval matters, Sparta war, and Rome virtue. The author of *the Spirit of the Laws*[12] has shown with what art *the legislator directs the system of institutions toward these objects.* But if the legislator makes a mistake and takes a principle other than that which arises from the nature of things and one tends toward slavery while the other tends toward freedom, one toward wealth and the other toward population, one to peace and the other to conquests, the laws will be seen to become imperceptibly weaker, the constitution will be changed, and the state will not cease to suffer agitation until it is either destroyed or changed and invincible nature has regained its empire.

---

12. The edition of *Spirit of the Laws* to which Bastiat might have had access was *Œuvres de Montesquieu, avec éloges, analyses, commentaires, remarques, notes, réfutations, imitations,* par MM Destutt de Tracy, Villemain, et al. (Paris, 1827), in eight volumes. The editor was Victor Destutt de Tracy, the son of Antoine Destutt de Tracy, who had earlier written an extensive commentary on the *Spirit of the Laws* for Thomas Jefferson, which Jefferson had published in 1811, *A Commentary and Review of Montesquieu's* Spirit of Laws.

But if nature is sufficiently invincible to regain its domination, why does Rousseau not admit that it did not need such a legislator to *take* this domination from the outset? Why does he not admit that by obeying their own initiative men will of their own accord *turn toward* trade on broad and accessible shorelines without a Lycurgus, a Solon, or a Rousseau interfering at the risk of *making a mistake?*

Be that as it may, we can understand the awesome responsibility that Rousseau places on inventors, teachers, leaders, legislators, and the manipulators of societies. This is why he is very demanding with regard to them.

> He who dares to undertake to teach a people must feel that he is, so to say, capable of changing human nature and transforming each individual who, of himself, is a perfect and solitary whole, into a part of a greater whole from which this individual receives totally or in part his life and being; he must be capable too of changing the constitution of man in order to strengthen it and substituting an incomplete and moral existence for a physical and independent one which we have all received from nature. In a word, he needs to remove from man his own forces in order to give him some that are foreign to him. . . .

Poor human race, what will Rousseau's disciples do with your dignity? *Raynal:*

> The climate, that is to say the sky and the soil, is the first rule of the legislator. *Its* resources dictate his duty to him. First of all, it is *its* local situation that he must consult. A people cast upon a seacoast will have laws that relate to navigation. . . . If the colony is concerned with the land, a legislator must provide for both its type and level of fertility. . . .
>
> It is above all in the distribution of property that the wisdom of the legislation will shine through. In general and in all the countries of the world, when a colony is founded, land must be given to each man, that is to say, a sufficient amount to each person to provide for a family. . . .
>
> In an uncivilized island that *one* would people with children, *one* would only have to leave the seeds of truth to blossom in the development of reason. . . . But when *one* establishes a people that is already old in a new country, the art lies in *leaving* to it *only* those harmful opinions and habits from which it cannot be cured and corrected. If *one* wants to prevent them from being passed on, *one* will supervise the second generation through the communal and public education of its children. A prince or legislator should never found a colony without sending wise men in advance to educate the young. . . . In a new colony every facility

is open to the precautions of the legislator who wishes to *purify the blood and manners of a people*. If he has genius and virtue, the lands and men he will have in his hands will inspire in his soul a plan for society which a writer would outline only in a vague manner subject to unstable hypotheses that vary and complicate one another with an infinite number of circumstances that are too difficult to forecast and combine.

Does he not appear to hear a teacher of agriculture say to his pupils, "The climate is the farmer's first rule? *Its* resources dictate *his* duties. It is *its* local situation that he has to consult. If the farm is on a clay soil, he has to take these steps. If he has to deal with sand, this is what he has to do. All facilities are available to the farmer who wishes to clear and improve his soil. If he is clever, the land and fertilizers he has in his hands will inspire in him an operating plan that a teacher will be able to outline only in a vague manner subject to unstable hypotheses that vary and complicate one another with an infinite number of circumstances that are too difficult to forecast and combine."

But, O sublime writers, please remember on occasion that this clay or sand, this compost of which you so arbitrarily dispose, is made up of men, your equals, who are intelligent and free beings like you, who, like you, have received from God the faculty of sight, foresight, thought, and making judgments for themselves!

*Mably:* (He takes the laws to be rusty from age, security to be neglected, and continues thus:)

> In these circumstances, you have to be convinced that the springs of government have been loosened. *Give them* renewed tension [Mably is addressing the reader] and the ill will be cured. . . . Think less of punishing faults than of encouraging the virtues *you need*. This way, you will restore the vigor of youth to *your republic*. Free peoples have lost their freedom because they did not know this! But if the ill has progressed so far that ordinary magistrates cannot remedy it effectively, *turn to* an extraordinary group of magistrates with a short tenure and considerable power. The citizens' imagination in such circumstances needs to be struck.

And more in this vein for twenty volumes.

There was a time when, under the influence of such teaching, which is the foundation of classical education, everyone wanted to place himself outside and above humanity in order to arrange it, organize it, and set it up according to his views.

*Condillac:*[13]

My Lord, make yourself out to be a Lycurgus or a Solon. Before continuing to read further, amuse yourself by giving laws to some uncivilized tribe in America or Africa. Settle these nomadic men in sedentary houses; teach them to feed their herds and work at developing the social qualities that nature has given them. Order them to start practicing the duties of humanity. Use punishment to poison the pleasures promised by passion and you will see that these savages will lose a vice and gain a virtue with each article of your legislation.

All peoples have had laws. But few of them have been happy. Why is this so? It is because legislators have almost always ignored the fact that the object of society is to unite families through a common interest.

The impartiality of laws lies in two things: establishing equality in the wealth and equality in the dignity of citizens.... As your laws establish greater equality, they will become dearer to each citizen.... How will avarice, ambition, sensuality, laziness, idleness, envy, hatred, and jealousy operate in men who are equal in fortune and dignity and in whose eyes the laws will give no opportunity of disrupting equality? [The idyll follows.]

What you have been told about the republic of Sparta should give you greater enlightenment on this question. No other state has ever had laws that conformed more to the order of nature and equality.[14]

It is not surprising that the seventeenth and eighteenth centuries considered the human race to be inert matter that waits, receives everything—form, face, stimulus, movement, and life—from a great prince, a great legislator, or a great genius. These centuries were fed on the study of antiquity and antiquity effectively offers us everywhere—in Egypt, Persia, Greece, and Rome—the sight of a few men manipulating at will a human race that is subjugated by force or imposture. What does that prove? It shows that because man and society can be improved, error, ignorance, despotism, slavery, and superstition must have existed in greater quantity at the dawn of time. The mistake of the writers I have quoted is not to have noted the fact but to have offered it as though it were a rule to be admired and imitated by future races.

13. Bastiat is wrong here. This passage, which he attributes to Condillac, is Mably's *Droits et devoirs,* p. 510.

14. (Paillottet's note) In the pamphlet *Baccalaureate and Socialism,* the author reveals the filiation of this very error through a series of similar quotations. (*OC,* vol. 4, p. 442, "Baccalauréat et socialisme.") [See also "Baccalaureate and Socialism," pp. 185–234 in this volume.]

Their mistake is to have accepted with an inconceivable lack of critical analysis and on the faith of puerile *conventionalism* what is unacceptable, that is to say, the grandeur, dignity, morality, and well-being of these artificial forms of society in the ancient world; to have failed to understand that time produces and propagates light; and that, as the light grows brighter, the force takes the side of the right and society takes possession of itself again.

And in fact, what is the political work we are witnessing? It is none other than the instinctive effort of all peoples to achieve liberty.[15] And what is liberty, this word that has the power of making all hearts beat faster and causing agitation around the world, if it is not the sum of all freedoms: freedom of conscience, teaching, and association; freedom of the press; freedom to travel, work, and trade; in other words, the free exercise of all inoffensive faculties by all men and, in still other terms, the destruction of all despotic regimes, even legal despotism, and the reduction of the law to its sole rational attribution, which is to regulate the individual law of legitimate defense or to punish injustice.

This tendency in the human race, it must be agreed, is grossly countered, particularly in our country, by the fatal disposition—the fruit of classical teaching—that is common to all political writers, to put themselves in a

---

15. (Paillottet's note) For a people to be happy, it is essential for the individuals that make it up to be farsighted and prudent and to have the confidence in one another that is rooted in security.

However, it can acquire these things only by experience. It becomes farsighted when it has suffered from lack of foresight, prudent when its temerity has suffered frequent punishment, etc., etc.

The result of this is that freedom always begins by being accompanied by the misfortunes that follow the unconsidered use made of it.

At the sight of this, some men stand up and demand that freedom should be forbidden.

"The state," they say, "should be farsighted and prudent on behalf of everyone."

In response to which I ask the following questions:

1. Is this possible? Can an experienced state arise from an inexperienced nation?
2. In any case, is this not to stifle experience in the bud?

If government prescribes individual acts, how can an individual learn from the consequences of his acts? Will he remain subject to trusteeship in perpetuity?

And the state, having ordered everything, will be responsible for everything.

This will constitute a hotbed of revolution and revolutions with no outcome, since they will be carried out by a people who, by forbidding experience, have been forbidden to progress. (*Idea drawn from the manuscripts of the author.*)

position outside the human race in order to sort it out, organize it, and institute it according to their lights.

For while society agitates to achieve freedom, the sole thought of the great men who put themselves at its head and who are imbued with the principles of the seventeenth and eighteenth centuries is to bend it to suit the philanthropic despotism of their social inventions and to have it, as Rousseau says, bear docilely the yoke of public felicity as they have conceived it.

We saw this clearly in 1789. Scarcely had the legal former regime been destroyed when the new form of society was made to bear other artificial systems all based on the agreed concept: the omnipotence of the law.

*Saint-Just:*

The legislator holds sway over the future. It is up to him to *want what is good*. It is up to him to make men what he *wants* them to be.

*Robespierre:*

The function of the government is to direct the physical and moral forces of the nation toward the purpose behind its institution.

*Billaud-Varennes:*

It is *necessary* to re-create the people to whom we wish to restore freedom. Since it is *necessary* to destroy former prejudices, change long-standing habits, improve depraved affections, restrict superfluous needs, and root out inveterate vices, strong action and a fervent drive are needed. . . . Citizens, in Sparta the inflexible austerity of Lycurgus became the unshakeable foundation for the republic; the weak and trusting character of Solon plunged Athens once again into slavery. This parallel encapsulates the entire science of the government.

*Le Peletier:*

Considering how far the human race has degenerated, I am convinced of the need to carry out total regeneration and, if I may put it this way, to create a new people.

As you can see, men are nothing other than vile material. It is not up to them to *want what is good;* they are incapable of this. It is up to the legislator, according to Saint-Just. Men are only what he *wants* them to be.

According to Robespierre, who echoes Rousseau literally, the legislator begins by designating the purpose for which the *nation is established.* Thereafter, all the government has to do is to direct all *physical and moral forces* toward this aim. The nation itself always remains passive in all this, and Billaud-Varennes teaches us that it should have only the prejudices, habits, affections, and needs that are authorized by the legislator. He goes so far as to say that the inflexible austerity of one man is the foundation of the republic.

We have seen that, where evil is so great that ordinary magistrates cannot remedy it, Mably recommended dictatorship in order to make virtue flourish. "Turn to an extraordinary group of magistrates," he says, "whose tenure will be short and whose power will be considerable. They need to have a strong impact on citizens' imaginations." This doctrine has not been lost. Listen to what Robespierre says:

> The principle of republican government is virtue, and its means, while it is becoming established, is terror. In our country, we want to substitute morality for selfishness, probity for honor, principles for customs, duty for the proprieties, the empire of reason for the tyranny of fashion, a scorn of vice for a scorn of misfortune, pride for insolence, greatness of spirit for vanity, a love of glory for a love of money, good people for good company, merit for intrigue, genius for a finely turned phrase, truth for brilliance, the attraction of happiness for the boredom of sensuality, the greatness of man for the small-mindedness of the great, a people that is magnanimous, powerful, and happy for a people that is likable, frivolous, and wretched, in a word, all the virtues and all the miracles of a republic for all the vices and absurdities of the monarchy.[16]

At what height above the rest of humanity Robespierre sets himself here! And note the circumstance in which he is speaking. He does not limit himself to expressing a wish for a major regeneration of the human heart; he does not even expect that this will be the result of a proper system of government. No, he wants to achieve this by himself, and through terror. The speech from which this puerile and plodding heap of antitheses is taken aimed to set out the *moral principles that ought to direct a revolutionary government.* Note that when Robespierre comes forward to request a dictatorship, it is not just to repel foreigners and combat factions but really to achieve the triumph of his own moral principles through terror, and this prior to the application of the

16. The edition of the writings of Robespierre to which Bastiat very likely would have had access was titled *Œuvres de Maximilien Robespierre,* a three-volume edition of Robespierre's collected works. It was published in the late 1830s as the French socialist movement was beginning to grow on the eve of the revolution of 1848.

Constitution. His pretension is to root out from the country, through terror, nothing less than *selfishness, honor, customs, the proprieties, fashion, vanity, a love of money, good society, intrigue, brilliance of mind, sensuality, and wretchedness.* It is only after he, Robespierre, has accomplished these *miracles,* as he quite rightly calls them, that he will allow the law to regain its empire. Oh, you poor people who think you are so great, who hold humanity to be so insignificant, who want to reform everything, reform yourselves and that task will suffice.

However, in general, reformers, legislators, and political writers do not ask to exercise an immediate despotism over the human race. No, they are too moderate and philanthropic for that. They demand only the despotism, absolutism, and omnipotence of the law. The only thing is that they aspire to make the law.

To show how universal this strange disposition of minds has been in France, not only would I have had to copy out the entire works of Mably, Raynal, Rousseau, and Fénelon, and long quotations from Bossuet and Montesquieu, I would also have had to copy the entire minutes of the sessions of the Convention. I will refrain from doing so and merely refer the reader to them.

We can be sure that this idea was very attractive to Bonaparte. He embraced it with fervor and put it energetically into practice. Since he considered himself to be a chemist, all he saw in Europe was a source of material on which to experiment. However, this material showed itself to be a powerful reagent. When he was three quarters disillusioned on Saint Helena, Bonaparte appeared to acknowledge that there was a certain amount of initiative in peoples and he seemed to be less hostile to freedom. However, this did not stop him from giving the following lesson to his son in his will, "To govern is to spread morality, education, and well-being widely."

Is it still necessary to use fastidious quotations to show where Morelly, Babeuf, Owen, Saint-Simon, or Fourier takes his source? I will limit myself to offering the reader a few extracts of the book by Louis Blanc on the organization of work.[17]

"In our project, society receives its drive from government." (Page 126)

In what does the drive that authority gives society consist? In imposing the project of M. Louis Blanc.

On the other hand, society is the human race.

17. Blanc, *L'Organisation du travail.*

Therefore, in the end, the human race receives its inspiration from M. Louis Blanc.

Let him get on with it, people will say. Doubtless the human race is free to follow the *advice* of no matter whom. But this is not how M. Louis Blanc sees things. He thinks that his project should be converted into law and consequently be imposed by force by the government.

> In our project, the state gives only a legislative structure for labor production (excuse the *only*) in virtue of which productive activity can and ought to accomplish its task *in total freedom.* It (the state) merely places freedom on a slope (*that is all*) which it descends once it has been put there simply through the force of things and by a natural consequence of the *established mechanism.*

But what is this slope? "The one indicated by M. Louis Blanc." Does it not lead to an abyss? "No, it leads to happiness." Why then does society not put itself on the slope of its own accord? "Because it does not know what it wants and needs a *stimulus.*" Who will give it this stimulus? "The government." And who will give a stimulus to the government? "The inventor of the mechanism, M. Louis Blanc."

We will never escape this circle, that of a passive human race and one great man who sets it in motion through the intervention of the law.

Once on this slope, will society at least enjoy a measure of freedom? "Doubtless." And what is freedom?

> Let us say this once and for all: freedom consists not only in the right awarded but in the *power* given to man to develop and exercise his faculties under the rule of justice and the safeguard of the law.
>
> And this is not a worthless distinction: its meaning is profound and its consequences immense. For, when it is admitted that, in order to be truly free, man needs the *power* to exercise and develop his faculties, it follows that society owes a suitable education to each of its members, without which the human mind *cannot* flourish, together with the instruments of work, without which human activity *cannot* be given full scope. However, by whose intervention will society give each of its members a suitable education and the necessary tools of work if it is not through the intervention of the state?

Thus freedom is power. In what does this *power* consist? "In taking possession of education and the tools of work." Who will *dispense* education and *hand out* the tools? "Society, which *owes them to its members.*" Through whose intervention will society hand out tools to those who lack them? "Through the *intervention of the state.*" From whom will the state take them?

It is up to the reader to reply and to see where all this will lead.

One of the strangest phenomena of our time, which will probably astonish our descendants a great deal, is that the doctrine based on this triple hypothesis—the radical inertia of humanity, the omnipotence of the law, and the infallibility of the legislator—is the sacred cow of the party that proclaims itself exclusively democratic.

It is true that the party also calls itself *social.*

Insofar as it is democratic, it has boundless faith in the human race.

Since it is *social,* it ranks the human race lower than mud.

Is it a question of human rights, or of producing a legislator from its bosom? In this case, indeed, in its view the people know everything instinctively; they have admirable tact. *Their will is always right and the general will cannot err.* Suffrage cannot be too *universal.* No one owes society any guarantees. The will and capacity to make a good choice is always assumed. Can the people make a mistake? Are we not in the century of enlightenment? Well, then! Will the people always remain in a state of guardianship? Have they not won their rights by enough effort and sacrifice? Have they not provided sufficient proof of their intelligence and wisdom? Have they not become mature? Are they not in a position to judge for themselves? Do they not recognize their own interests? Is there a man or a class that dares to claim the right to take the people's place and make decisions and act on their behalf? No, no, the people want to be *free* and will be free. They want to run their own affairs and will do so.

However, once the legislator has freed himself from electoral meetings through the elections, oh, how he changes his language! The nation reverts to passiveness, inertia, and nothingness, and the legislator enters into possession of omnipotent powers. Invention, direction, inspiration, and organization are all up to him! All humanity has to do is go along with it; the hour of despotism has rung. And note that this is fatal; for the people who only recently were so enlightened, moral, and perfect now have no propensities, or if they have any, these are leading them all to degradation. And they should be left a shred of freedom! Are you not aware that, according to M. Considérant, *freedom inexorably leads to monopoly?* Are you not aware that freedom is competition and that competition, according to M. Blanc, *is a system of extermination for the people and a cause of ruin for the bourgeoisie?* That it is for this reason that peoples have been all the more exterminated and ruined the freer they are, as Switzerland, Holland, England, and the United States show? Are you not aware that, still according to M. Louis Blanc, *competition leads to monopoly* and that *for the same reason, a good bargain leads to high prices? That competition leads to the drying up of sources of consumption and propels production to become a devouring activity? That competition forces production to increase and consumption to decrease?* From which it follows that free peoples produce in order not to consume and that *competition is simultaneously oppression and dementia* and that it is absolutely essential for M. Louis Blanc to meddle with it.

What freedom, besides, can we leave men? Will it be freedom of conscience? But we will see them all take advantage of permissiveness to become atheists. Freedom of education? But fathers will hasten to pay teachers to teach their sons immorality and error; what is more, according to M. Thiers, if education were left to national freedom, it would cease to be national and we would raise our children according to the views of the Turks or Hindus, instead of which, through the legal despotism of the university, they have the good fortune to be raised according to the noble views of the Romans. Freedom to work? But this is competition, which leaves products unconsumed, exterminates the people, and ruins the middle classes. Freedom to trade? But we know only too well, and protectionists have demonstrated this ad nauseam, that men are ruined when they carry out free trade and that in order to become rich they should trade without freedom. Freedom of association? But according to socialist doctrine, freedom and association are mutually exclusive precisely because one takes freedom away from men only in order to force them to form associations.

You can thus see clearly that social democrats cannot, in all conscience, leave men any freedom, since by their very nature, and if these fine gentlemen did not put it right, they would all tend everywhere toward all forms of degradation and demoralization.

We are left guessing, if this is so, on what basis universal suffrage is being demanded so insistently on their behalf.

The pretensions of the organizers raise another question, which I have often asked them and to which, as far as I know, they have never replied. Since the natural tendencies of man are sufficiently bad for their freedom to have to be removed, how is it that those of the organizers are good? Are the legislators and their agents not part of the human race? Do they think they are formed from a different clay from the rest of mankind? They state that society, left to itself, rushes inexorably toward the abyss because its instincts are perverse. They claim to be able to stop society on this slope and redirect it to a better goal. They have therefore received from heaven a level of intelligence and virtues that place them outside and above humanity; let them show the justification for this. They wish to be *shepherds* and want us to be *sheep*. This arrangement assumes that they have superior natures, and we have every right to demand prior proof of this.

Note that what I am questioning is not their right to invent social combinations and propagate them, recommend them, and try them out on themselves at their own risk, but in particular their right to impose them on us through the law, that is to say, using public compulsion and finance.

I demand that the followers of Cabet, Fourier, and Proudhon, the academics and protectionists, renounce, not their specific ideas, but the idea that is common to them, which is to subject us by force to their causes and writings, to their social workshops, their "free" banks, their Greek and Roman systems of morality, and their hindrances to trade. What I demand from them is for us to be allowed to judge their plans and to refuse to join them, whether directly or indirectly, if we find that they run counter to our interests or are repugnant to our consciences.

For, apart from the fact that it is oppressive and plunderous, the call for bringing in the government and more taxes implies once again this damaging hypothesis, the infallibility of the organizer, and the incompetence of humanity.

And if humanity is incapable of making its own judgments, why are people talking to us about universal suffrage?

The contradiction in these ideas is unfortunately reflected in events, and while the French people have led all the others in winning their rights, or rather their political guarantees, they nevertheless remain the most governed, directed, administered, taxed, hobbled, and exploited of all peoples.

They are also the people where revolutions are most likely to happen, and this should be so.

As soon as you start with the idea, accepted by all our political writers and so energetically expressed by M. Louis Blanc in the following words, "Society receives its motive force from the government"; as soon as men consider themselves to be sensitive but passive, incapable of lifting themselves up by their own discernment and energy to any form of morality or well-being and reduced to expecting everything to be provided by the law; in a word, when they accept that their relationship with the state is that of sheep with their shepherd, it is clear that the responsibility of the government is immense. Good and evil, virtues and vices, equality and inequality, wealth and poverty all flow from it. It is responsible for everything, it undertakes everything, and it does everything, so therefore it answers for everything. If we are happy, the state rightfully claims our gratitude, but if we are unhappy we can blame only it. Does it not, in principle, dispose of our persons and our belongings? Is not the law omnipotent? When the state created the university monopoly, it undertook to meet the hopes of heads of families who were deprived of their freedom, and if these hopes have been dashed, whose fault is this? By regulating industry, the state undertook to make it prosper; otherwise the state would have been absurd to remove freedom from industry, and if industry suffers, whose fault is it? By interfering in adjusting the balance of trade by playing with the tariffs, the state undertook to make the stale trade flourish and if, far from flourishing, it dies, whose fault is that? By awarding the shipbuilders protection in exchange for their freedom, the government undertook to make them generate wealth, and if they become a financial burden, whose fault is this?

Thus, there is no suffering in the nation for which the government has not voluntarily made itself responsible. Should we be surprised therefore that each cause of suffering is a cause for revolution?

And what remedy are they proposing? They propose the indefinite widening of the domain of the law, that is to say, the responsibility of the government.

But if the government makes itself responsible for raising and regulating all earnings and cannot do this, if it makes itself responsible for giving assistance in every misfortune and cannot do this, if it makes itself responsible for ensuring all the pensions of all the workers and cannot do this, if it makes itself responsible for supplying all the workers with their working tools and cannot do this, if it makes itself responsible for allocating free credit to all those craving loans and cannot do this, if, according to the words we have with regret seen escape from the pen of M. de Lamartine, "The state has set itself the mission of enlightening, developing, enlarging, fortifying, spiritualizing, and sanctifying the souls of peoples," and it fails, do we not see with each disappointment, alas, that it is more than likely that a revolution is inevitable?

I repeat my thesis and say: the overriding question to be asked is where the dividing line between economic and political science[18] lies. It is this:

18. (Bastiat's note) Political economy precedes politics; politics states whether human interests are naturally harmonious or antagonistic, which political economy ought to know before establishing the attributes of government.

What is the law? What ought it to be? What domain does it cover? What are its limits? Consequently, where do the attributions of the legislator cease?

I have no hesitation in replying: *the law is the common power organized to obstruct injustice* and, in short, the law is justice.

It is not true that the legislator has absolute power over our persons and property, since they existed before him and his task is to surround them with guarantees.

It is not true that the mission of the law is to rule over our consciences, our ideas, our will, our education, our feelings, our work, our trade, our gifts, and our enjoyment.

Its mission is to ensure that in none of these areas does the right of one person override the right of another.

Because it wields the necessary sanction of coercion, the law can have as its legitimate domain only the legitimate domain of force, that is to say, justice.

And as each individual has the right to have recourse to force only in the case of legitimate defense, collective force, which is just the union of individual forces, cannot reasonably be applied in any other case.

Therefore, the law is solely the organization of the pre-existing individual right of legitimate defense.

The law is justice.

It is entirely wrong for it to be able to oppress persons or plunder their property, even for a philanthropic reason, since its mission is to protect them.

And let it not be said that it can at least be philanthropic provided that it refrains from any oppression or plunder; that is contradictory. The law cannot fail to act with regard to our persons or our property; if it does not guarantee them, it violates them by the very fact that it acts, the very fact that it exists.

The law is justice.

This is a statement that is clear, simple, perfectly defined and delimited, easy to understand, and easy to see, for justice is a given quantity that is unmovable and inalterable and does not allow any *ifs* or *buts*.

If you exceed these bounds, and make the law religious, fraternal, egalitarian, philanthropic, industrial, literary, or artistic, you will immediately be in the realm of the infinite, uncertainty, and the unknown and in an imposed utopia or, what is worse, in the host of utopias struggling to take over the law and impose themselves, for fraternity and philanthropy, unlike justice, do not have established limits. Where will you stop? Where will the law stop? One person, like M. de Saint-Cricq, will extend his brand of philanthropy only to certain sectors of industry and will demand of the law that it *disadvantage consumers in favor of producers*. Another, like M. Considérant, will take up the cause of the workers and claim from the law on their behalf an *assured MINIMUM, by way of clothing, accommodation, food, and everything necessary for the preservation of life*. A third, M. Louis Blanc, will say, correctly, that this is just a rough outline of fraternity and that the law ought to provide all the tools for work and education. A fourth will call to our attention that such an arrangement will still leave an opening for inequality and that the law should ensure that luxury, literature, and the arts reach the most far-flung hamlet. You will thus be led right up to *communism,* or rather, the legislation will be . . . what it already is: a battlefield for all forms of dreams and cupidity.

The law is justice.

Within this circle a simple, unshakable government is conceived. And I defy anyone to tell me how the thought of revolution or insurrection, or even a simple riot, could arise against a public authority that is limited to repressing injustice. Under a regime like this, there would be greater fulfillment, well-being would be spread more evenly, and as for the suffering that is endemic to the human race, no one would think of attributing it to the government, which would have had as little effect over suffering as it has on variations in the weather. Has anyone ever seen the people rise up against the court of appeal or burst into the chamber of a justice of the peace to demand a minimum wage, free credit, tools for work, favorable tariffs, or social workshops? They are fully aware that these arrangements are beyond the judge's powers and will learn at the same time that they are beyond the powers of the law.

But if you make the law based on the principle of fraternity and proclaim that all benefits and misfortunes flow from it, that it is responsible for all individual suffering and all social inequality, you will open the floodgates to an unending flow of complaints, hatred, unrest, and revolution.

The law is justice.

And it would be very strange if it could in fairness be anything else! Does justice not encapsulate right? Are all rights not equal? How then could the law intervene to subject me to the social designs of MM Mimerel, de Melun, Thiers, and Louis Blanc rather than subject these gentlemen to my designs? Does anyone believe that I have not received sufficient imagination from nature to invent a utopia of my own? Is it the role of the law to choose among so many illusions and assign public compulsion to serve just one of these?

The law is justice.

And let nobody say, as is constantly said, that if the law were thus designed to be atheist, individualistic, and with no substance it would make the human race in its image. That is an absurd deduction, only too worthy of this government obsession with seeing humanity in the law.

What then! Once we are free, does it follow that we would cease to act? Once we no longer receive our animation from the law, does it follow that we will be devoid of any stimulus? Once the law limits itself to guaranteeing us the free exercise of our faculties, does it follow that our faculties will be struck by inertia? Once the law no longer imposes forms of religion, systems of association, methods of teaching, procedures for working, instructions for trading, or rules for charitable work on us, does it follow that we will rush into atheism, isolation, ignorance, deprivation, and selfishness? Does it follow that we will no longer be capable of recognizing the power and goodness of God, form associations, help each other, love and assist our brothers in misfortune, examine the secrets of nature, and aspire to achieving the perfection of our being?

The law is justice.

And it is under the law of justice, under the regime of right, under the influence of freedom, security, stability, and responsibility that each person will attain his full value, the full dignity of his being, and that humanity will accomplish with order and calmness, doubtless with slowness but certainty, the progress which is its destiny.

I think that I have theory on my side, for whatever question I subject to reason—whether it concerns religion, philosophy, politics, or economics; whether it relates to well-being, morality, equality, right, justice, progress, responsibility, solidarity, property, work, trade, capital, earnings, taxes, population, credit, or government; at whatever point on the scientific horizon I place the point of departure of my research—I invariably reach this conclusion: the solution to the social problem is to be found in freedom.

And have I not also experience on my side? Take a look at the globe. What countries have the happiest, most moral, and most peaceful peoples? Those countries in which the law intervenes the least in private activity; in which the government is the least felt; in which individuality has the most vigor and public opinion the greatest influence; in which the administrative systems are the least in number and degree of complexity, the taxes the least heavy and the least unfair, popular discontent the least heated and the least justifiable; in which the responsibility of individuals and classes is the most active and, consequently, where habits are imperfect, they tend most indefatigably to improve; in which transactions, agreements, and associations are the least hindered; in which labor, capital, and the population are subject to the fewest artificial displacements; in which humanity obeys its proper leanings most readily; in which the thought of God prevails the most over the designs of men; those in a word that come the closest to the following state of affairs: all things to be achieved through man's free and perfectible spontaneous action, within the limits of what is right; nothing to be achieved by the law or by force other than universal justice.

It has to be said: there are too many great men in the world. There are too many legislators, organizers, founders of society, leaders of peoples, fathers of nations, etc., etc. Too many people put themselves above humanity in order to rule it and too many people think their job is to become involved with it.

People will say to me: you yourself are becoming involved, you who talk about it. That is true. But they will agree that it is for a very different reason and from a very different point of view, and while I am taking on those who wish to reform, it is solely to make them abandon their effort.

I am becoming involved with it not like Vaucanson with his automaton but like a physiologist with the human organism, in order to examine it and admire it.

I am becoming involved with it in the same spirit as that of a famous traveler.

He arrived among a savage tribe. A child had just been born and a host of fortune-tellers, warlocks, and quacks were crowding around it, armed with rings, hooks, and ties. One said, "This child will never smell the aroma of a pipe if I do not lengthen his nostrils." Another said, "He will be deprived of the sense of hearing if I do not make his ears reach down to his shoulders." A third said, "He will never see the light of the sun unless I make his eyes slant obliquely." A fourth said, "He will never stand upright if I do not make his legs curve." A fifth said, "He will never be able to think if I do not squeeze his brain." "Away with you," said the traveler. "God does His work well. Do not claim to know more than He does and, since He has given organs to this frail creature, leave those organs to develop and grow strong through exercise, experimentation, experience, and freedom."

God has also provided humanity with all that is necessary for it to accomplish its destiny. There is a providential social physiology just as there is a providential human physiology. The social organs are also constituted so as to develop harmoniously in the fresh air of freedom. Away with you, therefore, you quacks and organizers! Away with your rings, chains, hooks, and pincers! Away with your artificial means! Away with your social workshop, your phalanstery, your governmentalism, your centralization, your tariffs, your universities, your state religion, your free credit or monopolistic banks, your constraints, your restrictions, your moralizing, or your equalizing through taxes! And since the social body has had inflicted on it so many theoretical systems to no avail, let us finish where we should have started; let us reject these and at last put freedom to the test, freedom, which is an act of faith in God and in His work.

## → 10 ←
### *Property and Plunder*[1]

[vol. 4, p. 394. "Propriété et spoliation."
Originally published in the 24 July 1848
issue of *Le Journal des débats*.]

FIRST LETTER

*July 1848*

The National Assembly has been set an immense question, the answer to which is of the greatest interest to the prosperity and peace of France.[2] A new right is knocking on the door of the Constitution: the right to work. Not only is it demanding a place for itself, but also it claims to take, in all or in part, the place of the right to property.

M. Louis Blanc has already provisionally proclaimed this new right with the success we have seen.[3]

M. Proudhon claims the right to work in order to put paid to property.

M. Considérant claims it in order to strengthen it by making it legitimate.

Thus, according to these political writers, property carries within it something that is unjust and wrong, a germ of death. I pretend to demonstrate that it is truth and justice itself and that what it carries within itself is the very basis of progress and life.

---

1. The following five letters were formally addressed to *Le Journal des débats,* which is why Bastiat refers to them several times as "the articles." However, in his mind they were intended as letters to Victor Considérant. In them he explains his notions of rent, services, and value as they will be developed later in *Economic Harmonies.*

2. On 17 May 1848 the Constituent Assembly elected an eighteen-member commission to prepare a draft constitution (Considérant was among the members, but so was Tocqueville). It started by elaborating a preamble, the "declaration of rights and duties," in which the right to work was prominent. The final preamble, though, referred only to the duty of the republic to protect the citizens' work and to provide work, *within the limits of state resources,* for the needy.

3. Written at Blanc's initiative, the decree of 25 February 1848 stated: "The provisional government guarantees the existence of the worker through work."

They appear to believe that, in the combat about to take place, the poor have an interest in the triumph of the *right to work* and the rich in the defense of the right to *property*. I believe I can prove that property rights are essentially democratic and that everything that denies or violates them is fundamentally aristocratic and anarchical.

I hesitated to ask for space in a journal for a dissertation on social economy. The following may perhaps justify this attempt:

First of all, there is the seriousness and topicality of the subject.

Second, MM Louis Blanc, Considérant, and Proudhon are not merely political writers. They are also the heads of schools with a number of enthusiastic disciples, as is shown by their presence in the National Assembly. Their doctrines today exercise considerable influence, which I think disastrous, on the world of business; and, what is no less serious, they may be strengthened by concessions at odds with the orthodoxy of the masters of political economy.

Last, and why should I not admit it, something in the depths of my conscience tells me that at the heart of this burning controversy it might be given to me to cast an unexpected ray of light to illuminate the terrain on which the schools most in opposition may sometimes be reconciled.

This is enough, I hope, for these letters to be accepted by their readers.

First of all, I have to set out the criticism made of property.

In short, this is how M. Considérant explains it. I do not think I am distorting his theory by summarizing it.[4]

> All men legitimately possess the thing that their activity has created. They may consume it, give it, exchange it, and transmit it without any person, even the whole of society, having any concern with it.
>
> Landowners therefore legitimately possess not only the products they have created on the land but also the *added value* they have given to the land itself through farming.
>
> However, there is one thing that they have not created, which is the fruit of no work, and that is the ground in its natural state, the original capital and the productive power of the agents of nature. However, landowners have taken over this capital. In this lie usurpation, confiscation, injustice, and constant illegitimacy.

4. (Bastiat's note) See the small volume published by M. Considérant titled *Théorie du droit de propriété et du droit au travail* [*Theory of the Right to Property and the Right to Work*].

The human race has been put on this globe in order to live and develop itself. The *species* is therefore the usufructuary of the surface of the globe. However, this surface has now been confiscated by the minority at the expense of the majority.

It is true that this confiscation was inevitable, for how can it be cultivated if each person can exercise, as he sees fit and in total freedom, his natural rights, that is to say, the rights of savagery?

We should therefore not destroy property but legitimize it. How? We should do it by recognizing the *right to work*.

In fact, savages exercise their four rights (to hunt, fish, grow crops, and graze animals) only provided they work. It is therefore under the same proviso that society owes the proletariat the equivalent of the usufruct of which it has robbed them.

To sum up, society owes all the members of humanity, on condition that they work, a wage that puts them in a situation that can be reckoned equally favorable to that of savages.

Property will then be legitimate from all points of view, and the poor and the rich will be reconciled.

This is M. Considérant's entire theory.[5] He asserts that this question of property is very simple, since it can be solved with just a little common sense, but nevertheless no one before him had understood it at all.

This is not much of a compliment to the human race, but in compensation I can only admire the extreme modesty expressed in the author's conclusions.

What in effect is he asking of society?

---

5. (Bastiat's note) M. Considérant is not the only one to hold it, as is shown by the following passage taken from *The Wandering Jew,* by M. Eugène Sue:

> *Mortification* would express better the complete lack of the essentially vital things that an equitably balanced society ought to owe, yes, ought to owe all active and upright workers, since civilization has dispossessed them of any right to the land and they are born with only their arms as sole heritage.
>
> Savages do not enjoy the advantages of civilization, but at least they have as food the animals of the forest, the birds of the air, fish from the rivers, the fruits of the earth, and the trees of the wide forests to give them shelter.
>
> Civilized people, who are despoiled of these gifts of God and who regard property as holy and sacred, may therefore, in return for their hard daily labor that enriches the country, claim a wage that is enough to live healthily, neither more nor less.

That it acknowledge the right to work as equivalent for humanity's well-being to a usufruct of the land in its natural state.

And what value does he place on this equivalent?

He reckons it equivalent to the level at which the land in its natural state can keep savages alive.

Since there is approximately one inhabitant per square league, the owners of land in France can certainly legitimize their usurpation at very little cost. All they have to do is to undertake that thirty to forty thousand nonowners will continue to live side by side with them at the full level of the Eskimos.

But what am I saying? Why are we talking about France? In this system there is no longer any France and no longer any national property, since the *life tenancy* of the land belongs as of right to the whole human race.

Besides, I have no intention of examining M. Considérant's theory in detail, since that would take me too far. I wish only to attack what is weighty and consequential at the core of this theory, that is to say, the question of *rent*.

M. Considérant's system can be summarized thus:

An agricultural product exists through the combination of two actions:

The *action by a man,* or work, which creates the right to property,
And the *action of nature,* which ought to be free and which
    landowners can arrange to be turned unjustly to their advantage.
    This is what constitutes the usurpation of the rights of humanity.

If, therefore, I were to prove that men, in the course of their transactions, are mutually *paid only for their work* and that they do not contrive to have the *action of nature* included in the price of the items being exchanged, M. Considérant should consider himself to be totally satisfied.

M. Proudhon's complaints against property are absolutely identical.[6] "Property," he says, "will cease to be abusive through the mutual sharing of services." Therefore, if I demonstrate that men exchange only *services* with each other, never charging each other a sou for the use of the *forces of nature* that God has given to everyone free of charge, M. Proudhon, for his part, should agree that his utopia has been achieved.

These two political writers are not entitled to claim the *right to work*. It does not matter that they consider this famous right in such a diametrically

6. Proudhon is best known for his work *Qu'est-ce que la propriété?* (1841).

opposed light that, in M. Considérant's view, it ought to legitimize property while according to M. Proudhon it ought to put paid to it. It is still true that there will no longer be any question of this right, provided that it is clearly proved that, under the regime of property, men will exchange hardship for hardship, effort for effort, work for work, and *service for service,* with the contribution made by nature always provided *in addition to the bargain struck,* so that the forces of nature, intended to be *free of charge,* continue to be *free of charge* through all human transactions.

We can see that what is being contested is the legitimacy of *rent,* since it is supposed that this is, in whole or in part, an unjust payment that the consumer makes to the landowner, not for a personal service but for the advantages supplied by nature free of charge.

I have said that modern reformers can base themselves on the opinion of the leading economists.[7]

In fact, Adam Smith says that rent is often a reasonable interest payment for the capital spent on improving the land, and also that this interest is often *just a part of the rent.*

To which McCulloch makes this positive declaration:

> That which is properly called rent is the sum paid for the use of *the forces of nature and the inherent power of the land.* It is totally distinct from the sum paid for the buildings, fences, roads, and other improvements made to the land. Rent is therefore always a monopoly.

Buchanan goes so far as to say that "rent is a part of the revenue from consumers that goes into the pockets of landowners."

Ricardo says:

> A part of the rent is paid for the use of the capital that has been used to improve the quality of the land, constructing buildings, etc.; *the rest is paid for the use of the latent and indestructible powers of the land.*

Scrope says:

> The value of the land and the ability to draw a rent from it are the result of two circumstances: 1. *the appropriation of its natural powers,* and 2. the work devoted to improving it.

---

7. (Paillottet's note) This proposition is developed in more detail in chapters 5 and 9 of the *Economic Harmonies.* (*OC,* vol. 6, p. 140, "De la valeur," and p. 297, "Propriété foncière.")

With regard to the first circumstance, rent is a monopoly. It is a restriction to the usufructor of the gifts that the Creator has made to men to satisfy their needs. This restriction is just only to the extent that it is necessary for the common good.

Senior says:

The instruments of production are labor and the *agents of nature*. Once the agents of nature are appropriated, landowners *have themselves paid* for their use in the form of rent, which is compensation for no sacrifice whatever and is received by those who have neither worked nor made any advance payments, but who limit themselves to holding out their hands to receive the offerings of the community.

After having said that part of rent is the interest on capital, Senior adds:

The rest is taken by the owner of the agents of nature and consists of his reward, not for having worked or saved but simply for not having kept to himself what he could have kept to himself and for having allowed the gifts of nature to be used by others.

Certainly, when entering into an argument with men who proclaim a doctrine that is specious in itself, which is likely to give rise to hopes and favorable reactions from the suffering classes and which is based on authorities like these, it is not enough to close your eyes to the seriousness of the situation. It is not enough to cry disdainfully that you are facing dreamers, utopians, people that are crazy, or even members of factions. You have to study the question and settle it once and for all. It is worth a moment of dull work.

I believe that it will be settled satisfactorily for all if I prove that property not only leaves those that are labeled the proletariat the free usufruct of the agents of nature but even increases it by ten or a hundredfold. I dare to hope that the result of this demonstration will be a clear view of a few *harmonies* likely to satisfy intelligent minds and calm the pretensions of all the schools of economists, socialists, or even communists.[8]

8. (Paillottet's note) See the claim from M. Considérant that provoked this first letter at the end of this pamphlet together with F. Bastiat's reply.

## SECOND LETTER

What inflexible power logic has!

Rough conquerors share an island. They live from *rent* in leisure and luxury among hard-working and poor vanquished people. According to political economy, there is, therefore, a source of *value* other than work.

This being so, political economy sets about breaking down rent and floats this theory on the world:

"Rent is partly interest on capital spent. Another part stems from *the monopoly of the agents of nature that have been usurped and confiscated.*"

This strain of political economy from the *English school* very rapidly crossed the Channel. Socialist logic caught hold of it and told the workers, "Watch out! There are three elements in the price of the bread you eat. There is the labor of the workers, you owe them for this; there is the work of the landowners, you owe them for this; and there is the work of nature, for which you do not owe anything. What is being taken from you under this heading is a monopoly, as Scrope says; it is a tax imposed on the gifts that God has given you, as Senior says."

Political economy sees the danger of this distinction. In spite of this, political economy does not withdraw it but explains it: "True, in the social mechanism the role of the landowner is useful and necessary. People work for him and he pays them with the heat of the sun and the coolness of the dew. This has to be the way; otherwise there would be no crops grown."

"Never mind that," logic replies; "I have a thousand types of organization in reserve with which to eliminate injustice, which incidentally is never necessary."

Therefore, because of a false principle gathered from the *English school,* logic has breached landownership. Will it stop there? Do not be too ready to believe this. It would not be logic if this were so.

As logic said to farmers, "The law governing plant life cannot be property and generate profit"; it will say to manufacturers of woolen cloth, "The law of gravity cannot be property and generate profit."

To manufacturers of cotton sheeting, "The law of the elasticity of steam cannot be a property and generate profit."

To ironmasters, "The law of combustion cannot be property and generate profit."

To seamen, "The laws of hydrostatics cannot be property and generate profit."

To roofers, carpenters, and lumberjacks, "You use saws, axes, and hammers; you also contribute to your work the hardness of bodies and the resistance of environments. These laws belong to everyone and should not generate profit."

Yes, logic will go this far at the risk of overturning the entire system of society. Once it has denied landownership, it will deny the productivity of capital, continuing to use as its basis the fact that landowners and capitalists are charging payment for the use of the force of nature. For this reason it is important to prove that logic is starting from a false premise, that it is not true that in any art, trade, or industry the forces of nature are being charged for and that in this respect agriculture is not receiving special treatment.

There are things that are *useful* without any work intervening, such as the earth, the air, water, the light and heat of the sun, and the materials and forces that nature provides.

There are others, which become *useful only* because work has been carried out on these materials and has taken over these forces.

*Utility* is therefore sometimes due to nature alone, sometimes due to work alone, but nearly always due to the combined activity of work and nature.

Let others lose their way in definitions. For my part, I understand *utility* to be what everyone understands by this word whose etymology shows its meaning exactly, namely, that everything that *serves* a purpose, whether by its nature, by work, or by both, being *useful,* constitutes utility.

I call *value* the only part of *utility* that is communicated or added by work, so that two things are of equal value when those who have *worked on* them exchange them freely with each other. The following are my reasons for this:

What makes a man refuse an exchange? It is his knowledge that the item being offered to him would require less work from him than the item demanded from him. It is absurd to say to him, "I have worked less than you, but gravity helped me and I have included it in the calculation." He will reply, "I can also use gravity with work that is equal to yours."

When two men are isolated, if they work, it is to *provide a service to themselves.* Where an exchange is involved, each person is *providing a service* to the other and receives an *equivalent* service in return. If one of them is helped by some force of nature that is at the disposal of the other, this force will not be included in the bargain as the right to refuse will oppose this.

Robinson hunts and Friday fishes. It is clear that the quantity of fish exchanged for game will be determined by the work involved. If Robinson said to Friday, "Nature goes to a lot more trouble in making a bird than a fish, so give me more of your work than I will give you of mine since I am trading you in return a greater effort by nature. . . . " Friday would not fail to reply, "It is no more up to you than me to judge the efforts of nature. What should be compared is your work to mine, and if you wish to establish our relationship on the footing that I will work more than you on a regular basis, I will start to hunt and you can fish if you want to."

You can see that the generosity of nature in this hypothesis cannot become a monopoly unless violence is involved. You can also see that, while it is a significant factor in *utility,* it is not a factor in *value.*

I have pointed out in the past that metaphors are an enemy of political economy. Here I accuse metonymy of the same misdeed.[9]

Are people using language accurately when they say, "Water is *worth* two sous"?

It is said that a famous astronomer could not bring himself to say, "Ah, what a fine sunset!" Even in the presence of ladies he cried, in a strange form of enthusiasm, "Ah, what a fine sight is the rotation of the earth when the sun's rays strike it tangentially!"

This astronomer was accurate and ridiculous. An economist would be no less ridiculous if he said, "The work needed to go to fetch water from the spring is worth two sous."

The strange character of the paraphrase does not prevent its accuracy.

In effect, water is not *worth* anything. It has no *value* although it is *useful.* If we all had a constant spring near our doorstep, obviously water would have no *value* because it would not give rise to any exchange. But if it is a quarter of a league away and you have to go to fetch it, this is work and here you have the origin of *value.* If it is half a league away, it is double the work and therefore double the *value,* although its *utility* remains the same. In my view, water is a free gift of nature on condition that you go to fetch it. If I do it for myself, I am doing myself a service involving some work. If I entrust this to another, I am giving him the bother and I owe him a payment for service rendered. There are thus two occasions of work and two services that have to be compared and discussed. The gift of nature continues to be free.

9. (Paillottet's note) See chapter 22 of the first series of *Sophisms.* (*OC,* vol. 4, p. 115, "Métaphores.")

In fact, I consider that the *value* lies in the *work* and not in the water and that metonymy is being used as much when people say, "Water is worth two sous" as when they say, "I have drunk a bottle."

Air is a free gift of nature and has no *value*. Economists say, "It has no exchange value, but it has a use value." What language! Well, sirs, have you made it your work to turn people off science? Why not simply say, "It has no *value,* but it is *useful.*" It is *useful* because it *serves a purpose.* It has no *value* because nature has done everything and *work* nothing. If work has not entered into it, no one has any *service* to return, receive, or pay for. There is no effort involved nor any exchange to be made. There is nothing to compare; therefore there is no *value.*

But if you enter a diving bell and entrust a man with transmitting air to you by using a pump for two hours, he will be exerting himself by providing you with a service and you will have *to pay for this.* Will you be paying for the air? No, you will be paying for the work. Therefore, has the air acquired *value?* You can say so to abbreviate, if you like, but do not forget that it is *metonymy.* The air remains free and no human intelligence is capable of attributing *value* to it. If it has a value, it is that measured by the effort taken compared with the effort required to make the exchange.

A launderer is obliged to dry washing in a large building using the action of fire. Another is content to hang it out in the sun. This launderer takes less trouble; he is not nor can he be as demanding. He therefore does not make me pay for the heat of the sun's rays and I, as the consumer, benefit from this.

Therefore the major economic law is this:

Services are traded for other services.

*Do ut des; do ut facias; facio ut des; facio ut facias* (do this for me and I will do that for you). This is very trivial and common but is nonetheless the beginning, the middle, and the end of political economy.[10]

---

10. (Paillottet's note) "It is not enough for the value not to be in the material or in the forces of nature. It is not enough for it to be exclusively in *services.* It is also necessary for the services themselves not to have an exaggerated *value.* For what difference does it make to a poor laborer if the high price he pays for his wheat is because the landowner has himself paid for the productive powers of the soil or has paid excessively for his intervention?

"It is the job of competition to equalize the services on the basis of justice. It does this constantly." (*An unpublished thought by the author.*)

For a more developed treatment of *value* and *competition,* see chapters 5 and 10 of *Economic Harmonies.* (*OC,* vol. 6, p. 140, "De la valeur," and p. 349, "Concurrence.")

From these three examples we can draw the following general conclusion: the consumer pays for all the services received by him, all the trouble he is saved, and all the work he generates, but he enjoys free of charge the free gifts from nature and its powers that the producer has put to use.

Here are three men who have placed air, water, and heat at my disposal with only their work being paid for.

What then has been able to make people think that farmers who also make use of the air, water, and heat are making me pay the so-called *intrinsic value* of these *agents of nature?* That they are charging me alike for utility created and utility not created? That, for example, the price of wheat sold at 18 francs is broken down as follows:

12 fr. for the actual work     ⎫
3 fr. for the preceding work ⎬ legitimate property
                            ⎭
3 fr. for the air, rain, sun, and plant life,
    which are illegitimate property?

Why do all the economists in the English school believe that this last element has crept surreptitiously into the value of wheat?

## Third Letter

*Services are traded for other services.* I am obliged to make a heroic effort to resist the temptation of showing how simple, true, and fertile this axiom is.

Faced with it, what are all these subtle notions, use-*value* and exchange-*value, material and immaterial products, or the productive and unproductive classes?* Industrialists, lawyers, doctors, civil servants, bankers, merchants, seamen, soldiers, artists, workers, whichever of these we are, with the exception of rapacious men, we provide and receive *services.* However, as these mutual services are commensurate only with each other, it is in them alone that *value* resides and not in the free material and the free agents of nature they set in motion. Let nobody say, therefore, as is currently fashionable, that merchants are parasitical intermediaries. Does he or does he not have to make an effort? Does he or does he not save us work? Does he or does he not provide us with *services?* If he provides services, he creates value just as much as the manufacturer does.[11]

---

11. (Paillottet's note) On the question of intermediaries, see, in vol. 5, chapter 6 of the pamphlet *What Is Seen and What Is Not Seen,* and, in vol. 6, the beginning of chapter 16.

Just as the manufacturer by means of his steam engine uses the weight of the atmosphere and the expansion of gas to turn his thousand spindles, the merchant uses the direction of the wind and the fluidity of water to transport his products. But neither of these makes us pay for the forces of nature since the more they are assisted the more they are obliged to lower their prices. These things therefore remain what God wanted them to be, a free gift for the whole of humanity, except for the work put in.

Is this not equally true for farming? This is what I have to examine.

Let us suppose that there is a huge island inhabited by a few savages. One of these has the bright idea of concentrating on growing crops. He prepares for this at length as he knows that the enterprise will take up a great many days of work before it shows the slightest yield. He gathers provisions and manufactures crude instruments. At last he is ready and fences and clears a tract of land.

Two questions arise:

Does this savage contravene community rights?
Does he contravene his own interests?

Since there is a hundred thousand times more land than the community is capable of cultivating, he no more contravenes its interests than I contravene those of my fellow countrymen when I take a glass of water from the Seine to drink or a cubic foot of air from the atmosphere to breathe.

He does not contravene his own interests either. On the contrary, since he no longer hunts or hunts less, his companions have proportionally more space. What is more, if he produces more crops than he can consume, he will have a surplus to trade.

In trading, will he be exercising the slightest pressure on his fellow men? No, because they will be free to accept or refuse.

Will he be charging for the contribution of the earth, sun, and rain? No, because everyone, like him, has recourse to these agents of production.

Should he wish to sell his tract of land, what could he obtain for it? The equivalent of his work, that is all. If he said, "First of all, give me as much of your time as I have devoted to the operation and then another amount of your time for the value of the land in its natural state," people would answer, "There is land in its natural state next to yours; I can only repay you for your

----

(*OC*, vol. 5, "Ce qu'on voit et ce qu'on ne voit pas," chap. 6, p. 356, "Les Intermédiaires"; and vol. 6, p. 497, "De la population.")

time, since, for an equal amount of time, nothing stops me from putting myself in a position similar to yours." This is exactly the reply we would give to the water carrier who asks us for two sous for the value of his service and two for the value of the water, from which we can see that the earth and water have this in common: both are very *useful* but neither has any *value*.

If our savage wished to rent out his land, he would never obtain anything other than payment for his work in another form. The more exaggerated of his demands would always meet this inexorable reply, "There is more land on the island," a reply more decisive than that of the miller of Sans-Souci,[12] "There are judges in Berlin."[13]

Thus, at least at the beginning, the landowner who either sells the products of his land or his land itself or leases it is doing nothing more than provide and receive *services* on an equal footing. It is the services that are compared, and consequently have *value,* the value being attributed to the land only by abbreviation or *metonymy*.

Let us see what happens as the island becomes increasingly populated and farmed.

It is quite clear that the ease of procuring raw materials, subsistence, and *work* is increasing for everyone, without privileged advantage for anyone, as we can see in the United States. There, it is absolutely impossible for landowners to put themselves in a position that is more favorable than that of other workers since, because of the abundance of land, each person has the choice of taking up agriculture if it becomes more lucrative than other jobs.

---

12. See "Bastiat's Political Writings: Anecdotes and Reflections," pp. 414–15 in this volume.

13. (Bastiat's note) We have heard not so long ago a denial of the legitimacy of leasing land. Without going so far, many people find it hard to understand the durable nature of income from capital. "How," they say, "does capital once formed produce a never-ending income?" Here is an explanation of its legitimacy and durability using this example:

I have a hundred sacks of wheat, which I could use to live on while I carry out useful work. Instead of this, I lend them for one year. What does the borrower owe me? The total restitution of my hundred sacks of wheat. Is this all he owes me? In this case, I will have done him a service without receiving any. He therefore owes me, in addition to the simple restitution of my loan, a *service,* a payment that will be determined by the laws of supply and demand: this is *interest*. You can see that at the end of a year, I will have once more one hundred sacks of wheat to lend and so on, eternally. The interest is a small portion of the work that my loan has enabled my borrower to execute. If I have enough sacks of wheat to ensure that the interest is sufficient for me to live, I would be able to be a man of leisure without doing any harm to anyone and it would be easy for me to show that the leisure thus purchased is itself one of the springs of progress of society.

This freedom is enough to maintain the *balance between services*. It is also enough to ensure that the *agents of nature,* used in a great many industries as well as in agriculture, do not benefit producers as such but the general public who are the consumers.

Two brothers take leave of each other; one is going whaling, the other to clear land in the *far west.* They then trade oil for wheat. Does one take the *value* of the land more into account than the *value* of the whale? Comparison can be made only between services received and given. These services therefore are the only ones to have *value.*

This is so true that, when nature has been very generous with regard to the soil, that is to say, when the harvest is plentiful, the price of wheat decreases and *it is the fisherman who benefits from this.* When nature is generous with produce from the ocean, in other words, when catches are large, oil is cheap and *farmers benefit from this.* Nothing proves better that the free gifts of nature remain free for the masses than the fact that producers who bring goods to market are paid solely for the service they provide in doing so.

Therefore, for as long as there is an abundance of uncultivated land in the country, the balance will be maintained between mutual services; and any exceptional advantage to the landowner will be refused.

This would not be so if landowners succeeded in prohibiting any new land clearance. In this case, it is perfectly clear that they would be laying down the law to the rest of the community. As the population is growing, the need for subsistence is increasingly being felt and it is clear that they would be in a position to have their *services* remunerated at a higher price, which in normal speech would be expressed by the metonymy, *land has increased in value.* However, the proof that this iniquitous privilege would be conferring an *artificial value,* not to the matter but to the services, is the situation we are witnessing in France and in Paris itself. Through a procedure similar to the one we have just described, the law limits the number of brokers, currency exchange agents, notaries, and butchers, and what is the result? By enabling them to put a high price on their *services,* it creates for their benefit a capital that is not included in any material. The need for brevity produces the following statement, "This project, this practice, or this patent is *worth* so much," and the metonymy is obvious. The same applies to the land.

We have reached the final hypothesis, that in which the land in the entire island is subject to individual appropriation and farming.

In this case, it appears that the relative position of the two sectors will change.

In effect, the population continues to grow. It will take up all the occupations except for the one that has been filled. The latter's owner will then operate the law of trade! What limits *the value of a service* is never the goodwill of the person supplying it; it is when the person to whom it is being offered can either do without it, supply it himself, or ask for it from others. The propertyless man no longer has any of these alternatives. In former times, he would say to a landowner, "If you ask me for more than the payment for your work, I will grow my own crops!" and the landowner would be forced to give way. These days, a landowner would reply, "There is no more land in the country." Thus, whether we see value in things or in services, farmers will take advantage of the lack of any competition and, like landowners, will lay down the law to sharecroppers and farm laborers and in the long run to everyone.

This new situation has obviously one single cause, the fact that those who do not own land can no longer stem the demands of those that do by stating, "There is still land left to clear."

What, therefore, is needed to ensure that the balance between services is maintained and that the situation according to the current hypothesis immediately concurs with that of the previous one? One single thing: that another island rises up next to our island, or even better new continents that are not totally covered by agriculture.

If this happened, production would continue to develop and be distributed in fair proportions between agriculture and other industries without any possible oppression on either side, since if landowners said to craftsmen, "I will sell you my wheat at a price that exceeds the normal payment for the work," craftsmen would be quick to reply, "I will work for the landowners on the continent who are unable to make such demands."

Once this situation has happened, the proper guarantee for the masses lies in free exchange, that is, in the right of labor.[14]

14. (Paillottet's note) This theoretical situation has been examined again by the author in the final part of his letter to M. Thiers. See the last twelve pages of "Protectionism and Communism." (*OC*, vol. 4, p. 504, "Protectionisme et communisme," pp. 534–45 [the last twelve pages].) [See also "Protectionism and Communism," pp. 257–65, and "Anecdotes and Reflections," p. 410, in this volume.]

The *right of labor* constitutes freedom and property. Craftsmen are the owners of their labor, their services, or the price they earn from them in the same way that landowners own the soil. So true is this that, by virtue of this right, craftsmen can exchange their labor and services around the world for agricultural products and are *bound* to keep landowners in the position of equality I have previously described in which *services are exchanged for other services,* without the possession of the land itself conferring any more of a benefit independently of the land's being put to work than does the ownership of a steam engine or the simplest tool.

However, if by usurping legislative power, landowners prohibit the landless farm laborers[15] from working away from the land in return for subsistence, the equilibrium between services is broken. Out of respect for accuracy in political economy, I will not say that in this way they are artificially increasing the *value of the land or agents of nature,* but I will say that that they are artificially increasing the *value of their services.* With *less* work themselves, they are buying *more* work. They are committing oppression. They are behaving like all the monopolists with patents. They are behaving like all the landowners in the earlier period who prohibited land clearance. They are introducing into society a cause of inequality and poverty. They are changing the notions of justice and property and are digging an abyss under their feet.[16]

But what relief can nonlandowners draw from the proclamation of the *right to work?* How does this new right increase subsistence or the work distributed to the masses? Are not all forms of capital devoted to making work for people? Do they increase by passing through the coffers of the state? When it purloins capital from the people through taxes, does the state not eliminate as many sources of work on the one hand as it opens up on the other?

Furthermore, in whose favor are you claiming this right? According to the theory that revealed it to you, it would be to the advantage of anyone who no longer has a share in the usufruct of the land in its original state. But bankers, merchants, manufacturers, lawyers, doctors, civil servants, artists,

---

15. Bastiat uses the word *prolétaires,* which we have translated as "landless farm laborers."

16. (Paillottet's note) See chapters 9 and 13 of *Economic Harmonies* on land ownership. See also, in vol. 2, the second parable in the speech given on 29 September 1846 in Montesquieu Hall. (*OC,* vol. 6, p. 297, "Propriété foncière," and p. 430, "De la rente"; also see vol. 2, p. 238, "Second discours.")

and craftsmen are not landowners. Do you mean that those who own the land will all be required to provide work for all these citizens? But all participants create openings for one another. Is it your view that only the rich, whether landowners or not, have to come to the assistance of the poor? In this case, what you are talking about is *assistance* and not a right that takes its source from an appropriation of the land.

With regard to rights, the one that has to be insisted on, because it is incontestable, rigorous, and sacred, is the right to work. It is freedom and ownership, not only of the land but also of bodily strength, intelligent minds, faculties, and personality, that are violated if one class can forbid to others *the free exchange of services,* both domestic and foreign. As long as this freedom exists, landownership is not a privilege; like all the others, it is just the *ownership of a form of work.*

I need only to deduce a few consequences of this doctrine.

## FOURTH LETTER

The physiocrats used to say, "Only the land is productive." Certain economists have said, "Only work is productive."

When you see laborers bent over the furrow that they drench with their sweat, you can scarcely deny their contribution to the work of production. On the other hand, nature never rests. And the ray of sunshine that pierces the clouds and the clouds that the wind chases away and the wind that brings rain and the rain that dissolves fertilizing substances and these substances that develop the mystery that is life in young plants—all the known and unknown powers of nature—prepare the harvest while laborers seek solace from their weariness in sleep.

It is therefore impossible not to recognize that work and nature join forces in accomplishing the phenomenon of production. *Utility,* which is the basis on which the human race survives, results from this cooperation, and this is as true of almost all forms of industry as it is of agriculture.

However, in the exchanges carried out between men, there is one thing only that is and can be compared, and that is human labor, the services received and rendered. These services alone are mutually commensurable and therefore they alone can elicit payment. In them alone lies value and it is precisely accurate to say that in the final analysis man is the sole *owner* of his *own* work.

As for the portion of utility due to the contribution of nature, although this is genuine, although it is immensely greater than anything that man can accomplish, it is *free*. It is transmitted from hand to hand over and above the market and is properly speaking without value. And who could assess, measure, and determine the value of the natural laws that, since the world began, have acted to produce an effect when work solicits them? With what should they be compared? How should we *evaluate* them? If they had a value, they would be included in our accounts and inventories; we would have ourselves reimbursed for their use. And how could we manage to do this, since they are at the disposal of all under the same condition, that of work?[17]

Thus all useful production is the work of nature, which acts free of charge, and of labor, which is paid for.

However, in achieving the production of a given utility, these two elements, *human labor* and the *forces of nature,* are not in fixed and immutable proportions. Far from it. Progress consists in ensuring that the proportion of the *contribution from nature* increases constantly and reduces in the same proportion that of *human work* by taking its place. In other words, for a given quantity of utility, the free cooperation of *nature* increasingly tends to replace the burdensome cooperation of *work.* The *common* portion grows at the expense of the portion remunerated and *appropriated.*

If you had to transport a burden weighing one hundred kilograms from Paris to Lille without the intervention of any force of nature, that is to say, on the backs of men, you would need one month of hard labor. If, instead of taking this work on yourself, you gave it to another person, you would have to compensate him for an equal effort; otherwise he would not do it. The sled came on the scene, followed by the cart and then the railway. At each stage of progress part of the work is entrusted to the forces of nature with a corresponding reduction of the labor to be taken or paid for. Well, it is clear that any remuneration eliminated is a victory, not in favor of the person providing the service but of him who receives it, that is to say, the human race.

Before the invention of printing, a scribe could not copy the Bible in less than one year, and that was the measure of the remuneration he was entitled to claim. Today we can procure a Bible for five francs, which is scarcely the reward for one day's work. The *free* forces of nature have thus taken the

17. (Paillottet's note) On the objection drawn from a so-called taking over of the agents of nature, see letter 14 of *Free Credit,* and, in vol. 4, the last two pages of chapter 14. (*OC,* vol. 5, p. 312, "Gratuité du crédit," "Quatorzième lettre"; and vol. 4, p. 86, "Conflit de principes," pp. 89–90 [last two pages].)

place of paid force in the proportion of 299 parts out of 300. One part still represents human labor and remains *personal property;* 299 parts represent the *contribution of nature,* no longer paid for, and consequently are relegated to that which is free and common.

There is no tool, instrument, or machine that does not result in reducing the contribution of human labor, which can be seen either as the value of the product or as the basis of property.

This observation, which I agree is only imperfectly set out here, ought to rally the schools of thought, which so bitterly divide the arena of public opinion today, on the common ground of *property* and *liberty.*

Each school can be summarized in one axiom:

Economists' axiom: laissez-faire, laissez-passer.
Egalitarians' axiom: the mutuality of services.
Saint-Simonians' axiom: to each according to his ability, to each
    ability according to its works.
Socialists' axiom: the equal sharing of capital, talent, and work.
Communists' axiom: the common ownership of goods.

I will indicate (for I cannot do otherwise here) that the doctrine set out in the preceding lines meets all these priorities.

*Economists.* It is scarcely necessary to prove that economists are obliged to welcome a doctrine that comes so obviously from *Smith* and *Say* and is only a consequence of the general laws they discovered. *Laissez-faire, laissez-passer,*[18] is summarized by the word *freedom,* and I ask whether it is possible to conceive the notion of *property* without freedom. Am I the owner of my work, faculties, or physical powers if I cannot use them to provide *services* voluntarily undertaken? Do I not need to be *free* either to exercise my forces in isolation, which involves the need for exchange, or to join them with those of my fellows, which is *association* or exchange under another form?

And if freedom is hampered, is not property itself assailed? On the other hand, how will mutual *services* all have their full relative value if they are not exchanged freely and if the law forbids labor from being drawn to those best remunerated? Property, justice, equality, and the proper balance of services can obviously result only from freedom. It is also freedom that causes the contribution made by the forces of nature to become a *common* benefit, for

18. *Laisser-passer:* "Let us go about our affairs." See also "Bastiat's Political Writings: Anecdotes and Reflections," pp. 408–9 in this volume.

as long as a legal privilege grants me the exclusive exploitation of one of nature's powers, I ensure that I am remunerated not only for my work but also for the use of this power. I know how fashionable it is today to curse freedom. The century appears to have taken seriously the ironic refrain of our great songwriter:

> My heart in a burst of hatred
> Has taken its freedom.
> To hell with freedom!
> Down with freedom![19]

For my part, since I have always instinctively loved freedom, I will always defend it through reason.

*Egalitarians.* The *mutuality of services* they aspire to is exactly that resulting from a *property-owning* regime.

In appearance, men are the owners of the whole, the entire thing, of all the utility that this thing holds. In reality, they own only its *value,* that portion of utility communicated by work, since by selling it they can obtain payment only for the *service* they are providing. The representative of the egalitarians condemned property from the rostrum recently, restricting this word to what he called *usury,* the use of the soil, money, houses, credit, etc. But this *usury* is production and cannot be anything other than production. Receiving a service implies the obligation of reciprocating it. It is in this that the *mutuality of services* exists. When I lend something I have produced by the sweat of my brow and from which I might draw benefit, I am providing a *service* to the borrower, who also owes me a *service.* He will not provide me with one if he limits himself to giving me back the thing one year later. During this interval, he would have benefited from my labor to my detriment.

---

19. This verse comes from Pierre-Jean de Béranger's poem "La Liberté" ("Liberty"), which he wrote in January 1822 when he was imprisoned following the publication of his second volume of satirical songs and poems in 1821. It is ironic that, far from having his spirit broken by short periods of imprisonment, Béranger continued to defy the censors with his poems, which mocked the political and religious establishment. His published songs and poems were bestsellers and went through many editions. They often included sheet music to help members of the underground singing and drinking clubs enjoy his political songs.

"Liberty" can be found in a contemporaneous English edition of his works: Béranger, *Béranger's Songs of the Empire, the Peace, and the Restoration,* pp. 109–11. There is a French edition that includes the music for "La Liberté": Béranger, *Musique des chansons de Béranger. Airs notés anciens et modernes,* pp. 128–29.

If I obtained payment for something other than my work, the objection of the egalitarians would be specious. But this is not so. Therefore, once they are assured of the truth of the theory set out in these articles, if they are consistent, they will join us to support property and claim what completes or rather what constitutes it, freedom.

*Saint-Simonians. To each according to his ability, to each ability according to its works.*

This is also what the property-owning regime achieves.

We provide each other with services mutually, but these services are not proportional to the length or intensity of the work. They are not measured using a dynamometer or chronometer. Whether I have been busy for one hour or one day, it is of little concern to the person to whom I provide my service. What he looks at is not the trouble I go to but the trouble I save him.[20] To save effort and time, I seek to obtain help from *some power in nature.* As long as no one except me is capable of taking advantage of this power, I am giving others, for an equal amount of time, more output than they could provide for themselves. I am well paid and grow rich without damaging anyone. The natural power is used for my benefit alone and my ability is remunerated. *To each according to his capacity.* However, my secret is soon divulged. Imitators take over my process and competition obliges me to reduce my demands. The price of the product is decreased until my work receives only the normal pay for any similar work. The natural power is not thereby lost; it escapes my control but is recuperated by the entire human race which, from now on, will gain equal satisfaction from less work. Whoever exploits this power for his own use will need to take less trouble than in former times, and consequently anyone who exploits it on behalf of others will be entitled to less payment. If he wishes to increase his well-being, he will have no other option than to increase the amount of his work. *To each ability according to its works.* In the end, it is a question of *working better* or *working more,* which is the literal translation of the axiom for followers of Saint-Simon.

*Socialists. The equal sharing of capital, talent, and work.*

Equitable sharing results from the law: *Services are exchanged for other services,* provided that these exchanges are free, that is to say, provided that property is acknowledged and respected.

---

20. (Paillottet's note) On the *effort saved,* considered as the most important element of value, see chapter 5 of *Economic Harmonies.* (*OC,* vol. 6, p. 140, "De la valeur.")

First of all, it is perfectly clear that the person with the most talent provides more services for a given amount of work. From this it follows that he is readily paid more handsomely.

As for capital and labor, this is a subject that, I regret, I cannot discuss in detail here, since no other has been presented to the general public under more false and disastrous colors.

Capital is often represented as a devouring monster, as the enemy of labor. In this way, an irrational sort of antagonism has been fostered between two powers that, basically, have the same origin and the same nature and that contribute to and help each other and cannot do without each other. When I see labor growing angry with capital, I seem to be seeing starvation rejecting food.

I define capital thus: *materials, instruments, and provisions,* whose use is *free,* let us not forget, to the extent that nature has contributed to producing them and for which only the value, the fruit of work, is paid for.

To execute a useful work, you need *materials.* If it is at all complicated, you need *instruments.* If it takes a long time, you need *provisions.* For example, for a railway line to be built, society must have saved enough means of existence to keep thousands of men alive for several years.

Materials, instruments, and provisions are themselves the fruit of previous work, which has not yet been paid for. Therefore, when previous work and current work are combined for an end, a common work, they pay for each other; there is an exchange of work, an *exchange of services* in accordance with agreed conditions. Which of the two parties will obtain the better conditions? The one that needs the other less. We are faced here with the inexorable law of supply and demand, and complaining about it is puerile and contradictory. To say that work should be highly paid when there are many workers and a limited level of capital is to say that each person has to be paid all the more when capital resources are smaller.

For work to be in demand and well paid, it is therefore necessary for there to be a great deal of materials, instruments, and provisions in the country, in other words, a great deal of capital.

It follows from this that the basic interest of the workers is that capital should be built up quickly, that as a result of its prompt accumulation, materials, instruments, and provisions should be in active competition. Only this can improve the lot of the workers. And what is the essential condition for the accumulation of capital? It is that each person should be sure of being genuinely the *owner,* in the fullest sense of the word, of his work and savings.

Property, security, freedom, order, peace, and economy are the things that interest everybody—above all and to the greatest extent, the workers.

*Communists.* In every age, honest and benevolent hearts have been found—Thomas Mores,[21] Harringtons,[22] and Fénelons—who, distressed by the sight of human suffering and the inequality of living conditions, sought refuge in a *communist* utopia.

As strange as it may appear, I claim that the regime of property is increasingly achieving this utopia under our very eyes. This is why I said at the start that property is essentially democratic.

On what foundation does humanity live and develop? On everything that *serves a purpose,* on everything that is *useful.* Among the *useful* things, there are those in which there is no human work, air, water, or sunlight. For these, there is a total absence of payment and full communal ownership. There are others that become *useful* only following a combination of work and nature. *Utility* can therefore be broken down into parts. One part is provided by labor and only this is to be paid for, has value, and constitutes property. The other part is contributed by the agents of nature, and this remains free of charge and common to all.

Well, of these two forces that contribute to producing utility the second, the part that is free of charge and common to all, is increasingly replacing the first, which requires work and consequently is to be paid for. This is the law of progress. There is no man on earth who does not seek help from the forces of nature, and when he finds it he shares it with the entire human race by proportionally reducing the price of the product.

Thus, in each given product, the portion of utility that is *free of charge* gradually replaces the other portion which is to be *paid for*.

The *commonly owned* base thus tends to surpass the *appropriated* base in indefinite proportions, and it can be said that within humanity the domain of common ownership is expanding unceasingly.

On the other hand, it is clear that, under the influence of freedom, the portion of utility that remains to be paid for or that can be appropriated tends to be distributed in a way that is, if not rigorously equal, at least in proportion to the *services* supplied, since these services themselves are the measure of the payment.

It can thus be seen with what irresistible power the principle of property

21. Sir Thomas More.
22. James Harrington.

tends to achieve equality between men. First of all, it establishes a *common basis* that is constantly increased by each stage of progress and with regard to which equality is perfect, since all men are equal in the face of value that has been *eliminated,* in the face of a utility that has ceased to generate payment. All men are equal in the face of the portion of the price of books that the publisher has eliminated.

Subsequently, with regard to the portion of utility that corresponds to human work, care that must be taken, or skill, competition tends to establish a balance in the flow of payments and all that remains is the inequality that is justified by the actual inequality of the effort, fatigue, work, or skill, in a word, of the *services* supplied. And apart from the fact that inequality of this sort will always be just, who does not understand that without it all effort would instantly cease?

I can see the objection coming! People will say: "This is an example of economists' optimism. They live in a world of theory and do not deign to cast a glance at the facts. Where in reality are these egalitarian tendencies? Can we not see all over the world the lamentable sight of opulence side by side with poverty, ostentation with destitution, idleness with fatigue, and satiety with starvation?"

I do not deny this inequality, this destitution, this suffering. Who could deny them? However, I say, "Far from being the result of the principle of property, they can be attributed to the principle of plunder."

It remains for me to prove this.


## FIFTH LETTER

No, economists do not think that we are in the best of all worlds, as they are reproached for doing. They do not shut their eyes to the afflictions of society nor their ears to the groans of those who suffer. But they seek the causes of these sufferings and believe that they have discovered that among those on which society is capable of taking action, there is none more active or generalized than injustice. This is why what they call for in particular and above all is universal justice.

Men wish to improve their lot; that is their first law. In order for this improvement to take place, a prior task or *effort* is required. The same principle that propels men toward their well-being also incites them to avoid the effort that is its means. Before addressing their own work, they all too often have recourse to the work of others.

We can therefore apply to *personal interest* what Aesop said of language: nothing on earth has done more good or more evil. Personal interest creates everything that enables men to live and develop themselves; it stimulates work and gives rise to *property*. But at the same time it introduces to the earth all forms of injustice that, depending on their form, take a variety of names and can be summarized in one word, *plunder*.

*Property and plunder,* sisters with the same father, the savior and scourge of society, a genius for good and a genius for evil, powers that, right from the start, have been in conflict over the empire and the fate of the world!

It is easy to use this common origin of property and plunder to explain the facility with which Rousseau and his modern disciples have been able to calumniate and undermine the social order. All they needed to do was to show just one of the aspects of *personal interest.*

We have seen that men are by nature the owners of their work and that by transmitting this work from one to another they provide mutual *services* to each other.

This having been said, the general character of plunder consists in employing force or guile to change the equivalent value of services in our favor.

The variations of plunder are boundless, as are the resources of human sagacity. Two conditions are needed for services that are exchanged to be considered legitimately equivalent. The first is that the judgment of one of the contracting parties is not distorted by the maneuvers of the other. The second is that the transaction must be free. If a man succeeds in extorting a genuine service from a fellow man by making him believe that what he is giving him in return is also a genuine service whereas it is in fact illusory, there is plunder. This is all the more true if he has recourse to force.

We are initially led to believe that plunder takes place only in the guise of those forms of *theft* defined and punished by the Code. If this were so, I would be in effect giving too great a social importance to exceptional events that public conscience condemns and the law punishes. But sad to say, there is plunder that takes place with the consent of the law and that is carried out by the law with the consent and often the applause of society. It is this form of plunder alone that can take on enormous proportions sufficient to change the distribution of wealth in the body of society, paralyze for a considerable time the force for leveling which lies in freedom, create permanent inequality in living conditions, open the abyss of destitution, and spread around the world the flood of evil that superficial minds attribute to property. This is the plunder of which I am speaking when I say that it has been in conflict with its opposing principle for empire over the world since the beginning. Let us point out briefly just a few of its manifestations.

First of all, what is war, especially as it was understood in antiquity? Men formed an alliance, the nation as a body, and did not deign to apply their faculties to exploiting nature in order to obtain from it the means of existence. On the contrary, after waiting for other peoples to establish properties, they attacked them with fire and sword and stripped them periodically of their goods. The conquerors then gained not only the booty but also the glory, the songs of poets, the acclaim of women, national reward, and the admiration of posterity! It is true that a regime like this and universally accepted ideas of this nature were bound to inflict a great deal of torture and suffering and result in extreme inequality between men. Is this the fault of property?

Later, the plunderers became more refined. Putting the vanquished to the sword was, in their eyes, to destroy a treasure. Plundering only property was a transitory form of plunder; plundering men along with property was to organize permanent plunder. This led to slavery, which is plunder extended to its ideal limit, since slavery plundered the vanquished of all their current and future property, their work, their arms, their minds, their faculties, their affections, and their entire personality. It can be summarized thus: requiring man to provide all the services that force can wrench from him while rendering him none. This was the state of the world until an era that is not all that far from ours. This was the situation in particular in Athens, Sparta, and Rome, and it is sad to think that it is the ideas and customs of these republics that education is offering for our enjoyment and that we are absorbing through our every pore. We are like the plants that growers force to absorb colored water and that thus receive an artificial tint that cannot be effaced. And then we are surprised that generations educated in this way are incapable of founding an honest republic! Be that as it may, it can be agreed that here there was a cause of inequality that can certainly not be imputed to the regime of property as it has been defined in the preceding articles.

I will pass over *serfdom,* the *feudal regime,* and what followed it up to 1789. But I cannot prevent myself from mentioning the plunder exercised for so long through the abuse of religious influence. Receiving positive services from men and supplying them in return only with imaginary, fraudulent, illusionary, and derisory services is to rob them of their consent, it is true, an aggravating circumstance since it implies that the plunderers have begun by perverting the very source of all progress, human judgment. I will not stress this any further. Everybody knows that the exploitation of public credulity through the abuse of true or false religions has placed distance between the priesthood and the laity in India, Egypt, Italy, and Spain. Is this also the fault of property?

We come to the nineteenth century following great social iniquities that have imprinted a profound trace on the soil, and who can deny that time is needed to efface that trace even when through all our laws and relationships we now give prominence to the principle of property, which is none other than *freedom*, which is none other than the expression of *universal justice*? We should remember that *serfdom* these days covers half of Europe, that in France the feudal system received its death blow scarcely half a century ago, that it is in full splendor in England, that all nations are making unheard-of efforts to keep powerful armies in operation, which implies either that they are mutually threatening each other's property or that these armies are themselves just a large-scale plunder. Let us remember that all peoples succumb to the weight of debts whose origin lies in past folly. We should not forget that we ourselves are paying millions each year to prolong artificially the lives of colonies with slaves and more millions to prevent slave trading along the coasts of Africa (which has involved us in one of our greatest diplomatic problems) and that we are on the point of delivering one hundred million to planters to crown the sacrifices which this type of plunder has inflicted on us in so many forms.[23]

This is how the past binds us, no matter what we may say. We can disengage ourselves from it only gradually. Is it surprising that there is inequality between men, since the egalitarian principle, property, has been so little respected up to now? Where will the leveling of living conditions that is the ardent wish of our era and that characterizes it so honorably come from? It will come from simple justice, from the achievement of this law: *a service in return for a service*. In order for two services to be exchanged according to their genuine value, two things are needed by the contracting parties: enlightened judgment and freedom of transaction. If the judgment is not enlightened, people will accept, even freely, derisory services in return for genuine services. It is even worse if force intervenes in the contract.

This having been said, and acknowledging that there exists inequality between men whose causes are historic and that only time will efface, let us see

23. Slavery in the French colonies ended (again) in the revolution of 1848. See also the entry for "Slavery" in the Glossary of Subjects and Terms.

whether our century at least by giving prominence to *justice* everywhere will finally banish force and guile from human transactions, allow the equivalent nature of services to establish itself naturally, and cause the democratic and egalitarian cause of property to triumph.

Alas! I can see here so many incipient abuses, so many exceptions, and so many direct and indirect deviations appearing on the horizon of the new social order that I do not know where to begin.

First of all, we have privileges of all sorts. No one can become a lawyer, doctor, lecturer, currency exchange agent, broker, notary, solicitor, pharmacist, printer, butcher, or baker without encountering legal prohibitions. These are so many *services* that you are forbidden to provide; consequently those to whom authorization is given will charge a higher price for them to the extent that this privilege alone, without any work, often has a great deal of value. My complaint here is not that guarantees are required from those who supply these *services,* although truth to tell the effective guarantee is found in those who receive and pay for it. What is also necessary is for these guarantees not to have any exclusivity. You may demand of me that I know what you need to know to be a lawyer or doctor, but do not demand that I should have learned it in a particular town, in so many years, etc.

Next there is the artificial price, the additional value that people try to add to the majority of essential things such as wheat, meat, fabrics, iron, tools, etc., by playing with the tariffs.

Here there is obviously an effort to destroy the equivalence of services, a violent attack on the most sacred of all properties, that of men's strength and faculties. As I have already shown, when the soil of a country has been successively occupied, if the working population continues to grow, its right is to limit the claims of the landowner by working elsewhere or by importing its subsistence from abroad. This population has only work to give in exchange for products, and it is clear that if the former increases unceasingly, then should the second remain stationary, more work has to be provided in return for fewer products. This effect is shown by the decrease in earnings—the greatest misfortune when it is due to natural causes and the greatest crime when it results from the law.

Next come taxes. Tax-funded jobs have become a highly sought means of livelihood. We know that the number of positions in government services has always increased and that the number of candidates increases faster than the number of openings. Well, where is the candidate who asks himself if he will be providing the public with *services* equivalent to those he is expecting from them? Is this scourge anywhere near its end? How can we believe it when we see that public opinion itself presses to have everything done by the fictitious being we call the *state,* which means a *collection of salaried agents?* After judging all men without exception to be capable of governing the country, we declare them to be incapable of governing themselves. Soon there will be two or three salaried agents around each Frenchman, one to prevent him from working too much, a second to educate him, a third to supply him with credit, perhaps a fourth to hinder his transactions, etc., etc. Where will this illusion, the illusion that has led us to believe that the state is a person with an inexhaustible fortune independent of ours, take us?

People are beginning to realize that the government machine is expensive. But what they do not know is that the burden *inevitably* falls on them. They are led to believe that although up to now their share has been heavy, the Republic, while increasing the general burden, has the means of at least shifting the greater part of it to the shoulders of the rich. A disastrous illusion! Doubtless the situation may be reached where the tax collector calls upon one person rather than another and physically receives money from the hands of the rich. But all is not at an end once the tax has been paid. Work is done subsequently in society, there are reactions to the respective value of services, and it is unavoidable for this charge not to be distributed to everybody, including the poor, in the long run. The latter's real interest, therefore, is not that one class alone is afflicted, but that all classes are treated with consideration because of the solidarity that binds them.

Now, are there any signs that the time has come when taxes will be reduced?

I say this most sincerely: I believe that we are going down a path in which, under very gentle, very subtle, and very ingenious aspects, clad in the fine names of solidarity and fraternity, plunder is going to take on dimensions, the extent of which the imagination scarcely dares to envisage. This is how it will appear: under the denomination of *the state,* the massed group of citizens will be considered a real being with its own life and wealth, independent of the life and wealth of the citizens themselves. Each person will then call upon this fictional being to ask, one for education, one for work, one for credit, one for food, etc., etc. However, the state cannot give anything to citizens unless it has taken it from them to start with. The only effect of this intermediary is first of all a great waste of effort and then the complete destruction of the *equivalence of services,* for the effort of each person will be devoted to giving as little as possible to the treasury of the state and taking as much from it as possible. In other words, the public treasury will be pillaged. And can we not see something of this sort happening today? Which class is not clamoring for the favors of the state? It appears in itself to be the principle of life. Setting aside the countless hordes of its own agents, agriculture, factories, trade, the arts, theaters, the colonies, and shipping are expecting everything from it. It is required to clear land, irrigate it, set up colonies, teach, and even amuse us. Everyone is begging for a premium, a subsidy, a motivating payment, and above all for certain services, like education and credit, to be *free of charge*. And why not ask the state to make all services free of charge? Why not require the state to feed, quench the thirst of, provide lodgings for, and clothe all citizens free of charge?

One class had not been included in these mad pretensions,

> One poor servant girl at least remained to me
> Who was not infected with this foul air;[24]

and that was the people itself, the countless working class. However, here they are now in the crowd. They pay heavily to the treasury; by all that is just and in virtue of the principle of equality, they have the same rights to this universal dilapidation for which the other classes have fired the starting signal. We should profoundly regret that on the day on which their voices were heard it was to demand their share of the pillage and not that it be stopped. But was it possible for this class to be more enlightened than the others? Might it not be excused for being taken in by the illusion that is blinding us all?

However, because of the very fact that the number of applicants for government positions is now equal to the number of citizens, the error I am pointing out here cannot last long and people will soon, I hope, come to ask from the state only the services it is competent to provide: justice, national defense, public works, etc.

We are facing another cause of inequality, which is perhaps more active

---

24. These lines come from Molière's play *Les Femmes savantes* (1672). The long-suffering bourgeois gentleman Chrysale is complaining about his household of women who have discovered the joys of disputation, reasoning, and the quotation of verse but who neglect his needs. In these lines Chrysale is complaining to his sister Bélise: "Reasoning has become the norm throughout my house, and reasoning has banished reason. One servant burns my roast while reading some story, another dreams of some verses when I want a drink; finally I see how they have followed your example, I have servants but I am not served." (See *Œuvres complètes de Molière*, vol. 6, p. 145.)

than all the others, and that is the *war against capital*. The working class has only one way to free itself, through an increase in the nation's capital. Where capital increases faster than the population, two results infallibly occur, both of which contribute to improving the lot of the workers: products decrease in price and earnings rise. However, for capital to increase, it must above all have security. If it is frightened, it hides, takes flight abroad, is dissipated, and is destroyed. At this point, production stops and labor is offered at a knockdown price. The greatest of all misfortunes for the working class is therefore to let itself be carried along by beguilers into a war against capital, which is as absurd as it is disastrous. It is a constant threat of plunder, worse than plunder itself.

In short, if it is true, as I have endeavored to show, that freedom, the free disposal of property, and consequently the supreme consecration of the right to property; if it is true, as I have said, that this freedom invariably tends to bring about *a just equivalence of services,* and little by little equality, to bring everyone closer to the same constantly rising level, it is not property that is responsible for the distressing inequality that can still be seen around the world; it is its opposing principle, plunder, that has triggered wars, slavery, serfdom, the feudal system, the exploitation of public ignorance and credulity, privilege, monopolies, restrictions, public borrowings, commercial fraud, excessive taxes, and lastly the war against capital and the absurd pretension of each person to live and develop at the expense of all.

## CLAIM MADE BY M. CONSIDÉRANT AND F. BASTIAT'S REPLY

*Published by* Le Journal des débats *in its issue dated 28 July 1848.*

*Sir,*

In the serious discussions to come on the social question, I am determined to prevent the public from being given, as coming from me, opinions that are not mine, and to prevent my opinions being presented in a way that distorts and disfigures them.

I have not defended the principle of *property* for twenty years against the followers of Saint-Simon who denied the right of inheritance, against the disciples of Babeuf and Owen, and against all the varieties of communism, to let myself be depicted as being in the ranks of those who oppose the rights of property, whose logical legitimacy I believe I have established on foundations that are difficult to undermine.

I have not fought in the Luxembourg Palace against the doctrines of M. Louis Blanc, I have not on numerous occasions been attacked by M. Proudhon as one of the fiercest defenders of property only to allow M. Bastiat to paint me in your columns as forming, with these two social-ists, a sort of triumvirate *against property*, without my protesting.

Besides, since I do not wish to be obliged to claim your indulgence in in-serting lengthy tracts of my prose in your columns, and you doubtless agree with me in this, I am asking your permission to make a few observations to M. Bastiat before he goes any further, which will cut short the replies that he may oblige me to give him and perhaps even to eliminate them completely.

1. I would not like M. Bastiat, even when he thinks he is analyzing my thought accurately, to use, in inverted commas and as though quoting textu-ally from my pamphlet on the right of property and the right to work or any other of my writings, phrases of his own that, especially in the penultimate of the quotations he attributes to me, convey my ideas inaccurately. This is not a proper way to proceed, and it may even lead the person who uses it much further than he himself would wish. Abbreviate and analyze as you wish, that is your right, but do not give your analytical abbreviation the char-acter of a verbatim quotation.

2. M. Bastiat says: "They (the three socialists among whom I am in-cluded) appear to think that in the combat that is about to take place, the poor have an interest in the triumph of the *right to work* and the rich in defending the *right of property*." For my part, I do not believe and do not even believe that I *appear to believe* anything of the sort. On the contrary, I believe that the rich now have a more serious interest than the poor in the recognition of the right to work. This is the thought that dominates my entire article, published for the first time not today, but ten years ago, and written to give the men in government and landowners a salutary warning and at the same time defend property against the redoubtable logic of its op-ponents. Moreover, I believe that the right of property is just as much in the interests of the poor as of the rich, since I regard the denial of this right as a denial of the principle of individuality and would consider its elimination, in whatever form of society, to be the signal for a return to the primitive state, which to my knowledge I have never shown myself to favor.

3. Last, M. Bastiat says:

"Besides, I have no intention of examining M. Considérant's theory in detail. . . . I wish only to attack what is weighty and consequential at the basis of this theory, that is to say, the question of *rent*. M. Considérant's theory can be summarized thus. An agricultural product exists through the combination of two actions: the *action by a man*, or labor, which generates the right of property; and the *action of nature*, which ought to be free and which landowners turn unjustly to their advantage. This is what constitutes the usurpation of the rights of humanity."

I ask a thousand pardons of M. Bastiat, but there is not one word in my pamphlet that authorizes him to attribute to me the opinions that he so freely does here. As a rule I do not hide my thought, and when I think it is midday it is not my habit to say it is two o'clock. Therefore, let M. Bastiat, if he wishes to do me the honor of disparaging my pamphlet, oppose what I have written and not what he attributes to me. I have not written one word against *rent;* the question of *rent,* with which I am as familiar as everyone, does not appear at all in any shape or form, and when M. Bastiat quotes me as saying "that the *action of nature* ought to be free and that landowners turn it unjustly to their advantage and that is what, according to me, constitutes the usurpation of the rights of the human race," he again remains stuck in a domain of thought that I have not referred to in the slightest. He is attributing to me an opinion that I consider to be absurd and that is even diametrically opposed to the entire doctrine of my article. I am not complaining at all, in fact, that landowners enjoy the *action of nature,* what I am asking for, in the name of those who do not enjoy this, is the right to work that will enable them to be able, alongside landowners, to create products and to live by working, when property (whether agricultural or industrial) fails to give them the means to do so.

Besides, sir, I have no intention of indulging in a debate on my opinions with M. Bastiat in your columns. This is a favor and an honor not reserved to me. Let M. Bastiat therefore reduce my system to dust and ruin; I will think myself entitled to claim your hospitality for my comments only when, through a lack of understanding, he attributes to me doctrines for which I am not responsible. I am well aware that it is often easy to bring down people by attributing to them what you want instead of what they have said, and in particular one is more readily right when opposing *socialists* when one opposes them in a confused way and in general than when one takes each one to task for what he has put forward. But, whether right or wrong, I for my part insist on taking responsibility for no one other than myself.

M. Editor, the discussion that M. Bastiat has undertaken in your columns bears on subjects that are too sensitive and weighty for you not to be in agreement with me on this at least. I am confident therefore that you will agree that I am right to be upset and that you will in fairness give my complaint a clear and legible place in your columns.

*V. Considérant*
*Representative of the people*

Paris, 24 July 1848

M. Considérant is complaining that I have altered or distorted his opinion on property. If I have committed this fault I have done so involuntarily, and I can do no more in reparation than to quote his words.

After having established that there are two sorts of rights—natural rights, which express the relationships resulting from the very nature of beings or things, and conventional or legal rights, *which exist only to regulate false relationships*—M. Considérant continues thus:

"This having been said, we will say clearly that property as it has generally been constituted *in all the hardworking nations up to now,* is tarnished by illegitimacy and is contrary to right. . . . The human race has been placed on earth to live and develop there. The species is thus a usufructuary of the surface of the globe. . . .

"However, under the regime that constitutes property in all civilized nations, the common basis on which the species has right of usufruct has been invaded. It has been confiscated by the minority to the exclusion of the majority. Well then! If there were in fact one single man deprived of his right to a usufruct of the common fund by the nature of the regime of property, this deprivation on its own would constitute an infringement of rights, and the regime of property that endorsed it would certainly be unjust and illegitimate.

"Might not any man who was born into a civilized society with no possessions and who found the land around him confiscated say to those who preached respect for the existing regime of property by affirming the respect due to the rights of property, "My friends, let us understand one another and set things straight a little; I am much in favor of the rights of property and very ready to respect it with regard to others, on the sole condition that others respect it with regard to me. However, as a member of the human race, I am entitled to a usufruct of the fund that is the common property of the race and that nature, as far as I know, has not given to some to the detriment of others. In virtue of the regime of property that I found established on my arrival here, the common fund has been confiscated and is well guarded. Your regime of property is therefore founded on the plunder of my right to a usufruct. Do not confuse the right of property with the particular regime of property that I find is established by your artificial right.

"The current regime of property is therefore illegitimate and is based on fundamental plunder."

M. Considérant finally manages to set out the fundamental principle of the right of property in these terms:

"Every man possesses the thing that his work, intelligence, or more generally his activity has created."

To show the extent of this principle, Considérant gives the example of the first generation of men who farm an isolated island. The results of the work of this generation are divided into two categories.

"The first includes the products of the land that belonged to this first generation as usufructuaries, and that were increased, refined, or manufactured by its work and industry. These products, in their raw state or manufactured, consist either of consumer products or instruments of work. It is clear that these products belong in total and legitimate property to those who have created them through their activity. . . .

"Not only has this generation created the products we have just designated . . . but it has also created *added value* to the original value of the land through cultivation, the buildings, and all the basic and construction work it has carried out.

"This *added value* obviously constitutes a product, a value due to the activity of the first generation."

M. Considérant acknowledges that this secondary value is also a legitimate property. Then he adds:

"We can thus totally accept that, when the second generation comes onto the scene, it will find two types of capital on the earth:

"A. *The original or natural capital*, which has not been created by the men of the first generation, that is to say, the value of the land in its natural state.

"B. The *capital created* by the first generation, which includes 1. the products, goods, and instruments that have not been consumed and worn out by the first generation; 2. the *added value* that the work done by the first generation has added to the value of the land in its natural state.

"It is thus obvious and results clearly and essentially from the fundamental principle of the right of property established just now, that each individual of the second generation has an equal right to the original or natural capital, whereas he has no right to the other form of capital, the capital created by the first generation. Each individual of this first generation can thus dispose of his part of the created capital in favor of the particular individuals of the second generation of his choice, his children, friends, etc."

Thus, in this second generation, there are two types of individuals, those who inherit created capital and those who do not. There are also two types of capital, original or natural capital and created capital. The latter legitimately belongs to the heirs but the former legitimately belongs to everyone. *Each individual of the second generation has an equal right to the original capital.* Well, it has happened that the heirs to created capital have also seized the capital not created; they have invaded it, usurped it, and confiscated it. This is why and how the *current regime* of property is illegitimate, contrary to right and based on a fundamental plunder.

I may certainly be mistaken, but it seems to me that this doctrine exactly echoes, though in other terms, the doctrine of Buchanan, McCulloch, and Senior on *rent*. They too acknowledged the legitimate ownership of what has been created by work. However, they regard as illegitimate the usurpation of that which M. Considérant calls the *value of the land in its natural state* and what they call the *productive force* of the land.

Let us now see how this injustice can be put right.

"Primitive men in forests and savannahs enjoy four natural rights: hunting, fishing, the gathering of fruit, and grazing. That is the initial form taken by rights.

"In all civilized forms of society, men of the people, the working classes who inherit nothing and who own nothing, are purely and simply deprived of these rights. We thus cannot say that the initial right has changed its form here, since it no longer exists. The form has disappeared along with the substance.

"But under what form might the right be reconciled with the conditions of a hardworking society? The answer is easy. In primitive forms of society, in order to make use of his rights, man is *obliged to act*. The work of hunting, fishing, gathering fruit, and grazing is the condition governing the exercise of his rights. The initial right is thus only the *right to these forms of work*.

"Well then! Let a hardworking society that has taken possession of the land and removed from men their faculty of exercising their four rights at random and freely over the surface of the land, recognize the right to work of each individual in compensation for these rights that it has taken away from him. Then, in principle and subject to proper application, no individual would have anything to complain about. In effect, his initial right was the right to work exercised in what was the poor workshop constituted by nature in its natural state. His current right would be the same right exercised in a better equipped and richer workshop in which individual activity has to be more productive.

"The condition *sine qua non* for property to be legitimate is thus that society should recognize the *right to work* of the proletariat and that it should *ensure* that it has at least as much of the means of subsistence for the exercise of a given activity as this exercise would have procured for it in the natural state."

Now I leave the reader to judge whether I have changed or distorted M. Considérant's opinions.

M. Considérant considers himself to be a fierce defender of the *right to property*. Doubtless he is defending this right as he understands it, but he understands it in his own way and the question is to establish whether it is the right way. In any case, it is not the way of everybody.

He himself says that, *although it needed only a modicum of good sense to settle the question of property, it has never been properly understood.* I am fully allowed not to agree with this condemnation of human intelligence.

It is not only the theory that M. Considérant is accusing. I would yield it to him, thinking like him that in this matter as in many others, it has often been on the wrong track.

However, he also attacks the universal practice. He says clearly:

"Property, as generally constituted *in all hardworking nations up to the present,* is tarnished with illegitimacy and sins spectacularly against rights."

If, therefore, M. Considérant is a fierce defender of property, it is at least of a mode of property that is different from the one recognized and practiced by men since the dawn of time.

I am fully convinced that M. Louis Blanc and M. Proudhon also claim to defend property as they understand it.

I myself have no other pretension than to give an explanation of property that I believe to be true but that is perhaps false.

I believe that the ownership of land, as it is formed naturally, is always the fruit of work, that consequently it is based on the very principle established by M. Considérant, that it does not exclude the working classes from enjoy-ing the usufruct of the land in its natural state but on the contrary it multi-plies ten and a hundredfold this usufruct for them and thus is not tarnished with illegitimacy, and that all that undermines it in fact and in belief is as great a calamity for those who do not possess the land as for those who do.

This is what I would like to devote myself to proving, to the extent that this can be done in the columns of a journal.

*F. Bastiat*

# 11

# Baccalaureate and Socialism [1]

[vol. 4, p. 442. "Baccalaureate et socialisme." 1850. This article was written in early 1850 for a parliamentary commission looking into the question of the freedom of education. n.p.]

*Citizen Representatives*

I have submitted an amendment to the Assembly the object of which is *to eliminate university degrees.*[2] My health does not allow me to develop it from the rostrum. Allow me to have recourse to the pen.[3]

The question is extremely serious. As faulty as the law drawn up by your commission is, I believe that it would mark a signal improvement on the current condition of state education if it were amended as I propose.

University degrees have the triple disadvantage of *making teaching uniform* (uniformity is not unity) and of *freezing* it after having imprinted it with the *most disastrous orientation.*

If there is anything in the world that is progressive by nature it is teaching. What is it, in fact, other than the transmission from generation to genera-

---

1. From 1815 to the end of the Second Republic, freedom of education had been a recurrent theme in parliamentary debates. In early 1850, a bill put forward in 1849 by Frédéric de Falloux was debated in a commission presided over by Adolphe Thiers. Victor Hugo and Charles de Montalembert were among the members. Bastiat proposed a significant amendment but was unable to attend the debates for health reasons. This paper, a justification for the amendment, was sent to the commission. After serious, deep, and sometimes brilliant debates, the law was adopted on 15 March 1850, but without Bastiat's amendment.

2. "Baccalaureat," "licence," and "doctorat" were the degrees delivered by the universities only.

3. (Paillottet's note) Twenty years before, the author, in his initial article, had already pointed to the freedom of education as being one of the reforms that the nation should try to obtain. See the article titled "To the Electors of the *Département* of the Landes," in vol. 1. (*OC,* vol. 1, p. 217, "Aux électeurs du département des Landes.")

tion of the knowledge acquired by society, that is to say, a treasure that is relieved of its dross and increased every day?

How has it happened that teaching in France has remained uniform and stationary in medieval obscurity? Because it has been monopolized and enclosed by university degrees in an impassable circle.

There was a time when, to acquire any sort of knowledge, it was as necessary to learn Latin and Greek as it is for people in the Basque and lower Brittany regions to begin by learning French. Living languages had not been settled, printing had not been discovered, and the human spirit had not applied itself to penetrating the secrets of nature. To be educated was to know what Epicurus and Aristotle thought. In the higher ranks, people boasted that they could not read. One single class possessed and imparted education, the clergy. What could this education be like under these circumstances? Obviously it had to be limited to a knowledge of the dead languages, principally Latin. There were only Latin books; people wrote only in Latin; Latin was the language of religion, and the clergy could teach only what they themselves had learned, Latin.

We can understand, therefore, that in the Middle Ages teaching was limited to the study of the dead languages, most improperly called scholarly.

Is it natural, is it right that this should be so in the nineteenth century? Is Latin an essential instrument for the acquisition of knowledge? Is it in the writings left to us by the Romans that we can learn about religion, physics, chemistry, astronomy, physiology, history, law, morality, industrial technology, or social science?

To know a language, like knowing how to read, is to possess an instrument. And is it not strange that we should spend our entire youth mastering an instrument that is no longer any use, or very little use, since there is nothing we are more in a hurry to do, once we have begun to know it, than to forget it? Alas, why can we not forget the impressions left on us by this disastrous study just as quickly?

What would we say if, at Saint-Cyr, while initiating our young people into modern military science, we taught them only to throw stones with a sling?

The law of our land has decided that the most honorable careers will be closed to anyone who has not obtained a baccalaureate. What is more, it has decided that in order to obtain it students have to stuff their heads with Latin texts to such an extent that nothing else enters. So, what is the result according to common agreement? It is that our young people *have calculated the minimum work strictly required to gain a pass mark* and they stop there. You object to this and you complain bitterly about it. Well, do you not see that this is the cry of public awareness, a public that refuses to have a useless effort imposed on it?

Teaching an instrument that, as soon as you know it, no longer gives out any sound, is a very strange anomaly! How has it lasted up to our time? The explanation lies in a single word: *monopoly.* Monopoly is constructed in such a way that it renders immobile everything it touches.

For this reason, I would have liked the Legislative Assembly to achieve freedom, that is to say, progress in teaching. It has now been decided that this will not happen. We will not have total freedom. May I be allowed to make an effort to save a shred of it?

Freedom may be considered from the point of view of people and in relation to subjects taught—*ratione personae et ratione materiae*[4]—as lawyers say, to eliminate the competition between methods is no less an attack on freedom than to eliminate competition between men.

There are those who say: "The teaching profession will be free, since anyone may enter it." That is a great illusion.

The state, or more precisely the party, the faction, the sect, or the man who briefly and even very legally takes control of government influence, may give teaching any direction he pleases and fashion at will all intelligent minds through the single mechanism of degrees.

Give a man the power to confer degrees and, while leaving yourself free to teach, the teaching will in fact be carried out in servitude.

I, as the father of a family, and the teacher with whom I join forces for the education of my son may well believe that a proper education consists in knowing what things are and what they produce, both in the realm of physics and in the realm of morals. We may think that a person is best educated if he has the most accurate knowledge of phenomena and is most conversant with the cycle of cause and effect. We would like to base teaching on this foundation. But the state thinks otherwise. It thinks that to be learned is to be able to scan the verses of Plautus and to quote the opinions of Thales and Pythagoras with regard to fire and air.

So what does the state do? It tells us: "Teach your pupil whatever you like, but when he is twenty, I will have him interrogated on the opinions of

---

4. "By reason of his person and relevant reasons." This phrase relates to a jurisdiction's competence to judge a person or a material offence.

Pythagoras and Thales, I will have him scan the verses of Plautus, and if he is not schooled enough in these matters to prove to me that he has devoted his entire youth to them, he cannot be a doctor, lawyer, magistrate, consul, diplomat, or teacher."

This being so, I am obliged to bow to the state, since I cannot take the responsibility on myself to bar my son from such fine professions. You may well say that I am free; I insist that I am not, since you reduce me to making my son, at least in my opinion, a pedant, perhaps a *frightful little orator,* and most certainly a turbulent troublemaker.

It would be bearable if only the knowledge required for the baccalaureate related in some slight way to the needs and interests of our era, if only it was merely useless; but what is required is deplorably disastrous! Distorting the human mind is the problem that seems to have been set and that the bodies to which the monopoly of teaching has been allocated have settled on. This is what I will try to demonstrate.

Since the start of this debate, the university and the clergy have been throwing accusations at each other like so many balls. "You are perverting our youth with your philosophical rationalism," say the clergy. "You are dulling its wits with your religious dogmatism," replies the university.

Arbitrators then come forward and say: "Religion and philosophy are sisters. Let us merge free examination and authority. University and clergy, you have taken turns in having the monopoly. Share it and let us have an end to this."

We have heard the venerable bishop of Langres[5] rudely identify the university thus: "It is you who have given us the socialist generation of 1848."

And M. Crémieux hastened to respond to the chastisement in these words: "It is you who have raised the revolutionary generation of 1793."

If there is any truth in these allegations, what should we conclude from them? That the two forms of teaching have been disastrous not because of what separates them but because of what they have in common.

Yes, I am convinced of this. There is one common factor in these two forms of teaching, the abuse of classical studies, and it is in this that both have perverted the judgment and morality of the country. They differ in that one emphasizes the religious element while the other emphasizes the philosophical one, but these elements, far from having caused the harm they are

5. Pierre Louis Parisis.

reproached for, have lessened it. We are indebted to them for not being as barbaric as the barbarians unceasingly put up by Latinism for us to imitate.

Let me make a supposition that is a bit stretched, but that will help my thought to be understood.

I imagine, then, that somewhere in the Antipodes there is a nation that, because it hates and despises work, has based its entire means of existence on the successive pillage of all the neighboring tribes and on slavery. This nation has established a policy, a moral code, a religion, and public opinion in line with the cruel purpose that is sustaining and developing it. Since France has given the clergy the monopoly on education, the clergy finds nothing better to do than to send all French young people to visit this nation, to live its way of life, be inspired by its sentiments, share its enthusiasms, and breathe its ideas as their own air. The thing is that the clergy takes care to ensure that each student goes with a small volume titled *The Gospels*. The generations brought up in this way return to their home country and a revolution breaks out; I leave you to imagine the role they will play in it.

When it sees this, the state snatches the monopoly on teaching from the clergy and hands it over to the university. Faithful to its traditions, the university also sends its young people to the Antipodes to visit the nation that pillages others and possesses slaves, after supplying them, however, with a small volume titled *Philosophy*. Scarcely have five or six generations raised this way returned to their native soil than a second revolution breaks out. Trained in the same school as their predecessors, they show themselves their worthy emulators.

In this way, war breaks out between the monopolists. "It is your small book that did all the damage," says the clergy. "It is yours," replies the University.

Well no, sirs, your small books had nothing to do with all of this. What did the damage was the strange idea, thought out and carried out by both of you, of sending young French people whose future lay in work, peace, and freedom, to become imbued and permeated with and saturated in the sentiments and opinions of a nation of brigands and slaves.

My contention is this: The subversive doctrines that have been given the name of *socialism* or *communism* are the fruit of classical teaching, whether it is dispensed by the clergy or by the university. I add that the baccalaureate imposes classical teaching by force even on the so-called free schools that will, people say, arise as a result of the law. It is for this that I demand that university degrees be eliminated.

Much praise has been heaped on Latin as a means of developing intelligence; this is pure *conventionalism*. The Greeks, who did not learn Latin, did not lack intelligence, and we do not see that French women lack it any more than they lack common sense. It would be strange if the human spirit could gain strength only by deforming itself; and will people never understand that the highly problematic advantage that is alleged, if it exists, is very dearly bought with the redoubtable disadvantage of having the soul of France penetrated by the language of the Romans, their ideas, their sentiments, their opinions, and a caricature of their behavior?

Since the time when God pronounced this decree over men: "By the sweat of thy brow shalt thou eat bread," they have found existence to be so great and absorbing an affair that, depending on the means they use to achieve it, their behavior, habits, opinions, moral code, and social systems necessarily manifest wide-ranging differences.

A people that lives by hunting cannot resemble one that lives by fishing, nor can a pastoral nation resemble a nation of seafarers.

However, these differences are nothing in comparison with that which has to characterize two peoples, one of which lives from work and the other from theft.

For between huntsmen, fishermen, shepherds, farm laborers, traders, and manufacturers, there is this common factor, that they all seek to satisfy their needs through the action they carry out on things. What they wish to subject to their rule is nature.

But the men who base their means of existence on pillage exercise their action on other men; what they ardently aspire to dominate are their fellow men.

For men to exist, it is absolutely necessary for this action on nature, which we call work, to be carried out.

It may be that the fruits of this action benefit the nation that carries it out. It is also possible that they come across another people, either indirectly or through force, who rule over the people who do the work.

I cannot develop this line of thinking in detail here, but if you care to think about it, you will be convinced that between two conurbations of men situated in such opposing conditions, everything has to be different: behavior, habits, judgments, organizations, moral codes, and religions, and this is so far true that the very words intended to express the most basic relationships, such as those for family, property, freedom, virtue, society, government, republic, or people, cannot represent the same ideas in both cases.

A nation of warriors will soon understand that the family will weaken military devotion (we feel this ourselves since we forbid our soldiers to have families). However, the population must not die out. How do we solve the problem? As Plato did in theory and Lycurgus in practice, by *promiscuity*. Plato and Lycurgus, however, are names we are accustomed to pronounce only with reverence.

As for property, I challenge you to find an acceptable definition of this in the whole of antiquity. We, for our part, say: "Men are the owners of themselves and consequently of their faculties and, following this, of the products of their faculties." But could the Romans conceive of such a notion? As the owners of slaves, were they able to say: "Man belongs to himself"? As they despised work, were they able to say: "Man is the owner of the product of his faculties"? This would have been to base a whole society on collective suicide.

On what then did antiquity base property? On the law, a disastrous idea, the most disastrous ever introduced into the world, since it justifies the use and abuse of anything it pleases the law to declare *property,* even the fruits of theft and even the theft of men.

In these barbaric present times, freedom could not be better understood. What is freedom? It is the sum total of freedoms. To be free, under one's own responsibility, to think and act, to speak and write, to work and trade, to teach and learn, that alone is to be free. Can a disciplined nation with the prospect of an endless battle conceive freedom thus? No, the Romans prostituted the word to mean a certain audaciousness in the internecine struggles that the sharing of plunder triggered between them. The leaders wanted everything, and the people demanded their share. This gave rise to storms in the Forum, the retreats to the Aventine Mountain, the agrarian laws, the interventions by the tribunes, and the popularity of conspirators. This also gave rise to this maxim: *Malo periculosam libertatem,*[6] etc., which has passed into our language and which I inscribed in adornment on all my schoolbooks:

> O Freedom! How your storms
> Attract great hearts!

Fine example, sublime precepts, precious seed to be sown in the souls of French youth!

What should we say about Roman morals? And I am not referring here

---

6. *Malo periculosam libertatem* [*quam quietam servitutem*]: "I prefer the tumult of liberty [to the quiet of servitude]."

to relationships between father and son, husband and wife, shop owner and customer, master and servant, or man and God, relationships that slavery all on its own could not fail to transform into a tissue of turpitude; all I wish to concentrate on here is that which is called the estimable side of the republic, *patriotism*. What is this patriotism? The hatred of foreigners. To destroy all civilization, stifle all progress, put the entire world to fire and the sword, and chain women, children, and the elderly to the triumphal chariots: in that lay glory and virtue. It is to these atrocities that the marble of sculptors and the songs of poets were devoted. How many times have our young hearts beat with admiration and alas with emulation at this sight! This is how our teachers, venerable priests full of years and charity, prepared us for a Christian and civilized life; so great is the power of *conventionalism!*

The lesson has not been lost, and doubtless it is from Rome that we have this maxim that is right for theft and wrong for work: *One people loses what another gains,* a maxim that still governs the world.

To give us an idea of the Roman moral code, let us imagine an association of men in the center of Paris. The association hates work and is intent on procuring possessions for itself through guile and force, and is thus at war with society. There is no doubt that within this association a certain moral code and even a high degree of virtue will soon evolve. Courage, perseverance, dissimulation, prudence, discipline, constancy in misfortune, profound secrecy, cultivation of points of honor, and devotion to the community will doubtless be the virtues that necessity and general opinion would develop in these brigands. This was true of buccaneers and also true of the Romans. It will be said of the Romans that the grandeur of their enterprise and its immense success has shrouded their crimes in a sufficiently glorious veil to transform them into virtues. And it is for this very reason that this school is so pernicious. It is not abject vice but vice crowned with splendor that pleases the spirit.

Finally with regard to *society,* the ancient world has bequeathed to the new world two erroneous notions that undermine it and that will continue to undermine it for a long time.

The first: that *society is a state separate from nature and born of a contract.* This idea was not as erroneous in past times as it is currently. Rome and Sparta were indeed two associations of men with a common and determined goal, pillage, and they were not exactly societies, but rather armies.

The second, a corollary of the first: that *law creates rights* and that, consequently, the legislator and humanity have the same relationship with each other as the potter and clay. Minos, Lycurgus, Solon, and Numa constructed the systems of society in Crete, Sparta, Athens, and Rome. Plato was the constructor of imaginary republics that were to serve as models for future *teachers of peoples* and *fathers of nations*.

So, and note this well, these two ideas form the special character and distinctive stamp of *socialism* in the unfavorable sense of the word and as a common label for all social utopias.

Whoever, not knowing that the social body is a set of natural laws, like the human body, dreams of creating an artificial form of society, and sets out to manipulate the family, property, rights, and humanity to suit his will, is a socialist. He is not engaging in physiology but in statuary. He does not observe; he invents. He does not believe in God but in himself. He is not a scholar; he is a tyrant. He is not serving mankind; he is making use of it. He is not studying its nature; he is changing it in accordance with Rousseau's advice.[7] He is drawing inspiration from antiquity and following on from Lycurgus and Plato. And, to sum it up, he has certainly obtained his *baccalaureate*.

People will tell me that I am exaggerating, that it is not possible for our studious youth to draw such deplorable opinions and sentiments from glorious antiquity.

And what do you want them to draw there, other than what is there? Make an effort of memory and remind yourself of your turn of mind when you left school and entered the wide world. Did you not burn with a desire to imitate the ravagers of the land and the agitators in the Forum? For my part, when I see the society of today cast young people in the tens of thousands into the mold of the Brutuses and the Gracchi, only to launch them, incapable of any honest work (*opus servile*), into the crowd and onto the street, I am astonished that they withstand the test. For a classical education is not only reckless enough to plunge us into Roman life, it does so while accustoming us to becoming enthusiastic about it, to considering it as a fine ideal for humanity, a sublime type that is placed too high for modern souls but which we should strive to imitate without ever claiming to attain it.[8]

7. (Bastiat's note) "He who dares to undertake to teach a people must consider himself capable of changing human nature, in a manner of speaking . . . , of altering the physical and moral constitution of man, etc." [This passage comes from *Du contrat social,* bk. 2, chap. 7, "The Legislator."]

8. (Paillottet's note) See pp. 365 and 380 of this volume. (*OC,* vol. 4, "La Loi," and pp. 365 and 380.)

Is the objection raised that socialism has permeated the classes who do not aspire to the baccalaureate?

I will reply, with M. Thiers:[9]

> Secondary education teaches ancient languages to the children of the affluent classes. . . . It is not just the words that are being taught to children when they are taught Greek and Latin, it is noble and sublime things (plunder, war, and slavery), it is the history of humanity through images that are simple, great, and *indelible*. . . . Secondary education shapes what are known as the enlightened classes of a nation. But, while the enlightened classes are not the nation in its entirety, they characterize it. Their vices, qualities, and good and evil tendencies are very soon those of the entire nation; they create the people themselves through the contagion of their ideas and sentiments.[10]

(Very good.)

Nothing is more true and nothing explains better the disastrous and artificial deviations of our revolutions.

"Antiquity," adds M. Thiers, "let us dare to say to a century proud of itself, *is the most beautiful thing in the world*. Let us leave children in antiquity, sirs, as in a *calm, peaceful, and healthy* refuge that is destined to keep them fresh and pure."

The calm of Rome! The peace of Rome! The purity of Rome! Oh! If the lengthy experience and remarkable good sense of M. Thiers has not been able to preserve him from such a strange fascination, how do you expect our ardent youth to stand up to it?[11]

9. In 1844 Thiers battled against a bill instituting a degree of freedom in secondary education. He was in favor of a system where "the youth would be thrown into a mold and cast according to the effigy of the state." According to him, any free educational establishment should be under the tight control of the university.

10. (Bastiat's note) Report by M. Thiers on the law on secondary education, 1844.

11. (Paillottet's note) Distance contributes not a little to giving antique figures an aura of greatness. If Roman citizens are mentioned to us, we do not normally conjure up a vision of a brigand intent on acquiring plunder and slaves at the expense of peaceful peoples. We do not visualize him going about half naked, hideously dirty in muddy streets. We do not come across him whipping a slave who shows a bit of initiative and pride until the brigand draws blood or kills him. We prefer to conjure up a fine head set on a bust brimming with force and majesty and draped like an ancient statue. We prefer to contemplate this person as he meditates on the high destiny of his fatherland. We seem to see his family around the hearth honoring the presence of the gods, with his wife preparing a simple meal for the warrior and casting a confident and admiring look on the

In the last few days, the National Assembly has witnessed a comic dialogue, certainly worthy of Molière's brush.

M. Thiers, addressing M. Barthélemy Saint-Hilaire from the rostrum without a smile: "You are wrong, not from the artistic but *from a moral point of view,* to prefer Greek to Latin, in particular for the French nation, which is a Latin nation."

M. Barthélemy Saint-Hilaire, also without a smile: "What about Plato!"

M. Thiers, still without a smile: "It has been a good thing and is a good thing to nurture Greek and Latin studies. I prefer Latin *for a moral reason.* But people have also wanted these poor young people to learn German, English, the exact sciences, physical sciences, history, etc."

*To know what is the case,* that is evil. To become imbued with Roman behavior, that is morality!

M. Thiers is neither the first nor the only one to have succumbed to this illusion, I almost said to his mystification. May I be allowed to point out in a few words the deep-rooted impression (and what an impression!) that a classical education has made on literature, the moral code, and the politics of our country?

It is a picture that I have neither the leisure nor the aspiration to complete, for which writer would not have to be summoned to appear? Let us be content with a sketch.

I will not go back as far as Montaigne. Everybody knows that he was as Spartan in his vague intentions as he was far from this in his tastes.

As for Corneille, of whom I am a sincere admirer, I think he has rendered a sad service to the minds of the century by shrouding in fine verses and giving an appearance of sublime grandeur to sentiments that are forced, extravagant, fierce, and antisocial, such as the following:

> But to wish to immolate the thing you love in public,
> To devote oneself to combating another part of oneself
>
> .    .    .    .    .    .
>
> Such virtue belongs only to us . . .
> Rome has chosen my arm, I ask no questions,

---

brow of her husband and the children and paying attention to the words of an old man who whiles the hours away reciting the exploits and virtues of their father. . . .

Oh! How many illusions would be dissipated if we could evoke the past, wander in the streets of Rome, and see at close hand the men whom we admire from afar in such good faith! (*Unpublished draft by the author, shortly before 1830.*)

> With a joy that is as full and sincere
> As when I married the sister, I will fight the brother.[12]

And I admit that I feel disposed to share Curiace's sentiment by applying it not to a particular fact but to the entire history of Rome, when he says:

> I thank the gods that I am not Roman
> To retain still some remnant of humanity.

*Fénelon:* These days *communism* horrifies us because it frightens us, but did not a long-standing attention to the ancients make a communist of Fénelon, a man whom modern Europe rightly regards as the finest example of moral perfection? Read his *Telemachus,* the book that people are quick to put into the hands of children. In it you will see Fénelon adopting the traits of wisdom itself to teach legislators. And along what lines does he organize his model form of society? On the one hand, the legislator thinks, invents, and acts; on the other, society, impassive and inert, allows itself to be acted upon. The moral motivation, the principle of action, is thus wrested from all men to be vested in a single man. Fénelon, the precursor of the boldest of our modern organizers, decides on the food, accommodation, clothing, games, and occupations of all the inhabitants of Salente. He tells them what they will be allowed to eat and drink, on what plan their houses should be built, how many rooms they should have, and how they will be furnished.

He says . . . but I will allow him to use his own words:

> Mentor set up magistrates to whom merchants accounted for their assets, profits, expenditure, and enterprises. . . . Besides, there was total freedom of trade . . . He forbade all the goods from foreign countries that might introduce opulence and ease. . . . He cut off a remarkable number of merchants who sold fashioned fabrics. . . . He regulated the clothes, food, furniture, size, and decoration of houses for all the different statuses.
>
> Arrange social condition by birth, he told the king . . . those of first rank after you will be clad in white, . . . those in the second rank in blue, . . . the third, in green, . . . the fourth in dawn yellow, . . . the fifth in pale red or pink, . . . the sixth in linen gray . . . and the seventh, who will be the lowest of the people in a color that is a mixture of yellow and white. These will be the clothes of the seven different conditions of free men. All

---

12. The verses quoted by Bastiat are from Corneille's play *Horace* (1640). See also the entry for "Corneille, Pierre," in the Glossary of Persons.

the slaves will be clad in brownish gray. One[13] will never allow any change, either of the nature of the fabric or of the lines of the clothes.

He regulated the food eaten by citizens and slaves in the same way.

He then eliminated all soft and effeminate music.

He provided examples of simple, graceful architecture. He wanted each house of a certain standing to have a drawing room and peristyle with small rooms for all the *people who were free.*

Where other things were concerned, Mentor's moderation and frugality did not stop him from authorizing all the large buildings intended for horse and chariot racing, or for *wrestling and boxing.*

Mentor considered that painting and sculpture were arts that could not be abandoned, but he did not wish many men in Salente to devote themselves to them.

Do we not recognize in this an imagination inflamed by the reading of Plato and the example of Lycurgus that is amusing itself by carrying out experiments on men as though they were base matter?

And let no one justify such wild fancies by saying that they are the fruit of excessive benevolence. This is just as true of all constructors and undoers of society.

*Rollin:* There is another man, almost equal to Fénelon in intellect and feeling and more involved than Fénelon in education, and that is Rollin. Well then! To what abject intellectual and moral depths did a lengthy study of the classics reduce this good man, Rollin! We cannot read his books without being overcome by sadness and pity. We do not know whether he is a Christian or a pagan, so impartial is he between God and the gods. The miracles of the Bible and the legends of heroic times evoke the same credulity in him. On his placid face we see the shadows of warlike passion constantly flicker; all he can speak of are javelins, swords, and catapults. For him, as for Bossuet, one of the most interesting social problems is knowing whether the Macedonian phalanx was better than the Roman legion. He praises the Romans for pursuing only sciences that had domination as their objective: eloquence, politics, and war. In his eyes, all other forms of knowledge are sources of corruption and are good only for turning men toward peace. For this reason he banishes them carefully from his colleges, to the applause of

13. (Bastiat's note) The shapers of societies are sometimes modest enough not to say, "I will do this," "I will dispose of this." They readily use this impersonal but equivalent form: "One will do this," "One will not allow this."

M. Thiers. His only objects of veneration are Mars and Bellona, with just a passing thought for Christ. He is a sad plaything of the *conventionalism* that a classical education has caused to be predominant; he is so predisposed to admire the Romans that, where they are concerned, simply refraining from the greatest abominations is considered by him to be on a par with the greatest virtues. Alexander for having regretted that he assassinated his best friend and Scipio for not having enticed a wife from her husband are proof in his eyes of inimitable heroism. In short, while he has made a *walking contradiction* of each of us, he is certainly the perfect example of this.

It is clear that Rollin was enthusiastically in favor of communism and Spartan institutions. We should do him justice, however; his admiration is not total. He takes this legislator to task, with appropriate circumspection, for having stamped his work with four minor blemishes:

1. Idleness
2. Promiscuity
3. Infanticide
4. The mass murder of slaves

These four reservations once entered, this gentleman returns to the path of classical conventionalism and sees in Lycurgus not a man but a god, and finds his policy perfect.

The intervention of the legislator in everything appears to Rollin to be so essential that in all seriousness he congratulates the Greeks for the fact that a man named *Pelasge* came to teach them to eat acorns. Before that, he says, they grazed on grass like animals.

Elsewhere, he says:

"God was obliged to give the Romans a world empire as a reward for their great virtues, which only appear to be real. He would not have been just if He had awarded a lesser prize to these virtues, which are not actually real."

Do we not clearly see conventionalism and Christianity in conflict in Rollin, a poor soul in torment? The spirit of this utterance is the spirit of all the works of the founder of teaching in France. Contradicting oneself, making God contradict himself, and teaching us to contradict ourselves is Rollin in a nutshell, and the baccalaureate in a nutshell.

If promiscuity and infanticide awaken Rollin's scruples with regard to Lycurgus's institutions, he is enthusiastic about everything else and even finds the means of justifying theft. This is how he does it. The stroke employed is curious and close enough to my subject to be worth mentioning.

Rollin begins by stating in principle that the law creates property—a disastrous principle common to all constructors of society, and one that we will soon be finding in the mouths of Rousseau, Mably, Mirabeau, Robespierre, and Babeuf. Well, since the law is the justification for property, can it not also be the justification for theft? What can be opposed to this reasoning?

"Theft was allowed in Sparta," says Rollin, while "it was severely punished by the Scythians. The reason for this difference is clear; it is because the law, *which alone decides on the ownership and use of assets,* in the case of the Scythians, had granted an individual no rights over the assets of another, whereas the law, in the case of the Spartans, did the exact opposite."

Next, this good fellow, Rollin, in the heat of his plea in favor of theft and Lycurgus, invokes the most incontestable of authorities, that of God:

"Nothing is more commonplace," he says, "than similar rights awarded over the assets of others; this is how God not only gave the poor the authority to pick grapes in the vineyards and glean in the fields and carry off entire sheaves, but He also gave any passersby without distinction the freedom to enter the vineyards of others as often as they chose and to eat as many grapes as they wanted *in spite of the vineyard owner.* God Himself gave the first reason for this. It is that the land of Israel was His and that the Israelites enjoyed the use of it only on this burdensome condition."

People will doubtless say that this was Rollin's personal doctrine. That is exactly what I am saying. I am trying to show to what state of moral infirmity the habitual study of the frightful form of society in classical times can reduce the finest and most honest minds.

*Montesquieu:* It has been said of Montesquieu that he rediscovered the just credentials of the human race. He is one of the great writers whose every sentence has the force of authority. God forbid that I should wish to diminish his fame! But what should we not think of a classical education if it has succeeded in misleading this noble intelligence to the extent of causing him to admire the most barbarous of institutions in antiquity?

> The ancient Greeks, imbued with the need for the peoples who lived under a popular government to be raised *in virtue,* established singular institutions to inspire it. The laws of Crete were the origin for those of Sparta and those of Plato corrected them.
>
> I would ask people to give some attention to the extent of the genius needed by these legislators to see that, by upsetting all the accepted customs, by confusing all the virtues, they were revealing *their wisdom* to the universe. Lycurgus, combining robbery with the spirit of justice, the most

severe slavery with the heights of freedom, the most atrocious sentiments with the greatest moderation, gave stability to his city. He appeared to remove all its resources from it, its arts, trade, money, and city walls. People had ambition there with no hope of being better off; *they had natural sentiments and they were neither child, husband, nor father there.* Even modesty was removed from chastity. It is along these paths that Sparta was led to *greatness and glory,* but with such infallibility in its institutions that nothing was obtained from it by winning battles if it was not possible to remove its policies. (*Spirit of Laws,* book 4, chapter 8)[14]

*Those who will wish* to found similar institutions will establish the common ownership of assets as in Plato's republic, the respect that he demanded for the gods, the separation from foreigners in order to preserve behavior, and with the city carrying out trade and not the citizens. They will supply our arts without our luxury and our needs without our desires. . . .

Montesquieu explains in these words the great influence that the ancients attributed to music:

I believe that I can explain this: You have to get it into your head that in Greek towns, especially those *whose principal object* was war, all work and all the occupations that might lead to earning money were regarded as *unworthy of a free man.* "Most arts," said Xenophon, "corrupt the body of those that exercise them. They oblige people to sit in the shade or close to the fire; such people have no time either for their friends or for the republic." It was only in the *corruption* of some democracies that craftsmen managed to become citizens. This is what Aristotle teaches us, and he claims that a good republic will never give them the right of citizenship.

Agriculture was still a *servile activity,* and it was normally a conquered people that carried it out: the Helots in Sparta, the Periecians in Crete, the Penestes in Thessalonia, and other enslaved peoples in other republics.

In sum, all commercial exchange was infamous in the eyes of the Greeks. *It would have implied that a citizen had rendered services to a*

---

14. Montesquieu, *L'Ésprit des lois.* The edition of *L'Ésprit des lois* to which Bastiat might have had access was *Œuvres de Montesquieu, avec éloges, analyses, commentaires, remarques, notes, réfutations, imitations.* The editor was Victor Destutt de Tracy, the son of Antoine Destutt de Tracy, who had written an extensive commentary on *L'Ésprit des lois* for Thomas Jefferson. Jefferson had it published in 1811: *A Commentary and Review of Montesquieu's* Spirit of Laws.

*slave,* a tenant, or a foreigner, and the very idea *shocked the spirit of free-dom in Greece.* Thus Plato, in his *Laws,* wanted a citizen who engaged in commercial exchange to be punished.

The situation in the Greek republics was therefore very embarrassing: it was thought improper for citizens to work in trade, agriculture, or the arts, yet also wrong for them to be idle. An acceptable occupation was identified in the exercises relating to gymnastics and *to war.* The polity gave them no other choices. The Greeks, therefore, have to be regarded as a society of athletes and warriors. However, these activities, so suited to producing people that were hard and barbarous, needed to be tempered by others that made their behavior gentler. Music, which reaches the spirit through the organs of the body, was very suited to this. (*Spirit of Laws,* book 5)[15]

This is the notion that a classical education gives us of freedom. This is now how it teaches us to understand equality and thrift:

Although in a democracy genuine equality is the soul of the state, this is, however, so hard to establish that punctilious conformity in this regard is not always suitable. All that is necessary is for a tax to be established that reduces or sets the differences at a given level, following which it is up to specific laws to equalize, so to speak, inequalities, through the charges it imposes on the rich and the relief it grants to the poor. (*Spirit of Laws,* book 5, chapter 6)[16]

In a good democracy, it is not enough for tracts of land to be equal; they have to be small as in Roman times. . . .

Since equality in wealth encourages thrift, thrift maintains equality in wealth. Although these things are different, they are such that one cannot exist without the other. (*Spirit of Laws,* chapter 6)[17]

The Samnites had a custom which, in a small republic, and especially in a situation like theirs, was bound to produce *admirable effects.* All the young men were gathered together and judged. The one declared the best of all took any girl he wanted as his wife, the runner-up then made his choice, and so on down the line. . . . It would be difficult to imagine a reward that was nobler or greater, less of a burden to a small state, and more capable of affecting either sex.

15. Ibid.
16. Ibid.
17. Ibid.

The Samnites were descendants of the Spartans, and Plato, whose institutions are simply the perfection of the laws of Lycurgus, produced a law that was more or less similar. (*Spirit of Laws,* book 7, chapter 16)[18]

*Rousseau:* No man has had such influence on the French Revolution as Rousseau. "His work," says Louis Blanc, "was on the table of the Committee of Public Safety." "These paradoxes," he says elsewhere, "which his century took to be literary daring, were shortly to resound in the nation's assemblies in the form of dogmatic truths that *cut like a sword.*" And in order for the moral bond linking Rousseau to antiquity not to be overlooked, the same panegyrist adds, "His style recalled the touching and fiery language of a *son of Cornelia.*"

Besides, who does not know that Rousseau was the most fervent admirer of the ideas and behavior conventionally attributed to the Romans and Spartans? He himself said that reading Plutarch made him what he was.

His first article was directed against human intelligence. In the very first pages he exclaimed:

> Can I forget that it was in the bosom of Greece that this city, as famous for its *happy ignorance* as for the *wisdom* of its laws, was seen to rise, this republic of *demigods rather than men,* so superior did their virtues seem to be over those of humanity? Oh Sparta! The eternal opprobrium of a vain doctrine! While the vices encouraged by the fine arts were introduced into Athens, while a tyrant so carefully assembled the works of the prince of poets, you cast out from your walls the arts and artists, the sciences and scholars! (*Discourse on the Re-establishment of the Sciences and Arts*)[19]

In his second work, *Discourse on the Inequality of Conditions,* he railed with even greater vehemence against all the bases of society and civilization. This is why he believed himself to be the mouthpiece of ancient wisdom:

> I will picture myself in the Lyceum in Athens, repeating *my masters'* lessons, with Plato and Xenocrates as my judges and the human race as my audience.[20]

The predominant idea in this famous discourse may be summarized thus: The most terrible fate awaits those who, unfortunate enough to be born after

18. Ibid.

19. Rousseau, "Discours: Si le rétablissement des sciences et des arts a contribué a épurer les mœurs," in *Du Contrat social et autres œuvres politiques,* pp. 8–9.

20. Rousseau, "Quelle est l'origine de l'inégalité parmi les hommes," in *Du contrat social et autres œuvres politiques,* p. 40.

us, add their knowledge to ours. The development of our faculties has already made us very unhappy. Our fathers were less unhappy, as they were more ignorant. Rome was close to perfection; Sparta had achieved it, as far as perfection is compatible with a social state. But the real good fortune for man is to live in the woods, alone, naked, with no bonds, no affections, no language, no religion, no ideas, no family, and in short in a state in which he is so close to an animal that it is highly unlikely that he stands upright and that his hands are not feet.

Unfortunately, this golden age has not lasted. Men have gone through an intermediate phase, which nevertheless has not been without its charms:

> For as long as they were content with their rustic cabins, for as long as they were content with sewing their clothes of skins with bone needles, adorning themselves with feathers and shells, painting their bodies in a variety of colors ... for as long as they occupied themselves only with work that *a single person* could do, they lived free, healthy, good, and happy.[21]

Alas, they were not able to stop at this first degree of culture:

> From the moment that a man *needed help from another* [here is society making its disastrous appearance]; as soon as it was seen to be useful for one person to have enough provisions for two, equality disappeared, property was introduced, and work became necessary. . . .
> Metallurgy and agriculture were the two arts whose invention brought about this great revolution. For the poet, it is gold and silver, for the philosopher, it is *iron* and *wheat* that civilized men and *caused the perdition of the human race.*[22]

It was therefore necessary to escape from the *state of nature* to enter into *society*. This gave rise to the third of Rousseau's works, the *Social Contract*.

It is not part of my subject to analyze this work here. I will limit myself to pointing out that Greek and Roman ideas are echoed on each page.

Since society is a pact, each person has the right to make his own stipulations.

> It is up to those who associate, and to them alone, to regulate the conditions of society.[23]

21. Ibid., pp. 72–73.
22. Ibid., p. 73.
23. Rousseau, "Du contrat social," in *Du contrat social et autres œuvres politiques,* p. 259.

But that is not easy.

How will they regulate them? Will it be by common accord, by sudden inspiration? ... How will a blind throng, who often do not know what they want, carry out on their own such a grand and difficult enterprise as a system of legislation? ... This is why a legislator is needed.[24]

Thus, universal suffrage is conjured away in practice as soon as it is acknowledged in theory.

For how will this legislator act, when *in all respects, he has to be an extraordinary man who, since he is daring to undertake the establishment of a people, has to consider himself capable of changing human nature and of modifying man's physical and moral constitution, who must,* in short, *invent the machine* of which men are the material.

Rousseau clearly proves here that the legislator cannot count either on force or persuasion. How does he solve this problem? By deception.

This is what forced the fathers of nations of all eras to have recourse to the intervention of heaven and to honor the gods for their own wisdom ... This sublime reason, which rises above common souls, is the one whose decisions are placed by the legislator in the mouths of the immortals in order for divine authority to sweep along those whom human prudence might not move. But it is not given to everyone to make the gods speak.[25] (*The gods! The immortals!* A classical reminiscence)

Like Plato and Lycurgus, his masters, like the Spartans and Romans, his heroes, Rousseau gave the words *work* and *freedom* a meaning that expressed two incompatible ideas. In the social state a choice had to be made, either to renounce freedom or to die of hunger. There was, however, a solution to the problem and that was slavery.

As soon as a people provides itself with representatives, it is no longer free, it no longer exists!
    In Greece, all the people had to do, they did it themselves. They were constantly assembled on the square; *slaves did their work; their great preoccupation was freedom.* Once they no longer had the same advantages, how were they to retain the same rights? You value your material advantage more than your freedom and you fear slavery far less than destitution.

24. Ibid., pp. 259–60.
25. Ibid., pp. 262–63.

What! Freedom is maintained only with the support of servitude? Perhaps. The two extremes meet. Everything outside nature has its disadvantages, and civil society more than the rest. There are situations so unfortunate that you can save your freedom only at the expense of that of others, and in which citizens can be in the fullest sense free only if slaves are in the fullest sense enslaved. This was the situation in Sparta. For you, a modern people, you do not have slaves, you are yourselves slaves, etc.

This is genuine classical conventionalism. The ancients were propelled into procuring slaves for themselves by their brute instincts. But since it is a rank preconception, a college tradition, to find everything they did beautiful, subtle reasoning on the quintessence of freedom is attributed to them.

The contrast that Rousseau established between the state of nature and the social state is as disastrous to private as to public morals. According to this mode of thinking, society is the result of a pact that gives rise to the law which, in turn, creates justice and morality out of nothing. In the state of nature there is neither morality nor justice. Fathers have no duty to their sons nor sons to their fathers, husbands to their wives nor wives to their husbands.

It follows from this that if the social pact, once concluded, is dissolved, everything collapses with it: society, law, morality, justice, and duty. "Each person," says Rousseau, "is entitled to his original rights and regains his natural freedom while losing the conventional freedom for which he renounced it."[26]

However, it should be noted that very little is needed to dissolve the social pact. This happens every time an individual breaks his undertakings or refuses the jurisdiction of a particular law. If a condemned man escapes when society tells him, "It is expedient for you to die," if a citizen refuses to pay taxes, if an accountant puts his hand into the public till, *at that very instant* the social contract is broken, all moral duty ceases, justice no longer exists, and fathers, mothers, children, and spouses owe nothing to each other. Each person has an unlimited right to anything that takes his fancy; in short, the entire population reverts to a state of nature.

I leave you to imagine the ravages that doctrines like this would have in revolutionary times.

They are no less disastrous for private morals. What young man entering the world with enthusiasm and ambition does not say to himself, "The im-

26. Rousseau, "Du contrat social," in *Du contrat social et autres œuvres politiques,* p. 243.

pulses of my heart are the voice of nature, which is never wrong. The institutions that bar my route come from men and are only arbitrary conventions to which I have not contributed. By crushing these institutions underfoot, I will have the twin pleasure of satisfying my leanings and thinking myself a hero."

Do I have to remind you here of this sad and painful page of the *Confessions*?[27]

> My third child was therefore placed in the orphanage along with the two others. This also happened for the next two, since I have had five in all. This arrangement seemed to me to be so good that if I did not boast about it, it was solely out of deference to their mother . . . By entrusting my children to state education . . . I considered myself to be a member of Plato's republic!

*Mably:* No quotations are needed to demonstrate the Greek and Roman mania of Abbé Mably. A narrow-minded man, with a soul more straight-laced and a less-sensitive heart than Rousseau, he also had ideas that allowed for a reduced range of temperaments and of intellectual content. This made him overtly platonic, that is to say, communistic. Convinced, like all the classicists, that humanity is the raw material for manufacturers of institutions, he preferred to be one of the manufacturers rather than part of the raw material. Consequently he set himself up to be a legislator. As such, he was first called upon to establish Poland and he does not appear to have succeeded in this. Next, he offered Anglo-Americans the black broth of the Spartans, which he could not persuade them to adopt. Outraged by this blindness, he foretold the fall of the Union and gave it no more than five years of existence.

May I be allowed to interject a reservation here? By quoting the absurd and subversive doctrines of such men as Fénelon, Rollin, Montesquieu, and Rousseau, I certainly do not wish to state that we do not owe pages full of reason and morality to these great writers. However, what is mistaken in their books arises from classical conventionalism and what is true arises from another source. It is precisely my thesis that teaching which is exclusively based on Greek and Latin literature makes us all *living contradictions*. It draws us violently back to a past that it glorifies down to its very horrors,

---

27. *The Confessions of Jean-Jacques Rousseau* was first published in 1782, after his death in 1778. An edition Bastiat might have used was *Les Confessions de J.-J. Rousseau. Avec les notes de Musset-Pathay et de Petitain.*

while Christianity, the spirit of the century, and a fund of good sense that never loses its rights show us an ideal for the future.

I will spare you Morelly, Brissot, and Raynal, who justify—what am I saying?—who praise to the skies war, slavery, clerical imposture, the community of possessions, and idleness. Who could fail to see the impure source of such doctrines? This source, I really must name it again, is the classical education that is imposed on us all by the baccalaureate.

It is not only into literary works that the *calm, peaceful, and pure* ancient world has poured its poison, but also into those of legal experts. I defy anyone to find in any of our lawyers anything that approaches a reasonable notion of the right to property. And what can legislation from which such a notion is absent be like? Recently I happened to open the *Treatise on the Law of Nations* by Vattel.[28] I saw that the author had devoted a chapter to examining the following question: *Is it permissible to carry off women?* It is clear that the legend of the Romans and Sabines has bequeathed to us this precious morsel. After having weighed the *pros* and *cons* with the utmost seriousness, the author opted for the affirmative. He owed this to the glory of Rome. Were the Romans ever wrong? A form of *conventionalism* forbids us to think this; they are Romans and that is enough. Burning, pillaging, or kidnapping, anything that comes from them is *calm, peaceful, and pure*.

Will it be claimed that these are only personal opinions? Our society would be very fortunate if the uniform action of a classical education reinforced by the approbation of Montaigne, Corneille, Fénelon, Rollin, Montesquieu, Rousseau, Raynal, and Mably did not contribute to shaping the general opinion. This is what we will see.

In the meantime, we have proof that the communist idea took hold not only of a few individuals but also of certain public bodies, wholesale, including the most learned and influential. When the Jesuits wanted to organize a social order in Paraguay,[29] what plans did their previous studies suggest to them? Those of Minos, Plato, and Lycurgus. They established communism, which in turn did not fail to produce its sorry consequences. The Indians were reduced to several degrees below the state of savages. In spite of this, such was the inveterate predisposition of the Europeans in favor of communist institutions, constantly presented as being examples of perfection, that

28. Bastiat is referring to Vattel's *Le droit des gens, ou principes de la loi naturelle* (1758).

29. See "The Law," p. 128, note 10, in this volume.

the happiness and virtue of these nameless beings (for they were no longer men) who were vegetating under the wing of the Jesuits were praised far and wide.

Did Rousseau, Mably, Montesquieu, and Raynal, these great extollers of ideological crusades, check the facts? Not in the slightest. Could Greek and Latin literature be mistaken? Could anyone go wrong with Plato as a guide? Therefore, the Indians in Paraguay were happy or ought to have been, under pain of being unhappy against all the rules. Azara, Bougainville, and other travelers set off under the influence of these preconceived ideas to admire these marvels. First of all, in spite of the sorry reality being glaringly obvious, they could not believe it. They nevertheless had to accept the evidence and finally recorded, to their great regret, that communism, an attractive illusion, is an appalling reality.

The logic is rock solid. It is perfectly clear that the authors I have just quoted did not dare to take their doctrine to its limit. Morelly and Brissot took it upon themselves to repair their inconsistency. As true followers of Plato, they openly preached the community of possessions and women and this, let us note, by constantly quoting the examples and precepts of this fine ancient world that everyone is supposed to admire.

Such was the state to which education as imparted by the clergy had reduced public opinion in France with regard to family, property, freedom, and society when the Revolution broke out. The causes of the Revolution probably had no connection with a classical education, but can we doubt that this form of education contributed a host of mistaken ideas, sadistic feelings, subversive utopias, and deadly experimentation? Read the speeches made in the Legislative Assembly and the Convention. They are in the language of Rousseau and Mably. They are just tirades in favor of, and invocations and exclamatory addresses to, Fabricius,[30] Cato, the two Brutuses, the Gracchi, and Catiline. Is an atrocity going to be committed? There is always the example of a Roman to glorify it. What education has instilled in the mind is translated into act. Sparta and Rome are agreed on as models and so they must be imitated or parodied. One person wants to establish the Olympic Games, another the agrarian laws, and a third black broth in the streets.

I cannot hope to make a comprehensive commentary here on a question worthy of an accomplished pen devoting something more to it than a pam-

---

30. Gaius Fabricius Luscinus.

phlet: "On the influence of Greek and Latin literature on the spirit of our revolutions." I have to limit myself to a few outlines.

Two great figures dominate the French Revolution and appear to personify it, Mirabeau and Robespierre. What was their doctrine on property?

We have seen that peoples who, in antiquity, had based their means of existence on depredation and slavery were unable to give property its proper principle. They were obliged to consider it a conventional fact and based it on the law, which enabled them to include slavery and theft in it, as Rollin so naively explains.

Rousseau had also said, "Property is a human convention and institution, whereas freedom is a gift of nature."

Mirabeau professed the same doctrine: "Property," he said, "is a *social creation*. Laws do not just protect or maintain property; *they give rise to it,* determine it, and give it the rank and scope that it occupies in the rights of citizens."[31]

And when Mirabeau expressed himself thus, it was not to establish a theory. His real aim was to commit the legislator to limiting the exercise of a right that was within his discretion, since he had created it.

Robespierre echoed Rousseau's definitions.

In defining freedom, this primary need of man, the most sacred of the rights he *holds from nature,* we have rightly said that its limit is the right of others. Why have you not applied this principle to property, *which is a social institution,* as though the laws of nature were less inviolable than the *conventions* of men?[32]

Following this preamble, Robespierre moves on to the definition.

Property is the right held by each citizen to enjoy and dispose of possessions that are guaranteed to him *by the law.*[33]

Here then is the clear opposition between freedom and property. They are two rights whose origin is different. One comes *from nature;* the other is a *social institution.* The first is *natural,* the second *conventional.*

---

31. An edition of Mirabeau's work that Bastiat might well have used would be the eight-volume *Œuvres de Mirabeau* (1834–35).

32. This quotation is from "Discours de Robespierre sur la propriété." See Robespierre, *Œuvres de Maximilien Robespierre,* vol. 3, pp. 352–53.

33. Ibid., p. 353.

But who makes the law? The legislator. He can therefore give the exercise of the right to property the conditions that suit him, since he confers it.

Robespierre also hastens to deduce the *rights of labor,* the *right to assistance,* and *progressive taxes* from his definition.

> Society is obliged to provide for the subsistence of all of its members, either by procuring work for them or by assuring the means of existence for those who cannot work.
>
> The assistance required for indigence is a debt of the rich to the poor. *It is up to the law* to determine the manner in which this debt must be settled.
>
> Citizens whose income does not exceed what is necessary for their subsistence are exempted from contributing to public expenditure. The others have to support them progressively, in accordance with the extent of their wealth.[34]

Robespierre, said M. Sudre, thus adopted all the measures that, in the minds of their inventors as in reality, constitute the transition from property to communism. By applying Plato's *Treatise on Laws,* he was unconsciously moving toward the achievement of the social state as described in Plato's book called the *Republic.*

(We know that Plato wrote two books, one—the *Republic*—to point out ideal perfection, the community of possessions and women, and the other—the *Treatise on Laws*—to teach the means of transition.)

Robespierre may be considered, besides, as an admirer of the *calm, peaceful, and pure* ancient world. His speech, even on property, abounds in such declamations as "Aristide would not have envied the treasures of Crassus!"[35] "Fabricius's thatched cottage is no whit less enviable than Crassus's palace!" etc.[36]

In principle, once Mirabeau and Robespierre decided to give the legislator the power to determine the extent of the right of property, it mattered little where they decided it was appropriate to draw the line. It might have suited them to go no further than the right to work, the right to assistance, and progressive taxes. However, others, more consistent, did not stop there. If the law that creates property and disposes of it can move one step to-

34. Ibid., p. 354.
35. Marcus Licinius Crassus.
36. From "Discours de Robespierre sur la propriété." See Robespierre, *Œuvres de Maximilien Robespierre,* vol. 3, pp. 351–52.

ward equality, why can it not move two? Why would it not achieve absolute equality?

For this reason, Robespierre was surpassed by Saint-Just, as had to happen, and Saint-Just by Babeuf, as had to happen too. This path has just one logical terminus. It was highlighted by the divine Plato.

Saint-Just, . . . but I am becoming mired in the question of property and forgetting that I have undertaken to show how a classical education has perverted all moral notions. Assuming that the reader will believe me when I say that Saint-Just surpassed Robespierre along the path to communism, I will return to my subject.

First of all, you have to know that Saint-Just's errors were due to a study of the classics. Like all men of his time and ours, he was imbued with classicism. He thought he was a Brutus. Kept far from Paris by his party, he wrote:

Oh god! Must Brutus languish, forgotten, far from Rome? My decision has been made, however, and if Brutus does not kill the others, he will kill himself.[37]

Kill! It appears that this is the destiny of man here below.

All Greek and Latin scholars agree that the principle of a republic is *virtue* and God alone knows what they mean by this word! This is why Saint-Just wrote:

A republican government has virtue as its principle, if not terror.[38]

There is another dominant opinion in the ancient world: that work is something squalid. Saint-Just condemned it in these words:

37. This passage probably comes from a speech that Saint-Just gave in the National Convention. His collected works were published in Paris in 1834: *Œuvres de Saint-Just, représentant du peuple* à *la Convention Nationale*.

38. In 1831 a book titled *Fragments sur les institutions républicaines, ouvrage posthume de Saint-Just* was published. The book contained "fragments" on republican institutions by the Jacobin politician Louis Antoine de Saint-Just. The title page had a quotation from Montesquieu's *L'Ésprit des lois,* bk. 3, chap. 3: "The politic Greeks, who lived under a popular government, knew no other support than virtue: the modern inhabitants of that country are entirely taken up with manufacture, commerce, finances, opulence, and luxury." Bastiat quotes from Fragment Three, "Un gouvernement républicain a la vertu pour principe; sinon, la terreur. Que veulent ceux qui ne veulent, ni vertu, ni terreur?" It is interesting to note that this book was copublished by the Guillaumin publishing house, which in the 1840s was to specialize in publishing the works of the French political economists, including books and pamphlets by Bastiat.

Having a job is not the attribute of a proper citizen. The hand of man is made only for the land and for arms.

And it was so that no one would be able to abase himself by carrying out a trade that Saint-Just wished to distribute land to everyone.

We have seen that, according to the views of the ancients, the legislator is to humanity what the potter is to clay. Unfortunately when this idea dominates, everyone wants to be the potter and no one wants to be clay. We can well imagine that Saint-Just saw himself in the leading role:

> The day I am convinced that it is impossible *to give* the French manners that are gentle, sensitive, and inexorable toward tyranny and injustice, I will stab myself.
>
> If there were manners, all would be well. Institutions are needed to purify them. To reform manners, we have to begin by meeting the requirements of need and personal interest. Some land has to be given to everyone.[39]
>
> The children are clothed in cotton all the year round. They sleep on rush mats for eight hours. They are fed in the community and live only on roots, fruit, vegetables, bread, and water. They are allowed to eat meat only after the age of sixteen.
>
> Men aged twenty-five will be obliged to declare each year in the temple the names of their friends. He who abandons his friend without good reason will be banished![40]

In this way, Saint-Just, echoing Lycurgus, Plato, Fénelon, and Rousseau, attributes to himself more rights and powers over the manners, feelings, wealth, and children of the French than all the French have as a group. How small humanity is compared to him! Or rather it lives only in him. His brain is the brain and his heart the heart of the human race.

This was, therefore, the course stamped on the revolution by Greek and Latin conventionalism. Plato pointed out the ideal. In the seventeenth and eighteenth centuries, both clergy and laity began to celebrate this marvel. When the time came for action, Mirabeau took the first step, Robespierre the second, Saint-Just the third, Antonelle the fourth, and Babeuf, more logical than all his predecessors, stood to attention at the final step, absolute communism, pure Platonism. I ought to quote his writings here but will

---

39. See Saint-Just, *Fragments sur les institutions républicaines,* p. 58.
40. Ibid., pp. 58–59.

limit myself to saying that he signed them *Caius Gracchus,*[41] which is highly characteristic.

The spirit of the Revolution from the point of view that concerns us can be summed up in a few quotations. What did Robespierre want? "To raise men's souls to the height of the republican virtues of the peoples of the ancient world" (3 nivôse year III).[42] What did Saint-Just want? "To offer us the happiness of Sparta and Athens" (23 nivôse year III). He also wanted "all citizens to carry beneath their tunic Brutus's dagger" (idem). What did the bloodthirsty Carrier want? "That all young men in future should envisage the live coals of Scaevola, the hemlock of Socrates, the death of Cicero, and the sword of Cato." What did Rabaut Saint-Etienne[43] want? "Following the principles of the Cretans and Spartans, the state should take control of man from the cradle and even before birth" (16 December 1792). What did the Quinze-vingts[44] section want? "A church to be consecrated to freedom and an altar to be raised on which a perpetual fire would burn, maintained by young vestals" (21 November 1794 nivôse). What did the entire Convention want? "Our communes to include only Brutuses and Publicolas in the future" (19 March 1794).

All these sectarians were nevertheless of good faith, and this made them all the more dangerous, since sincerity in error is fanaticism and fanaticism is a formidable power, especially when it acts upon masses prepared to suffer its action. Widespread enthusiasm in favor of a social stereotype cannot always be without issue, and public opinion, whether enlightened or misled, is nonetheless the ruler of the world. When one of these fundamental errors, such as the glorification of the ancient world lodged through teaching in all brains with the first glimmers of intelligence, is established there in a state of *conventionalism,* it tends to pass from minds to actions. Should a revolution then ring out the time to undertake experiments, who knows under what terrible name the person who appeared a hundred years earlier under the name of Fénelon would appear? Had he set his ideas out in a novel he would die for them on the scaffold; were he a poet, he would make himself a martyr; had he amused society, he would overturn it.

41. See the entry for "Gracchi" in the Glossary of Persons.
42. See the entry for "Republican calendar" in the Glossary of Subjects and Terms.
43. Jean-Paul Rabaut.
44. The Hospice des Quinze-vingt was originally an almshouse for the blind and later transformed into a workshop for inmates. Bastiat is referring to the administration in charge.

However, in reality, there is a power that is superior to the most universal conventionalism. When education has deposited in the social body a disastrous seed, the social body has in it a force for self-preservation, a *vis medicatrix*,[45] which makes it rid itself over time, and through suffering and tears, of the harmful germ.

Therefore, when communism had sufficiently terrified and compromised society, a reaction became inevitable. France started to retreat into despotism. In its ardor it might have made little even of the legitimate conquests of the Revolution. It had the consulate and the empire. But alas! Do I need to show that the infatuation with Rome followed France into this new phase? The ancient world is forever there to justify all forms of violence. From Lycurgus to Caesar, how many models there are to choose from! Therefore, and I am here borrowing M. Thiers's language, "We who, after being Athenians with Voltaire and fleetingly wishing to be Spartans under the Convention, became the soldiers of Caesar under Napoléon." Can we fail to see the stamp that our devotion to Rome has left on this period? And, goodness me, this stamp is everywhere. It is in the edifices, the monuments, the literature, and the very fashions of imperial France. It is in the ridiculous names imposed on all our institutions. It is doubtless not an accident that we saw *consuls, an emperor, senators, tribunes, prefects, senatus-consultes, eagles, Trajan columns, legions, Champs de Mars* [Martian fields], *prytaneums* [military schools], and *lycées* spring up everywhere.

The conflict between the revolutionary and counterrevolutionary principles seemed to be bound to end with the July Days in 1830. Since that time, the intellectual forces of this country have turned toward the study of social matters, which is nothing if not natural and useful. Unfortunately, the university gives the first impetus to the progress of the human mind, and it is still directing the mind toward the poisoned sources of the ancient world, to the extent that our unfortunate country is reduced to repeating its past and experiencing the same trials. It seems that it is condemned to go round in the circle of utopia, experimentation, reaction—literary Platonism, revolutionary communism, military despotism—Fénelon, Robespierre, Napoléon! Can things be any different? Instead of seeking to discover and reveal the natural laws of society, the young generation from whom the ranks of literature and journalism are recruited is content to take over as a basis this Greco-Roman axiom: *Social order is a creation of the legislator.* A dreadful

45. A "healing power."

point of departure, which opens a career of unlimited scope to the imagination and is nothing but the eternal spawning of *socialism*. For, if society
is an invention, who would not want to be the inventor? Who would not
want to be Minos, Lycurgus, Plato, Numa, Fénelon, Robespierre, Babeuf,
Saint-Simon, Fourier, Louis Blanc, or Proudhon? Who does not think it
glorious to *establish a people*? Who does not delight in the title of *Father of
the Nations*? Who does not aspire to combine the family and property like
chemical elements?

But to give rein to fantasy elsewhere than in the columns of a journal,
you have to hold power and occupy the focal point to which all the threads
of public power lead. It is the essential preamble to any experimentation.
Each sect, each school, will therefore do its utmost to remove the dominant
school or sect from the government, and thus, under the influence of classical teaching, social life can be only an interminable sequence of struggles
and revolutions whose object is to settle the question of which utopian will
have the power to carry out experiments on the people as though they were
base material!

Yes, I accuse the baccalaureate of shaping, as though wantonly, all French
youth for socialist utopias and social experimentation. And doubtless that is
the reason for a very strange phenomenon, the incapacity to refute socialism
shown by the very people who think they are threatened by it. Men from the
bourgeoisie, landowners and capitalists, the systems of Saint-Simon, Fourier,
Louis Blanc, Pierre Leroux, and Proudhon, are only doctrines, after all. You
say they are wrong. Why do you not refute them? Because you have drunk
from the same cup, because frequent reading of the ancients and your conventional liking for everything that is Greek or Roman has inoculated you
with socialism.

"Your mind is somewhat infatuated with it."

The leveling of your wealth as a result of tariffs, your law on government
assistance, your calls for free education, your subsidies to encourage industry,
your centralization, your faith in the state, your literature, your theater, everything demonstrates that you are socialists. You differ from the apostles in
degree but you are on the same slope. This is why, when you feel yourself to
be outdistanced, instead of refuting these beliefs—which you do not know
how to do and which you cannot do without condemning yourselves—you
wring your hands, tear out your hair, call for retrenchment, and exclaim pite-
ously, "*France is going to the dogs.*"

No, France is not going to the dogs. What is happening is that while you are concentrating on your sterile lamentations, the socialists are refuting themselves. Their sages are in open warfare. We have seen the end of the Fourierist phalanxes, and of the triad, and of the national workshop, and your leveling of conditions by law will die in the same way. What will still be there? *Free credit.* Why do you not show how absurd it is? Alas, it is you who invented it. You preached it for a thousand years. When you were unable to stifle personal interest, you regulated it. You taxed it to the *maximum,* giving rise to the thought that *property is a creation of the law,* which is exactly the view of Plato, Lycurgus, Fénelon, Rollin, and Robespierre and which is, and I am not afraid to state this, the essence and quintessence not only of socialism but of communism. Do not sing the praises to me therefore of a form of education that has taught you nothing of what you need to know and which leaves you astounded and struck dumb when faced with the first illusion it has pleased a madman to imagine. You are not capable of opposing error with truth; at least let the errors mutually destroy each other. Be careful not to gag the utopians, thus placing their propaganda on the pedestal of persecution. The minds of the working masses, if not the middle classes, have become absorbed with the major social questions. They will solve them. They will eventually find other definitions for *family, property, freedom, justice,* and *society* than those your education has given you. They will overcome not only the socialism that speaks its name but also the socialism that is unaware of what it is. They will kill off your universal intervention of the state, your centralization, your artificial unity, your system of protection, your official philanthropy, your laws on usury, your barbarous diplomacy, and your monopolized system of education.

This is why I state that France is not going to the dogs. It will emerge from the combat happier, more enlightened, better organized, greater, freer, more moral, and more religious than you have made it.

After all, and note this well, when I rail against classical studies, I am not asking for them to be *forbidden;* I am asking only that they should not be *imposed.* I am not calling on the state to align everyone with my views but to say, "Do not subject me to the opinion of others." There is a great difference, and everyone should be quite clear on this.

M. Thiers, M. de Riancey, M. de Montalembert, and M. Barthélemy Saint-Hilaire consider that the Roman atmosphere is excellent for shaping the hearts and minds of the young. So be it. Let them immerse their children in it; I leave them free to do this. But they should leave me free also to keep my children away from it as from pestilent air. You gentleman who would regulate us, what you consider to be sublime I consider odious; what satisfies your consciences frightens mine. Well then, follow your inspirations but allow me to follow mine. I am not constraining you; why do you constrain me?

You are perfectly convinced that from the social and moral point of view, the finest ideal is in the past. For my part, I see it in the future. "Let us dare to say this to a century that is proud of itself," said M. Thiers. "The ancient world *is what is finest in the world*." For my part, I have the good fortune not to share this sorry opinion. I use the term *sorry* because this opinion implies that, because of a fatal law, humanity is constantly deteriorating. You situate perfection at the dawn of time while I situate it at the end. You believe society to be retrograde; I consider it to be progressive. You believe that our opinions, ideas, and manners should be cast in the classical mold as far as possible; in vain do I study the social order of Sparta and Rome, all I find in it are violence, injustice, imposture, perpetual wars, slavery, turpitude, erroneous policy, erroneous morals, and an erroneous religion. What you admire, I abhor. But in the end, you keep your judgment and leave me mine. We are not here as lawyers, on the one hand pleading in favor of a classical education and on the other against, before an assembly responsible for making a decision that will conflict either with my conscience or with yours. I am asking the state only for neutrality. I am asking for freedom both for you and for me. I have at least the advantage of impartiality, moderation, and modesty over you.

Three sources of education are going to open up: the state, the clergy, and the teachers who claim to be free.

What I am asking for is that these teachers should be free in effect to try out new and fruitful avenues in their career. Let the university teach what is dear to it, Greek and Latin. Let the clergy teach what it knows, Greek and Latin. Let them both produce Platonists and tribunes, but do not let them stop us from forming, through other processes, men for our country and our century.

For if this freedom is forbidden to us, what bitter derision it will be when you come forward to say to us at every moment, "You are *free!*"

During the session on 23 February, M. Thiers came to tell us for the fourth time:

I will forever repeat what I have already said: The freedom established by the law we have drafted is freedom in accordance with the Constitution.

> I challenge you to prove otherwise. Prove to me that it is not free-
> dom; for my part I uphold the view that no other is possible.
> In former times, no one could teach without the authority of the gov-
> ernment. We have eliminated prior authorization; anyone can teach.
> In former times it was said: "Teach this, do not teach that." Today we
> say: "Teach anything you wish to teach."

It is a painful thing to hear such a challenge addressed to us and to be condemned to silence. If the weakness of my voice did not forbid me to take the rostrum, I would have replied to M. Thiers.

Let us then see what this freedom that you say is so sincere amounts to, from the point of view of teachers, fathers of families, and society in general.

By virtue of your law, I found a college. With the cost of board and lodging, I have to purchase or rent premises, provide for feeding the students, and pay the teachers. However, next door to my college there is a lycée. It does not have to concern itself with premises and teachers. The taxpayers, *including me,* pay for these. It can therefore lower the cost of board and lodging to the extent that it makes my enterprise impossible. Is this freedom? One resource remains to me, however; that is to give instruction that is so much better than yours, so sought after by the public that it comes to me in spite of the relative expensiveness that you have forced on me. But now we meet and you say to me, "Teach whatever you like, but if you stray from my syllabus, all forms of professional career will be closed to your pupils." Is this freedom?

Now I am imagining that I am the father of a family and enroll my sons in a free institution. Into what position am I put? As a father, I pay for the education of my children without any help from anyone. As a taxpayer and Catholic, I am paying for the education of other people's children since I cannot refuse to pay the tax that subsidizes the lycées; nor can I even excuse myself during Lent from casting a coin into the friar's collection box to support the seminaries. In this, at least, I am free; but am I free with regard to taxes? No, no, tell me that you are acting in *solidarity* in the socialist meaning of the word, but do not pretend to be furthering freedom.

And that is just the short side of the question. Here is something more serious. I give preference to free education since your official type of education (to which you make me contribute without drawing any benefit from it) appears to me to be communist and pagan. My conscience is averse to my sons' being indoctrinated with Spartan and Roman ideas which, in my view at least, are nothing other than glorified violence and robbery. Consequently, I am obliged to pay board and lodging for my sons and taxes for the sons of others. And what do I then find? I find that your mythological and warlike teaching has been indirectly imposed on free colleges through the ingenious mechanism of your degrees and that I have to bend my conscience to suit your views under pain of making my children pariahs of society. You have told me four times that I am free. You may tell me this a hundred times, and a hundred times I will answer, "I am not."

Be inconsistent since you cannot avoid it, and I will concede that in the current state of public opinion, you will not be able to close the official colleges. But set a limit to your inconsistency. Do you not complain every day about the attitudes of the young? About their socialist tendencies? About their estrangement from religious ideas? About their passion for warlike expeditions, a passion so fierce that, in our deliberating assemblies, it is scarcely permissible to utter the word *peace,* and the most ingenious oratorical precautions have to be taken to mention *justice* when it comes to foreign parts? Such deplorable dispositions doubtless have a cause. At the worst, is it not possible that your mythological, platonic, warlike, and factious form of education has something to do with this? I am not telling you to change it, however; that would be to expect too much of you. But I tell you: Since you allow so-called *free* schools to spring up next to your lycées in conditions that are already very difficult, allow them, at their risk and peril, to try the paths of Christianity and science. The experiment is worth trying. Who knows? Perhaps it will mark progress. And you want to snuff it out at birth!

Last, let us examine the question from the point of view of society, and first of all let us note that it would be strange for society to be free with regard to teaching if teachers and fathers of families were not.

The first sentence of M. Thiers's report on secondary education in 1844 proclaimed this terrible truth:

"State education is perhaps the greatest interest of a civilized nation and, for this reason, *is the greatest object of the ambition of the parties.*"[46]

It appears that the conclusion to be drawn from this is that a nation that does not want to be the prey of the parties has to hasten to suppress *state* education, that is to say, *by the state,* and to proclaim freedom of education. If

---

46. From vol. 6, chap. 129, "Rapport sur le report de loi relatif à l'instruction secondaire, déposé le 13 juillet 1844 à la Chambre des Députés," in Thiers, *Discours parlementaires: Troisième partie,* p. 450.

there is a form of education entrusted to the government, the parties would have one more reason to seek to take hold of power since, at the same time, they would be taking hold of education, *the greatest object of their ambition*. Does the hunger to rule not arouse enough covetousness already? Does it not engender enough conflicts, revolutions, and disorders? And is it wise to stir it up further through the bait of such high influence?

And why do the parties seek to direct study? Because they know this saying by Leibnitz, "Make me the master of education and I will take charge of changing the face of the world." Education by government is therefore education by one party, by a sect that is temporarily triumphant; it is education for the benefit of one idea, one exclusive approach. "We have fashioned the Republic," said Robespierre; "It remains for us to fashion republicans," an attempt that was repeated in 1848. Bonaparte wanted to fashion only soldiers, Frayssinous fanatics, and Villemain mere talkers. M. Guizot would fashion only Doctrinaires, Enfantin mere followers of Saint-Simon, and someone who resented seeing humanity degraded in this way, if ever he were in the position of saying "*I am the state,*" would perhaps be tempted to fashion only economists. What then! Will we never see the danger of giving parties the opportunity of imposing their views, I mean their errors, *by force,* universally and uniformly, whenever they snatch power? For forbidding by law any view other than the one with which you yourself are infatuated is indeed coercion.

Claims and intentions of this nature are essentially monarchical, although no one has more resolutely displayed them than the republican party, since they are based on the premise that those governed are made by those who govern, that society belongs to the government, which has to fashion it in its image, whereas, according to our citizen rights, so dearly bought, power is only an emanation of society, one of the manifestations of its thought.

For my part, I cannot conceive a vicious circle more absurd, especially in the mouths of republicans, than this: As the years go by, through the mechanism of universal suffrage, national thought will be incarnate in the magistrates and then these magistrates will fashion national thought to suit their will.

This doctrine implies the following two assertions: National thought wrong, governmental thought infallible.

And if this is so, you republicans, immediately restore autocracy, state education, legitimacy, divine right, and irresponsible and infallible absolute power, all institutions that have a common basis and that emanate from the same source.

If there is in the world one infallible man (or sect), let us hand over to him not only education but all the powers and make an end of it. If not, let us become enlightened as best we can, but let us not give up.

Now, I will repeat my question: from the social point of view, does the law we are discussing achieve freedom?

In former times, there was one university. Its permission was needed in order to teach. It imposed its ideas and methods, and people were obliged to operate through it. In Leibnitz's view it was thus the ruler over generations, and doubtless this was the reason that its head took the revealing title *grand master.*

Now all of this has been overturned. The university will henceforward have just two attributions: 1. the right to dictate what knowledge is needed to obtain degrees, and 2. the right to block innumerable careers to those who do not follow this avenue.

People will say that such power is almost nothing. I, on the other hand, say that this nothing is all.

This leads me to say something about a word that has often been used in this debate: *unity,* since many people consider the baccalaureate as a means of stamping a single direction on all minds that, if not reasonable and useful, is at least uniform, and for this reason a good thing.

Those who admire unity are very numerous, and this is understandable. Providence has decreed that we all have faith in our own judgment, and we believe that there is just one valid opinion, that is to say, ours. We therefore think that the legislator can do no better than to impose this on all, and for greater safety we all want to be the legislator. However, legislators succeed one another in office, and what happens? At each changeover one form of unity replaces another. State education thus favors uniformity by taking each period into consideration in isolation, but if successive periods are compared—for example, the Convention, the Directoire, the empire, the restoration, the July Monarchy, and the Republic—we find diversity and, what is worse, the most subversive of all forms of diversity, that which produces visible changes in the intellectual field, as though on a stage, depending on the caprices of the person controlling the effects. Will we forever allow national intelligence and public awareness to descend to this level of degradation and indignity?

There are two types of unity. One is a point of departure. It is imposed by force by those who temporarily control it. The other is a result, the supreme consummation of human perfectibility. It is the result of the natural gravitation of human intelligence toward truth.

The principle of the first type of unity is scorn for the human race, and its instrument is despotism. Robespierre was a unitarian when he said, "I have fashioned the Republic, I will set out to fashion republicans." Napoléon was a unitarian when he said, "I love war and will make all Frenchmen into warriors." Frayssinous was a unitarian when he said, "I have one belief and will bend all consciences to this belief through education." Procrustes was a unitarian when he said, "Here is a bed; I will shorten or stretch anyone who exceeds or does not reach its dimensions." The baccalaureate is unitarian when it says, "Life in society will be forbidden to anyone who has not followed my syllabus." And let no one claim that the Supreme Council can change this syllabus each year, since we certainly cannot imagine a circumstance that would make matters worse. What then! The entire nation is to be considered as clay that the potter smashes when he is not happy with the shape he has given it?

In his report in 1844, M. Thiers showed that he was a fervent admirer of this type of unity, while at the same time regretting that it conformed little to the genius of modern nations.

> A country in which freedom of education does not reign would be one in which the state, driven by absolute determination and wishing to cast its young people in the same mold and strike them in its effigy as though they were coins, would not permit any diversity in the system of education and, for a period of several years, would make all children wear the same type of clothes, eat the same type of food, and subject them to the same type of studies and the same type of exercises, bend them, etc.[47]
>
> Let us refrain from speaking ill of this claimed prerogative of the state to impose unity of character on the nation and from regarding it as inspired by tyranny. It might almost be said, on the contrary, that this strong determination of the state to make all its citizens conform to a common type is in proportion to the patriotism of each country. It was in the ancient republics in which the fatherland was most adored and best served that it displayed the most stringent exactions with regard to the behavior and spirit of its citizens. . . . And we who, in the past century, have displayed all the aspects of human society, we who, having

47. Ibid., p. 458.

been Athenians with Voltaire, fleetingly wished to be Spartans under the Convention and the soldiers of Caesar under Napoléon, if there was one moment during which we thought of imposing the yoke of the state on education in an absolute manner, it was under the National Convention at the time of the greatest exaltation of patriotism.[48]

Let us give credit to M. Thiers. He does not suggest that we follow such examples. "We should not," he said, "either imitate them or undermine them. It was a delirium but one arising from patriotism."

It remains no less true that M. Thiers here shows that he continues to adhere to the judgment he made. "The ancient world is what is finest in the world." He shows a secret predilection for absolute state despotism, an instinctive admiration for the institutions of Crete and Sparta, which gave the legislator the power to cast all young people in the same mold, to strike them in its effigy of the state, like coins, etc., etc.

And I cannot refrain from pointing out at this juncture, as it is fully part of my subject, the traces of classical *conventionalism* which make us admire as virtue in the ancient world that which was the result of the hardest and most immoral of necessities. The ancients whom we exalt, and I cannot repeat this too often, lived from piracy and would not have touched a tool for anything in the world. The entire human race was their enemy. They had condemned themselves to perpetual warfare and to the situation of always having to conquer or perish. This being so, there was and could be only one occupation, that of a soldier. The community had to devote itself to developing military qualities uniformly in all of its citizens, and its citizens subjected themselves to this *unity*, which guaranteed their existence.[49]

48. Ibid., p. 459.
49. (Paillottet's note) In the outline from which we borrowed the preceding note [p. 194, note 11], the author examines these two questions:

1. Whether self-renunciation is a political motivation preferable to personal interest;
2. Whether ancient peoples, especially the Romans, practiced this renunciation better than modern peoples do.

Bastiat opts for the negative for both, as we would guess. Here is one of his reasons with regard to the latter:

When I sacrifice part of my wealth to build walls and a roof that will protect me from thieves and the weather, it cannot be said that I am driven by self-renunciation but that on the contrary I am endeavoring to preserve myself.
   In the same way, when the Romans sacrificed their internal divisions in favor

224 BACCALAUREATE AND SOCIALISM

But what is there in common between these barbarous times and modern times?

With what precise and clearly determined aim would all citizens be struck in the same effigy, like so many coins, today? Is it because they are all destined to follow a variety of careers? What would be the reason for casting them in the same mold? *And who will hold the mold?* This is a terrible question, which should make us think. *Who will hold the mold?* If there is a mold (and the baccalaureate is one), everyone will want to hold the handle: M. Thiers, M. Parisis, M. Barthélemy Saint-Hilaire, me, the Reds, the Whites, the Blues, and the Blacks.[50] We would therefore have to fight to

of their security, when they risked their lives in combat, when they subjected themselves to the yoke of an almost unbearable discipline, they were not practicing self-renunciation; on the contrary they were embracing the sole means they had of preserving themselves and escaping the extermination with which they were threatened by the reaction of other peoples to their violence.

I know that several Romans demonstrated great personal abnegation and devoted themselves to saving Rome. But there is an easy explanation for this. The interest that determined their political organization was not their only motive. Men accustomed to conquering together, to hating everything foreign to their association, had to have an exalted degree of national pride and patriotism. All warlike nations, from primitive hordes to civilized peoples who make war only accidentally, experience patriotic exaltation. This is all the more true of the Romans, whose very existence was a constant war. This exalted national pride, combined with the courage born of warlike customs, the scorn of death it inspired, the love of glory, and the desire to live on in posterity, had frequently to produce shining actions.

For this reason, I do not say that no virtue can arise in a society that is purely military. I would be contradicted by events, and the bands of brigands themselves offer us examples of courage, energy, devotion, a scorn of death, generosity, etc. However, I claim that, like these bands of robbers, robber nations, from the point of view of self-renunciation, do not win out over hardworking peoples, and I add that the enormous and constant vices of the former cannot be effaced by a few shining actions, which are perhaps unworthy of the name of virtue, since they occur to the detriment of humanity. [Unpublished article by the author, shortly before 1830.]

50. In many societies colors are associated with different political points of view. It is possible that the term "Reds" refers to supporters of the army or the emerging socialists; "Whites" refers to supporters of the monarchy; "Blues" refers to the liberals; and "Blacks" refers to supporters of the church.

The novelist Stendhal (1783–1842) moved in Saint-Simonian circles in the 1820s and wrote a witty satire of the Saint-Simonians titled *D'un nouveau complot contre les industriels* (1825). He is also the author of *Le Rouge et le noir* (The Red and the Black) settle this initial question, which would constantly resurface. Is it not easier to break the fatal mold and proclaim freedom honestly?

Especially since freedom is the terrain in which genuine unity germinates and is the environment that makes it fertile. The effect of competition is to stimulate good methods, reveal them and make them universal, and eliminate bad ones. It has to be admitted that the human mind is naturally more disposed to the truth than to error, to good than to evil, to what is useful than to what is harmful. If this were not true, if a fall were to be naturally reserved for the truth and triumph for the false, all our efforts would be in vain; humanity would be inevitably propelled, as Rousseau believed, toward a fatal and progressive degradation. We would have to say, with M. Thiers, "*The ancient world is what is finest in the world,*" which is not only an error but blasphemy. Properly understood, the interests of men are harmonious and the light that enables men to understand them shines with an ever more brilliant glow. Therefore, individual and collective efforts, experience, stumbling and even deceptions, competition—in a word, freedom—make men gravitate toward this form of unity that is an expression of the laws of their nature and the achievement of the general good.

What has made the *liberal* party fall into this strange contradiction of failing to recognize freedom, dignity, and the ability of man to grow in perfection and instead preferring an artificial unity that is static, degrading, and imposed in turn by all the despotic regimes to the benefit of the most diverse dispensations?

There are several reasons for this. First, the party itself has also received the Roman impress of a classical education. Are its leaders not holders of the baccalaureate? Second, it hopes that this precious instrument, this intellectual *mold,* the object of all desires, according to M. Thiers, will fall, by way of political vicissitudes, into its hands. Last, the requirements of defense against unjust aggression from Europe in '92 have not inconsiderably contributed to making the idea of a powerful unity popular in France.

However, of all the motives that have persuaded liberalism to sacrifice

---

(1831), in which the hero, Julien Sorel, was torn between a life in the army (the red) and a life in the clergy (the black). Stendhal's use of colors to depict different ideological groups was common in the 1820s and probably was shared by Bastiat. See also "The Concepts of 'Industry' and 'Plunder' (Spoliation)" in "Bastiat's Political Writings: Anecdotes and Reflections," pp. 409–10 in this volume; and the entries "Saint-Hilaire, Jules Barthélemy," "Saint-Simon, Claude Henri de Rouvroy," and "Thiers, Adolphe," in the Glossary of Persons.

freedom, the most powerful is the fear that the encroachments of the clergy have inspired in liberalism with regard to education.

I do not share this fear but I understand it.

Consider, says liberalism, the situation of the clergy in France, its scholarly hierarchy, its strong discipline, its militia of forty thousand members, all unmarried and occupying the leading role in each commune in the country. Consider the influence that the clergy owes to the nature of its functions, which it draws from the word that it causes to resound without contradiction and with authority from the pulpit and which it murmurs in the confessional. Consider the links that bind it to the state through the religious budget, the links that subject it to a religious head who is simultaneously a foreign king, the help it receives from a fervent and devoted congregation, the resources it gains from the alms it distributes. Consider the fact that it regards as its first duty to take control of education and tell me whether, under these conditions, freedom of education is not just a delusion.

A volume would be needed to discuss this mighty question and all those questions relating to it. I will limit myself to one consideration and say this:

Under a free regime, *it is not the clergy who will conquer education but education that will conquer the clergy. It is not the clergy who will strike the century in its effigy, but the century that will fashion the clergy in its image.*

Can we have any doubt that education stripped of university shackles and divorced, through the elimination of degrees, from classical conventionalism, will launch itself down new and fruitful paths under the spur of rivalry? Free institutions, which will laboriously start up between lycées and seminaries, will feel the need to give the human mind its proper food, that is to say, the science of what things are and not the science of what was said about them two thousand years ago. "Ancient times are the childhood of the world," said Bacon, "and in truth it is our time that is ancient, since the world has acquired knowledge and experience as it has grown old." The study of the works of God and nature in the moral and physical order, this is true education; this is what will be dominant in free institutions. The young people who receive this education will show themselves to be superior through the force of their intelligence, the sureness of their judgment, and their practical aptitude in life to the *frightful little talkers* that the university and clergy will have saturated with doctrines that are as false as they are outmoded. While the first group will be prepared to assume the social functions of our time, the others will be reduced at first to forgetting what they have learned, if they can, and then learning what they ought to know.

When faced with these results, fathers of families will tend to prefer free schools, full of sap and life, to these other schools, which are succumbing to the slavery of routine.

What will happen then? The clergy itself, still wishing to retain its influence, will have no other recourse than to substitute the teaching of things for the teaching of words, the study of positive truths for that of conventional doctrines, and substance for the superficial.

However, in order to teach you have to know, and in order to know you have to learn. The clergy will thus be obliged to change the direction of its own studies, and this renovation will be introduced all the way up to the seminaries. Well, do you think that a different diet will not produce different temperaments? For, let us be clear, it is not a question here of changing the subject only but also the method of clerical teaching. Knowledge of the works of God and nature is acquired by other intellectual processes than that of theogony. Observing facts and their sequence is one thing; admitting a text that is taboo without examination and drawing its consequences is quite another. When science replaces intuition, examination is substituted for authority and the philosophical method for the dogmatic. A different aim requires a different procedure, and other procedures give the mind other habits.

There is therefore no doubt that the introduction of science into the seminars, the infallible result of the freedom of teaching, will have the effect of modifying these institutions, right down to their intellectual habits. And I am convinced that therein lies the dawn of a great and desirable revolution, which will achieve religious unity.

I said not long ago that classical *conventionalism* made us into living contradictions, French by necessity and Romans by education. Could it not also be said that from the religious point of view we are living contradictions?

We all feel in our heart of hearts an irresistible magnet that draws us toward religion, and at the same time we feel intellectually a no less irresistible force that repels us from it; and it is a point of fact that this is all the more true the more the mind is cultured, so that a great doctor was able to say: *Litterati minus credunt.*[51]

Oh what a sad sight it is! For some time now, above all, we have heard deep groans on the dilution of religious beliefs and, what is strange, the very people who have let the last spark of faith die out in their soul are the most

51. "Learned men are those who have the least faith."

willing to find doubt impertinent . . . in others. "Submit your reason," they told the people, "or all will be lost. It is right for me to defer to mine since it is of a particular temper, and to observe the Decalogue I do not need to believe it has been revealed. Even when I drift away from it a little, not much harm is done; for you on the other hand it is different, you cannot infringe it without imperiling society . . . and my peace of mind."

This is how fear seeks refuge in hypocrisy. People do not believe but pretend to do so. While skepticism forms the basis, calculated religiosity rises to the surface and here is a new form of *conventionalism,* of the worst kind, to dishonor the human mind.

However, not everything in this language is hypocritical. Although people do not believe everything or practice anything, there is deep in people's hearts, as Lamennais said, a root of faith that never dries up.

Where has this bizarre and dangerous situation come from? Might it not be that institutions, practices, and rites that intelligent reflection cannot admit, whatever people say, have been mingled over time with the religious, primordial, and fundamental truths to which all sects and schools by common consent have adhered? And have these human additions no other support in the actual minds of the clergy than the dogmatism through which they attach them to the primordial and uncontested truths?

Religious unity will come about, but only when every sect has abandoned the parasitic institutions to which I am referring. Let us remember that Bossuet made good use of them when he debated with Leibnitz on the means of bringing all the various Christian confessions back to unity. Will what appeared to be possible and good to the great seventeenth-century doctor be seen as being too daring by the doctors of the nineteenth century? Whatever happens, by implanting other intellectual habits in the clergy, freedom of teaching will doubtless be one of the most powerful instruments of the great religious renovation that alone can satisfy consciences and save society.[52]

So great is the need of societies for a moral code that the body that makes itself the guardian and dispenser of this code in the name of God acquires unlimited influence over them. However, experience has shown that nothing perverts men more than unlimited influence. There comes a time, therefore, when far from the priesthood remaining merely the instrument of re-

---

52. (Paillottet's note) See *Justice and Fraternity,* pages 316 and 317. (*OC,* vol. 4, p. 298, "Justice et fraternité.") [See also "Justice and Fraternity," pp. 73–74 in this volume.]

ligion, it is religion that becomes the instrument of the priesthood. At this point a fatal antagonism comes into the world. Faith and intelligence, from opposing sides, pull everything over to them. Priests unceasingly add to sacred truths errors that they proclaim as no less sacred, thus offering the lay opposition solid reasons and arguments that are increasingly serious. The former seeks to pass on falsehood with truth while the latter undermines the truth by falsehood. Religion becomes superstition and philosophy incredulity. Between these two extremes, the masses are shrouded in doubt, and it can be said that humanity is going through a critical period. Nevertheless, the abyss becomes ever deeper and the struggle continues not only between individuals but also within the conscience of every man, with a variety of outcomes. If political upheaval strikes terror into society, it finds refuge in faith, out of fear; a sort of hypocritical religiosity gains the upper hand, and priests consider themselves the victors. But no sooner has calm returned, no sooner have priests tried to turn victory to their advantage than intelligence reclaims its rights and resumes its work. When will this anarchy end then? When will intelligence and faith form an alliance? When faith is no longer a weapon, when priests return to what they ought to be, an instrument of religion, and abandon the outward show that interests them in favor of the fundamentals that interest humanity. When this happens, it will not be enough to say that religion and philosophy are sisters; they will have to be said to be merged in unity.

But I will come down from these elevated heights and, returning to university degrees, I ask myself whether the clergy will be very averse to abandoning the routine paths of classical teaching, which, incidentally, they are in no way obliged to do.

It would be amusing if Platonic communism, paganism, the ideas and behavior shaped by slavery and piracy, Horace's *Odes,* and Ovid's *Metamorphoses* were to find their ultimate defenders and teachers in the priests of France! It is not my place to give them advice, but they will doubtless allow me to quote an excerpt from a journal which, unless I am mistaken, is written by ecclesiastics:

> Who then, among the doctors of the church, are the apologists of pagan teaching? Is it Saint Clement, who wrote that secular science is like fruit and jam that should be served only at the end of a meal? Is it Origen, who wrote that in the golden cups of pagan poetry there is deadly poison? Is it Tertullian, who called the pagan philosophers the patriarchs of the heretics, *Patriarchae hereticorum?* Is it Saint Irenaeus, who declared

that Plato was the seasoning for all heresies? Is it Lactantius, who noted that the well-read men of his day were those who had the least faith? Is it Saint Ambrose, who said that it was very dangerous for Christians to be concerned with lay oratory? Finally, is it Saint Jerome, who in his letter to Eustochia strongly condemned the study of the pagans, saying: "What is there in common between light and darkness? What agreement can there be between Christ and Baal? What has Horace to do with the Psalms or Virgil with the Gospels?" Saint Jerome, who so bitterly regretted the time he devoted in his youth to the study of pagan letters: "How unfortunate I was, I denied myself food in order not to abandon Cicero; as soon as morning broke, I had Plautus in my hands. If on occasion, withdrawing into myself, I began to read the prophets, their style seemed to me to be crude and, because I was blind, I denied the light."

But let us listen to Saint Augustine:

The studies through which I came to read the writings of others and to write what I think, were nevertheless much more useful and much more solid than those that I was later obliged to pursue, which concerned the adventures of I do not know which Aeneas and which made me weep over the fate of Dido, dying of love, while, forgetting my own faults, I was myself finding death in this disastrous literature. . . . However, these are the follies that are called *fine and honest letters: Tales dementiae honestiores et uberiores litterae putantur.*[53] . . . Let these *merchants of fine literature* upbraid me. I am not afraid of them, and I am concentrating on extricating myself from the evil paths I have followed. . . . It is true that from these studies I have retained many expressions that are useful to know, but *all of this can be learned elsewhere than in such frivolous literature* and children should be led down less dangerous paths. But who dares resist you, you cursed torrent of custom! Is it not to follow your course that I was made to read the story of Jupiter who simultaneously held the thunderbolt and committed adultery? We know that this cannot be reconciled, but with the help of this false thunderbolt we reduce the horror inspired by adultery and encourage young people to imitate the actions of a criminal god.

53. From Augustine's *Confessions* 1.13. The full Latin passage reads, "Tali dementia honestiores et uberiores litterae putantur quam illae quibus legere et scribere didici." [Madness like this is thought a higher and a richer learning than that by which I learned to read and write.]

And notwithstanding this, oh infernal torrent, every child is cast into your waters, and this culpable custom is made into a great event. This is carried out publicly under the gaze of magistrates for an agreed salary. . . . It is the wine of error that drunken teachers offered us in our childhood; they chastised us when we refused to drink it and we could not appeal against their sentence to any judge who was not as drunk as they were. My soul was thus the prey of impure minds, for there is not just one way of offering sacrifice to devils.[54]

Adds the Catholic article, are not this eloquent lamentation, this bitter criticism, these unbending reproaches, these touching regrets, and this judicious advice as relevant to our century as to the century for which Saint Augustine was writing? Have we not retained in the name of classical education the same system of study against which Saint Augustine speaks out with such force? Has this torrent of paganism not flooded the world? Do we not cast thousands of children into its waters each year, children who lose their faith, their code of behavior, human feelings and dignity, their love of freedom, and a knowledge of their rights and duties, and who emerge imbued with false ideas of paganism, its false moral code, and its virtues no less than with its vices and profound scorn for humanity?

And this frightful moral disorder does not arise from the corruption of individual will abandoned to its own devices. No, it is imposed by law through the mechanism of university degrees. M. de Montalembert himself, while regretting that the study of the literature of the ancient world was not sufficiently intense, quoted the reports of university inspectors and deans. They were unanimous in recording the resistance, and I would almost say revolt, of public feeling against such an absurd and disastrous tyranny. All note that French young people calculate with mathematical accuracy what they are obliged to learn and what they are allowed not to know in terms of classical studies, and they stop just at the limit at which they will gain their required grades. Is this also true of other branches of human knowledge, and is it not common knowledge that, for ten places, there are a hundred candidates, all of whom have degrees superior to those required for

54. Bastiat is quoting from St. Augustine, *The Confessions,* chap. 16: "He Disapproves of the Mode of Educating Youth, and He Points Out Why Wickedness Is Attributed to the Gods by the Poets."

the courses? Let the legislator therefore take into account public reason and current views.

Is it a savage, a tribesman from the Vosges or one of the Gepids, who would dare to speak up here? Does he fail to see the supreme beauty of the literary monuments bequeathed to us by the ancient world or the services rendered to the cause of civilization by Greek democracies?

Certainly not; he would not fail to repeat that he was not requiring the law to ban but just not to impose. Let it leave citizens free. They would be capable of recasting history in its true colors, admiring what is worthy of admiration, attenuating that which warrants scorn, and freeing themselves of the classical *conventionalism* that is the disastrous scourge of modern society. Under the influence of freedom, natural sciences, and secular literature, Christianity and paganism will be able to occupy their rightful share in education; and in this way, harmony, which is the condition for the establishment of order in both consciences and society, will be established between ideas, the code of behavior, and personal interest.

## LIBERTY, EQUALITY[55]

Words have their changing fortunes just as men do. Here are two that man has made divine or cursed in turn, so that it is very difficult for philosophers to speak about them calmly. There was a time when he who dared to examine the sacred syllables would have risked his head, since examination implies doubt or the possibility of doubt. Today, on the contrary, it is not prudent to mention them in a certain place, and that place is the one from which the laws that govern France are issued! Thank heaven I have to deal only with liberty and equality from the economic point of view. That being so, I hope that the title of this chapter will not have too painful an effect on the reader's nerves.

But how has it happened that the word *liberty* sometimes makes hearts beat faster, arouses enthusiasm in peoples, and is the signal for actions of the utmost heroism, while in other circumstances it appears to emerge from the hoarse throats of the populace only to spread discouragement and terror far

55. (Paillottet's note) In the first few months of 1848, the author, who was working on the second volume of the *Harmonies,* began a chapter titled "Liberty, Equality" for this volume. Shortly afterward, he abandoned this plan and never finished it. We have printed this fragment here since it is in tune with the idea of the article we have just read.

and wide? Doubtless it does not always have the same meaning and does not whip up the same idea.

I cannot stop myself believing that our entirely Roman education has something to do with this anomaly....

For many years, the word *liberty* has struck our young ears, bearing a meaning that cannot be adjusted to modern behavior. We make it the synonym of national supremacy abroad and of a certain equity at home for the sharing of conquered loot. This sharing was in effect a great subject of dissent between the Roman people and the Senate and, when this dissent is recited, our young people always take the side of the people. Thus it is that the combats between the Forum and liberty end by forming an indissoluble association of ideas in our minds. To be free is to struggle and the region of liberty is that of storms....

Were we not slow to leave school to thunder in public places against *foreign savages* and *avaricious nobles?*

How can liberty when understood this way fail to be in turn an object of enthusiasm or terror for a working population?...

Peoples have been and are still so oppressed that they have not been able to achieve liberty except through struggle. They resign themselves to it when they feel oppression clearly, and they surround the defenders of liberty with their homage and gratitude. However, the struggle is often long and bloody, a blend of triumphs and defeats; it can generate scourges that are worse than oppression.... When this happens, the people, tired of combat, feel the need to draw breath. They turn against the men who exact from them sacrifices beyond their strength and start to doubt the magic word in the name of which they are being deprived of security and even liberty....

Although struggle is necessary to achieve liberty, let us not forget that liberty is not a struggle, any more than soldiers presenting arms is a maneuver. Writers, politicians, and speakers imbued with the Roman philosophy make this mistake. The masses do not. Combat for its own sake repels them, and it is in this that they justify the profound saying: There is someone with more wit than the witty, and this person is *everyone*....

A common fund of ideas links the words *liberty, equality, property, and security* to one another.

*Liberty,* whose etymology is *weights and scales,* implies the ideas of justice, equality, harmony, and balance, which excludes combat and which is exactly the opposite of the Roman interpretation.

On the other hand, liberty is generalized *property.* Do my faculties belong to me if I am not free to make use of them, and is not slavery the most total negation of property as it is of liberty?

Finally, liberty is *security,* since security is also property that is guaranteed not only in the present but also in the future.

Since the Romans, and I stress this, lived from plunder and cherished liberty, since they had slaves and cherished liberty, it is clear that the idea of liberty was in their eyes in no way incompatible with the ideas of theft and slavery. This must therefore be true of all our generations who have been to school, and these are the ones who are governing the world. In their minds the ownership of the product of our faculties or the ownership of the faculties themselves has nothing to do with liberty and is an asset that is infinitely less precious. For this reason theoretical attacks on property scarcely move them. Far from it; so long as the laws go about this with a certain symmetry and with an aim that is overtly philanthropic, this form of communism attracts them. . . .

You should not believe that these ideas disappear when the first fires of youth die down and when you have grown out of the urge to upset the tranquillity of the city as the Roman tribunes used to do, when you have had the good fortune to take part in four or five insurrections and have ended up choosing a state, working, and acquiring *property.* No, these ideas do not pass away. Doubtless, people value their property and defend it with energy but take little account of the property of others. If it is a case of violating it, provided that this is carried out through the intervention of the law, they have not the slightest scruple in doing so. The concern of us all is to curry favor with the law, to attempt to put ourselves in its good graces, and if it smiles on us we ask it quickly to violate the property or the liberty of others for our benefit. This is done with charming naïveté, not only by those who proclaim themselves to be communists or communitarians but also by those who claim to be fervent devotees of property, by those who are roused to fury by the mere mention of the word *communism,* by brokers, manufacturers, shipowners, and even by the archetypal property owners, those who own land. . . .

# 12

## *Protectionism and Communism*

[vol. 4, p. 504. "Protectionisme et communisme." January 1849.
This article is Bastiat's response to Adolphe Thiers's book
*De la propriété*, which appeared in the fall of 1848. n.p.]

*To M. Thiers*[1]
*Sir,*

Do not be ungrateful to the February revolution. It surprised you, offended you perhaps, but it also prepared you as an author, orator, and privy councillor[2] for unexpected triumphs. Among these successes, there is one that is certainly very extraordinary. In the last few days the following appeared in *La Presse:*

"The association for the defense of national work (formerly the Mimerel Committee) has just sent a circular to all its correspondents to announce that a subscription had been set up to support the distribution in the workshops of M. Thiers's book on property. The association itself is buying five thousand copies."

I would have liked to have been present when your eyes saw this flattering announcement. A flash of malicious joy must have shone in them.

It is very true to say that the ways of God are as unerring as they are mysterious. For if you are ready for a moment to agree that when it is generalized, protectionism becomes communism (something which I will shortly endeavor to demonstrate), just as carp fry become adult carp provided that God keeps them alive, it is already very strange that a champion of protec-

---

1. Thiers's book *De la propriété* was published in the fall of 1848 under the auspices of the Central Committee of the Association for the Defense of National Work, a vehicle for protectionist doctrines. The association apparently took no offence at Thiers's claim that "everyone is entitled to dispose completely and freely of the products of his work." Bastiat shows below that the latter proposition contradicts protectionist doctrines.

2. (Paillottet's note) At the time this article appeared, in January 1849, M. Thiers was very highly regarded at the Elysée.

tionism poses as a destroyer of communism; but what is even more strange and consoling is that a powerful association, which was formed to propagate the communist principle both theoretically and practically (to the extent that the association considered it profitable for its members), should now devote half of its resources to destroy the evil that it has done with the other half.

I repeat, this is a consoling sight. It reassures us that the truth will inevitably triumph, since it reveals that the first and true propagators of subversive doctrines, terrified by their success, are now concocting both the antidote to the poison and the poison in the same dispensary.

It is true that the latter assumes that the communist and prohibitionist principles are identical, and perhaps you do not accept this identity, although to tell the truth I cannot think it possible that you could have written four hundred pages on property without being struck by this. Perhaps you think that a little effort devoted to commercial freedom or rather *free trade*, impatience with sterile discussion, the ardor of combat, and the energy of the struggle have shown me the errors of my adversaries under a magnifying glass, as happens only too often to us polemicists. Doubtless it is my imagination that is inflating the theory of *Le Moniteur industriel* to the dimensions of that of *Le Populaire*, in order to more easily be right about it. Is it likely that major manufacturers, honest landowners, rich bankers, and clever statesmen unwittingly and unintentionally made themselves the initiators and apostles of communism in France?

Why not, may I ask? There are many workers, brimming with a sincere belief in the *right to work*, who are consequently communists without knowing it or wishing it and who would not allow people to consider them such. The fact is that in all classes interest directs the will, and the will, as Pascal said, is the major organ of credit. Under another name, many industrialists, highly honest people incidentally, treat communism as it is always treated, that is to say, on the condition that only other people's property will be shared out. But as soon as this principle is gaining ground and it becomes a matter of releasing their own assets to be shared out, then, oh dear! communism repels them! They distributed *Le Moniteur industriel*, and now they are distributing the book on property. To be surprised by this, you would need to have no knowledge of the human heart and its secret recesses and of how easily it makes itself a skillful deceiver.

No, sir, it is not the heat of the struggle that has caused me to see the prohibitionist doctrine in this light, since, on the contrary, it is because I saw it in this light before the struggle that I became involved.[3] Please believe me, expanding our foreign trade a little, an incidental result that is certainly not to be sniffed at, has never been my decisive reason for this. I believed and still believe that property is involved in this question. I believed and still believe that our customs duties, because of the spirit in which they were drawn up and the arguments used to defend them, have made a breach in the very principle of property through which all the rest of our legislation threatens to drive.

Considering the state of people's minds, it seemed to me that a form of communism that—I have to say this to be fair—is unaware of itself and its effects was about to overwhelm us. It seemed to me that this form of communism (for there are several forms) was taking advantage very logically of the prohibitionist arguments and limiting itself to insisting on its implications. It is therefore in this domain that I considered it useful to combat this form of communism, since it was arming itself with the sophisms put about by the Mimerel Committee and since there was no hope of overcoming this form of communism as long as these sophisms were left unrefuted and triumphant in the public outlook. It is from this point of view that we took our stance in Bordeaux, Paris, Marseilles, and Lyons when we founded the Association pour la liberté des échanges (free-trade association). Commercial freedom, considered in its own right, is doubtless a precious asset for nations, but all in all if we had had only this in view, we would have given our association the title of Association for Commercial Freedom, or even more politically apposite, *for the gradual reform of duties.* But the term *free trade* implies the *freedom to dispose of the fruits of your work,* in other words, *property,* and this is the reason that we preferred it.[4] Of course we knew that this term would raise difficulties. It affirmed a principle, and this being so it was bound to cause all the advocates of the opposing principle to join the ranks of our opponents. What is more, it was extremely repugnant to people, even those best disposed to support us, that is to say, the merchants, who were then more concerned with reforming the tariffs than overcoming

3. (Paillottet's note) See in vol. 1 the letters addressed to M. de Lamartine in January 1845 and October 1846 and in vol. 2 the article titled *Du Communisme,* dated 27 June 1847. (*OC,* vol. 1, p. 406, "Un Économiste à M. de Lamartine," and p. 452, "Seconde Lettre à M. de Lamartine"; and vol. 2, p. 116, "Du Communisme.")

4. (Paillottet's note) See in vol. 2 the article titled *Free Trade* dated 20 December 1846. (*OC,* vol. 2, p. 4, "Le Libre-Échange.")

communism. Le Havre, while sympathizing with our views, refused to come under our banner. People everywhere told me, "We are more likely to obtain a lessening of the duties on our products by not parading absolute demands." I replied, "If this is your sole view, take action through your Chambers of Commerce." I was also told, "The term *free trade* terrifies and makes success less likely." This was perfectly true, but I drew my strongest argument for its adoption from the very fear conjured up by this term. The more it terrifies people, I said, the more it proves that the notion of property is losing its hold in people's minds. The prohibitionist doctrine has distorted ideas, and distorted ideas have produced protectionism. Obtaining an accidental improvement in customs duties by stealth or the goodwill of the minister is to alleviate an effect, not destroy the cause. I therefore continued to use the term *free trade,* not out of spite but because of the obstacles that it was bound to create for us, obstacles that revealed the sickness of people's minds and thus proved beyond doubt that the very foundations of social order were being threatened.

It was not enough to indicate our aim by means of a term; the term needed to be defined. That is what we did, and I quote here, as supporting evidence, the first act or manifesto of this association:

At the time of joining forces to defend a great cause, the undersigned feel the need to set out their *beliefs* and to proclaim the *aim, limits, means,* and *spirit* of their association.

Trade is a natural right like property. Any citizen who has created or acquired a product must have the option of either using it immediately or selling it to another person on the earth's surface who is free to give him in exchange the object of his preference. Depriving him of this faculty, when he has not used it to contravene public order and proper behavior, and solely to satisfy the convenience of another citizen, is to legitimize plunder and contravene the law of justice.

It also violates the conditions of order, since what order can there be within a society in which each branch of production, supported by the law and public forces, seeks its success through the oppression of all the others?

This is to misunderstand the providential design which rules human destiny as shown in the infinite variety of climate, seasons, and natural forces and the aptitudes and goods that God has so unequally shared out between men with the sole aim of uniting them through trade in the bonds of universal fraternity.

It is to oppose the development of public prosperity, since he who is not free to trade is not free to choose his work and is obliged to give a false orientation to his efforts, faculties, capital, and the agents nature has made available to him.

Last, it is to compromise peace between nations since it disrupts the relationships that unite them and that make wars impossible by making them too costly.

The aim of the Association is therefore *la liberté des échanges.*

The undersigned do not contest the right of society to establish taxes on goods that cross the border in order to cover common expenditure, provided that they are determined solely in view of the needs of the treasury.

However, as soon as the tax loses its fiscal character and aims to repel foreign goods, to the detriment of the tax system itself, in order to raise the price of a similar national product artificially and thus hold the community to ransom for the benefit of a particular group, protectionism or rather plunder instantly becomes manifest and *this* is the principle the Association aims utterly to discredit in people's minds and remove totally from our laws, independently of any form of reciprocity and arrangements in force elsewhere.

Although the Association is pursuing the total destruction of the protectionist regime, it does not follow that it is asking for a reform of this nature to be achieved overnight and result from a single vote. Even to retrace one's steps from evil to good and from an artificial state of affairs to a natural situation, precautions may be required as a matter of prudence. Such details of execution are part of the powers of the state; the mission of the Association is to spread knowledge of and popularize the principle.

As for the means it intends to use, it will never seek these elsewhere than in constitutional and legal avenues.

Last, the Association is independent of all political parties. It is at the service of no industry, sector, or part of the national territory. It embraces the cause of eternal justice, peace, union, free communication, and fraternity among all men and the cause of general interest, which is confused everywhere and in all aspects with that of the *public as a consumer.*

Is there one word in this manifesto that does not reveal a burning desire to strengthen or even reestablish the notion of property, corrupted by a regime of restriction, in people's minds? Is it not plain that in the manifesto commercial interest is secondary and social interest primary? Note that the duty in itself, whether good or bad from an administrative or fiscal point of view, is of little concern to us. But as soon as it acts *intentionally* in a protectionist manner, that is to say, as soon as it reveals a tendency to plunder and the negation in principle of the right to property, we fight against it, not as a customs duty but as a system. It is the idea of this system, we argue, that we are endeavoring to discredit utterly in people's minds in order to make it disappear from our laws.

Doubtless the question will be asked why, with regard to a general matter of this importance, we have limited the struggle to the domain of a specific question.

The reason is simple. It was necessary to oppose one association by another and recruit interests and soldiers into our army. We were fully aware that between prohibitionists and free traders the polemic could not be prolonged without its shaking up and finally resolving all the moral, political, philosophical, and economic questions that relate to property, and since the Mimerel Committee had compromised this principle by pursuing just one specific aim, we had to hope to raise the principle by pursuing in our turn the specific and opposing aim.

But what does it matter what I may have said or thought in previous times? What does it matter that I may have glimpsed or thought that I had glimpsed a certain link between protectionism and communism? The essential is to know whether this link exists. That is what I am going to examine.

Doubtless you remember the day when, with your natural skill, you caused M. Proudhon to utter this admission that has become famous: "Give me the right to work and I will yield you the right of property." M. Proudhon did not hide that in his view these two rights are incompatible.

If property is incompatible with the right to work and if the right to work is based on the same principle as protectionism, what ought we to conclude other than that protectionism is itself incompatible with property? In geometry, it is held to be an incontrovertible truth that two entities equal to a third are equal to each other.

However, it has happened that an eminent orator, M. Billault, believed it to be his duty to support the right to work on the rostrum. This was not easy in view of the admission let slip by M. Proudhon. M. Billault fully understood that having the state intervene to equalize wealth and level situations was to embark on the slippery slope to communism, and what did he say to persuade the National Assembly to violate the whole basis of property? He simply told you that what he was asking you to do you were already doing through your customs duties. His claim does not go beyond a somewhat wide application of doctrines that are accepted and applied by you. These are his words:

Cast a glance on our customs duties. Through their prohibitions, differential taxes, subsidies, and various arrangements, society is helping, supporting, slowing down, or speeding up all the forms of national work [very good]. Society not only holds the balance between French work, which it protects, and foreign work, but in our homeland various forms of industry still see it constantly intervening between them. Listen to the never-ending claims before the courts by one industry against another, for example, industries that use iron complaining against the protection given to French iron against foreign iron, those that use flax or spun cotton protesting against the protection given to French yarn against foreign yarn, and so on. Society [*he should have said the government*] thus finds itself closely involved in all the struggles and difficulties of work. It actively intervenes in it on a daily basis both directly and indirectly, and the first time you have customs problems you will see that whether you like it or not you will be obliged both to take sides and sort out the rights of each of the interests.

The argument that it is the debt owed by society to destitute workers that causes the government to intervene in the question of work is therefore not a valid one.

And please note that in his argumentation, M. Billault had no thought of subjecting you to bitter irony. He is not a free trader in disguise taking pleasure in making the lack of consistency of the protectionists palpable. No, M. Billault is himself a *bona fide* protectionist. He aspires to having wealth leveled by the law. To this end, he considers the action of customs duties useful, and when he encounters the right to property as an obstacle he leaps over it, just as you do. He is then shown the right to work, which is a second step in the same direction. He next encounters the obstacle of the rights of property and leaps over it once more. However, on turning around, he is totally surprised to see that you are no longer following him. He asks you why. If you reply:

I accept in principle that the law may violate property, but I find it inconvenient for it to do this under the guise of the right to work,

M. Billault would understand you and would discuss with you this secondary question of opportuneness. But you counter him with the actual principle of property. This surprises him and he thinks he has the right to say to you:

> Do not play the good apostle now, and if you reject the right to work, let it at least not be by basing yourself on the rights of property, since you are violating this right by means of your customs duties whenever it suits you.

He might add with good reason:

> Through protectionist duties you often violate the property of the poor for the benefit of the rich. Through the right to work you will be violating the property of the rich for the benefit of the poor. By what misfortune have you been overcome by scruples this late in the day?[5]

Between M. Billault and you, therefore, there is just one difference. Both of you are treading the same path, that of communism. The only thing is that you have taken one step and he has taken two. In this respect, in my view at least, you have the advantage. However, you lose it from the point of view of logic. For since, like him, you are walking with your back turned from property, it is amusing to say the least that you pose as its champion. This is an inconsistency that M. Billault has been able to avoid. But alas! It is only for him to fall in turn into a depressing battle of words! M. Billault is too enlightened not to sense, at least dimly, the danger of each of his steps along a path that leads to communism. He does not lay himself open to ridicule by posing as the champion of property just when he is violating it, but how does he think of justifying himself? He invokes the favorite axiom of those who want to reconcile two irreconcilable things: *There are no principles*. Property, communism, let us take a bit from anywhere we choose depending on the circumstances.

> In my view, the pendulum of civilization, which swings from one principle to the other depending on the needs of the moment, but which always records a step forward, will return to the need for government action after strongly inclining toward the absolute freedom of individualism.

---

5. (Paillottet's note) This thought, by which, according to the author, M. Billault was able to strengthen his argument, was shortly to be adopted by another protectionist. It was developed by M. Mimerel in a speech delivered on 27 April 1850 to the General Council for Agriculture, Industry, and Trade. See a passage from his speech quoted in this volume in the article *Plunder and Law*. (*OC,* vol. 5, p. 1, "Spoliation et loi"; passage begins on p. 11.) [See also "Plunder and Law," p. 174 in this volume.]

There is therefore nothing new under the sun; there are no principles since *the pendulum has to swing from one principle to the other depending on the needs of the moment.* Oh, metaphor! Where would you lead us if we gave you your head![6]

As you so judiciously said from the rostrum, not everything can be said, and still less written, all at once. It should be clearly understood that I am not examining here the economic aspect of the protectionist regime. I am not looking to see whether, from the point of view of national wealth, it does more good than harm or more harm than good. The only point I wish to prove is that it is nothing other than a manifestation of communism. MM Billault and Proudhon have begun the demonstration. I will try to complete it.

First of all, what is meant by *communism?* There are several ways, if not of achieving communality of property, at least of trying to achieve it. M. de Lamartine counted four. You think that there are at least a thousand, and I agree with you. However, I think that they can all be divided into three general categories, of which just one, in my opinion, is genuinely dangerous.

First of all, two or more men can envisage pooling their work and lifestyle. As long as they do not seek to infringe security, restrict freedom, or usurp the property of others, either directly or indirectly, if they do harm, they harm themselves. The tendency of these men will always be to achieve their dreams in distant deserts. Anyone who has thought about these things knows that those who are unfortunate will perish in torment, the victims of their illusions. In these days communists of this type have called their illusionary Elysian Fields Icaria,[7] as if they had had the gloomy premonition of the terrible outcome to which they were being driven. We must weep for their blindness and should warn them if they were likely to listen to us, but society has nothing to fear from their illusions.

Another form of communism, and decidedly the most brutal, is this: make a heap of all the assets that exist and share them out *ex aequo.*[8] This is plunder that has become a dominant and universal rule. It is the destruction not only of property but also of work and the very motivation that stimulates men to work. This form of communism is so violent, absurd, and monstrous that in truth I cannot really think it is dangerous. This is what I

---

6. (Paillottet's note) See this volume, p. 94, chapter 18, of *Sophisms.* (*OC,* vol. 4, p. 94, chap. 18, "Il n'y a pas de principes absolus.")

7. See the entry for "Cabet, Étienne," in the Glossary of Persons.

8. "On equal footing."

said some time ago to a large assembly of voters, the majority of whom belonged to the suffering classes. An outburst of murmuring greeted my words.

I showed surprise. "What!" it was said; "M. Bastiat dares to say that communism is not dangerous! He must be a communist! Well, we thought as much, since communists, socialists, and economists are all tarred with the same brush as the rhyme shows." I had some trouble extricating myself from this fix. But this very interruption proved the truth of my statement. No, communism is not dangerous in its most naïve form, that of pure and simple plunder; it is not dangerous when it causes dread.

I hasten to say that while protectionism may and should be assimilated to communism, it is not to the form I have just described.

But communism also has a third form.

Causing the state to intervene, giving it the mission of evening out profits and balancing wealth by taking from some without their consent in order to give to others with no retribution, making it responsible for carrying out the work of leveling through plunder, this is definitely communism. Neither the procedures practiced by the state to do this nor the fine names used to adorn this idea change this. Whether direct or indirect means are used to achieve this, through restriction or taxes, through customs duties or the right to work, whether equality, solidarity, or fraternity is invoked, this does not change the nature of things. Plundering property is no less plunder because it is accomplished legally, in an orderly fashion, systematically, and through the implementation of the law.

I add that this is the form of communism that is truly dangerous in our time. Why? Because in this form we see it always ready to invade everything. And look! One person asks the state to supply the *tools of their trade* free of charge to artisans and workers; this is inviting it to seize them from other artisans and workers. Another wants the state to lend interest free; it cannot do this without violating property. A third claims free education at all levels. Free! That means at taxpayers' expense. A fourth demands that the state subsidize associations of workers, theaters, artists, etc. But such subsidies embody an equal level of income withheld from those who have legitimately earned it. A fifth will not rest until the state has artificially raised the price of a product for the benefit of those selling it, but this is to the disadvantage of those who buy it. Yes, in these terms there are very few people who in one way or another are not communists. You are one, M. Billault is one, and I fear that in France we are all such to a greater or lesser extent. It seems as though intervention by the state reconciles us with plunder by attributing responsibility for it to everyone, that is to say, to no one, with the result that people can enjoy the property of others with a perfectly clear conscience. Did not the honest M. Tourret, one of the most upright men to sit on a ministerial bench, start his exposition of the reasons for the draft law on advance payments to agriculture in this way: "It is not enough to give education to encourage the arts; it is also necessary to provide the tools of the trade"? Following this preamble, he submitted to the National Assembly a draft law whose first article went as follows:

> Article I: In the 1849 budget, a credit of ten million has been opened for the minister of agriculture and trade, intended to make advance payments to landowners and associations of owners of rural assets.

Admit that if legislative language were concerned with accuracy, this article should have been drafted thus:

> During 1849 the minister of agriculture and trade is authorized to take ten million from the pockets of workers who have great need of it and *to whom it belongs* in order to put it in the pockets of other workers who also need it and *to whom it does not belong*.

Is this not a communist act, and when generalized does it not constitute communism?

Take a manufacturer who would die rather than steal a sous. He does not have the slightest scruple in submitting the following request to the legislature: "Enact a law that raises the price of my cloth, iron, or coal and makes it possible for me to hold my purchasers to ransom." Since the reason on which he bases his request is that he is not happy with his profit as provided by freedom to trade or free trade (which I state is the same thing, whatever people say),[9] and since we are all discontented with our profit and inclined to call upon the legislature, it is clear, at least to me, that if the legislature

---

9. Bastiat contrasts the expression "l'échange libre" (which we have translated as "freedom to trade") with "le libre-échange" (which we have translated as "free trade"). By January 1849, when he wrote this article, the expression "le libre-échange" had acquired a particular meaning. It had become associated with the Association pour le libre-échange (The Free Trade Association), which he helped found, and with the journal *Le Libre-échange* (Free Trade), which he edited, and the movement for free trade in France, which he led.

does not hasten to say, "That is none of my business; I am not responsible for violating property but for guaranteeing it," I say that we are clearly in the throes of communism. The means of implementation used by the state may differ, but they all have the same aim and follow the same principle.

Supposing that I come to the bar of the National Assembly and say,

> I carry out a trade and do not think that my profit is sufficient. For this reason, I ask you to issue a decree that authorizes the tax collectors to exact just one little centime from each family in France for my benefit.

If the legislature accepts my request, it could be seen as just an isolated example of legal plunder, which is not enough to warrant being called communism. However, if every Frenchman, one after another, made the same request, and if the legislature examined these requests with the avowed aim of achieving equality of wealth, it is in this principle and its effects that I see, and you will not fail to see, communism.

That the legislature makes use of customs officers and tax collectors, direct or indirect taxation, or restrictions or premiums to put its ideas into practice is of little importance. Does it consider itself entitled to *take* and to *give* without compensation? Does it think that its mission is to balance profits? Does it act in accordance with this belief? Does the majority of the public approve and encourage this method of acting? In this case, I say that we are on the downward slope to communism, whether we are aware of this or not.

And if I am told: "The state is not acting in favor of everyone, but only in favor of a few sectors," I will answer: "It has then found the means to make communism itself worse still."

I am aware, sir, that doubt can be cast on these deductions by creating confusion of a very facile sort. People will quote quite legitimate administrative facts, cases in which state intervention is as equitable as it is useful; then, establishing an apparent analogy between these cases and those against which I am protesting, they will put me in the wrong and they will tell me: "Either you ought not to see communism in protectionism or you ought to see it in all government action."

This is a trap into which I do not wish to fall. For this reason I am obliged to look for the exact circumstance that confers a communist character on state intervention.

What is the purpose of the state? Which matters ought citizens to entrust to collective compulsion? Which ought they to reserve to private activity? Answering these questions would be to give a course in politics. Fortunately, I do not need to do this to solve the problem that concerns us.

When citizens, instead of providing a service to themselves, transform it into a public service, that is to say, when they consider it apposite to pool resources to have work done or to procure *joint* satisfaction for themselves, I do not call this *communism*, since I do not see in it the element that gives the latter its special character: *leveling through plunder*. It is true that the state *takes* through taxation but *gives back* by means of services. This is a particular but legitimate form of the basis of all types of society: *exchange*. I will go further. By entrusting a particular service to the state, citizens may be doing something that is an advantage or a disadvantage. It is advantageous if, by this means, the service is provided better or cheaper. It is disadvantageous if it is not, but in none of these cases do I see the principle of communism. In the first case the citizens have succeeded, and in the second they have made a mistake, but that is all, and while communism is an error it does not follow that every error is the result of communism.

In general, economists are very distrustful of government intervention. They see in it all sorts of disadvantages: a downgrading of freedom, energy, foresight, and individual experience, which are the most valuable bases of society. It often happens, therefore, that they oppose such intervention. But it is not at all from this point of view and for this reason that they reject protectionism. Let no one therefore use as an argument against us our predilection, which is perhaps too pronounced, for freedom; and let no one say: "It is not surprising that these men reject the protectionist regime since they reject state intervention in everything."

First of all, it is not true that we reject it in everything. We allow that it is the state's mission to maintain order and security, to ensure respect for people and property, and to curb fraud and violence. As for the services whose sphere is, so to say, production, we have no other rule than this: Let the state be responsible for it if there is a proven economizing of resources for the masses. But for goodness' sake, in calculating this include all the innumerable disadvantages of work monopolized by the state.

Then, I am bound to repeat, it is one thing to vote against a new function given to the state on the basis that, all things being considered, it is a disadvantage and constitutes a national loss; it is quite another thing to vote against this new function because it is illegitimate and plunderous and because it grants to the government a new mission to do precisely what its original mission was designed to prevent and punish. Well, we hold against what is called the protectionist regime both these types of objection, but the second outweighs the first by far in our determination to wage a bitter war on it, of course by legal means.

Thus, for example, let people submit to a local council the question of whether it is better to allow each family to collect its water requirements a quarter of a league away or whether it is preferable for the authority to levy a subscription to bring the water to the village square. I would have no objection *in principle* to an examination of this question. The calculation of the advantages and disadvantages for all would be the sole element in the decision. A mistake may be made in the calculation, but the error itself, though it would lead to a loss of property, would not constitute a systematic violation of that property.

But should the mayor propose to ride roughshod over one enterprise for the benefit of another, to forbid clogs in order to benefit shoemakers or something similar, then I would tell him that it was no longer a calculation of advantages and disadvantages: it would be political corruption and an abusive hijacking of public compulsion. I would say to him, "You who are the trustee of public authority and power to punish plunder, how do you dare to apply them to the protection and systematic operation of plunder?"

Should the mayor's intention triumph, if I were to see as a result of this precedent all the businesses in the village agitating to solicit favors at the expense of each other, and if in the midst of this noisy and unscrupulous ambition I see the very notion of property sink without trace, I would be free to think that, to save it from shipwreck, the first thing to do would be to point out what was iniquitous in the measure that was the initial link in this abominable chain.

It would not be difficult, sir, for me to find passages in your book that agree with my subject and are in line with my views. To tell the truth, I would have only to open it at random. Yes, harking back to a children's game, if I stick a pin into this book, I would find on the page selected by fate an implicit or explicit condemnation of the protectionist regime and proof that this regime is in principle identical with communism. And why should I not demonstrate this proof? Here I go. The pin has selected page 283; on it I read:

> It is therefore a serious error to attack competition and not to have seen
> that while the nation is a producer, it is also a consumer, and that if it re-

ceives less on the one hand (which I deny and you will deny it yourselves a few lines further down) and pays less on the other, there remains, for the benefit of all, the difference between a system that restrains human activity with a system that urges it ever forward down the path, telling it never to stop.

I challenge you to say that this does not apply just as much to the competition that takes place above the Bidassoa[10] as to that which occurs above the Loire. Let us make another stab with the pin. That's it; here we are, on page 325.

> Rights either exist or they do not. If they exist, they lead to absolute consequences. . . . There is something else: if the right exists, it exists at all times; it is fully operational today, yesterday, tomorrow, the day after, in summer as in winter, not when it suits you to declare it valid but whenever it suits the worker to invoke it.

Would you claim that an ironmaster has an indefinite and perpetual right to prevent me from indirectly producing two hundredweight of iron in my workplace, which is a vineyard, for the advantage to him of directly producing just one in his factory, which is a forge? This right also exists or it does not. If it exists, it is fully operational today, yesterday, tomorrow, the day after, in summer as in winter, not when it suits you to declare it valid but whenever it suits the *ironmaster* to invoke it!

Let us tempt fate again. It has selected page 63, on which I read the following aphorism:

> Property does not exist if I cannot *give it away* as well as *consume* it.

We, for our part, say: "Property does not exist if I cannot *trade* it as well as *consume* it." And allow me to add that the *right to* exchange is at least as precious, as socially important, and as characteristic of property as the *right to give it away*. It is to be regretted that in a book intended to examine property from every angle, you thought it necessary to devote two chapters to giving, which is not in danger, and not one line to exchange, which is so shamelessly violated under the very authority of the laws of the country. Another jab of the pin. Oh! It brings us to page 47.

> The first property owned by man lies in his person and faculties. There is a second, less close to his being but not less sacred, in the product of

10. A river in the Basque country between France and Spain.

these faculties that embraces everything known as his worldly goods and that society has the greatest interest in guaranteeing him, since without this guarantee there would be no work, and without work, no civilization, not even the necessities but deprivation, plunder, and barbarity.

Well, sir, let us elaborate on this text, if you will.

Like you, I see property first in the *free disposal* of man's person, followed by his faculties and finally the product of these faculties, which proves, let it be said in passing, that from a certain point of view freedom and property merge.

I would scarcely dare to say, like you, that the ownership of the product of our faculties is less closely linked to our being than that of the faculties themselves. Physically this is unquestionable, but if a man is deprived of his faculties or their products, the result is the same, and this result is known as *slavery*—a fresh proof of the natural identity of freedom and property. If I use force to appropriate all the work of a man for my benefit, this man is my slave. He is also my slave if, while letting him work freely, I find a way through force or guile to take possession of the fruit of his work. The first type of oppression is more odious, the second cleverer. Since it is a known fact that work done freely is more intelligent and productive, the masters have said to themselves, "Let us not usurp the faculties of our slaves directly, but let us seize the richer product of their faculties operating freely and give this new form of servitude the fine title of *protection*."

You also say that society has an interest in *guaranteeing* property. We agree; the only thing is that I go further than you, and if by *society* you mean the *government,* I say that its sole duty with regard to property is to *guarantee* it; if the government attempts to *level* property, the government is by this very action violating property instead of guaranteeing it. This is worth examining.

When a certain number of men who cannot live without work and property pool their resources to pay for a *common force,* obviously their aim is to work and enjoy the fruit of their work in total security and not to put their faculties and property at the mercy of this force. Even if no government, properly called, has yet formed, I do not believe that individual persons can have their *right to defense*—that is, the right to defend their persons, faculties, and property—challenged.

Without claiming to philosophize here on the origin and extent of the prerogatives of governments, a huge subject very likely to daunt me in my weakness, I ask that you allow me to put an idea before you. It seems to me that the prerogatives of the state can consist only in the codification of *pre-existing* personal rights. For my part, I cannot conceive of a *collective right* that is not rooted in *individual right* and does not presuppose it. Therefore, to know whether the state is legitimately endowed with a right, the question must be asked whether this right exists in individuals by virtue of their organization and in the absence of any form of government. It is on the basis of this idea that I rejected the right to work a few days ago. I said, "Since Peter does not have the right to force Paul directly to give him work, he is no more entitled to exercise this alleged right through the intervention of the state, since the state is only the *common force* created by Peter and Paul at their expense with a clear aim, which can never be to make something just that is not just. This is the touchstone I use to judge between the *guarantee* and the *leveling* of property by the state. Why has the state the right to *guarantee* everyone his property, even by force? Because this right preexists in each individual. The *right of legitimate defense* of individual entities, the right to employ force if need be to repel attacks directed against their persons, faculties, and assets, cannot be challenged. It is accepted that, since it is within each citizen, this individual right can take a collective form and make the common force legitimate. And why should the state not have the right to *level* property? Because in order to do so it has to take away from some and give to others. Well, since none of the thirty million French citizens have the right to take by force on the pretext of achieving equality, it is difficult to see how they can invest this right in the common force.

And note that the prerogative of *leveling* is destructive of the right of *guarantee*. Take savages. They have not yet founded a government. But each of them has the *right of legitimate defense,* and it is not difficult to see that this is the right that will become the basis of the *legitimate common force.* If one of these savages has devoted his time, energy, and intelligence to making himself a bow and arrow and another wishes to steal these from him, the entire sympathy of the tribe will be with the victim, and if the cause is brought before the elders to be judged, the plunderer will unfailingly be condemned. Only one step further is needed to organize a common force. But, I ask you, has this force the task, at least the legitimate one, of regularizing the act of him who defends his property as of right, or the act of him who violates the property of others in defiance of this right? It would be very strange if the collective force were to be based not on individual right but on its constant and systematic violation! No, the author of the book I have before me cannot be supporting a thesis like this. But it is not enough for the author not to support the thesis; he ought perhaps to have contested it. It is not enough to attack this crude and absurd form of communism, which a few sectarians advocate in leaflets that are decried. It might have been a good thing to unveil and stigmatize this other bold and subtle form of communism, which by simply corrupting the just notion of the prerogatives of the state has insinuated itself into some of the branches of our legislation and threatens to invade them all.

For, sir, it is really unquestionable that by operating the customs duties, through the so-called protectionist regime, governments are carrying out the monstrosity of which I have just spoken. They are deserting the right of legitimate defense that preexists in each citizen and is the source and reason of their own purpose, in order to appropriate an alleged right to level through plunder, a right that previously resided in no one and thus cannot exist communally either.

But what is the use of stressing these general ideas? What is the use of demonstrating here the absurdity of communism since you have done this yourself (except for one of its manifestations, and in my view the most threatening in practice) much better than I am able to do?

Perhaps you will tell me that the principle of the protectionist regime does not oppose the principle of property. Let us look at the procedures of this regime.

There are two of these: subsidies[11] and restrictions.

With regard to the subsidy, this is evident. I dare to challenge anyone to claim that the last stage of the system of premiums, taken to its limit, is not absolute communism. Citizens work in the shelter of the common force, which is responsible, as you say, for *guaranteeing* to each his own, *suum cuique*. But now the state with the most philanthropic intentions in the world is undertaking a quite new and different task, which in my view is not just exclusive but destructive of the first. It is pleased to make itself the judge of profit, to decide which activities are not being remunerated enough and which get too much. It is pleased to set itself up as the *leveler* and, as M. Billault says, to swing the pendulum of civilization to the opposite side from *freedom and individualism*. As a result, it is levying a contribution from

---

11. Customs gave subsidies to some exporters in order to encourage—or maintain in existence—a specific sector of production. In practice, these subsidies covered the taxes levied on raw materials used by the said industries for the exported products.

the entire community to hand out presents in the form of premiums to the exporters of a particular type of product. Its claim is to be encouraging industry. It should say *one* industry at the expense of *all* the others. I will not stop at showing that it stimulates suckers at the expense of fruit-bearing branches, but I ask you, by going down this path, is it not authorizing every producer to come forward to claim a premium as long as he provides proof that he does not have as much income as his neighbor? Has the state the proper function of listening to and assessing all these requests and acceding to them? I do not think so, but those who believe this must have the courage to clothe their thought in its controlling detail and to say: "The government is not responsible for guaranteeing property but for leveling it. In other words, property does not exist."

I am dealing here only with a question of principle. If I wanted to scrutinize the economic effects of subsidies for exports, I would show them in their most ridiculous light since they are just a free gift made by France to foreigners. It is not the sellers who receive it but the purchaser by virtue of this law that you yourself have noted in connection with taxes: the consumer finally bears all the charges, just as he receives all the advantages of production. For this reason, the most mortifying and mysterious thing possible has happened to us with regard to these premiums. A few foreign governments have reasoned thus: "If we raise our entry duties to a figure equal to the premium paid by French taxpayers, it is clear that nothing will change for our consumers since the cost price for them will be the same. Goods reduced by five francs at the French border will pay five francs more at the German border. This is an infallible way of making the French treasury responsible for our public expenditure." But other governments, I am assured, have been even more ingenious. They said to themselves, "The premium given by France is really a gift made to us, but if we raise the duty, there is no reason for more of these goods to enter our country than in the past; we ourselves are setting a limit on the generosity of these excellent Frenchmen. On the other hand, let us abolish these duties provisionally; let us encourage an unprecedented influx of their cloth in this way, since each meter brings with it a totally free gift." In the first case, our premiums have been to the foreign tax authorities; in the second, they have benefited the ordinary citizens but on a wider scale.

Let us move on to restriction.

I am an artisan, a carpenter, for example. I have a small workshop, tools, and some materials. All of these are unquestionably mine, since I have made them or, what amounts to the same thing, I have purchased and paid for them. What is more, I have vigorous arms, some intelligence, and a great deal of goodwill. These are the funds with which I have to provide for my needs and those of my family. Note that I cannot produce anything that I need directly, whether iron, wood, bread, wine, meat, fabric, etc., but I can produce their *value*. In the end, these things have, so to say, to emerge in another form from my saw and my plane. My interest is to receive honestly as great a quantity as possible for each quantity of my work. I say "honestly" since I do not wish to violate either the property or the person of anyone. However, I have no wish to see anyone violating either my property or my freedom. I and other workers who agree on this point impose sacrifices on ourselves and give up part of our work to men known as civil servants, since we give them the specific function of guaranteeing our work and its proceeds from all forms of attack, whether from within or from without.

With these arrangements in place, I am getting ready to put my intelligence, arms, saw, and plane to work. Naturally, my eyes are constantly fixed on those things that are necessary for my existence. These are the things I have to produce indirectly by creating their *value*. The problem for me is to produce them as advantageously as possible. Consequently I cast a glance over the world of *values,* summed up in what is known as the current price. From the data on the current price I note that the means for me to have the greatest possible quantity of fuel, for example, for the smallest quantity of work is to make an item of furniture and deliver it to a Belgian who in return will give me coal.

However, there is in France a worker who is looking for coal in the bowels of the earth. It so happens that the civil servants whose salary both the miner and I are contributing to in order for each of us to have our freedom to work and the free disposal of our products maintained (which is property), it so happens, I repeat, that these civil servants have conceived another idea and have given themselves a different purpose. They have decided that they ought to *equalize* my work and that of the miner. Consequently, they have forbidden me to heat myself with Belgian coal; and when I go to the border with my item of furniture to collect my coal, I find that these civil servants are preventing the coal from entering, which is the same thing as preventing my item of furniture from leaving. I therefore say to myself: "If we had not thought of paying civil servants to spare us the trouble of defending our property ourselves, would the miner have had the right to go to the border and forbid me a profitable trade on the pretext that it is better for him that this trade not be concluded?" Certainly not. If he had made such an unjust attempt, we would have fought on the spot, he driven by his unjust claim and I fired up by my right of legitimate defense. We had cast our votes and paid a civil servant precisely to avoid fights like this. How, therefore, is it that I find the miner and the civil servant in agreement to restrict my freedom and hard work in order to reduce the sphere in which my talents may be exercised? If the civil servant had taken my side, I would understand his right; it would derive from mine, since legitimate defense is a genuine right. But where has he drawn the right to help the miner in his injustice? I learn from all this that the civil servant has changed his role. He is no longer a simple mortal invested with his own rights delegated to him by other men who, in consequence, possessed them. No. He is a being superior to humanity, drawing his rights from himself, and among his rights, he arrogates to himself that of leveling profits and keeping the balance between all forms of position and condition. All very good, say I; in this case I will overwhelm him with claims and requests as soon as I see someone richer than me anywhere in this country. He will not listen to you, I am told, for if he listened to you he would be a communist and he does not forget that his mission is to *guarantee* property, not to level it.

What chaos and confusion reigns in the facts! And how can you expect chaos and confusion not to reign in men's minds? You may well be fighting against communism; as long as you are seen to accommodate, cherish, and flatter it in that part of the legislation it has invaded, your efforts will be in vain. It is a snake that, with your approval and care, has slipped its head into our laws and behavior, and now you are indignant at seeing its tail show itself in turn!

It is possible, sir, that you will make me a concession. Perhaps you will tell me the "protectionist regime is based on the principle of communism. It is contrary to law, property, and freedom. It ejects the government from its path and invests it with arbitrary attributions that have no rational basis. All this is only too true, but the protectionist regime is useful; without it the country would succumb to foreign competition and be ruined."

This would lead us to examine restriction from an economic point of view. Setting aside any consideration of justice, right, equity, property, and freedom, we would have to settle the question of pure utility, the question of what is purchasable, so to speak; and you will agree that this is not my subject. Incidentally, take care that in using utility to justify a contempt for right, you are in effect saying: "Communism, plunder, although condemned by justice, may nevertheless be accepted as being expedient." And you will agree that an admission like this would be full of danger.

Without seeking to solve the economic problem here, I ask you to allow me one assertion. I declare that I have subjected the advantages and disadvantages of protectionism, from the sole point of view of wealth, to arithmetical calculation, setting aside any consideration of a higher order. I also declare that I have reached the following result: that any restrictive measure has one advantage and two disadvantages, or, if you prefer, one profit and two losses, with each of these losses being equal to the profit and thus giving rise to a clear and definite loss, which provides the consoling proof that, in this as in many other things, and I dare say in everything, utility and justice agree.

True, this is just a statement, but it can be proved mathematically.

What causes public opinion to err on this point is that the profit due to protectionism is visible to the naked eye, whereas of the two equal losses it brings in its wake one is infinitely divided between the citizens and the other is visible only to the eye of an investigative mind.

Without claiming to do this demonstration here, I ask you to allow me to outline its basis.

Two products, A and B, have a normal value of 50 and 40 in France. Let us suppose that in Belgium A is worth only 40. This being so, if France is subject to a restrictive regime, she will be able to enjoy the use of A and B by diverting a quantity equal to 90 from her total output since she will be reduced to producing A directly. If she were free, this amount of effort, equal to 90, would come to: 1. the production of B, which she would deliver to Belgium to obtain A; 2. the production of another B for herself; and 3. the production of some good C.

It is this part of the effort made available in the second case for the subsequent production of C, that is to say the creation of a new good equal to 10, without France thereby being deprived of either A or B, that is difficult to understand. Substitute iron for A; wine, silk, and Parisian articles for B; and loss of wealth for C; you will always find that restriction limits national well-being.[12]

Do you wish to abandon this heavy algebra? I am happy to. You will not

---

12. (Paillottet's note) See in vol. 2 the articles titled "One Profit for Two Losses" and "Two Losses for One Profit." (*OC,* vol. 2, p. 377, "Un profit contre deux pertes," and p. 384, "Deux pertes contre un profit.")

deny that while the prohibitionist regime has achieved some good for the coal industry, it is only by raising the price of coal.[13] You will not deny either that this excess price from 1822 to the present has caused every person who uses this form of fuel a higher expenditure for each such usage, in other words, that this excess price represents a *loss*. Can it be said that the producers of coal, in addition to the interest on their capital and the ordinary profits to the industry, have received *excess profit* through restriction that is equivalent to this loss? If that were the case, protection, while remaining unjust, odious, plundering, and communistic, would be at least *neutral* from the purely economic point of view. It would then deserve to be equated to plunder of the basic kind, which displaces wealth without destroying it. But you yourself declare on page 236 "that the mines in the Aveyron, in Alais, Saint-Etienne, Creuzot, and Anzin, the best known, have not produced an income of 4 percent of the capital committed!" In order for capital in France to yield 4 percent, no protection is needed. Where then is the profit here to compensate for the loss described above?

This is not all. There is another form of national loss here. Since through the relative increase in price of the fuel all the users of coal have lost money, they have had to restrict their other forms of consumption proportionally and the total of national production has of necessity been reduced by this measure. This is the loss that is never included in the calculations since it is not obvious.

Allow me one more observation that to my surprise has not struck others more. It is that protection applied to the products of agriculture is shown in all its odious iniquity with regard to those known as the Proletariat while causing damage in the long run to landowners themselves.

Let us imagine a South Sea island whose land has become the private property of a certain number of inhabitants.

Let us imagine that on this territory that has been appropriated and marked out there is a proletarian population that is constantly increasing, or tending to increase.[14]

---

13. The cost of French coal after extraction was on average 9.76 francs per ton. France imported one-third of its consumption of coal from the United Kingdom and Belgium. The import duty was 6 francs for the British coal and 3 francs for the Belgian coal coming by land.

14. (Paillottet's note) See in this volume the third letter of the article titled "Property and Plunder," pp. 407ff. (*OC*, vol. 4, p. 394, "Propriété et spoliation," pp. 407ff.) [See also "Property and Plunder," p. 157 in this volume.]

This latter class will never be able to produce *directly* the things that are essential to life. They will need to sell their labor to men who are in a position to supply them in exchange with food and even materials of work: cereals, fruit, vegetables, meat, wool, flax, leather, wood, etc.

Obviously it is in their interest that the market in which these things are sold be as wide as possible. The more they are faced with a greater abundance of these agricultural products, the more they will receive for each given quantity of their own output.

Under a free regime, a fleet of boats will be seen going to seek foodstuffs and materials on neighboring islands and continents and carrying in payment manufactured products. The owners will benefit from all the prosperity they have the right to expect. A just balance will be maintained between the value of industrial production and that of agricultural production.

However, in these circumstances, the landowners of the island make the following calculation: If we prevented the proletarians from working for foreigners and receiving in exchange subsistence and raw materials, they would be obliged to call upon us. As their number is growing unceasingly and the competition between them is increasingly active, they would rush to obtain the portion of food and materials remaining for sale after we had taken what we needed, and we could not fail to sell our products at a very high price. In other words, the balance will be upset between the relative value of their work and ours. They would devote a greater number of hours of labor to our satisfaction. Let us therefore pass a law forbidding this trade that is hampering us, and to execute this law let us create a body of civil servants, for the payment of which the proletariat will be taxed along with us.

I ask you, would this not be the utmost oppression, a flagrant violation of the most precious of all freedoms, of the first and most sacred of all property?

However, and note this well, it would perhaps not be difficult for landowners to have this law accepted as a benefit by the workers. They would not fail to tell them:

"We have not done this for ourselves, honest creatures, but for you. Our interest concerns us little; we are thinking only of yours. Through this wise measure, agriculture will prosper. We the landowners will become rich, which will enable us to give you a great deal of work and pay you a good wage. Without it we will be reduced to destitution, and what will become of you? The island will be flooded with subsistence goods and materials of work from abroad, your ships will be constantly at sea; what a national catastrophe! It is true that abundance would reign around you, but would you be part of it? Do not say that your wages would be maintained and increased, because foreigners would do nothing save increase the number of people demanding what you produce. What makes you sure that they will not take the fancy of delivering you their products for nothing? If this happened, you would die of starvation surrounded by abundance, since you would no longer have either work or a wage. Believe us, accept our law gratefully. Increase and multiply; what is left of provisions on the island beyond what we consume will be delivered to you for your work, of which, in this way, you will always be sure. Above all, do not allow yourself to think that this is a war of words between you and us in which your freedom and property are at risk. Never listen to those that tell you so. Take it as fact that the real conflict is between you and foreigners, those barbarous foreigners, may God curse them, who obviously want to exploit you by offering you deceitful transactions that you are free to accept or reject."

It is not unlikely that a speech such as this, suitably seasoned with sophisms on money, the balance of trade, national production, agriculture that feeds the nation, the prospect of war, etc., etc., would be hugely successful and would gain approval for the oppressive decree by those oppressed themselves, if they were consulted. This has happened before and will happen again.

But the prejudices of landowners and the proletariat do not change the nature of things. The result will be a population that is destitute, hungry, ignorant, corrupted, and devastated by starvation, illness, and vice. The result will also be the dreadful shipwreck in people's minds of the notions of right, property, freedom, and the proper attributes of the state.

And what I would like to be able to demonstrate here is that the punishment will shortly reach the landowners themselves; they will have prepared their own ruin by ruining the consuming public, since, in this island, the increasingly indigent population will be seen to fall upon the poorest food. Sometimes they will eat chestnuts, sometimes corn, at other times millet, buckwheat, oats, and potatoes. They will forget the taste of wheat and meat. Landowners will be totally astonished to see agriculture decline. They will in vain agitate, form themselves into agricultural associations, and eternally hark back to the famous adage, "Make forage; with forage you have cattle, with cattle, fertilizer, and with fertilizer, wheat." They will in vain create new taxes to distribute subsidies to producers of clover and alfalfa; they will always be thwarted by the obstacle of a destitute population incapable of paying for meat and consequently of giving the slightest impetus to this hackneyed circle. They will end by learning at their own expense that it is better to be subject to competition and face rich customers than to have a monopoly and be faced with a ruined customer base.

This is why I say: "Not only is prohibition communism, but it is the worst kind of communism. It starts by subjecting the faculties and work of the poor, their sole property, to the discretion of the rich, it leads to a clear loss for the masses and ends by enveloping the rich themselves in the common ruin. It invests the state with the singular right to take from those with little in order to give to those with a great deal; and when, by virtue of this principle, the disinherited people of the world invoke the intervention of the state to achieve a leveling in the opposite direction, I really do not know what the state will be able to reply. In any case, the initial and best response would be to renounce oppression.

But I am eager to finish with these calculations. After all, what is the state of the debate? What are we saying and what do you say? There is one point, a capital point, on which we agree: that the intervention of the legislator to level wealth by taking from some what is needed to gratify others is *communism,* the death of all work, all forms of saving, all well-being, all justice, and all society.

You notice that this disastrous doctrine is invading journals and books in all its forms, in a word, the field of intellectual speculation; and you attack it there vigorously.

For my part, I think I see that it had previously penetrated legislation and the practical world with your consent and assistance, and it is here that I am striving to combat it.

I would next draw your attention to the inconsistency into which you would fall if, while combating the prospect of communism, you were to treat it in action with consideration or, even worse, encourage it.

If your reply is: "I am acting in this way because although communism carried out by customs duties is opposed to freedom, property, and justice, it is nevertheless in accord with general utility and this consideration makes me discount by comparison all others." If this is your answer, do you not feel that you are destroying in advance the entire success of your book, limiting its range, depriving it of its force, and acknowledging that communists of all shades are right, at least with regard to the philosophical and moral aspects of the question?

And then, sir, could a mind as enlightened as yours accept the hypothesis of radical antagonism between utility and justice? Would you like me to be frank? Rather than venture such a subversive and impious statement, I would prefer to say, "This is a particular question in which, at first sight, it seems to me that utility and justice are in conflict. I am glad that all men who have spent their lives examining it in detail think otherwise; I have doubtless not studied it enough." I have not studied it enough! Is this such a painful admission that, to avoid making it, people rush into inconsistency to the extent of denying the wisdom of providential laws which govern the development of human societies? For what more formal negation of divine wisdom is there than to deduce the essential incompatibility of justice and utility! It has always appeared to me that the most cruel form of anguish that can afflict an intelligent and conscientious mind is to stumble at this limit. What side should you join, in fact, what decision should you take in the face of an alternative like this? Should you support utility? This is the path taken by men who consider themselves to be practical. But unless they cannot put two ideas together, they are doubtless appalled at the consequences of systemic plunder and iniquity. Will those who embrace the cause of justice resolutely, whatever it costs, say: "Do what you have to do, whatever the consequences"? This is what honest souls prefer, but who would want to take the responsibility of plunging his country and humanity into destitution, desolation, and death? I defy anyone who is convinced of this antagonism to make up his mind.

I am mistaken. People will decide, and the human heart is so made, that interest will be put before conscience. This is borne out by facts, since everywhere that the protectionist regime has been thought to favor the well-being of the people it has been adopted in spite of any consideration of justice, and then its consequences have occurred. Belief in property has been wiped out. In the spirit of M. Billault it has been said, "Since property has been violated by protection, why should it not be violated by the right to work?" Others after M. Billault will take a third step, and still others behind them a fourth, until communism has taken hold.[15]

Good and sound minds like yours are appalled at the steepness of this slope. They strive to climb back up it and in fact do climb back up, as you have done in your book, to the protectionist regime, which supplies the first and only practical momentum of society on the fatal decline, but in the pres-

---

15. (Paillottet's note) See in vol. 5 the final pages of the pamphlet titled "Plunder and Law." (*OC*, vol. 5, p. 1, "Spoliation et loi," final pages 13–15.) [See also "Plunder and Law," final pages 275–76 in this volume.]

ence of this living negation of the right to property, if instead of this maxim of your book: "Rights either exist or they do not; if they exist they lead to absolute consequences," you substitute this sentence: "Here is a special case in which the national good requires the sacrifice of right," then immediately everything that you believed gave force and reason to your work would be only weakness and inconsistency.

For this reason, sir, if you wish to complete your work, you have to give an opinion on the protectionist regime, and to do this it is essential that you start by solving the economic problem; one has to find out about the alleged usefulness of this regime. For even supposing I obtained from you its condemnation from the point of view of justice, this would not be enough to kill the regime. I repeat, men are so made that when they think they are placed between *real good* and *abstract justice,* the cause of justice is in great danger. Do you want palpable proof of this? This is what happened to me.

When I arrived in Paris, I found myself in the company of so-called democratic and socialist economists in whose circles, as you know, the words *principle, selflessness, sacrifice, fraternity, right,* and *union* are widely used. Wealth is examined from top to bottom as something that is, if not despicable, at least secondary to the point at which, since we take great account of it, we ourselves are seen as being cold economists, egoists, individualists, bourgeois and heartless men whose only God is Mammon.[16] "Good!" I said to myself. "Here are noble hearts with whom I have no need to discuss the economic point of view, which is very subtle and requires more application than Parisian political writers are in general able to give to a study of this nature. With these people, however, the question of interest cannot be an obstacle; either they believe, on the faith of divine wisdom, that interest is in harmony with justice, or they will sacrifice it very willingly, since they thirst after selflessness. If, therefore, they allow that free trade is an abstract right, they will resolutely flock to its banner." Following this, I addressed my appeal to them. Do you know what their answer was? Here it is:

> Your free trade is a splendid utopia. It is based on right and justice, it achieves freedom, it consecrates property, and its consequence will be the union of peoples and the reign of fraternity between men. You are right a thousand times in principle, but we will fight you to the death

16. (Paillottet's note) See in vol. 2 most of the articles under the heading "Polemic Against the Journals," especially the article titled "The Democratic Party and Free Trade." (*OC,* vol. 5, pp. 81–164; and p. 93, "Le Parti démocratique et le libre-échange.")

and by every means because foreign competition will be fatal to national production.

I took the liberty of addressing this reply to them:

I deny that foreign competition would be fatal to national production. In any case, if this were so, you would be positioned between interest, which, according to you, is on the side of restriction; and justice, which, by your own admission, is on the side of freedom! Well, when I, a venerator of the golden calf, call upon you to make a choice, how is it that you, the advocates of abnegation, trample principles underfoot to cling to interest? Do not therefore speak out so fiercely against a motive that governs you as it governs simple mortals.

This experience warned me that, above all, this daunting problem has to be resolved: Is there harmony or antagonism between justice and utility? And consequently the economic aspect of protectionism has to be scrutinized, for since the advocates of fraternity themselves were giving ground over the alleged loss of money, it was becoming clear that it is not enough to remove any doubt concerning universal justice as an ideal; it is also necessary to justify that unworthy, abject, despicable, and despised, albeit all-powerful, motive, interest.

This is what gave rise to a small thesis in two volumes which I am taking the liberty of sending you with this letter,[17] since I am convinced, sir, that if, like the economists, you judge the protectionist regime severely from the moral point of view and if we differ only with regard to its usefulness, you will not refuse to examine carefully the question whether these two major elements in any definitive conclusions are mutually exclusive or are in agreement.

This harmony exists, or at least it is as obvious to me as sunlight. May it also be revealed to you! It would be then that in applying your eminently persuasive talent to fighting communism in its most dangerous manifestation, you would deliver it a mortal blow.

Look at what is happening in England. It would seem that if communism were to find a soil that favored it anywhere, it would be in Britain. There, with feudal institutions everywhere causing extreme deprivation and

17. (Paillottet's note) These two small volumes, which the author indeed sent to M. Thiers, were the first and second series of the *Sophisms*. (*OC,* vol. 4, "Sophismes économiques," p. 1, "Première série," and p. 127, "Deuxième série.")

extreme opulence to confront each other, such conditions ought to have prepared people's minds for infection by false doctrines. And yet, what do we see? While these false doctrines caused unrest on the continent, they did not even ripple the surface of English society. Chartism[18] was not able to take root. Do you know why? Because the association, which for ten years has debated protectionism, has triumphed over it only by shining a strong light on the principle of property and on the rational functions of the state.

Doubtless, if unmasking protectionism is to attack communism for the same reason and because of their close connection, both may also be struck a blow by following the opposite approach from yours. Restriction could not survive very long faced with a proper definition of the right of property. This being so, if one thing surprised me and made me rejoice, it was to see the Association for the Defense of Monopolies[19] devote its resources to distributing your book. This is a highly striking sight and consoles me for the uselessness of my past efforts. This resolution from the Mimerel Committee will doubtless oblige you to increase the number of editions of your work. In this case, allow me to point out to you that in its present state the book has one major gap. In the name of science, in the name of truth, and in the name of public good, I beg you to fill this gap and call upon you to reply to the following two questions:

1. Is there any incompatibility in principle between protectionism and the right to property?
2. Is it the function of government to guarantee to each person the free exercise of his faculties and the free disposal of the fruit of his work, that is to say, property, or is it the government's function to take from some to give to others so as to level out profits, opportunities, and well-being?

Ah, sir, if you reach the same conclusions as me, if through your talent,

---

18. *Chartism* was an English working-class movement that was active from 1838 throughout the 1840s. It took its name from the so-called People's Charter of 1838, which called for the following: full manhood suffrage for those over twenty-one, the removal of the requirement that members of Parliament own a certain minimum of property, the payment of a salary for members of Parliament, the annual election of Parliament, and the creation of equally sized constituencies.

19. Bastiat is being sarcastic here. He is calling the protectionist Association for the Defense of National Work the "Association for the Defense of Monopolies." This association was headed by Pierre Mimerel and Antoine Odier.

reputation, and influence you caused these conclusions to become dominant in public opinion, who can calculate the extent of the service you would be rendering to French society? We would see the state limit itself to its purpose, which is to guarantee to each person the exercise of his faculties and the free disposal of his goods. We would see the state divest itself of both its colossal, illegitimate attributions and the terrifying responsibility they entail. It would limit itself to repressing the abuses of freedom, which is to achieve freedom itself. It would ensure justice for all and would no longer promise wealth to anyone. Citizens would learn to distinguish between what is reasonable to ask of it and what is puerile. They would no longer burden it with claims and demands. They would no longer accuse it of causing their misfortunes. They would not pin illusionary hopes on it, and in the enthusiastic pursuit of good that is not the state's to dispense, they would not be seen at each disappointment to accuse the legislator and the law, change the men and the forms of government, and pile institution on institution and rubble on rubble. We would see the universal fever for mutual plunder through the extremely expensive and risky intervention of the state die out. Once it is limited in its objectives and responsibility, simple in its action, with low expenditure, and no longer burdening those it governs with the cost of their own chains, and is enjoying the support of public good sense, the government would have a solid base, which in our country has never been its lot, and we would finally have resolved this most pressing problem: *the closing forever of the abyss of revolutions.*

## → 13 ←

### *Plunder and Law* [1]

[vol. 5, p. 1. "Spoliation et loi." This pamphlet was first published in the 15 May 1850 issue of *Le Journal des économistes*.]

#### *To Those Who Favor Protectionism in the General Council of Manufacturers*

Sirs, let us converse for a moment in a moderate and friendly way.

You do not wish political economy to believe in and teach free trade.

This is as if you were saying, "We do not want political economy to concern itself with society, exchange, value, right, justice, or property. We recognize two principles only, oppression and plunder."

Can you imagine political economy without society? Society without exchange? Exchange without a means of evaluation between the two objects or two services being exchanged? Can you imagine this rate, known as *value*, as anything other than a result of the *free* agreement of the people doing the exchanging? Can you imagine that a product is *worth* another if, in the exchange, one of the parties is not *free?* [2] Can you imagine free agreement between the parties without freedom? Can you imagine that one of the contracting parties could be deprived of freedom, unless one contracting party is being oppressed by the other? Can you imagine exchange between an oppressor and an oppressed party without the equivalence value of the

---

1. (Paillottet's note) On 27 April 1850, following a very curious discussion, printed in *Le Moniteur*, the General Council on Agriculture, Industry, and Trade issued the following wish:

> That political economy should be taught by teachers paid by the government, not only from the theoretical point of view of free trade but also and above all from the point of view of events and the legislation that governs French industry.

Bastiat was replying to this wish in *Plunder and Law*, first published in the issue of *Le Journal des économistes*, dated 15 May 1850.

2. (Paillottet's note) See the theory of value in chapter 5 of *Economic Harmonies*. (*OC*, vol. 6, chap. 5, p. 140, "De la valeur.")

services being distorted and therefore without rights, justice, and ownership being very seriously infringed?

What do you want? Tell me frankly.

You do not want trade to be free!

Do you therefore want trade not to be free?

Do you therefore want it to be carried out under the influence of oppression? For if it were not carried out under the influence of oppression, it would be carried out under the influence of freedom and that is what you do not want.

Admit it, what is worrying you is right and justice; what is worrying you is ownership—not yours, of course, but that of others. You find it difficult to accept that others are free to dispose of their property (the only way to be an owner); you want to dispose of your property . . . and theirs.

You then require economists to draft into a body of doctrine this jumble of absurdity and monstrosity in order to establish the theory of plunder for your use.

However, this is just what they will never do, for in their view plunder is a principle of hatred and unrest, and if there is a more particularly hateful form for it to take on, it is above all the *legal form*.[3]

---

3. (Paillottet's note) The author had expressed this opinion three years previously in the issue of the journal *Le Libre échange* dated 28 November 1847. In reply to *Le Moniteur industriel,* he had said:

We would ask the reader to forgive us if we become casuists for a moment. Our opponents oblige us to put on our doctor's mortarboard. This is apposite since it often pleases them to refer to us as *doctors.*

An *illegal* act is always *immoral* for the sole reason that it disobeys the law, but it does not follow that it is *immoral* in itself. When a mason (we apologize to our colleague for drawing his attention to such a small point) exchanges his earnings from a hard day's work for a length of Belgian cloth, his action is not intrinsically immoral. It is not the action that is immoral in itself; it is the violation of the law. And the proof of this is that, should the law be changed, no one would find anything wrong with this exchange. It is not immoral in Switzerland. But what is immoral in itself is immoral everywhere and at all times. Will *Le Moniteur industriel* claim that the morality of acts depends on their time and place?

If some acts can be *illegal* without being *immoral,* others are *immoral* without being *illegal.* When our colleague changes our words by trying to find a meaning in them that is not there, when certain people, after privately declaring that they are in favor of freedom, write and vote against it, when a master makes his slave work by beating him, it is possible that the Code is not violated, but

Here, M. Benoît d'Azy, I must take you to task. You are a moderate, impartial, and generous man. You do not set store by your interests and wealth; you are the one who constantly proclaims this. Recently at the General Council you said: "If the rich needed only to give up what they had for the people to be rich, we would all be ready to do it." (Oh yes! That is true!) And yesterday at the National Assembly: "If I thought that it was up to me to give all workers the work they needed, I would give all I owned to achieve this good act . . . which is unfortunately impossible."

Although the pointlessness of the sacrifice occasions in you the great sorrow of not performing it and has you echoing the words of Basile, "Money! Money! I despise it . . . but I am keeping it," surely no one will doubt such striking generosity of mind, whatever its impotence. It is a virtue that likes to shroud itself in a veil of modesty, especially when it is purely inactive and negative. For your part, you do not miss an opportunity to display it in front of the entire country from the pedestal of the rostrum in the Luxembourg

---

the consciences of all honest men are revolted. It is at the head of this category of actions that we place these restrictions. A Frenchman says to another Frenchman who is his equal or ought to be, "I forbid you to buy Belgian cloth because I want you to be obliged to come to my shop. That may upset you but it suits my purpose. You will lose four but I will gain two and that is enough." We would say that this action is immoral. If someone makes so bold as to bring it about himself forcibly or by means of the law, this does not change the character of the act. It is immoral by nature, in essence; it would have been so ten thousand years ago and would be in the Antipodes or on the moon, since whatever *Le Moniteur industriel* says, the law, which can do a great deal, cannot, however, turn something that is bad into good.

We are not even afraid to say that the contribution of the law increases the immorality of the act. If it were not involved, if for example the manufacturer had his restrictive wishes executed by those in his pay, the immorality would be blindingly obvious to *Le Moniteur industriel* itself. What then! Because this manufacturer was able to spare himself this effort, because he was able to appropriate the services of public compulsion and saddle those oppressed with part of the costs of repression, what was immoral has become meritorious!

It is true that the people thus trampled on may imagine that it is for their good and that oppression results from an error common to both oppressors and those oppressed. This is enough to justify the intention and remove from the act the odiousness that it would otherwise have. Where this happens, the majority approves of the law. We have to accept this and would never say otherwise. However, nothing will stop us from telling the majority that in our opinion, it is mistaken.

Palace to the Legislative Palace. This proves that you cannot contain its outbursts although you contain its effects, with regret on your part.

But when it comes to it, no one is asking you to give up your wealth, and I agree that it would not solve the social problem.

You would like to be generous, but you cannot do it to any good purpose. What I venture to ask you is to be just. Keep your wealth, but allow me to keep mine. Respect my property as I respect yours. Is this too bold a request that I am making?

Let us suppose that we were in a country in which free trade held sway, where everyone was able to dispose of his work and property. Does your hair stand on end? Calm yourself; this is only a hypothesis.

We are therefore all just as free as each other. There is indeed a rule of law, but this law, entirely impartial and just, far from undermining our freedom, guarantees it. It comes into action only if we try to exercise oppression, either you of me or I of you. There is public enforcement, there are magistrates and gendarmes, but all they do is to carry out the law.

This being so, you are an ironmaster and I am a hatmaker. I need iron for my own use or for my production. Naturally I ask myself, "How can I procure the iron I need for the least amount of work?" In view of my situation and knowledge, I discover that the best solution for me is to make hats and deliver them to a Belgian who will give me iron in return.

However, you are an ironmaster, and you say to yourself, "I know how to make this rascal (referring to me) come to my company."

Consequently, you adorn your belt with sabers and pistols, arm your many employees, go to the border, and there, when I am on the point of carrying out my exchange, you shout, "Stop, or I will blow your brains out!" "But, my lord, I need iron." "I have some to sell." "But, my lord, yours is very expensive." "There are reasons for this." "But, my lord, I also have reasons for preferring cheaper iron." "Well then, see what is going to decide between your reasons and mine. You fellows, take aim!"

In short, you prevent Belgian iron from entering the country and at the same time you prevent my hats from leaving.

Given the free society we have assumed, you cannot deny that this is a clear act of oppression and plunder on your part.

I therefore quickly call on the law, a magistrate, and public enforcement. They all intervene; you are judged, condemned, and justly punished.

But all this gives you a bright idea.

You say to yourself: "I have been very stupid to go to so much trouble.

What, exposing myself to killing or being killed! Making a journey! Taking my employees with me! Incurring huge expense! Making myself out to be a robber! Deserving to be condemned by the country's courts! All this to oblige a lowly hatmaker to come to my workshop to buy iron at my price! If only I could win over the law, the magistrates, and public enforcement so that they serve my interests! If only I could have them carry out at the border the odious act I was going to do myself!"

Excited by this attractive prospect, you get yourself elected to office and you get legislation enacted with the following provisions:

Article 1: A tax will be levied on everybody (and in particular on my cursed hatmaker).

Article 2: With the product of this tax, we will pay men to guard the border well, in the interests of ironmasters.

Article 3: The guards will ensure that no one can trade hats or other goods with Belgians in return for iron.

Article 4: Ministers, public prosecutors, customs officers, tax collectors, and jailers will be responsible, in their respective domains, for carrying out this law.

I agree, sir, that in this form plunder would be infinitely gentler, more lucrative, and less dangerous for you than in the form you originally envisaged.

I agree that it would have a very pleasant side for you. You would certainly be able to laugh up your sleeve, since you would have burdened me with the entire expense.

However, I assert that you would have introduced into society the basis of ruin, immorality, unrest, hatred, and constant revolution; you would have opened the door to all forms of socialist and communist experimentation.[4]

You will doubtless consider my hypothesis very bold. Well then! Turn it round against me! I am quite willing, given my love of proof.

I am now a worker and you are still an ironmaster.

It would be an advantage for me to acquire the tools of my trade cheaply or even free. However, I know that there are axes and saws in your workshop.

---

4. (Paillottet's note) See "Protectionism and Communism" in vol. 4. (*OC*, vol. 4, p. 504, "Protectionisme et communisme.") [See also "Protectionism and Communism," p. 235 in this volume.]

Therefore, with no further ado, I enter your shop and take everything that I want.

But you, using your right of legitimate defense, initially repel force with force. You then call upon the assistance of the law, magistrates, and public enforcement to have me thrown into prison, and you have acted rightly.

"Oh, dear!" I say to myself, "I have been stupid to do this. When you want to benefit from other people's property, it is not *in spite of* but *by virtue of* the law that you should act if you are not an imbecile. Consequently, since you have become a protectionist, I will become a socialist. As you have arrogated to yourself the right to profit, I invoke the right to work, or to the tools of my trade.

What is more, in prison I read my Louis Blanc and I know this doctrine by heart: "What the proletariat need to throw off their yoke are the tools of their trade, and the function of the government is to give them the tools." And also: "Once you agree that in order to be genuinely free, man needs the power to exercise and develop his faculties, it follows that society owes each one of its members both education, without which the human mind cannot develop, and the tools of his trade, without which human activity cannot forge a career for itself. But by whose intervention will society give each one of its members a suitable education and the tools of his trade that he needs if it is not by the intervention of the state?"[5]

Therefore, I, too, storm the doors of the Legislative Palace, even at the cost of causing a revolution in my country. I corrupt the law and make it accomplish the very act for which it had hitherto punished me, for my benefit and at your expense.

My decree is based on yours.

Article 1: A tax will be levied on all citizens and especially on ironmasters.

Article 2: With the product of this tax, the state will pay an armed body titled the *Fraternal Gendarmerie*.

Article 3: The fraternal gendarmes will enter stores that sell axes, saws, etc., seize these instruments, and distribute them to the workers who want them.

5. (Bastiat's note) *Organization of Work,* pages 17 and 24 of the introduction [Blanc, *L'Organisation du travail*].

As you can see, sir, through this clever arrangement I will no longer run the risk nor incur the expense, opprobrium, or scruples of plunder. The state will rob for me as it does for you. There will be two of us playing the game.

It remains to be seen what will become of French society if my second hypothesis comes true, or at least what it has become following the almost complete realization of the first.

I do not want to deal here with the question from the point of view of economics. People believe that when we demand free trade, we are solely driven by a desire to leave labor and capital free to take the most advantageous route. People are mistaken. This is only a secondary consideration for us. What wounds us, what distresses us, and what terrifies us about the protectionist regime is that it is the negation of rights, justice, and property; that it turns the law, which should guarantee property and justice, against them; and that it thus overturns and corrupts the conditions of the existence of society. And it is on this aspect of the question that I call on you to meditate most seriously.

What therefore is the law or at least what ought it to be? What is its rational and moral mission? Is it not to hold accurately the balance between all forms of right, all forms of freedom, and all forms of ownership? Is it not to ensure that justice reigns over all? Is it not to prevent and eliminate oppression and plunder, wherever they are found?

And are you not appalled by the immense, radical, and deplorable innovation that is introduced into the world on the day on which the law is made responsible for carrying out itself the crime whose punishment was its mission? The day on which it turns against freedom and ownership, both in principle and deed?

You deplore the symptoms exhibited by modern society. You bewail the unrest that reigns in institutions and in ideas. But is it not your principles that have corrupted everything, both in institutions and ideas?

What! The law is no longer a refuge for the oppressed but the arm of the oppressor! The law is no longer a shield but a sword! The law no longer holds in its august hands a set of scales but false weights and false keys. And you want society to be properly organized!

It is your principles that have written the following words on the pediment of the Legislative Chamber: "Whoever acquires any influence here may obtain his share of legal plunder here."

And what has happened? Each class has rushed to the doors of this palace shouting, "For me, too, I want my share of plunder!"

Following the February revolution, when universal suffrage was proclaimed, I hoped for a moment that its great voice would be heard to say: "No more plunder for anyone, justice for all!" And in that lay the true solution of the social problem. This did not happen; protectionist propaganda had for centuries past effected too deep a change in sentiments and ideas.

No, by bursting into the National Assembly, each class came to make the law an instrument of plunder for itself according to the principles you uphold. They demanded progressive taxes, free credit, the right to work, the right to state assistance, guaranteed interest rates, a minimum rate of pay, free education, subsidies to industry, etc., etc.; in short, each wanted to live and develop at other people's expense.

And under what authority have these claims been levied? Following precedents you set yourselves. What sophisms were invoked? Those that you have been propagating for centuries. Like you, people have been talking of *leveling the conditions of work.*[6] Like you, people have spoken out against *anarchical competition.* Like you, people have scorned *laissez-faire,* that is to say, *freedom.* Like you, people have said that the law should not limit itself to being just but should come to the aid of tottering industries, protect the weak from the strong, ensure profits for individuals at the expense of the community, etc., etc. In short, as M. Charles Dupin said, socialism has come to put the theory of plunder into practice. It has done what you do and what you want teachers of political economy to do, with you and for you.

It is no good your being clever, you people who support restriction; it is no good softening the tone, boasting of your hidden generosity or winning over your opponents through appealing to sentiment; you will not stop logic from being logic.

You will not stop M. Billault from saying to the legislator, "You are giving favors to some people; you must give them to everyone."

You will not stop M. Crémieux from saying to the legislator, "You are making manufacturers richer; you must make the proletariat richer."

You will not stop M. Nadeau from saying to the legislator, "You cannot refuse to do for the suffering classes what you do for those that are privileged."

You will not even stop M. Mimerel, your leader of the chorus, from saying to the legislator, "I demand twenty-five thousand francs worth of subsidies for workers' retirement funds," and developing his motion thus:

6. See *OC,* vol. 4, p. 27, "Égaliser les conditions de production" (Sophism no. 4).

Is this the first example of this nature that our legislation is offering? Will you establish a system in which the state is able to encourage everything, open science courses at its expense, subsidize fine arts, give grants to theaters, provide higher education, a wide variety of leisure pursuits, enjoyment of the arts, and rest in old age to the classes that are already favored by wealth, and give all this to those who have not experienced deprivation, making those who have nothing pay for their part in this deprivation, refusing them everything, even the essential items of life? . . .

Sirs, our society in France, our behavior, and our laws are so organized that the intervention of the state, as regrettable as you may think it, is found everywhere, and nothing appears stable or long-lasting if the state does not play a part in it. It is the state that makes Sèvres porcelain and the Gobelins tapestries. It is the state that exhibits periodically and at its expense the works of our artists and our manufacturers. It is the state that rewards our stockbreeders and our fishing fleets. All this costs a great deal; this is yet another tax that everyone pays; everyone, let that be understood! And what direct benefit do the people gain from this? What direct benefit do your porcelains, tapestries, and exhibitions give them? We can understand this principle of resisting what you call a state of being carried along, although only yesterday you voted for grants for flax. We can understand this on condition that the weather is considered and above all on condition that impartiality is clearly evident. If it is true that, through all the means I have just indicated, the state has appeared up till now to come to the aid of the comfortably off classes rather than those less favored, *it is essential for this appearance to disappear.* Will this be by closing the Gobelins factory or forbidding exhibitions? Certainly not but by *giving the poor a direct share in this distribution of benefits.*"[7]

In this long list of favors granted to a few at the expense of all, you will note the extreme reticence with which M. Mimerel glosses over customs favors,[8] even though they are the most explicit expression of legal plunder. All the speakers who supported or contradicted him were equally reticent. That is very clever! Perhaps they hoped that by *giving the poor a direct share in this distribution of benefits,* they would preserve the great iniquity from which they benefit but never mention.

7. (Bastiat's note) The issue of *Le Moniteur* dated 28 April 1850.
8. As indicated in "Protectionism and Communism," p. 252, note 11, in this volume customs gave subsidies to some exporters in order to encourage—or maintain in existence—a specific industrial sector.

They are deluding themselves. Do they believe that once they have achieved partial plunder through the institution of customs, other classes will not want, through other institutions, to achieve universal plunder?

I am fully aware that you always have a sophism at the ready; you say: "The favors that the law grants us are not intended for industrialists, but for industry. The products they enable us to skim off at the expense of consumers are just a deposit in our hands."[9]

"They make us rich, it is true; but our wealth, which enables us to spend more and increase the size of our businesses, falls like fertile dew on the working class."

This is your language, and what I deplore is that your dreadful sophisms have corrupted the public mind enough for them to be quoted today to support all the processes of legal plunder. The suffering classes also say: "Let us take the goods of others through law. We will be more comfortably off; we will buy more wheat, more meat, more cloth, more iron and what we will have received through taxes will return as a beneficial rain on capitalists and landowners."

However, as I have already said, I am not discussing today the economic consequences of legal plunder. When the supporters of protectionism are ready, they will find me ready to examine the *ricochet sophism*[10,11] which, besides, can be quoted for all sorts of theft and fraud.

Let us limit ourselves to the political and moral effects of trade that is deprived of freedom by the law.

I say this, the time has come to establish finally what the law is and what it ought to be.

If you make the law the safeguard of freedom and property for all citizens, if it is limited to the organization of the individual right of legitimate defense, you will found on justice a government that is rational, uncompli-

---

9. (Bastiat's note) The issue of *Le Moniteur* dated 28 April. See the opinion of M. Devinck.

10. (Paillottet's note) This is implicitly refuted in chapter 12 of the first series and chapters 4 and 12 of the second series of "Sophisms." (*OC,* vol. 4, chap. 12, p. 74, "La Protection élève-t-elle le taux des salaires?"; chap. 4, p. 160, "Conseil inférieur du travail," and chap. 12, p. 213, "Le Sel, la poste, la douane.")

11. *Ricochet sophism* is best translated as "the sophism of indirect consequences." The allusion is to the sophists, who pretend that there are very beneficial, indirect consequences to some duties for which they are asking.

cated, economical, understood by all, loved by all, useful to all, supported by all, given responsibility that is perfectly defined, highly restricted, and endowed with unshakeable solidity.

If, on the other hand, you make the law an instrument of plunder in the interest of particular individuals and classes, each one at first would want to make the law and each would then want to make it to his advantage. There would be a throng at the gates of the Legislative Palace, a bitter battle within it, anarchy in people's minds, the wreck of all morality, violence in the institutions representing various interests, fierce electoral battles, accusations, recriminations, jealousy, inextinguishable hatred, public enforcement in the service of unjust greed instead of containment of greed, the concept of right and wrong obliterated from people's minds just as the concept of justice and injustice is obliterated from all consciences, a government that is responsible for each person's existence and that is bowed under the weight of such responsibility, political convulsions, and fruitless revolutions and ruins on which all forms of socialism and communism will be tried out. These are the scourges that corruption of the law will not fail to unleash.

Consequently, oh you supporters of prohibition, these are the scourges to which you have opened the door by using the law to stifle free trade, that is to say, to stifle the right to property. Do not speak out against socialism; you are promoting it. Do not speak out against communism; you are promoting it. And now you are asking us economists to provide you with a theory that proves you are right and justifies you! Heavens above! Do it yourselves.[12]

---

12. (Paillottet's note) In this response to the protectionists, which he addressed to them on his departure for the Landes, the author, obliged to give his views rapidly on the rational domain of legislation, felt the need to set them out in more detail. He did this a few days later during a short stay in Mugron when he wrote *The Law,* a pamphlet included in this volume. (*OC,* vol. 4, p. 342, "La Loi.") [See also "The Law," p. 107 in this volume.]

[vol. 5, p. 16. "Guerre aux chaires
d'économie politique." June 1847. n.p.]

We know with what bitterness men who restrict the trade of others for their
own advantage complain that political economy stubbornly refuses to extol
the merit of these restrictions. Although they do not hope to obtain the
elimination of science, at least they pursue the dismissal of those who teach
it, retaining from the Inquisition this wise maxim, "If you wish to get the
better of your opponents, then shut their mouths."

We were therefore not surprised to learn that to mark the draft law on the
organization of the university, they addressed to the minister of education a
lengthy memorandum, from which we quote a few excerpts here:

"Do you really mean it, minister? Do you wish to introduce the teaching
of political economy in the university! Is this a deliberate act to discredit
our privileges?"

"If there is one venerable maxim, it is most assuredly this: In any country,
education ought to be in harmony with the principle of government. Do you

1. The teaching of political economy (essentially liberal) began rather late in France.
From 1815 Jean-Baptiste Say taught at the Athénée and then at the Conservatoire na-
tional des arts et métiers. Under the July Monarchy, two chairs were created: one at the
Collège de France, in 1831, occupied first by Say and then by Pellegrino Rossi and Michel
Chevalier; the other was created at the École des ponts et chaussées in 1846. It was oc-
cupied by Joseph Garnier.

2. (Paillottet's note) Three years before the demonstration that triggered the preceding pamphlet [Paillottet is referring to "Plunder and Law"], the removal of professors
and the abolition of chairs of political economy had been formally requested by the
members of the Mimerel Committee, who shortly afterward softened their position and
limited themselves to claiming that the theory of protectionism should be taught at the
same time as that of free trade.

Bastiat used the weapon of irony to combat this revised proposal, now surfacing for
the first time, in the issue of the journal *Le Libre-échange* dated 13 June 1847.

think that in Sparta or Rome the treasury would have paid teachers to speak out against the plunder resulting from war or against slavery? And you want to allow restrictionism to be discredited in France!"[3]

"Nature, sir, has so ordained things that society can exist only on the products of work, and at the same time it has made work burdensome. This is why in all eras and in all countries an incurable propensity for mutual pillage has been noted in men. It is so pleasant to lay the burden on one's neighbor and keep the payment for oneself!"

"War is the first means that people thought of. There is no shorter and simpler way of seizing other people's property."

"Then followed slavery, which is a more subtle means, and it has been proved that reducing prisoners to servitude instead of killing them was a major step toward civilization."

"Last, the passage of time has substituted for these two crude means of plunder another that is more subtle and for this very reason has much more likelihood of lasting, especially since its very name, *protection,* is admirably suited to dissimulating its odious aspect. You are not unaware of the way names can sometimes deceive us in regard to the bad side of things."

"As you see, minister, preaching against protectionism in modern times or against slavery in ancient times is exactly the same thing. It always undermines social order and upsets the peace of mind of a very respectable class of citizens. And if pagan Rome showed great wisdom and a farsighted spirit of conservation in persecuting the new sect that arose within its midst to proclaim aloud the dangerous words *peace* and *fraternity,* why should we have any more pity for professors of political economy? However, our customs are so gentle and our moderation so great that we do not require you to deliver them to the wild beasts. Forbid them to speak and we will be satisfied."

"Or at least, if they are so intent on speaking, can they not do this with a degree of impartiality? Can they not trim science a bit to suit our wishes? By what quirk of fate have professors of political economy all agreed to turn the weapon of reason against the protectionist dispensation? If this has certain disadvantages, surely it also has advantages since it suits us. Might our professors not gloss over the disadvantages a bit more and highlight the advantages?"

"Besides, what are scholars for if not to make science? What stops them

3. (Paillottet's note) This is the origin of *Baccalaureate and Socialism,* which will become even more apparent in the following pages. (*OC,* vol. 4, p. 442, "Baccalauréat et socialisme.") [See also "Baccalaureate and Socialism," p. 185 in this volume.]

from inventing a form of political economy specially for us? Obviously it is a case of ill will on their part. When the Sacred Inquisition of Rome found it impious that Galileo had the earth rotating, this great man did not hesitate to have it immobile again. He even declared it to be so on his knees. It is true that as he rose, it is said that he murmured, '*E pur si muove.*'[4] Let our professors declare publicly and on their knees that *freedom is worth nothing,* and we will pardon them if they mutter, on condition that they do it with clenched teeth, '*E pur è buona.*'"[5]

"But second, we want to push moderation still further. You will not disagree, minister, that we must be impartial first and foremost. Well then! Since there are two conflicting doctrines in the world, one whose motto is 'Leave trade alone' and the other 'Prevent trade,' for goodness' sake keep the balance equal and have one taught as well as the other. Give the order that our political economy should be taught in this way."

"Is it not very discouraging to see science always on the side of freedom, and should it not share its favors a little? No, no sooner is a chair instituted than, like the head of the Medusa, we see the face of a *free trader* appear."

"In this way, J. B. Say set an example that MM Blanqui, Rossi, Michel Chevalier, and Joseph Garnier were quick to follow. What would have become of us if your predecessors had not taken great care to limit this disastrous form of teaching? Who knows? This very year we would have had to endure cheap bread."

"In England, Adam Smith, Senior, and a thousand others caused the same scandal. What is more, Oxford University instituted a chair of political economy and appointed ... whom? A future archbishop,[6] and lo and behold, his grace started to teach that religion agreed with science in condemning the part of our profits that arose from a protectionist regime. So what happened? Little by little, public opinion was won over, and before two years were out, the English had the misfortune of being free to buy and sell. May they be ruined as they well deserve!"

"The same thing happened in Italy. Kings, princes, and dukes, both great and small, were imprudent enough to tolerate the teaching of economics without laying an obligation on professors to reconcile science with protectionism. A host of professors, men like Genovesi and Beccaria, and in

4. "And yet it moves."
5. "And yet it is good."
6. (Paillottet's note) Mr. Whately, the archbishop of Dublin, who founded a chair of political economy there, held the professorship at Oxford.

our time M. Scialoja, as might be expected, began to preach freedom; and here we have Tuscany free to trade and there we have Naples cutting swathes through its customs duties."

"You know the results achieved in Switzerland by the intellectual movement that has always directed men's minds toward economic knowledge there. Switzerland is free and seems to be situated in the center of Europe, like light on a chandelier, deliberately to embarrass us. For when we say, 'The result of freedom is to ruin agriculture, trade, and industry,' people do not fail to point Switzerland out to us. For a time, we did not know what to answer. Thank goodness *La Presse* solved our problem by supplying us with this invaluable argument, '*Switzerland can cope because it is small.*'"

"The curse of science is threatening to let loose the same plague on Spain. Spain is the very home of protection. And just see how it has prospered! And not counting the treasure she has drained from the New World and the richness of her soil, her prohibitionist policy is sufficient to explain the degree of splendor that she has achieved. However, Spain has professors of political economy, men like La Sagra and Florez Estrada, and so we find the minister of finance, M. Salamanca, aiming to raise Spain's credit and increase her budget just through the power of free trade."

"Last, minister, what more do you want? In Russia, there is only one economist and he is in favor of free trade."[7]

"As you can see, the conspiracy of all the world's scholars against the fettering of trade is flagrant. And what interest is urging them on? None. If they preached protectionism, they would be no leaner, no worse off. It is therefore pure wickedness on their part. This unanimity holds the greatest dangers. Do you know what people will say? Seeing them so closely in agreement, people will end up believing that what unites them in the same belief is the same reason that causes all the geometers around the world since Archimedes to think the same way regarding the square of the hypotenuse."

"When therefore, minister, we beg you to have two contradictory doctrines taught impartially, it can be only a secondary request on our part, since we can guess what will happen, and he whom you make responsible for teaching restriction may well, through his study, be brought to the path of freedom."

"The best thing is to outlaw science and scholars once and for all and return to the wise traditions of the empire. Instead of instituting new chairs

---

7. Bastiat is probably referring to Henri-Frédéric Storch.

of political economy, abolish those—fortunately they are few—that are still standing. Do you know how political economy has been defined? *The science that teaches workers to keep what belongs to them.* It is quite clear that a good quarter of the human race would be lost if this disastrous science happened to spread."

"Let us hold on to a good and harmless classical education. Let us fill our young people with Greek and Latin. What harm will it do us if they scan the hexameters of the *Bucolics*[8] on the tips of their fingers from morning to night? Let them live with Roman society, with the Gracchi and Brutus, within a Senate in which war is constantly discussed and a Forum in which the question of plunder is constantly to the fore; let them become imbued with the sweet philosophy of Horace:

> Tra la la la our youth
> Tra la la la is shaped there.

"What need is there to teach them the laws of production and trade? Rome teaches them to despise work, *servile opus,* and not to recognize as legitimate any other trade than the *vae victis* of the warrior who owns slaves. In this way, we will have a young generation well prepared for life in our modern society. There are indeed a few small dangers. Our young people will be somewhat republican, they will have strange ideas on freedom and property, and in their blind admiration for brute force they will perhaps be found to be somewhat disposed to find fault with the whole of Europe and to deal with political questions in the street by throwing cobblestones. This is inevitable, and frankly, minister, thanks to Titus Livy we have all more or less paddled in this rut. After all, these are questions that you can easily overcome with a few good gendarmes. But what gendarmerie can you call out against the subversive ideas of economists, the daring people who have inscribed at the top of their program this atrocious definition of property: When a man has produced something by the sweat of his brow, since he has the right to consume it, he has the right to exchange it?[9]

"No, no, with people like this, it is a waste of time to resort to rebuttal."

"Quick, a gag, two gags, three gags!"

8. This is a reference to the *Eclogues,* or *Bucolics,* of the Roman poet Virgil (70–19 B.C.). The *Eclogues* were pastoral poems depicting a rural Arcadia but set during a time of land confiscations by the Roman state.

9. (Paillottet's note) See the declaration of the principles of [Free Trade] Society in *Le Libre-échange* in vol. 2. (*OC,* vol. 2, p. 1, "Déclaration.")

[vol. 5, p. 407. "Paix et liberté ou le budget
républicain." February 1849. n.p.]

A program! A program! That is the cry that rises from all sides to the cabinet.[2]

How do you understand home affairs? What will your foreign policy be? Through what major measures do you mean to raise revenue? Are you undertaking to remove from us the triple plague that appears to be hovering over our heads: war, revolution, and bankruptcy? Will we at last be able to devote ourselves in some degree of security to work, enterprise, and major undertakings? What have you drawn up to ensure for us the *tomorrow* you promised to all citizens the day you took the helm of our affairs?

This is what everyone is asking, but alas! the minister makes no reply. What is worse, he appears to be systematically determined not to say anything.

What should we conclude from this? Either the cabinet has no plan, or, if it has one, it is hiding it.

Well then, I say that, in either case, the cabinet is failing in its duty. If it is hiding its plan, it is doing something it has no right to do, since a government plan does not belong to the government but to the public. We are the ones interested in the plan, since our well-being and security depend on it. We ought to be governed not according to the hidden intentions of the government but according to intentions that are known and approved. It

---

1. (Paillottet's note) A pamphlet published in February 1849. One month earlier in *Le Journal des débats,* the author had written an article that we are copying at the end of *Peace and Freedom* because it is on the same subject.

2. On the very day of his election as president of the Republic, Louis-Napoléon Bonaparte appointed a cabinet. It was headed by Odilon Barrot and included a number of outstanding personalities, among them two well-known liberals, Hyppolite Passy (finance) and Léon Faucher (public works and the interior).

is up to the cabinet to set out, propose, and take the initiative, up to us to judge it, accept or refuse it. But in order to judge, we need knowledge. He who climbs onto the driving seat and takes the reins is declaring by this very act that he knows or thinks he knows the destination to be reached and the route that must be taken. At the very least he should not keep destination and route a secret from the travelers when these travelers form the whole of a great nation.

If there is no plan,[3] let him judge for himself what he must do. In all eras government calls for an idea, and this is especially true today. It is very clear that we can no longer follow the same old ruts, the ruts that have already overturned the coach in the mud three times. The *status quo* is impossible and tradition inadequate. Reforms are needed, and although the words have a hollow ring, I will say, "We need something new," not something new that undermines, overturns, and terrifies, but something new that maintains, consolidates, reassures, and rallies.

Therefore, in my ardent desire to see a genuine republican budget appear, and discouraged by government silence, I remembered the old proverb, "If you want something done properly, do it yourself," and to be sure of having a program I drew one up. I submit it to the public's good sense.

And first of all, I have to tell you in what spirit it was conceived.

I love the Republic, and, to make an admission that may surprise some people,[4] I add that I like it much better than on 24 February.[5] These are my reasons.

Like all political writers, even those from the monarchical school, including Chateaubriand among others, I believe that a republic is the natural form of normal government. The people, the king, and the aristocracy are three powers that can coexist only during their conflict. This conflict has armistices known as charters. Each power stipulates in these charters a part that relates to its victories. It is in vain that theoreticians have intervened and said, "The height of art is to settle the attributions of the three jousters in such a way that they counter each other mutually." The nature of things or-

3. There is a misprint in Paillottet's edition, where "plan" is printed as "pain" (bread). We have checked it against the original pamphlet, "Paix et liberté ou le budget républicain" (Paris: Guillaumin, 1849), p. 6.

4. (Paillottet's note) On the political views of the author, see in vol. 1 his articles and political manifestos published on the occasion of the elections (*OC,* vol. 1, p. 506, "Profession de foi électorale de 1848," and p. 507, "Profession de foi électorale de 1849.")

5. Revolution of 1848.

dains that during and because of the truce one of the three powers strengthens and grows in stature. The conflict starts once more and then comes lassitude resulting in a new charter, one that is slightly more democratic, and so on until the republican regime triumphs.

However, it may happen that once the people have achieved self-government they govern themselves badly. They suffer and long for a change. The exiled claimant takes advantage of the opportunity and reascends the throne. At this, the conflict, the truces, and the reign of the charters starts again, to terminate once more in a republic. How many times can this experiment be repeated? This is what I do not know. But what is certain is that it will be final only when the people have learned to govern themselves.

Now, on 24 February, like many others, I had grounds to fear that the nation was not prepared to govern itself. I was fearful, I admit, of the influence of Greek and Roman ideas, which are imposed on all of us by the university monopoly, ideas that radically exclude all justice, order, and freedom and that have become even more false in the authoritative theories of Montesquieu and Rousseau. I also feared the terror of weak souls and the blind admiration of others, inspired by the memory of the First Republic. I said to myself, "As long as these unfortunate associations of ideas last, the peaceful reign of democracy over itself is not assured."

But events did not bear out these forecasts. The Republic was proclaimed; to return to a monarchy, there would have to be a revolution, perhaps two or three, since there are several claimants.[6] What is more, these revolutions would be only the prelude to a new revolution, since the final triumph of the republican format is the necessary and inexorable law of social progress.

May heaven preserve us from such calamities! We are in a Republic, so let us remain there; let us remain there, since sooner or later it will return; let us remain there, since to extricate ourselves from it would be to return to the era of upheavals and civil wars.

However, for the Republic to be maintained, the people have to love it. It has to put down innumerable deep roots in the universal goodwill of the masses. Confidence needs to be born again, production must flourish, capi-

---

6. After the revolution of 1848, there were a number of claimants to ruling France: on the royalist side was the grandson of Charles X, the duc de Bordeaux, who later become comte de Chambord; and the grandson of Louis-Philippe, comte de Paris. Then, of course, there was also Louis-Napoléon Bonaparte, the nephew of Napoléon Bonaparte, who would eventually become emperor in 1851.

tal has to be built up, and earnings have to be increased; life must become easier, and the nation become proud of its work and show it off to the rest of Europe, resplendent in its genuine grandeur, justice, and moral dignity. Let us therefore inaugurate the policy of peace and freedom.

Peace and freedom! It is certainly not possible to aspire to two more-elevated objects in the social order. But what can they have in common with the cold, stark figures of a mere budget document?

In fact, the link is as close as it can possibly be. A war, the threat of war, or a negotiation that might lead to war, these come into being only by virtue of some small article inscribed in this weighty volume, the terror of the taxpayer. Similarly, I challenge you to imagine a form of oppression, a limitation of citizens' freedom, or a chain around their arms or necks that is not born of a budget for state revenue and does not subsist because of it.

Show me a people who are fed on unjust ideas of their foreign domination, oppressive influence, preponderance, and irresistible power, who meddle in the affairs of neighboring nations, constantly menacing or being menaced, and I will show you a people bowed down with taxes.

Show me a people who have endowed themselves with institutions of such a nature that citizens cannot think, write, print, teach, work, trade, or assemble together without a mob of civil servants coming to hinder their movements, and I will show you a people bowed down with taxes.

For I can see quite clearly how it costs me nothing to live in peace with everyone. But I cannot conceive of what I would have to do to expose myself to continuous squabbles without being subject to enormous expenses either to attack or to defend myself.

And I also see quite clearly how it costs me nothing to be free, but I cannot understand how the state could take action against me in a way that is disastrous to my freedom if I had not begun by handing over to it, *at my expense,* the costly instruments of oppression.

Let us therefore seek economy in expenditure. Let us seek it because it is the only means to satisfy the people and make them like the Republic and keep a check on the spirit of turbulence and revolution through the goodwill of the masses. Let us seek economy, and peace and freedom will be given to us as a bonus.

Such economy is like personal interest. Both are vulgar motives, but they engender principles that are nobler than they.

The precise and current aim of financial reform is to restore the balance between revenue and expenditure. Its ulterior aim, or rather its effect, is to restore public credit. Last, another, more important aim that it has to achieve in order to merit the fine title of *reform* is to conciliate the people, make the institutional structure popular, and thus spare the country new political upheavals.

While I appreciate from these various points of view the systems that have been developed, I cannot prevent myself from considering them either very incomplete or illusory.

A word on two of these systems, one from practical-minded people and the other from utopians.

I begin by declaring that I have the most profound respect for the knowledge and experience of financiers. They have spent their lives studying the mechanisms of our financial systems, they know all their aspects; and if it were only a question of achieving the balance that is virtually the exclusive objective of their pursuit, perhaps there would be nothing better to do than to entrust them with this already very difficult task. By snipping away at our expenditure, by increasing our revenue a little, I would like to think that in three or four years' time they would lead us into that longed-for haven known as a *balanced budget*.

However, it is clear that the basic thought that governs our financial mechanism would remain the same, short of a few improvements to the details. Now, the question I am asking is this: by remaining under the sway of this basic thought, by replastering our system of contributions, so profoundly shaken up by the February revolution, do we have the three or four years ahead of us that separate us from this famous balance? In other words, does our financial system, even stripped of a few abuses, carry within itself the conditions that ensure its longevity? Is it not Aeolus's sack[7] and does it not contain wind and tempests within it?

If it is precisely from this system that all the upheavals arose, what are we to expect from its simple restoration?

Financiers, and by this I mean those for whom the fine ideal of reestablishing things, except for a few details, as they were before February, these men, may I say, want to build on sand and go around in a vicious circle. They do not see that the old system they are advocating, far from basing an abun-

---

7. Aeolus is a Greek mythical figure who is mentioned in Homer's *Odyssey* as the guardian of the winds. Aeolus gives the hero Odysseus the favorable winds he will need in order to sail safely back to Ithaca. He also gives Odysseus a tightly sealed leather bag containing "the adverse winds," which would hinder his journey.

dant flow of public revenue on the prosperity of the working classes, aims at swelling the budget by drying up the source that feeds it.

Apart from the fact that this is a radical vice from the financial point of view, it is also a frightful political danger. What! You have just seen what an almost mortal blow a revolution has given to our finances; you can have no doubt that one, if not the only, cause of this upheaval is the alienation of the people's hearts generated by the weight of taxes, and the aim to which you are aspiring is to return us to our starting point and to drag the coach painfully to the summit of the fatal slope!

Even if a revolution had not taken place, even if it had not awoken in the masses new hopes and demands, I believe in all truth that your plans would be unachievable. But is it not the case that what would have been prudent before February has now become a necessity? Do you believe that your three or four years of effort devoted to the exclusive pursuit of balanced budgets can pass peacefully if the people see nothing on the horizon other than new taxes and if the Republic is visible to them only through the increased ruthlessness of tax collectors. And if, from the fruit of their work, increasingly less well paid, they have to hand over to the state and its agents an increasingly large part? No, do not expect this. A new upheaval will come and cut short your cold, pedantic work; and then, I ask you directly, what will happen to the *balance* and the *credit* that, in your eyes, are the apogee of the art and the end product of all intelligent effort?

I therefore believe that the *practical* men have completely lost sight of the third aim (and the first in importance) that I have assigned to financial reform, that is to say, to relieve taxpayers and ensure that the Republic is loved.

We had proof of this recently. The National Assembly reduced the salt tax and the tax on letters. Well, then! Not only do the financiers disapprove of these measures, they also cannot get it into their heads that the Assembly has acted in accordance with its own will. They still assume in all good faith that it was the victim of surprise and they detest it, so great is their repugnance for any notion of reform.

Please God, I do not wish to insinuate by that that the financiers' cooperation should be rejected! Whatever *new idea* may emerge, it can scarcely be implemented other than with the assistance of their extremely useful experience. However, it is probable that it will not arise in their minds. They have lived too long with the vicissitudes of the past for that. If, before the campaigns in Italy, Napoléon had used thirty years of his life to study and apply all the combinations of the old strategy, do people believe that he would have been struck with the inspiration that caused a revolution in the art of war and gave such luster to French arms?

Next to this school so full of age and experience, one which will offer valuable resources in execution but which will never, I fear, produce the *fertile idea* that France is waiting for to achieve its salvation, glory, and security, there is another school or rather an almost infinite number of other schools, whose ideas, if they can be reproached in any respect, at least cannot be so for their lack of originality. I have no intention of examining all the systems that they have brought to light. I will limit myself to saying a few words about the thought that appeared to me to dominate in the manifesto of the so-called *advanced* republicans.

This manifesto appears to me to be based on a vicious circularity even more blatant than that of the financiers. To tell the truth, it is simply a perpetual and puerile contradiction to tell the people "The republic is going to perform a miracle for you. It will free you from all of this heavy responsibility that burdens the human condition. It will take charge of you in the cradle, and after leading you, at its expense, from the nursery to the infant school, from the infant school to primary school, from primary school to secondary and special schools, from there to the workshop, and from the workshop to the almshouse, it will take you to your grave without your having needed, in a word, to take care of yourself. Do you need credit? Do you lack the tools of your trade or work? Do you want education? Has an accident occurred in your field or your workshop? The state is there, like an opulent and generous father, to provide and fix everything. What is more, it will extend its solicitude to the entire world by virtue of the dogma of solidarity, and should you take the fancy to go and sow your ideas and political views far and wide it will always maintain a great army ready to enter the campaign. That is its mission—it is a vast one—and the state asks nothing from you to accomplish it. Salt, wines and spirits, the post office, city tolls, contributions of all sorts, it will renounce everything. A good father gives to his children but asks nothing of them. If the state does not follow this example, if it does not fulfill the double and contradictory duty that we are pointing out to you, it will have betrayed its mission, and all you will need to do is to overthrow it."

It is true that to hide these glaring impossibilities, they add, "Taxes will be transformed; they will be taken from the *excess wealth* of the rich."

But the people have to know that this is just one more illusion. To impose on the state exorbitant attributions and persuade the public that it can meet these with the money taken from the *surplus wealth* of the rich is to give vain hope to that public. How many rich people are there in France? When it was necessary to pay two hundred francs to have the right to vote, the number of electors was two hundred thousand, and of this number perhaps half did not have this surplus wealth. And people now wish to assert that the state can fulfill the immense mission it has been given by limiting itself to taxing the rich! It will be enough for two hundred thousand families to hand over to the government the *surplus part* of their wealth for it to lavish all sorts of benefits on eight million families that are less well off. However, people do not see one thing, which is that a tax system thus constituted would yield scarcely enough to provide for its own collection.

The truth is, and the people should never lose sight of this, that public contributions will always and of necessity be directed toward the most general objects of consumption, that is to say, the most popular. This is precisely the reason that should incite the people, if they are prudent, to restrict public expenditure, that is to say, the action, attributions, and responsibilities of the government. They should not expect the state to provide for them since they are the ones that provide for the state.[8]

Others place great hopes in the discovery of other sources of taxation. I am far from claiming that there is nothing to be gained from this avenue, but I submit the following observations to the reader:

1. All previous governments were passionately fond of taking a great deal from the public in order to be able to spend a great deal. It is scarcely probable that, where taxes are concerned, any valuable mine that is easy to exploit would have escaped the genius of the tax department. If it has been restrained by something, it can have been only the fear of national rejection.

2. If new sources of taxes cannot be found without upsetting habits and arousing discontent, would the moment be well chosen, after a revolution, to try this type of experiment? Would it not compromise the Republic? Let us work out the effect produced on taxpayers by this news: the National Assembly has just made you subject to taxes hitherto unknown to you and before which the monarchy retreated!

3. From the current and practical points of view, looking for and discovering new taxes is a certain means of doing nothing and neglecting the body

8. (Paillottet's note) See the pamphlet, *The State,* vol. 4, page 327. (*OC,* vol. 4, p. 327, "L'État.") [See also "The State," p. 93 in this volume.]

for its shadow. The National Assembly has only two or three months to live. In the meantime, it has to produce the budget. I leave it to the reader to draw his own conclusions.

After having referred to the most fashionable and the most unacceptable approaches, it remains for me to point out the one I would like to see triumph.

Let us first of all set out the financial situation we have to face.

We are in a situation of deficit (for the word *shortage* now falls short). I will not seek the exact figure of this deficit. I do not know how our accounts are kept; what I do know is that never, ever, do two official sets of figures for the same item agree. Be that as it may, the disease is serious in the extreme. The last budget (volume 1, page 62) contains this item of information:

| | |
|---|---|
| Former overdrafts (another pretty word) | |
| for 1846 and earlier | 184,156,000 francs |
| Budget for 1847 | 43,179,000 |
| Indemnity for the savings banks | 38,000,000 |
| Budget for 1848 | 71,167,000 |
| Budget for 1849 | 213,960,534 |
| Total overdraft | 550,462,534 francs |

This is the result of past budgets. Thus, the damage will constantly increase in the future if we do not succeed either in increasing revenue or in decreasing expenditure, not only in order to align them but also to find surplus revenue to absorb the previous overdrafts gradually.

It is no use hiding this from oneself; any other way leads to bankruptcy and its consequences.

And what makes the situation more difficult is the consideration that I have already indicated and that I stress with all my strength, namely, if a remedy is wholly or partially sought in a tax increase, which is what comes naturally to mind, this will generate a revolution. Well, although the financial effect of revolutions, to mention only these, is to increase expenditure and dry up the sources of revenue (I will refrain from a demonstration), instead of avoiding a catastrophe this procedure is likely only to precipitate it.

I will go further. The difficulty is even greater, since I assert (or at least this is my deepest conviction) that even all the existing taxes cannot be maintained without setting up the most terrible odds against us. A revolution has been achieved; it has proclaimed itself to be democratic and the democracy wants to experience the benefits. It may be right or wrong, but that is the way things are. Woe to the government, woe to the country if this idea is not constantly present in the minds of the people's representatives!

Now that the problem has been set out, what ought we to do?

For on the other hand, if expenditure can be reduced, there are limits to these reductions. They should not go so far as to disorganize services, as this would cause revolutions to occur from the other end of the financial spectrum.

What, then, ought we to do?

This is what I think. I set out my thought in all its naïveté at the risk of raising the hackles of all financiers and practitioners.

Reduce taxes. Reduce expenditure in an even greater proportion.

And, to clad this financial thought in its political formula, I add:

Liberty within. Peace without.

This is the entire plan.

You protest! "It is as contradictory," you say, "as the Montagnards' manifesto.[9] It encompasses a vicious circle that is at least as obvious as those you have previously pointed out in the alternative measures."

I deny this; I grant you only that the attempt is bold. But first, if the gravity of the situation has been clearly established and second, if it has been proved that traditional means will not extricate us, it seems to me that my thought has at least some right to be considered by my colleagues.

May I therefore be allowed to examine my two proposals, and would the reader be so good as to suspend his judgment and perhaps his verdict, remembering that these proposals form an indivisible whole?

First of all, there is a truth that should be remembered, since it is not sufficiently taken into account: it is that, because of the nature of our tax system, which is based predominantly on indirect taxation, that is to say, consumption taxes, there is a very close connection, an intimate relationship, between general prosperity and the prosperity of public finances.

This leads us to the following conclusion: it is not strictly accurate to say that relieving taxpayers will inevitably undermine revenue.

If, for example, in a country like ours the government, driven by an excess of fiscal zeal, raised taxes to the point of destroying consumers' purchasing power, if it doubled or tripled the market price of essentials, if it made the materials and tools of the trade even more expensive, if, as a result, a considerable section of the population was reduced to depriving itself of every-

---

9. See the entry for "La Montagne" in the Glossary of Subjects and Terms.

thing and living on chestnuts, potatoes, buckwheat, and corn, it is clear that the drastic shortfall in revenue might be attributed with some reason to the sharply increased taxation itself.

And in such circumstances it is also clear that the real means, the rational means of making public finances flourish, would not be to deal further blows to general wealth but on the contrary to allow it to grow; this would not be to tighten taxation but to relax it.

In theoretical terms, I do not believe that this can be queried. Through successive increases, taxation may reach the point at which what is added to its rate is bound to reduce its yield. When this point is reached, it is as vain, as crazy, and as contradictory to look for an increase in revenue by an increase in taxes as it would be to wish to raise the liquid in a manometer by means whose result would be to reduce the heat in the boiler.[10]

This having been said, we have to know whether, in fact, our country has not reached this point.

If I examine the principal objects of universal consumption from which the state exacts its revenue, I find them burdened with such exorbitant taxes that the acquiescence of taxpayers can be explained only by force of habit.

To say that a few of these taxes are tantamount to confiscation would be to understate the case.

First of all, take sugar and coffee. We could procure these at a low cost if we were free to seek them in the markets to which our interests direct us. However, in the clearly defined aim of closing off trade with the world to us, the tax authorities subject us to a heavy fine when we commit the crime of trading with India, Havana, or Brazil. If we, docilely bowing to its will, limit our trade to what three small rocks lost in the midst of the oceans are able to supply, we then pay, it is true, much more for sugar and coffee, but the mollified tax authorities take from us only approximately 100 percent of their value in the form of taxes.

This is called profound political economy. Note that acquiring the small rocks has cost us rivers of blood and tons of gold, interest on which will burden us for eternity. As compensation, we also pay tons of gold to keep them.

---

10. Here and on the following pages, Bastiat describes, then justifies through the English experience, the phenomenon known today as the *Laffer Curve*. The idea behind the so-called Laffer Curve (named after the economist Arthur Laffer) is that a cut in tax rates will lead to greater economic output, which over time increases the overall size of the tax base.

In France there is a product that is quintessentially national and whose use is inseparable from popular habits. To restore the strength of workers, nature has given meat to the English and wine to the French; this wine can be procured everywhere at eight or ten francs a hectoliter, but the tax authorities intervene and tax you at the rate of fifteen francs.

I will say nothing about the tax on *tobacco*, which public opinion is ready to accept. It is no less true that this substance is taxed at several times its value.

The state spends five centimes or ten at the most to carry a letter from one point in the territory to another. Until recently, it obliged you to rely upon it; subsequently, when it had you in its grip, it made you pay eighty centimes, one franc, and one franc twenty for what cost it five centimes.

Shall I mention *salt?* It has been clearly established in a recent debate that salt can be produced in unlimited quantities in the southeast of France for fifty centimes. The tax authorities inflicted a duty of thirty francs on it. Sixty times the value of the product! And you call that a tax! I *contribute* at a rate of *sixty* because I possess *one!* I would earn 6,000 percent by abandoning my property to the government!

It would be worse if I mentioned the customs. Here the government has two clearly defined aims: the first, to raise the price of goods, to deny industry the materials it needs, and to increase the hardships of life; the second to amalgamate and increase taxes to such an extent that the tax authorities do not receive anything, recalling the following remark from a dandy to his tailor on the subject of a pair of breeches: "If I can get into them, I will not take them."

Last, the exorbitantly high level of these taxes cannot fail to stimulate a spirit of fraud. When this happens, the government is obliged to surround itself with several armies of civil servants, to arouse suspicion in the entire nation and invent all sorts of interventions and procedures, which all paralyze production and drain the budget.

This is our tax system. We have no means of expressing its consequences in figures. But when, on the one hand, we study this mechanism and on the other we note that it is impossible for a major section of the population to become consumers, can we not ask ourselves whether these two facts are in a cause and effect relationship? Can we not ask ourselves whether we will set this country and its finances on their feet again by continuing down the same path, assuming that public disaffection leaves us the time? Truly, I consider that we are a little like a man who, having painfully emerged from an abyss into which his foolhardiness has plunged him several times, can think of nothing better than to put himself on the same spot from which he started and to follow the same rut with a little more determination.

In theory, everyone will agree that taxes may be raised to such an inordinate degree that it is impossible to add anything to them without freezing general wealth creation so that it compromises the public treasury itself. This theoretical possibility has in fact made itself felt in such a striking way in a neighboring country that I ask to be able to use this example, since if the phenomenon was not acknowledged to be possible, my entire dissertation and all my subsequent conclusions would be worthless and without effect. I know that in France those who seek lessons from British experiments are not very welcome; we prefer to carry out experiments at a cost to ourselves. But I beg the reader to admit for an instant that, on both sides of the Channel, two and two make four.

A few years ago, England found herself financially speaking in a very similar situation to the one we are in. For several consecutive years, each budget ended in a deficit, to such an extent that daring and drastic means had to be envisaged. The first one that occurred to financiers was—you can guess—to increase taxes. The Whig cabinet did not spend much time on invention. It limited itself purely and simply to deciding that a surtax of 5 percent would be added to taxes. Its reasoning was this: "If 100 shillings of tax provide us with 100 shillings of revenue, 105 shillings of tax will provide us with 105 shillings of revenue, or at least 104 or 104½ shillings, since we have to allow for a slight drop in consumption." Nothing seemed more mathematically assured. However, at the end of one year, they were astonished to have gathered, not 105 or 104 and not even 100, but only 96 or 97.

It was then that this cry of pain escaped from aristocratic breasts: "It is finished. We can no longer add even a farthing to our civil list. We have reached the limit of profitable taxation.[11] We have no further resources since *taxing more* is to *receive less*."

The Whig cabinet was overturned immediately. Other competent means had to be tried out. Sir Robert Peel stood forward. He was certainly a practical financier. This did not stop him from producing the sort of reasoning which, pronounced by a novice like me, seemed subtle and perhaps absurd. "Since taxation has created the destitution of the masses and since in turn

---

11. (Bastiat's note) We have got [reached] the bounds of profitable taxation. (*Peel*) [This note is in English in the original.]

the destitution of the masses has limited the yield of taxation, it is a strict consequence, although one that appears paradoxical, that to make revenue prosper taxes have to be reduced. Let us try, therefore, to see whether the tax authorities, which have lost out by being too greedy, will not gain by being generous." Generosity in the tax authorities! That would certainly be a new experience! It would be one well worth examining. Would the financiers not be happy to discover that generosity itself could sometimes be lucrative? It is true that in this case, generosity ought to be called *interest properly understood*. So be it. Let us not bicker over words.

Sir Robert Peel therefore began to cut taxes repeatedly. He allowed wheat, cattle, wool, and butter to be imported in spite of the clamors of the landlords, thinking with apparent reason that the people are never better fed than when there is a great deal of food in the country, a proposition that elsewhere is considered to be seditious. Soap, paper, swill, sugar, coffee, cotton, dyes, salt, the post, glass or steel, everything workers use or consume was subjected to reform.

However, Sir Robert, who is not a hothead, was perfectly aware that although a system like this had to react favorably on the exchequer by stimulating public prosperity, it could do so only in the long term. On the other hand, the deficits, shortfalls, or overdrafts, whatever you want to call them, were current and pressing. To abandon, even provisionally, part of the revenue would have made the situation worse and undermined credit. A difficult period had to be endured, made even more so by the enterprise itself. Thus, reducing taxes was just half of Sir Robert's system, as it is just half of the one I am putting forward in all humility. It has been seen that the essential complement of mine[12] consists in reducing expenditure in an even greater proportion. The complement of the Peel system was closer to financial and fiscal traditions. He thought of how to find another source of revenue, and *income tax* was decreed.

Thus, in the face of deficits, the first thought had been to make taxes *heavier* and the second was to *transform* them, to ask payment from those able to pay. This was progress. Why should I not have the pleasant idea that *reducing expenditure* would be even more decisive progress?

12. (Bastiat's note) I say *mine* to keep things short, but I must not pose as its inventor. The editor in chief of *La Presse* has published several times the basic idea that I am echoing here. What is more, he has produced its application successfully. *Suum cuique* ["to each his own"].

I am obliged, in spite of the slowness it imposes on me, to examine the following question briefly: Has the British experiment been successful? I must do this, for what would be the use of an example that has failed, if not to avoid imitating it? This is certainly not the conclusion to which I wished to lead the reader. However, many people claim that Sir Robert Peel's enterprise was disastrous, and their claim is all the more seemingly plausible since, precisely from the day that tax reform was inaugurated, a long and terrible commercial and financial crisis occurred to afflict Great Britain.

But first of all, I must point out that even if the recent economic disasters might be attributed at least in part to Sir Robert Peel's reform, people should not be able to argue against the one I am proposing, since these two reforms differ signally. What they have in common is this: they seek the ulterior increase of revenue in the prosperity of the masses, that is to say, in the reduction of taxes as far as levels are concerned. How they differ is in this: Sir Robert Peel arranged the resources for facing up to the difficulties of transition through the *establishment of a new tax*. The resources I am calling for come through a *steep reduction in expenditure*. Sir Robert was so far from orienting his ideas in this direction that, in the very document in which he set out his financial plan before an attentive England, he was requesting a considerable increase in subsidies for the development of military and naval forces.

However, since the first part of these two systems merge in that they aim to establish the ample funding of the public treasury over the long term by relieving the working classes, is it not obvious that a reduction in expenditure or the pure and simple abolition of taxes is more in harmony with this thinking than shifting the tax?

I cannot help thinking that the second element of Peel's plan was such as to contradict the first. Doubtless it did a great deal of good to spread the tax burden better. But when all is said and done, when you know a little about this subject, when you have studied the natural mechanism of taxes, their rebounds and repercussions, you know full well that what the tax authorities require from one class is paid for the most part by another. It is not possible for English workers not to have been affected, either directly or indirectly, by *income tax*. Thus, though they were relieved on the one hand, they were to a certain extent afflicted on the other.

But let us leave these considerations aside and examine whether, in the face of the clear facts that explain the English crisis so naturally, it is possible to attribute it to the reform. The eternal false reasoning of those who are determined to incriminate something involves them in attributing to it all the evils that happen in the world. *Post hoc, ergo propter hoc.*[13] The preconceived idea is and always will be the scourge of reason since, by its very nature, it flees the truth when it has the misfortune of glimpsing it.

England has had other commercial crises than the one it has just gone through. All have been explained by obvious causes. Once she was seized by a fever of ill-conceived speculation. Immense amounts of capital deserted production and went down the road of American loans and the mining of precious metal. The result was great upheaval in industry and finance. On another occasion, the harvest failed and the consequences are easy to imagine. When a considerable portion of the work of an entire nation has been directed toward the creation of its own subsistence, when the people have ploughed, harrowed, sown, and watered the earth with sweat for a year to make the harvest grow, if, at the time it is due to be gathered in, it is destroyed by a plague, they are faced with two alternatives: either to die of hunger or to import unexpectedly and rapidly huge amounts of food products. All the ordinary operations of production have to be interrupted in order for the capital involved in them to be freed to meet this gigantic and unexpected operation that cannot be postponed. What a waste of energy! What a loss of assets! And how can a crisis not result? This also happens when the cotton crop fails in the United States, for the simple reason that the factories cannot be as active in operation when they lack cotton as when they have it and it is never with impunity that stagnation spreads to the manufacturing districts of Great Britain. Insurrections in Ireland and unrest on the continent that disrupt British trade and reduce consumer power in its customers are also obvious causes of financial hindrance, difficulty, and disturbance.

The economic history of England teaches us that just one of these causes has always been enough to trigger a crisis in that country.

Well, it so happened that just at the moment when Sir Robert Peel introduced the reform, all these plagues occurred to afflict England at the same time and with a degree of intensity that had hitherto been unknown.

The result was great suffering for the people and the immediate broad-

13. "After this, therefore because of this."

casting of the *preconceived idea:* You see! It is the reform that is crushing the people!

However, I put the question: Was it really the financial and commercial reform that led to two successive losses of harvest in 1845 and 1846 and forced England to spend two billion to replace the wheat lost?

Was it really the financial and commercial reform that caused the destruction of the potato harvest in Ireland for four years and forced England to feed a starving people at its own expense?

Was it really the financial and commercial reform that ruined the cotton crop in two successive years in America, and do people believe that maintaining import taxes would have been an effective remedy?

Was it really the financial and commercial reform that gave rise to and developed *railway mania*[14] and suddenly removed two or three billion from productive and customary work to throw them into enterprises that could not be completed, a folly that, according to all observers, has done more *current* harm than all the other plagues combined?

Was it really the financial and commercial reform that lit the fires of revolution on the continent and reduced the absorption of all sorts of British products?

Ah, when I think of the unheard-of alliance of destructive agents working together in a common direction, this tightly woven fabric of disasters of all sorts, accumulated by a fate without precedent in a limited space of time, I cannot help thinking, contrary to the *preconceived idea:* "What would have become of England, its power, its greatness, and its wealth, if Providence had not raised up a man at this precise and solemn moment? Would not everything have been swept away in a terrible convulsion?" Yes, I sincerely believe that the reform, blamed for the misfortunes in England, neutralized part of them. And the English people understand this, since although the most sensitive part of this reform, free trade, has been subjected right from its inception to the most difficult and unexpected tests, popular faith in it has not been shaken, and at the time I am writing this the work begun is continuing and progressing toward its glorious fulfillment.

14. *Railway mania* refers to an investment bubble in the mid 1840s for the building of railways in England. The Bank of England lowered interest rates, thus stimulating a boom in railway investment by private companies. Hundreds of acts of Parliament were passed authorizing such companies to build new railway lines. When the Bank of England raised interest rates in late 1845, the speculative nature and economic unsoundness of these investments were exposed, which led to a crash in the market in 1846.

Let us therefore return from across the strait, and may confidence accompany us; there is no need to leave it on the other side of the Channel.

We are facing the revenue budget. The Assembly has already lowered the tax on salt and the carriage of letters. In my opinion, it should do the same for wines and spirits. Under this heading, I consider that the state should agree to lose fifty million. As far as possible it should spread the remaining tax over the whole of the wine consumed. People will understand that thirty to forty million spread over forty-five million hectoliters will be much easier to pay than one hundred million concentrated on a quantity three times less. The expenses and above all the hindrances resulting from the current collection system will also have to be reduced.

The state should also agree to reduce duties on sugar and coffee considerably. Increased consumption will solve the fiscal and colonial questions simultaneously.

Another great and popular measure would be the abolition of city tolls.[15] On this subject, I have been struck by the advantage that might be drawn from an opinion put forward by M. Guichard. Everyone acknowledges that an *income tax* would be just and in accordance with proper principles. If people hesitate, it is because of the problems of executing it. There is great fear, which I think is justified, of the heavy responsibility that the importunate investigations essential for this tax would bring to bear on the state. It is not a good thing for a republican government to appear to taxpayers to be an avid inquisitor. In local districts, wealth is known about. It can be assessed within the family and if its holders were given the choice of establishing income tax with the specific aim of replacing city tolls, it is likely that this transformation, based on justice, would be received favorably. In the long run, France would thus be preparing a register of wealth held in movable assets and the means of leading its tax system down the path of truth. I do not think that a measure of this sort, which would also have the advantage of triggering decentralization, would be beyond the means of a clever statesman. It would certainly not have made Napoléon retreat.

15. Many cities, bridges, and rivers in the medieval and early-modern period imposed tolls, or *péage,* on travelers and the goods they were transporting for sale. By the eighteenth century the tolls had became so onerous that they impeded the free flow of goods within a state like France. The physiocrats advocated their abolition as a means of creating free trade, and this was partially achieved during the French Revolution as part of the policy of rationalizing and centralizing the nation state. Bastiat is referring here to those local and city tolls that still remained.

I am obliged to say something about the customs; and to shelter myself from the prejudices that I can see arising from here, I will consider them only from the fiscal point of view, since in any case it is just a question of the budget. It is not that I am not strongly tempted to make a sortie toward *freedom of exchange,* but will I not be compared to the brave general who was famous for his predilection for the care of horses? Wherever on the intellectual horizon you place the point of departure of the conversation, whether on chemistry, physics, astronomy, music, or the navy, you will see him rapidly mounting the *saddle horse* and you will be obliged to mount it behind him. We all have our pet subjects, our hobbyhorses in a Shandyan[16] style. My pet subject, and why should I not admit it, is freedom, and if it so happens that I defend freedom to trade in particular, it is because, of all the freedoms, it is the one most misunderstood and most compromised.

Let us therefore examine the customs services from the fiscal point of view; and may the reader pardon me if, escaping tangentially, I touch a little on the questions of right, property, and freedom.

One of the most sincere and clever protectionists in this country, M. Ferrier,[17] admitted that, if one wished to retain a fiscal character for the customs, it would be possible to draw twice the revenue for the treasury. It raises about one hundred million; therefore, independently of the charge imposed on us as consumers by protectionism, it makes us lose one hundred million as taxpayers. For it is perfectly clear that what the tax authorities refuse to recover by means of the customs services, it has to raise through other taxes. This mechanism is worth the trouble of examination.

Let us suppose that the treasury requires one hundred. Let us also suppose that, if foreign iron could enter on payment of a reasonable duty, it would provide the revenue with five. However, a sector of industrialists claims that it would be to its advantage for foreign iron not to be admitted. Taking their side, the law decrees prohibition, or what amounts to the same thing, a prohibitive duty. Consequently, any opportunity to raise a tax is deliberately sacrificed. The five do not come in and the treasury is left with only ninety-five. But since we have accepted that it needs one hundred, we have to agree to its taking five from us in some other way, on salt, the post, or tobacco.

---

16. Bastiat is probably making a reference to the novel *The Life and Opinions of Tristram Shandy,* by Laurence Sterne, published in 1759.

17. See p. 292, note 10.

And what happens for iron also happens for all imaginable forms of consumer products.

In the face of this strange dispensation, what is the situation of the *consumer-taxpayer?*

It is this:

1. He pays considerable taxes, which are intended to maintain a huge army of employees at the frontier, an army that is established there on the instigation of and for the account and benefit of ironmasters or any other privileged person whose business it is furthering.

2. He pays a higher than market price for iron.

3. He is forbidden to make the thing in exchange for which the foreigner would have delivered his iron, for to prevent an asset from being imported is also to prevent by the same measure another asset from being exported.

4. He pays a tax to fill the void at the treasury, for to prevent an import from entering is to prevent tax being collected, and since the needs of the tax authorities are established, should a tax fail to be collected, it has to be replaced by another.

This certainly is a strange position for a *consumer-taxpayer* to be in. Is it more unfortunate than ridiculous or more ridiculous than unfortunate? It might be a problem to answer this.

And what is the reason for all of this? For an ironmaster to reap from his work and capital no extraordinary profit but only to enable him to experience even greater difficulties in production!

When then will decisions be taken in matters like this in consideration of the majority and not the minority? The interest of the majority, this is the economic rule that never goes wrong since it merges with justice.

One thing has to be clearly agreed upon, which is that in order for protection to be just without ceasing to be disastrous, it would need at least to be equal for all. However, is this possible, even in the abstract?

Men trade products with each other, or products in return for services, or services for services. It may even be asserted that, as products have *value* only because of the services they generate, everything is reduced to the *mutuality of services.*

Well, the customs service can obviously protect only the types of service whose value is incorporated in material products that can be stopped or seized at the frontier. It is radically incapable of protecting the direct

*services* provided by doctors, lawyers, priests, magistrates, soldiers, traders, men of letters, artists, or artisans, who already constitute a considerable part of the population, by raising the value of the services. It is
equally powerless to protect men who let out their work, since they do
not sell products, but provide services. Here then we have all workers or
journeymen excluded from the alleged benefits of protectionism. But
while protection is of no benefit to them, it damages them, and here we
have to identify clearly the counterblow that those protected should feel
themselves.

The only two classes protected, and to a very unequal degree, are manufacturers and farmers. These two classes see the customs as providential,
and nevertheless we are witnesses to the fact that they never cease to bewail
their distress. It must be that protection is not as effective for them as they
had hoped. Who would dare to say that agriculture and manufacturing are
more prosperous in those countries most protected, such as France, Spain,
or the Roman states, than in those nations that have held their freedom
less cheap, such as the Swiss, the English, the Belgians, the Dutch, and the
Tuscans?

What is happening with regard to protection is something similar or
rather identical to what we have confirmed just now in connection with
taxes. In the same way that there is a limit to profitable taxation, there is
a limit to profitable protection. This limit is the complete destruction
of the ability to consume, a destruction that protection tends to bring,
like taxes. The tax authorities prosper with the prosperity of taxpayers.
In the same way, the *value* of an industry is based only on the wealth
of its customers. From that it follows that, when the tax authorities or a
monopoly seek to develop themselves by means whose inevitable effect
is to ruin consumers, both enter the same vicious circle. There comes a
time when the more they increase the level of tax, the more they reduce
the yield. Those who are protected cannot assess the state of depression
that weighs upon their industry, in spite of the favors of the protectionist
dispensation. As in the case of the tax authorities, they seek a remedy in
making these arrangements even more extreme. In the end they should
ask themselves whether it is not the favors themselves that are oppressing
them. They should contemplate the half or two-thirds of the population
that is reduced, as a result of these unjust favors, to doing without iron,
meat, cloth, or wheat, building carts with branches of willow, clothing

themselves in homespun, eating millet like birds or chestnuts like less poetic creatures![18]

Since I have let myself be drawn into this discussion, allow me to end it
with a sort of apologue.

In a royal park, there was a host of small *ponds,* all communicating with
one another through underground conduits, so that the water had the invincible tendency to reach a uniform level. These reservoirs were supplied
by a large canal. One of them, slightly more ambitious, wanted to attract
to itself a major part of the supply intended for all. This should not have
caused much of a problem in view of the inevitable leveling that would have
followed the attempt, if the means thought up by the greedy and reckless
reservoir had not led to an inevitable loss of liquid in the supply canal. We
can guess what happened. The level decreased everywhere, even in the favored reservoir. It said to itself, since in apologues, there is nothing that does
not speak, even reservoirs: "It is very strange, I draw to myself more water
than before; I succeed for a fleeting moment in raising myself above the
level of my peers and yet I see with distress that we are all moving, I along
with the rest, toward total desiccation." This reservoir, doubtless as ignorant
of hydraulics as it was of morals, closed its eyes to two circumstances: the
first being the underground communication of all the reservoirs with each
other, an invincible obstacle to its being able to benefit exclusively and permanently from its injustice; the other being the general loss of liquid inherent in the means it had thought up, which was to lead inevitably to a general
and continuous lowering of the level.

Well, I say that the social order also exhibits these two circumstances and
that those who do not take them into account are reasoning incorrectly. First
of all, between all forms of production, there are hidden communications,
transmissions of work and capital, which do not allow one of them to raise
its normal level above the rest indefinitely. Second, in the means thought up
to carry out the injustice, that is to say, in protectionism, there is the radical
ill that it generates an unredeemable loss of total wealth; and from these two
circumstances, it follows that the level of well-being decreases everywhere,
even within the industries that are protected, like the level of the water in
the greedy and stupid reservoir.

18. (Paillottet's note) See the chapter titled "Expensive, Cheap" in vol. 4, p. 163, *Economic Sophisms,* second series. (*OC,* vol. 4, p. 163, "Cherté, bon marché.")

I was fully aware that free trade would divert me from my path. Ob-sessions! Obsessions! Your sway is irresistible! But let us return to the tax authorities.

I will say to those who support protectionism: In view of the press-ing needs of the Republic, will you not agree to set a limit to your greed? What! When the treasury is in desperate straits, when bankruptcy threatens to engulf your wealth and security, when the customs service offers a truly providential means of rescue by being able to fill the public coffers without causing harm to the masses, but on the contrary, relieving them of the weight oppressing them, will you remain inflexible in your selfishness? On your own initiative, at this solemn and decisive moment, you ought to make the sac-rifice, as you call it and which you sincerely believe it to be, of part of your privileges on the altar of the fatherland. You would be rewarded by public esteem and, I dare to forecast this, what is more you will also gain by way of material prosperity.

Therefore, is it too much to ask you to substitute duties of 20 to 30 per-cent for prohibition, which has become incompatible with our constitu-tional law? A reduction by half of the duties on iron and steel, those sinews of production; on coal, on which industry, so to speak, feeds; on wool, flax, and cotton, the materials used by labor; and on wheat and meat, the basis of strength and life?

But I see that you are becoming reasonable,[19] you welcome my humble request, and we can now cast a glance, both morally and financially, at our now properly *rectified* budget.

First of all, here are many things that have at last come within the reach of the hands or lips of the people: salt, letter post, wines and spirits, sugar, coffee, iron, steel, fuel, wool, flax, cotton, meat, and bread! If we add to this list the abolition of city tolls and the profound modification if not the total abolition of the terrible law of recruitment, a terror and plague in our coun-tryside, I ask you, will the Republic not have sunk its roots in all the fibers of popular adhesion? Will it be easy to shake? Will it require five hundred thousand bayonets to be the terror of the parties . . . or their hope? Shall

---

19. (Paillottet's note) In the pamphlet titled *Plunder and Law* [see "Plunder and Law," p. 266 in this volume], we have seen that the author was not slow to acknowledge how far he was mistaken in imagining that the protectionists had become reasonable. However, it is true that, at the start of 1849, they showed themselves to be much more amenable than they were one year later.

we not be protected from these terrible upheavals with which, it seems, the very air is charged right now? Might we not conceive the justified hope that a feeling of well-being and the awareness that the power has at last firmly entered into the path of justice will regenerate production, confidence, security, and credit? Is it an illusion to think that these beneficial causes will react on our finances more surely than a surfeit of taxes and hindrances might?

And, as for our current, immediate financial situation, let us see how it will be affected.

Here are the reductions that will result from the proposed system:

| | |
|---|---|
| 2 million, post | |
| 45 million, salt | |
| 50 million, wines and spirits | |
| 33 million, sugar, coffee, so . . . . . . . . . . . . . . . . . . . . . . . . . . | 130,000,000 |
| It is not too much to hope for 30 million more to be deducted through an increase in general consumption and by the customs carrying out their fiscal responsibilities, so . . . . . . . . . . . . . . . . . . . . . . . . . . . . . | 30,000,000 francs |
| Total of the loss of revenue caused by the reform . . . . . . . . | 100,000,000 francs |

——A loss that should decrease, by its very nature, from year to year.*

To decrease taxes (which does not always mean decreasing revenue), this is then the first half of the financial program of the Republic. You will say: "This is very bold, faced with the deficit." And I will reply: "No, this is not boldness, it is prudence. What is bold, what is reckless and senseless is to continue down the path that brings us closer to the abyss. See where you are! You have made no secret of it, indirect taxes are causing you worry, and as for direct taxes themselves, you count on collecting them only if you employ a *militia*. Are we in the world of taking aim and military sallies? How could things have reached this stage? Here are one hundred men; they all pay a subscription to set up, for their security, an apparatus of enforcement, a *common force* of their own. Little by little, this common force is diverted from its purposes and it is made responsible for a host of unreasonable functions. Because of this, the number of men who live off this subscription increases, the subscription itself increases, and the number of those paying it decreases. Discontent and disaffection arise and what will be done? Return the common force to its original purpose? That would be too commonplace and, people say, too bold. Our statesmen are cleverer; they think of decreasing still further the number of those paying to increase the number of those being paid. We need new taxes, they say, to maintain the military and new militias to collect the new taxes! And people do not see a vicious circle in this! We thus reach the fine situation in which half of the citizens will be occupied in repressing and holding the other half to ransom. This is what is known as wise and practical policies. All the rest is just utopia. Give us a few years more, say the financiers; allow us to push the system to its limits and you will see that we will at last achieve the famous balanced budget that we have been pursuing for so long and that has been upset precisely by the procedures that we have been following for the last twenty years.

It is therefore not as paradoxical as it appears at first glance to take an opposite course and to seek a balance through the reduction of taxes. Will such balance be less worthy of its name because instead of seeking it at 1.5 billion we achieve it at 1.2?

But this first part of the republican program makes a commanding appeal to its essential complement: *a reduction in expenditure*. Without this complement, the system is utopian, I agree. With this complement, I challenge anyone, other than those involved, to dare to say that it does not go right to the heart of the matter, and by the path that holds the least danger.

I add that the reduction in expenditure must be greater than the revenue; without this, we would be pursuing the leveling in vain.

Finally, it has to be said, a group of measures like these cannot provide all the results we have the right to expect of them in a single financial year.

We have seen, with regard to revenue, that to instill in it this *force for growth* whose basis lies in general prosperity, we had to begin by reducing it. This means that time is needed to develop this force.

This is equally true for expenditure; its reduction can be only gradual. Here is one reason for this, among others.

When a government has raised its expenditure to a level that is swollen and burdensome, this means in other words that many lives depend on its prodigality and feed on it. The idea of achieving savings without upsetting anyone carries a contradiction within it. To use sufferings as an argument against reform, which of necessity implies these sufferings, is to totally reject any act of reparation and to say: "Because an injustice has been introduced into the world, it is proper for it to be perpetuated forever." This is an eternal sophism of those who idolize abuse.

However, from the truth that individual suffering is the necessary consequence of any reform, it does not follow that it is not the legislator's duty to alleviate it as far as he can. For my part, I am not one of those who hold that, when a member of society has been attracted by society to a career, when he has grown old in it and made it his specialty, when he is incapable of earning his living from another occupation, society should be able to cast him out, with neither hearth nor home. Any loss of particular employment therefore imposes on society a temporary responsibility on grounds of humanity and, in my view, of strict justice.

It follows from this that the modifications made to the expenditure budget cannot produce results immediately, any more than those made to the revenue budget. They are germs whose nature is to develop, and the overall scheme involves a decrease of expenditure from year to year by way of specific reductions and revenue that increases from year to year in parallel with general prosperity, so that the final result ought to be a balanced budget or a surplus.

As for the alleged disaffection that might reveal itself in the very numerous sector of public servants, I have to confess that, with the gradual changes that I have just mentioned, I am not afraid of this. Besides, this scruple is strange. As far as I know, it has never stopped massive destitutions after each revolution. And yet, what a difference there is! To dismiss an employee in order to give his job to another is more than upsetting his interest, it is wounding his dignity and his acute sense of right. But when the abolition of an occupation, fairly managed, results in the loss of jobs, it may cause harm but will not enrage. The wound is less sharp, and the person affected by it is consoled by consideration of the public good.

I needed to put these reflections before the reader when speaking about deep reforms, which would of necessity lead to the laying off of many of our fellow citizens.

I will not review all the articles of expenditure that I consider it to be useful and good policy to cut. The budget reflects nothing but politics. It swells or decreases depending on whether public opinion requires more or less from the state. What good would it do to show that the elimination of such and such a government department would lead to this or that major saving if the taxpayer himself prefers the department to the saving? There are reforms that have to be preceded by lengthy debates and a slow preparation of public opinion, and I do not see why I should go down a path in which it is clear that public opinion would not follow me. This very day the National Assembly took the decision to draw up the first budget of the Republic. It has a short and very limited time only in which to do this. With a view to setting out a reform that is immediately practicable, I have to turn away from the general and philosophical considerations that I first thought of putting before the reader. I will limit myself to indicating them.

What postpones any radical financial reform to a far distant future is that in France people do not like freedom. They do not like feeling responsible for themselves and have no confidence in their own dynamism; they feel reassured only when they feel the pressure of government pulling strings on all sides, and it is precisely these pullings of strings that are so expensive.

If, for example, people had faith in the freedom of education, what would need to be done other than abolishing the *public education budget?*

If people really valued freedom of conscience, how would they achieve it other than by abolishing the *budget for religious practice?* [20]

If people understood that farming is improved by farmers and trade by traders, they would come to the conclusion that the *budget for agriculture and commerce* is superfluous and is something that the most advanced nations are careful not to inflict on themselves.

If, on a few points, like surveillance, the state needs to intervene with regard to education, religious practice, or commerce, an extra division in the ministry of the interior would be enough; we do not need three ministries to do this.

Thus, freedom is the first and most fertile source and spring of savings.

However, this spring is not made for our lips. Why? Solely because public opinion rejects it. [21]

Our children will therefore continue, under the monopoly of the university, to quench their thirst on false Greek and Roman ideas, to be imbued

20. (Bastiat's note) The treaty passed between our fathers and the clergy is an obstacle to this very welcome reform. Justice above all.

21. (Paillottet's note) This blindness of public opinion saddened the author for a long time, and as soon as an attempt to consolidate the blindfold over the eyes of our fellow citizens came to his attention, he felt the need to combat it. However, in his retreat in Mugron, he lacked the means to publish his writing. The following letter, therefore, written by him many years ago has remained unpublished to the present day.

*To M. Saulnier*
*Editor of* La Revue britannique

*Dear Sir,*

You have instilled transports of joy in all those who find the word *economics* absurd, ridiculous, unacceptable, bourgeois, and shifty. *Le Journal des débats* extols you, the president of the council quotes you, and the favors of government are waiting for you. However, what have you done, sir, to merit so much apwith the warlike and revolutionary spirit of Latin authors, to scan the licentious verses of Horace, and to become unsuited to modern life in society. We will continue not to be free and as a result to pay for our servitude, since peoples can be held in servitude only at great expense.

We will continue to see farming and commerce languish and succumb under the yoke of our restrictive laws and, what is more, pay the cost of this torpor, for all the hindrances, regulations, and useless formalities can be carried out only by agents of government enforcement, and the agents of the state can live only through the budget.

And, it must be repeated, the harm is without a remedy that can currently be applied, since public opinion attributes to oppression all the intellectual and industrial development that this oppression has not succeeded in stifling.

An idea that is as strange as it is disastrous has taken hold of people's minds. When it is a question of politics, people assume that the social en-

---

plause? You have established through figures (and everyone knows that figures never lie) that it costs the *citizens* of the United States more than the *subjects* of France to be governed. This gives rise to the rigorous consequence (rigorous for the people in effect) that it is absurd to wish to place limits on the lavishness of power in France.

But, sir, and I ask your pardon and that of the economic research centers, your figures, assuming they are correct, do not seem to me to be unfavorable to the American government.

In the first place, to establish that one government spends more than another does not give any information on their relative goodness. If one of them, for example, is administering a nascent nation that has all its roads to build, all its canals to dig out, all its towns to pave, and all its public establishments to create, it is natural that it spends more than one that has scarcely more to do than maintain its existing establishments. Well, you know as well as I do, sir, that spending that way is to save and capitalize. If it were done by a farmer, would you be confusing the investments that an initial establishment requires with his annual expenditure?

However, this major difference in situation leads, according to your figures, to an additional expenditure of only three francs for each citizen of the union. Is this excess genuine? No, according to your own data. This may surprise you, since you have set at thirty-six francs the contribution by each American and thirty-three francs that of each Frenchman. Well, 36 = 33 + 3 is good arithmetic . ——Yes, but in political economy, thirty-three is often worth more than thirty-six. See for yourself. Money, in comparison with labor and goods, is not as valuable in the United States as it is in France. You yourself set a day's pay at four francs fifty centimes in the United States and at one franc fifty centimes gine, if I can call it this, is in accordance with individual interest and opinion. We cling to Rousseau's axiom, "*The general will cannot err.*" And on this basis, we decree *universal suffrage* with enthusiasm.

However, from all other points of view, we adopt exactly the opposite hypothesis. We do not accept that the driving force of progress lies in individuality, in its natural yearning for well-being, a yearning that is increasingly

----

in France. The result, I believe, is that an American pays thirty-six francs with eight days' work, whereas a Frenchman needs twenty-two days' work to pay thirty-three francs. It is true that you say that people buy forced labor from each other in the United States for three francs and that consequently the price of a day's work ought to be set at three francs there. ——There are two answers to this. Forced labor is bought in France for one franc (for we also have forced labor, about which you do not speak) and then, if a day's work in the United States is worth only three francs the Americans no longer pay thirty-six francs since, to reach this figure, you have raised to four francs fifty centimes all the days that these citizens devote to fulfilling their military obligations, their forced labor, their jury service, etc.

This is not the only subtle difference you have used to raise the annual contribution of each American to thirty-six francs.

You impute to the government of the United States expenses that it is not concerned with in the slightest. To justify this strange method of proceeding, you say that these expenses are no less borne by the citizens. But is it not a question of determining which are the voluntary expenses of the citizens and which are the expenditures of the government?

A government is instituted to fulfill certain functions. When it exceeds its attributions, it has to appeal to the citizens' purses and thus reduce the portion of revenue that was freely at their disposition. It becomes simultaneously a plunderer and oppressor.

A nation that is wise enough to oblige its government to limit itself to guaranteeing security to each person and that spends only what is absolutely essential to this consumes the remainder of its revenue in accordance with its particular talents, its needs, and its inclinations.

But in a nation in which the government interferes in everything, nothing is spent by itself and for its own benefit, but it is spent by the government and for the government, and if the French public thinks as you do, sir, if it cares little that its wealth goes through the hands of functionaries, I do not lose the hope that one day we will all be lodged, fed, and clothed at the state's expense. These are things that cost us something and, according to you, it is of little importance whether we procure them through taxation or through direct purchase. The importance that our ministers give this opinion convinces me that we will soon have clothes produced by them, just as we have priests, lawyers, teachers, doctors, horses, and tobacco of their fashioning.

*Yours, etc.*
*Frédéric Bastiat*

enlightened by intelligence and guided by experience. No. We start off from the concept that mankind is divided into two: first, there are individuals who are inert and deprived of any dynamism or stimulus to progress or who obey depraved impulses which, left to themselves, reduce them to absolute evil; and second, there is a collective being, a common force, the government in short, to which is attributed inborn knowledge, a natural passion for good, and the mission to change the direction of individual tendencies. We assume that, if they were free, men would avoid all forms of education, religion, or production or, what is worse, that they would seek out education to attain error, religion to end up in atheism, and work to consummate their ruin. This being so, it is necessary for individuals to be subject to the regulatory action of the collective being, which, however, is none other than the coming together of these individuals themselves. Well, I ask you, if the natural inclinations of all the *fractions* tend toward evil, how will the natural inclinations of the *whole* tend toward good? If all the innate forces of man are directed toward nothingness, on what will the government, made up of men, take its point of support in order to change this direction?[22]

Be that as it may, as long as this strange theory remains in force, we will have to give up freedom and the convenient economies that it brings. We ought to pay for our chains when we love them, given that the state never gives us anything for nothing, not even irons.

The budget is not only the whole of politics, it is also in many respects the moral code of the people. It is the mirror in which, like Renaud, we might see the image and punishment of our preconceived ideas, our vices, and our wild pretensions. Here again, there are torrents of wrong expenditure that we are reduced to leaving to run, since they are caused by leanings which we are not ready to abandon; what would be more unreal than to wish to neutralize an effect while the cause continues to exist? I will mention, among other things, what I do not fear to call, even if the word sounds harsh, the *spirit of begging*, which has spread to all classes, the rich as much as the poor.[23]

22. (Paillottet's note) See, in vol. 4, the pamphlet titled *The Law*, in particular the passage on pages 381 to 386. (*OC*, vol. 4, "La Loi," pp. 381–86.) [See also "The Law," p. 107 in this volume.]

23. (Paillottet's note) Among the author's manuscripts we find the following thought, which refers to the particular subject he is dealing with here:

"Why are our finances in a mess?"

Certainly, in the circle of private relations, the French character does not fear comparison with regard to independence and pride. God forbid that I should cast a slur on my own country and even less that I should calumniate it! However, I do not know how it has happened that the same men who, even when pressed by distress, would blush to hold out a hand to their fellow men, lose all their scruples when the state intervenes and averts the gaze of their consciences from the contemptibility of such action. As soon as the request is not addressed to individual largesse, as soon as the state is the intermediary of the work, it appears that the dignity of the supplicant is spared, that begging is no longer shameful nor plunder an injustice. Farmers, manufacturers, traders, shipowners, artists, singers, dancers, men of letters, civil servants of all sorts, entrepreneurs, suppliers, or bankers, everyone in France wants something, and everyone expects the budget to provide. And soon the whole nation en masse has joined in. One person wants positions, another pensions, a third premiums, a fourth subsidies, a fifth inducements, a sixth restrictions, a seventh credit, and an eighth work. The whole of society is rising up to snatch a share of the budget in one form or another, and in its Californian fever it forgets that the budget is not a *Sacramento* where nature has deposited gold; the budget contains only what this mendicant society has itself put into it. Society forgets that the generosity of the government can never equal its avidity since, on the basis of this largesse, it has to keep back enough to pay for the twin services of tax collection and distribution.

In order to give these rather abject arrangements the authority and appearance of regularity, they have been attached to what is known as the principle of *solidarity,* a word that, used in this way, means nothing other than the effort of all the citizens to despoil each other through the costly intervention of the state. However, it can be understood that once the *spirit of mendacity* becomes systematized and almost an administrative science, imagination knows no bounds with regard to ruinous institutions.

But, I agree, we can do nothing at the moment in this respect and I end with this question: When the spirit of begging is taken to the point at which

---

"Because, for the representatives, there is nothing easier than to vote for an item of expenditure and nothing harder than to vote for an item of revenue."

"If you prefer it, because salaries are very pleasant and taxes very hard."

"I know another reason."

"Everyone wants to live at the state's expense, and we forget that the state lives at the expense of everyone."

it incites the entire nation to plunder the budget, do people not think that it compromises political security even more than public resources?

For the same reason, another considerable saving is still insuperably forbidden to us. I refer to Algeria. We have to yield and pay until the nation has understood that to transport one hundred men to a colony and at the same time transport ten times the capital that would maintain them in France is to relieve nobody and to tax everyone.

Let us therefore seek our means of salvation elsewhere.

The reader will acknowledge that, for a utopian, I am easy to deal with when it comes to retrenchment. *There are many more and even better examples that I could mention.* Restrictions to our most precious freedoms, the mania for seeking special treatment, an infatuation with a disastrous conquest: in all this I have given way to public opinion. Let it now allow me to take my revenge and to be slightly radical with regard to foreign policy.

For finally, if public opinion intends to close the door to any reform, if it has decided in advance to keep everything that exists and to allow for no change whatever in anything that relates to our expenditure, my whole argument will crumble and all financial plans will be powerless; all that remains to us is to leave the people to bow down under the weight of taxes and walk with lowered heads toward bankruptcy, revolution, disorganization, and social conflict.

In talking about our foreign policy, I will start by clearly establishing the following two proposals, outside of which I make so bold as to say there is no salvation.

1. The recourse to brute force is not necessary and damages the influence of France.
2. The recourse to brute force is not necessary and damages our internal and external security.

As a consequence of these two proposals there arises a third, which is: We have to disarm on land and sea as quickly as possible.

False patriots! Enjoy yourselves to the full. There was a day on which you called me a *traitor* because I demanded freedom; what will happen now that I am invoking peace?[24]

Here again, public opinion is an obstacle to the first item. It has been sat-

---

24. (Paillottet's note) An allusion to the inept accusation made against the free traders that they had sold themselves to England.

urated by the following words: *national greatness, power, influence, prepon-derance,* and *dominance.* France is repeatedly told that she must not retreat from the rank that she occupies among the nations; her pride having been addressed, it is now time to turn to her interest. She is told that she must show evidence of strength to support useful negotiations, that the French flag must be displayed on every ocean to protect our trade and control distant markets.

What is all of that? An inflated balloon that a pinprick will be enough to deflate.

Where is influence today? Is it at the mouths of cannon or the points of bayonets? No, it is in ideas, institutions, and the sight of their success.

Peoples affect each other through the arts, literature, philosophy, journalism, trading transactions, and above all by example, and if they also act on occasion through constraint and threats, I cannot believe that this type of influence is likely to develop the principles that encourage humanity to progress.

The rebirth of literature and the arts in Italy, the revolution of 1688 in England, and the Declaration of Independence in the United States have doubtless contributed to the outburst of generosity that enabled our fathers to accomplish such great things in 1789. In all this, where do we see the hand of brute force?

People say: "The triumph of French arms at the turn of this century has broadcast our ideas everywhere and left the imprint of our politics on the entire surface of Europe."

But do we know, can we know what would have happened in other circumstances? If France had not been attacked, if the revolution pushed to the brink by resistance had not slipped into a bloodbath, if it had not ended up in military despotism, if, instead of grieving, terrifying, and disrupting Europe, it had shown it the sublime sight of a great people peacefully accomplishing its destiny, with rational and beneficial institutions ensuring the good fortune of its citizens, is there anyone who would assert that an example like this would not have aroused the ardor of the oppressed and weakened the aversions of oppressors in our vicinity? Is there anyone who would say that the triumph of democracy in Europe would not now be further advanced? Let us calculate therefore all the waste of time, just ideas, wealth, and genuine force that these major wars have cost democracy and take account of the doubts they have raised for a quarter of a century about popular rights and about political truth!

And then, how is it that there is not enough impartiality in the depths of our national conscience to understand how much our pretensions to impose an idea by force wound the hearts of our brothers abroad? What! We, the most sensitive people in Europe, we who, rightly, would not allow the intervention of an English regiment even if it were to erect a statue to freedom on the soil of our country and teach us social perfection itself! When we all, up to the old rubble of Koblenz,[25] are in agreement on this point, that we would need to unite to break the grip of the foreign hand that comes bearing arms to interfere in our sorry debates, it is we who constantly have this irritating word on our lips: *preponderance,* and we do not know how to show freedom to our brothers other than with a sword in our hand aimed at their breasts! How have we come to imagine that the human heart is not the same everywhere, that it does not everywhere have the same pride or the same horror of dependence?

But last, where is this illiberal preponderance that we pursue so blindly and, in my view, with such great injustice, and have we ever seized hold of it? I can see the efforts clearly but not the results. I can see clearly that for a long time we have had a huge army and naval power that crush the people, ruin workers, generate disaffection, and drive us to bankruptcy. They threaten us with terrible calamities on which the very eyes of imagination tremble to gaze. I see all of this, but I cannot see preponderance anywhere, and if we have any weight in the destiny of Europe it is not through brute force but in spite of it. Proud of our prodigious military state, we have quarreled with the United States[26] and we yielded; we have had arguments relating to Egypt and we yielded; from year to year we have made promises to Poland and Italy and not kept them. Why? Because the deployment of our forces has provoked a similar deployment throughout Europe. Once this happened, we could no longer doubt that the slightest combat concerning the most futile cause might threaten to take on the proportions of a world war, and

25. German city to which some aristocrats had emigrated after 1790. They had tried to organize a counterrevolutionary army under the prince de Condé. See also the entry for "Bourbon, Louis Joseph de," in the Glossary of Persons.

26. Some American vessels were seized irregularly between 1806 and 1812. In July 1831, the French government agreed to pay twenty-five million francs to the United States. In April 1834, the parliament had not yet ratified the agreement! Following a complaint by President Jackson and a mediation by Great Britain, a new agreement was signed in 1834.

humanity as well as prudence has enjoined statesmen to decline any such responsibility.

What is remarkable and very instructive is that the people who have pushed this pretentious and cantankerous policy the furthest, the English, who have led us on by their example and perhaps made it a hard necessity for us, have reaped the same disappointments from it. No nation has gone so far as they in laying exclusive claim to regulate the balance of power in Europe, and this balance has been compromised ten times without their moving. The English arrogated to themselves the monopoly of colonies, and we have taken Algiers and the Marquise Islands without their moving. It is true that in this they may have been suspected of having, with apparent ill humor but secret joy, seen us attach two balls and chains to our feet. They claimed to be the owners of Oregon and the patron of Texas, and the United States have taken Oregon, Texas, and part of Mexico to cap it all, without their reacting. All this proves to us that, while the minds of governments are full of war, those of the governed are full of peace, and as for me, I do not see why we should have carried out a democratic revolution if not to ensure the triumph of a spirit of democracy, the working democracy which indeed pays the costs of a military system but can only ever draw from it ruin, danger, and oppression.

I therefore believe that the time has come when the entire genius of the French Revolution must come together, make its presence felt, and glorify itself solemnly through one of these acts of greatness, loyalty, progress, self-belief, and confidence in its strength, on the likes of which the sun has never shone. I believe that the time has come when France should resolutely declare that it sees the solidarity of peoples in the linking of their interests and the communication of their ideas and not in the interjection of brute force. And to give this declaration irresistible weight—for what is a mere manifesto, however eloquent it is?—I believe that the time has come for it to dissolve this brute force itself.

If our beloved and glorious country took the initiative in Europe of carrying out this revolution, what would its consequences be?

First of all, to enter into my subject, here at one fell swoop our finances would be in balance. Here is the first part of my reform immediately put into practice. Taxes would be relieved. Work, confidence, well-being, credit, and consumption would reach down to the masses. The republic would be loved, admired, and consolidated through the strength given to institutions by public support. The threatening ghost of bankruptcy would be banished from people's thoughts. Political upheavals would be a thing of the past. At last, France would be happy and glorious among nations, with the irresistible force of her example shining all around her.

Not only would the achievement of the democratic task inflame hearts abroad at the sight of this spectacle, but the spectacle itself would also certainly make that achievement easier. Elsewhere, as in our country, it is difficult to make people love revolutions that result in new taxes. Elsewhere, as in our country, people feel the need to break out of this circle. Our threatening attitude is, for foreign governments, a continuing reason or pretext for extracting money from their people and for raising a soldiery. How much easier would the work of regeneration be made all over Europe if it could be accomplished under the influence of tax reforms, which are fundamentally questions of approval and disapproval and questions of life and death for new institutions!

What are the objections to this?

National *dignity*. I have already indicated the reply to this. Is it to benefit their dignity that France and England, after being crushed by taxes to finance their military might, have always refused to do what they have announced they would? In this manner of understanding national dignity, there is a trace of our Roman education. At the time when peoples lived from plunder, it was important for them to inspire terror far and wide at the sight of their mighty armies. Is this also true for those who base their progress on work? The American people are reproached for a lack of dignity. If this is true, it is at least not so in American foreign policy, to which a tradition of peace and nonintervention gives such an imposing character of justice and grandeur.

*Everyone at home, everyone for himself* is the policy of selfishness, that is what people will say. A terrible objection if it had any common sense. Yes, everyone at home, *when it comes to brute force,* but let the influence of moral strength, intellectual and economic, emanating from each national center freely mingle and their contact give out light and fraternity for the benefit of the human race. It is very strange that we are accused of selfishness, we who always support expansion against restriction. Our code is this: "The least possible contact between governments, the most contact possible between peoples." Why? Because contact between governments compromises peace, whereas contact between peoples guarantees it.

*Security abroad*. Yes, I agree that there is an interlocutory question to be resolved. Are we or are we not threatened with invasion? There are some who sincerely believe that there is danger. Other kings, they say, are too interested in extinguishing the revolutionary flame in France not to flood it with their soldiers if France disarms. Those who think this way are right to demand that our forces be maintained. However, they have to accept the consequences. If we maintain our forces, we cannot reduce our expenditure significantly and we should not reduce taxes; it would even be our duty to increase them, since budgets are settled in deficit each year. If we increase our taxes there is one thing of which we are not sure, and that is that we will increase our revenue; one thing, however, on which there is no possible doubt is that we will generate disaffection, hatred, and resistance in this country, and we will have ensured security abroad only at the expense of security at home.

For my part, I would not hesitate to vote in favor of disarmament, since I do not believe there will be invasions. Where will they come from? Spain? Italy? Prussia? Austria? That is impossible. There remain England and Russia. England! She has already tried the experiment, and twenty-two billion of debt on which workers are still paying the interest is a lesson that cannot be lost. Russia! That is just an illusion. Contact with France is not what she is seeking but rather what she is avoiding. And if Emperor Nicholas thought of sending two hundred thousand Muscovites to us, I sincerely believe that what it would be best for us to do would be to welcome them, have them taste the sweetness of our wines, show them our streets, our shops, our museums, the happiness of our people, and the gentleness and equitableness of our penal laws, following which we would say to them: "Retrace your path to your steppes as quickly as possible and tell your fellow men what you have seen."

*Protection for trade.* People say, "Do we not need a powerful navy to open out new routes for our trade and control distant markets?" Truly the ways of government toward trade are strange. They start by hindering it, hampering it, restricting it, and stifling it at huge expense. Then if a fraction of it escapes, that same government becomes deeply attached to such few crumbs as have succeeded in passing through the nets of the customs service. We want to protect traders, they say, and to do this we will seize 250 million from the public in order to cover the oceans with ships and cannon. But first of all, 99 percent of French trade is carried out with countries in which our flag has never appeared nor will ever appear. Have we got trading posts in England, the United States, Belgium, Spain, the Zollverein, or Russia? This must therefore concern Mayotte and Nosibé;[27] that is to say, more is being taken away from us in taxes in francs than we are receiving in centimes through this trade.

And then, what is controlling the markets? Just one thing: *low prices*. Send products that cost five sous more than similar products from England or Switzerland anywhere you like and ships and cannon will not ensure that you sell them. Send products that cost five sous less there and you will not need cannon or ships to sell them. Do we not know that Switzerland, which does not have a single boat, unless there are some on its lakes, has even ousted from Gibraltar some English fabrics, in spite of the guard that is on watch at its gates? If, therefore, *low prices* are the true protectors of trade, how does our government go about achieving them? First of all, it raises the cost of raw materials, all tools of the trade, and all consumer products through customs duties; then, to compensate, it burdens us with taxes on the pretext of sending its navy to seek outlets. This is barbarism, the most barbaric barbarism, and it will not be long before people say: "The French in the nineteenth century had very strange trading systems; they ought at least to have refrained from considering themselves to be in the *century of enlightenment*."

*Balance of power in Europe.* We need an army to keep a watch on the balance of power in Europe. The English say the same, and balance becomes what the wind of revolution makes it. The subject is too wide-ranging for me to tackle it here. I will say just a little about it. "Let us mistrust metaphor," said Paul-Louis,[28] and he was very right. Here it is, as presented to us on three occasions in the form of balances. First of all, we have the *balance of the European powers,* then the *balance of powers,* and finally the *balance of trade.* Volumes would be needed to list the evils that have resulted from these alleged balances, and I am just writing an article.

*Internal security.* The worst enemy of logic, after metaphor, is the vicious circle. Well, here we are encountering one vicious in the highest degree. "Let us crush the taxpayers in order to have a great army, and then let us have a great army to contain the taxpayers." Is this not the position we are in? What internal security can we expect from a financial system whose effect is to generate general disaffection and whose result is bankruptcy and its

---

27. Mayotte is part of French overseas territory and belongs to the Comoro Islands, off the northwest coast of Madagascar. Nosibé is a town on the northern side of Madagascar.
28. Paul-Louis Cornier.

political consequences? I myself believe that if we allowed the workers to breathe, if they had the feeling that all that could be done for them was being done, the disruptors of public peace would have very few grounds for disturbance at their disposal. Certainly the National Guard, the police, and the gendarmerie would be enough to contain them. And last, we have to take account of the terrors that are specific to the age in which we are living. They are very natural and very justified. Let us strike a bargain with them and allocate two hundred thousand men to them until times improve. You can see that my devotion to my point of view does not make me either absolutist or stubborn.

Let us now sum up the situation.

We have formulated our program thus: "reduce taxes—reduce expenditure in a greater proportion."

This is a program that is bound to lead to balance, not via the path of distress, but via that of general prosperity.

In the initial part of this article, we have proposed to abolish various taxes, thus involving a loss of one hundred million in revenue, compared with the budget presented by the cabinet. Our program will therefore be fulfilled if the preceding considerations result in a reduction of expenditure in excess of a hundred million.

However, apart from the cuts that would be manageable in various services if only we had a little faith in freedom, cuts that I am not requesting out of respect for a misguided public opinion, we have the following *items:*

1. *The costs of collection.* As soon as indirect taxes are reduced, the incitement to fraud will be blunted. Fewer hindrances will be needed, fewer annoying formalities, less inquisitorial surveillance, in a word, fewer employees. What can be done in this respect just in the Customs Service alone is huge—let us say, ten million.

2. *The administrative costs of criminal justice.* In the entire physical universe, there are no two facts that are more closely connected than *destitution* and *crime.* If the effect of the implementation of our plan has the necessary result of increasing the well-being and work of the people, it is inevitable that the costs of pursuing, repressing, and punishing miscreants will be reduced.—*For the record.*

3. *Assistance.* The same must be said for assistance, which should decrease because of the increase in well-being.—*For the record.*

4. *Foreign affairs.* The policy of nonintervention, the one our fathers ac-

claimed in 1789, the one that Lamartine would have inaugurated were it not for the pressure of circumstances beyond his control, the one that Cavaignac would have been proud to carry out, this policy leads to the abolition of all the embassies. This is little from the financial point of view. It is a great deal from the political and moral point of view.—*For the record.*

5. *The army.* We have allowed two hundred thousand men for the contingencies of the moment. That makes two hundred million. Let us add fifty million for unforeseen events, withdrawals, payments for being on call, etc. Compared with the official budget, the savings are one hundred million.

6. *The navy.* One hundred thirty million are being requested. Let us allow eighty million and return fifty million to the taxpayers. Trade will be all the more prosperous.

7. *Public works.* I am not a great partisan, I admit, of savings whose result is the slumbering or death of committed capital. However, we must bow to necessity. We are being asked for 194 million. Let us remove thirty million.

Without much effort, we will thus obtain, in round figures, two hundred million of savings in expenditure, against one hundred million in revenue. We are thus on the path to balance, and my task is fulfilled.

That of the cabinet and the National Assembly, however, is just beginning. And here, in closing, I will spell out my entire thinking.

I believe that the proposed plan, or any other based on the same principles, can on its own save the Republic, the country, and society. All the parts of this plan are linked together. If you take only the first, to reduce taxes, you will be advancing toward revolution through bankruptcy. If you take just the second, to reduce expenditure, you will be advancing toward revolution through destitution. By adopting the plan in its entirety, you will simultaneously avoid bankruptcy, destitution, and revolutions, and on top of this, you will do the people good. It therefore forms a complete system, which has to stand or fall in its entirety.

However, I fear that a unitary and methodical plan cannot spring from nine hundred brains. Nine hundred projects may well emerge, which will clash with each other, but not one project that will triumph.

In spite of the goodwill of the National Assembly, the opportunity will be missed and the country lost if the cabinet does not take the initiative vigorously.

However, the cabinet is rejecting this initiative. They presented their budget, which does nothing for the taxpayer and leads to a frightful deficit.

They then said: "We do not have to issue an overall view, and we will discuss the details when the time comes." In other words, "We are handing over the destiny of France to chance or rather to probabilities that are as terrifying as they are certain."

And why is this when the cabinet is made up of competent men, patriots and financiers? It is doubtful whether any other government could have accomplished the work of common salvation better.

They are not even trying. Why? Because they have entered office with a *preconceived idea. A preconceived idea!* I should have placed you, as the scourge of all reasoning and conduct, far ahead of the metaphor and the vicious circle!

The government has said to itself, "We cannot do anything with this Assembly, since we will not have a majority!"

I will not examine all the disastrous consequences of this preconceived idea here.

When it is believed that an Assembly is an obstacle, the wish to dissolve it is very close.

When one wishes to dissolve an Assembly, one is very close to taking steps to achieve this purpose.

In this way, great efforts have been made to do harm just at the time when it was so urgent to devote them to doing good.

Time and strength have been worn out in a deplorable conflict. And, I say this with my hand on my heart, in this conflict the cabinet was in the wrong.

For after all, to base their action or rather their inertia on the premise "We will not have a majority," they needed at least to put forward something useful and then wait for a refusal to cooperate.

The president of the Republic traced a wiser path when he said on the day of his installation, "I have no reason to believe that I will not agree with the National Assembly."

On what, therefore, did the cabinet base themselves when they set the point of departure of their policy in an opposing direction in advance? On the fact that the National Assembly had shown sympathy for the candidature of General Cavaignac.

However, the cabinet members have thus not understood that there is one thing that the Assembly places a hundred and a thousand times above General Cavaignac! That is the will of the people, expressed through universal suffrage, by virtue of a constitution formulated by the will of the people itself.

For my part, I say that, to express its respect for the will of the people and the constitution, our twin anchors of salvation, the Assembly might have been easier with Bonaparte than with Cavaignac himself.

Yes, if the government, instead of starting by promoting the conflict, had come to the Assembly to say, "The election of 20 December[29] puts an end to the period of agitation of our revolution, and now let us concentrate in concert on the good of the people and administrative and financial reform," I say with certainty that the Assembly would have followed them enthusiastically since it has a passion for good and cannot have any other.

Now the opportunity has been lost, and if we do not secure its rebirth, woe to our finances and woe to the country for centuries to come.

Well then! I believe that if each person forgets his complaints and represses his bitterness, France can still be saved.

Ministers of the Republic, do not say: "We will act later; we will look for reforms with another Assembly." Do not make such statements, for France is on the brink of an abyss. She does not have the time to wait for you.

A government frozen, made rigid by inertia! That has never been seen before. And what a time you have chosen to present us with this sight! It is true that the country—ruined, wounded, and bruised—does not blame you for its suffering. All its prejudices are turned against the National Assembly; this is certainly a circumstance that is as convenient as it is rare for a cabinet. But do you not know that any false prejudice is fleeting? If, through a vigorous initiative, you had formally warned the Assembly and it refused to follow you, you would have been justified and the country would have been right. But you did not do this. Sooner or later, its eyes will inevitably be opened, and if you continue to put nothing forward, try nothing, and direct nothing and later the state of our finances becomes irreparable, the prejudice of the day may well absolve you, but history will never absolve you.

It has now been decided that the National Assembly will produce the budget. But will an assembly of nine hundred members, left to its own devices, be able to accomplish such a complex work, one that requires such a high degree of agreement between all its parts and components? From the parliamentary tumult there may well emerge a few fumblings, impulses, and aspirations; a financial plan will not emerge.

This at least is my conviction. If it enters the mind of the cabinet to leave the reins loose at the mercy of chance, reins that have assuredly not been en-

29. A slight mistake: the election took place on 10 December.

trusted to it for this purpose, if its members are resolved to remain impassive and indifferent spectators of the vain efforts of the Assembly, the Assembly should refrain from undertaking a work that it cannot accomplish alone and should decline any responsibility for a situation that it has not caused.

But this will not happen. No, France will not have to go through this disaster too. The cabinet will take the initiative incumbent on it energetically, with no mental reservations and in a spirit of selflessness. It will present a plan for financial reform based on this twin principle: reduce taxes—reduce expenditures in an even greater proportion. And the Assembly will vote for it with enthusiasm, without dragging matters out and becoming bogged down in the details.

To relieve the people, make the Republic loved, base security on popular approval, make good the deficit, raise confidence, breathe new life into work, restore credit, diminish deprivation, reassure Europe, bring about justice, freedom, and peace, and offer the world the sight of a great people who have never been better governed than when they are governed by themselves: is there nothing in this to awaken the noble ambition of a government and arouse the soul of the man who carries the heritage of the name Napoléon! A heritage that, in spite of the glory surrounding it, has two jewels that shine by their absence, peace and freedom!

## Consequences of the Reduction of the Salt Tax
(*Le Journal des débats*, 1 January 1849)

The immediate reduction of the salt tax has disoriented the cabinet in one respect, with good reason. It is being said that we are seeking new taxes to fill the gap. Is this really what the Assembly wanted? Reductions would be only a game and one of these unfortunate games in which everyone loses. What is the meaning of their vote, then? It is this: expenditure is constantly rising; there is just one means of forcing the state to reduce expenditure, and that is to make it absolutely impossible for the state to do otherwise.

The means the Assembly has adopted is heroic, we must agree. What is still more serious is that the reform of the salt tax was preceded by the reform of the postal services and will probably be followed by the reform of wines and spirits.

The government is disoriented. Well then! For my part, I say that the Assembly could not put it in a better position. This is a wonderful, and one might say providential, opportunity to go down a new path, to put an end to false philanthropy and warlike passions and, converting its failure into triumph, to deliver security, confidence, credit, and prosperity from a vote that appeared to compromise it and at last to found a republican politics on these two great principles, peace and freedom.

Following the resolution from the Assembly, I was expecting, I must admit, the president of the Council to ascend the rostrum and make a speech along these lines:

"Citizen Representatives,

"Your vote yesterday has shown us a new path; more than this, it *obliges* us to go down it.

"You know how much the February revolution aroused illusory hopes and dangerous theorizing. These hopes and systems, clad in the false colors of philanthropy and entering this chamber in the form of draft laws, were directed at nothing less than destroying freedom and swallowing up the public wealth. We did not know which way to turn. Rejecting all these projects was to upset public opinion in a temporary state of exaltation; accepting them was to compromise the future, violate all rights, and distort the attributions of the state. What were we to do? Procrastinate, compromise, accommodate error, give partial satisfaction to the utopians, enlighten the people through the hard lesson of experience, and create administrative departments with the ulterior purpose of abolishing them later, which is not easy to do. Now, thanks to the Assembly, we are at ease. Do not come any longer to ask us to monopolize education or credit, finance agriculture, favor certain industries, and turn charitable giving into a system. We have finished with the harmful tail of socialism. Your vote has delivered the death blow to its dreaming. We no longer even have to discuss it, for where would discussion lead, since you have removed from us the means to carry out these dangerous experiments? If someone knows the secret of carrying out official philanthropy with no money, let him come forward; here are our portfolios, we will hand them over to him with joy. As long as they remain in our hands, in the new situation that has been established for us, it remains for us only to proclaim freedom as the basis of our domestic policy, freedom for the arts, sciences, agriculture, industry, work, trade, the press, and teaching, for freedom is the only system compatible with a reduced budget. The state needs money to regulate and oppress. No money, no regulation. Our role, with very little expenditure, will henceforward be limited to repressing abuses, that is to say, preventing one citizen's freedom from being exercised at the expense of another's.

"Our foreign policy is no less clearly marked and *obligatory*. We were making compromises and we were still fumbling; now we are irrevocably directed, not only by choice but also by necessity. Happy, a thousand times happy that this necessity imposes on us exactly the policy that we would have adopted by choice. We are resolved to reduce our military posture. You should clearly note that there is nothing to discuss in this regard; we have to act, for we have the choice of disarmament or bankruptcy. It is said that one should choose the lesser of two evils. Here, according to us, the only choice is between an immense good and a terrible evil and, in spite of this, even yesterday the choice was not an easy one for us. False philanthropy and warlike passions stood in our way, and we had to take them into consideration. Today they have forcibly been reduced to silence, for whatever people say about passion failing to reason, it nevertheless cannot lack reason to the point of demanding that we wage war with no money. We have therefore come to this rostrum to proclaim disarmament as a fact, and consequently that nonintervention is the basis of our foreign policy. Let nobody speak to us any longer of preponderance and dominance; let nobody point to Hungary, Italy, and Poland as fields of glory and carnage. We know what can be said for or against armed propaganda when we have the choice. But you will not disagree that when you no longer have it, controversy is superfluous. The army will be reduced to what is necessary to guarantee the independence of the country, and at the same time all nations may henceforward count on their independence as far as we are concerned. Let them carry out their reforms as they will; let them undertake only that which they can accomplish. We will let them know loudly and clearly that none of the parties that divide them can count on the support of our bayonets. What am I saying? They do not even need our protestations, since these bayonets will be returned to their sheaths or rather, for added security, they will be converted into ploughshares.

"I can hear interruptions coming down from these benches; you are saying: 'This is the policy of everyone at home, everyone for himself.' Even yesterday we might have discussed the value of this policy, since we were free to adopt another. Yesterday, I would have quoted reasons. I would have said, 'Yes, everyone at home, everyone for himself, as long as it is a matter of brute force.' This is not to say that the links between peoples will be broken. Let us have philosophical, scientific, artistic, literary, and trade relations with everyone. Through this, humanity will become enlightened and make progress. However, I do not want relations at the point of a sword and the barrel of a gun.

It is a strange abuse of words to say that families that get on well with one another conduct their lives according to the principle "Every man's home is his castle" simply because they don't visit each other *armed to the teeth*.[30] Besides, what would we say if, to end our differences, Lord Palmerston sent us English regiments? Would not our cheeks flush with indignation? How is it therefore that we refuse to believe that other peoples also cherish their dignity and independence? This is what I would have said yesterday, for when there is a choice between two policies, the one that is preferred has to be justified by the giving of reasons. Today, I am merely invoking necessity, since we no longer have any option. The majority, who have refused us the revenue in order to oblige us to reduce expenditure, would not be so inconsistent as to impose a ruinous policy on us. If anyone, knowing that the taxes on the post, salt, and wines and spirits are going to be reduced considerably, knowing that we are facing a deficit of five hundred million, still has the temerity to proclaim the clear need for armed propaganda, or who, threatening Europe, obliges us, even in peacetime, to undertake ruinous efforts, let him stand up and take this portfolio. As for us, we will not assume the shame of such puerility. Therefore, from today onward, the policy of nonintervention is proclaimed. From today onward, measures will be taken to dismiss part of the army. From today onward, orders will go out to abolish useless embassies.

"Peace and freedom! This is the policy that we would have adopted by conviction. We would thank the Assembly for having made it an absolute and clear necessity for us. It will ensure the salvation, glory, and prosperity of the republic and will ensure that history will retain our names."

Here, it seems to me, is what the current cabinet ought to have said. Its words would have received the unanimous approval of the Assembly, France, and Europe.

30. It is not clear what Bastiat is saying here. He uses part of a French proverb, "chacun chez soi et les vaches seront bien gardées" (each in their own home and the cows will be well guarded). One might compare it to the English idea of "good fences make good neighbors," but we have used the proverb "every man's home is his castle" to be closer to Bastiat's idea about the role of force and coercion in disrupting social bonds.

## Discourse on the Tax on Wines and Spirits[1,2]

[vol. 5, p. 468. "Discours sur l'impôt des
boissons." 12 December 1849. n.p.]

*Citizen Representatives,*

I wanted to discuss the question of the tax on wines and spirits as it appears to me to exist in the understandings of all of you, that is to say, from the point of view of financial and political necessity. I thought, in effect, that necessity was the only reason invoked to support the retention of this tax; I believed that in your eyes it brought together all the features by which economic science teaches us to recognize bad taxes. I believed that it had been accepted that this tax is unjust and inequitable and that its collection involved extremely tedious and annoying formalities. However, since the reproaches directed against this tax by all statesmen since its inception are now being disputed, I will say a few quick words about it.

First of all, we claim that the tax is unjust and base our claim on the following: Here are parcels of land that are side by side and subject to a land tax, a direct tax. These parcels are classified and compared with each other and taxed in accordance with their value. Subsequently, each person may

---

1. (Paillottet's note) This unprepared talk was delivered to the Legislative Assembly on 12 December 1849.
2. Inherited from the First Empire, taxes on alcoholic beverages had three components:

> 1. A "circulation" duty
> 2. A retail tax
> 3. An "entrance duty," when the drink was introduced into a city of more than four thousand inhabitants.

These taxes were very unpopular and were abolished in May 1849 by the Assembly; however, in December the minister of finance proposed to reestablish them as part of an attempt to balance the budget.

grow anything he wants on them; some grow wheat, others pasture, yet others carnations and roses, and others vines.

Well then, of all these products, there is one and only one that, once it has entered into circulation, is subject to a tax that yields 106 million to the treasury. All the other agricultural products are free from this tax.

It might be said that the tax is useful and necessary, and this is not the subject with which I wish to deal, but it cannot be said that it is not unjust from the owner's point of view.

It is true that it is said that the tax does not fall on the producer. I will examine this later.

We then say that the tax is badly distributed.

In fact, I was very surprised that this has been disputed, since . . . (interruption)

*A member on the right:* Speak a little louder!

*The president:* Will the Assembly be silent please?

*M. F. Bastiat:* I am even ready to abandon this argument in the interest of speed.

*Various voices:* Speak! Speak!

*M. F. Bastiat:* The matter seems to me to be so clear, it is so obvious that the tax is badly distributed that, truly, it is embarrassing to demonstrate this.

When we see, for example, that a man who, in an orgy, drinks six francs' worth of champagne pays the same tax as a worker who needs to restore his strength for work and drinks six sous' worth of ordinary wine, it is impossible to say that there is no inequality, no monstrousness in the distribution of the tax on wines and spirits. (Hear! Hear!)

Calculus has almost been used to establish that the tax is negligible, that these are fractions of a centime and ought not to be taken into account. In this way, a class of citizens has been burdened with 106 million of an iniquitous tax by being told: "This is nothing. You should consider yourselves fortunate!" The men who invoke this argument ought to be telling you: "We are operating such and such an industry, and we are so convinced that the tax, by being split up, cannot be felt by the consumer on whom it falls that we are subjecting ourselves to the indirect tax and to the "exercise"[3] in the case of the industry we are involved with. The day when these men come to the rostrum to say this, I will say: "They are sincere in their defense of the tax on wines and spirits."

---

3. The "exercise" was a control carried out by the tax officials at the wholesalers.

But anyhow here are some figures. In the Department of the Ain, the average wholesale price of wine is eleven francs, and the average retail sales price in forty-one francs. This is a considerable difference; it is obvious that he who is able to buy wine wholesale pays eleven francs and that he who is obliged to purchase it retail pays forty-one francs. Between eleven and forty-one francs the difference is thirty francs. (Interruption.)

*A member on the right:* It is not the tax that causes this difference; this is the same for all goods.

*The president:* M. de Charencey has done his calculations; allow the speaker to do his own.

*M. F. Bastiat:* I could quote other *départements,* but I have taken the first on the list. Doubtless, there is profit to the salesman, but the tax is a considerable proportion of this difference.

In the last two days, efforts have been made to prove such extraordinary things that I really would not be surprised if efforts were made to prove that the tax harmed no one, neither the producer nor the consumer. But if this is so, let us tax everything, not just wines but *all* products!

I then say that the tax is very costly to collect. I will not quote figures to prove this; figures can be used to prove a great many things. When figures are quoted on this rostrum, people think they are giving them great authority by saying: "These are official figures." However, official figures mislead just like the others; it all depends on the use made of them.

The fact is that when we see functionaries, and well-paid ones, operating across the entire territory of France in order to collect this tax, we are quite justified in our belief that its collection is very expensive.

Last, let us note that the collection of this tax is accompanied by tedious and annoying formalities. This is a point that the speakers who preceded me on this rostrum have not dealt with. This does not surprise me since all or nearly all of them come from *départements* that do not grow vines. If they lived in our *départements,* they would know that the complaints of vineyard owners against the tax on wines and spirits are directed less against the tax itself, its magnitude, than against these annoying, anger-provoking, and dangerous formalities, which are seen as so many traps set at every stage under their feet. (Approval from the left.)

Everyone understands that when this extraordinary thought, this immense utopia—for it was immense then—was conceived, namely, establishing a duty on the circulation of wines without a prior inventory being carried out, everyone, I say, understands that, in order to ensure its collection, it was necessary to conceive a code of the most severely preventive kind, even to the point of harassment, since otherwise how would they have done it? It was necessary that, for a cask of wine to circulate openly in a commune there had to be an employee to determine whether it was in accordance with the rules or not. That cannot be done without an army of employees and a host of irritating interventions against which, I repeat, the taxpayers complain even more than against the tax itself.

The tax on wines and spirits has another very serious consequence, which I have not heard pointed out on this rostrum.

The tax on wines and spirits has caused a disturbance in that great economic phenomenon that is known as the division of labor. In former times, vines were grown in soils that were suited to them, on the slopes of hills and on gravel. Wheat was grown on the plateaus and flat open fields and on alluvial soil. In the beginning an inventory[4] was devised, but this method of tax collection caused an uprising among all the landowners. They invoked the rights of property and, as there were three million of them, they were listened to. The burden was then cast onto the café owners and, as there were only three hundred thousand of them, it was declared that, in principle, the property of three hundred thousand men was not property to the same extent as that of three million men although, as it happens, property has always had only the one basis, in my opinion.

But what was the result for the landowners? I believe that the landowners themselves bear the weight of the fault and injustice they then committed. Since they enjoyed the privilege of consuming their products without paying tax, it transpired that, either to avoid the tax or to avoid in particular and above all the formalities and risks to which its collection subjects people, the owners of flat, open fields and alluvial soils all wanted to have vines on their property for their own consumption. In the *département* that I represent here, or at least in the major part of this *département,* I can state positively that there is not one sharecropping farm on which there are not sufficient vines planted for the family's consumption. These vines produce very bad wine, but this offers the immense advantage of being free from the intervention of indirect taxes and all the risks attached to inspections.

This fact explains to a certain extent the increase in the numbers of vines planted that has been pointed out. This increase is often set against the com-

4. The inventory was drawn up in order to check the honesty of producers' declarations of crops.

plaints of the landowners, who claim to be the victims of injustice; and the landowners appear to be told: "This injustice does not count; it is nothing, since vines are being planted in France."

First of all, I would like someone to quote me an industry that, in the period from 1788 to 1850, the space of sixty-two years, has not expanded in this proportion. I would like to know, for example, if the coal, iron, and cloth industries have not expanded in this proportion. I would like to know if there is any industry of which it can be said that it has not grown by a quarter in the space of sixty years. Would it be so very surprising that, following its natural development, the industry most firmly rooted in our soil, the industry that is able to provide the entire universe with its products, should increase by this amount? However, this increase, sirs, is provoked by the law itself. It is the law that causes people to dig up vines on the hill slopes and plant them in the flat fields to avoid the vexations of indirect taxation. That is a huge and obvious disturbance.

I ask you to allow me to draw your entire attention to a fact that is almost local in character, since it concerns only a single district, but is of major importance, at least in my eyes, since it is linked to a general law.

This fact, sirs, will also be useful in replying to the argument brought to this rostrum when, invoking the authority of Adam Smith, it was said that the tax always falls on the consumer, with the implication that, for the last forty years, all the owners of vineyards in France have been wrong to complain and ignorant of what they have been talking about. Yes, I am one of those who believe that tax falls on the consumer, but I also add this aside: it is in the long term, with the passage of time, when all the properties have changed hands following economic arrangements that take a long time to be concluded, that this great result is achieved, and for all the time that this revolution lasts, suffering may be great, enormous. I will give you an example.

In my district,[5] which is a vine-growing one, there used to be great prosperity. There was general well-being. Vines were grown and the wine was consumed in the local area, in the surrounding plains where vines were not grown, or abroad in northern Europe.

Suddenly, the customs war on the one hand, the war of city tolls on the

5. Saint-Sever.

other, and the amalgamation taxes[6] came along and depreciated the value of this wine.

The region of which I am speaking was cultivated in its entirety, especially with regard to vines, by sharecroppers. Sharecroppers retained one half and the landowner the other half of the product. The areas of the sharecropper farms were cultivated in such a way that a sharecropper and his family were able to live on the value of the half quantity of wine that remained to them, but when the value of the wine depreciated, the sharecropper was no longer able to live on his share. He then went to his landowner and told him: "I can no longer cultivate your vines if you do not feed me." The landowner gave him corn to live on and then, at the end of the year, he took the entire harvest to reimburse himself for his advance. Since the harvest was not enough to cover the advance, the contract was modified, not before the notary but in practice; the landowner had workers to whom he gave their food only in corn, as a total payment for their work.

However, a way out of this situation had to be found, and this is how the revolution was carried out. The sharecropping farms were expanded; that is to say, two were formed out of three or one out of two. Then, by grubbing up a few fields of vines and by growing corn in their place, it was said: "The sharecropper can live on this corn and the landowner will no longer be obliged to give him extra corn to ensure his subsistence."

Over all the communes, people thus saw houses being torn down and sharecropping farms destroyed. Consequently, as many families as sharecropping farms were destroyed; depopulation became rife, and in the last twenty-five years the number of deaths has exceeded that of births.

Doubtless, when the revolution is fully completed, when the landowners have bought for ten thousand francs what used to cost them thirty thousand francs, when the number of sharecroppers is reduced to the level of the means of subsistence that the region is able to provide, then I believe that the population will no longer be able to blame the tax on wines and spirits. The revolution will be complete, and the tax will fall on the consumer; however, this revolution will be achieved at the price of suffering that will have endured for one or two centuries.

I ask whether it is for this that we are making laws. I ask whether we

---

6. The "amalgamation taxes" were a combination of taxes introduced by Napoléon under the name "droits réunis."

raise taxes to torment the population, to oblige them to shift work from the hill slopes to the flat fields and from the flat fields to the hill slopes. I ask whether this is the aim of legislation. For my part, I do not think so.

Sirs, however much we attack the tax and say that it is inequitable, vexatious, costly, and unjust, there is one reason before which everyone bows his head; that reason is necessity. It is necessity that is invoked. It is necessity that obliges you to bring to this rostrum words that justify the tax. It is necessity and only necessity that determines your action. Financial problems are feared, as are the results of a reform (for I may properly call it a reform) whose immediate consequence would be to withhold one hundred million from the public treasury; it is therefore about necessity that I wish to speak.

Sirs, I admit that necessity exists and is very insistent. Yes, the balance sheet, not of France but of the French government, can be summed up in very few words. For the last twenty or twenty-five years, taxpayers have been supplying the treasury with a sum that, I believe, has doubled in this period. Successive governments have found ways to devour the original sum, the surplus supplied by taxpayers; to add a public debt of one or two billion to it; to reach at the start of the year a deficit of five or six hundred million; and finally to start the next year with an assured overdraft of three hundred million.

This is the position we are in. I believe that it is well worth the trouble to ask what the cause of this situation is and whether it is prudent in the face of this cause to tell us that the best thing to do is to restore things to the state they were in before, to change nothing or hardly anything in our financial system, or else to change imperceptibly, either with regard to revenue or to expenditure. I seem to see an engineer who has started a locomotive and caused a catastrophe, who then discovers where the fault lay and, without taking any other action, puts it back on the same rails and runs the same risk a second time. (Approval from the left.)

Yes, necessity exists but it is double. There are two necessities.

Finance minister, you mention only one necessity, but I will point out another, one that is extremely serious. I consider that it is even more serious than the one about which you are talking. This necessity is encapsulated in a single phrase: the February revolution.

There occurred, following abuses (since I call abuses everything that has led our finances into the state they are in now), an event; this event is sometimes said by people to have been a surprise. I do not think it was a surprise.

It is possible that the external event was the result of an accident that would have been stopped. . . .

*M. Barthélemy Saint-Hilaire:* Delayed!

*Several other members on the left:* Yes! Yes! Delayed!

*M. Bastiat:* But the general causes are not at all fortuitous. It is just as though you were saying to me, when a passing breeze causes fruit to fall from its tree, that if we could have prevented the breeze from blowing, the fruit would not have fallen. Yes, but on one condition and that is that the fruit was not rotten and gnawed. (Approval from the left.) This event happened, this event has given political power to the entire mass of the population; that is a serious event.

*M. Fould, minister of finance:* Why did the provisional government not abolish the tax on wines and spirits?

*M. Bastiat:* It did not consult me, it did not submit a draft law to me and I was not called upon to give it advice; however, we have a draft here, and in rejecting your draft I am in a good position to tell you the reasons on which I base my reasoning. I base my reasoning on this: not one but two necessities weigh upon you. The second necessity, as imperious as the first, is to do justice to all citizens. (Agreement from the left.)

Well then! I say that following the revolution that has occurred, you ought to be concerned with the political state in which France finds itself and the fact that this political state is deplorable; allow me the word. I do not attribute this to the men governing it now; it goes back a long way.

Do you not see that in France a bureaucracy that has become an aristocracy is devouring the country? Industry is dying out and the people are suffering. I am fully aware that the people are seeking a remedy in wild utopias, but this is no reason for opening the door to these by leaving flagrant injustices to exist such as those I have been pointing out on this rostrum.

I believe that not enough attention is being paid to the state of suffering that exists in this country and to the causes of this suffering. These causes are rooted in the 1.5 billion raised in a country that cannot pay this sum.

I would ask you to have a very mundane thought, but for goodness' sake, I often indulge in one. I ask myself what has happened to my childhood and school friends. And do you know what the answer is? Out of twenty, there are fifteen who are civil servants, and I am convinced that if you do the calculation, you will reach the same result. (Approving laughter from the left.)

*M. Bérard:* That is what causes revolutions.

*M. Bastiat:* I also ask myself another question and it is this: taking them one by one, in all honesty, are they giving the country a genuine service worth what the country is paying them? And almost always I am obliged to reply: that is not the case.

Is it not deplorable that this huge amount of labor and intelligence has been withdrawn from the genuine production of the country to supply civil servants who are useless and almost always harmful? For when it comes to civil servants, there is no halfway house: if they are not very useful indeed, they are harmful; if they do not uphold the freedom of citizens, they stifle it. (Approval from the left.)

I say that this calls for necessary, nay absolutely imperative action by the government. What is the plan being proposed to us? I say frankly, if the minister had come and said: "The tax must be maintained for a short while, but here is a financial reform that I am putting forward. This is the plan in its entirety, but a certain period is needed for it to be accomplished. We need four or five years; we cannot do everything at once," I would have understood this necessity and I might have acceded to it.

But nothing of the sort has happened. We are being told: "Let us reestablish the tax on wines and spirits." I do not even know whether we are not being made to feel that the salt tax and the postal tax will be reestablished.

As for your reductions in expenditure, they are derisory: three thousand or four thousand soldiers more or less; however, it will be the very same financial system which in my view cannot last much longer in this country without ruining it. (New burst of approval from the left.)

Sirs, it is impossible to discuss this subject without doing so from this point of view: will France be ruined within a very short space of time? For I will be so bold as to ask the minister of finance how long he thinks he can prolong this system. It is not enough to reach the end of the year with an approximate balance between revenue and expenditure; we have to know if this can continue.

However, with this in mind, I really do have to discuss the question of tax in general. (Signs of impatience from the right.)

*A number of voices:* Speak! Speak!

*The president:* You have the floor.

*M. Bastiat:* I believe, sirs, that I have the right to come here on my own authority to express ideas, even absurd ones. Other speakers have come here to put forward their ideas and I make so bold as to believe that their ideas were no clearer than mine. You heard them patiently; you did not welcome

M. Proudhon's plan for general liquidation any more than M. Considérant's phalanstery, but you listened to them. You went even further; M. Thiers spoke for you all to say that whoever thought he had an idea of any use was under an obligation to bring it to this rostrum. Well then! When people say: "Speak!" when something of a challenge is thrown down, it must at least be listened to. (Hear! Hear!)

Sirs, we have lately spent a great deal of time on the tax question. Should taxes be direct or indirect?

A short time ago we heard indirect taxes being praised.

Well! For my part, I am raising my voice against indirect taxes in general.

I believe that there is a law of taxation which dominates the entire question, and which I encapsulate in this formula: the inequality of taxation lies in its mass. By that I mean that the lighter a tax is, the easier it is to spread it equitably. On the other hand, the heavier it is, the more likely it is, in spite of the good intentions of the legislator, to be spread inequitably and, as may be said, the more it tends to become regressive, that is to say, to burden citizens in inverse proportion to their ability to pay. I believe that this is a serious and inevitable law, and its consequences are of such importance that I ask your permission to clarify it.

I will suppose for the sake of argument that France has been governed for a long time according to my proposals, which would consist in the government's keeping each citizen within the limits of his rights and of justice and abandoning everything else to the responsibility of each person. This is my starting point. It is easy to see that in this case France could be governed with two hundred or three hundred million. It is clear that if France were governed with two hundred million, it would be easy to establish a single, proportional tax. (Murmurs.)

This hypothesis of mine will become reality. The only question is whether it will do so by virtue of the foresight of the legislator or by way of age-old political convulsions. (Approval from the left.)

The idea is not mine; if it was, I would distrust it, but we see that all the peoples of the world are more or less happy depending on whether they approach or distance themselves from the achievement of this idea. It has been achieved more or less totally in the United States.

In Massachusetts there are no taxes other than direct taxes that are unique and proportional. Consequently, if this be so, and it is easy to understand it since I am elucidating only the principle, nothing would be easier than to ask citizens to pay a proportional part of the assets they accumulate. This would be so inconsequential that no one would be tempted, at least to any great extent, to hide his wealth in order to escape it.

This is the first part of my axiom.

However, if you ask citizens to pay, not two hundred million but five hundred, six hundred, or eight hundred million, then as you increase taxes, direct taxes will escape your control and it is clear that you will reach a stage when a citizen would rather take up his gun than pay the state half his wealth, for example.

*A member:* As in the Ardèche.

*M. Bastiat:* So you will not be paid. What will you do then? You will have to turn to indirect taxes; this is what happens wherever major expenditure is wanted. Everywhere, as soon as the state wants to give citizens all sorts of benefits, such as education, religion, or a moral code, people are obliged to pay that state considerable indirect taxes.

Well then! I say that when you go down this path, you become mired in tax inequality. Inequality always stems from the indirect taxes themselves. The reason for this is simple. If expenditure were kept within certain limits, some indirect taxes which infringe equality but which would not arouse a feeling of injustice might certainly be found, because these would be luxury taxes; however, when the wish is to raise a great deal of money, then the schema I am assuming will operate leads to the articulation of a true principle, to the effect that the best tax is the one that affects the most generally consumed objects. This is a principle that all our financiers and statesmen acknowledge. And in fact, it is very consequent in the case of governments bent on taking as much money as possible from the people, but in this case the price is the most glaring inequality.

What is an object of mass consumption? It is one that the poor consume in the same proportion as the rich. It is an object on which workers spend all their earnings.

Thus, a currency trader earns five hundred francs a day, a worker earns five hundred francs a year, and justice would like the currency trader's five hundred francs to produce as much for the treasury as the worker's five hundred francs. But this does not happen, for the currency trader will buy drapes, bronzes, and luxury items with his money, that is to say, objects of limited consumption that are not taxed, whereas the worker buys wine, salt, or tobacco, that is to say, objects of mass consumption that are weighed down by taxes. (Murmurs and various interruptions.)

*M. Lacaze:* If the currency trader did not buy these objects, he would not give the worker a living.

*M. Bastiat:* Would the abolition of the tax on wines and spirits prevent the currency trader from buying bronzes and drapes? No financier will contradict my argument. Under indirect taxation, a system that I disapprove of, it is all too reasonable to tax only the objects of the greatest mass consumption. In this way you start charging for the air we breathe with a tax on doors and windows, followed by salt, then wines and spirits and tobacco, and finally everything within the reach of everyone.

I say that these arrangements cannot last in the face of universal suffrage. I add that he who does not see necessity from this point of view too, and sees only the necessity to which I have just alluded, is very blind and very imprudent. (Lively approval from the left.)

I have another reproach to make to indirect taxes, and that is that they create precisely the necessities people have been talking to you about, financial ones. Do you think that if each citizen were asked for his part of the contribution directly, if he were sent a tax demand showing not only the figure of what he owed for the year but the details of his contributions (for this is easy to break down: so much for the administration of justice, so much for the maintenance of public order, so much for Algeria, so much for the expedition to Rome, etc.), do you believe that this would mean that the country was not well governed?[7] M. Charencey told us not long ago that with indirect taxes the country was sure to be well governed. Well then, I, for my part, say the opposite. With all these taxes misappropriated through guile, the people suffer, complain, and put the blame everywhere—capital, property, the monarchy or the Republic—when it is the tax that is the guilty party. (That is true! That is true!)

This is why the government, forever finding new facilities, has increased

---

7. (Paillottet's note) It can be said that taxpayers cry out instinctively against the weight of taxes, for few of them know exactly what it costs them to be governed. We are fully aware of our share of land tax, but not what consumer taxes take from us. I have always thought that nothing would be more favorable to progress in our constitutional knowledge and behavior than a system of *individual accounts,* through which each person would know the amount and destination of his contribution.

While waiting for the minister of finance to distribute to each of us each year, together with our direct tax demand, our current account with the treasury, I have endeavored to design a form with the 1842 budget to hand.

expenditure so much. When has it stopped? When has it said: "We have excess revenue; we are going to abolish taxes." It has never done this. When we have too much, we seek ways of using it up, and this is how the number of civil servants has increased to an enormous figure.

We have been accused of being Malthusian; yes, I am a Malthusian with regard to civil servants. I am fully aware that they have followed perfectly the great law that populations reach the level of the means of subsistence. You have contributed eight hundred million; public civil servants have devoured eight hundred million. If you gave them two billion, there would be enough civil servants to devour this two billion. (Approval from several benches.)

A change in a financial system brings of necessity a similar change in the political system, for a country cannot follow the same policy when the population gives it two billion as when it gives it only two hundred or three hundred million. And here you will perhaps find that I am in profound dis-

---

Here is the account of M. N——, a landowner paying five hundred francs of direct taxes, which implies a revenue of twenty-four hundred to twenty-six hundred francs at the most.

THE PUBLIC TREASURY'S CURRENT ACCOUNT WITH M. N.

| DEBIT. *Sums received from M. N. in 1843* | fr. | c. |
|---|---|---|
| Through direct taxes | 500 | 00 |
| Registration, stamps, domain | 504 | 17 |
| Customs and salt | 158 | 00 |
| Forestry and fishing | 30 | 10 |
| Indirect taxes | 206 | 67 |
| Post | 39 | 00 |
| University products | 2 | 50 |
| Sundry products | 21 | 87 |
| | 1,162 | 31 |

| CREDIT. *Sums paid in the interest of M. N.* | fr. | c. |
|---|---|---|
| Interest on the public debt | 353 | 00 |
| Civil list | 14 | 00 |
| Distribution of justice | 20 | 00 |
| Religion | 36 | 00 |
| Diplomacy | 8 | 00 |
| State education | 16 | 00 |
| Secret expenditure | 1 | 00 |
| Telegraphs | 1 | 00 |
| Subsidies to musicians and dancers | 3 | 00 |

agreement with very many members sitting on this side (on the left). For anyone who is serious, the obligatory consequence of the financial theory I am developing here is obviously this: since no one wants to give a great deal to the state, people have to know how to ask very little of it. (Agreement.)

It is clear that you have the profound illusion in your head that there are two factors in society: first, the men who make it up, and second, a fictional being known as the state or the government to which you attribute a cast-iron moral code, a religion, credit, and the ability to spread benefits widely and provide assistance. It is very clear that in this case you are placing yourselves in the ridiculous position of men who say, "Give us something without taking anything from us," or "Stay in the disastrous system in which we are at the moment."

We have to learn to renounce these ideas. We have to know how to be men and say to ourselves, "We are responsible for our existence and we will assume it." (Hear! Hear!) Once again today, I received a petition from in-

| CREDIT. *Sums paid in the interest of M. N.* | fr. | c. |
|---|---|---|
| The needy, sick, and handicapped | 1 | 10 |
| Aid to refugees | 2 | 15 |
| Subsidies to agriculture | 00 | 80 |
| to deep-sea fishing | 4 | 00 |
| to manufacturing | 00 | 23 |
| Stud farms | 2 | 00 |
| Sheep pens | 00 | 63 |
| Aid to colonists | 00 | 87 |
| to those suffering from fire and flood | 00 | 90 |
| Departmental services | 72 | 00 |
| Prefects and subprefects | 7 | 20 |
| Roads, canals, bridges, and ports | 52 | 60 |
| Army | 364 | 00 |
| Navy | 114 | 00 |
| Colonies | 26 | 00 |
| Tax collection and administration | 150 | 00 |
| TOTAL | 1,251 | 48 |

Between the *debit* of 1,162 francs 31 centimes and the *credit* of 1,251 francs 48 centimes, the difference is 89 francs 17 centimes. This balance means that the treasury has spent 89 francs 17 centimes more on behalf of M. N—— than it has received from him. However, M. N—— should be reassured; Messrs. Rothschild and company were willing to advance this sum and M. N—— will have to pay only the interest in perpetuity, that is to say, to pay in the future 4 to 5 francs a year more. (*Unpublished sketch dated 1843.*)

habitants of my region in which vineyard owners say, "We are not asking any of that from the government; let them leave us alone, let them leave us free to act and work. This is all we ask of them; let them protect our freedom and our security."

Well then! I believe that there is a lesson there, provided by the poor vineyard owners, which should be listened to in the largest towns. (Hear! Hear!)

The domestic politics that this financial system would oblige us to enter is obviously the politics of freedom, for, and you should note this, freedom is incompatible with overbearing taxation, whatever anyone says.

I have read a saying by a very famous statesman, M. Guizot, and I quote: "Freedom is too precious an asset for a nation to haggle over it."

You know, when I read this sentence a long time ago now, I said to myself, "If ever this man governs the country, he will ruin not only the finances but also the freedom of France."

And indeed, I ask you to note, as I said just now, that the public services are never neutral; if they are not essential, they are harmful.

I say that there is radical incompatibility between excessive taxation and freedom.

The maximum of taxation is servitude, for a slave is a man from whom everything has been taken, even the freedom of his arms and faculties. (Hear! Hear!)

I put it to you, if the state did not pay for religion,[8] for example, at our expense, would we not have freedom of religious practice? If the state did not pay for university education at our expense, would we not have freedom of public education? If the state did not pay the numerous members of a bureaucracy at our expense, would we not have communal and departmental freedom? If the state did not pay customs officers at our expense, would we not have freedom of trade? (Hear! Hear! A prolonged swell.)

For what have the men in this country lacked the most? A little self-confidence and a feeling of responsibility. It is not very surprising that they have lost this; they have been accustomed to losing it through being governed. This country is overgoverned; that is what is wrong.

The remedy is for the country to learn to govern itself, for it to learn to distinguish between the essential attributions of the state and those it has usurped at our expense from private activity.

This is the nub of the problem.

---

8. Catholic and Protestant priests and Jewish rabbis were paid by the state (until 1905).

As for me, I say, "The number of things included in the essential attributions of the government is very limited: to ensure order and security, to keep each person within the limits of justice, that is to say, to repress misdemeanors and crimes, and to carry out a few major public works of national utility. These are, I believe, its essential attributions, and we will have no peace, no financial wherewithal, and we will not destroy the hydra of revolution if we do not regain, little by little if you like, this limited governance toward which we should be aiming. (Hear! Hear!)

The second condition of such governance is that we have to want peace sincerely, for it is obvious that not only war but even the spirit of war or warlike tendencies are incompatible with a system like this. I am fully aware that the word *peace* sometimes causes an ironic smile to pass along these benches, but truly I do not believe that serious men can treat this word ironically. What! Will we never learn from experience?

Since 1815, for example, we have been maintaining numerous armies, huge armies, and I am able to say that it is precisely these great military forces that have led us in spite of ourselves into adventures and wars, in which we would certainly not have become involved if we had not had these huge forces behind us. We would not have had the war with Spain in 1823;[9] we would not have had the expedition to Rome last year; we would have let the pope and citizens of Rome reach an agreement on their own if our military structures had been limited to more modest proportions.[10] (A variety of reactions.)

*A voice from the right:* In June, you were not upset that we had the army!

*M. Bastiat:* You quote the month of June as an answer. I tell you, for my part, that if you had not had these huge armies, you would not have had the month of June. (Prolonged hilarity on the right. Lengthy agitation.)

*A voice from the right:* It is as though you were saying that there would have been no thieves if there were no gendarmes.

*M. Bérard:* But it was the civil servants in the national workshops who caused the month of June.

*M. Bastiat:* My reasoning follows the speculative idea of a well-governed France, a France almost ideally governed, in which case I am free to believe

9. After the pronunciamento of 1 January 1822, and the ensuing troubles, France, mandated by the Verona Congress (October 1822), conducted a military intervention in Spain.

10. The National Assembly sent troops to restore the pope in Rome while protecting the new republic. Nevertheless, the new Roman republic fell after a month of fighting. Bastiat, however, makes a mistake: this happened in April 1849, not in 1848.

that we would not have had the disastrous days in June, just as we would not have had 24th February 1848, 1830, nor perhaps 1814.

Be that as it may, freedom and peace are the two pillars of the proposals I am developing here. And please note that I am not presenting these only as being good in themselves but as being required by the most pressing necessity.

At present there are people who are concerned, and rightly so, about security. I too am concerned and as much as anyone else; it is an asset that is as precious as the two others. But we are in a country that is accustomed to being governed to such an extent that no one can imagine that there can be a little order and security with less regimentation. I believe that it is precisely in this excessive government that the cause of almost all the troubles, agitations, and revolution lies, of which we are the sorry onlookers and on occasion the victims.

Let us see what this implies.

Society is thus divided into two parts: those who exploit and those who are exploited. (Nonsense! Lengthy interruption.)[11]

*A voice from the right:* A distinction like this will not bring peace back.

*M. Bastiat:* Sirs, there must be no misunderstanding. I am not alluding in the slightest either to property or to capital. I am talking only about 1.8 billion that is paid on the one hand and received on the other. I was perhaps mistaken to say *those who are exploited* since, in this 1.8 billion there is a considerable portion that goes to men who provide very genuine services. I therefore withdraw this expression. (Mutterings at the foot of the rostrum.)

*The president:* Silence, sirs! You are there only on condition that you keep silent more than all the others.

*M. Bastiat:* I want to have it noted that this state of affairs, this manner of existing, this immense expenditure of the government must always be justified or explained in some way. Consequently, this aspiring of the government to do everything, run everything, and govern everything was naturally bound to give rise to a dangerous thought in the country, with the lowest stratum of the population expecting everything from the government and expecting the impossible from this government. (Hear! Hear!)

We are discussing vineyard owners; I have seen vineyard owners on days

11. See "Note on the Translation," pp. xi–xiv, and "Bastiat's Political Writings: Anecdotes and Reflections," pp. 401–15, both in this volume.

when it hails, days on which they are ruined. They weep but do not blame the government. They know that there is no connection between the hail and the government. However, when you lead the population to believe that all the misfortunes that are not as sudden as hail are the fault of the government, when the government itself allows this to be believed since it receives a huge tax revenue only on condition that it does some good for the people, it is clear, when things have reached this stage, that you have constant revolution in the country since, because of the financial system I spoke of just now, the good that the government is able to do is nothing in comparison to the harm it does itself through the contributions it extorts.

The people then, instead of feeling better, are more unfortunate; they suffer and blame the government and there is no lack of men in the opposition to tell them, "Look at the government that has promised you this and that . . . , which should have reduced all taxes and showered you with benefits. See how this government keeps its promises! Put us in its place and you will see how differently we will act!" (General hilarity. Signs of approval.) The government is then overturned. However, the men who gain power find themselves in exactly the same situation as those who preceded them. They are obliged to withdraw all their promises gradually. They tell those who urge them to carry out their promises, "The time has not yet come, but you can count on it that the situation will improve, count on exports, count on future prosperity." But since in reality they do no better than their predecessors, there are even more complaints against them; they end up being overthrown, and the people go from one revolution to another. I do not believe that a revolution is possible where the only relationship between a government and its citizens is the guarantee of security and freedom for all. (Hear! Hear!) Why do people revolt against a government? Because it breaks its promises. Have you ever seen the people revolt against magistrates, for example? Their mission is to hand down justice and they do this; nobody thinks of asking any more of them. (Hear! Hear!)

You should convince yourselves of one thing, and that is that a love of order, security, and tranquillity is not exclusive to any one person. It exists and is inherent in human nature. Ask all those who are discontented, among whom there are doubtless a few agitators. God knows, there are always exceptions. But ask men from all classes and they will all tell you how terrified they are these days to see order being compromised. They love order; they love it to the extent of making great sacrifices for it, sacrifices of opinion and sacrifices of freedom; we see this every day. Well then! This sentiment would be strong enough to maintain security, especially if contrary opinions were not constantly being encouraged by the incorrect constitution of the government.

I will add just one word with regard to security.

I am not an experienced legal expert, but I truly believe that if the government were contained within the limits I have mentioned, and all the force of its intelligence and capacity were to be directed toward this particular point: to improve citizens' conditions of security, immense progress might be made in this direction. I do not believe that the art of repressing misdemeanors and vice, restoring morals, and reforming prisoners has made all the progress it might. I do say and do repeat that if the government aroused less jealousy on the one hand and fewer prejudices on the other and concentrated all its force on civil and penal improvements, society would have everything to gain thereby.

I will stop there. I am so profoundly convinced that the ideas I have brought to this rostrum fulfill all the conditions for a government program, that they reconcile so fully freedom, justice, financial necessity, the need for order, and all the great principles that nations and humanity support; this conviction of mine is so firm that I find it hard to believe that this project can be called utopian. On the contrary, I think it likely that if Napoléon, for example, returned to earth (exclamations from the right) and was told, "Here are two systems: one aims to restrict and limit the attributions of the government and as a result, taxes, while the other aims to extend the attributes of government indefinitely and as a result, taxes, following which France will have to be made to accept amalgamation taxes,"[12] I am convinced and will indeed assert that Napoléon would say that the true utopia lies on the latter side, since it was much more difficult to establish combined taxes than it would be to enter the system I have just proclaimed from this rostrum.

Now I will be asked why I immediately reject the tax on wines and spirits today. I will tell you. I have just set out the theoretical dispensation that I would like the government to espouse. But since I have never seen a government exercise on itself what it considers to be a sort of semisuicide by cutting back all the attributions not essential to it, I consider myself obliged to compel it to and I can do this only by refusing it the means of continuing down a disastrous path. It is for this reason that I voted for the reduction in the salt

12. See p. 333, note 6.

tax, it is for this reason that I voted for postal reform, and it is for this reason that I will vote against the tax on wine and spirits. (Agreement on the left.)

It is my profound conviction that if France has faith and confidence in herself, if she is certain that no one will come to attack her once she decides not to attack others, it will be easy to decrease public expenditure to an enormous extent and, even with the abolition of the tax on wines and spirits, there will be enough not only to balance revenue and expenditure but also to reduce public debt. (A host of signs of approval.)

## → 17 ←
### *The Repression of Industrial Unions*[1]

[vol. 5, p. 494. "Coalitions industrielles." 17 November 1849. This article was part of the debate in the Chamber on 17 November 1849. n.p.]

*Citizen Representatives,*

I come to support the amendment of my honorable friend M. Morin; but I cannot support it without also examining the commission's draft. It is impossible to discuss M. Morin's amendment without involuntarily, so to speak, entering into the general discussion, and this obliges us to discuss the commission as well.

In effect, M. Morin's amendment is more than a modification of the principal proposal; it compares one set of arrangements with another, and we cannot come to a decision without doing this comparison.

Citizens, I am not bringing any partisan spirit to this discussion, nor any preconceived ideas based on class, and I will not speak to enflamed feelings. In any case, the Assembly can see that my lungs cannot battle with parliamentary storms; I need its most benevolent attention.

To help our understanding of the commission's proposals, allow me to

---

1. (Paillottet's note) Articles 413, 415, and 416 of the penal code punished unions between employers and those between workers, though in a very inequitable way. [Paillottet may be mistaken here, as Bastiat refers to Article 414, not 413, in the course of his speech.] A proposal to abrogate these three articles had been sent back by the Legislative Assembly for examination by a commission [presided over by M. de Vatismenil] that judged the abrogation inadmissible and considered that it was essential to maintain the repressive dispositions, while amending them to make them impartial.

This aim, it is fair to say, was not achieved by the amendments formulated. M. Morin, a manufacturer and representative for the Drôme, convinced that the only basis on which a proper agreement might be established between workers and employers was equality before the law, wished to amend the conclusions of the commission in accordance with this principle. The amendment that he presented was supported by Bastiat during the session on 17 November 1849.

recall a few words by the honorable recorder, M. de Vatismenil. He said, "There is a general principle in Articles 44 *et seq.* of the penal code, and it is this: A union, either between employers or between workers, constitutes a misdemeanor on one condition, which is that there should have been an attempt at executing it, or the actual start thereof." This is what the law says and it answers immediately the observation made by the honorable M. Morin. He has told you, "Workers will not be able to get together therefore and meet their employer to discuss honorably with him (this is the expression he used), to discuss honorably with him the subject of their wages!"

"Pardon me, but they will be able to meet," added M. de Vatismenil. "They will absolutely, either by all coming together or by appointing committees to negotiate with their employers. There is no difficulty with this; the misdemeanor, according to the terms of the Code, begins only with an attempt to set up the union or the actual start of its activities, that is to say, when, after having discussed the conditions and in spite of the spirit of conciliation that employers, in their own interest, always bring to this type of affair, the workers tell them, 'But, after all, since you are not going to give us all we are asking, we are going to withdraw and, *through our influence, influence that is well known and that is based on the identity of interest and comradeship,* we are going to persuade all the other workers in other workplaces to stop work.'"

After reading this, I ask myself where the misdemeanor lies, for in this Assembly, I consider that there cannot be what might be called a systematic majority or minority on a question like this. What we all want is to stop misdemeanors. What we are all seeking to achieve is not to introduce into the Penal Code fictitious and imaginary misdemeanors in order to have the pleasure of punishing them.

I ask myself where the misdemeanor lies. Does it lie in the union, in the stoppage of work, or in the influence to which allusion is made? It is said that it is the union itself that constitutes the misdemeanor. I admit that I cannot accept this proposition since the word *union* is synonymous with association. It has the same etymology and the same meaning. When you disregard the aim, it sets itself and the means it employs; *union* cannot be considered a misdemeanor, and the recorder himself senses this, since when replying to M. Morin, who asked whether workers could discuss wages with employers, the honorable M. de Vatismenil said, "They certainly will be able to; they will be able to present themselves individually or all together and to appoint committees." Well, to appoint committees they certainly need to agree, to act in concert, and to associate; they have to form a union. Strictly speaking, the misdemeanor therefore does not lie in the very fact of the union.

Nevertheless, some people would like to see it that way, then say: "There must be a start of operations." But can the opening operations of an innocent action make this action guilty? I do not think so. If an action is wrong in itself, it is clear that the law can move against it only if operations have begun. I will even say: "It is the opening of operations that causes the action to exist." Your language on the other hand amounts to this: "To look is a misdemeanor, but it becomes a misdemeanor only when someone starts to look." M. de Vatismenil himself acknowledges that we cannot look for the thoughts that inspire guilty actions. Well, when an action is innocent in itself and is manifested only in innocent facts, it is clear that such an action is not incriminating and can never change its nature.

Now what is meant by the words, "start of operations"?

A union may reveal itself, may start operating in a thousand different ways. No, we are not concerned with these thousand ways; we are concentrating on the stoppage of work. In this case, if it is the stoppage of work that is necessarily the start of the union's operations, then you have to say that the stoppage of work is of itself a misdemeanor; let us therefore punish the stoppage of work and say that the stoppage of work will be punished. Whoever refuses to work at a rate that does not suit him will be punished. If this is so, then your law will be sincere.

But are there any consciences able to accept that the stoppage of work in itself, independently of the means used, is a misdemeanor? Does a man not have the right to refuse to sell his work at a rate that does not suit him?

The answer will be given that this is true when it concerns an individual, but not true when it concerns a group of men in association.

But, sirs, an action that is innocent in itself does not become criminal because it is multiplied by a certain number of men. When an action is wrong in itself, I can see that, if this action is carried out by a certain number of individuals, it can be said that there has been aggravation; but when it is innocent in itself, it cannot become guilty because it is carried out by a large number of individuals. I cannot therefore see how it can be said that the stoppage of work is a guilty act. If one man has the right to say to another, "I will not work under such and such a condition," two or three thousand men have the same right; they have the right to withdraw. That is a natural right which ought to be a legal right as well.

However, people want to add a veneer of guilt to the stoppage of work, so how are they going to manage it? The following words are slipped into parentheses, "Since you are not giving us what we ask, we are going to withdraw our labor; we are going to act *through influences that are well known* and that stem from the identity of interests and comradeship. . . ."

This then is the crime; it is the *influences that are well known,* it is violence and intimidation; there lies the crime, and it is there that you should attack. Indeed, it is there that the amendment of the honorable M. Morin attacks. How can you refuse him your votes?

But then another chain of reasoning is brought before us, which says the following:

"The union includes the two characteristics that enable it to be classified as a crime. Union in itself can be condemned and it then produces disastrous consequences, disastrous for the worker, for the employer, and for society as a whole."

First of all, the fact that the union can be condemned is exactly the point on which we disagree, the point that needs to be proven, *quod erat demonstrandum.* It can be condemned depending on the aim it sets itself and especially depending on the means it employs. If the union limits itself to the force of inertia or passivity, if the workers act in concert, have reached an agreement, and say, "We do not want to sell our product, which is labor, at such and such a price; we want such and such an amount, and if you refuse we will go home, or seek work elsewhere," it seems to me that it cannot be said that this is an action that can be condemned.

However, you claim that it is disastrous. Here, in spite of all the respect I profess for the talent of the recorder, I believe that he has embarked on an avenue of reasoning that is at least highly confused. He says, "The stoppage of work damages the employer, as it is troublesome for an employer if one or more of his workers withdraw their labor. It damages his business with the result that the worker undermines the freedom of the employer and consequently infringes Article 13 of the Constitution."

In fact, that is a total reversal of ideas.

What! I am standing before an employer, we discuss the price, the one he is offering me does not suit me, I commit no act of violence and withdraw, and you tell me that it is I who am undermining the freedom of the employer because I am damaging his business! Take care lest what you are proclaiming is none other than slavery. For what is a slave if not a man obliged by law to work under conditions that he rejects? (*On the left:* Hear! Hear!)

You ask the law to intervene because it is I who am violating the property of the employer. Do you not see that, on the contrary, it is the employer that is violating mine? If he calls upon the law to ensure that his will is imposed on me, where is freedom or equality? (*On the left:* Hear! Hear!)

Do not tell me that I am mutilating your argument, for it is contained in its entirety in the report and in your speech.

You then say that when the workers form a union they harm themselves, and you use this basis to say that the law should prevent the stoppage of work. I agree with you that in the majority of cases, the workers do themselves damage. But it is precisely for this reason that I want them to be free, since freedom will teach them that they are damaging themselves, whereas you want to draw the conclusion that the law must intervene and shackle them to the workshop.

However, you are setting the law on a road that is very wide and extremely dangerous.

Every day, you accuse the socialists of wanting to have the law intervene in all circumstances and wanting to remove personal responsibility.

Every day, you complain that, wherever there is misfortune, suffering, or pain, people constantly call upon the law and the state.

For my part, I do not want the law to be able to say to a man who stops work and consequently consumes part of his savings, "You must work in this workshop even though you have not been granted the price you are asking for." I do not accept this theory.

Last, you say that he is damaging society in its entirety.

There is no doubt that he is damaging society, but the same reasoning applies. A man considers that by ceasing to work he will obtain a better rate of pay in eight or ten days' time. Doubtless this is a loss of output for society, but what do you want to do? Do you want the law to remedy everything? That is impossible; we would then have to say that a trader who is waiting for a better time to sell his coffee or sugar is damaging society. We would then have to be calling upon the law and the state incessantly!

One objection was made to the commission's draft that I believe was treated very lightly, too lightly for such a serious subject. It was said: "What is this all about? There are employers on the one hand and workers on the other; it is a question of settling wages. Obviously what is desirable is that, since wages are settled by the free play of supply and demand, demand and supply should be as free or, if you wish, as constrained as each other. There are only two ways for this to happen: either we should leave unions perfectly free, or we should abolish them entirely.

An objection is made to you, and you agree with it, that it is perfectly impossible for your law to keep an equitable balance, that since the unions of the workers are constantly being formed on a grand scale and in broad daylight, they are easier to detect than the associations of employers.

You admit the difficulty, but you also add, "The law does not pay attention to such details." I reply that it ought to do so. If the law can repress an alleged crime only by carrying out the most flagrant and enormous injustices against an entire class of workers, then it needs to pay attention. There are a thousand similar cases in which the law has indeed paid attention.

You yourself admit that, by dint of your legislation, supply and demand are no longer equal players since a union of employers cannot be prosecuted, and it is obvious why: two or three employers have lunch together and form a union, and nobody knows anything about it. A workers' union will always be detected because it is formed in broad daylight.

Since the one escapes your law while the other does not, its inevitable result is that supply is affected where demand is not and, insofar as it acts, it alters the natural level of earnings systematically and continuously. It is this that I cannot approve. I say that since you cannot draft a law that applies equally to all relevant interests, and since you cannot treat them equally, leave them their freedom, which subsumes equality.

But while it was not possible to achieve equality in the commission's draft, is it at least theoretically possible? Yes, and I believe, indeed I am certain, that the commission has made a great effort to achieve at least apparent equality. It has, however, not yet succeeded, and to be convinced of this you need only compare Article 414 with Article 415, the one relating to the employers with the one relating to the workers. The first is excessively simple; no mistake can be made. Both the law when it prosecutes and the delinquent when he defends himself will be perfectly aware of what they are doing.

"The following will be punished: 1. Any association between those who give employment to workers that tends to force wages down, if there has been an attempt at such or if such a process has begun."

I draw your attention to the word *force,* which gives great latitude to employers to defend themselves. They will say: "It is true that two or three of us have had a meeting. We adopted measures to bring about a decrease in earnings, but we have not tried to force this through." This is a very important word, which is not found in the following article.

In fact, the next article is extremely elastic; it does not include just one fact, it includes a huge number of them.

"Any union of workers in order to stop work at the same time, to prohibit work in the workshops, to prevent anyone from entering them before or after certain times and in general to suspend, prevent, or make work more expensive (the word *force* is absent), if there is an attempt at such or if such a process has begun, etc."

And if it were said that I am finding fault with the use of the word *force,* I would call the commission's attention to the importance that it itself gave to this word. (Murmurs.)

*A member on the left:* The right is not allowing silence. When correct things are being said, they always interrupt. Tell us a story and you will be listened to.

*M. Frédéric Bastiat:* In its wish to achieve a certain equality, at least theoretically, since it is impossible in fact, the commission had two avenues it might have taken with regard to the expressions *unjustly* and *abusively* contained in Article 414.

Obviously they had either to delete these words, which open a wide breach for the defense of employers from Article 414, or they had to include them in Article 415 to offer the same opportunity to workers. The commission preferred to delete the words *unjustly* and *abusively.* On what did it base this decision? It based its decision precisely on the fact that, immediately after these words came the verb *force* and this word is underlined five times on just one page of its report, which proves that it attached great importance to it. Indeed it expressed itself very categorically on this, in the following terms:

"When a set of measures contrary to the law has been established to force a decrease in earnings, it is impossible to justify it. An event of this nature is of necessity *unjust* and *an abuse,* for to *force* earnings down is to produce a decrease which is not the result of the circumstances of the industry concerned and of free competition, but rather the outcome of a pact as illegal as it is contrary to humanity. It thus follows that the use of the words *unjustly* and *abusively* is contrary to common sense."

Thus, how has the deletion of the words *unjustly* and *abusively* been justified? By the claim that their use constituted a pleonasm; the word *force* replaces all of this.

However, sirs, in the case of the workers, the word *force* was not included, so that the workers from now on do not have the same opportunity to defend themselves. All that is now stated is that they may not increase earnings, with nothing now said about *unjustly or abusively forcing* them up. Here again there is a fault, at least in the drafting, and an inequality that is grafted on to the much more serious inequality of which I spoke just now.

Such, sirs, is the commission's approach, one that in my view is faulty in every respect, faulty in theory and faulty in practice, a system that leaves us in total uncertainty as to what constitutes the offence. Is it the union, is it the stoppage of work, is it the abuse, or is it force? We do not know at all. I challenge anyone, the most logical of minds, to see where impunity begins or ends. You say to me, "The union is criminal. However, you may appoint a committee." I am not sure, though, that I can appoint a committee and send delegates to it when your report is full of considerations according to which the union is the very essence of the offence.

The next thing I want to say is that, in practice, your law is full of in-equalities; it does not apply exactly and proportionally to both parties whose antagonism you wish to remove. This is a singular way to remove antago-nism between two parties: treating them in an unequal manner!

As for M. Morin's proposal, I will not spend much time on it. It is per-fectly clear and perfectly lucid. It is based on an unshakeable principle, one accepted by everyone: freedom of action and repression of abuses. No intel-ligent mind would fail to support such a principle.

Ask the first person you see, whoever you like, whether the law is unjust or partial when it is content to repress intimidation and violence. Everyone will tell you that these are real crimes. Besides, the laws are drafted for the ignorant as well as for scholars. The definition of a misdemeanor must per-suade the intelligent, it must satisfy every conscience; when the law is read, people should say: "Yes, that is a crime." You talk about a respect for the law; this is an integral part of respect for the law. How do you expect a law that is unintelligent and unintelligible to be respected? That is impossible. (Approval from the left.)

What is happening here, sirs, appears to draw importance from the per-fect analogy between what has happened in another country, England, of which M. de Vatismenil spoke yesterday and which has such great experience of unions, conflict, and difficulties of this nature. I believe that this experi-ence is worth consulting and bringing to the rostrum.

Mention has been made of the numerous and formidable unions that have come into being since the abrogation of the law or laws, but you have heard nothing of those that took place before. These unions should have been mentioned as well, since in order to evaluate the two systems the sys-tems have to be compared.

Before 1824,[2] England was ruined by so many unions, which were so ter-

2. The law of 1800 forbade workers' unions. They nonetheless developed as secret societies and routinely practiced violent action. Violence increased by 1822, caused by

rible and forceful, that this scourge gave rise to thirty-seven statutes in a country in which, as you know, antiquity is, so to speak, part of the law, and in which even absurd laws are respected solely because they are ancient. The country must have been very worried and tormented by this evil for it to have decided to pass thirty-seven statutes, one after the other, in a very short space of time, each more forceful than the last. Well then! What happened next? They did not manage to contain the evil, which continued to worsen. One fine day, they said: "We have tried very many approaches and thirty-seven statutes have been passed. Let us try to see whether we might succeed through very simple means, justice and freedom." I would like this reasoning to be applied to a great many questions, and we would find that their solution is not as difficult as we think; but in the end on this occasion, this reasoning was formulated and acted upon in England.

Thus, in 1824 a law was effected on the basis of Mr. Hume's proposals, proposals that resembled closely those advocated by MM Doutre, Greppo, Benoît, and Fond.[3] It was for the complete and total abrogation of what had hitherto existed. Justice in England found itself disarmed when faced by unions, even against violence, intimidation, and threats, facts that, however, are aggravating to the union. To such behavior one can apply only laws that relate to threats and the accidental skirmishes that take place in the streets. So one year later, in 1825, the minister of justice requested a special law that would leave unions totally free but increase the penalty incurred for ordinary violence; that in a nutshell is the whole basis of the 1825 law.

Article 3 says: "Anyone who, through intimidation, threats, or violence, etc. . . . will be punished by imprisonment and a fine, etc., . . ."

The words *intimidation, threats,* and *violence* return in each sentence. The word *union* is not even mentioned.

There then follow two other extremely remarkable articles, which would probably not be accepted in France because they are virtually encompassed in this maxim: anything that the law does not forbid is allowed.

---

a sharp increase in food prices (43 percent in two years). A parliamentary commission, headed by Joseph Hume, proposed a radical modification authorizing unions but forbidding coercion or violence. The law was enacted in 1824. Unions flourished anew, but some violent demonstrations erupted again in Glasgow, Dublin, and London. A new law was enacted in 1825. It confirmed the freedom of association, but limited it through more specific definitions of offences.

3. The deputies, all former workers, who put before the Assembly the initial proposal to abrogate Articles 414, 415, and 416 of the penal code (see p. 348, note 1).

They say: "Those who organize a meeting, those who form a union and who seek to influence the level of wages, those who enter into verbal or written agreements, etc., . . . will not be subject to this penalty."

In a word, the widest and most complete freedom is expressly granted in it.

I say that there is some analogy in the situation, for what the commission is proposing is the former English system, that of the statutes. The proposal by M. Doutre and his colleagues is the one proposed by Mr. Hume, which abolished everything and which allowed no aggravation for concerted violence, although it cannot fail to be known that violence meditated by a certain number of men offers more danger than the individual acts of violence committed in the street. Last, the proposals made by the honorable M. Morin perfectly match the ones that were effected by the definitive law in England in 1825.

Now you are being told: "Since 1825, England is not at ease in this system." She is not at ease! But I, for my part, find that you are giving an opinion on this question without going into it in sufficient detail. I have traveled in England several times and have asked a large number of manufacturers about this question. Well then, I can state that I have never met anyone who did not applaud this development and who was not highly satisfied that England in this respect had dared to look freedom in the face. And perhaps it is because of this that later, with regard to many other questions, she dared again to look freedom in the face.

You refer to the union in 1832,[4] which in effect was a formidable union, but you have to be careful and not present the facts in isolation. That year, there was a shortage and wheat cost ninety-five shillings a quarter; there was a famine and that famine lasted several years. . . .

*The recorder, M. de Vatismenil:* I referred to the union in 1842.

---

4. As Bastiat notes, many conservatives opposed the right of workers to voluntarily form *trades unions* (or "labor unions" in American English), but he argued that the right to associate belonged to factory owners as well as to the people who worked in their factories as long as there was no resort to violence by either party. In England, trades unions had been severely repressed until 1824 and were not fully decriminalized until 1867. The 1830s saw several efforts to create a nationwide association of trades unions, the first being the National Association for the Protection of Labour, which was formed in 1830 and which at its peak a few years later had joined together some 150 unions with a combined membership of twenty thousand to thirty thousand. Robert Owen also attempted something similar with his Grand National Consolidated Trades Union in 1834.

*M. Bastiat:* There was a famine in 1832 and another, more severe one in 1842.

*The recorder:* I spoke about the union in 1842.

*M. Bastiat:* My argument applies even more strongly to 1842. What happens in years of shortage like these? The income of nearly all the population is used to buy the things necessary for their subsistence. Manufactured products are not bought, the workshops have no work, and a great many workers have to be laid off; there is competition for work and earnings are reduced.

Well then, when earnings suffer a significant decrease at the same time that there is a dreadful famine, it is not surprising that in a country with total freedom unions are formed.

This is what happened in England. Was the law changed for this reason? Not at all.

The causes of the unions were seen, but they were braved out. Threats and violence were punished wherever they occurred, but nothing else was done.

You have been presented with a terrible picture of these associations and it has been said that they tend to become political.

Sirs, at the time of which I am speaking, a major question was being debated in England, and this question was being inflamed still further by circumstances, the dearth. There was conflict between the industrial population and the landowners, that is to say the aristocracy, who wanted to sell wheat as expensively as possible and, to do this, prohibited foreign wheat. What happened? The unions, which were recently jokingly called *trades unions* and which enjoyed freedom of union, saw that all the efforts made by their unions had not succeeded in raising the level of wages.[5]

*A voice:* Which is a bad thing.

*M. Bastiat:* You say it is a bad thing. On the contrary, I say that it is a very good thing. The workers saw that the level of earnings did not depend on the employers, but on other social laws, and they said to themselves, "Why don't our wages rise? The reason is simple; it is because we are forbidden to work for foreigners or at least to receive foreign wheat in payment for our work. We are therefore mistaken in blaming our employers; we ought to be blaming the aristocratic classes, who not only own the land but also

---

5. This section and the following ones refer to the position of Richard Cobden and the Anti–Corn Law League. See also the entry for "Anti–Corn Law League" in the Glossary of Subjects and Terms.

make the law, and we will have an influence on earnings only when we have reconquered our political rights."

*On the left:* Hear! Hear!

*M. Bastiat:* Truly, sirs, to find something extraordinary in the conduct—so simple and natural—of the English workers, is almost to bring a protest against universal suffrage in France to this rostrum. (More agreement from the left.)

The result of this was that English workers have learned a great lesson through freedom. They have learned that raising or lowering wages does not depend on the employers; and right now England has experienced two or three very difficult years as a result of potato blight, failed harvests, and the railway mania, and also because of the revolutions that have desolated Europe and closed the outlets for her industrial products. Never had she experienced crises like these. However, there has been not one instance of reprehensible union behavior and not a single act of violence. The workers have abandoned all this as a result of their experience, and this is an example to bring before our country and to meditate on. (Approval from the left.)

Last, there is one consideration that strikes me and that is more important than any of this. You want the laws to be respected, and you are very right in this, but you should not extinguish in men the sense of justice.

Here are two systems before you, the commission's and M. Morin's.

Imagine that alternatively, by virtue of both one and the other system, workers are prosecuted. So here we have workers prosecuted by virtue of the present law on unions; they do not even know what is being asked of them. They believed they had the right, up to a certain point, to form a union and to act in concert, and you yourselves will acknowledge this to some degree. They say: "We have devoured our pay; we are ruined. It is not our fault but that of society, which is ill-treating us, the employers, who are harassing us, and the law, which is prosecuting us." They come before the courts in a very irritated mood; they project themselves as victims, and not only do they resist, but those who are not being prosecuted also sympathize with them. Young people, ever ardent, and political writers side with them. Do you think that this is a very flattering or favorable position for justice in our country?

On the other hand, prosecute workers on the basis of M. Morin's proposals. Bring them before the court and let the public prosecutor say: "We are not prosecuting you because you have formed unions, you were perfectly free to do so. You have asked for an increase in wages and we have said nothing. You have acted in concert and we have said nothing. You have wished to stop work and we have said nothing. You have sought to act by persuading your comrades and we have said nothing. However, you have used arms, violence, and threats and so we have brought you before the courts."

The worker whom you prosecute will bow his head because he will realize his wrong and will acknowledge that the justice of his country has been impartial and just. (Hear! Hear!)

I will end, sirs, with another consideration, which is this:

In my view, there is now a host of heated questions among the working classes on the subject of which, I am deeply and intimately convinced, the workers are making a mistake, and I draw your attention to this point. Whenever a revolution breaks out in a country in which there are a series of classes one above the other and in which the top class has arrogated to itself certain privileges, it is the second in rank that reaches the top; it naturally invokes the feelings of right and justice to gain help from the others. The revolution is carried out, and the class that was second in line reaches the top. Most often it does not take long to build up privileges for itself. This happens for the third in line and then the fourth. All this is odious, but it is always possible as long as there is a class below that can bear the costs of the privileges that are being disputed.

However, it so happened that in the February revolution it was the entire nation, the entire people, right to the very lowest of its masses, that has been able or that may be able to govern itself, through elections and universal suffrage. And then in a spirit of imitation, which I deplore but which I think is somewhat natural, the people thought that it might cure its grievances by also establishing special privileges for itself—since I consider the *right to credit,* the *right to work,* and many other such claims as privileges in the proper sense of the word.[6] (Murmuring.)

And in fact, sirs, they might be granted if beneath them or within reach of them there were another class even more numerous, three hundred million Chinese, for example, who could bear the cost. (Approving laughter.)

6. Bastiat's pamphlet *Capital and Rent* (*OC,* vol. 5, p. 23, "Capital et Rente") appeared in February 1849 and aroused the anger of the anarchist socialist writer Pierre-Joseph Proudhon, who attacked it vehemently in his journal *Le Peuple.* Bastiat requested the right to reply to Proudhon's criticism of an individual's right to charge interest, and there was a back and forth of articles in the journal until Proudhon suddenly ended the exchange. A short time later Bastiat published the exchange along with a new conclusion by himself in the book *Gratuité du crédit* (1850) (*OC,* vol. 5, p. 94, "Gratuité du crédit").

But this does not exist. Therefore, every privilege will have to be paid for by the men of the people, without any possible profit to themselves, through a complicated system and, on the contrary, by suffering all the losses caused by the system.

So the Legislative Assembly may be called upon to combat these claims to privilege, which should not be treated too lightly since, after all, they are sincere. You will be obliged to struggle. How will you struggle advantageously if you reject the working class when they are asking only for something that is reasonable, when they are purely and simply asking for justice and freedom? I believe that you will gain great strength by proving your impartiality here. People will listen to you more and you will be regarded as the tutors of all the classes, and in particular this class, if you show yourselves to be totally impartial and just toward it. (Lively approval from the left.)

To sum up, I reject the commission's draft because it is just an expedient, and the character of any expedient is weakness and injustice. I support M. Morin's proposal because it is based on a principle, and only principles have the power to satisfy people's minds, to win over their hearts, and to unite all serious minds. We have been asked: "Do you wish then to proclaim freedom to satisfy a platonic love of freedom?" For myself, I reply: "Yes. Freedom may cause a few problems for nations but freedom alone will enlighten them, raise them up, and improve their moral life. Without freedom there is only oppression and, mark well, you friends of order, that the time has passed, if ever it existed, when the union of classes, a respect for law, the security of interests, or the tranquillity of peoples could be based on oppression."

# ⟶ 18 ⟵

## *Reflections on the Amendment of*
## *M. Mortimer-Ternaux*[1]

[vol. 5, p. 513. "Réflexions sur l'amendement
de M. Mortimer-Ternaux." 1 April 1850. This
article was part of the debate in the Legislative
Assembly on 1 April 1850. n.p.]

*To All Democrats*

No, I am not mistaken; I feel a democratic heart beating within my breast.
How is it then that so often I find myself in opposition to these men who
proclaim themselves to be the sole representatives of democracy?

We need, however, to make sure we understand one another. Has this
word two opposing meanings?

For my part, I consider that there is a link between the aspiration that
drives all men toward their physical, intellectual, and moral advancement and the faculties with which they have been endowed to pursue this
aspiration.

This being so, I would like each man to have responsibility for the free
disposition, administration, and control of his own person, his acts, his family, his business dealings, his associations, his intelligence, his faculties, his
work, his capital, and his property.

This is how freedom and democracy are understood in the United States.
Each citizen jealously guards his ability to remain his own master. This is

---

1. (Paillottet's note) At the session of the Legislative Assembly on 1 April 1850, during
the discussions on the budget for state education, M. Mortimer-Ternaux, a representative of the people, put forward as an amendment a reduction of three hundred thousand
francs in expenditure on lycées and secondary schools, the establishments frequented by
the children of the middle classes.

On this question, the representatives of the extreme left voted with the extreme right.
When put to the vote, the amendment was defeated by a small majority.

The very next day, Bastiat published, in a daily news sheet, the opinion on this vote
that we are printing.

how the poor hope to rise out of poverty and how the rich hope to retain their wealth.

And in truth, we see that in a very short space of time this regime has enabled the Americans to achieve a degree of energy, security, wealth, and equality that has no peer in the annals of the human race.

However, there as everywhere, there are men who have no scruples in undermining the freedom and property of their fellow citizens for their own advantage.

This is why the law intervenes, with the sanction of the common force, to anticipate and repress this dissolute tendency.

Each person contributes to maintaining the force in proportion to his wealth. This is not, as has been said, a *sacrifice of one part of one's freedom to preserve the other*. On the contrary, it is the simplest, most just, most effective, and most economical way of guaranteeing the freedom of all.

And one of the most difficult problems of politics is to remove from those in whom the common force is vested the opportunity to do themselves what they are responsible for preventing.

It would appear that French democrats see things in a very different light.

Doubtless, like American democrats, they condemn, reject, and stigmatize the plunder that citizens might be tempted to indulge in on their own behalf against one another, such as any attack on property, work, and freedom by one individual to the detriment of another individual.

But they consider this plunder, which they reject between individuals, as a means of gaining equality and consequently they entrust it to the *law*, the *common force*, which I thought had been instituted to prevent plunder.

Thus, while American democrats, having entrusted to the common force the task of punishing individual plunder, are deeply concerned by the fear that this force might itself become a plunderer, in the case of French democrats, making this force an instrument of plunder appears to be the very basis and spirit of the system they advocate.

They give these arrangements the grandiose titles of organization, association, fraternity, and solidarity. In doing this, they remove any scruples from the most brutal of appetites.

"Peter is poor, Mondor is rich. Are they not brothers? Do they not share solidarity? Should they not be put in association and organized? This being so let them share, and everything will be for the best. It is true that Peter should not take anything from Mondor; that would be iniquitous. But we will pass laws and create forces that will be responsible for the operation. In this way, Mondor's resistance will become factious and Peter's conscience will remain clear."

In the course of this legislature, there have been occasions on which plunder has been presented in a particularly hideous light. Those occasions are when the law has operated for the benefit of the rich to the detriment of the poor.

Well then! Even in these cases we have seen the Montagne applaud. Might this not be because what they want above all is to ensure this principle for themselves? Once legal plunder of the poor for the benefit of the rich has become part of the system, with the support of the majority, how will we be able to reject legal plunder of the rich for the benefit of the poor?

Oh unfortunate country, in which the sacred forces, which ought to have been instituted to ensure the rights of each person, are perverted so that they themselves violate these rights!

Yesterday, we witnessed a scene in the abominable and disastrous comedy in the Legislative Assembly that might well be titled *The Comedy of Fools*.

This is what happened:

Every year, three hundred thousand children reach the age of twelve. Out of these three hundred thousand children, perhaps ten thousand enter state secondary schools and lycées. Are their parents all rich? I do not know. But what can be stated categorically is that they are the richest in the nation.

Naturally, they have to pay the costs of board, education, and care for their children. However, they find this very expensive. Consequently, they have requested—and it has been granted to them—that the law, through the taxes on wines and spirits and salt, should take money from the millions of poor parents in order for the said money to be distributed to them, the rich parents, as grants, bonuses, indemnities, subsidies, etc.

M. Mortimer-Ternaux has asked for a monstrosity like this to cease, but his efforts have failed. The extreme right finds it very pleasant to have the poor pay for the education of the rich, and the extreme left finds it very politically astute to seize an opportunity like this to have the system of legal plunder passed and approved.

This makes me ask myself, "Where are we going? The Assembly must be governed by a few principles; it must either be wedded to justice everywhere and for all, or else it will be thrown into the system of legal and mutual plunder to the point where all the conditions of life are totally equal, that is to say, communism."

Yesterday, it declared that the poor would pay taxes to relieve the rich.

With what impudence will it reject the taxes that will shortly be put forward to assail the rich to relieve the poor?

For my part, I cannot forget that, when I presented myself to the electors, I said to them:

"Would you approve a system of government which consisted in this: You will have the responsibility for your own lives. You will expect from your work, efforts, and energy the means to feed and clothe yourself, house yourself, get lighting, and achieve prosperity, well-being, and perhaps wealth. The government will have dealings with you only to guarantee you protection against any disorder or unjust aggression. On the other hand, it will ask from you only the minimal taxes essential for accomplishing this task."

And everyone cried out, "We do not ask for anything else from it."

*Now, what would my position* be if I had to present myself once more to these poor laborers, honest artisans, and courageous workers and say to them:

"You pay more taxes than you expected. You have less freedom than you hoped for. This is partly my fault since I strayed from the philosophy of government for which you elected me and on 1 April I voted for an increase in the tax on salt and wines and spirits in order to come to the aid of a small number of our fellow countrymen who send their children to state secondary schools."

Whatever happens, I hope never to put myself in the sad and ridiculous position of having to say things like this to the men who gave me their trust.

→ 19 ←

*Parliamentary Conflicts of Interest* [1,2]

[vol. 5, p. 518. "Incompatibilités parlementaires."
March 1850. n.p.]

We have translated the title of this pamphlet as "Parliamentary Conflicts of
Interest" (and related occurrences of the word *incompatibilités* as "conflicts
of interest") instead of retaining the literal English translation, which presents some awkwardness. In the context of this pamphlet, Bastiat is referring to the matter of civil servants who have been elected to the Chamber
of Deputies and whether or not they should continue to fulfill their work
commitments to the state while they serve in the Chamber. Bastiat argued
that it was "incompatible" for them to do both.]

*Citizen Representatives,*
I urge you to give some attention to this article.
"Is it a good thing to exclude certain categories of citizen from the Na-
tional Assembly?"

---

1. (Paillottet's note) This article, published in March 1849, was reprinted in 1850, a
few months before the author's death. [Toward the end of Bastiat's life, his health was
failing to the point where he could no longer speak in the Chamber, and so in March
1849 he distributed his would-be speech in pamphlet form to his friends and colleagues.]
The views he developed in it were deeply rooted in his mind, as can be seen in his "Letter
to M. Larnac" dating from 1846 in vol. 1, as well as in the article written in 1830 titled
"To the Electors of the *Département* of the Landes." (*OC,* vol. 1, p. 480, "À M. Larnac,
député des Landes," and vol. 1, p. 217, "Aux électeurs du département des Landes.")
2. Bastiat distributed this pamphlet to his colleagues, in March 1849, during the debate on the draft of an electoral bill prepared by a commission of fifteen members directed by Adolphe Billault. A prior discussion had taken place in June 1848. At that time
Bastiat had proposed the following amendment, which was rejected: "Civil servants who
are elected deputies will not exercise their function during their mandates.... No deputy
will be appointed to public functions during his mandate."

"Is it a good thing to make high political office seem dazzling in the eyes of deputies?"

These are the two questions that I will deal with now. The constitution itself has not raised more important ones.

However, a very strange thing has happened: one of these questions, the second one, was decided without discussion.

Should the government recruit in the Chamber? England says yes and is in trouble because of this. America says no and is thereby doing well. In '89 we adopted the American way of thinking; in 1814 we preferred the English way. Between authorities of this stature, there is, it would appear, good reason for caution. However, the National Assembly has plumped for the system of the restoration imported from England and has done this without discussion.

The author of this article had put forward an amendment. In the time he took to mount the steps of the rostrum, the question was decided. "I propose," he said. "The Chamber has voted," shouted the president. "What! Without allowing me to . . ." "The Chamber has voted." "But nobody was aware of this!" "Consult the office; the Chamber has voted."

Certainly on this occasion, the Assembly will not be reproached for being systematically dilatory!

What should we do? Grab the attention of the Assembly before the final vote. I am doing this in writing in the hope that a more-experienced voice will come to my assistance.

Besides, for the ordeal of a verbal discussion, the lungs of a stentor would be needed to address attentive hearers. Decidedly, the safest thing is to put it in writing.

Citizen deputies, from the depths of my soul and conscience, I believe that section 4 of the electoral law must be redrafted. As it is, it will lead to anarchy. There is still time, let us not bequeath this scourge to the country.

The issue of conflicts of interest raises two profoundly separate questions that have nevertheless often been confused.

Will the position of deputy in the National Assembly be open or closed to those whose careers are in the civil service?

Will a civil service career be open or closed to deputies of the people?

These are certainly two separate questions that have no connection with one another, so much so that solving one does not prejudice in any way the solution of the other. The position of deputy may be open to civil servants without the civil service being open to deputies and vice versa.

The law that we are discussing is very severe with regard to the admission of civil servants to the Chamber and very tolerant with regard to the admission of deputies of the people to high political office. In the first case, I consider that it has let itself be drawn into base radicalism. On the other hand, in the second, it is not even prudent.

I will not hide the fact that, in this article, I have reached quite different conclusions.

To move from public office to the Chamber there should be no exclusion, but adequate precautions should be taken.

To move from the Chamber to public office there should be total exclusion.

Respect for universal suffrage! Those it elects people's deputies should *be* representatives and *remain* such. No exclusion to entry but total exclusion to exit. That is the principle. We will see that this is in line with the public good.

§1.   *May electors have themselves represented by civil servants?*

My reply is yes, except that it is up to society to take adequate precautions.

I encounter an initial difficulty here, one that appears to place an insurmountable rejection in advance in the path of anything I might say. The constitution itself proclaims the principle of the conflict of interest between any paid civil *service* job and a mandate to represent the people. However, as the report says, it is not a question of eluding this principle but of applying it, since henceforth it will be fundamental.

I ask whether it is not being too subtle to get round the word *service* as used in the Constitution and say: "What it intends to exclude is not the person nor even the civil servant but the service and the danger that it might bring into the Legislative Assembly. Provided, therefore, that the service does not enter and remains outside, even if it is resumed at the end of the legislative term by the person appointed to it, the intention of the Constitution is upheld."

The National Assembly has thus interpreted Article 28 [3] of the Constitution with regard to the army, and since I must necessarily extend this inter-

---

3. Article 28 of the Constitution stipulated, "Any paid public function is incompatible with the mandate of people's representative. No member of the National Assembly may be assigned or promoted to salaried public functions whose incumbents are appointed by the executive power. Exceptions will be determined by an organic law."

pretation to all civil servants, I have reason to believe that I will be allowed not to be diverted by the rejection that the report is placing in my path.

What I am asking, in effect, is this: That any elector should be eligible. That electoral colleges may have themselves represented by anyone who has deserved their confidence. But if the choice of the electors falls upon a civil servant, it is the man and not the job that enters the Chamber. The civil servant will not, for all that, lose his previous rights and job titles. He will not be expected to make the sacrifice of a genuine property acquired through long and useful work. Society has only to make a few trivial demands and should be content with adequate safeguards. In this way, the civil servant will be removed from the influence of executive power; he will not be allowed promotion or dismissed from office. He will be made safe from the pushing and pulling between hope and fear. He will not be able to exercise his erstwhile functions or collect his payments for them. In a word, he will be a representative, and only a representative, throughout the duration of his mandate. His life in public service will, so to speak, be suspended and as though absorbed by his life in parliament. This is what was done for the military, through the distinction made between rank and actual function. Why should this not also be done for magistrates?

Let us note this clearly: *conflict of interest,* taken in the meaning of *exclusion,* is an idea that in the nature of things had to be put forward and popularized under the former regime.

At that time, no indemnity was given to deputies who were not civil servants, but they could use the job of deputy as a stepping-stone to lucrative office. On the other hand, civil servants elected as deputies continued to receive their salaries. To tell the truth, they were paid not as civil servants but as deputies, since they no longer fulfilled their duties, and if the minister was displeased with the way they voted, he could, by removing them from their position as deputies, deprive them of all their salary.

The results of a combination like this had to be and, indeed, were deplorable. On the one hand, candidates who were not civil servants were very rare in the majority of districts. The electors were *free* to choose, yes, but the extent of their choice did not exceed five or six people. The first condition of eligibility was considerable wealth.[4] If a man who was merely prosperous

4. To be eligible one had to pay personal income taxes at least equal to five hundred francs, which drastically limited the number of potential candidates.

stood for election, he was rejected with some reason, since he was suspected of having ulterior motives, which were not forbidden by the charter.

On the other hand, civil service candidates came in droves. It was very simple. First, they were granted an indemnity. Second, the job of deputy was for them an assured means of rapid advancement.

When you think that the battle for portfolios, the inevitable consequence of the ease of access to ministries for deputies (a huge subject that I will deal with in the following paragraph), as I say, when you think that the battle for portfolios generated coalitions within parliament that were systematically organized to overthrow the cabinet, that the cabinet could resist only with the help of a majority that was equally systematic, compact, and devoted, it is easy to understand what this double facility given to men of position to become deputies, and for deputies to become men of position, would lead to.

The result had to be and was that the civil service departments were converted into a form of exploitation, the government absorbed the domain of private activity, our freedoms were lost, our finances were ruined, and corruption descended increasingly from high parliamentary levels to the lowest levels of the electorate.[5]

In circumstances like these, we should not be surprised that the nation becomes attached to the principle of conflict of interest as though it were a lifeline. Everyone remembers that the rallying cry of honest electors was, "No more civil servants in the Chamber!" And the manifesto of the candidates carried the words, "I promise not to accept either office or favors."

However, has the February revolution changed nothing in this state of affairs, one that both explained and justified the current of public opinion?

First, we have universal suffrage, and obviously the influence of the government on the elections is going to be much weakened, if indeed it retains any at all.

Second, no government purpose will be served by its securing the election by preference of civil servants who are totally removed from its influence.

What is more, we have an equal salary paid to all the deputies, a circumstance which, just on its own, changes the situation completely.

In fact, we do not need to fear, as in the past, that there will be a lack of

5. Corruption was one of the plagues of the July Monarchy, more particularly under the Guizot government. On 18 July 1847, in a resounding speech, Lamartine announced, "The revolution of public conscience, the revolution of contempt."

candidates for election. We have more to fear from difficulties arising from having far too many to choose from. It will therefore be impossible for civil servants to overrun the Chamber. I add that they will have no incentive to do so, since the job of deputy will no longer be for them a means of achieving success. In former times, civil servants welcomed candidacy as a piece of luck. Today they can accept it only as a genuine sacrifice, at least from the point of view of their career.

Changes so profound in the respective situations of the two sets of people are also likely, I think, to change the view we had formed of *conflict of interest,* under the influence of quite different circumstances. I believe that we should envisage the real principle and common good, not in the light of the ancient charter but in that of the new constitution.

Conflict of interest as a synonym for exclusion has three major disadvantages:

1. First, it is a huge disadvantage to restrict the choices open to *universal suffrage.* Universal suffrage is a principle that is as jealous as it is absolute. When an entire population has enveloped a councillor of the Court of Appeal, for example, with esteem, respect, confidence, and admiration, when its members have faith in his enlightenment and virtues, do you think it will be easy to make them understand that they have the option to entrust to anyone they like other than this worthy magistrate the task of correcting their legislation?

2. It is no less exorbitant to attempt to deprive a complete class of citizens of their finest political right and the noblest reward of lengthy and loyal service, a reward given by electors exercising free choice. The question might almost be raised as to what extent the National Assembly has this right.

3. From the point of view of practical usefulness, it is blindingly obvious that the level of experience and enlightenment has to be very low in a chamber that is renewed every three years and from which all men who are highly experienced in public affairs are excluded. What! Here we have an assembly that has to deal with the navy and the army too, in which there is not a single naval or army officer! We have to deal too with civil and criminal legislation and in the Assembly there will not be a single magistrate!

It is true that army and naval officers are admitted, through a law that has nothing to do with the matter and for reasons that do not relate to the fundamentals of this question. But this itself is a fourth and serious disadvantage to be added to the other three. The people will not understand that in a chamber in which laws are passed, the military is present and lawyers are absent just because in 1832 or 1834 a particular set of arrangements was introduced in the army. It will be said that such a shocking inequality should not be the result of an old and entirely contingent law. You were made responsible for drafting a comprehensive electoral law; this was worth doing and you ought not to bring a monstrous inconsistency into it under the cloak of an obscure article in the Military Code. Absolute *incompatibility* would have been better. It would at least have had the prestige of a principle.

A few words now on the precautions that I think society has the right to take with regard to civil servants who are elected as deputies.

People may try to get me to be inconsistent by saying: "Since you do not accept any limits to the choices open to universal suffrage, since you do not believe that a category of citizens can be deprived of their political rights, how can you accede to the idea that more- or less-restrictive precautions can be placed on some people while others are not subjected to them?"

These restrictions, it should be clearly noted, are limited to one thing: ensuring the independence and impartiality of the representative in the public interest and placing deputies who are civil servants on a totally equal footing with those who are not. When a magistrate accepts a legislative mandate, the law of the country should say to him, "Your parliamentary life is just beginning and, as long as it lasts, your judiciary life will be suspended." What in this is excessive or contrary to right principle? When the function is interrupted de facto, why should it not also be by law, since this has the additional advantage that it protects the civil servant from all pernicious influences? I do not want him subject to promotion or dismissal by the executive power, since, if he were to be, this would not be for actions relating to the service that he is no longer engaged in but as a result of the way he votes. Now who could accede to the executive power's rewarding or punishing votes? These safeguards are not arbitrary. Their aim is not to restrict the choices which go with universal suffrage or the political rights of one class of citizens, but on the contrary to make them universal, since without them we would necessarily face absolute conflict of interest.

A man who, in whatever degree, is part of the government hierarchy should straightforwardly accept that he is in a very different position from that of other citizens with regard to society, and notably so with respect to the subject before us.

The activities of the civil service and private industry have something in common and something that differentiates them. What they have in common is that both satisfy social needs. The latter protects us from hunger, cold, illness, and ignorance, the former from war, unrest, injustice, and violence. These are all services rendered for payment.

This, however, is what is different. Each person is free to accept or refuse private services or to receive them to the extent that suits him and to think about how much they cost. I cannot force anyone to buy my pamphlets, read them, or pay the price for them that the publisher would charge if he had the power to do so.

But everything that concerns the departments of the civil service is regulated in advance by law. It is not I who judge how much *security* I will buy and how much I will pay for it. Civil servants give me as much as the law prescribes that they should and I pay for it as much as the law ordains that I should. My free will counts for nothing.

It is therefore essential to know who will be drafting this bill.

Since it is in the nature of man to sell for as high a price as possible as many goods as possible, and those of the poorest-possible quality, it might be thought that we would be governed horribly and expensively if those who had the privilege of selling government products also had the privilege of determining their quantity, quality, and price.[6]

For this reason, faced with that vast organization that we call the government and that, like all organized bodies, is constantly seeking to grow, the nation, as represented by its deputies, decides for itself on which matters, to what extent, and at what price it wants to be governed and administered.

If, to settle these things, the nation chooses individually those who govern, it is greatly to be feared that it will, within a short time, be administered to within an inch of its life until its funds run out.

So I understand why men driven to extremes have thought of saying to the nation, "I forbid you to have yourselves represented by civil servants." This is absolute conflict of interest.

For my part, I am much inclined to say the same thing to the nation, but only as a piece of advice. I am not very certain of having the right to convert this advice into prohibition. Certainly, if universal suffrage is left free, this

---

6. (Paillottet's note) See pages 10 and 11 in vol. 4, chapter 17 in vol. 6, and pages 443ff. in this volume. (*OC,* vol. 4, "Abondance, disette," pp. 10 and 11; vol. 6, p. 535, "Services privés, service public"; and vol. 5, p. 407, "Paix et liberté ou le budget républicain," pp. 443ff.

means that it can make mistakes. Does it therefore follow that to anticipate its errors, we ought to deprive universal suffrage of its freedom?

However, what we do have the right to do, as those responsible for drafting an electoral law, is to ensure the independence of the civil servants that are elected as deputies and to put them on an equal footing with their colleagues, to protect them from the capriciousness of their superiors, and to regulate their position during their mandate insofar as this may be contrary to the public good.

This is the aim of the first part of my amendment.[7]

I think it reconciles everything.

It respects the rights of electors.

It respects the citizens' rights of civil servants.

It eliminates the special interest that in former times incited civil servants to become deputies.

It restricts the number of those who will seek to be elected as deputies.

It ensures the independence of those elected.

It leaves rights intact while abolishing abuses.

It raises the level of experience and education in the Chamber.

In a word, it reconciles principles with usefulness.

However, if the rule of conflict of interest is not in force *before* the election, it certainly must be *afterward*. The two parts of my amendment stand together, and I would prefer a hundred times to see it rejected as a whole than to have half of it accepted.

§2. *Can deputies become civil servants?*

At every period, when a question of *parliamentary reform* has arisen, people have felt the need to bar careers in the civil service to deputies.

This was based on the following reasoning, which is in fact highly conclusive: The people who are governed elect representatives to supervise, control, limit, and, if necessary, prosecute those who govern. In order to carry out this mission, they have to retain their full independence with regard to

---

7. During the discussion of the March 1849 law, on 26 February, Bastiat had indeed proposed an amendment that he justified in this way: "Deputies should be only deputies, and should not be appointed to any position by the executive power. If it so happened that some exceptions were found to be justified, a minister's position should never be such an exception, as the greatest plague of a government is the possibility for a deputy to become a minister."

the executive. If the executive were to enroll deputies in its ranks, the aim of the institution would miscarry. Such is the constitutional objection.

The moral objection is no less strong. What could be sadder than to see the deputies of the people betraying the confidence invested in them, one after the other, selling for their advancement both their votes and the interests of their constituents?

At first people hoped to reconcile everything through *reelection*.[8] Experience has shown the ineffectiveness of this palliative measure.

Public opinion therefore became strongly attached to this second aspect of conflict of interest, and Article 28 of the constitution is nothing other than the manifestation of its triumph.

However, public opinion has also always considered that there should be one exception to conflict of interest, and that, while it is wise to forbid lesser jobs to deputies, this should not be so for ministries, embassies, and what is known as *high political office*.

Thus, in all the plans for parliamentary reform that were produced before February, in that of M. Gauguier as in that of M. de Rumilly and that of M. Thiers, while Article 1 always set out the principle boldly, Article 2 invariably produced the exception.

To tell the truth, I think that nobody has entertained the thought that it could possibly be otherwise.

And, since public opinion, right or wrong, always ends up carrying the day, Article 79 of the draft electoral law is nothing more than a second manifestation of its triumph.

This article states:

"Article 79. The salaried public offices to which, *as exceptions* to Article 28 of the Constitution, the members of the National Assembly may be called for as long as the law is in effect, following selection by the executive power, are those of:

minister;
undersecretary of state;
senior commander of the National Guard of the Seine;
attorney general of the Supreme Court of Appeal;
attorney general of the Court of Appeal of Paris;
prefect of the Seine."

8. Under the July Monarchy, any deputy who accepted a remunerated public function had to return to his electors to get their permission to combine the two functions.

Public opinion does not change overnight. It is therefore with no hope of present success that I am addressing the National Assembly. It will not delete this article of the law. However, I am carrying out a duty, since I can see (and I only hope I am wrong!) that this article will cover our unfortunate country in ruins and debris.

I certainly do not have such faith in my own infallibility that I would trust my views when they are in opposition to those of the general public. May I therefore be allowed to shelter behind authorities who are not to be despised.

Ministers who are deputies! This is a very English import. It is from England, the cradle of representative government, that this irrational and monstrous combination has come. However, it should be noted that in England the entire representative regime is just an ingenious method of putting and retaining power in the hands of a few parliamentary families. In the spirit of the British constitution, it would have been absurd to shut off access to power to members of Parliament, since this constitution has the precise objective of delivering this to them. And we will soon see, however, what hideous and terrible consequences this departure from the simplest indications of common sense has had.

But on the other hand, the founders of the American republic wisely rejected this source of trouble and political upheaval. Our fathers did the same in 1789. I am not therefore in the process of supporting a purely personal view or an innovation with neither precedent nor authority.

Like Washington, Franklin, and the authors of the '91 constitution,[9] I cannot stop myself from seeing in the *eligibility of deputies for ministerial posts* a constant cause of unrest and instability. I do not think that it is possible to imagine an alliance that is more destructive of any effectiveness and any continuity in the action of the government, or a harder pillow for the heads of kings or presidents of republics. Nothing on earth seems to me to be more likely to arouse a partisan spirit, ferment factional conflict, corrupt all the sources of information and publicity, distort the action of the rostrum and the press, mislead public opinion after having whipped it up, make true facts unpopular in order to make falsehood popular, hinder administrative processes, stir up national hatred, provoke foreign wars, ruin public finances, wear down and discredit governments, discourage and corrupt those being

9. The 1791 Constitution stipulated that ministers had to be chosen by the king outside the Assembly.

governed, and, in a word, falsify all the stimuli of a representative regime. I
know of no social scourge that can be compared to that, and I believe that if
God Himself sent us a constitution by one of His angels, all it would need
is for the National Assembly to insert Article 79 for this divine work to
become the scourge of our country.

This is what I propose to demonstrate.

I warn you that my line of argument is a long syllogism based on this
premise, taken as read: *"Men love power.* They adore it with such fervor that
to conquer or retain it, there is nothing they would not sacrifice, even the
tranquillity and happiness of their country."

This universally observed truth will not be contested in advance. But
when, from consequence to consequence, I have led the reader to my conclusion—that access to government must be closed to deputies—it may be
that the reader will return to my starting point, not having found any broken
link in my chain of reasoning, and say to me, *"Nego majorem,*[10] you have not
proved the *attraction of power."*

In this case I will stubbornly stand by my unproven thesis. Proof! Just
open the annals of the human race at random! Consult ancient or modern
history, whether sacred or profane, and ask yourself where all these wars of
race, class, nations, or families came from! You will always receive the invari-
able answer: the thirst for power.

This having been said, does the law not act blindly and rashly in the extreme when it offers candidacy for a position of power to the very men it
makes responsible for checking, criticizing, accusing, and judging those who
hold it? I am no more suspicious than the next man of the sentiment of this
or that person, but I distrust the human heart when it is placed by a reckless
law between duty and self-interest. In spite of the most eloquent speeches in
the world on the purity and disinterestedness of the magistrates, I would not
like to have my small savings in a country in which a judge is able to decree
its confiscation in his own favor. In the same way, I pity the minister who has
to say to himself: "The nation forces me to report to men who really want
to replace me and who can do so provided they can find fault with me." Just
go and prove your innocence to judges like these!

But it is not just the minister who is to be pitied; it is above all the nation.
A terrible conflict is about to break out and this will provide the challenge.

---

10. "The major premise is untrue."

What is at stake is its tranquillity, its well-being, its moral code, and even the true standing of its ideas.

The salaried high offices to which, as exceptions to Article 28 of the Constitution, the members of the National Assembly may be called during the life of this legislature, following selection by the executive power, are those of ministers.

Oh, this is a peril so great and palpable that, if we did not have experience in this respect, if we were reduced to *a priori* judgment, or simple common sense, we would not hesitate for a minute.

Allow me to imagine that you have no concept of a representative regime. You, a new Astolphus,[11] are being transported to the moon and you are told: "Out of all the nations that people this world, here is one that does not know what tranquillity, calm, security, peace, and stability are." "Does it not have a government?" you ask. "Oh, there is none more governed in the universe," comes the reply, and to find one that is governed as much, you would have to travel around all the planets to no avail, except perhaps the earth. The government there is immense, dreadfully overbearing, and spendthrift. Five out of six of the people with some sort of education work for the state there. But at last those being governed there have won a precious right. They periodically elect deputies who draft all the laws, hold the purse strings, and oblige the government to obey their decisions, either in its actions or in its expenditures. "Oh! What splendid order, what a wise economy ought to result from this simple mechanism!" you cry. "Certainly this people has to have found, or will find, by trial and error, the exact point at which the government will achieve the greatest benefits at least cost. Why then are you telling me that everything is in trouble and confusion under such a marvelous regime?" "You ought to know," replies your guide, "that if the inhabitants of the moon, or the lunatics, have a prodigious love of being governed, there is one thing that they love even more prodigiously and that is to govern. So, they have introduced into their wonderful constitution a tiny article, lost in the midst of all the others, that says: "The representatives combine the faculty of overthrowing ministers with that of replacing them. Consequently, if parties, systematic opposition groups, or coalitions are

---

11. A character from the then-famous poem "Orlando furioso," by Ludovico Ariosto (1474–1533). Orlando has lost his mind. Astolphe cures him with a bottle brought back from the moon and given to him by Saint John the Evangelist.

formed in parliament, which by dint of noise and clamor and exaggerating and distorting all the questions manage to make the government unpopular and overthrow it through the blows delivered by a majority that has been suitably prepared to do this, the leaders of these parties, opposition groups, and unions, will *ipso facto* be *ministers,* and, while these heterogeneous elements are quarreling among themselves for power, the overthrown ministers, who have become simple representatives once again, will proceed to foment intrigues, alliances, and new opposition groups and unions." "Good heavens!" you cry; "since this is so, I am not surprised that the history of this people is just the history of a frightful and constant upheaval!"

But let us return to the moon, fortunate if, like Astolphus, we can take back to it a small vial of common sense. We will pay homage to anyone involved during the third reading[12] of our electoral law.

I request leave to stress once again my *a priori* argument. Only this time we will apply it to existing situations, which are occurring as we watch.

There are in France some eighty parliaments on a small scale. They are known as General Councils. The reports sent by prefects to General Councils are similar in many respects to those sent by ministers to the National Assembly. On the one hand there are agents mandated by the public, who decide in its name to what extent and at what cost they intend to be governed. On the other, an agent of the executive power studies the measures to be taken, has them accepted if he can, and once they are, sees that they are carried out. This is a procedure that is carried out repeatedly nearly a hundred times a year under our eyes, and what does it teach us? Certainly the hearts of general councillors are formed from the same clay as those of the representatives of the people. There are few of them who do not want to become prefects as much as deputies want to become ministers. However, the idea does not even cross their minds, and the reason for this is simple: the law has not made the post of councillor a stepping-stone to the prefecture. However ambitious men are (and nearly all of them are), they pursue, *per fas et nefas,*[13] only what it is possible to attain. Faced with total impossibility, desire fades away for lack of sustenance. We see children cry-

---

12. Article 41 of the Constitution stipulated that no law could be voted before three deliberations had taken place at intervals of more than five days. The third deliberation of the draft of electoral legislation took place from 11 to 14 March 1849.

13. "Through right and wrong."

ing for the moon, but when reason takes over, they no longer think about it. This is directed at those who tell me, "Do you then believe that you can root out ambition from men's hearts?" Certainly not, and I do not even want to. However, what is very possible is to divert ambition from a given path by abolishing the bait that had rashly been placed there. You can erect greasy poles as much as you like; no one will climb them if there is no prize at the top.

It is clear that if a systematic opposition group or an equal coalition of the red and white were to form in General Councils, it might well overthrow the prefect, but it would not install the leaders in his place. What is also certain, and experience has borne this out, is that as a result of this impossibility, coalitions like this do not form in them. The prefect puts forward his plans; the Council discusses them, assesses them among its membership, and estimates their intrinsic value from the point of view of the general good. I am ready to accept that one person may let himself be influenced by local considerations and another by his own personal interest. The law cannot reform the human heart; it is up to the electors to allow for this. But it is very true that nobody systematically rejects the proposals of a prefect solely to check him, to thwart him, or to overthrow him and take his place. This senseless conflict, for which the country pays the cost in the end, this conflict that is so frequent in our legislative assemblies that it is their very history and life, is never witnessed in the assemblies of the *départements;* do you want to see it occur there? There is a simple way of doing this. Constitute these tiny parliaments along the lines of the big one; introduce into the law that organizes the General Councils a little article drafted thus:

"If a measure, whether good or bad, put forward by the prefect is rejected, he will be removed from office. The member of the Council who has led the opposition will be nominated in his place and will distribute to his companions of fortune all the major activities of the *département:* general tax collection, the management of direct and indirect contributions, etc."

I ask the question: out of my nine hundred colleagues, is there a single one who would dare to vote for a dispensation like this? Would he not think he was making the country a most disastrous gift? Could one choose anything better if one had decided to watch it die under the grip of factions? Is it not certain that this article alone would totally throw the spirit of General Councils into confusion? Is it not certain that these hundred enclaves in which calm, independence, and impartiality reign would be converted into so many arenas of conflict and intrigue? Is it not clear that each proposal put forward by the prefect would become a battlefield of personal conflict instead of being studied for its own sake and for its effect on the public good? Would each person not seek only opportunities for his own advantage? Now, let us assume that there are journals in the *département;* would the warring parties not devote every effort to win them over to their side? Would not the controversy between these journals be tinged with the passions that agitate the council? Would all the questions not be brought before the public changed and distorted? When there are elections, how can a public that has been misled or circumvented judge matters correctly? Do you not see, moreover, that corruption and intrigue, whipped up by the heat of the conflict, will know no bounds?

These dangers strike and terrify you. Representatives of the people, you would let your right hand burn sooner than vote in an organization for the General Councils that was as absurd and anarchical as this. And yet, what are you going to do? You are going to deposit this destructive scourge, this dreadful solvent, in the constitution of the National Assembly when you reject it with horror in assemblies of the *département.* In Article 79 you are going to proclaim out loud that you will be saturating the heart of the social body with this poison, from which you are protecting its veins.

You say: "That is very different. The attributions of General Councils are very limited. Their discussions have no great importance; politics are banished; they do not give laws to the country; and, after all, the position of prefect is not a very attractive object of greed.

Do you not understand that each of your alleged objections places as many more conclusive reasons that are just as clear as day within my reach? What! Will the struggle be less bitter, will it inflict less harm on the country because the arena is larger, the theater more elevated, the battlefield more extensive, the whipping up of passions more lively, the prize for the combat more desired, the questions that serve the war machine more burning, more difficult, and hence more likely to mislead the feelings and judgment of the multitude? While it is distressing when public opinion makes a mistake with regard to a neighborhood path, is it not a thousand times worse when it makes a mistake with regard to questions of peace or war, financial order or bankruptcy, public order or anarchy?

I say that Article 79, whether applied to General Councils or National Assemblies, amounts to *disorder that has intentionally been organized* according to the same design, in the first case on a small scale and in the second case on an immense one.

But let us cut short the monotonous enumeration of reasons by a call on experience.

In England, it is from members of Parliament that the king always chooses his ministers.

I do not know whether the principle of the separation of functions is stipulated, at least on paper, in that country. What is certain is that not even a shadow of this principle is revealed by the facts. All of the executive, legislative, legal, and spiritual powers are lodged in one class to its own advantage, and that is the oligarchic class. If it encounters a limitation, this is due to public opinion, and the limitation is very recent. For this reason, the English people have up to now not so much been governed as exploited, as is shown by taxes of two billion and debts of twenty-two billion. If its finances have been better managed in the recent past, England has not the combination of powers to thank for this but public opinion, which, even though deprived of constitutional means, exercises great influence, and also the common prudence of those who carry out this exploitation and who decided to stop just when they were about to become engulfed, along with the entire nation, in the abyss opened up by their rapacity.

In a country in which all the branches of government are just parts of a single exploitative system that benefits the parliamentary families, it is not surprising that ministries are open to members of Parliament. It would be surprising if this were not the case, and it would be even more surprising if this curious organization were imitated by a people that claims to govern itself, and what is more, govern itself well.

Be that as it may, what result has it produced in England itself?

No doubt people are expecting me to give the history of the coalitions that have caused disruption in England. This would amount to an account of its entire constitutional history. However, I cannot refrain from recalling a few of its details.

When Walpole was prime minister, a coalition was formed. It was led by Pulteney and Carteret for the *dissident Whigs* (those for whom Walpole had not succeeded in finding positions) and by Windham for the Tories who, suspected of Jacobite sympathies, were condemned to the sterile honor of acting as auxiliaries to all forms of opposition.[14]

---

14. The terms *Whigs* and *Tories* had appeared by 1640 in the English political vocabulary. While they are still in use today, they were formally replaced in the early nine-

It was in this coalition that Pitt the Elder (subsequently Lord Chatham) began his brilliant career.

Since the Jacobite spirit, which was still deep rooted, was capable of giving France an opportunity to cause a powerful diversion in case of hostilities, Walpole's policy favored peace. The coalition, therefore, was for war.

"To put an end to a system of corruption that subjected Parliament to the desires of the government and to replace Walpole's *timid* and exclusively peace-loving policy in foreign relations with one that has *greater pride* and more dignity": this was the twin aim that the coalition set for itself. I leave you to imagine what it said about France.

You cannot play with impunity with the patriotic sentiments of a people who sense their strength. The coalition spoke so freely and so loudly to the English of their humiliation that they ended up believing it. They called raucously for war. This broke out on the occasion of a *right of inspection*.[15]

Walpole loved power just as much as his adversaries did. Rather than lose it, he claimed to lead the operations. He put forward a subsidies bill and the coalition rejected it. The coalition wanted war but refused the means of waging it. This was how it saw the matter: a war fought without adequate resources would be a disaster; we would then be able to say: "It is the fault of the minister who has waged it half-heartedly." When a coalition places a country's honor on one side of the scales and its own success on the other, it is not the country's honor that wins the day.

This conspiracy succeeded. The war was unsuccessful, and Walpole fell from power. The opposition, minus Pitt, came into power; but, made up of heterogeneous elements, it could not agree. During this internal struggle, England was always beaten. A new coalition formed. Pitt was its driving force. He turned against Carteret. With him, he favored war; against him he wanted peace. He called him *an appalling minister and a traitor* and reproached him for subsidizing Hanoverian[16] troops. A few years later, we find these two men, now firm friends, sitting side by side in the same council. Pitt said of Carteret, "I am proud to say that I owe what I am to his patronage, friendship, and what he taught me."

---

teenth century by the terms *liberals* and *conservatives*. See also the entry for "Whig and Tory" in the Glossary of Subjects and Terms.

15. Spain granted permission to England to send a commercial vessel to her American colonies once a year but kept the right to inspect English vessels to avoid smuggling.

16. Bastiat is referring to the fact that the troops of King George II (elector of Hanover) were subsidized by the English government.

In the meantime, the new coalition brought on a ministerial crisis. The Pelham brothers[17] were ministers. A fourth coalition was formed by Pulteney and Carteret. They overthrew the Pelhams. However, they themselves were overthrown three days later. While Parliament was in the throes of these intrigues the war continued, and the Pretender,[18] who took advantage of the situation, made advances in Scotland. But this consideration did not rein in personal ambition.

Pitt finally regained a somewhat modest official position. He was *of the governing party* for a few days. He approved everything he had criticized, including the subsidy to the Hanoverians. He criticized everything he had approved, including resistance to the *right of inspection* invoked by the Spanish, which he had used as a pretext to foment the war, a war that itself had just been a pretext for overthrowing Walpole. "Experience has matured me," he said; "I have now gained the conviction that Spain is within its rights." At last peace was concluded with the Treaty of Aix-la-Chapelle, which restored things to the state they were in before and did not even mention the right of inspection that had inflamed Europe.

Then came a fifth coalition against Pitt. This was unsuccessful. Then a sixth that had one particular characteristic: it was directed by one-half of the cabinet against the other half. Pitt and Fox[19] were indeed ministers, but both wanted to be prime minister. They joined forces but were soon to oppose one another. In fact, Fox rose and Pitt fell, and Pitt lost no time in fomenting a seventh coalition. Finally with the help of circumstances (these circumstances were the ruin and humbling of England), Pitt succeeded in his efforts. He was to all intents and purposes prime minister. He was to have four years before him to make himself immortal, since *John Bull* began to be disgusted with all these conflicts.

At the end of four years, Pitt fell victim to parliamentary intrigue. His adversaries got the better of him all the more easily by constantly throwing his old speeches in his face. An interminable series of ministerial crises followed. It reached the point where Pitt, who had regained power in the midst of these vicissitudes and thought he was doing Frederick the Great much honor by offering him an alliance, received this crushing reply from him: "It is very difficult to enter into an agreement of any stature with a country

---

17. Thomas Pelham-Holles and Henry Pelham.
18. Charles Edward Stuart.
19. Henry Fox.

that, as a result of continual changes in its government, offers no guarantee of continuity and stability."

But let us leave the venerable Chatham to wear out his final days in these sorry conflicts. Here comes a new generation, other men with the same names, another Pitt,[20] another Fox,[21] who, in matters of eloquence and genius, were no less worthy than their predecessors. However, the law remained the same. *Members of Parliament could become ministers.* For this reason we are going to find the same coalitions, the same disasters, and the same immorality.

Lord North[22] was the head of the cabinet. The opposition boasted a host of illustrious names: Burke, Fox,[23] Pitt,[24] Sheridan, Erskine, etc.

Early in his career, Chatham had encountered a peace-loving government and had naturally clamored for war. The second Pitt entered Parliament during the war; his role was to clamor for peace.

North resisted the son just as Walpole had resisted the father. The opposition achieved a peak of violence. Fox went so far as to demand North's head.

North fell and a new government was formed. Burke, Fox, and Sheridan were included in it, but Pitt was not. Four months later there was a fresh shuffle, which brought Pitt into the government and removed Sheridan, Fox, and Burke. With whom do you think Fox was to form an alliance? With North himself! What a strange sight! Fox first of all wanted peace because the government was warlike. Now he wanted war because the government was peace loving. It is easy to see that war and peace were purely parliamentary strategies.

As absurd and odious as this coalition was, it succeeded. Pitt fell and North was summoned to the palace. However, individual ambition had reached such a point that it was impossible to put an end to the governmental crisis. It lasted two months. Messages from the two Houses, petitions by the citizens, and the embarrassment of the king had no effect. The members of Parliament who were candidates for ministerial office did not back down from their demands. George III thought of throwing such a heavy crown to the winds, and I believe that this period was the origin of the dreadful ill-

20. William Pitt (the Younger).
21. Charles James Fox.
22. Frederick North.
23. Charles James Fox.
24. Pitt the Younger.

ness that afflicted him later on. In truth this was enough to make him lose his head.[25]

At last agreement was reached. Fox became minister, leaving North and Pitt in opposition. A new crisis, new difficulties. Pitt triumphed and, in spite of the fury of Fox, who had become the head of another coalition, managed to maintain his position. Fox could no longer contain himself and launched into coarse insults. Pitt replied, "Sympathetic as I am with the position of the honorable gentleman who has just spoken, with the torture of his dashed hopes, his illusions that have been destroyed, and his ambition that has been disappointed, I declare that I would consider myself inexcusable if the outbursts of a mind crushed by the weight of devouring regret were to arouse in me any other emotion than that of pity. I declare that they do not have the power to provoke my anger nor even my scorn."

I will stop there. In truth, this story would be endless. If I have quoted illustrious names, it is certainly not for the vain pleasure of denigrating great reputations. I thought that my argument would be given even more force by including them. If a rash law could humiliate men such as the Pitts and the Foxes to this extent, what would it not have done to more common mortals, such as Walpole, Burke, and North?

What should be noted above all is that England was the plaything and victim of these coalitions. One led to a ruinous war, the other to a humiliating peace. A third caused the failure of the plan conceived by Pitt for justice and reparation in favor of Ireland.[26] How much suffering and shame would have been spared England and humanity by this plan!

What a sad sight is that of statesmen abandoned to the shame of perpetual contradiction! Chatham, when in opposition, taught that the slightest sign of commercial prosperity in France was a calamity for Great Britain. Chatham, when a minister, concluded a peace with France and pronounced that the prosperity of one people is beneficial to all the others. We are accustomed to seeing in Fox a defender of French ideas. Doubtless he was, when Pitt was making war on us. But when Pitt negotiated the treaty of 1786,[27]

25. After 1788 George III started to display signs of mental illness.

26. Pitt the Younger attempted until his death to eliminate discrimination against Catholics.

27. The Eden-Rayneval Treaty (from the names of the two negotiators), a commercial treaty finally signed in 1788.

Fox said in as many words that hostility was the natural state of things, the normal situation with regard to relations between the two peoples.

Unfortunately, these changes in views, which were only strategic maneuvers for the coalitions, were taken seriously by the people. This is why we have seen them pleading for peace or war in turn at the whim of the leader who was popular at the time. In this lies the great danger of coalitions.

We might rightly say that for the last few years these types of maneuver are so decried in England that their statesmen no longer dare to indulge in them. What does that prove, other than that, because of their disastrous effects, they have finally opened the eyes of the people and molded their experience? I am well aware that man is naturally liable to progress, that he always ends by becoming enlightened, if not by farsightedness, at least by experience, and that a corrupt institution loses its effectiveness for harm in the long run as a result of doing harm. Is this a reason for adopting such an institution? Besides, it should not be believed that England escaped this scourge a long time ago. We have seen the country suffering its ill effects within our lifetimes.

In 1824, as the state of the finances was hopeless, a clever minister, Huskisson, thought of a great reform which was very unpopular at the time. Huskisson had to content himself with carrying out a few experiments in order to prepare and enlighten public opinion.

At the time, there was a young man in Parliament, who was deeply versed in economics and who understood the full greatness and extent of this reform. If, as a member of Parliament, his access to government had been barred, he would have had nothing better to do than to help Huskisson in his difficult enterprise. But there was also a fatal Article 79 in the English constitution. And Sir Robert Peel, for it was he, said to himself: "This reform is fine, and it is I and I alone who will accomplish it." However, to do this, he had to be a minister. To be a minister, he had to overthrow Huskisson. For Huskisson to be overthrown, he had to be made unpopular. To make him unpopular, Sir Robert had to decry the work that he admired deep in his heart. This is what Sir Robert set out to do.

Huskisson died without achieving his idea. Finances were desperate. A heroic solution had to be conceived. Lord John Russell put forward a bill that started and implied the said reform. Sir Robert did not scruple to oppose it furiously. The bill failed. Russell advised the king to dissolve Parliament and call for an election, so grave was the situation. Sir Robert filled England with protectionist arguments, which were contrary to his convictions but essential to his plans. The old preconceived ideas prevailed. The new House of Commons overthrew Russell, and Peel entered the government *with the express mission of opposing any reform.* You can see that he was not afraid to take the longest way round.

However, Sir Robert had counted on help that was not slow to appear, public affliction. Since his careful attentions had delayed the reform, the state of finances had naturally gone from bad to worse. All the budgets had resulted in terrifying deficits. Because foodstuffs had not been able to enter Great Britain, the country experienced famine accompanied, as is always the case, by criminal acts, debauchery, illness, and death. Affliction! Nothing is more propitious to make a people fickle. Public opinion, supported by a powerful league, demanded freedom. The situation had reached the point that Sir Robert wanted. He then betrayed his past, his constituents, and his parliamentary party; and one fine day he proclaimed that he had become converted to political economy and carried out himself the very reform which, to England's great misfortune, he had delayed for ten years with the sole aim of robbing others of the glory of its achievement. He gained this glory but paid dearly for it through being abandoned by all his friends and having to suffer pangs of conscience.

We also have our *constitutional history,* in other words, the history of our portfolio war, a war that throws our country into turmoil and often corrupts it altogether. I will not spend much time on this; it would just be an echo of what has already been read, with changes in the names of the players and a few of the stage details.

The point to which I want above all to draw the reader's attention is not so much the deplorable nature of the maneuvers of parliamentary coalitions as the most dangerous aspect of one of their effects: the popularization of injustice and absurdity for a while and the rendering unpopular of truth itself.

One day, M. de Villèle noticed that the state had a little credit, and that he could borrow at 4½ percent. We then had heavy debt with interest that cost us 5 percent. M. de Villèle thought of putting the following proposal to the state's creditors: agree from now on to receive only the interest at today's rate for all transactions or take back your capital; I am ready to give it back to you. What was more reasonable and just, and how many times has France really asked for such a simple measure since then?

However, in the Chamber there were deputies who wanted to become ministers. Their natural role, therefore, was to find fault with M. de Villèle in anything and everything. They thus decried the *conversion* with so much noise and intensity that France wanted no truck with it at any price. It appeared that to give back a few million to the taxpayers was to tear out their entrails. When the upright M. Laffite, imbued by his financial experience to the extent of forgetting his role as a coalition member, decided to say: "After all, there is an advantage in the conversion," he was instantly denounced as a renegade, and Paris no longer wanted him as its deputy. Imagine making a just decrease in the interest paid to stockholders unpopular! Since coalitions have achieved this tour de force, they will surely achieve a good many others. Such being the case, at present we are still paying for this lesson and what is worse, we do not appear to be benefiting from it.

But here is M. Molé in power. Two men of talent entered the Chamber under the governance of the new charter, which also has its Article 79. This article whispered in the ear of one of our two deputies these seductive words: "If you can manage to demolish M. Molé by making him unpopular, one of you will take his place." And our two champions, who have never been able to agree on anything, agreed perfectly about heaping floods of unpopularity on M. Molé's head.

What terrain did they choose? Matters concerning foreign affairs. This was about the only one on which the two men of opposing political opinions were able to agree for a moment. Besides, it was perfectly suited to the aim they had in mind. "The government is cowardly and traitorous, and it is humiliating the French flag. We ourselves are the true patriots and defenders of national honor." What is better calculated to debase your opponent and raise yourself in the eyes of a public that is so well known to be sensitive to points of honor? It is true that if this exalted feeling of patriotism is pushed too far in the masses, it may result initially in scuffles and then in universal conflagration. However, this was just a secondary consideration in the eyes of a coalition; the essential lay in seizing power.

At the time of which we are speaking, M. Molé had found France bound by a treaty that included, if I am not mistaken, the following clause which I quote: "When the Austrians leave the legations,[28] the French will leave Ancona." Well, once the Austrians left the legations, the French left Ancona.

28. A reference to the countries that the French had formally administered. Molé was minister of foreign affairs during the July Monarchy (1836) and was instrumental in withdrawing the French garrison from the Italian city of Ancona, where the French had been since it was first occupied in 1797, at which time Ancona declared itself to be a revolutionary municipality. Until Italy became a unified nation state, Austria and France were the dominant European powers in the northern part of Italy.

Nothing in the world was more natural and just. Unless it is claimed that the glory of France lies in violating treaties and that she has been given promises so that she can deceive those with whom she negotiates, M. Molé was right a thousand times.

However, it was precisely on this question that MM Thiers and Guizot, supported by a public opinion that had been misled, succeeded in overthrowing him. And it was on this occasion that M. Thiers professed the famous doctrine on the value of international undertakings that has made him an impossible man since it has done nothing less than make France itself an impossible nation, at least among civilized peoples. But the essence of coalitions is to create future embarrassment and obstacles for those who enter into them. The reason for this is simple. While people are in systematic opposition, they declare sublime principles and fierce patriotism and clothe themselves in outraged austerity. When the hour of success sounds, they enter the government, but they are obliged to leave all declamatory baggage outside the door and humbly follow the policy of their predecessors. This is why the public conscience loses any faith it has. The people see a policy that they have been taught to find despicable being continued. They say sadly to themselves, "The men who gained my confidence through their fine speeches in opposition never fail to betray it when they become ministers." Fortunately, they do not add: "From now on, I will be calling upon men of action, not speechmakers."

We have just seen MM Thiers and Guizot aim the batteries of Ancona against M. Molé in parliament. I could now demonstrate how other coalitions have disparaged M. Guizot using the batteries of Tahiti,[29] Morocco,[30] and Syria.[31] But the story would really become tedious if I did. It is always the

29. In 1842 Tahiti was a French protectorate. Following incidents with English ships, Admiral Dupetit-Thouars transformed it into a territory of "direct sovereignty" and expelled the British consul George Pritchard, a Protestant minister hostile to the French, chiefly on account of their Catholicism. This created tension between London and Paris. The latter disavowed the admiral on 24 February 1844.

30. A brief conflict opposed France to Morocco in 1844 because Morocco refused to sign the Treaty of Tangiers, which allowed cruisers of the signatory states to control merchant ships in order to check for slaves. This "right of search" did not fail to raise trouble between France and England for a while, as English cruisers, outnumbering those of other nations, exerted a de facto police of the seas. For "right of search," see also the entry for "Slavery" in the Glossary of Subjects and Terms.

31. France supported Mehemet Ali, pasha (governor) of Egypt, in his views on Syria, part of the Ottoman Empire. England and Russia supported the sultan.

same. Two or three deputies from a variety of parties, often opposed to one another and often irreconcilable, get it into their heads that they ought to be ministers whatever happens. They calculate that all these parties together would be able to form a majority or very close to one. Therefore they form a coalition. They do not bother with serious administrative or financial reform that would lead to public good. No, they would not agree on this. Besides, the role of a coalition is to attack men violently and abuses tepidly! Destroy abuse! That would be to reduce the inheritance to which they aspire! Our two or three leaders pitch their camp firmly on questions relating to foreign affairs. Their mouths are full of the words: national honor, patriotism, the greatness of France, and physical and moral superiority. They whip up the journals and then public opinion; they exalt it, inflame it, and overexcite it, now on the question of the Egyptian pasha, then on the right of search, and yet again on questions raised by someone such as Pritchard.[32] They lead us right up to the brink of war. Europe is racked by anxiety. Armies are increased on all sides and budgets with them. "Just a little more effort," says the coalition; "The government must fall or Europe has to be in flames." The government does indeed fall, but the armies remain, as do the budgets. One of the happy victors joins the government; the two others remain on the wayside and go on to form a new coalition with the overthrown ministers that uses the same intrigues to achieve the same results. If anyone thinks of saying to the newly appointed government, "Now reduce the army and the budget," they will reply, "What! Do you not see how often the danger of war arises in Europe?" And the people chorus: "They are right." So the burden increases with each government crisis until it becomes unbearable and the artificial perils abroad are replaced by the genuine ones at home. And the government says: "We have to arm half of the nation to keep the other half in check." Whereupon the people, or at least that part of the people who still have something to lose, say: "It is right."

Such is the sorry sight that France and England are offering to the rest of the world, to the extent that many people with common sense have been brought to the point of asking themselves whether a representative regime, however logical in theory, is not by its very nature a cruel hoax. That de-

32. The "right of search" refers to the disputed and resented policy of the British navy of stopping and searching suspected slave ships on the high seas. See also the entry for "Slavery" in the Glossary of Subjects and Terms.

pends. Without Article 79, it lives up to the hopes that gave it birth, as is proved by the example of the United States. With Article 79, it is just a series of illusions and disappointments for the people.

And how could it be otherwise? Men have dreamed of greatness, influence, wealth, and glory. Who does not dream of these on occasion? Suddenly the wind of election blows them into the legislative arena. If the constitution of their country tells them, "You are entering here as a deputy and you will remain a deputy," what good would it do them, I ask you, to torment, hinder, decry, and overturn those in power? However, far from speaking to them thus, the constitution tells one of them, "The government needs to increase its following and has high political office in its gift, which I do not forbid you to accept," and another, "You have daring and talent; there is the ministers' bench. If you succeed in removing the incumbents, your place will be on it."

At this point, infallibly, the floods of angry accusations begin, the unheard-of efforts to gain the support of a fleeting popularity, and the grand display of unattainable principles when the person is on the attack or abject concessions when he is on the defensive. There is nothing but traps and counter-traps, feints and counterfeints, mines and countermines. Politics becomes mere strategy. Operations are carried out outside and in offices, commissions, and committees. The slightest accident in parliament, the election of the treasurer of a parliamentary assembly, is a signal that makes hearts beat fast through fear or hope. No greater interest would be aroused if it were a question of the Civil Code itself. The most unlikely elements form alliances and the most natural alliances dissolve. Here, a partisan spirit forms a coalition. There, the undercover skill of one minister causes the downfall of another. If a matter arises concerning a law on which the well-being of the people depends but which does not involve a *question of confidence,* the Chamber is deserted. On the other hand, any event that occurs that carries within it general conflagration is always welcome if it offers a terrain on which assault ladders may be raised. Ancona, Tahiti, Morocco, Syria, Pritchard, the right of inspection or fortifications,[33] any of these is a good excuse, provided that the coalition can gain enough strength from it to overthrow the cabinet. At this point we are drenched in this type of stereotyped lamentations, "At home, France is suffering, etc., etc., while abroad, France is humiliated, etc., etc." Is this true? Is it false? Nobody cares. Will this measure make us

33. Following the 1840 diplomatic crisis, the government had fortifications built around Paris.

quarrel with Europe? Will it oblige us to keep five hundred thousand men constantly on the ready? Will it stop the march of civilization? Will it create obstacles for any future government? That is not the point. Basically, just one thing is of interest: the fall or triumph of a particular name.

And do not think that this political perversity affects only base hearts within parliament, hearts that are consumed by ignoble ambition, the commonplace lovers of well-paid positions. No, it attacks over and above all the highest minds, noble hearts, and powerful intellects. To tame men like these, it needs only Article 79 to awaken in the depths of their consciences, in place of the trivial thought: *You will achieve your dreams of wealth,* this much more dominant idea: *You will achieve your dreams for the public good.* Lord Chatham had shown evidence of great disinterest, and M. Guizot has never been accused of worshipping the golden calf. We have seen these two men in coalitions, and what did they do there? Everything that a thirst for power and, perhaps worse, a thirst for riches might suggest. The display of sentiments they did not have, clothing themselves in ferocious patriotism of which they did not approve, generating embarrassment for the government of their country, making negotiations of the highest importance fail, inciting journalism and public views to follow the most perilous paths, creating problems for their own future government through all of this, and preparing themselves in advance for shameful retractions: that is what they did. Why? Because the tempting demon, hidden in the form of an Article 79, had whispered in their ear these words, whose seductive power it has known from the beginning: "*Eritis sicut dii;*[34] overturn everything in your path, but achieve power and you will be the providence of the people." And the deputy, succumbing to this, makes speeches, sets out doctrines, and carries out actions of which his conscience disapproves. He says to himself: "I have to do this to make my way. Once I have reached government, I will be able to return to my genuine ideas and my true principles."

There are therefore very few deputies who are not diverted by the prospect of government from the straight line that their constituents were entitled to see them pursue. Here again, if the war for portfolios, this scourge which the fabulist might have included in his sorry list between plague and famine, if only this war for portfolios was limited to the chamber of the national palace! But the field of battle has gradually expanded right up to and beyond the borders of our country. Warlike masses are everywhere; only

34. "You shall be as gods."

their leaders remain in the Chamber. They know that, in order to reach the body of the fort, they have to start by conquering the outer works—journalism, popularity, public opinion, and electoral majorities. It is therefore fatal for all these forces, to the extent that they support or oppose the coalition, to become impregnated and imbued with the passions that are aroused in parliament. Journalism from one end of France to the other no longer discusses; it pleads a case. It argues for and against each law and each measure, not on the basis of what good or harm they contain but solely from the point of view of the assistance they might provide temporarily to this or that champion. The government press has only one motto: *E sempre bene*,[35] and the press for the opposition, like the old woman in the satire, lets the following word be read on her petticoat: *Argumentabor*.[36]

When journalism has thus decided to mislead the general public and mislead itself, it is able to accomplish some surprising miracles of this sort. Let us recall the *right of inspection*.[37] For I do not know how many years this treaty was carried out without anyone taking any notice. However, since a coalition needed a strategic expedient, it unearthed this unfortunate treaty and used it as the basis of its operations. Within a short time, with the help of journalism, the coalition succeeded in making every Frenchman believe that it had only one clause, which stated: "English warships will have the right to inspect French commercial ships." I have no need to relate the explosion of patriotism that a notion like this was bound to generate. It reached a point at which we still cannot understand how a world war could have been avoided. I remember at this time finding myself in a circle of many people who were fulminating against this odious treaty. Someone thought of asking, "How many of you have read it?" It was fortunate for him that his audience had no stones to hand or he would inevitably have been stoned.

Besides, the involvement of the journals in the war for portfolios and the role they play in it was revealed by one of them in terms that deserve to be quoted here (*La Presse* dated 17 November 1845):

"M. Petetin describes the press as he understands it and as he likes fondly to imagine it. In good faith, does he believe that when *Le Constitutionnel*, *Le Siècle*, etc., attack M. Guizot and when in turn *Le Journal des débats* takes

35. "All is well."
36. "It will be argued." [Nicolas Boileau-Despréaux (1636–1711), Satire X, *Œuvres* (1821), vol. 1, p. 293.]
37. See the entry for "Slavery" in the Glossary of Subjects and Terms.

on M. Thiers, these papers fight solely for the idea in its essence, for truth, stimulated by the internal needs of conscience? Defining the press in this way is to paint it as one imagines it, not to paint it as it is. It costs us nothing to declare this, for if we are journalists we are less so by vocation than by circumstance. Every day we see the press in the service of human passions, *rival ambitions, ministerial alliances, parliamentary intrigue,* a wide variety and the most diverse of political calculations and those that are the least noble; we see it associating closely with these. But we rarely see it in the service of ideas, and when by chance a journal happens to take hold of an idea, *it is never for itself, it is always as a governmental instrument of defense or attack.* He who is writing these lines is speaking from experience. Every time he has tried to make journalism leave the partisan rut for the open fields of ideas and reform, the path of the healthy application of economic science to public administration, he has found himself alone, and has had to acknowledge that, *outside the narrow circle drawn by the assembled letters of four or five individuals,* there was no possible discussion, and no politics."

In truth, I do not know to what demonstration to turn if the reader is not scandalized and appalled by such a terrible admission?

Finally, just as the evil, having escaped parliament, invaded journalism, through journalism it invaded the whole of public opinion. How could the general public not be misled when, day after day, *La Tribune* and *La Presse* concentrated on allowing only false glimmers, false judgments, false quotations, and false assertions to reach it?

We have seen that the terrain on which ministerial battles normally take place is first of all the question of foreign affairs, followed by parliamentary and electoral corruption.

With regard to foreign affairs, everyone understands the danger of this incessant work undertaken by coalitions to whip up national hatred, inflame patriotic pride, and persuade the country that foreigners are thinking only of humiliating them and the executive power only of betraying them. I trust I may be allowed to say that this danger is perhaps greater in France than anywhere else. Our civilization has made work a necessity for us. It is our means of existence and progress. Production develops through security, freedom, order, and peace.

Unfortunately, university education is in flagrant contradiction with the needs of our time. By making us live throughout our youth the life of the Spartans and Romans, it fosters in our souls the sentiment common to children and barbarians, an admiration for brute force. The sight of a fine regiment, the sound of a flourish of trumpets, the appearance of the machines invented by men to break each other's arms and legs, or the strutting of a drum major, all put us in a state of ecstasy. Like barbarians, we believe that *patriotism* means a *hatred of foreigners*. As soon as our intelligence begins to grow, it is nourished solely with military virtues, the great policies of the Romans, their profound diplomacy, and the strength of their legions. We learn our morals from Livy. Our catechism is Quintus Curtius and our enthusiasm is offered, as an ideal of civilization, a nation that founded its means of existence on the methodical plundering of the entire world. It is easy to understand how the efforts of parliamentary coalitions, which are always directed toward war, find us so eager to support them. They could not sow on a field that is better prepared. For this reason, in the space of a few years we came on three occasions within a whisker of clashing with Spain, Morocco, Turkey, Russia, Austria, and England. What would have become of France if calamities like these had not been averted with great difficulty and almost in spite of what she was doing? Louis-Philippe fell, but nothing will stop me from saying that he rendered the world an immense service by maintaining the peace. How much sweat this success worthy of the blessings of nations cost him! And why (this is the heart of my thesis)? Because at a given time peace no longer had public opinion on its side. And why did it not have public opinion on its side? Because it did not suit the newspapers. And why did it not suit them? Because it was inconvenient for some deputy, who aspired to a ministry. And why in the end was it inconvenient for this deputy? Because accusations of weakness and treason have been, are, and always will be the favorite weapon of deputies who aspire to portfolios and need to overthrow those who hold them.

The other point on which coalitions normally attack the government is corruption. In this respect, during the last regime, it was quite easy for them. However, do coalitions not make corruption itself inevitable, so to speak? The government, being attacked on a matter on which it is in the right—such as, for example, when people want to incite it to start an unjust war—initially defends itself using reason. However, it soon realizes that reason is powerless and that it has broken itself against systematic opposition. What recourse has it left in these circumstances? To create at all costs for itself a solid majority and to oppose one *prejudice* with *another*. This was Walpole's defensive weapon and that of M. Guizot. I hope I will not be accused of presenting an apology or justification for corruption here. However, I will say this: given the state of the human heart, coalitions make corruption inevitable. The opposite implies contradiction, for if the government were honest, it would fall. It exists; therefore it corrupts. The only cabinets that have ever been stable to any extent were those which created a majority for themselves in spite of this: those of Walpole, North, Villèle, and Guizot.

And now let the reader imagine a country in which the major political meetings, chambers, and electoral bodies are under pressure, on the one hand from the maneuvers of systematic opposition, backed up by a journalism sowing hatred, lies, and warlike ideas, and on the other by government maneuvers instilling venality and corruption in the very fibers of the social body! And this has been going on for centuries! And this is becoming the permanent situation of the representative regime! Should we be surprised if honest people end up by losing all trust in it? It is true that from time to time we see leaders change their role. However, an event like this serves only to substitute universal and indelible skepticism for the last vestiges of trust.

I must close. I will end with a consideration of the greatest importance.

The National Assembly has established a constitution. We ought to give it the most profound respect. It is the lifeline of our purposes. However, this is not a reason to close our eyes to the dangers that it may present by virtue of its claims as a work of human construction, especially if, in this conscientious scrutiny, we set ourselves the aim of banishing from all its ancillary institutions anything that is likely to germinate a disastrous seed.

Everyone will agree, I think, that the danger of our constitution is to bring face to face two powers which are or may think they are rivals and equals because both take advantage of the universal suffrage from which they arise.[38] Already the possibility of irreconcilable conflict is alarming many minds and has given rise to two very distinct theories. Some claim that the February revolution against the former executive power has not felt able to propose a reduction in the preponderance of the legislative power. On the contrary, the chairman of the Council claimed that, although in previous times the government had to withdraw in the face of majorities, this was not the case today. Be that as it may, any sincere advocate of security or stability ought to hope ardently that no actual opportunity for this conflict of power will occur and that the danger, if it exists, will remain latent.

---

38. The 1848 Constitution did not provide any means for resolving a conflict between the president of the republic and the Assembly. The president could not dissolve the Assembly; the Assembly could not overthrow the president (short of extraordinary circumstances).

If this is so, will we with light hearts establish a clear cause of artificial government crises within the electoral law? Faced with the huge constitutional difficulty confronting and appalling us, will we organize parliamentary strife before going our own ways, as though to increase at whim the opportunities for conflict?

Let us therefore meditate on this: what were known as *government crises* in former times will now be called *struggles for power* and will take on gigantic proportions because of this. We have already seen this, even though the constitution has scarcely been in existence for two months, and without the admirable moderation of the National Assembly we would now be in the eye of a revolutionary storm.

Certainly, this is a powerful reason for avoiding the creation of artificial causes of *government crises*. Under the constitutional monarchy, they did a great deal of harm, but in the end a solution was found. The king could dissolve the Chamber and go to the country. If the country condemned the opposition, the result arose from a new majority and the harmony of powers was reestablished. If the country condemned the government, this also resulted from a majority and the king could not refuse to give way.

Now, the question no longer arises between the opposition and the government. It arises between the legislative power and the executive power, both with a mandate for a specific duration[39]; that is to say, it arises between two expressions of universal suffrage.

Once again, I am not seeking to determine who should give way, but am limiting myself to saying, "Let us accept the ordeal if it occurs naturally, but let us not be so imprudent as to cause it to arise artificially several times a year.

Well, drawing on the lessons of the past, I ask the question: is not a declaration that representatives may aspire to portfolios an invitation to foment coalitions, increase the number of government crises, or, to express it better, struggles for power? I ask my colleagues to reflect on this.

Now I will deal with two objections.

It has been said: "You read a great deal into the eligibility of deputies to enter government. To hear you it would appear that, without this, the republic would be a paradise. By closing the door of power to deputies, do you think that you can extinguish all passions? Have you yourself not declared that in England coalitions have become impossible as a result of their

---

39. The president was elected for four years; the Assembly, for three years.

unpopularity, and have we not seen Peel and Russell lend each other loyal support?"

The argument can be summed up thus: Because there will always be evil passions, let us conclude that sustenance for the most harmful of all should be included in the law. That with time and because they cause harm repeatedly, coalitions will wear out, I believe. There is no scourge about which as much can be said, and this is a singular reason for sowing the seed of coalition government in our laws. Superfluous wars and burdensome taxes, the fruit of coalitions, have taught England to scorn them. I do not say that after two or three centuries, at the cost of similar calamities, we might not learn the same lesson. The question is to know whether it is better to reject a bad law or to adopt it on the basis that the excessive harm it does will generate a reaction toward good in a hundred years.

It has also been said: to forbid governmental posts to deputies is to deprive the country of all of the great talents that are revealed in the National Assembly.

For my part, I say that forbidding governmental posts to deputies is, on the contrary, to keep the great talents in the service of the general good. To show the prospect of power to a man of genius who is a representative is to lead him on to do a hundred times more harm as a member of a coalition than he would ever do good as the member of a cabinet. It would be to turn his very genius against public tranquillity.

Besides, do we not delude ourselves by imagining that all the great talents are in the Chamber? Do we not believe that, in the entire armed forces, there is no one who would make a good minister of war and in the entire judiciary no one who would make a good minister of justice?

If there are men of genius in the Chamber, let them stay there. They will exercise a good influence on the majorities and the government, especially since they will no longer have any interest in exercising a bad one.

Besides, even if the objection had any value, it would give way before the immeasurably greater dangers of coalition that are the inevitable consequence of the article that I oppose. Do we hope to find a solution that has no disadvantages at all? Let us be capable of choosing the lesser of two evils. The following is a singular form of logic and one used by all sophists: Your proposal has a *tiny* disadvantage and mine has immense ones. We therefore must reject yours because of the *tiny* disadvantage it has.

Let us sum up this dissertation, which is both too long and too short.

The question of parliamentary conflicts of interest is at the very heart of the Constitution. For the last year, we have not turned over a question that is more in need of being resolved correctly.

The solution that is in line with justice and the public good appears to me to be based on two principles that are clear, simple, and incontrovertible:

1. For entering the National Assembly there should be no exclusion, but precautions should be taken with regard to civil servants.

2. For moving from representative seats to political office, there should be total exclusion.

In other words:

All electors are eligible.

All representatives must remain representatives.

All this is found in the amendment that I have formulated thus:

1. Civil servants elected as deputies will not lose their rights and titles and cannot be either promoted or dismissed from these. They cannot exercise their functions nor receive salaries for these for the entire duration of their mandate.

2. A deputy cannot accept any public office, especially that of a *minister*.

# Bastiat's Political Writings:
## Anecdotes and Reflections

*In* the present volume, we focus on Bastiat's political writings, most of which were written in the 1840s on behalf of the various political campaigns in which Bastiat was involved. Not surprisingly, Bastiat was greatly affected, both personally and in his political outlook, by those campaigns and the people and events associated with them: his early activity in the free-trade movement; his burgeoning contact with the Parisian-based political economists in the Société d'économie politique;[1] his political activity as an elected member of the Constituent Assembly and then the Legislative Assembly during the revolutionary years of 1848 and 1849; and his struggles in the Chamber of Deputies, in the periodical press, and on the streets against the growing socialist movement.

During our work on this translation of Bastiat's political writings, we have come across interesting and sometimes unexpected material about the life and ideas, the colleagues and opponents, of Bastiat. Thus, in this essay I have gathered information about Bastiat and his political and intellectual milieu; much of the material is of a personal and anecdotal nature, and as such will, we hope, provide an added dimension to our understanding of the man and his ideas and complement the translation and the accompanying notes.

## THE LAW-ABIDING REVOLUTIONARY

In a review of a collection of letters Bastiat wrote to the Cheuvreux family, the young economist Gustave de Molinari reminisced about his revo-

---

1. The Société d'économie politique became the main organization that brought like-minded classical liberals together for discussion and debate. See Breton, "The Société d'économie politique of Paris (1842–1914)," pp. 53–69.

lutionary activities with Bastiat in 1848.[2] Bastiat was then forty-seven and
Molinari twenty-nine. Molinari notes that the February revolution forced
the young radical liberals to "replace our economic agitation [for free trade]
with a politico-socialist agitation," which they did on 24 February, the same
date that Molinari and a young friend decided to start a new magazine to be
called *La République*. The prime minister at the time, François Guizot, was
forced to resign on 23 February, and a provisional government was formed
on 26 February. (Thus, Molinari and his friend tried to start their new
journal the day after the revolution broke out.) Molinari asked Bastiat if he
would join him as co-editor; Bastiat agreed to do so with the understanding
that they would abide by the censorship laws, which at the time called for
approval by the government before publication took place. Molinari wryly
noted that Bastiat told them that "we may be making a revolution but revolutions do not violate the laws!"

The three of them proceeded to the Hôtel de Ville in order to have their
hastily written screed approved by the government, but the building was in
complete turmoil with armed revolutionaries milling about. They wisely decided that the provisional government was "otherwise occupied," and Bastiat
consented to publish the journal without prior approval. In Montmartre,
on their way to the printer, they came across another would-be revolutionary who was hawking a journal that had already taken the name *La République*—such was the competition at the time for catchy titles. The three
decided on the spot to rename their journal *La République française* and had
five thousand copies printed and distributed. Like most periodicals at the
time, *La République française* lasted a very short while, but it did include a
number of "striking" articles penned by Bastiat directed at the working class,
who were pushing the revolution in an increasingly socialist direction. As
Molinari notes, their journal "was decidedly not at the peak of the events"
that were swirling about them, and it soon folded.

Undaunted, Molinari and Bastiat decided to launch another journal, this
time directed squarely at working people, to be called *Jacques Bonhomme*, a
wordplay on the nickname given to the average working Frenchman. Molinari and Bastiat joined with Charles Coquelin, Alcide Fonteyraud, and
Joseph Garnier to launch the new journal in June 1848, just before the June

2. Molinari wrote a book review of the collection of letters Bastiat wrote to the
Cheuvreux family in *Le Journal des économistes*. See Molinari, "Frédéric Bastiat: *Lettres
d'un habitant des Landes*."

Days uprising (23–26 June). On 21 June the government, because of out-of-control expenses, decided to close the so-called National Workshops, which were a government program to provide state-subsidized employment to unemployed workers. This action was promptly followed by a mass uprising in Paris to protest the decision, and troops were called in to suppress the protesters, causing considerable loss of life. During this time, Bastiat sent Molinari and the editorial committee an article he had written titled "Dissolve the National Workshops!" which appeared on the front page of the very last issue of *Jacques Bonhomme.*

*Jacques Bonhomme* seems to have lasted for only four issues (June–July 1848), its lifespan abruptly truncated when Bastiat and his colleagues wisely decided to shut it down because the troops were shooting people in the streets of Paris.

## The State as the "Great Fiction"

Bastiat's essay *L'État* (The State) is probably his best-known work in English. In this volume we are reprinting a draft of his essay that appeared in the 11–15 June 1848 issue of *Jacques Bonhomme,* about a week before the shootings of the rioters began in Paris and shortly before the journal was forced to close. The essay was written to appeal to people on the streets of Paris and to attempt to woo them away from the spread of socialist ideas. Three months later Bastiat rewrote the piece, and it appeared in the 25 September 1848 issue of *Le Journal des débats,* where it was featured on the front page of the journal's four very densely printed pages.[3]

Bastiat's famous definition of the state is given in the pamphlet: "The state is the great fiction by which everyone endeavors to live at the expense of everyone else."[4] Bastiat's theory of the state was taken up for discussion in some detail in a meeting of the Société d'économie politique, of which Bastiat was a member, on 10 January 1850.[5]

In the meeting, the liberal economist Louis Wolowski defended a more expansive role for the state but was challenged by Bastiat and other mem-

---

3. Bastiat, "L'État," *Le Journal des débats,* 25 September 1848, pp. 1–2. See also "The State," p. 93 in this volume.

4. See "The State," p. 97, in this volume.

5. Société d'économie politique, "Séance du 10 janvier 1850," in *Annales de la société d'économie politique.*

bers of the society. Bastiat's pamphlet stirred up so much interest that future meetings of the society were set aside for futher discussion of the matter.

The entry "L'État" by Charles Coquelin (who attended the January meeting) in the *Dictionnaire de l'économie politique* (1852)[6] quoted so extensively from Bastiat's pamphlet that one could say that the dictionary entry was half written by him—an indication of the influence that Bastiat's ideas had on the closely knit circle of political economists. Even fifty years later the reverberations of Bastiat's ideas were still being felt. At a meeting of the society on 5 August 1899, the topic for discussion was Bastiat's acclaimed definition of the state with the additional topic, "Is this always the case, and what will it become in the future?"[7]

## BASTIAT'S PUBLISHER, THE LIBRAIRIE DE GUILLAUMIN

Bastiat, like most of those involved in the free-trade and classical liberal circles, had his books published by Gilbert Guillaumin's publishing firm, Librairie de Guillaumin et Cie, a publishing dynasty that lasted from 1835 to around 1910. Guillaumin's firm had become the focal point for the classical liberal movement in France, eventually developing into the major publishing house for classical liberal ideas in nineteenth-century France.[8]

Gilbert-Urbain Guillaumin (1801–64) was orphaned at the age of five and brought up by his uncle. He came to Paris in 1819 and worked in a bookstore before founding his publishing firm in 1835. Guillaumin became active in liberal politics after the revolution of 1830 brought the July Monarchy to power and made contact with a number of free-market economists. In addition to his publishing firm, Guillaumin helped found *Le Journal des économistes* in 1841 and the Société d'économie politique in 1842. Bastiat was a regular contributor to *Le Journal des économistes* before his death at the end of 1850, and he was a regular attendee of the monthly meetings of the Société d'économie politique, which often debated his books and ideas.

Guillaumin's firm published hundreds of books on economic issues, making its catalog a virtual who's who of the liberal movement in France. The firm's 1866 catalog listed 166 separate book titles, not counting journals and other periodicals. For example, Guillaumin published the works of Quesnay,

---

6. Coquelin, "L'État," in the *Dictionnaire de l'économie politique.*
7. Letort, "Société d'économie politique: Réunion du 5 août 1899."
8. See Garnier, "Nécrologie. Guillaumin. Ses funérailles—sa vie et son œuvre"; and Levan-Lemesle, "Guillaumin, éditeur d'économie politique 1801–1864."

Turgot, Jean-Baptiste Say, Dunoyer, Bastiat, Molinari, and many others, including translations of works by Hugo Grotius, Adam Smith, Jeremy Bentham, Thomas Malthus, David Ricardo, John Stuart Mill, and Charles Darwin. The 1849 Guillaumin catalog was five pages long, and Bastiat's "Petits Pamphlets" were prominently displayed on page 3. The first and second series of his *Economic Sophisms* could be purchased for four francs each, and *The State* for only forty centimes. There was also an announcement of Bastiat's forthcoming work *Economic Harmonies*. In the 1866 Guillaumin catalog (now thirty-three pages long) one could purchase the newly announced volume seven of the Paillottet edition of Bastiat's *Œuvres complètes* for three francs.

By the mid-1840s Guillaumin's home and business had become the focal point of the classical liberal lobby in Paris, which debated and published material opposed to a number of causes that they believed threatened liberty in France: statism, protectionism, socialism, militarism, and colonialism. After Guillaumin's death in 1864, the firm's activities were continued by his oldest daughter, Félicité, and after her death the firm was handed over to his youngest daughter, Pauline. The Guillaumin firm continued in one form or another from 1835 to 1910, when it merged with the publisher Félix Alcan. The business was located at 14 rue de Richelieu, in a central part of Paris not far from the Seine, the Tuileries Gardens, the Louvre, the Palais Royal, the Comédie Française, and the Bibliothèque Nationale de France.

The crowning glory of the Guillaumin publishing firm in the mid-nineteenth century was the two-volume, double-columned, two-thousand-page *Dictionnaire d'économie politique,* which Guillaumin co-edited with Charles Coquelin.[9] The dictionary contains a number of articles written by Bastiat, and the spirit of his ideas pervades throughout. By its sheer size, breadth, and scope, the *Dictionnaire d'économie politique* is truly one of the cornerstones of nineteenth-century classical liberal scholarship.

BASTIAT'S EDITOR AND EXECUTOR,
PROSPER PAILLOTTET (1804–78)

Prosper Paillottet[10] was a successful businessman who was drawn to Bastiat's free-trade association, the Association pour la liberté des échanges, in the mid-1840s, joining it in its earliest days. Paillottet eventually became a

9. Coquelin, *Dictionnaire de l'économie politique.*
10. For some details on Paillottet's life see Passy, "Nécrologie. Prosper Paillottet."

firm friend of and companion to the ailing Bastiat, caring for him when he was very ill in Italy. Paillottet was with Bastiat during his last few days and formed the Société des amis de Bastiat (Society of the Friends of Bastiat) only five days after Bastiat's death in order to preserve his papers and drafts and to edit his collected works.

Paillottet made his living in the jewelry business, and his modest wealth enabled him to devote most of his energies to philanthropic causes. He was vice president of the Labor Tribunal (Conseil des prud'hommes) and a member of the Commission for the Encouragement of Workers' Associations (Conseil de l'encouragement aux associations ouvrières) and of the recently formed Société d'économie politique (meetings of which Bastiat also attended). Paillottet was very active in the Association pour la liberté des échanges, even learning English in order to help Bastiat translate material on or by the Anti–Corn Law League. Much of this material probably ended up in Bastiat's book on the English Anti–Corn Law League, *Cobden et la Ligue, ou l'agitation anglaise pour la liberté du commerce* (1845), which consisted mostly of translations of Anti–Corn Law League pamphlets, newspaper articles, and speeches.[11]

As Bastiat's health worsened during 1850, Paillottet became his virtual secretary, editor, and research assistant, assisting with the editing and publishing of Bastiat's pamphlet *Property and Plunder* and the second edition of *Economic Harmonies,* which was published by the Société des amis de Bastiat.[12]

On his deathbed Bastiat authorized Paillottet to collect his manuscripts and papers and to publish them in his complete works, the first edition of which appeared in 1854–55, with a second edition in 1862–64. The various volumes of the series remained in print for much of the nineteenth century.[13] In Paillottet's edition, which forms the basis of our translation, the reader is guided by the frequent and often intriguing footnotes and comments inserted by Bastiat's close friend throughout the volumes.

Paillottet wrote several articles and book reviews of his own that appeared in *Le Journal des économistes.* Two of those articles were published separately

---

11. Bastiat's introduction to this book lays out his thoughts on Cobden's free-trade movement and its relevance for France. (*OC,* vol. 3, p. 1, "Introduction.")

12. Bastiat, *Harmonies économiques.*

13. Bastiat, *Œuvres complètes de Frédéric Bastiat.*

in book form:[14] an essay on intellectual property rights,[15] and a translation of a religious work by William Johnson Fox, who had been a popular orator in the Manchester League and a Unitarian minister.[16]

## THE CONCEPT OF INDIVIDUALISM

In nineteeth-century France the word *individualism* had strong negative connotations, and Bastiat seemed to share some of the contemporary reservations about embracing the term to describe his own philosophy.[17] Nevertheless, by the end of the century he was definitely categorized by his free-market heirs as one of the leading members of the French school of individualism.

The term *individualism* was coined by conservative counterrevolutionary theorists in the early nineteenth century to criticize the Enlightenment's overemphasis on the rights of individuals at the expense of crown, church, and community. This idea had manifested itself, Edmund Burke and Joseph de Maistre believed, in the excesses of the French Revolution and had also been taken up by Saint-Simon and other French socialist thinkers in the 1820s and 1830s in order to contrast the more "socially responsible" rule by a technocratic elite (Saint-Simon) or by "the people" themselves (Louis Blanc) with the economic and political order created by the free market, in which individuals subordinated all broader social concerns to their own narrow selfish interests.

Many French free-market political economists were aware of the writings of Adam Smith and other members of the Scottish Enlightenment, who argued that the reverse was in fact the case: that human beings were naturally sociable and that their search for private benefits resulted in the creation of public benefits (Bernard de Mandeville) as if "an invisible hand" (Adam Smith) were guiding their activity. This more-positive view of individualism (even though Bastiat was wary of directly adopting the word) lies at the heart of his notion of "economic harmony," which was the title of his magnum opus (*Economic Harmonies*). Bastiat rejected the idea that there

14. Paillottet, *Des Conseils de prud'hommes,* and *De l'encouragement aux associations ouvrières.*

15. Paillottet, *De la propriété intellectuelle.*

16. Paillottet, *Des idées religieuses.*

17. See Lukes, *Key Concepts in the Social Sciences: Individualism;* and Schatz, *L'Individualisme économique et social.*

were only three means by which society could be organized: authority (of the church and the state), individualism, or fraternity (under socialism). The proper distinction according to Bastiat was between coerced association (whether by church or state or by "the people") and voluntary association (which lay at the heart of his idea of the free market).

Liberal conservatives, on the other hand, like Alexis de Tocqueville writing in the late 1830s, worried that the democracy unfolding in America would result in a form of individualism that would weaken the ability of intermediate institutions to reduce its deleterious effects. Later in the century attitudes to individualism had changed significantly. In the entry on "Individualism" in the *Nouveau dictionnaire de économie politique* (1891–92), a clear distinction is made between "egoism" (which is rejected) and "individualism" (which was a legitimate reaction against socialism, militarism, and statism). Among the individualists the author mentioned approvingly were Wilhelm von Humboldt, Böhm-Bawerk, Karl Menger, Eugen Richter from the Austro-German school; Jeremy Bentham, Adam Smith, Herbert Spencer, Henry Sumner Maine from the Anglo-Scottish school; and Jean-Baptiste Say, Charles Dunoyer, Gustave de Molinari, and of course Bastiat from the French school.[18]

## THE IDEA OF *LAISSEZ-FAIRE*

Bastiat is now seen as one of the leading advocates of the idea of *laissez-faire* in the nineteenth century, yet the origin of the term is surrounded by controversy.[19] In English the phrase "laissez-faire" has come to mean the economic system in which there is no regulation of economic activity by the state. Other terms have also been used to mean the same thing, such as the "Manchester School" or "Cobdenism," thus linking this policy prescription to the ideas of Richard Cobden and the Anti–Corn Law League.

The origins of the term *laissez-faire* are not clear. One account attributes the origin to the merchant and physiocrat Vincent de Gournay (1712–59), who used a slightly longer version of the phrase, "laissez faire, laissez passer"

18. Bouctot, "Individualisme," in *Nouveau dictionnaire de économie politique,* vol. 2, pp. 64–66.
19. Other manifestations of the term were "laissez faire, laissez passer"; "laissez-nous faire"; and "Laissez-nous faire. Ne pas trop gouverner." See Oncken, *Die Maxime laissez faire et laisser passez.*

(let us do as we wish, let us pass unrestricted) to describe his preferrred government economic policy. Another physiocrat, Anne-Robert-Jacques Turgot (1727–81), attributes the phrase "laissez-nous faire" (let us do as we wish) to the seventeenth-century merchant Legendre, who used the phrase in an argument with the French minister of finance Colbert about the proper role of government in the economy. Yet a third physiocrat, François Quesnay (1694–1774), combined the term with another phrase: "Laissez-nous faire. Ne pas trop gouverner" (Let us do as we wish. Do not govern us too much) to make the same point.

A contemporary of Bastiat, Joseph Garnier (1813–81), in the entry for "laissez faire, laissez passer" in the *Dictionnaire de l'économie politique,* explained *laissez-faire* to mean "laissez travailler" (leave us free to work as we wish) and *laissez passer* to mean "laissez échanger" (leave us free to trade as we wish).[20] By all these measures, Bastiat is certainly an advocate of laissez-faire in the fullest sense.

## The Concepts of "Industry" and "Plunder" (Spoliation)

Bastiat got many of his ideas from reading a number of classical liberal theorists who were active during Napoléon's empire and the restoration, most notably the economist Jean-Baptiste Say (1767–1832) and the lawyers and journalists Charles Comte (1782–1837) and Charles Dunoyer (1786–1862). The latter developed an "industrialist theory" of history in which the class of *industriels* played an important role.[21] According to this school of thought there were only two means of acquiring wealth: by productive activity and voluntary exchanges in the free market (*l'industrie,* which included agriculture, trade, factory production, and services, etc.) or by coercive means (or "plunder," such as conquest, theft, taxation, subsidies, protection, transfer payments, and slavery).

Anybody who acquired wealth through voluntary exchange and productive activities belonged to a class of people collectively called *les industrieux.* In contrast to *les industrieux* were those individuals or groups who acquired their wealth by force, coercion, conquest, slavery, or government privileges.

20. Garnier, "Laissez faire, laissez passer" in Coquelin, *Dictionnaire de l'économie politique,* vol. 2, p. 19.

21. See Hart, *Class, Slavery, and the Industrialist Theory of History in French Liberal Thought, 1814–1830.*

The latter group was seen as a ruling class, or as "parasites" and plunderers, who lived at the expense of *les industrieux*.[22] A parallel group of thinkers who shared many of these views developed around Henri Saint-Simon, who advocated rule by a technocratic elite rather than the operations of the free market as did Say, Comte, Dunoyer, and Bastiat.

In contrast to Bastiat's use of the term *industry* is his use of the word *la spoliation* (or plunder), which was a key idea in his pamphlet "Propriété et spoliation," which we have translated as "Property and Plunder."[23]

It was the latter principle that had come to prominence during the revolution of 1848, exemplified in the National Workshops and the "right to work" movement, the opposition to which occupied a considerable amount of Bastiat's time as a deputy.

## THE RIGHT TO WORK VS THE RIGHT OR FREEDOM OF WORKING

The "right to work" (*le droit au travail,* which one might translate in English as the "right to a job") had been a catch phrase of the socialists throughout the 1840s. What they meant by this term was that the state had the duty to provide work for all men who demanded it. In contrast, the classical liberal economists called for the "right of working," or the "freedom to work" (*la liberté du travail,* or *le droit de travailler*), by which they meant the right of any individual to pursue an occupation or activity without any restraints imposed upon him by the state. The latter point of view was articulated by Charles Dunoyer in his *De la liberté du travail* and by Bastiat in many of his writings. The socialist perspective was provided by Louis Blanc in *L'Organisation du travail* and *Le Socialisme, droit au travail* and by Victor Considérant in *La Théorie du droit de propriété et du droit au travail*.

Matters came to a head in May 1848, when a committee of the Constituent Assembly was formed to discuss the issue of "the right to work" just prior to the closing of the state-run National Workshops, which prompted widespread rioting in Paris. In a veritable "who's who" of the socialist and liberal movements of the day, a debate took place in the Assembly and was

22. See Dunoyer, *L'Industrie et la morale considérées dans leurs rapports avec la liberté.* See also the entries for "Say, Jean-Baptiste"; "Comte, Charles"; and "Dunoyer, Barthélémy-Pierre-Joseph-Charles," in the Glossary of Persons.
23. See "Property and Plunder," pp. 147–84 in this volume.

duly published by the classical liberal publishing firm of Guillaumin later in the year along with suitable commentary by such leading liberal economists as Léon Faucher, Louis Wolowski, Joseph Garnier, and, of course, Bastiat.[24] Here is the beginning of the "opinion" Bastiat wrote for the volume, in which he distinguished between the right to work (*droit au travail,* where "work" is used as a noun and thus might be rendered as the "right to a job") and the "right to work" (*droit de travailler,* where "work" is used as a verb):

*My dear Garnier,*

You ask for my opinion of the "right to a job" (*droit au travail*), and you seem to be surpised that I did not present it on the floor of the National Assembly. My silence is due solely to the fact that when I asked for the floor, thirty of my colleagues were lined up before me.

If one understands by the phrase "right to a job" (*droit au travail*) the right to work (*droit de travailler*) (which implies the right to enjoy the fruit of one's labor), then one can have no doubt on the matter. As far as I'm concerned, I have never written two lines that did not have as their purpose the defense of this notion.

But if one means by the "right to a job" that an individual has the right to demand of the state that it take care of him, provide him with a job and a wage by force, then under no circumstances does this bizarre thesis bear close inspection.

First of all, does the state have any rights and duties other than those that already exist among the citizens? I have always thought that its mission was to protect already existing rights. For example, even if we abstract the state away from consideration, I have the right to work (*droit de travailler*) and to dispose of the fruit of my work. My fellow citizens have the same rights, and we have in addition the right to defend them even by the use of force. This is why we have the community, the communal force. The state can and ought to protect us in the exercise of these rights. It is its collective and regularized action that is substituted for individual and disordered action, and the latter is the raison d'être for the former.[25]

---

24. See *Le Droit au travail à l'Assemblée Nationale.* See also Faucher, "Droit au travail" in Coquelin, *Dictionnaire de l'économie politique,* vol. 1. pp. 605–19.

25. *Le Droit au travail à l'Assemblée Nationale,* pp. 373–74.

WE can see clearly in these passages that Bastiat has a strong view of individual rights, that they exist prior to the formation of the state, that the state exists only to protect these preexisting rights, and that if state force is used to do anything else then it steps outside of its just boundaries. It was precisely this expansion of illegitimate state power that Bastiat was battling during the revolution in 1848 and 1849.

## CLASSICAL LIBERAL VS SOCIALIST UTOPIAS

An important part of the classical liberal critique of socialism was its analysis of the utopian vision many socialists had of a future community where their ideals of common ownership of property, the equality of economic conditions, state-planned and state-funded education, and strictly regulated economic activity for the "common good" were practiced. Bastiat makes many references in his writings to the ideas and proposed communities of people like Fénelon, Saint-Simon, Fourier, and Owen.

In an article titled "Utopie," by Hippolyte Passy,[26] which summed up the thinking of the liberal political economists on this topic just two years after Bastiat's death, Passy stated that Bastiat had provided the key insight into the differences between the socialists' vision and the economists' vision of the future of society: the socialist vision was a "factice," or artificial one, with an order imposed by a ruling elite, party, or priesthood; while the liberal vision was a "natural," or spontaneous, one that flowed "harmoniously" from the voluntary actions of individuals in the marketplace. Given the harshness of the economists' rejection of socialist utopian schemes,[27] it is rather ironic that the classical liberals also had their utopian moments. One could mention Condorcet's vision of a fully liberal and enlightened future in his *Tenth Stage: The Future Progress of the Human Mind* (1795),[28] Charles Comte's and Charles Dunoyer's idea of the "industrial stage" of economic development

---

26. Passy, "Utopie," in Coquelin, *Dictionnaire de l'économie politique*, vol. 2, pp. 798–803.

27. See also Reybaud, *Études sur les réformateurs contemporains*.

28. See Condorcet's *Esquisse d'un tableau historique des progrès de l'esprit humain, suivie de Réflexions sur l'esclavage des nègres*. (This is a French edition to which Bastiat might have had access.)

(1820s), and Gustave de Molinari's vision of a fully privatized society where there was no role left for the state (1849).[29]

## THE CAUSE OF BASTIAT'S UNTIMELY DEATH

It is not entirely clear what killed Bastiat on Christmas Eve 1850 in Rome. Originally Bastiat had been sent to Pisa by his doctor because of the "better air" there compared with the damp of Paris. We know that Bastiat suffered from a throat condition of some kind and that he lost his ability to speak (a considerable handicap for an elected politician). It was not uncommon for people in his era to die ahead of their time because of serious ailments like tuberculosis (or consumption), but it is also possible that he suffered from throat cancer. According to the minutes of a meeting of the Société d'économie politique, we are given some pieces of information about his condition.[30]

Bastiat had been an enthusiastic member of the Société d'économie politique, and as the minutes of the society's meetings show, he attended regularly. His last attendance was the meeting of 10 September 1850, when he came to say farewell to his colleagues before leaving to spend the winter in Italy on his doctor's advice. He and his colleagues must have known that this was the last time they would see each other, as Bastiat had been ill for some time; he had been getting worse as he struggled to finish the second part of the *Economic Harmonies,* and indeed he passed away on 24 December later that year. The following comments in the minutes suggest that Bastiat's illness might have been cancer of the throat and not consumption:

> M. Frédéric Bastiat, representative of the people, came to this meeting in order to say farewell to the members of the society. Accepting the wise advice of his doctor Andral, M. Bastiat was going to spend the winter in Pisa in order to improve his health which had changed because of the Paris climate and his excessive work load: at this moment he was suffering from a persistent sore throat [*mal de gorge persistant*], which

---

29. Molinari first presented his ideas on the private provision of public goods in an article in *Le Journal des économistes* in February 1849, which sparked a very spirited debate in the Société d'économie politique. He was still arguing for a variation of this idea fifty years later. See Molinari, "De la production de la sécurité," *Les Soirées de la rue Saint-Lazare,* and *Esquisse de l'organisation politique et économique de la société future.*

30. "Séance du septembre 1850."

has caused him to completely lose his voice. We hope that the brilliant author of the *Sophisms* and the *Economic Harmonies,* enjoying the better Italian climate, will be able to soon finish the second volume of the latter work, which is already well advanced.

### SPEAKING TRUTH TO POWER: "THE MILLER OF SANS-SOUCI"

In his writings Bastiat makes many references to literary works in order to make his political and economic points. He often quoted the playwright Molière as well as the more contemporary poet and playwright François Andrieux (1759–1833). Andrieux had been a member of the liberal Girondin group during the Revolution before taking up a number of academic positions under Napoléon. Bastiat was particularly interested in Andrieux's tale "The Miller of Sans-Souci," which was read at a public meeting of the institute on 15 Germinal an 5 (4 April 1797).

The story is about a German who had the courage to speak the truth to power, namely, Frederick the Great. One might say that Bastiat is the Frenchman of his day who had the courage to speak some unpalatable truths to power, in his case the socialists and interventionists who had come to power during the revolution of 1848. Bastiat refers to this tale several times in his writings, and it is not hard to see why it became one of his favorite anecdotes.[31]

The liberal republican Andrieux depicts an entrepreneurial mill owner who is determined to keep his property when ordered to hand it over to the state in order to satisfy the whim of Frederick the Great, who wishes to expand the size of his palace. Not only does Frederick take the name of the mill, "Sans-Souci," as the name for his palace, but he also wants to tear down the mill and its large rotating blades in order to have a clear view of the countryside. The mill owner refuses, saying that he does not want to sell the mill and the property to anybody, that his father is buried there, that his son was born there, and that the mill is as valuable to him as Potsdam is to the Prussian emperor.

Frederick slyly replies that if he wanted to he could seize the miller's property, as he was the "master." The resolute and fearless miller says to Frederick's face, "You? Take my mill? Yes, (you might) if we didn't have judges in Berlin." Frederick smiles at the thought that his subjects really believed that

---

31. See "Property and Plunder," p. 159 in this volume.

justice existed under his reign and tells his courtiers to leave the miller alone. Andrieux concludes his tale with a reflection on the nature of the power of emperors, reminding his readers that the warrior Frederick had seized Silesia and put Europe to the torch: "These are the games princes play. They respect a miller but steal a province." [32]

This story is quite similar to one related by St. Augustine in Book 4 of *The City of God*, where a pirate who had been seized and brought before Alexander the Great asks Alexander what is the real difference between a pirate and an emperor apart from the scale of their actions? The pirate asks the emperor, "What thou meanest by seizing the whole earth; but because I do it with a petty ship, I am called a robber, whilst thou who dost it with a great fleet art styled emperor." [33]

Bastiat despised the teaching of classical Latin authors to the youth of France because such authors were slave owners and warriors and thus, in Bastiat's mind, had the moral philosophy of plunderers and conquerors. However, Bastiat was never shy about quoting from more-contemporary authors like Andrieux, who had a more-relevant moral, political, or economic story to tell about individuals who courageously stood up to the state to protect their liberty and their property. Bastiat was one of those individuals who, in the extraordinary times in which he lived, did exactly this, until he lost both his voice and then his life.

*David M. Hart*

32. "The Miller and Sans-Souci" first appeared in *Contes et opuscules en vers et en prose* (1800) and was reprinted in *Œuvres de François-Guillaume-Jean-Stanislas Andrieux,* vol. 3, pp. 205–8.

33. Augustine, *City of God,* bk. 4, ch. 4, in *St. Augustin's City of God and Christian Doctrine.*

# Glossary of Persons

ALI, MEHEMET (1769–1849). Governor of Egypt who introduced reforms in Egypt in order to modernize the state along European lines. He nationalized the land, created a state monopoly in foreign trade and a network of war industries, and conscripted peasants to work in the cotton factories.

ANTONELLE, PIERRE ANTOINE, marquis d' (1747–1817). Journalist, politician, and president of the tribunal that judged and condemned Marie Antoinette.

AZARA, DON FELIX (1746–1811). Spanish explorer and geographer.

AZY, PAUL BENOÎT D' (1824–98). Deputy and metallurgical industrialist.

BABEUF, FRANÇOIS (alias "Gracchus") (1760–97). Radical author, minor state official, and agitator during the French Revolution. Babeuf's ideas were an early form of communism (i.e., equality of ownership in all things, government distribution of goods and planning of the economy, equalization of salaries and wages, and a common state-sanctioned public education).

He adopted the alias "Gracchus" in honor of the brothers who attempted to introduce land-reform legislation in ancient Rome. Babeuf survived many intrigues and court cases before finally being convicted and executed for his role in the Conspiracy of the Equals during the Directory. This movement was part of an uprising against the government's attempt to end the system of large subsidies for the supply of food to the city of Paris. The subsidies enabled food to be sold at fixed, artificially low prices. (See also the entry for "Gracchi" in this glossary.)

BACON, SIR FRANCIS (1561–1626). English philosopher, statesman, and author. Bacon was trained as a lawyer but made a name for himself as one of the clearest exponents of the scientific method at the dawn of the scientific revolution in the sixteenth and early seventeenth centuries. He argued that knowledge about the natural world could be best acquired through direct observation, experiment, and the testing of a hypothesis. His best-known works include *The Advancement of Learning* (1605), *Novum Organum* (1620), and *New Atlantis* (1626).

BARBÈS, ARMAND (1809–70). Left-wing republican radical, follower of Babeuf, and friend of the socialist revolutionary Auguste Blanqui. Barbès was part of a plot in 1839 to overthrow Louis-Philippe during the July Monarchy. He was initially condemned to death, but the intervention of Victor Hugo changed the verdict to imprisonment. Barbès was released only as a result of the outbreak of the 1848 revolution. In May 1848, soon after his release, he was engaged in another plot against the government for which he was imprisoned. He was amnestied in 1854 and went into voluntary exile.

BASILE. Character in Beaumarchais' play (and later, Mozart's opera) *The Barber of Seville.*

BEAUMARCHAIS, PIERRE-AUGUSTIN, baron de (1732–99). French playwright. Beaumarchais was a watchmaker and a court musician before he turned to writing plays. He is best known for having dared to publish Voltaire and two antiaristocratic plays of his own — *The Barber of Seville, or the Useless Precaution* (1775), and *The Marriage of Figaro or the Follies of a Day* (1784). During the American Revolution he acted on behalf of the French crown to supply guns and other weapons to the American revolutionaries.

BECCARIA, MARQUIS DE (Cesar Bonesana) (1738–94). Italian jurist and philosopher raised in France. His treatise on crimes and punishments, *Dei delitti e delle pene* (1764), which stated the principle that the accused should be considered innocent until proven guilty, was translated into many languages.

BÉRANGER, PIERRE-JEAN DE (1780–1857). Béranger was a liberal poet and songwriter who rose to prominence during the Restoration period with his funny and clever criticisms of the monarchy and the church. His antics got him into trouble with the censors, who imprisoned him for brief periods in the 1820s. His material was much in demand in the singing societies, or "goguettes," which sprang up during the Restoration and the July Monarchy as a way of circumventing the censorship laws and the bans on political parties.

After the appearance of his second volume of songs, in 1821, Béranger was tried and convicted and sentenced to three months' imprisonment in Sainte-Pélagie, where he wrote the "La Liberté" (Liberty) in January 1822. Another bout of imprisonment (this time nine months in La Force) followed in 1828, when his fourth volume was published. Many of the figures who came to power after the July revolution of 1830 were friends or acquaintances of Béranger's, and it was assumed he would be granted a sinecure in recognition of his critiques of the old monarchy. However, he refused all government appointments in a stinging poem that he wrote in late 1830 called "Le Refus" (The Refusal). In April 1848, at the age of sixty-eight, Béranger was overwhelmingly elected to the Constituent Assembly, in which he sat for a brief period before resigning.

Béranger mixed in liberal circles in the 1840s in Paris, when he joined Bastiat's Free Trade Society and the Society of Political Economy. He was invited to attend the welcome dinner held by the latter to honor Bastiat's arrival in Paris in May 1845 but was unable to attend.

BÉRARD, AUGUSTE (1783–1859). Politician who started his political career in 1827. Liberal deputy during the restoration and July Monarchy. He was a constitutional monarchist who played an important role in the 1830 July revolution which brought Louis Philippe to power.

BILLAUD-VARENNES, JEAN (1756–1839). Member of the Convention and of the Committee of Public Safety, he was at first a supporter of Robespierre, then an opponent who contributed to his fall.

BILLAULT, ADOLPHE (1805–63). Deputy, lawyer, and mayor of Nantes. Billault also served in other capacities, such as undersecretary of state for agriculture and commerce under Thiers in 1840. In 1848 he was elected to the Constituent Assembly but was not reelected in 1849. He became a strong supporter of Louis-Napoléon's bid to become emperor and served as his minister of the interior. In his political and economic views he was a follower of Saint-Simon.

BLANC, LOUIS (1811–82). Journalist and historian who was active in the socialist movement. Blanc founded the journal *La Revue du progrès* and published therein articles that later became the influential pamphlet *L'Organisation du travail* (1839). During the 1848 revolution he became a member of the temporary government, promoted the National Workshops, and debated Adolphe Thiers on the merits of the right to work in *Le Socialisme; droit au travail, réponse à M. Thiers* (1848).

In 1847 Blanc began work on a multivolume history of the French Revolution, *Histoire de la Révolution française,* two volumes of which had appeared when the February revolution of 1848 broke out. A second edition of fifteen volumes appeared in 1878.

BLANQUI, JÉRÔME ADOLPHE (1798–1854). Liberal economist and brother of
the revolutionary socialist Auguste Blanqui. Jérôme Blanqui became director
of the prestigious École supérieure de commerce de Paris and succeeded Jean-
Baptiste Say to the chair of political economy at the Conservatoire national
des arts et métiers. He was elected deputy representing the Gironde from 1846
to 1848. Among his many works on political economy and sociology are the
*Encyclopédie du commerçant* (1839–41), *Précis élémentaire d'économie politique*
(1842), and *Les Classes ouvrières en France* (1848).

BONAPARTE, NAPOLÉON (1769–1821). French general, first consul of France
(1799–1804), emperor of the French (1804–15). Although Napoléon's
conquests of Europe were ultimately unsuccessful (Spain 1808; Russia
1812; Waterloo, Belgium, 1815), he dramatically altered the face of Europe
economically, politically, and legally (the Civil Code of 1804).

   Many European countries suffered huge economic losses from
Napoléon's occupation and the looting of museums and churches.
Napoléon introduced a new form of economic warfare, the "continental
system" (1807), which was designed to cripple Britain by denying its goods
access to the European market. It was partly in response to these and other
measures that Jean-Baptiste Say wrote his *Traité d'économie politique* (1803).
Politically, Napoléon introduced harsh censorship in order to stifle his
liberal critics and weakened parliamentary institutions in order to rule
in his own right. Benjamin Constant and Madame de Staël were two of
his sharpest critics. See in particular the former's *Principes de politiques
applicables à tous les gouvernements* (1815). Constant also wrote a devastating
critique of Napoléon's militarism in *De l'esprit de conquête et de l'usurpation,
dans leurs rapports à la civilisation européen* (1813).

BOSSUET, JACQUES BÉNIGNE (1627–1704). Bishop of Meaux, historian,
and tutor to the dauphin (son of Louis XIV). Bossuet was renowned
for his oratory and classical writing style, which was used as a model for
generations of French schoolchildren. In politics he was an intransigent
Gallican Catholic, an opponent of Protestantism, and a supporter of the
idea of the divine right of kings.

BOUGAINVILLE, LOUIS ANTOINE DE (1729–1814). French mathematician,
navigator, and explorer. He directed an expedition around the world in
1766, related in his 1771 book *Voyage autour du monde*. He took part in the
American War of Independence under Admiral de Grasse.

BOURBON, LOUIS JOSEPH DE (1736–1818). Prince de Condé from 1740 to
his death. He fled France after the fall of the Bastille in 1789 and formed
an army of counterrevolutionary émigrés in the German city of Koblenz

between 1791 and 1801, fighting first with the Austrians and then with the English. After the restoration of the Bourbon monarchy in 1815 he returned to Paris, where he served in the royal household of Louis XVIII.

BOYER-FONFRÈDE, HENRI (1788–1841). Liberal publicist, economic journalist, and supporter of the July Monarchy. He founded *L'Indicateur* and wrote *Questions d'économie politique* (1846).

BRISSOT DE WARVILLE, JACQUES PIERRE (1754–93). Member of the Girondin faction in the French Revolution and one of many Girondins who were executed during the Terror. (See also the entry for "Girondins" in the Glossary of Subjects and Terms.) Brissot studied law and became a writer and a journalist. He was active in a number of liberal reformist groups, such as the abolitionist organization the Société des amis des noirs (which he founded). During the Revolution he was elected to the Legislative Assembly and then the National Convention. He opposed the execution of the king.

BRUTUS, LUCIUS JUNIUS (ca. 500 B.C.). Ancestor of Marcus Junius Brutus, who assassinated Julius Caesar. According to legend, Lucius led a revolt against the last king of Rome, Tarquinius, thus founding the republic of Rome. He was appointed one of the first consuls of Rome.

BRUTUS, MARCUS JUNIUS (ca. 85–42 B.C.). Roman senator who had been brought up on Stoic philosophy by his uncle, Cato the Younger. Brutus participated in the assassination of Julius Caesar and because of this was regarded by many in the eighteenth and nineteenth centuries as the model of the tyrannicide.

BUCHANAN, DAVID (1779–1848). Journalist and economist. Buchanan edited and annotated an 1814 edition of Adam Smith's *Inquiry into the Nature and Causes of the Wealth of Nations.* Buchanan's notes on Smith were included in the French translation of Smith's *Wealth of Nations* published by Guillaumin in 1843.

BURKE, EDMUND (1729–97). English political philosopher whom many consider to have laid the foundations of modern conservative political thought. Although he supported the American colonies in the revolution against the British crown, he strongly opposed the French Revolution, the rise of unbridled democracy, and the growing corruption of government. Burke was a member of Parliament from 1765 to 1794 and served under Rockingham. His major works include *The Sublime and the Beautiful* (1757), *Reflections on the Revolution in France* (1790), and *Thoughts and Details on Scarcity* (1795).

CABET, ÉTIENNE (1788–1856). Lawyer and utopian socialist who coined the word "communism." Between 1831 and 1834 he was a deputy in the Chamber, until he was forced into exile in Britain, where he came into contact with Robert Owen.

Cabet advocated a society in which the elected representatives controlled all property that was owned in common by the community. He promoted his views in a journal called *Le Populaire* and in a book about a fictitious communist community called Icarie, *Voyage et aventures de lord William Carisdall en Icarie* (1840). In 1848 Cabet left France in order to create such a community in Texas and then at Nauvoo, Illinois, but these efforts ended in failure. The naming of his utopian community after the figure from Greek mythology Icarus, who failed in his attempt to flee the island of Crete by flying with wax wings too close to the sun, was perhaps unfortunate.

CARLIER, PIERRE. Head of the Paris police in 1830 and 1848. Named prefect of police in 1849.

CARRIER, JEAN-BAPTISTE (1756–94). French revolutionary. One of the most bloodthirsty participants in the Terror, he was guillotined in December 1794.

CARTERET, JOHN, second earl of Granville (1690–1763). British ambassador to Sweden (1719), secretary of state (1721–24 and 1742–44), and lord president of the Privy Council (1751–63). Granville's family owned one-eighth of the province of Carolina in America, which they lost during the American Revolution.

CATILINA, LUCIUS (109–62 B.C.). Roman patrician. His conspiracy against the Senate was denounced by Cicero.

CAVAIGNAC, EUGÈNE (1802–57). General, deputy, minister of war, head of the executive. He crushed the workers' uprising of June 1848. He was a candidate in the presidential election of 10 December but obtained only 1,448,000 votes against 5,434,000 for Louis-Napoléon.

CHARENCEY, CHARLES DE (1773–1838). An army officer who became a captain in the Royal Guard. He was also an elected deputy, 1822–30, and a member of the State Council, 1828–38.

CHATEAUBRIAND, FRANÇOIS RENÉ, vicomte de (1768–1848). Novelist, philosopher, and supporter of Charles X. He was minister of foreign affairs from 28 December 1822 to 6 June 1824. A defender of freedom of the press and Greek independence, he refused to take the oath to King Louis-Philippe after 1830. He spent his retirement writing his *Mémoires d'outre-tombe* (1849–50).

CHEVALIER, MICHEL (1806–87). Liberal economist, alumnus of the École polytechnique, and minister of Napoléon III. Initially a Saint-Simonist, Chevalier was imprisoned for two years (1832–33). After a trip to the United States, he published *Lettres sur l'Amérique du Nord* (1836), *Histoire et description des voies de communications aux États-Unis et des travaux d'art qui en dependent* (1840–41), and *Cours d'économie politique* (1845–55). He was appointed to the chair of political economy at the Collège de France in 1840 and became a senator in 1860. He was an admirer of Bastiat and Cobden and played a decisive role in the free-trade treaty of 1860 between France and England (Chevalier was the signatory for France, while Cobden was the signatory for England).

COBDEN, RICHARD (1804–65). Founder of the Anti–Corn Law League. Born in Sussex to a poor farmer's family, Cobden was trained by an uncle to become a clerk in his warehouse. At twenty-one, he became a traveling salesman and was so successful that he was able to acquire his own business, a factory making printed cloth. Thanks to his vision of the market and his sense of organization, his company became very prosperous. Nevertheless, at the age of thirty, he left the management of the company to his brother in order to travel. He wrote some remarkable articles in which he defended two great causes: pacifism, in the form of nonintervention in foreign affairs, and free exchange.

From 1839, he devoted himself exclusively to the Anti–Corn Law League and was elected as member of Parliament for Stockport in 1841. Toward the end of the 1850s, he was asked by the government to negotiate a free-trade treaty with France. His French counterpart was Michel Chevalier, a minister of Napoléon III and a friend and admirer of Bastiat. The treaty (the Cobden–Chevalier Treaty) was signed by Cobden and Chevalier in 1860.

COMTE, CHARLES (1782–1837). Lawyer, liberal critic of Napoléon and then of the restored monarchy, son-in-law of Jean-Baptiste Say. One of the leading liberal theorists before the 1848 revolution, he founded, with Charles Dunoyer, the journal *Le Censeur* in 1814 and *Le Censeur européen* in 1817 and was prosecuted many times for challenging the press censorship laws and criticizing the government. He encountered the ideas of Say in 1817 and discussed them at length in *Le Censeur européen*. After having spent some time in prison he escaped to Switzerland, where he was offered the Chair of Natural Law at the University of Lausanne before he was obliged to move to England. In 1826 he published the first part of his magnum opus, the four-volume *Traité de législation,* which very much influenced the thought of Bastiat, and in 1834 he published the second part, *Traité de la propriété.* Comte was secretary of the Académie des sciences morales et politiques and was elected a deputy representing La Sarthe after the 1830 revolution.

CONDÉ, PRINCE DE. (See the entry for "Bourbon, Louis Joseph de," in this glossary.)

CONDILLAC, ÉTIENNE BONNOT, abbé de (1714–80). Priest, philosopher, economist, and member of the Académie française. Condillac was an advocate of the ideas of John Locke and a friend of the encyclopedist Denis Diderot. In his *Traité des sensations* (1754), Condillac claims that all attributes of the mind, such as judgment, reason, and even will, derive from sensations. His book *Le Commerce et le gouvernement, considérés relativement l'un à l'autre* (1776) appeared in the same year as Adam Smith's *Wealth of Nations.*

CONSIDÉRANT, VICTOR PROSPER (1808–93). Follower of the socialist Fourier and advocate of the "right to work," a movement to which Bastiat was greatly opposed. Considérant was author of *Principes du socialisme: Manifeste de la démocratie au XIXe siècle* (1847) and *Théorie du droit de propriété et du droit au travail* (1845).

COQUELIN, CHARLES (1802–52). One of the leading figures in the political economy movement (*Les Économistes*) in Paris before his untimely death. Coquelin was selected by the publisher Guillaumin to edit the prestigious and voluminous *Dictionnaire de l'économie politique* (1852) because of his erudition and near-photographic memory. He also wrote dozens of articles for the *Dictionnaire.* Coquelin was very active in the free-trade movement, becoming secretary of the Association pour la liberté des échanges, writing articles for Bastiat's journal *Le Libre-échange,* and later taking over the editor's role when Bastiat had to resign because of ill health. Coquelin also wrote dozens of articles and book reviews for *Le Journal des économistes.* During the Revolution of 1848 Coquelin was active in forming a debating club, Le Club de la liberté du travail (The Club for Free Labor), which took on the socialists before the club was violently broken up by opponents. Coquelin, along with Bastiat, Fonteyraud, Garnier, and Molinari, started a small revolutionary magazine, *Jacques Bonhomme,* which was written to appeal to ordinary people. Unfortunately it lasted only a few weeks in June before it, too, was forced to close. Coquelin wrote about transport, the linen industry, the law governing corporations, money, credit, and banking (especially free banking, of which he was probably the first serious advocate).

CORNEILLE, PIERRE (1606–84). Playwright who, along with Molière and Racine, helped define French classical tragedy in the seventeenth century. In some of his tragedies, such as *Horace* (1640), he exalted the virtues of idealized Roman heroes.

CORNELIA AFRICANA (190–100 B.C.). Daughter of Scipio Africanus and mother of Tiberius Sempronius Gracchus and Gaius Sempronius Gracchus.

CORNIER, PAUL-LOUIS (1772–1825). Author of pamphlets in which he harassed the government of Louis XVIII, who ruled 1814–24.

CRASSUS, MARCUS LICINIUS (115–53 B.C.). Wealthy Roman consul and member of the first triumvirate with Pompey and Caesar.

CRÉMIEUX, ADOLPHE (1796–1880). Lawyer active in freemason and Jewish circles. He was appointed minister of justice in the new republican government, which formed after the revolution of 1848. Crémieux was first elected deputy in 1841 and served until his resignation in 1850 because of his opposition to Louis-Napoléon. He did not return to politics until the 1870 revolution, when he again served as minister of justice.

CURIACE. Character in Corneille's play *Horace*.

DECIUS, GAIUS MESSIUS QUINTUS (201–51). Emperor of Rome. Decius was notorious for attempting to increase the power of the Roman state by strengthening the military and, most significantly, for persecuting Christians by forcing them to sacrifice to Roman deities.

DESTUTT DE TRACY, ANTOINE (1754–1836). One of the leading intellectuals of the 1790s and early 1800s and a member of the ideologues (a philosophical movement not unlike the objectivists, who professed that the origin of ideas was material, not spiritual). In his writings on Montesquieu, Tracy defended the institutions of the American republic, and in his writings on political economy he defended laissez-faire. During the French Revolution he joined the third estate and renounced his aristocratic title. During the Terror he was arrested and nearly executed. Tracy continued agitating for liberal reforms as a senator during Napoléon's regime. One of his most influential works was the four-volume *Éléments d'idéologie* (first published in 1801–15) (Tracy coined the term *ideology*).

Volume four of *Éléments d'idéologie,* titled *Traité de la volunté,* was translated by Thomas Jefferson and appeared in English under the title *Treatise of Political Economy* in 1817. It was then republished in France in 1823 under the same title, *Traité d'économie politique.* Tracy also wrote *Commentaire sur l'ésprit des lois* (1819), which Thomas Jefferson translated and brought to the United States.

DIODORUS (Diodorus Siculus) (first century B.C.). Greek historian who wrote a universal history of the Greeks from the early tribes of Hellas to Alexander the Great and the rise of Julius Caesar.

DUNOYER, BARTHÉLÉMY-PIERRE-JOSEPH-CHARLES (1786–1862). Dunoyer was a journalist; an academic (a professor of political economy); a politician; the author of numerous works on politics, political economy, and history; a founding member of the Société d'économie politique (1842); and a key figure in the French classical liberal movement of the first half of the nineteenth century, along with Jean-Baptiste Say, Benjamin Constant, Charles Comte, Augustin Thierry, and Alexis de Tocqueville. He collaborated with Comte on the journals *Le Censeur* and *Le Censeur européen* during the end of the Napoleonic empire and the restoration of the Bourbon monarchy. Dunoyer (and Comte) combined the political liberalism of Constant (constitutional limits on the power of the state, representative government); the economic liberalism of Say (laissez-faire, free trade); and the sociological approach to history of Thierry, Constant, and Say (class analysis and a theory of historical evolution of society through stages culminating in the laissez-faire market society of "industry"). His major works include *L'Industrie et la morale considérées dans leurs rapports avec la liberté* (1825), *Nouveau traité d'économie sociale* (1830), and his three-volume magnum opus *De la liberté du travail* (1845). After the revolution of 1830 Dunoyer was appointed a member of the Académie des sciences morales et politiques, worked as a government official (he was prefect of L'Allier and La Somme), and eventually became a member of the Council of State in 1837. He resigned his government posts in protest against the coup d'état of Louis-Napoléon in 1851. He died while writing a critique of the authoritarian Second Empire; the work was completed and published by his son Anatole in 1864.

DUPIN, CHARLES (1784–1873). Liberal deputy. Dupin was also an alumnus of the École polytechnique, a naval engineer, and a professor of mechanics at the Conservatoire national des arts et métiers, where he taught courses for working people. He is one of the founders of mathematical economics and the statistical office (Bureau de France).

ENFANTIN, BARTHÉLEMY PROSPER (1796–1864). Wine merchant, banker, and manager of the Paris–Lyon railroad. In the early 1840s he was appointed to the Scientific Commission of Algeria, which looked into matters concerning the French colonization of that country. His earliest political activity was to join the nationalist and liberal secret society, the Carbonari (the "charcoal burners"), which included La Fayette and Lord Byron among its members. Enfantin came into contact with the ideas of Saint-Simon and, with Olinde Rodrigues and Bazard, founded the utopian socialist school of the Saint-Simonians, which advocated a form of socialism in which industrial society would be managed by an elite of scientists and engineers. By the time of the July revolution their "doctrine" had become a veritable "religion," with Enfantin as one of its "high priests." (See also the entry for "Saint-Simon, Claude Henri de Rouvroy, comte de," in this glossary.)

ERSKINE, THOMAS, first baron Erskine (1750–1823). Lawyer and Whig member of Parliament who served as lord chancellor of Great Britain 1806–7. He made a name for himself in the 1780s and 1790s by defending radical authors such as Thomas Paine against charges of libel.

ESTRADA, ANTONIO FLOREZ (1769–1853). Spanish jurist, economist, and liberal constitutionalist politician. His best-known work is a *Tratado de economica politica* (1828). Upon Bastiat's death in 1850 Estrada was elected a corresponding member of the Institute to fill Bastiat's vacancy.

FALLOUX DU COUDRAY, FRÉDÉRIC ALFRED PIERRE, VICOMTE DE (1811–86). Deputy, minister of education (20 December 1848 to 31 October 1849), and author of a law on freedom of education.

FAUCHER, LÉON (1803–54). Journalist, writer, deputy for the Marne, and twice appointed minister of the interior. Faucher became an active journalist during the July Monarchy, writing for *Le Constitutionnel* and *Le Courrier français*. He was one of the editors of *La Revue des deux mondes* and *Le Journal des économistes*. Faucher was appointed to the Académie des sciences morales et politiques in 1849 and was active in the Association pour la liberté des échanges. He wrote on prison reform, gold and silver currency, socialism, and taxation. One of his better-known works is *Études sur l'Angleterre* (1856).

FÉNELON (François de Salignac de la Motte-Fénelon) (1651–1715). Archbishop of Cambrai and tutor to the young duke of Burgundy, the grandson of Louis XIV. After the revocation of the Edict of Nantes (which had granted toleration for Protestants in France), Fénelon was one of several high-ranking clergy sent to convert recalcitrant Protestants to Catholicism.

He wrote a collection called *Dialogue des morts et fables* (1700), and *Les Aventures de Télémaque* (1699), which was a thinly veiled satire of the reign of Louis XIV and a critique of the notion of the divine right of kings.

FIGARO. Character in Beaumarchais' play *The Barber of Seville* and later in his play *The Marriage of Figaro* (both later became operas by Rossini and Mozart, respectively).

FONTENAY, ROGER-ANNE-PAUL-GABRIEL DE (1809–91). Member of the Société d'économie politique and an ally of Bastiat in their debates in the Société on the nature of rent. Fontenay worked with Prosper Paillottet in editing the *Œuvres complètes* of Bastiat and was a regular contributor to *Le Journal des économistes* right up to his death. In a work published soon after Bastiat's death in 1850, *Du revenu foncier* (1854), Fontenay describes himself and Bastiat as forming a distinct "French school of political economy," tracing its roots back to Jean-Baptiste Say and including Antoine Destutt de Tracy, Charles Comte, and especially Charles Dunoyer, in contrast with the "English school" of Adam Smith, Thomas Malthus, and David Ricardo. The main difference between the two schools was on the issue of rent from land: Bastiat and Fontenay denied that there was any special "gift of nature" that made up the rents from land, instead arguing that all returns on investments (whether capital, interest, or rent) were the result of services provided by producers to consumers.

FONTEYRAUD, HENRI ALCIDE (1822–49). Fonteyraud was born in Mauritius and became professor of history, geography, and political economy at the École supérieure de commerce de Paris. He was a member of the Société d'économie politique and one of the founders of the Association pour la liberté des échanges. Because of his knowledge of English he went to England in 1845 to study at first hand the progress of the Anti–Corn Law League. During the revolution of 1848, he campaigned against socialist ideas with his activity in the Club de la liberté du travail and, along with Bastiat, Coquelin, and Molinari, by writing and handing out in the streets of Paris copies of the broadside pamphlet *Jacques Bonhomme*. Sadly, he died very young during the cholera epidemic of 1849. He wrote articles in *La Revue britannique* and *Le Journal des économistes,* and he edited and annotated the works of Ricardo in the multivolume *Collection des principaux économistes*. His collected works were published posthumously as *Mélanges d'économie politique,* edited by J. Garnier (1853).

FOULD, ACHILLE (1800–1867). Banker and deputy who represented the *départements* of Les Hautes-Pyrénées in 1842 and La Seine in 1849. He was close to Louis-Napoléon, lending him money before he became emperor, and then serving as minister of finance, first during the Second Republic and then under the Second Empire (1849–67). Fould was an important part of the imperial household, serving as an adviser to the emperor, especially on economic matters. He was an ardent free trader but was close to the Saint–Simonians on matters of banking. (For the Saint-Simonians, see the entry for "Saint-Simon, Claude Henri de Rouvroy, comte de," in this glossary.)

FOURIER, FRANÇOIS-MARIE CHARLES (1772–1837). Socialist and founder of the phalansterian school (Fourierism). Fourierism consisted of a utopian, communistic system for the reorganization of society. The population was to be grouped in "phalansteries" of about eighteen hundred persons, who would live together as one family and hold property in common. Fourier's main works include *Le Nouveau monde industriel et sociétaire* (1829) and *La Fausse industrie morcelée répugnante et mensongère et l'antidote, l'industrie naturelle, combinée, attrayante, véridique donnant quadruple produit* (1835–36). Many of Fourier's ideas appeared in his journal *Phalanstère, ou la réforme industrielle*, which ran from 1832 to 1834.

FOX, CHARLES JAMES (1749–1806). Leading Whig political leader in the last decades of the eighteenth century in England. He supported parliamentary reform, civil and religious liberty, the American and French revolutions, and the abolition of slavery. He had a very public split with Edmund Burke over Britain's war against the French Republic, with Fox advocating a negotiated peace and settlement. Fox expressed his strong criticism at the loss of civil liberties in Britain as a result of the war against the French Republic, for example, the suspension of habeas corpus in 1794. In one of his last major speeches in the House of Commons shortly before his death he spoke in support of the bill to abolish the slave trade.

FOX, HENRY, LORD HOLLAND (1705–74). Whig member of Parliament, Secretary of War (1746–55), and father of Charles James Fox.

FRAYSSINOUS, DENIS-ANTOINE-LUC, comte de (1765–1841). Strong defender of the Catholic Church in France until he was forced into retirement by Napoléon's arrest of the pope and his conquest of Rome in 1809. He returned to Paris with the restoration of the Bourbon monarchy after 1815, serving as court preacher to King Louis XVIII. During the restoration he was made a bishop, elected to the Académie française, and created a peer of France. With the coming to power of King Charles X in 1824, Frayssinous became minister of education and religious worship (1824–28). After the July revolution of 1830 he retired to Rome. He was noted for his work *Les vrais principes de l'église gallicane sur le gouvernement ecclésiastique* (1818), written in support of the French state's concordat with the pope (1817).

FULCHIRON, JEAN-CLAUDE (1774–1859). Poet and dramatist before
becoming a deputy representing the Rhône. He was first elected to office
in 1831 during the July Monarchy and served in the Chamber of Deputies
until he was made a peer in 1845. His best-known work is his three-volume
set of books about his travels in Italy, *Voyages dans l'Italie méridionale*
(1840–42).

GARNIER, JOSEPH (1813–81). Professor, journalist, politician, and activist
for free trade and peace. He arrived in Paris in 1830 and came under the
influence of Adolphe Blanqui, who introduced him to economics and who
eventually became his father-in-law.

   Garnier was a pupil, professor, and then director of the École supérieure
de commerce de Paris, before being appointed the first professor of political
economy at the École des ponts et chaussées in 1846. Garnier played a
central role in the burgeoning free-market school of thought in the 1840s
in Paris. He was one of the founders of the Association pour la liberté des
échanges and the chief editor of its journal, *Libre-échange;* he was active in
the Congrès de la paix; he was one of the founders, along with Guillaumin,
of *Le Journal des économistes,* of which he became chief editor in 1846;
he was one of the founders of the Société d'économie politique and was
its perpetual secretary; and he was one of the founders of the 1848 liberal
broadsheet *Jacques Bonhomme.*

   Garnier was acknowledged for his considerable achievements by being
nominated to join the Académie des sciences morales et politiques in 1873
and to become a senator in 1876. He was the author of numerous books
and articles, among which are *Introduction à l'étude de l'économie politique*
(1843); *Richard Cobden, les ligueurs et la ligue* (1846); and *Congrès des amis
de la paix universelle réunis à Paris en 1849* (1850). He edited Malthus's
*Essai sur le principe de population* (1845); *Du principe de population* (1857);
and *Traité d'économie politique sociale ou industrielle* (1863).

GAUGUIER, JOSEPH (1793–1865). Soldier in Napoléon's army, an industrialist,
and deputy (1831–42). He unsuccessfully proposed parliamentary reform in
1832 and 1834.

GENOVESI, ANTONIO (1712–69). Italian priest, philosopher, and economist.
He was appointed to the first chair of political economy at the University
of Naples in 1754 and was a supporter of free trade. His main book in
economics is *Lezzioni di commercio e di economica civile* (1705).

GIRARDIN, SAINT-MARC (1801–73). Literary critic, professor of French
poetry at the Sorbonne, and deputy. He served as a councillor of state and
was minister of education in 1848.

GOUDCHAUX, MICHEL (1797–1862). Banker and opponent of the July Monarchy, during which time he was the chief financial writer for the opposition journal *Le National*. After the 1848 revolution he was elected deputy representing the *département* of La Seine in the National Assembly. He also served as minister of finance in General Cavaignac's government, where he fought with Thiers over tax policy in the finance committee. Goudchaux's political career came to an end in 1849, when he was not elected to the Legislative Assembly. During the Second Empire Goudchaux raised money to help republicans who had been proscribed by Napoléon III.

GRACCHI. TIBERIUS GRACCHUS (162–133 B.C.) and GAIUS GRACCHUS (154–121 B.C.). Brothers and Roman patricians who both held the office of tribune at different times. They attempted to introduce significant land reform in ancient Rome. In response to an economic crisis they proposed to limit the size of the land holdings of aristocratic owners and distribute parcels of land to the poor. They failed to achieve this and were crushed by force. They have been seen by socialists as precursors of the modern socialist movement. Babeuf even adopted the pseudonym "Gracchus" in homage to them.

GUILLAUMIN, GILBERT-URBAIN (1801–64). French editor and founder of his own publishing firm in 1835. (For a fuller account of Guillaumin's life, see "Bastiat's Political Writings: Anecdotes and Reflections," pp. 404–5.)

GUIZOT, FRANÇOIS (1787–1874). Academic and politician. Guizot served as minister of the interior, then minister of education (1832–37), ambassador to England in 1840, foreign minister, and prime minister, becoming in practice the leader of the government from 1840 to 1848. He was born to a Protestant family in Nîmes, and his father was guillotined during the Terror. As a law student in Paris the young Guizot was a vocal opponent of the Napoleonic empire. After the restoration of the monarchy, Guizot was part of the Doctrinaires, a group of conservative and moderate liberals. He was professor of history at the Sorbonne from 1812 to 1830, publishing *Essai sur l'histoire de France* (1824), *Histoire de la Révolution d'Angleterre* (1826–27), *Histoire générale de la civilisation en Europe* (1828), and *Histoire de la civilisation en France* (1829–32).

He was elected deputy in 1829 and became very active in French politics after the 1830 revolution, supporting constitutional monarchy and a limited franchise. During his political life, he promoted peace abroad and liberal conservatism at home, but his regime, weakened by corruption and economic difficulties, collapsed with the monarchy in 1848. He retired to Normandy to spend the rest of his days writing history and his memoirs such as *Histoire parlementaire de France* (1863–64) and *Histoire des origines du gouvernement représentif en Europe* (1851).

HARRINGTON, JAMES (1611–77). Leading English republican political theorist of the seventeenth century. His views on voting by ballot and the rotation of office were considered radical in his day. Harrington's work was influential in the eighteenth century as Jefferson and the founding fathers discovered in his writings on an independent gentry and the right to bear arms a useful antidote to the claims of the British monarchy. His most famous work is *The Commonwealth of Oceana* (1656).

HORACE (Quintus Horatius Flaccus) (65–8 B.C.). One of the leading Latin poets during the rule of Augustus. He was the son of a freed slave and served in the army of Brutus (one of the assassins of Caesar), but was reduced to poverty when his family farm was confiscated. His poetry, especially his odes, had enormous influence in the Renaissance, on Shakespeare, and in the eighteenth century. A well-known line from one of his odes is "dulce et decorum est pro patria mori" (how sweet and fitting it is to die for one's country).

HUGO, VICTOR (1802–89). Poet, novelist, dramatist, and politician who wrote some of the most important literary works of nineteenth-century France. His works include the novels *Les Misérables* (1862) and *The Hunchback of Notre Dame* (1831). Hugo was a conservative Catholic in his youth but had become more liberal minded by the time he was elected deputy (1848–50). During the 1848 revolution, he became a republican and a free thinker, which contributed to his forced exile after the coup d'état of Louis-Napoléon Bonaparte (2 December 1851). Hugo went into exile in Jersey and then Guernsey, where he remained until the 1870 revolution. He could have returned to France after an amnesty in 1859 but chose to remain in Guernsey, realizing that if he returned he would have to temper his criticisms of the emperor. Soon after his return to Paris he was elected to the National Assembly and then the Senate.

HUME, JOSEPH (1777–1855). Member of Parliament elected in 1812. Leader of the liberal reformists, he played a major role in the repeal of laws forbidding machinery export and emigration and in the emancipation of Catholics.

HUS, JAN (1370–1415). Czech Catholic priest and dean of the Prague faculty of theology. A follower of Luther, he was an ardent supporter of church reform. He was burned as a heretic.

HUSKISSON, WILLIAM (1770–1830). British member of Parliament who served from 1796 to 1830. He rose to the post of secretary to the treasury 1804–9 and later president of the Board of Trade (1823–27). Huskisson introduced a number of liberal reforms, including the reformation of the Navigation Act, a reduction in duties on manufactured goods, and the repeal of some quarantine duties. As president of the Board of Trade he played an important role in persuading British merchants to support a policy of free trade.

LACAZE, JOSEPH BERNARD (1798–1874). Lawyer who studied and practiced in the United States before returning to France. He was elected deputy for the Hautes-Pyrénées (1848–51) where he voted with the right. He was a senator in the Second Empire.

LAFFITE, JACQUES (1767–1844). Banker and entrepreneur, born in Bayonne. He was elected deputy in 1816 and was prime minister from 1831 until March 1832. He was a friend of the Bastiat family.

LAMARTINE, ALPHONSE DE (1790–1869). Poet and statesman. As an immensely popular romantic poet, he used his talent to promote liberal ideas. He was a member of the provisional government and minister of foreign affairs in June 1848. After he lost the presidential elections of December 1848 against Louis-Napoléon, he retired from political life and went back to writing.

LAMENNAIS, FÉLICITÉ, ABBÉ DE (1782–1854). Priest, deputy, and journalist. Known for his four-volume *Essai sur l'indifférence en matière de religion* (1821–23), he was a strong critic of the Gallican Church and an ardent defender of the pope.

LA SAGRA, RAMON (1798–1871). La Sagra studied natural history and became the director of the Botanical Gardens in Cuba. He became interested in political economy in 1840 when he lectured at the Ateneo de Madrid. La Sagra was an advocate of the ideas of Proudhon, supporting his idea of a people's bank with a book called *Banque du peuple* (1849).

LEDRU-ROLLIN, ALEXANDRE (1790–1874). Lawyer, deputy (1841–49), owner of the newspaper *La Réforme,* minister of the interior of the provisional government of February 1848, and then member of the executive commission. He had to yield his powers to General Cavaignac in June 1848. In 1849 he organized a demonstration against the foreign policy of Louis-Napoléon, the new president of the Republic. He was exiled and came back to France only in 1870.

LE PELETIER DE SAINT-FARGEAU, LOUIS-MICHEL (1760–93). Deputy to the Constituent Assembly, of which he became the president in 1790. A nobleman sharing revolutionary ideas, he was assassinated for having voted for the death of Louis XVI.

LEROUX, PIERRE (1798–1871). Prominent member of the Saint-Simonian group of socialists and founder of *Le Globe,* a review of the Saint-Simonists. Like Bastiat, he was a journalist during the 1840s and was elected to the Constituent Assembly in 1848 and to the Legislative Assembly in 1849. The most developed exposition of his ideas can be found in *De l'humanité* (1840) and also in *De la ploutocratie, ou, Du gouvernement des riches* (1848).

LOUIS-PHILIPPE, DUC D'ORLÉANS (1773–1850). Last French king during the July Monarchy (1830–48), abdicating on 24 February 1848. He served in the French army before going into exile in 1793. His exile lasted until 1815, when he was able to return to France under the restoration of the monarchy (King Louis XVIII was his cousin). During his exile he visited Switzerland, Scandinavia, the United States, and Cuba before settling in England. When the July revolution overthrew King Charles X in 1830, Louis-Philippe was proclaimed the new "king of the French." Initially, he enjoyed considerable support from the middle class for his liberal policies, but he became increasingly conservative and was ousted in the February 1848 revolution.

LUSCINUS, GAIUS FABRICIUS. Elected consul 282 B.C.–278 B.C.

LYCURGUS OF SPARTA (8th century B.C.). Mythical Greek legislator to whom were attributed the severe laws of Sparta. These laws enshrined the virtues of martial order, simplicity of family and personal life, and shared communal living. His counterpart in Athens was Solon. (See the entry for "Solon" in this glossary.) In the eighteenth century it was common among social theorists to regard Athens and Sparta as polar opposites, with Athens representing commerce and the rule of law and Sparta representing war and authoritarianism.

MABLY, GABRIEL BONNOT, abbé de (1709–95). Elder brother of Condillac and an enormously popular writer on political, legal, and economic matters in his own right. He trained as a Jesuit and briefly entered religious orders. Mably was an admirer of Plato and Sparta, both, in his opinion, models for political and economic institutions. In economics, Mably was an advocate for ending private property and for the redistribution of property by the state in order to achieve equal ownership for all; thus he may be considered an early communist thinker. Mably was best known for his work *Entretiens de Phocion, sur le rapport de la morale avec la politique* (1763); and the *Observations sur le gouvernement et les lois des États-unis d'Amérique* (1784).

MARET, HUGUES-BERNARD, duc de Bassano (1763–1839). Served as an ambassador during the Revolution and was minister of foreign affairs under Napoléon.

McCULLOCH, JOHN RAMSAY (1789–1864). Leader of the Ricardian school following the death of Ricardo. He was a pioneer in the collection of economic statistics and was the first professor of political economy at the University of London in 1828. He wrote *The Principles of Political Economy: With a Sketch of the Rise and Progress of the Science.*

MELUN, ARMAND, vicomte de (1807–77). Politician, philanthropist, and Catholic social reformer. He was elected deputy in 1843 and took up the cause of improving the social condition of workers by founding the Société d'économie charitable and the journal *Les Annales de la charité* (1847). Although he was instrumental in establishing private charities for his cause, he also was an active proponent of state intervention, because only the state, in his view, "was in a position to reach all miseries."

MENTOR. Tutor of Telemachus.

MIMEREL DE ROUBAIX, PIERRE (1786–1872). Textile manufacturer and politician who was a vigorous advocate of protectionism. He was elected deputy in 1849; appointed by Napoléon III to the Advisory Council and to the General Council of Agriculture, Industry, and Trade; and named senator in 1852. He founded the protariff Association for the Defense of Domestic Industry, whose journal was *Le Moniteur industriel.* He also headed a businessmen's association called the Mimerel Committee, which was a focus for Bastiat's criticisms of protectionism. It was the Mimerel Committee that called for the firing of free-market professors of political economy and for the abolition of their chairs. The committee later moderated its demands and called for the equal teaching of protectionist and free-trade views.

MINOS. Son of Zeus and Europa and the king of Crete in Greek mythology. After his death he became a judge of the dead in Hades and is sometimes depicted serving this function in later literary works, such as those by Virgil and Dante.

MIRABEAU, GABRIEL HONORÉ RIQUETI, comte de (1749–91). Eldest son of the economist Victor Riqueti. He was a soldier as well as a diplomat, journalist, and author who spent time in prison or in exile. During the French Revolution he became a noted orator and was elected to the Estates General in 1789 representing Aix and Marseilles. In his political views he was an advocate of constitutional monarchy along the lines of Great Britain. He is noted for his *Essai sur le despotisme* (1776) and several works on banking and foreign exchange.

MOLÉ, LOUIS MATHIEU, comte de (1781–1855). Former prefect and minister of justice under Napoléon and under Louis XVIII. Rallying to Louis-Philippe, he was head of the government and minister of foreign affairs in 1836. Accused by some deputies of being little more than a spokesman for the king, he resigned in 1839 and led a moderate opposition against Guizot. A deputy in 1848 and 1849, he quit political life after the coup of 1851.

MOLINARI, GUSTAVE DE (1819–1912). Born in Belgium but spent most of his working life in Paris, where he became the leading representative of the laissez-faire school of classical liberalism in France in the second half of the nineteenth century. His liberalism was based on the theory of natural rights (especially the right to property and individual liberty), and he advocated complete laissez-faire in economic policy and an ultraminimal state in politics. In the 1840s he joined the Société d'économie politique and was active in the Association pour la liberté des échanges. During the 1848 revolution he vigorously opposed the rise of socialism and published shortly thereafter two rigorous defenses of individual liberty in which he pushed to its ultimate limits his opposition to all state intervention in the economy, including the state's monopoly of security. During the 1850s he contributed a number of significant articles on free trade, peace, colonization, and slavery to the *Dictionnaire de l'économie politique* (1852–53) before going into exile in his native Belgium to escape the authoritarian regime of Napoléon III. He became a professor of political economy at the Musée royale de l'industrie belge and published a significant treatise on political economy (*Cours d'économie politique,* 1855) and a number of articles opposing state education. In the 1860s Molinari returned to Paris to work on *Le Journal des débats,* becoming editor from 1871 to 1876. Toward the end of his long life, Molinari was appointed editor of the leading journal of political economy in France, *Le Journal des économistes* (1881–1909). Molinari's more important works include *Les Soirées de la rue Saint-Lazare* (1849), *L'Évolution économique du dix-neuvième siècle: Théorie du progrès* (1880), and *L'Évolution politique et la Révolution* (1884).

MONTAIGNE, MICHEL EYQUEM DE (1533–92). One of the best-known and most-admired writers of the Renaissance. His *Essays* (first published in 1580) were a thoughtful meditation on human nature in the form of personal anecdotes infused with deep philosophical reflections. Montaigne was brought up with Latin as his first language and went on to study law, serving in the Bordeaux parliament from 1557 to 1570 and then as mayor of Bordeaux from 1581 to 1585. He was a close friend of Étienne de la Boétie, who wrote *Discours de la servitude volontaire* (1576), in which he explores why the majority too often willingly capitulates to the demands of a tiny ruling minority. In the religious controversies of his day Montaigne was a moderate Catholic.

MONTALEMBERT, CHARLES FORBES, comte de (1810–70). French publicist and historian. Montalembert was born and educated in England before moving to France. In 1830 he joined forces with Lamennais to write for the journal *L'Avenir* and to promote liberal Catholicism, but he split with Lamennais after 1834; when the pope condemned liberal Catholicism, Montalembert chose to submit to the will of the pope on this issue. He supported a free, Catholic alternative to the state monopoly of education and was arrested and fined for his activities. During the 1848 revolution he was elected to the Constituent Assembly as a moderate republican. He is known for his work *Des devoirs des catholiques sur la question de la liberté de l'enseignement* (1843).

MONTESQUIEU, CHARLES LOUIS DE SECONDAT, baron de (1689–1755). One of the most influential legal theorists and political philosophers of the eighteenth century. He trained as a lawyer and practiced in Bordeaux before going to Paris, where he attended an important enlightened salon. His ideas about the separation of powers and checks on the power of the executive had a profound impact on the architects of the American constitution. His most influential works are *L'Esprit des lois* (1748), *Les Lettres persanes* (1721), and *Considérations sur les causes de la grandeur des Romains et de leur décadence* (1732).

MORE, SIR THOMAS (1478–1535). English lawyer, privy councillor, and speaker of the House of Parliament before he ran afoul of the Anglican Church by refusing to acknowledge Henry VIII as the sole head of the church. He was beheaded for refusing to compromise his Catholic beliefs. He is famous for his political work *Utopia* (1516), in which there was no private property, widespread use of slaves, and an internal passport required for travel. See also "Classical Liberal vs Socialist Utopias," in "Bastiat's Political Writings: Anecdotes and Reflections," pp. 412–13.

Morelly (ca. 1717–78). Novelist and political philosopher. In his *Code de la nature, ou le véritable esprit des lois, de tout temps négligé ou méconnu* (1755), he advocated a form of utopianism in which society was ruled by an enlightened despot, private property had been abolished, and marriage and police were no longer required in a state of absolute equality. He influenced the thinking of Babeuf, Saint-Simon, and Marx.

Morin, Étienne-François-Théodore (b. 1814). Textile manufacturer and the elected representative for the *département* of La Drôme in the Constituent Assembly in 1848 and then in the Legislative Assembly in 1849. He published many works on jurisprudence and political economy, being best known for his *Essai sur l'organisation du travail et l'avenir des classes laborieuses* (1845). Morin was a staunch defender of freedom of association for both manufacturers and the workers. He believed that such association would promote both their interests, provided that no one used any coercion or violence.

Mortimer-Ternaux, Louis (1808–72). Jurist and member of the Council of State, a French institution giving advice on draft bills and acting as a court of final appeal on administrative matters. He was a deputy from 1842 until Louis-Napoléon's coup d'état in 1857.

Nadaud, Martin (1815–98). Stonemason and follower of the socialist Étienne Cabet. He was elected deputy in 1849, during the 1848 revolution, but fled to Britain after Louis-Napoléon's coup d'état of 2 December 1851. Nadaud was again elected deputy as a moderate republican in 1876 during the Third Republic.

Necker, Jacques (1732–1804). Swiss-born banker and politician who served as the minister of finance under Louis XVI just before the French Revolution broke out. His private financial activities were intertwined with the French state when he served as a director of the monopolistic French East India Company and made loans to the French state. In 1775 he wrote a critique of Turgot's free-trade policies in *L'Essai sur la législation et le commerce des grains*. In 1776 he was appointed director general of French finances until his dismissal in 1781. He served again in this position from 1788 to 1790. As minister of finance he tried to reform the French taxation system by broadening its base and removing some of its worst inequalities. Needless to say, in this he largely failed. His daughter, Germaine Necker (de Staël), became a famous novelist and historian of the French Revolution.

North, Frederick, second earl of Guilford (1732–93). Member of Parliament, 1754 to 1790; chancellor of the exchequer, 1767 to 1782; and prime minister during most of the period of the American War of Independence.

NUMA POMPILIUS (ca. 715–672 B.C.). Legendary king of Rome. Inspired by the nymph Egeria, he organized Roman religious institutions.

ODIER, ANTOINE (1766–1853). Swiss-born banker and textile manufacturer who came to Paris to play a part in the French Revolution, siding with the liberal Girondin group. He was president of the Chamber of Commerce of Paris, deputy (1827–34), and eventually a peer of France (1837). Bastiat crossed swords with him because of his membership in the protectionist Association for the Defense of Domestic Industry.

OWEN, ROBERT (1771–1858). Successful manufacturer, philanthropist, and socialist theoretician. He made his fortune with a cotton mill in New Lanark in Manchester. The reforms he introduced in his factory became the model for creating "villages of cooperation," which culminated in the establishment of a model community, New Harmony, in Indiana, in 1824. Owen spent his own money in order to improve the fate of his workers and based his model community on the ideas of mutual cooperation, community of property, consumer cooperatives, and trade unions. His best-known works are *A New View of Society* (1813) and *Report to the County of Lanark of a Plan for Relieving Public Distress* (1821).

PAILLOTTET, PROSPER (1804–78). Editor of *Les Œuvres complètes de Frédéric Bastiat* and friend of Bastiat's. See also "Bastiat's Editor and Executor, Prosper Paillottet (1804–78)," in "Bastiat's Political Writings: Anecdotes and Reflections," pp. 405–7.

PARISIS, PIERRE LOUIS (1795–1865). Bishop of Langres and deputy. After 1850, he became a member of the Conseil Supérieur de l'Instruction.

PASCAL, BLAISE (1623–62). French mathematician and philosopher whose best-known work, *Pensées,* appeared only after his death.

PASSY, FRÉDÉRIC (1822–1912). Nephew of Hippolyte Passy, who was cofounder of the Société d' économie politique (1842) and wrote numerous articles in *Le Journal des économistes*. Frédéric was a supporter of free trade and the ideas of Richard Cobden and Bastiat. Passy was a cabinet minister and then professor of political economy at Montpellier. He wrote an introduction to one of the Guillaumin editions of the works of Bastiat. He was active in the French peace movement and helped found the Ligue internationale et permanente de la paix. For his efforts he received the first Nobel Peace Prize (1901, with Henri Dunant, one of the founders of the Red Cross). He wrote many books on economics and peace, including *Notice biographique sur Frédéric Bastiat* (1857) and *Pour la paix: notes et documents* (1909).

PEEL, SIR ROBERT (1788–1850). Served as Home Secretary under the Duke of Wellington (1822–27) and was prime minister twice (1834–35, 1841–46). He is best known for creating the Metropolitan Police Force in London, the Factory Act of 1844 which regulated the working hours of women and children in the factories, and the repeal of the Corn Laws in May 1846. The latter inspired Bastiat to lobby for similar economic reforms in France.

PELHAM-HOLLES, THOMAS, first duke of Newcastle (1693–1768). Secretary of state from 1724 to 1754 and prime minister from 1754 to 1756 and 1757 to 1762. His brother, Henry Pelham (1696–1754), was a member of Parliament and succeeded Walpole as chancellor of the exchequer in 1743.

PÉTETIN, ANSELME (1807–73). Moderate republican lawyer, journalist, and director of the Imperial (or Royal) Press 1850–60. He was appointed the Prefect of Haute-Savoiè in 1860.

PITT, WILLIAM (the Elder), first earl of Chatham (1708–78). Whig member of Parliament from 1735 to 1766, leader of the House of Commons from 1756 to 1761, prime minister from 1766 to 1768, and earl of Chatham from 1766 to 1778. He was a popular figure for his propriety in managing funds when he was paymaster of the armed forces and for prosecuting the war against Spain and France during the Seven Years' War. He successfully conducted a two-front war on the continent, seized several French colonies in Africa and the Carribean, and defeated the French in North America. Despite the French defeat, Britain was left with significant debt, which had repercussions later during the War of Independence in the American colonies.

PITT, WILLIAM (the Younger) (1759–1806). Son of William Pitt the Elder. He became a member of Parliament in 1781, chancellor of the exchequer in 1782, and prime minister from 1783 to 1801 and from 1804 to 1806. Pitt was a Tory and a strong opponent of the French Revolution.

PROUDHON, PIERRE JOSEPH (1809–65). Political theorist, considered to be the father of anarchism. Proudhon spent many years as a printer and published many pamphlets on social and economic issues, often running afoul of the censors. He was elected to the Constituent Assembly in 1848 representing La Seine. In 1848 he became editor in chief of a number of periodicals, such as *Le Peuple* and *La Voix du peuple,* which got him into trouble again with the censors and for which he spent three years in prison, between 1849 and 1852. He is best known for *Qu'est-ce que la propriété? Ou recherches sur le principe du droit et du gouvernement* (1841), *Système des contradictions économiques* (1846), and several articles published in *Le*

*Journal des économistes*. His controversy with Bastiat on the subject appears in the form of letters between Bastiat and Proudhon (*OC,* vol. 5, p. 94, "Gratuité du crédit").

Pulteney, William (1684–1764). A Whig member of Parliament who served as secretary of war 1714–17; was made a peer, the Earl of Bath, in 1742; and was a member of the "Patriot Whigs" who opposed Walpole.

Rabaut de Saint-Étienne, Jean-Paul (1743–93). Son and grandson of a minister. He actively defended the rights of non-Catholics. A member of the Girondins, he was guillotined in 1793.

Raynal, Guillaume-Thomas-François, abbé (1713–96). Enlightened historian who wrote on the Dutch Stadholderate and the English Parliament. His most famous work was the eight-volume *Histoire philosophique et politique, des établissements et du commerce des européens dans les deux Indes* (1770), which went through some thirty editions by 1789, was put on the Index in 1774, and was publicly burned. The book was found objectionable because of its treatment of religion and colonialism and its advocacy of the popular right to consent to taxation and to revolt, among other things. Its sometimes incendiary treatment of the slave trade became canonical in the debate over abolition of slavery, which it did much to spur.

Riancey, Henri Leon Camusat de (1816–70). Lawyer and journalist. He became a deputy in 1849. He defended Catholic and legitimist causes.

Ricardo, David (1772–1823). English political economist born in London of Dutch-Jewish parents. He joined his father's stockbroking business and made a considerable fortune on the London Stock Exchange. In 1799 he read Adam Smith's *Wealth of Nations* (1776) and developed an interest in economic theory. He met James Mill and the Philosophic Radicals in 1807, was elected to Parliament in 1819, and was active politically in trying to widen the franchise and to abolish the restrictive Corn Laws. He wrote a number of works, including *The High Price of Bullion* (1810), on the bullion controversy, and his treatise *On the Principles of Political Economy and Taxation* (1817).

Robespierre, Maximilien de (1758–94). Lawyer and one of the best-known figures of the French Revolution. Robespierre represented Arras in the Estates General before entering the National Convention in 1792. He was an active member of the Société des amis de la constitution (Society of Friends of the Constitution) (the Jacobin Club) and became leader of the Montagnard faction. He was a fierce opponent of the liberal Gironde faction, and in his position as leader of the Committee of Public Safety (1793) he had arrested and executed many members of this group during the Terror. Robespierre was also active in introducing a new civic religion, the Cult of Reason and the Supreme Being, to replace traditional religion. Eventually the Terror turned on its own supporters and Robespierre was himself executed in July 1794. In his political thinking, Robespierre was strongly influenced by the writings of Rousseau, and in 1793 he supported a new declaration of the rights of man that subordinated private property to the needs of "social utility."

ROLLIN, CHARLES (1661–1741). Professor of history and literature and eventually president (*recteur*) of the University of Paris. He was also the author of treatises on literature and a defender of classical studies.

ROSSI, PELLEGRINO (1787–1848). Italian-born professor of law and political economy, poet, and in his final days diplomat for the French government. Rossi lived in Geneva, Paris, and Rome. He moved to Switzerland after the defeat of Napoléon, where he met Germaine de Staël and the duc de Broglie. He founded with Sismondi and Etienne Dumont the *Annales de législation et de jurisprudence*. After the death of Jean-Baptiste Say, Rossi was appointed professor of political economy at the Collège de France in 1833, and in 1836 he became a member of the Académie des sciences morales et politiques. In 1847 he was appointed ambassador of France to the Vatican but was assassinated in 1848 in Rome. He wrote *Cours d'économie politique* (1840) and numerous articles in *Le Journal des économistes*.

ROUSSEAU, JEAN-JACQUES (1712–78). Swiss philosopher and novelist who was an important figure in the Enlightenment. In his novels and discourses he claimed that civilization had weakened the natural liberty of mankind and that a truly free society would be the expression of the "general will" of all members of that society. He influenced later thinkers on both ends of the political spectrum. He is best known for his book *Du contrat social* (The Social Contract)(1761); he was also the author of, among other works, the autobiographical *Les Confessions* (1783) and the novels *Julie, ou la nouvelle Héloïse* (1761) and *Émile, ou l'éducation* (1762).

RUMILLY, LOUIS GAUTHIER DE (1792–1884). Lawyer and deputy (1830–34 and 1837–40). He unsuccessfully presented a project for parliamentary reform in 1840.

RUSSELL, LORD JOHN (1792–1878). Member of Parliament, leader of the Whigs, and several times a minister. He served as prime minister from 1846 to 1852 and from 1865 to 1866.

SAINT-CRICQ, PIERRE LAURENT BARTHÉLEMY, comte de (1772–1854). Protectionist who was made director general of customs in 1815, president of the Trade Council, and then minister of trade and colonies in 1828.

SAINT-HILAIRE, JULES BARTHÉLEMY (1805–95). Businessman, journalist, deputy, and professor of ancient philosophy. Saint-Hilaire became interested in politics in the late 1820s in order to oppose the conservative reign of King Charles X (1824–30). He wrote articles for a number of newspapers and journals, such as *Le Globe, Le National,* and *Le Courrier français.* He was elected to the Constituent Assembly after the outbreak of the 1848 revolution and served as a deputy until he resigned soon after the coup d'état of Louis-Napoléon in 1851. He renounced politics and turned to ancient philosophy, becoming professor of Greek and Latin philosophy at the Collège de France, spending much of the rest of his life translating Aristotle.

SAINT-JUST, LOUIS ANTOINE DE (1767–94). Close friend and colleague of Robespierre. Saint-Just suffered the same fate as Robespierre, execution by guillotine in July 1794. He served in the National Guard and was elected to the Legislative Assembly (but denied his seat because of his young age), and then to the Convention, where he joined the Montagnard faction. Saint-Just became a member of the Committee of Public Safety in 1793 and was active in military affairs on the committee's behalf. He was much influenced by Rousseau and supported the creation of an austere and egalitarian republic.

SAINT-SIMON, CLAUDE HENRI DE ROUVROY, comte de (1760–1825). Writer and social reformer. Saint-Simon came from a distinguished aristocratic family and initially planned a career in the military. He served under George Washington during the American Revolution. When the French Revolution broke out in 1789, he renounced his noble status and took the simple name of Henri Saint-Simon.

Between 1817 and 1822 Saint-Simon wrote a number of books that laid the foundation for his theory of "industry" (see "Bastiat's Political Writings: Anecdotes and Reflections," pp. 409–10), by which he meant that the old regime of war, privilege, and monopoly would gradually be replaced by peace and a new elite of creators, producers, and industrialists.

His disciples, such as Auguste Comte and Olinde Rodrigues, carried on his work with the Saint-Simonian school of thought. Saint-Simon's views developed in parallel to the more-liberal ideas about "industry" espoused by Augustin Thierry, Charles Comte, and Charles Dunoyer during the same period (see the entries for "Comte, Charles," and "Dunoyer, Charles," in this glossary). What distinguished the two schools of thought was that Saint-Simonians advocated rule by a technocratic elite and state-supported "industry," which verged on being a form of socialism, while the liberal school around Comte and Dunoyer advocated a completely free market without any state intervention whatsoever, which would thus allow the entrepreneurial and "industrial" classes to rise to a predominant position without coercion. Saint-Simon's best-known works include *Réorganisation de la société européenne* (1814), *L'Industrie* (1817), *L'Organisateur* (1819), and *Du système industriel* (1821).

SAY, JEAN-BAPTISTE (1767–1832). Leading French political economist in the first third of the nineteenth century. Before becoming an academic political economist quite late in life, Say apprenticed in a commercial office, working for a life insurance company; he also worked as a journalist, soldier, politician, cotton manufacturer, and writer. During the revolution he worked on the journal of the ideologues, *La Décade philosophique, littéraire et politique,* for which he wrote articles on political economy from 1794 to 1799.

In 1814 he was asked by the government to travel to England on a fact-finding mission to discover the secret of English economic growth and to report on the impact of the revolutionary wars on the British economy. His book *De l'Angleterre et des Anglais* (1815) was the result. After the defeat of Napoléon and the restoration of the Bourbon monarchy, Say was appointed to teach economics in Paris, first at the Athénée, then as a chair in "industrial economics" at the Conservatoire national des arts et métiers, and finally as the first chair in political economy at the Collège de France.

Say is best known for his *Traité d'économie politique* (1803), which went through many editions (and revisions) during his lifetime. One of his last major works, the *Cours complet d'économie politique pratique* (1828–33), was an attempt to broaden the scope of political economy, away from the preoccupation with the production of wealth, by examining the moral, political, and sociological requirements of a free society and how they interrelated with the study of political economy. In 1823 Say published a second, unauthorized edition of the *Cours* with extensive notes criticizing Storch's ideas on immaterial goods (many of which Bastiat was to take up in *Economic Harmonies*). Storch replied with an additional volume in 1824, *Considérations sur la nature du revenu national.*

SCIALOJA, ANTONIO (1817–77). Italian economist and professor of political economy at the University of Turin. He was imprisoned and exiled during the 1848 revolution. His major economic works were *I principi della economia sociale esposti in ordine ideologico* (1840); *Trattato elementare di economia sociale* (1848); and *Lezioni di economia politica* (1846–54). He also wrote many works on law. The first book was translated into French as *Les Principes de l'économie exposé selon des idées* (1844).

SCROPE, GEORGE POULETT (1797–1876). Economist, member of Parliament, and fellow of the Royal Society. He was an opponent of the Malthusian theory of population, believing that agricultural production, if unhindered, would always outpace population growth; an advocate of free trade and of parliamentary reform; and an advocate of freer banking using paper currency but following the principles of the Scottish free-banking school. His major theoretical work was *Principles of Political Economy* (1833).

SENIOR, NASSAU WILLIAM (1790–1864). British economist who became a professor of political economy at Oxford University in 1826. In 1832 he was asked to investigate the condition of the poor and, with Edwin Chadwick, wrote the *Poor Law Commissioners' Report* of 1834. In 1843 he was appointed a correspondent of the Institut de France. In 1847 he returned to Oxford University. During his life he wrote many articles for the review journals, such as the *Quarterly Review,* the *Edinburgh Review,* and the *London Review.* His books include *Lectures on Political Economy* (1826) and *Outline of the Science of Political Economy* (1834).

SERRES, OLIVIER DE (1539–1619). Pioneering French agronomist who is best known for introducing the growing of silk to France. His best-known work is *Le Théâtre d'agriculture et mésnage des champs* (1600).

SHERIDAN, RICHARD (1751–1816). Irish playwright and poet who enjoyed a successful career in the London theater. From 1780 to 1812, he was also a member of Parliament, where he gave many memorable speeches. His best-known work is the play *The School for Scandal* (1777).

SMITH, ADAM (1723–90). Leading figure in the Scottish Enlightenment and one of the founders of modern economic thought with his work *The Wealth of Nations* (1776). He studied at the University of Glasgow and had as one of his teachers the philosopher Francis Hutcheson. In the late 1740s Smith lectured at the University of Edinburgh on rhetoric, belles-lettres, and jurisprudence; those lectures are available to us because of detailed notes taken by one of his students. In 1751 he moved to Glasgow, where he was a professor of logic and then moral philosophy. His *Theory of Moral Sentiments* (1759, translated into French in 1774) was a product of this period of his life.

Between 1764 and 1766 he traveled to France as the tutor to the duke of Buccleuch. While in France Smith met many of the physiocrats and visited Voltaire in Geneva. As a result of a generous pension from the duke, Smith was able to retire to Kirkaldy to work on his magnum opus, *The Wealth of Nations,* which appeared in 1776 (French edition in 1788). Smith was appointed in 1778 as commissioner of customs and was based in Edinburgh, where he spent the remainder of his life. In 1843 an important French edition of the *Wealth of Nations* was published by Guillaumin with notes and commentary by leading French economists such as Blanqui, Garnier, Sismondi, and Say. The most complete edition of Smith's works is the *Glasgow Edition of the Works and Correspondence of Adam Smith,* originally published by Oxford University Press (1960) and later by Liberty Fund in paperback (1982–87).

SOBRIER, MARIE JOSEPH (1825–54). A radical socialist revolutionary and journalist. He was a member of the Robespierre-inspired Society of the Rights of Man. During the 1848 revolution he edited a radical Montagnard journal *La Commune de Paris* between March and June 1848 with the assistance of George Sand and Eugène Sue. He was arrested and imprisoned for inciting riots in May 1848 and later pardoned by Napoléon III.

SOLON (ca. 640–558 B.C.). Athenian political leader and legislator who contributed to the birth of Athenian democracy with his legendary constitutional and economic reforms.

STORCH, HENRI-FRÉDÉRIC (1766–1835). Russian economist of German origin who was influenced by the writings of Adam Smith and Jean-Baptiste Say. He was noted for his work on the economics of unfree labor (particularly that of serfdom), the importance of moral (human) capital to national wealth, comparative banking, and the greater wealth-producing capacity of industry and commerce compared with agriculture. Storch studied at the universities of Jena and Heidelberg before returning to Russia, where he taught, worked in various positions in education and government administration, and became a corresponding member of the Saint Petersburg Academy of Sciences. He was chosen to teach various members of the Russian royal family (tutor to the daughters of Tsar Paul I and then appointed by Alexander I to teach political economy to the grand dukes Nicholas and Michael). He became a state councillor in 1804 and head of the Academy's statistical section. In 1828 he was promoted to the rank of private councillor and appointed vice president of the Academy of Sciences, offices that he held until his death. His major theoretical work was his six-volume *Cours d'économie politique, ou exposition des principes qui déterminent la prospérité des nations* (1815), which was based upon the lectures he gave the grand dukes.

STUART, PRINCE CHARLES EDWARD (1720–88). Son of James III and the Stuart claimant to the throne after William of Orange came to power in 1688. Known as Bonnie Prince Charlie to his Scottish supporters, he attempted to gain the throne by stirring up a revolt in the Scottish highlands but was decisively beaten at the Battle of Culloden in 1746.

SUDRE, ALFRED (1820–1902). Economist and political writer. He was author of *Histoire du communisme ou Réfutation historique des utopies socialistes* (1848), which was highly regarded by the reviewer in *Le Journal des économistes.*

SUE, EUGÈNE (1804–57). Son of a surgeon in Napoléon's army and himself a surgeon in the French navy. He served in Spain in 1823 and at the Battle of Navarino in 1828. Sue was active in the romantic and socialist movements and represented the city of Paris in the Assembly of 1850. He was forced into exile for his opposition to Louis-Napoléon. He wrote many novels on social questions and is best known for his ten-volume work, *Le Juif errant* (The Wandering Jew) (1844–45).

TANNEGUY DUCHÂTEL, CHARLES MARIE, comte (1803–67). Member of the Doctrinaires (conservative liberals) during the July Monarchy. He served as minister of public works, agriculture, and commerce (1834–36), minister of finance (1836–37), and minister of the interior (1840–48). He was regarded as economically informed (tending toward Malthusianism) and sympathetic to liberal reform.

TELEMACHUS. Mythological son of Odysseus and Penelope and a central character in Homer's *Odyssey.*

THIERS, ADOLPHE (1797–1877). Lawyer, historian, politician, and journalist. While he was a lawyer he contributed articles to the liberal journal *Le Constitutionel* and published one of his most famous works, the ten-volume *Histoire de la Révolution française* (1823–27). He was instrumental in supporting Louis-Philippe in July 1830 and was the main opponent of Guizot. Thiers defended the idea of a constitutional monarchy in such journals as *Le National.*

After 1813 he became successively a deputy, undersecretary of state, minister of agriculture, and minister of the interior. He was briefly prime minister and minster of foreign affairs in 1836 and 1840, when he resisted democratization and promoted some restrictions on the freedom of the press. During the 1840s he worked on the twenty-volume *Histoire du consulat et de l'empire,* which appeared between 1845 and 1862. After the 1848 revolution and the creation of the Second Empire he was elected a deputy representing Rouen in the Constituent Assembly.

Thiers was a strong opponent of Napoléon III's foreign policies. After Napoléon's defeat Thiers was appointed head of the provisional government by the National Assembly and then became president of the Third Republic until 1873. Thiers wrote some essays on economic matters for *Le Journal des économistes,* but his protectionist sympathies did not endear him to the economists.

TOURRET, CHARLES GILBERT (1795–1858). Moderate republican and minister of agriculture and commerce in Cavaignac's government during the 1848 revolution. He sided with the socialists in the Assembly by supporting workers' cooperatives and state loans to the unemployed. However, he voted with Bastiat and the other liberals against the right-to-work legislation.

TRISMEGISTUS (Hermes Trismegistus). Commonly considered to be some sort of combination of the Greek god Hermes and the Egyptian god Thoth, both of whom were gods of writing and of magic in their respective cultures, although it is arguable if there ever was an actual figure called Hermes Trismegistus.

TURGOT, ANNE ROBERT JACQUES, baron de Laulne (1727–81). Economist of the physiocratic school, politician, reformist bureaucrat, and writer. During the mid-1750s Turgot came into contact with the physiocrats, such as Quesnay, du Pont de Nemours, and Vincent de Gournay (who was the free-market intendant for commerce). Turgot had two opportunities to put free-market reforms into practice: when he was appointed Intendant of Limoges in 1761–74; and when Louis XVI made him minister of finance between 1774 and 1776, at which time Turgot issued his six edicts to reduce regulations and taxation. His works include *Éloge de Gournay* (1759), *Réflexions sur la formation et la distribution des richesses* (1766), and *Lettres sur la liberté du commerce des grains* (1770).

VATISMENIL, ANTOINE LEFEBVRE DE (1789–1860). Lawyer, magistrate, and minister of public education in 1830 and deputy in 1849.

VATTEL, EMER DE (1714–67). One of the foremost theorists of natural law in the eighteenth century. His writings were widely read in the American colonies and had a profound impact on the thinking of the framers of the American constitution. His most famous work is *The Law of Nations, or, Principles of the Law of Nature* (1758).

VAUCANSON, JACQUES DE (1709–82). French inventor who was famous for creating automata that could play musical instruments to entertain the nobility. He was best known for his machines "The Flute Player" and "The Duck." Vaucanson turned his hand to more-practical subjects by trying to automate the weaving of silk.

VIDAL, FRANÇOIS (b. 1812). Vidal was the editor of *La Démocratie pacifique, La Presse,* and *La Revue indépendante.* His major work *De la repartition des richesses, ou de la justice distributive en économie sociale* (1846), on the redistribution of wealth, was reviewed critically by Bastiat in *Le Journal des économistes* (vol. 14, p. 248). Again in *Le Journal des économistes* (vol. 16, pp. 106ff.), Bastiat also replied to five letters by Vidal that originally appeared in *La Presse.* During the 1848 revolution Vidal was secretary of the Luxembourg Commission under Louis Blanc which managed the National Workshops and other matters related to state support for unemployed workers.

VILLÈLE, JEAN-BAPTISTE, comte de (1773–1854). Leader of the ultralegitimists during the Restoration. He was minister of finance in 1821 and prime minister from 1822 until his resignation in 1828. He was instrumental in getting passed in 1825 an Indemnification Law for nobles who had been dispossessed during the Revolution, and a Law of Sacrilege for affronts to the Church.

VILLEMAIN, ABEL FRANÇOIS (1790–1870). A prolific author and professor of French literature at the Sorbonne in 1816. He initially supported the Doctrinaires but became more liberal with his defense of freedom of the press during the government crackdown in the late 1820s. He supported the July revolution in 1830 and was appointed minister of education 1839–1844. He supported legislation which allowed the number of private schools to increase on condition that they submit to greater government regulation.

VOLTAIRE (François-Marie Arouet) (1694–1778). One of the leading figures of the French Enlightenment. He first made a name for himself as a poet and playwright before turning to political philosophy, history, religious criticism, and other literary activities. He became notorious in the 1760s for his outspoken campaign against abuses by the Catholic Church and the use of state torture in the Calas Affair. Voltaire wrote a number of popular works, including *Lettres philosophique* (1734), in which he admired the economic and religious liberties of the English; his philosophic tale *Candide* (1759); his pathbreaking work of social history *Le Siècle de Louis XIV* (1751); his *Traité sur la tolérance* (1763); and the *Dictionnaire philosophique* (1764), which contained his criticisms of religion and superstition.

WALPOLE, ROBERT, Earl of Oxford (1676–1745). Whig politician who served from 1701 (when he was first elected to Parliament) until his resignation in 1742. From 1721 to 1742 he was first lord of the treasury and prime minister. He narrowly escaped financial ruin when the South

Sea Bubble collapsed in 1720, as a result of speculation in its stock. The company had assumed much of the British National Debt in return for lucrative trading monopolies in South America.

WHATELY, RICHARD (1787–1863). Archbishop of Dublin and professor of political economy at the University of Oxford, where he was an important member of Nassau Senior's group. Whately wrote many works of theology before turning to political economy. He was an opponent of the Ricardian school and is considered to be an early adherent to the subjective theory of value. He published his Oxford lectures delivered in Easter Term 1831 as *Introductory Lectures on Political Economy* (1832). He also wrote a popular work designed to introduce young readers to ideas about money: *Easy Lessons on Monetary Matters* (1849).

WINDHAM, WILLIAM (1750–1810). Viceroy of Ireland and member of Parliament in 1784. He was also secretary of state for war under Pitt the Younger.

WOLOWSKI, LOUIS (1810–76). Lawyer, politician, and economist of Polish origin. His interests lay in industrial and labor economics, free trade, and bimetallism. He was a member and the president of the Société d'économie politique. In 1848 he represented La Seine in the Constituent and Legislative assemblies, and during the 1848 revolution he was an ardent opponent of the socialist Louis Blanc and his plans for labor organization.

# Glossary of Places

ADOUR. River flowing through the Landes. It permitted the transportation of goods from the Chalosse, the part of the *département* in which Bastiat lived, to the port of Bayonne, from which they could be exported. With time, sand deposits made navigation more and more difficult.

ARMAGNAC. Region in southwest France, adjacent to the *département* of Landes. A major industry of Armagnac is grape growing and wine production, including the distilling of a brandy called "Armagnac."

CHALOSSE. Part of the Landes *département* in which Bastiat had his home. It covers several counties.

GIRONDE. *Département* in the Aquitaine region in southwest France, immediately to the north of the *département* of Landes, on the Atlantic coast. The Gironde contains the port city of Bordeaux and is famous for its wines. Because a number of liberal-minded deputies were sent to Paris from this region during the French Revolution, they were given the name Girondins. (See also the entry for "Girondins" in the Glossary of Subjects and Terms.)

LANDES. *Département* in the southwest of France, where Bastiat spent most of his life.

MUGRON. A small town in the Landes overlooking the Adour River, where Bastiat lived from 1825 to 1845. At the time it was a significant commercial center, with a port on the Adour River and about two thousand inhabitants (fifteen hundred now). Today, Mugron has a street, a square, and a plaza named after Bastiat.

SAINT-SEVER. Major vine-growing district of the Landes.

# Glossary of Subjects and Terms

ANTI–CORN LAW LEAGUE (Corn League, or League). Founded in 1838
by Richard Cobden and John Bright in Manchester. The initial aim of the
League was to repeal the law restricting the import of grain (Corn Laws),
but it soon called for the unilateral ending of all agricultural and industrial
restrictions on the free movement of goods between Britain and the rest of
the world. For seven years they organized rallies, meetings, public lectures,
and debates from one end of Britain to the other and managed to have
proponents of free trade elected to Parliament. The Tory government
resisted for many years but eventually yielded on 25 June 1846, when
unilateral free trade became the law of Great Britain.

ASSOCIATION POUR LA LIBERTÉ DES ÉCHANGES (Free Trade
Association). Group founded in February 1846 in Bordeaux. Bastiat was
the secretary of the Board, presided over by François d'Harcourt and having
among its members Michel Chevalier, Auguste Blanqui, Joseph Garnier,
Gustave de Molinari, and Horace Say.

LE BIEN PUBLIC. Journal founded by Lamartine at the end of 1843 "to serve
as the organ of the serious but not radical opposition," as he stated in his
Récapitulation. Extrait du bien public (1844), which was taken from Le Bien
public, 21 November 1844.

COLLÈGE DE FRANCE. Institution created under François I in 1529 to deliver
advanced teaching not yet available at the universities. It grants diplomas,
chiefly in engineering.

CONSERVATOIRE NATIONAL DES ARTS ET MÉTIERS. Public institution
of higher education created by Abbé Grégoire in 1794. It is intended for
people already engaged in professional life and grants diplomas, chiefly in
engineering.

CONSTITUENT ASSEMBLY. After the overthrow of Louis Philippe on
24 February 1848, an election was held on 23 April to elect a Constituent
Assembly which would draw up a new constitution. The election was

454 GLOSSARY OF SUBJECTS AND TERMS

by universal male suffrage and involved nearly eight million Frenchmen. Bastiat was successful in this election, representing the *département* of the Landes. A Constitution Committee of Twelve was appointed to draw up the constitution, which was approved 739 to 30 on 4 November 1848.

*LA DÉMOCRATIE PACIFIQUE: JOURNAL DES INTÉRÊTS DES GOUVERNEMENTS ET DES PEUPLES.* Fourierist journal, launched and edited by Victor Considérant. The journal advocated the creation of "harmonious communities." It ran from 1843 to 1851.

DÉPARTEMENT. French administrative division. *Départements* are the equivalent of counties and enjoy a certain administrative autonomy.

DOCTRINAIRES. Group of liberal constitutional monarchists who emerged during the restoration of the French monarchy, between 1815 and 1830. They included such people as Pierre Paul Royer-Collard, François Guizot, Élie Decazes, and Maine de Biran, and the journals in which they wrote included *Le Constitutionnel* and *Le Journal des débats*. The aim of the Doctrinaires was to steer a middle course between an outright return to the pre-1789 status quo (supported by the Legitimists) and a republic based on full adult suffrage (supported by the socialists and the radical liberals). The Doctrinaires supported King Louis XVIII, the constitution of 1814, and a severely restricted electorate of wealthy property owners and taxpayers who numbered barely one hundred thousand people. Their main principles were articulated by François Guizot in *Du gouvernement représentatif et de l'état actuel de la France* (1816).

*LES ÉCONOMISTES* (The Economists). Self-named group of liberal, free-trade political economists. Bastiat and his colleagues believed that, because their doctrine was founded on natural law and a scientific study of the way markets and economies worked in reality, there could be only one school of economics (just as there could be only one school of mechanics or optics). On the other hand, the opponents of free markets (such as the followers of Fourier, Robert Owen, Étienne Cabet, Louis Blanc, Pierre Proudhon, and Pierre Leroux) had as many schools of socialist thought as they could imagine different ways in which society might be restructured or reorganized according to their utopian visions.

FEBRUARY REVOLUTION. See the entry for "Revolution of 1848" in this glossary.

FOURIERISM. See the entry for "Fourier, François-Marie Charles," in the Glossary of Persons.

FOURIERIST. See the entry for "Fourier, François-Marie Charles," in the Glossary of Persons.

GENERAL COUNCIL. Chamber in each French *département* that deliberates on subjects concerning that *département.* It has one representative per county (twenty-eight at the time for the Landes *département,* thirty-one today), elected for nine years (six years today). Its functions have varied over time. Bastiat was elected general councillor in 1833 for the county of Mugron, a post he held until his death. At that time, the Council deliberations had to be approved by the prefect.

GENERAL COUNCIL ON AGRICULTURE, INDUSTRY, AND TRADE. Created by a decree of 1 February 1850, the Council resulted from the merger of three councils (respectively agriculture, industry, and commerce) that were separate up to then. It had 236 members: 96 for agriculture, 59 for industry, 73 for commerce, and 8 for Algeria and the colonies. Its role was to enlighten the government on economic matters. The first session took place from 7 April to 11 May 1850 in the Luxembourg Palace and was opened by the president of the Republic.

GIRONDINS. Group of liberal-minded and moderate republican deputies and their supporters within the Legislative Assembly (1791–92) and National Convention (1792–95) in the early phase of the French Revolution. They got their name from the fact that many of the deputies came from the Gironde region in southwest France, near the major port city of Bordeaux. An important meeting place for the Girondins, where they discussed their ideas and strategies, was the salon of Madame Roland (1754–93). Other members of the group included Jean Pierre Brissot, Pierre Victurnien Vergniaud, Charles Barbaroux, Thomas Paine, and the marquis de Condorcet.

In their bitter rivalry with other groups within the Jacobin group (in particular Robespierre and the Montagnard faction), they disputed the proper treatment and punishment of the deposed king, the war against Austria, and the other monarchical powers that threatened France with invasion, and how far the radical policies of the Revolution needed to be pushed. Eventually they lost out to the radical Jacobins around Robespierre, and many of them were imprisoned and executed during the Terror.

JACOBITES. Supporters of James II, overthrown in 1688, of his son James III, and of his grandson Charles Edward. The 1688 revolution had organized the succession to the throne in such a way as to prevent any return of the Stuarts, that is, of a Catholic monarchy. Many Tories, though, were suspected of Jacobite sympathies.

JACQUES BONHOMME. Short-lived biweekly paper in June 1848, written by Bastiat. See also "Bastiat's Political Writings: Anecdotes and Reflections," pp. 402–3.

LE JOURNAL DES DÉBATS. Journal founded in 1789 by the Bertin family and managed for almost forty years by Louis-François Bertin. The journal went through several title changes and after 1814 became *Le Journal des débats politiques et littéraires*. The journal likewise underwent several changes of political positions: it was against Napoléon during the First Empire; under the second restoration it became conservative rather than reactionary; and under Charles X it supported the liberal stance espoused by the Doctrinaires. It ceased publication in 1944.

LE JOURNAL DES ÉCONOMISTES. Journal of the Société d'économie politique, which appeared from December 1841 until the fall of France in 1940. It was published by the firm of Guillaumin (1841–42), which also published the writings of most of the liberals of the period. *Le Journal des économistes* was the leading journal of the free-market economists (known as "les économistes") in France in the second half of the nineteenth century. It was edited by Adolphe Blanqui (1842–43), Hippolyte Dussard (1843–45), Joseph Garnier (1845–55), Henri Baudrillart (1855–65), Joseph Garnier (1866–81), Gustave de Molinari (1881–1909), and Yves Guyot (from 1910). Bastiat published many articles in the journal, many of which were later published as pamphlets and books, and his works were all reviewed there. There are fifty-eight entries under Bastiat's name in the table of contents of the journal for the period 1841 to 1865.

JULY MONARCHY. See the entry for "Revolution of 1848" in this glossary.

JULY REVOLUTION. See the entry for "Revolution of 1848" in this glossary.

JUNE DAYS. See the entry for "Revolution of 1848" in this glossary.

MIMEREL COMMITTEE. See the entry for "Mimerel de Roubaix, Pierre," in the Glossary of Persons.

LE MONITEUR. See the entry for "*Le Moniteur industriel*" in this glossary.

LE MONITEUR INDUSTRIEL. Periodical created in July 1835. It became the stronghold of protectionists and Bastiat's bête noire.

LES MONTAGNARDS. See the entry for "La Montagne" in this glossary.

LA MONTAGNE (The Mountain). Comprising a group of deputies (Montagnards) favorable to a "democratic and social republic." The Manifesto of the Montagnards, issued on 8 November 1848, presented the program of Ledru-Rollin and in general expressed the ideas of the

Montagnards. The name comes from the first general assemblies of the revolution, in which the deputies professing these ideas sat in the highest part of the assembly, "the mountain."

*LE NATIONAL*. Liberal paper founded in 1830 by Adolphe Thiers to fight the ultrareactionary politics of the duc de Polignac (ultraroyalist politician who served in various capacities, such as prime minister, during the restoration of the Bourbon monarchy). *Le National* played a decisive role during the "three glorious days" and contributed to the success of Louis-Philippe. Its readership considerably exceeded the number of its subscribers (around three thousand).

PHALANSTERY. Self-sustaining community of the followers of the utopian socialist Charles Fourier. He envisaged that new communities of people would spring up in order to escape the injustices of free-market societies and industrialism. He called his new self-supporting communities "phalanxes," which would consist of about sixteen hundred people who would live in a specially designed building called a "phalanstère," or "phalanstery." A number of communities modeled on his ideas were set up in North America—in Texas, Ohio, New Jersey, and New York. Fourier's ideas had some influence in French politics during the revolution of 1848 through the activities of Victor Considérant and his "right to work" movement. See also the entry for "Fourier, François-Marie Charles," in the Glossary of Persons.

PHYSIOCRATS. Group of French economists, bureaucrats, and legislators who came to prominence in the 1760s and included such figures as François Quesnay (1694–1774), Anne-Robert-Jacques Turgot (1727–81), Mercier de la Rivière (1720–94), Vincent de Gournay (1712–59), Mirabeau (1715–89), and Pierre Samuel du Pont de Nemours (1739–1817). They are best known for coining the expression "laissez-faire" as a summary statement of their policy prescriptions. (See also the discussion of laissez-faire in "Bastiat's Political Writings: Anecdotes and Reflections," pp. 408–9.)

As the word *physiocracy* suggests (the rule of nature or natural law), the physiocrats believed that natural laws governed the operation of economic events and that rulers should acknowledge this fact in their legislation. They further believed that agricultural production was the source of wealth and that all barriers to its expansion and improvement (such as internal tariffs, government regulation, and high taxes) should be removed. The strategy of the physiocrats was to educate others through their scholarly and journalistic writings as well as to influence monarchs to adopt rational economic policies via a process of so-called "enlightened despotism." This strategy met with very mixed results, as Turgot's failed effort to deregulate the French grain trade in the 1770s attests.

*LE POPULAIRE.* Newspaper propagating the communist ideas of Étienne Cabet.

*LA PRESSE.* Widely distributed daily newspaper, created in 1836 by journalist, businessman, and politician Émile de Girardin (1806–81). Girardin was one of the creators of the modern press and author of, among many works, the brochure *Le socialisme et l'impôt* (1849), in which he advocated a single tax on capital and revenue.

REPUBLICAN CALENDAR. New calendar adopted by the National Convention in October 1793 as part of a reorganization of all aspects of French society. The calendar would be based on months with three ten-day weeks and a renaming of the days and months of the year. Thus 3 Nivôse Year III is 23 December 1794, and 23 Nivôse Year III is 12 January 1795. Many of the names of the months are quite poetic and have become associated with significant historical events: Brumaire, or "fog" (October–November); Nivôse, or "snowy" (December–January); Ventôse, or "windy" (February–March); Germinal, or "germination" (March–April); and Thermidor, or "summer heat" (July–August). The calendar was scrapped by Napoléon in 1805, soon after he became emperor.

REVOLUTION OF 1848 (also "February revolution"). Because France went through so many revolutions between 1789 and 1870, they are often distinguished by reference to the month in which they occurred. Thus we have the "July Monarchy" (of 1830), when the restored Bourbon monarchy of 1815 was overthrown in order to create a more liberal and constitutional monarchy under Louis-Philippe; the "February revolution" (of 1848), when the July Monarchy of Louis-Philippe was overthrown and the Second Republic was formed; the "June Days" (of 1848), when a rebellion by some workers in Paris who were protesting the closure of the government-subsidized National Workshops work-relief program was bloodily put down by General Cavaignac; the "18th Brumaire of Louis-Napoléon," which refers to the coup d'état that brought Louis-Napoléon (Napoléon Bonaparte's nephew) to power on 2 December 1851 and that ushered in the creation of the Second Empire—the phrase was coined by Karl Marx and refers to another date, 18 Brumaire in the revolutionary calendar, or 9 November 1799, when Napoléon Bonaparte declared himself dictator in another coup d'état. Bastiat was an active participant in the 1848 revolution, being elected to the Constituent Assembly on 23 April 1848 and then to the Legislative Assembly on 13 May 1849.

*LA REVUE BRITANNIQUE.* Monthly review that was founded in 1825 by Sébastien-Louis Saulnier (1790–1835). Its full title read *Revue britannique. Receuil international. Choix d'articles extraits des meilleurs écrits périodiques*

*da la Grande-Bretagne et de l'Amérique, complété sur des articles originaux.*
It contained many articles on economic matters, such as the article in the
6th series, vol. 1, published in 1846, which was an unattributed piece on
"La ligue anglaise" (Anti–Corn Law League), which might have been by
Bastiat. It ceased publication in 1901.

RIGHT OF INSPECTION. See the entry for "Slavery" in this glossary.

SAINT CYR. Leading French military academy (École spéciale militaire de
Saint-Cyr). It was founded by Napoléon in 1803 in order to train officer
cadets. During Bastiat's lifetime there was some contention over the school's
motto. During Napoléon's rule (1803–15) the motto was "ils s'instruirent
pour vaincre" (they study in order to win [or conquer]). The restored
monarch, Louis XVIII, changed the motto to "ils s'instruirent pour la
défense de la patrie" (they study in order to defend the country). After
the 1848 revolution and during the Second Empire (1852–70) the original
wording used by Napoléon was reinstated.

SAINT-SIMONISTS (or Saint-Simonians). See the entry for "Saint-Simon,
Claude Henri de Rouvroy," in the Glossary of Persons.

SLAVERY (slave trade, right of inspection). Slavery did not have a strong
presence within France, but it played a major role in the French Caribbean
colonies, such as Saint-Dominique (Haiti). Under the influence of
the ideas of the French Revolution, slavery was abolished in 1794 and
a number of freed blacks were elected to various French legislative
bodies. Napoléon reintroduced slavery in 1802 and fought a bloody but
unsuccessful war in order to prevent a free black republic from emerging in
Haiti.

In 1807, under pressure from such abolitionists as William Wilberforce
and Thomas Clarkson, Britain passed an act that abolished the slave trade,
much of which was carried in British vessels. The United States followed
suit in 1808 with a similar ban. This had significant implications for the
southern states of the United States and the French Caribbean, where
slavery remained firmly in place. The British Navy patroled the oceans,
insisting upon a "right of inspection" to look for slaves being carried
from Africa to the Caribbean and to punish those involved in the trade
as pirates. This policy was a serious bone of contention between Britain
and France, as the latter viewed the British policy as interference in their
sovereign right to engage in trade and shipping. Slavery was abolished
in the British Caribbean in 1833, again in the French colonies during
the 1848 revolution, and in the United States in 1865 (the Thirteenth
Amendment).

Société d'agriculture, commerce, arts, et sciences du département des Landes (Society for Agriculture, Trade, Arts, and Sciences of the *Département* of the Landes). Founded in 1798, the society, of which Bastiat was a member, included landowners with large holdings and people from the liberal professions.

Société d'économie politique (Society of Political Economy). Refounded in late 1842 after a false start in early 1842 and had its first monthly meeting at a restaurant in November 1842. It was attended by Joseph Garnier, Adolphe Blaise, Eugène Daire, Gilbert-Urbain Guillaumin, and a fifth member who soon dropped out because he was a supporter of tariffs. Its first president was Charles Dunoyer, who served from 1845 to 1862, and Joseph Garnier was made permanent secretary in 1849. Its membership in 1847 was about fifty and grew to about eighty at the end of 1849. It is not known when Bastiat joined the society, but he is first mentioned in the minutes for August 1846, when the society hosted a banquet in honor of Richard Cobden, and Bastiat was one of several members of the society to make a formal toast to "the past and present defenders of free trade in the House of Lords and the House of Commons." A summary of its monthly meetings was published in *Le Journal des économistes.*

Tory. See the entry for "Whig and Tory."

Whig and Tory. Before the establishment of modern, organized, ideologically based political parties in the nineteenth century, there were less-formal groups or alliances that associated for short-term political benefit. In the late seventeenth, eighteenth, and early nineteenth centuries there emerged in Britain groupings called Whigs and Tories.

   The Whigs emerged in the late seventeenth century during the struggle of the Protestants, constitutional monarchists, and landed interests to prevent a newly invigorated Catholic Stuart monarchy from gaining power in 1678–81. This group was led by the Earl of Shaftesbury. By the 1830s and 1840s the Whigs had adopted the policies of free trade, the abolition of slavery, and Catholic emancipation. The origin of the name is probably from a term of abuse and criticism coined by their opponents—a "whiggamor" is a Scottish Gaelic word for cattle drover.

   The Tories originally supported the Catholic Scottish claimant to the English throne in 1680 but later became staunch defenders of the established Anglican Church and the interests of the court. They opposed all forms of religious dissent and extension of the suffrage. Their name, too, probably came from their opponents—*tóraidhe* is an Irish word that means "outlaw."

WINE AND SPIRITS TAX. The wine and spirits tax was eliminated by the revolutionary parliament of 1789 but progressively reinstated during the empire. It comprised four components: (1) a consumption tax (10 percent of the sale price); (2) a license fee paid by the vendor, depending on the number of inhabitants; (3) a tax on circulation, which depended on the *département;* and (4) an entry duty for the towns of more than four hundred inhabitants, depending on the sale price and the number of inhabitants. Being from a wine-producing region, Bastiat had always been preoccupied by such a law, which was very hard on the local farmers.

ZOLLVEREIN. German customs union that emerged in 1834 when the southwestern German states of Baden and Württemberg joined the Prussian customs union. The Prussian state and its territories had created an internal customs union in 1818 following the economic turmoil of the Napoleonic wars and the increase in size of Prussian-controlled territory. It was based upon the relatively low Prussian customs rate, which meant that the expanded German customs union created a significant trading zone within the German-speaking part of Europe with a relatively low external tariff rate and the hope of increasing deregulation of trade within the trading zone.

# Bibliographical Note on the Works Cited in This Volume

*In* the text, Bastiat cites or alludes to many literary, political, and economic works. We have listed these works with a full citation in the bibliography of primary sources. In the glossaries, if a work is cited, we have given only the title of the work and the date when it was first published, so that its historical context might be appreciated, for example, Rousseau, *The Social Contract* (1762); the bibliography, however, might cite a different edition, depending on the source or reason for the citation.

In the bibliography of primary sources, we have tried, if possible, to cite editions published during Bastiat's lifetime that he might well have used. For example, the third edition of the complete works of Rousseau appeared in seventeen volumes in 1830–33: *Œuvres complètes de J.-J. Rousseau, avec les notes de tous les commentateurs.* The edition by Hiard of *The Social Contract* might have also been used by Bastiat: *Du contrat social, ou principes du droit politique.* Or, for example, a three-volume collected works of Maximilien Robespierre was published in the late 1830s as the French socialist movement was beginning to grow on the eve of the 1848 revolution. This is the edition Bastiat most likely had access to: *Œuvres de Maximilien Robespierre, avec une notice historique et des notes, par le citoyen Laponneraye.*

Bastiat was often quite cavalier in citing the sources he used, not providing page references let alone identifying the chapters. Where we have been able to locate the quotation, we have given the book number, chapter number, and the title of the chapter. Sometimes we have been able to locate the exact edition of a work Bastiat used, and in those instances, we have provided page numbers to that work.

If we have not been able to locate the exact edition of a work Bastiat used but have found the exact location of the quotation in a different (sometimes, modern) edition, we have cited and provided the page numbers to that work. For example, in the chapter "Baccalaureate and Socialism," Bastiat quotes often from Rousseau. We have been able to locate many of those quotations, with page numbers, in a 1975 edition of Rousseau's works, *Du contrat social et autres œuvres politiques.*

For background information about key concepts and biographical details of political figures and authors we have frequently consulted *Le Diction- naire de l'économie politique* (1852–53). Bastiat was closely connected to the group of classical liberal political economists in Paris during the 1840s: he was a member of the Société d'économie politique (founded 1842); he wrote many articles for *Le Journal des économistes* (founded 1841); he published his books and pamphlets with the Guillaumin publishing house (which also published *Le Journal des économistes* and the *Dictionnaire*); he wrote two key articles for the *Dictionnaire,* "Abondance" (Wealth) and "Loi" (Law); and he was quoted in many other articles, most notably in the key article in the *Dictionnaire,* "L'État" (The State).

In some cases Bastiat does not quote an author or authors directly but paraphrases their ideas in his own words. For example, in a speech in the Chamber of Deputies he might refer to his socialist opponents as "they" and "quote" a number of their ideas in a paragraph in which he paraphrases their thoughts. In cases like this we have made no effort to track down and cite the source of each of these individual ideas or thoughts.

# Bibliography

## PRIMARY SOURCES

### WORKS BY BASTIAT

The works by Bastiat listed below represent not only the sources used for this translation but also those cited in the text, notes, and glossaries.

*Economic Harmonies*. Edited by W. Hayden Boyers and translated by George B. de Huszar. Irvington-on-Hudson, N.Y.: Foundation for Economic Education, 1979.

*Economic Sophisms*. Translated by Arthur Goddard. Irvington-on-Hudson, N.Y.: Foundation for Economic Education, 1968.

"L'État." *Journal des débats* (25 September 1848), pp. 1–2.

*L'État. Maudit argent*. Paris: Guillaumin, 1849.

*Harmonies économiques: Augmentée des manuscrits laissés par l'auteur, Publiée par la Société des amis de Bastiat*. Edited by Prosper Paillottet and Roger de Fontenay. 2nd ed. Paris: Guillaumin, 1851.

*Lettres d'un habitant des Landes, Frédéric Bastiat*. Edited by Mme Cheuvreux. Paris: A. Quantin, 1877.

*Œuvres complètes de Frédéric Bastiat, mises en ordre, revues et annotées d'après les manuscrits de l'auteur*. Paris: Guillaumin, 1854–55, 1st ed.; 1862–64, 2nd ed.; 1870–73, 3rd ed.; 1878–79, 4th ed.; 1881–84, 5th ed.; if there was a sixth edition, the date is unknown; 1893, 7th ed.

The editions of Bastiat's *Œuvres complètes* that were used in making this translation are as follows:

Vol. 1: *Correspondance et mélanges* (2nd ed. of 1862)

Vol. 2: *Le Libre-échange* (2nd ed., 1862)

Vol. 3: *Cobden et la Ligue ou l'agitation anglaise pour la liberté des échanges* (2nd ed., 1864)

Vol. 4: *Sophismes économiques. Petits pamphlets I* (3rd ed., 1873)

Vol. 5: *Sophismes économiques. Petits pamphlets II* (3rd ed., 1873)

Vol. 6: *Harmonies économiques* (2nd ed., 1864)

Vol. 7: *Essais, ébauches, correspondance* (2nd ed., 1864)

*Selected Essays on Political Economy.* Translated by Seymour Cain. Irvington-on-Hudson, N.Y.: Foundation for Economic Education, 1975.


WORKS BY OTHER AUTHORS
CITED IN THE TEXT, NOTES, AND GLOSSARIES

We list here the works by other authors mentioned in the text, notes, and glossaries. Although not exhaustive, these works represent many primary sources that were important during Bastiat's time.

Andrieux, Jean Stanislas. *Contes et opuscules en vers et en prose; suivis de poésies fugitives.* Paris: Renouard, 1800.
———. *Œuvres de François-Guillaume-Jean-Stanislas Andrieux.* Vol. 3. Paris: Chez Nepveu, Librairie, 1818.
*Annales de la Société d'économie politique.* Publiées sous la direction de Alph. Courtois Fils, secrétaire perpétuel. Vol. 1: 1846–53. Paris: Guillaumin, 1889.
Augustine. *The Confessions and Letters of St. Augustin, with a Sketch of His Life and Work.* Volume 1 of *A Select Library of the Nicene and Post-Nicene Fathers of the Christian Church,* edited by Philip Schaff. 14 vols. Buffalo: Christian Literature Co., 1886.
———. *St. Augustin's City of God and Christian Doctrine.* Volume 2 of *A Select Library of the Nicene and Post-Nicene Fathers of the Christian Church,* edited by Philip Schaff. 14 vols. Buffalo: Christian Literature Co., 1887.
Béranger, Pierre-Jean de. *Béranger's Songs of the Empire, the Peace, and the Restoration.* Translated by Robert B. Brough. London: Addey and Co., 1856.
———. *Chansons.* Paris: Baudouin frères, 1827.
———. *Musique des chansons de Béranger. Airs notés anciens et modernes.* Septième edition, augmentée de la musique des nouvelles chansons et de trois airs avec accompagnement de piano, par Halévy et Mme. Mainvielle-Fodor. Paris: Perrotin, 1858.
Blanc, Louis. *Histoire de la Révolution française.* Paris: Langlois et Leclercq, 1847.
———. *Histoire de la Révolution française.* 2nd ed. 15 vols. Paris: Lacroix, 1878.
———. *L'Organisation du travail. 5. édition, revue, corrigée et augmentée d'une polémique entre M. Michel Chevalier et l'auteur, ainsi que d'un appendice indiquant ce qui pourrait être tenté dès à présent.* Paris: Au bureau de la Société de l'industrie fraternelle, 1848. [The first edition of Blanc's book appeared in 1839 and went through many editions during the 1840s, with each edition having corrections and additions. The fifth edition appeared in 1848 with a polemical exchange between Michel Chevalier and Blanc. In 1850 the ninth edition appeared.]
———. *Le Socialisme; droit au travail, réponse à M. Thiers.* Paris: M. Levy, 1848.

Boileau-Despréaux, Nicolas. *Œuvres de Boileau Despréaux, avec un commentaire par M. de Saint-Súrin.* Tome premier, *Satires* (Paris: J-J. Blaise, 1821).

Bouctot, Georges. "Individualisme." In *Nouveau dictionnaire d'économie politique,* edited by Léon Say and Joseph Chailley. 2 vols. 2nd ed. Paris: Guillaumin, 1900. Vol. 2, pp. 64–66.

Comte, Charles. *Traité de la propriété.* 2 vols. Paris: Chamerot, Ducollet, 1834. [Brussels edition, H. Tarlier, 1835. A second, revised edition was published in 1835 by Chamerot, Ducollet of Paris in 4 vols. A revised and corrected third edition was published in 1837 by Hauman, Cattoir of Brussels.]

———. *Traité de legislation, ou exposition des lois générales suivant lesquelles les peuples prospèrent, dépérissent ou restent stationnaire.* 4 vols. Paris: A. Sautelet, 1827; Paris: Chamerot, Ducollet, 1835 (2nd ed.); Brussels: Hauman, Cattoir, 1837 (3rd ed.).

Condorcet, Marie-Jean-Antoine-Nicolas Caritat, marquis de. *Esquisse d'un tableau historique des progrès de l'esprit humain, suivie de Réflexions sur l'esclavage des nègres.* Paris: Masson et fils, 1822.

Considérant, Victor Prosper. *Théorie du droit de propriété et du droit au travail.* Paris: Librairie phalanstérienne, 1848.

Constant, Benjamin. *Political Writings.* Translated and edited by Biancamaria Fontana. Cambridge: Cambridge University Press, 1988.

Coquelin, Charles, and Gilbert-Urbain Guillaumin, eds. *Dictionnaire de l'économie politique, contenant l'exposition des principes de la science, l'opinion des écrivains qui ont le plus contribué à sa fondation et à ses progrès, la bibliographie générale de l'économie politique par noms d'auteurs et par ordre de matières, avec des notices biographiques et une appréciation raisonnée des principaux ouvrages,* publié sur la direction de MM Charles Coquelin et Guillaumin. Paris: Librairie de Guillaumin et Cie., 1852–53. 2 vols. 2nd ed., 1854; 3rd ed., 1864; 4th ed., 1873.

Corneille, Pierre. *Horace, tragédie en cinq actes. Édition classique.* Paris: Librairie Classique d'Eugène Belin, 1847.

Courcelle-Senueil, Jean-Gustave. "Prestations." In volume 2 of *Dictionnaire de l'économie politique.* 2 vols. Paris: Librairie de Guillaumin et Cie., 1852–53.

Destutt de Tracy, Antoine. *A Commentary and Review of Montesquieu's "Spirit of the Laws": To which are annexed, Observations on the Thirty-First Book by the late M. Condorcet; and Two letters of Helvetius, On the Merits of the Same Work.* Translated by Thomas Jefferson. Philadelphia: William Duane, 1811.

*Le Droit au travail à l'Assemblée Nationale. Recueil complet de tous les discours prononcés dans cette mémorable discussion par MM Fresneau, Hubert Delisle, Cazalès, Gaulthier de Rumilly, Pelletier, A. de Tocqueville, Ledru-Rolin, Duvergier de Hauranne, Crémieux, M. Barthe, Gaslonde, de Luppé, Arnaud (de l'Ariège), Thiers, Considérant, Bouhier de l'Ecluse, Martin-Bernard, Billault, Dufaure, Goudchaux, et Lagrange (texts revue par les orateurs), suivis de l'opinion de MM Marrast, Proudhon, Louis Blanc, Édition Laboulaye et Cormenin; avec des observations inédites par MM Léon Faucher, Wolowski, Fréd. Bastiat, de Parieu, et une introduction et des notes par M. Joseph Garnier.* Paris: Guillaumin, 1848.

Dunoyer, Charles. *De la liberté du travail; ou, Simple exposé des conditions dans lesquelles les forces humaines s'exercent avec le plus de puissance.* Paris: Guillaumin, 1845.

———. *Economisti classici italiani. Scrittori classici italiani di economia politica.* 50 vols. Edited by Pietro Custodi. Milan: G. G. Destefanis, 1803–16.

———. *L'Industrie et la morale considérées dans leurs rapports avec la liberté.* Paris: A. Sautelet, 1825.

———. *Nouveau traité d'économie sociale.* Paris: A. Sautelet, 1830.

Fénelon (François de Salignac de la Motte-Fénelon). *Œuvres complètes de Fénelon.* Paris: Gauthier frères, 1830; 1848–52.

Fonteyraud, Henri Alcide. *Mélanges d'économie politique. La Ligue anglaise pour la liberté du commerce. Notice historique sur la vie et les travaux de Ricardo.* Edited by J. Garnier. Paris: Guillaumin, 1853.

Fourier, François-Marie Charles. *La Fausse industrie morcelée répugnante et mensongère et l'antidote, l'industrie naturelle, combinée, attrayante, véridique donnant quadruple produit.* 2 vols. Paris: Bossange père, 1835–36.

———. *Le Nouveau monde industriel et sociétaire, ou, invention du procédé d'industrie attrayante et naturelle, distribuée en séries passionnées.* Paris: Bossange Père, 1829.

Garnier, Joseph. "Nécrologie. Guillaumin. Ses funérailles—Sa vie et son œuvre." *Journal des économistes* 45 (January–March 1865): 108–21.

Guizot, François. *Du gouvernement représentatif et de l'état actuel de la France.* Paris: Maradan, 1816.

Lamartine, Alphonse de. *Récapitulation. Extrait du bien public.* Paris: Chassipollet (Mâcon), 1844.

McCulloch, John Ramsay. *The Principles of Political Economy: With a Sketch of the Rise and Progress of the Science.* Edinburgh: W. and C. Tait, 1825.

Mirabeau, Honoré-Gabriel Riqueti, comte de. *Œuvres de Mirabeau, précédées d'une notice sur sa vie et ses ouvrages, par M. Merilhou.* 8 vols. Paris: Lecointe et Pougin, 1834–35.

Molière (Jean-Baptiste Poquelin). *Œuvres complètes de Molière, avec une notice par M. L. B. Picard.* 6 vols. Paris: Baudouin frères, 1827.

Molinari, Gustave de. *Cours d'économie politique.* Paris: Guillaumin, 1855.

———. "De la production de la sécurité." *Journal des économistes* (February 1849): 277–90.

———. *Esquisse de l'organisation politique et économique de la société future.* Paris: Guillaumin, 1899.

———. *L'Évolution économique du dix-neuvième siècle: Théorie du progrès.* Paris: C. Reinwald, 1880.

———. *L'Évolution politique et la Révolution.* Paris: C. Reinwald, 1884.

———. "Frédéric Bastiat: *Lettres d'un habitant des Landes.*" *Journal des économistes* 4th series, no. 7 (July 1878): 60–70.

———. *Les Soirées de la rue Saint-Lazare: Entretiens sur les lois économiques et défense de la propriété.* Paris: Guillaumin, 1849.

Montesquieu, Charles Louis de Secondat, baron de. *L'Esprit des lois.* In *Œuvres de Montesquieu, avec éloges, analyses, commentaires, remarques, notes, réfutations, imitations,* edited by MM Destutt de Tracy, Villemain. 8 vols. Paris: Dalibon, 1827.

Oncken, August. *Die Maxime laissez faire et laisser passez, ihr Ursprung, ihr Werden. Ein Beitrag zur Geschichte des Freihandelslehre.* Bern: K. J. Wyss, 1886.

Paillottet, Prosper. *De la propriété intellectuelle: Études par MM Frédéric Passy, Victor Modeste et P. Paillottet; avec une préface de M. Jules Simon.* Paris: E. Dentu, 1859.

———. *De l'encouragement aux associations ouvrières, voté par l'Assemblée constituante.* Paris: Guillaumin, 1849.

———. *Des conseils de prud'hommes.* Batignolles: Hennuyer, 1847.

———. *Des idées religieuses, par William Johnson Fox, 15 conférences.* Translated by P. Paillottet. Paris: G. Baillière, 1877.

Passy, Frédéric. "Nécrologie. Prosper Paillottet." *Le Journal des économistes* (January–March 1878): 285–89.

Passy, Hippolyte. "Utopie." In *Dictionnaire de l'économie politique,* edited by Charles Coquelin and G.-U. Guillaumin. Vol. 2, 1852–53, pp. 798–803.

Proudhon, Pierre Joseph. *Qu'est-ce que la propriété? Ou recherches sur le principe du droit et du gouvernement.* Paris: Prévot, 1841.

———. *Système des contradictions économiques.* Paris: Guillaumin, 1846.

Reybaud, Louis. *Études sur les réformateurs contemporains, ou socialistes modernes: Saint-Simon, Charles Fourier, Robert Owen.* 2 vols. Paris: Guillaumin, 1849.

Ricardo, David. *The High Price of Bullion.* London: John Murray, 1810.

———. *On the Principles of Political Economy and Taxation.* London: J. Murray, 1817.

———. *The Works and Correspondence of David Ricardo.* Indianapolis: Liberty Fund, 2004.

Robespierre, Maximilien. *Œuvres de Maximilien Robespierre, avec une notice historique et des notes, par le citoyen Laponneraye (précédées de Considérations générales, par Armand Carrel, Mémoires de Charlotte Robespierre sur ses deux frères.* 3 vols. Paris, Chez l'editeur, 1834–40.

Rousseau, Jean-Jacques. *Les Confessions de J.-J. Rousseau. Avec les notes de Musset-Pathay et de Petitain.* Paris: Firmin-Didot frères, 1844.

———. *Du contrat social et autres œuvres politiques.* Introduction by Jean Ehrard. Paris: Garnier frères, 1975.

———. *Œuvres complètes de J.-J. Rousseau, avec les notes de tous les commentateurs.* 17 vols. Paris: A. Aubrée, 1830–33.

———. *The Political Writings of Jean-Jacques Rousseau.* Edited from the original manuscripts and authentic editions, with introductions and notes by C. E. Vaughan. 2 vols. Cambridge: Cambridge University Press, 1915.

Saint-Just, Louis Antoine de. *Fragments sur les institutions républicaines, ouvrage posthume de Saint-Just, précédé d'une notice par Ch. Didier.* Paris: Techener and Guillaumin, 1831.

———. *Œuvres de Saint-Just, représentant du peuple à la Convention Nationale.* Paris: Prévot, 1834.

Say, Jean-Baptiste. *Cours complet d'économie politique pratique.* Paris: Rapilly, 1828–33.

———. *De l'Angleterre et des anglais.* Paris: A. Bertrand, 1815.

———. *Œuvres complètes.* Edited by André Tiran et al. Paris: Economica, 2006.

———. *Traité d'économie politique.* Paris: Déterville, 1803.

———. *A Treatise on Political Economy; or the Production, Distribution, and Consumption of Wealth.* Edited by Clement C. Biddle. Translated by C. R. Prinsep from the 4th ed. of the French. Philadelphia: Lippincott, Grambo, 1855.

Say, Léon, and Joseph Chailley, eds. *Nouveau dictionnaire d'économie politique.* 2 vols. Paris: Guillaumin, 1891–92.

"Séance du 10 septembre 1850." In *Annales de la société d'économie politique,* pp. 124–26.

Senior, Nassau William. *Lectures on Political Economy.* [Place and publisher unknown], 1826.

———. *Outline of the Science of Political Economy.* London: B. Fellowes, 1834.

Smith, Adam. *Inquiry into the Nature and Causes of the Wealth of Nations, in Three Volumes. With notes, and an Additional Volume, by David Buchanan.* Edinburgh: Oliphant, Waugh & Innes, 1814.

———. *Recherches sur la nature et les causes de la richesse des nations, par Adam Smith, traduction du Germain Garnier, entierement rev. et cor. et precedée d'une notice biographique par M. Blanqui . . . avec les commentaires de Buchanan, G. Garnier, MacCulloch, Malthus, J. Mill, Ricardo, Sismondi; augm. de notes inedites de Jean-Baptiste Say, et d'eclaircissements historiques par M. Blanqui.* 2 vols. Paris: Guillaumin, 1843.

Stendhal. *D'un nouveau complot contre les industriels.* Paris: Sautelet, 1825.

———. *D'un nouveau complot contre les industriels, suivi de Stendhal et la querelle de l'industrie.* Édition établie, annotée et présentée par Michel Crouzet. Jaignes: La Chasse au Snark, 2001.

———. *Le Rouge et le noir. Chronique du XIXe siècle.* 2 vols. Paris: Levasseur, 1831. 2nd edition.

Sue, Eugène. *Le Juif errant*. Paris, 1845.

Thiers, Adolphe. *De la propriété*. Paris: Paulin, 1848.

———. *Discours parlementaires de M. Thiers, publiés par M. Calmon: Troisième partie (1842–45)*. Paris: Calmann-Lévy, 1880.

———. *Histoire de consulat et de l'Empire*. 20 vols. Paris: Paulin, 1845–62.

———. *Histoire de la Révolution française*. 10 vols. Paris: Lecointe et Durey, 1823–27.

Vattel, Emer de. *Le droit des gens, ou Principes de la loi naturelle, appliqués à la conduite et aux affaires des nations et des souverains*. 2 vols. Paris: J.-P. Aillaud, 1838.

## Secondary Sources

The works listed below were consulted in compiling the glossaries and notes.

Baylen, Joseph O., and and Norbert J. Gossman, eds. *Biographical Dictionary of Modern British Radicals*. Sussex, U.K.: Harvester Press, 1979.

Bramsted, E. K., and K. J. Melhuish, eds. *Western Liberalism: A History in Documents from Locke to Croce*. London: Longman, 1978.

Breton, Yves. "The Société d'économie politique of Paris (1842–1914)." In *The Spread of Political Economy and the Professionalisation of Economists: Economic Societies in Europe, America and Japan in the Nineteenth Century,* edited by Massimo M. Augello and Marco E. L. Guidi. London: Routledge, 2001.

*L'Économie politique en France au XIXe siècle*. Sous la direction de Yves Breton et Michel Lutfalla. Paris: Economica, 1991.

*Frédéric Bastiat, Œuvres économiques, textes présentés par Florin Aftalion*. Paris: Presses Universitaires de France, Collection Libre Échange, 1983.

French-language version of Wikilibéral: http://www.wikiliberal.org/wiki/Accueil.

Gray, Alexander. *The Socialist Tradition: Moses to Lenin*. London: Longmans, 1963.

Hart, David M. *Class, Slavery, and the Industrialist Theory of History in French Liberal Thought, 1814–1830: The Contribution of Charles Comte and Charles Dunoyer*. Ph.D. Diss., King's College, Cambridge, 1993.

Hayek, F. A. *The Counter-revolution of Science*. Glencoe, Ill.: Free Press, 1952.

Langer, William L., ed. and comp. *An Encyclopedia of World History: Ancient, Medieval, and Modern. Chronologically Arranged*. 5th ed. Boston: Houghton Mifflin, 1972.

Letort, Charles. "Société d'économie politique: Réunion du 5 août 1899." *Journal des économistes* 39 (July–September 1899): 257–63.

Levan-Lemesle, Lucette. "Guillaumin, éditeur d'économie politique 1801–1864." *Revue d'économie politique,* 95ᵉ année, no. 2 (1985): 134–49.

Lukes, Steven. *Key Concepts in the Social Sciences: Individualism*. Oxford: Basil Blackwell, 1973.

Newman, Edgar Leon, and Robert Lawrence Simpson, eds. *Historical Dictionary of France from the 1815 Restoration to the Second Empire.* 2 vols. Westport, Conn.: Greenwood Press, 1987.

O'Brien, D. P. *The Classical Economists.* Oxford: Clarendon Press, 1978.

*The Online Library of Liberty:* http://oll.libertyfund.org. Liberty Fund: Indianapolis, 2010.

Potier, Jean-Pierre, and André Tiran, eds. *Jean-Baptiste Say: Nouveaux regards sur son œuvre.* Paris: Economica, 2003.

Roche, George Charles, III. *Frédéric Bastiat: A Man Alone.* New Rochelle, N.Y.: Arlington House, 1971.

Rothbard, Murray N. *An Austrian Perspective on the History of Economic Thought.* 2 vols. Vol. 1: *Economic Thought before Adam Smith.* Vol. 2: *Classical Economics.* Auburn, Ala.: Ludwig von Mises Institute, 2006.

Rude, Fernand. *Stendhal et la pensée sociale de son temps.* Brionne: Gérard Monfort, 1983.

Russell, Dean. *Frédéric Bastiat: Ideas and Influence.* Irvington-on-Hudson, N.Y.: Foundation for Economic Education, 1969.

Schatz, Albert. *L'Individualisme économique et social.* Paris: Armand Colin, 1907.

Yolton, John W., et al., eds. *The Blackwell Companion to the Enlightenment.* Introduction by Lester G. Crocker. Oxford: Blackwell, 1995.

# Index

NO

This book is set in Adobe Garamond, designed by Robert Slimbach in 1989. The face is based on the refined array of the typefaces of French punchcutter, type designer, and publisher Claude Garamond. These faces combine an unprecedented degree of balance and elegance and stand as a pinnacle of beauty and practicality in sixteenth-century typefounding.

Claude Garamond (ca. 1480–1561), a true Renaissance man, introduced the apostrophe, the accent, and the cedilla to the French language.

This book is printed on paper that is acid-free and meets the requirements of the American National Standard for Permanence of Paper for Printed Library Materials, z39.48-1992. ∞

*Book design by Barbara E. Williams, BW&A Books, Inc.*
*Oxford, North Carolina*
*Typography by Graphic Composition, Inc.*
*Athens/Bogart, Georgia*
*Printed and bound by Sheridan Books, Inc.*
*Chelsea, Michigan*